PUBLICATIONS OF THE AMERICAN FOLKLORE SOCIETY

BIBLIOGRAPHICAL SERIES

VOLUME X

1959

TRADITIONAL INDIA: STRUCTURE AND CHANGE

INDERA P. SINGH

I am a Jat of Panjab. My stick has bright nails on it.

TRADITIONAL INDIA:
STRUCTURE AND CHANGE

edited by

MILTON SINGER

PHILADELPHIA

THE AMERICAN FOLKLORE SOCIETY

1959

International Standard Book Number 292–73504–9
Library of Congress Catalog Card Number 58–59652

Second Printing, 1970

Distributed by the University of Texas Press
Printed in the United States of America

TO THE MEMORY OF ROBERT REDFIELD
FRIEND, TEACHER, AND COLLEAGUE

CONTENTS

PREFACE

BY MILTON SINGER

THE movement of modern nationalism in India, as in most other countries, has always shown a strong interest in the recovery or reinterpretation of India's traditional culture. With the achievement of national independence, this interest has received an official definition. Language, national history, archeological monuments, folk arts and crafts, classical music, dance, and drama have become symbols of a modern Indian identity alongside the national emblem, Five Year Plans, parliamentary institutions, and atomic installations.

The definition is selective and creative. A traditional culture, notably that of India, is far too varied and rich a growth to be displayed adequately in Republic Day celebrations. And not all cultural traditions will be thought suitable for display; some are perhaps thought best left to grow or wither in provincial obscurity. Those cultural traditions that become symbols of national identity undergo, by virtue of their new role, a sea change; they take on a life of their own, quite different from their life as regional and local traditions. They have become the chosen representatives of a national tradition.

Theoretically, any element of traditional culture is a potential candidate for selection, but in fact only a small number are so chosen at any given time. In this selective and creative process, cultural traditions take on a fluidity and self-consciousness that reflects constantly changing moods and aspirations, and changing conceptions of national identity. They reflect, too, the fact that a civilization is a process of becoming, as well as a state of being, as Nirmal Kumar Bose has remarked apropos the modern history of Bengal. Now this is not the way we ordinarily think of traditions; they are, ordinarily, the things that we take for granted, the unquestioned assumptions and the handed-down ways of our ancestors. But it has become a commonplace of modern history that even the most traditional societies are no longer sure of what it is they can take for granted. Confronted by swift currents of internal and external change, they have been compelled to restate themselves to themselves in order to discover what they have been and what it is they are to become. Their cultural traditions have become problematic hypotheses in an inquiry into the design for a meaningful and worthwhile life.

The professional student of culture and civilization may contribute something to this inquiry through an objective study of the variety and changes in cultural traditions, freed from the immediate necessity of choosing among them a single meaningful pattern of existence. It is with this aim in view that I undertook to collect the following symposium of studies of India's changing traditional culture. These studies have two major bonds of unity. One of these is the underlying unity and continuity of Indian civilization itself, which emerges cumulatively with the recurrence of basic themes in the different papers. The second unifying bond is that of method and concept in the study of civilizations. This does not derive from one particular academic discipline but represents rather a convergence of thought among anthropologists, linguists, folklorists, cultural historians, and orientalists who are working on related problems. Since my own thinking has been greatly stimulated by Robert Redfield, I should like to quote here his recent formulation of how a civilization may be conceived and studied as a "structure of tradition."[1] This is the leading idea which was the point of departure for my research in India and which gives unity to the present symposium. It also suggests a method for answering the question mooted in *Village India: Studies in the Little Community* (edited by McKim Marriott [Chicago, 1955]), that is, how are the culture and society of India's villages related to the Great Traditions of Indian civilization?

The word "tradition" connotes the act of handing down and what is handed down from one generation to another. It means both process and product. A civilization may be thought of, then, as a structure of tradition, that is, as a persisting form of arrangements for the handing down of cultural substance (idea and its products), within a great community, the community of that civilization, and as the characteristic processes for transmitting it. Just as we may think of a civilization as kinds of people in persisting forms of relationship, so we may think of it as kinds of things thought and done, with characteristic forms for communicating this substance from generation to generation, and from one part of the people to other parts.

In that local community which is and long has been within a civilization "the intellectual and often the moral life . . . is perpetually incomplete . . . to maintain itself peasant culture requires continual communication to the local community of thought originating outside of itself."[2] Local culture "is continually replenished by contact with products of intellectual and scientific social strata."[3] The local community within a civilization is ideationally, culturally, intellectually, and often morally, "heteronomous"—dependent on norms coming to it from without.

This is the way that the conception of the structure of tradition may first appear to the anthropologist who begins his work within the dependent and heteronomous local community. But to one who tries to look at a whole civilization, it begins to appear as that total structure of formed relationships for the communication of the tradition that is that civilization, throughout the length and breadth and the whole historic depth during which that civilization is recognizable as that civilization. How is so inclusive a conception to be further defined?

The fact (both societal and cultural), which appears at once to a mind that looks at civilizations and that entertains this question, is the large degree of distinction and separation between two aspects of knowledge, of what is thought and done, persistingly and characteristically. It is, concretely, the difference between layman and priest, between peasant and philosopher or theologian, between local mythology and universal sacred doctrine, between the spontaneous developments of idea in the untutored and the considered teaching of the reflective.

We may note the development of this distinction and separation as we go from the less civilized to the more civilized peoples. Among the Andamanese there seem to be no specialists in tradition—older men know more than younger, that is all; among the Maori a special esoteric learning was carried on through time by a few special priests; in Dahomey priests of the Sky Cult had a more refined and penetrating knowledge of deities than did other people; in the shrine-centers of the ancient Maya a priesthood, separated now from ordinary people by their secluded places of work and thought and by the development of a mathematical and calendrical knowledge incomprehensible to the farmer; the world civilizations developed their Brahmins, Mandarins or *imams* to expound, for the whole civilization, *dharma*, the Confucian ethic or the *dar-al-Islam*.[4]

We may then attend to this distinction and separation and make it the axis of the formed thought for civilization as a structure of tradition. Most abstractly and schematically a civilization is a form of relationship between these two components of tradition. "In a civilization there is a great tradition of the reflective few, and there is a little tradition of the largely unreflective many."[5] This assertion evokes a diagram: a wide band to represent the whole-civilizational great tradition in reciprocal communication, through centuries, with a great many local and popular traditions, represented by small squares or circles. This is a concept of cogitation. It is so very schematic that it cannot begin to represent the real complexity of these relationships. As soon as we get to work, as we begin to study the relations of local tradition to widespread, reflective Brahminical tradition in India, we are at so particular and so small a part of the whole civilization that we develop and complicate the diagram, converting the concept of cogitation into concepts of observation. Writing of the structure of religious tradition in India, Marriott and Cohn say: ". . . there are chains of specialists from the expert masters of authoritative texts down to semi-literate domestic priests; all may be classed as 'Brahman,' but generally they will belong to several different Brahman groups."[6] The real structure of tradition, in any civilization or part thereof, is an immensely intricate system of relationships between the levels or components of tradition, which we enormously oversimplify by referring to as "high" and "low" or as "great" and "little."

The part-whole dilemma. The undertaking to disclose the intricate system of relationships in the structure of tradition for a particular civilization confronts a problem of method: the part-whole dilemma. There are, in any civilization, clearly differentiated groups which "carry" variants of a common tradition. In India these variants are differentiated according to caste and class; religious communities; linguistic and regional groupings; age, sex, and family history; tribal, peasant, and urban levels of cultural development. Yet there is a firm conviction among most Indians and among many scholars of Indian civilization that there is an overarching unity and continuity of tradition in this diversity. The problem of method is not whether such a unity exists, but how to demonstrate it in the variants, if it exists. The strategem adopted in the present symposium is to look for clues to the structure of the whole tradition through intensive studies of selected parts of it. The particular studies have not been selected primarily because they represent good samples of the total structure, for we do not know what that is independently of the organization of the parts. It is true that these studies, although far from being a comprehensive survey, do, when taken together, represent a fairly wide range of variation with respect to regions, castes, and levels of cultural development. But this does not of itself give assurance that the total structure of tradition will be discovered in this range; it simply provides a check against premature generalization of the results of any individual study.

The positive reasons for selecting just these studies is that they particularize the generic conception of a structure of tradition to particular variants. This particularization is achieved through the use of two operational concepts, "the social organization of tradition" (Section I) and "cultural performances and cultural media" (Section II). In Section III both these modes of particularization are employed to study changes in the structure of tradition.

The Social Organization of Tradition. Redfield has defined "the social organization of tradition" as "the way in which elements of action are put together in any particular case of transmission of tradition."[7] It is a particularization in concrete activity at a particular time and place of the "social structure of tradition," i.e., "those persisting and important arrangements of roles and statuses appearing in such corporate groups as castes and sects, or in teachers, reciters, ritual-leaders of one kind or another, that are concerned with the cultivation and inculcation of the great tradition." The distinction between these two concepts is a specialized application to the study of cultural traditions of Raymond Firth's generic distinction between "social structure" and "social organization."[8]

Since concrete activities in particular times and places are the primary data of observation, "social organization" is the more operational concept and provides the data for constructing the more abstract and persistent "social structure." These concepts are applied in section I to four major social classes within Indian society and to a caste of professional genealogists and mythographers who link in their records and tales the local and the all-India traditions.

In the papers by Ingalls, Hitchcock, Kramrisch, and Lamb, each of the four major orders (or *varṇas*) of Indian society is shown to cultivate a distinctive variant of the Great Tradition, with special provisions for training and initiating the young, internal organization, and myths and legends which explain origins and justify function and status. The traditions of the Brahman, the merchant, and the craftman are traced historically across the span of Indian civilization; that of the warrior is described as a present day survival among Rājpūts in a North Indian village. In his comments on these four papers, Norman Brown calls attention to the functional significance of the disciplines and skills cultivated by each group: learning, war and administration, arts and crafts, trade, and the changing interrelation of these within the framework of Indian society.

While each of these four major classes cultivates its own distinctive part-tradition, one of the groups, the Brahmans, is also charged with keeping the literary and learned traditions for the others. The Brahmans are therefore the custodians par excellence of the great tradition of Indian society insofar as its literature and learning is concerned. But this function is not exclusively confined to Brahmans. There are also Jain and Liṅgāyat literati. There are in particular localities non-Brahman castes of genealogists and mythographers who do something similar for their clients. The Bāroṭs now use written books but are probably descended from bards and minstrels identified with the oral tradition. Their method of summarizing and condensing their genealogical charts when a new book is started is a striking example of how history is transformed into legend and myth, and illuminates what Kroeber called "the twilight zone of transition between handed-down memories and patterned imagination."[9] Because they link the local genealogies and legends of their clients to ancient and all-India culture heroes and deities, the Bāroṭs can help to raise the social status of their clients. This function seems to be limited, however, to those who aspire to the status of Rājpūts. For merchants and Brahmans, Bāroṭs are not considered essential, a fact which suggests specialization of types of historians and mythographers on the basis of subcastes. The necessity for such specialization among Bāroṭs exists today and limits the variety and distribution of subcastes any one Bāroṭ is able to serve. In addition to validating the claims of a client who aspires to Rājpūt status, the Bāroṭs have also performed other important social functions of standing surety for loans and property in trust, and of giving evidence in disputes, functions only indirectly related to their literary qualifications.

Cultural Performances, Cultural Media, and Cultural Structure. Since a tradition has a culture content carried by specific cultural media as well as by human carriers, a description of the ways in which this content is organized and transmitted on particular occasions through specific media offers a particularization of the structure of tradition complementary to its social organization. These particular instances of cultural organization, e.g., weddings, temple festivals, recitations, plays, dances, musical concerts, etc., I have called "cultural performances."[10] Indians, and perhaps all peoples, think of their culture as encapsulated in such discrete performances, which they can exhibit to outsiders as well as to themselves. For the outsider these can be conveniently taken as the most concrete observable units of the cultural structure, for each cultural performance has "a definitely limited time span, a beginning and an end, an organized program of activity, a set of performers, an audience, and a place and occasion of performance."

How a comparative analysis of cultural performances can be used as a method for studying the structure and changes of a cultural tradition, and particularly of the interactions of the Great and Little Traditions, is explained and illustrated in my paper on Madras in this volume. The method is analogous to the construction of the social structure of a tradition from the data provided by observation of its social organization, except that the data in this case are the cultural constituents of performances, i.e., the cultural media of song, dance, instrumental music, verbal texts, plots and themes, the scene of the performance, etc., rather than the statuses and roles that occur in the social organization. Performers enter into both modes of analysis, as dramatis personae in the performances and as real people in the social organization. And just as we may abstract from social organization a generic social structure of persisting relations among roles and statuses, so we may abstract from cultural performances a generic cultural structure of persisting relations among media, texts, themes, and cultural centers.

These two ways of analyzing cultural traditions, one concentrating on societal elements and relations and the other on the cultural elements and relations, results in a double structure of tradition: a social structure derived operationally from the social organization of the tradition in particular instances, and a cultural structure derived operationally from concrete cultural performances. The parallelism, however, is only formal and methodological, for the data are different, and both kinds are required for the derivation of the structure of any cultural tradition. In Section II, however, the point of departure and the emphasis are clearly on cultural performances and on specific cultural media.

Textual and contextual analysis of oral and recorded traditions. Folklorists and linguists have generally concentrated on textual and thematic analyses of the oral media in cultural performances, particularly on folk oral literature, traditional tales, myths and legends, songs, sayings, and proverbs. Cultural anthropologists and ethnologists, on the other hand, have tended to describe complete cultural performances, particularly the major rites and ceremonies of the life cycle, in the context of a functioning society and culture. Culture historians of civilizations usually select some particular culture medium and its development—written literature, painting, music, or dance—for intensive study. Students of "popular culture" today deal chiefly with the "mass media" of print, radio, television, etc. To derive the cultural structure of any major living civilization such as that of India, it is necessary to employ all these different kinds of studies, for in these civilizations, the oral media, the written media, and the mass media coexist and interact in many different ways. Many of the cultural media have also been cultivated over long periods by specialists who have brought them to very refined and sophisticated levels of development.

Compared with Islam, China, and the West, the oral tradition in India has played a unique role. There, although writing was known from a very early date, the highest traditions of religion and culture were preserved chiefly by oral means. Even when texts were committed to writing, and later to print, the oral medium remained primary and most respected.[11] The papers by Ingalls and Brown indicate why and how this high oral tradition was transmitted. This circumstance may also explain why the Little and Great Traditions of Indian culture have been closer and in more continuous communication with each other through the media of recitation, dramatization, sculpture and painting, dance, and music than has been the case in China or Europe; it may help to explain as well the ease with which aspects of traditional cultural media and themes have been adapted to the modern mass media like the radio and the film.

The wide range of cultural performances and cultural media in Indian civilization and some methods of studying them are illustrated by several other papers in this symposium. Emeneau combines the methods of a classicist, a linguist, and an ethnologist to analyze the oral poetry of the tribal Todas. It is interesting that the marks of oral poetry which students of ancient Greek and other European poetry have discerned also apply to the poetry of the Todas. Some of these marks are also characteristic of the higher levels of traditional culture in India, e.g., the harmonious collation of verse, song, instrumental music and dance; the way in which fixed themes and formulae are combined with a free improvisation, the relevance of which to a particular context must be recognized by the audience; the way in which all the important events of life are celebrated on the spot with an appropriate song—"a rich verbification of Toda life," Emeneau calls it.

But while Toda poetry is the expression of the values and history of Toda culture in memorable speech, it does not allow, and does not attempt, generalization into universal human terms. It is at this point, Emeneau suggests, that it differs from the best European poetry, as well as from the best Indian poetry. Another difference implied in his account is the tendency for specialists in poetry and literature to develop at the higher levels of cultural development. Every Toda composes songs, although some are a little better at the art than others because they work a little harder at it. This is quite different from the professional bards and poets to whom authorship of the Homeric poems or of the *Mahābhārata* and *Rāmāyaṇa* is attributed.

The universally human is easier to find in the sophisticated Sanskrit tales which van Buitenen analyzes. His characterization of the hero of these tales—as a man intellectually resourceful, dependable, ever ready to relinquish his worldly possessions—not only brings to mind some basic cultural themes in Indian literature but also suggests a kinship with some culture heroes of Europe and America.

The analysis of the characteristics of the Indian culture hero or of the characteristics of Toda oral poetry is based to a large degree on textual analysis, although Emeneau also relates his analysis to Toda society and culture. In Hein's paper we have a detailed account of a particular kind of cultural performance, the Rām Līlā, in which the texts are described as integral and functioning components in the performance. Hein is a historian of religion, not an anthropologist, yet he has succeeded in combining the methods of the ethnologist, the folklorist, and the cultural historian to a remarkable degree in his description and analysis of one of the most popular forms of religious drama in India. From his account we clearly see how actors, audience, and literary *paṇḍits* cooperate to link folk and classic traditions into a living dramatic performance.

Hein suggests that the Rām Līlā, in the form described, is probably limited to North India and may have originated around Banaras, where it still thrives. Raghavan's paper describes some closely related religious dance dramas, as well as a rich variety of other types of cultural performances and culture media which have been developed in South India to bring the Sanskritic traditions to the masses.

Through the middle ages, at least, the most active cultural centers for such cultural performances were the temple, the *maṭh* (seat of a Hindu sect), and the court. In the modern period, as the Madras study tends to show, these centers give way to or must compete with the public theater and concert hall, the cinema, the radio, the village community stage, and the Republic Day celebration which is held in street parades, parks, and athletic fields. The types of performances and media have also been changing. Nevertheless it is surprising how many of the traditional performances and media which Raghavan's historical survey describes are still alive, even in modern cultural centers where they have also entered into the mass media and modern performances. McCormack's classification of the media of communication in Vīraśaiva religion shows how one South Indian sect freely combines both modern and traditional media to propagate its faith. And this mixture is quite typical, not only for religious propaganda but for secular as well.

Some Problems and Processes of Culture Change. *Urbanization and cultural change*. Changes in cultural performances, cultural media, and cultural centers give some indications of change in the total cultural structure and so may be used to study general trends and processes of cultural change. Such changes do not usually occur without accompanying changes in the social organization, and therefore need to be related in a complete study to societal changes. In the papers dealing specifically with problems of change in traditional culture, cultural and societal data are combined in varying degrees. The papers by Singer, Naik, Bose, Cohn, and Orans all deal with some aspect of the effects of urbanization on traditional culture. Although these authors' findings agree on some points, they differ on many others, the differences depending on the kind of urban environment, the particular group whose traditions are being considered, and the segment of culture being analyzed. For orthodox Brahmans in a metropolitan center like Madras, the demands of modern secular occupations and education make it difficult to observe their traditional ritual obligations and to cultivate sacred Sanskrit learning. These Brahmans have not turned their backs on the traditional culture, little or great, but have participated actively along with others in adapting popular devotional culture to urban media, and in reviving and reshaping classical dance, music, and Sanskrit studies.

In the once important commercial city of Surat on the West Coast, a group of lay Brahmans, the Anāvils, has also found ways to adapt and streamline their traditional religious practices in the city rather than abandon them. A cooperative purchasing of mattresses and ceremonial utensils made available to all members for marriage ceremonies and initiation rites, and a cooperative priest, are some of the new urban institutions this group has developed.

One of the general changes accelerated by urbanization is the abandonment of traditional occupations by different caste groups. Bose shows in his paper, however, that while there has been a general decrease in traditional occupations among all castes in West Bengal, this is not always a result of movement to the city nor does it always have the same effects. Because of general economic and political changes, there also has been a decrease in traditional occupations within villages and small towns, and these changes have occurred without change in residence or abandonment of caste endogamy. The data Bose presents also show a tendency of Brahmans and upper castes to pass into the higher professions and to maintain their relatively high literacy rate, and a tendency among the artisan castes to take up agriculture and skilled labor but to maintain their relatively low literacy rates.

That urban influences may result in a "traditionalization" as well as in "modernization" of culture is clearly suggested by Cohn's paper on the low-caste Camārs of Senapur village in Uttar Pradesh. The meager traditional culture of this group—Cohn describes it as a pale reflection of the upper-caste culture of the village—is being Sanskritized as Camārs visit city temples, participate in urban *bhajans*, and come under the influence of modern education and of the Siva Nārāyaṇ sect. It is interesting to see that the influence of the Ārya Samāj on Brahman villagers in rural Surat has been in the opposite direction—encouraging widow remarriage and discouraging the practice of child marriage and of the *śrāddha* ceremony.

In Orans' report on a tribal people in an industrial setting we have a meeting of the extremes: the traditional tribal culture of the Santals and one of the most industrialized cities in India, Jamshedpur, the site of the Tata Iron and Steel Company. To judge from Orans' observations, the Santals have taken rather easily to the urban industrial setting; they work in the factory and belong to the union and to political parties. Despite the brief period of association—Jamshedpur was founded only in 1911—some aspects of the urban industrial scene have already entered their traditional culture. They sing of the bright lights, the bus and the train, and of the Tata company, and see industrial employment as an acceptable alternative to living on the land: "Having a job at Tata is like having land, you can pass it on to your son."

Their traditional beliefs and practices concerning witchcraft are being changed in the city, although in a more indirect fashion than we might expect, as are the preferred forms of marriage and associated ceremonies. These later changes, too, proceed in several different directions simultaneously, e.g., the unarranged marriages which were cheapest and least esteemed in rural life have become more common and less stigmatized in the city. On the other hand, the more Hinduized forms of arranged marriage have also become popular with successful city Santals. As a result of this urbanizing influence, the Santals are beginning to feel a cultural identity wider than that of their own tribe, but they are not yet quite ready, Orans believes, to move into the Hindu fold.

One important kind of city that is not adequately represented in this symposium is the sacred city and shrine center. Two studies of such cities have recently been made, one of Wai in Maharastra by McKim Marriott, and the other of Gaya by Lalita P. Vidyarthi. Unfortunately reports of these studies were not available in time for inclusion here, but it is hoped that they will soon be published in another form.

Cultural processes and cultural structure. Industrialization and urbanization are not the only influences acting to change India's traditional culture. These are perhaps the most important of recent influences; in a civilization as old and experienced as that of India, however, one constantly feels "it has all happened before." Ingalls' description of the emergence of an urban śāstric tradition and of the secularization of Brahmans has its echoes in contemporary Madras, except that western education has replaced Sanskrit education as the pathway to power and prestige. Lamb's suggestion that the caste structure loosens in periods of prosperity and tightens in periods of economic distress gives a longer perspective on some contemporary trends.

The papers by Surajit Sinha, Kathleen Gough, and Indera Singh deal with cultural processes which are either recurrent or at least have strong parallels beyond the horizon of a particular time and place. Looking at Indian civilization from the bottom up, so to speak, Sinha attempts a comprehensive formulation of those structural characteristics and transformative processes which link the tribal cultures of peninsular India to the Hindu peasant culture and society and to the Great Tradition. These formulations represent a preliminary theoretical framework for a series of field studies which Sinha is conducting and the results of which he hopes to publish soon in monographic form.

Gough identifies several cults of the dead among the Nāyars of Southwest India which differ in degree of Sanskritization, and suggests a number of social psychological processes which relate these cults to characteristic features of family and social structure. Her account raises the very interesting question whether under modern conditions, as fellow factory workers and rivals for government jobs replace relatives as the dramatis personae, the social psychological processes also change in nature.

Singh's analysis of a Sikh village and of changing Sikh traditions in relation to dominant Hindu traditions illustrates a process of differentiation that is fairly characteristic in Indian civilization—the rise of dissenting sects. The Sikhs share with the Buddhists, the Jains, and the Śaivite and Vaiṣṇavite *bhakti* movements, an anti-caste sentiment which at the inception of the movement promises significant social and cultural changes but later mellows into some form of compromise with the orthodox position. In the Sikh village today, Singh finds upper castes and low castes clearly distinguished and not a single case of intermarriage. In the field of performances, Sikh festivals celebrating special Sikh heroes and saints have been added to traditional Hindu festivals.

The transformation of the Sikh ethos from an emphasis on nonviolence to an emphasis on martial values is a distinctive kind of change, and Singh quite properly calls attention to those values of the Sikh villagers which fit in with such an ethos—good health, manliness and physical prowess, good food and wine, independence and aggressiveness, leadership, etc. These certainly differ from the values usually regarded as dominant in Hinduism. Yet they are quite similar to the ethos of one strand of the Hindu tradition—the martial ethos of the warrior, which Hitchcock still finds among Rājpūts. And one wonders, as well, how far this ethos is characteristic of a particular region in North India. It would be useful to have further studies of the Sikhs, as well as of the Lingāyats, the Ārya Samāj, the Siva Nārāyaṇ and modern Muslim and Christian sects as agents of social and cultural change. Since membership in these sects usually cuts across several castes, they are relevant units for the study of social mobility and of "modernizing" as well as "traditionalizing" changes in India's cultural traditions. Such studies will need to compare the role of the sects in these processes with that of the castes on the one hand and the secular political and cultural movements on the other.

Traditional India and the New India. The Planning Commission of the Government of India has recently published an account of the principles and development programs of the Second Five Year Plan under the title *The New India, Progress Through Democracy*, (New York, 1958). The presentation is clear, persuasive, and optimistic. The book's title is adequately justified by the pictures—photographic, verbal, and statistical—of airplanes and fertilizer plants, hydroelectric dams and automobiles, of rising progress in agricultural development, industry, science and education, health and welfare services. The impression conveyed is of a dynamic, practical, and modern nation taking rapid strides to achieve justice, liberty, equality, and fraternity for its people.

The image of the "New India" here presented is wholly understandable; it recalls the history of other nations who have planned for progress, including that of the U. S. A., and evokes our active sympathies. Is it a true image? Certainly it is very different from the familiar image of a "spiritual" and "passive" India. It differs, as well, from the images of the travel posters, which show a maharaja on a caparisoned elephant and a tiger leaping over the Taj Mahal. The question of truth does not, however, resolve itself into a kaleidoscope of images, any one of which will come into view with a slight jar in perspective. Every nation has two faces, the "modern" and the "traditional," which are not always worn together on the same occasions. While extreme "modernists" and extreme "traditionalists" sometimes speak of irreconcilable conflict, there is, in fact, a mutual dependence between the two faces, as if the appearance of each were illuminated by the light reflected from the other. I do not refer merely to the ways in which modernizing reforms make use of traditional institutions and personnel or to the use of radios to broadcast temple prayers, although this is one aspect of the dependence. A deeper kind, however, is suggested by the juxtaposition by Nehru of two sentences in a speech laying the Second Five Year Plan before the Indian Parliament in 1956: "We are concerned with the shaping of the future of India. It is therefore with a sense of the burden of history upon me, upon us, upon this House, that I face this problem."[12]

From his other writings, and particularly from his *The Discovery of India*, we know that Nehru is a "modernist" who feels the "burden of history" not merely as an obstacle to progress which must be shaken off. The past is rather a burden because it is for him a living presence compelling his mind and heart which must be reconciled with the demands of reform. It is the same sense which prompted him to search for and discover "Mother India" in its history, ancient rivers and temples, in its many languages, philosophies, and religious epics, in its refined arts and illiterate villagers. The sense of the burden of history, in short, is the sense of cultural and group identity, which having become blurred and problematic under long periods of foreign rule and influence, now strives for self-clarification and direction.

This is the main justification, apart from the intrinsic or antiquarian interests of the subject, for undertaking a study of India's traditional culture. As a living heritage from the past, being transformed in the present, and projected creatively into the future, it is both the subject and object of the changes now going on. The cast and scene missing from the script of New India will be found in Traditional India.

CONTRIBUTORS

Nirmal Kumar Bose is Reader in Human Geography at the University of Calcutta, and also Lecturer in Social Anthropology in the Faculty of Political Science at the same institution. Graduated from Calcutta University with Geology Honors, he received his M.Sc. in Anthropology in 1925. He has done field work in prehistory in Orissa, and social anthropological fieldwork among the Juangs of Orissa and in villages of West and East Bengal. His work on the history of architecture has taken him throughout India. His publications include: *Cultural Anthropology* (1929); *Canons of Orissan Architecture* (1932); and *Excavations in Mayurbanj*. A Fellow of the National Institute of Science, he is also Anthropological Secretary of the Asiatic Society.

W. Norman Brown is Professor of Sanskrit at the University of Pennsylvania, and since its establishment in 1947 has been Chairman of the South Asia Regional Studies Department there. He received his Ph.D. in Sanskrit at Johns Hopkins University in 1916. For a number of years Brown was Chairman of the University of Pennsylvania's Oriental Studies Department. In addition to many articles, he is the author of a number of books including *The United States and India and Pakistan* (1953), and editor and part author of *India, Pakistan and Ceylon* (1951). Brown was most recently in India as a Fulbright Fellow in 1954-1955 and in 1956 when he was awarded an honorary degree at the anniversary celebrations of the University of Madras.

Bernard Cohn is presently Research Associate, Department of Anthropology, University of Chicago (on leave), and a Fellow of the Rockefeller Foundation at the School of Oriental and African Studies, University of London. He received his Ph.D. in anthropology at Cornell University in 1954. Fieldwork on which his thesis was based was done in Village Senapur, Jaunpur District, Uttar Pradesh, India, in 1952-1953. In 1957 he was Assistant Professor, College and Department of Anthropology, University of Chicago. Cohn was among the contributors to McKim Marriott, ed., *Village India* (Chicago, 1955), and to M. Singer, ed., *Introducing India in Liberal Education* (Chicago, 1957). His major scholarly concern is with the processes of social and cultural change in modern Indian society.

Murray B. Emeneau is Professor of Sanskrit and General Linguistics, and Chairman of the Department of Linguistics, at the University of California, Berkeley. He received his M.A. at Oxford University in 1935 and his Ph.D. at Yale University in 1931. Emeneau did fieldwork in South India (Nilgiris and Coorg) in 1935-1938. His published books are *Jambhaladatta's Version of the Vetālapañcavinśati*; *Union List of Printed Indic Texts and Translations in American Libraries*; *Kota Texts*; *Studies in Vietnamese Grammar*; and *Kolami, a Dravidian Language*, in addition to many published articles and reviews. His principal research interests are Sanskrit language and literature, Dravidian linguistics, and folktales of India.

Eleanor Kathleen Gough is, at present, Visiting Lecturer in the Department of Anthropology of the University of Michigan. She received her Ph.D. in Social Anthropology at Cambridge University (Girton College) in 1950. On the Malabar Coast (1947-1949) and in Tanjore, South India (1951-1953), she did intensive field studies of villages, focussing on changing political and economic structures of villages and on variations in religious and kinship institutions in different castes. She was among the contributors to McKim Marriott, ed., *Village India*, and has published several articles. The comparative study of economic, political, and kinship systems, and the functions of religious institutions in social structures and personalities, are her principal research interests.

Norvin Hein is Assistant Professor of Comparative Religion at Yale University. He received his B.D. degree at Yale and, in 1951, the Ph.D., from the Department of Religion. Hinduism is his teaching specialty. Hein taught English at Ewing Christian College, Allahabad, 1939-1942, was with the Army Y.M.C.A. of India 1942-43, and in 1949-50 did a field study of the indigenous dramas of Mathura District, supported by the American Council of Learned Societies. He expects soon to publish a full-length book on the religious dramas of Mathura. History of the western interpretation of Hinduism is Hein's current special research interest.

John T. Hitchcock, who received his doctorate from Cornell University, is Assistant Professor of Anthropology at the University of California, Los Angeles. Hitchcock has done fieldwork among the Ute Indians of North America, and in North India as a Ford Foundation Overseas Training and Research Fellow. While in India, from 1953 to 1955, he was Station Director of a Cornell University India Program station. In 1957-58 he was Acting Assistant Professor of Anthropology at the University of California, Berkeley.

Daniel H. H. Ingalls is Associate Professor of Sanskrit and Indian Studies, Harvard University; Editor, Harvard Oriental Series. He studied at Harvard: A.B., 1936, M.A., 1938, Society of Fellows (1938-41; 1946-49); and at the Sanskrit Research Institute, University of Calcutta, 1941. His travel includes India, 1941-42, Afghanistan 1943-44, India, 1952. Among Ingalls' publications are *Materials for the Study of Navya-Nyāya Logic* (Cambridge, 1951); and articles on Indian philosophy and Sanskrit literature.

Stella Kramrisch is Visiting Professor in the Department of Oriental Studies, University of Pennsylvania and Curator of Indian Art at the Philadelphia Museum of Art. She spent many years in India where she was Professor of Indian Art History at the University of Calcutta and visited and studied most of the important artistic monuments. She received her Ph.D. in the History of Art at the University of Vienna. She is the author of numerous works on Indian art and architecture, among them *The Hindu Temple*, 2 vols. (1946), and *The Art of India* (1954), in addition to many articles. She was editor of the Journal of the Indian Society of Oriental Art from 1932-1950.

Helen Lamb was, from 1952 until July, 1957, Research Associate on the India Project, Center for International Studies, Massachusetts Institute of Technology. She received her Ph.D. in Economics from Radcliffe College in 1943. During the years 1944-1946, Lamb worked for the Foreign Economic Administration. She has taught at Bennington, Sarah Lawrence, and Black Mountain Colleges. Her publications include, among others, *Economic Development of India* (Allahabad, 1954); and "The State and Economic Development in India" in *Economic Growth, Brazil, India, and Japan*, Kuznets, Moore, and Spengler, eds. (Durham, 1955).

William McCormack has been in India since October 1956, as a Junior Linguist in the research and training program jointly sponsored by the Deccan College, Poona, and the Rockefeller Foundation. He received the Ph.D. in Anthropology from the University of Chicago in June, 1956. In 1953-1954, McCormack studied village social organization in South India on a Ford Foundation Fellowship. He has published papers in *Man in India* and in *Economic Development and Cultural Change*.

T. B. Naik is Director of the Tribal Research Institute, Chhindwara, having been until 1954 Professor of Sociology in the Madhya Pradesh State Service, and in 1955-1956 a Lecturer in Indian Anthropology at the School of Oriental and African Studies, London. He received his Ph.D. in 1951. Naik has done fieldwork in Broach district, Bombay State, 1947-51; in South Gujarat, 1948-54; in the English Midlands in mid-1956; and in Central India from 1954 to the present. He published *The Bhils* in 1956, and has also published about twenty-five papers on the social anthropology of castes and tribes in Western and Central India. His principal current interests are social anthropology and ethnography, and social thought in Sanskrit literature, as well as development problems. Another major interest of Naik's is the teaching of the social sciences and the building up of institutions in this field.

Martin Orans is a graduate student at the University of Chicago, finishing work on his doctoral dissertation, which is based on his field studies in India, where he was a Ford Foundation Foreign Area Training Fellow. He received an M.A. in Anthropology at Chicago in 1953. Orans did field work in and about Jamshedpur, Singhbhum District, and in Mayurbhanj Division, Orissa. He contributed to the HRAF *Area Handbook on Cambodia*, and an article on the sickle-cell gene to the *American Anthropologist*, 58 (1956). Orans is interested in social anthropological studies of Asia, and his chief theoretical concern is with the relations between livelihood activities and other aspects of culture.

V. Raghavan is Professor and Head of the Department of Sanskrit, Madras University. He received his Ph.D. in 1935. He has been officially engaged at the University on the preparation of an up-to-date Catalogus Catalogorum of Sanskrit and allied authors, and for this has travelled extensively in India and Europe. Raghavan has published some 250 papers and twenty-five works, editions, expositions, translations, and histories. Among the latter are

New Catalogus Catalogorum, Volume I; *Bhoja's Śṛṅgāraprakāśa*; *Social Play in Sanskrit*; *Yantras or Mechanical Contrivances in Ancient India*; and *Indian Heritage* (an anthology of Sanskrit literature). He is a general secretary of the All-India Oriental Conference, and has received, among other honors, the Kane Gold Medal of the Bombay Asiatic Society for distinguished research. Raghavan's subjects of study include Sanskrit language and literature; traditional culture of India; historical and bibliographical studies; Sanskrit drama, religion, and philosophy; literary studies; Indian attitude and pattern of life; and the arts, especially music and dance.

Milton B. Singer is Paul Klapper Professor of the Social Sciences in the Department of Anthropology and in the College, University of Chicago. He received his Ph.D. at the University of Chicago in 1940. He travelled in India and Asia during 1954-55. He is co-author, with Gerhart Piers, of *Shame and Guilt, A Psychoanalytic and a Cultural Study* (1953), and with Robert Redfield of "The Cultural Role of Cities," *Economic Development and Cultural Change* (Chicago, 1954), also in *Man in India* (Ranchi, 1956), and co-editor with Robert Redfield of the series *Comparative Studies of Cultures and Civilization* (Chicago, 1953); and editor of *Introducing India in Liberal Education, Proceedings of a Conference* (Chicago, 1957). His special interests are the comparative study of civilization and, particularly, India, the relations of cultural anthropology to psychology, and philosophy of the social sciences. He is a Fellow of the American Anthropological Association and, for 1957-58, a Fellow at the Center For Advanced Study in the Behavioral Sciences.

Indera Paul Singh is a Lecturer to post-graduate classes in Anthropology at the University of Delhi, Delhi, India. He had his training in Anthropology first in Delhi (where he took his Master's degree in 1950) and later at Johann Wolfgang Goethe Universitat, Frankfurt/Main, Germany (1950-52). Back home in 1952, he assisted Oscar Lewis of Illinois University in his study of a North Indian Jāt Village. His major fields of interest in Cultural Anthropology are studies of peasant communities and culture change.

Surajit Sinha is Anthropologist, Department of Anthropology, Government of India, a post he has held since June 1, 1957. His Ph.D. is from Northwestern University, Evanston, 1956. Sinha did fieldwork among the Bhumij of Manbhum as University Research Scholar, University of Calcutta, from June, 1950, to December, 1951. He has been Anthropologist to the Refugee Rehabilitation Department, Government of West Bengal (his report on settlement possibilities in the Andaman Islands was published in monographic form), Lecturer in Anthropology at the University of Calcutta (January-April, 1953), and Research Associate at the University of Chicago, 1955-1956. His special interests include tribal ethrography of Peninsular India and the social organization of changing ethical aspirations and esthetic forms in primary civilizations.

Mysore Narasinhachar Srinivas is, and has been since 1951, Professor of Sociology at the M.S. University of Baroda. He received the Ph.D. in Sociology at Bombay in 1945, and the D. Phil. in Social Anthropology at Oxford in 1947. He was University Lecturer in Indian Sociology at Oxford, 1948-1951, a Simon Senior Fellow in Social Studies at Manchester, 1953-1954, a Rockefeller Fellow in the United States and United Kingdom in 1957. Srinivas did fieldwork in Coorg, 1940-1942; in Tamil and Telugu areas of South India, 1942-1944; and in Rampura Village, Mysore, 1948 and summer, 1952. He was awarded the Rivers Memorial Medal for anthropology in 1955. Srinivas' best-known work is *Religion and Society Among the Coorgs of South India* (Oxford, 1952). He edited *India's Villages* (Calcutta, 1955), and contributed to *Village India*, McKim Marriott, ed. His continuing chief research interests are South India, and the topics of social structure and change, ethics, modes of thinking, and religion. A. M. Shah and R. G. Shroff are students of Srinivas and have conducted the Study of the Bāroṭs under his direction.

Hans van Buitenen is the holder of a Post-Doctoral Fellowship at the University of Chicago. He received the Ph.D. degree in 1953 at Utrecht, the Netherlands. Van Buitenen has been Assistant (1951-1956) and Chief Assistant (1953) to the Chair of Indo-European philology at Utrecht University. In India, 1954-1956, he was Sub-Editor on the Sanskrit Dictionary on Historical Principles, an enterprise sponsored by the governments of Bombay State and of India. Receiving a Rockefeller Foundation Grant for study of Indian philosophy in 1956, Van Buitenen spent part of his time in India and nine months at Harvard with Daniel H. H. Ingalls. In 1955 he made film and sound recordings of a major Vedic sacrifice. Van Buitenen is the author of *Rāmānuja on the Bhagavadgītā* (the Hague, 1953; new edition to appear in Madras, 1958); *Rāmānuja's Vedārthasamgraha* (Poona, 1956); *Sprookjes van een Spook*, a popular translation of Vetāla stories, Leiden, 1952; and of some twelve philological and philosophical articles. His current interests are continuation of study of Vedānta speculation, studies in *upaniṣads* and early epic texts, and new approaches to the teaching of Indian philosophy and cultural history.

ACKNOWLEDGMENTS

Most of the contributors to this symposium have kindly abstracted from longer studies progress reports which deal with some aspect of the structure or change of traditional culture in India. We are grateful to them for this cooperation and look forward to the publication of their complete studies.

For the rectification of transliterations from Indian languages and for the preparation of the Index we are indebted to Hans van Buitenen.

The editor also wishes to express his appreciation to Thomas A. Sebeok, Editor of the JOURNAL OF AMERICAN FOLKLORE, for originally suggesting the idea for this symposium and for arranging to publish it. Shelby W. Thompson and Helen G. Singer have been helpful in preparing the manuscript for press.

The original research for some of these studies as well as publication of the symposium has been made possible through a grant from the Ford Foundation to the University of Chicago for the Program on Comparative Studies of Cultures and Civilizations, under the direction of Robert Redfield. A fellowship at the Center for Advanced Study in the Behavioral Sciences, Stanford, California, provided the time to collect, organize, and edit the symposium papers.

NOTES

1 From a lecture, "Civilizations as Cultural Structures?" delivered at the Center for Advanced Study in the Behavioral Sciences, Stanford, California, on 6 February 1958.

2 Robert Redfield, *Peasant Society and Culture* (Chicago, 1956).

3 George M. Foster, "What is Folk Culture?" *American Anthropologist,* IV, (1953).

4 Redfield, 1956.

5 Redfield, 1956.

6 Bernard S. Cohn and McKim Marriott, "Networks and Centers in the Integration of Indian Civilization," MS.

7 Robert Redfield, "The Social Organization of Tradition," *Far Eastern Quarterly,* XV (1955), 20-21; *Peasant Society and Culture,* pp. 101-102.

8 Raymond Firth, *Elements of Social Organization* (London, 1951), pp. 35ff.

9 A. L. Kroeber, *A Mohave Historical Epic,* Anthropological Records, Vol. 11, No. 2 (Los Angeles, 1951), p. 108.

10 Milton Singer, "The Cultural Pattern of Indian Civilization," *The Far Eastern Quarterly,* XV (1955), 27.

11 K. G. Ghurye, *Preservation of Learned Tradition in India,* (Bombay, 1950).

12 Quoted as the motto for *The New India* (New York, 1958).

University of Chicago
Chicago, Illinois

A NOTE ON THE TRANSCRIPTION OF INDIAN WORDS.

About a dozen languages from the three main linguistic families of India are quoted in the papers of the present volume. In the transcription the obtaining scholarly conventions have been followed. A very limited attempt has been made at standardization; so the nasalization of preceding vowel, rendered variously, is here represented by *ṃ*; *e* and *o* are long in Tamil as in Sanskrit transcription unless otherwise indicated. Generally the words are quoted in their standard forms unless dialectic forms are contextually relevant. Proper names of recent persons have been left unmarked and are retained in the accepted form—Gandhi, instead of *Gāṃdhī*; so are geographic names and names of streets. Very occasionally a common word, which may be considered to have become naturalized in English, has been retained in the Anglicized form: brahman for *brāhmaṇa;* the number of such words has been reduced to a minimum to avoid confusions.

Since the transcription is not phonetic but purely graphic, and is also not based on the English values of the vowels and consonants, it is not always a proper guide for pronunciation. Here follow a few general remarks which may serve as a rough guide. A bar over a vowel indicates length, except in the case of e and o which are long unmarked; for Santal and Toda different systems have been followed. An *a* is pronounced as the vowel in "but," *i* as in "bit," *u* as in "bull"; *ā*, *ī* and *ū* as in "calm," "routine," and "rule"; *e* as in "hay"; *o* as in "go"; *ai* as in "time" (Skt.) or "ever," *au* as in "cow" (Skt.) or "go." Interconsonantal *ṛ* represents a vocalic *r*, pronounced *ṛi* as in rich, but *ṛ* may also represent the retroflex consonant *ṛ* when followed or preceded by a vowel. A *c* represents *ch* as in "church," not *c* as in "cot"; *ś* and *ṣ* may both be pronounced as *sh*. Sub-dotted consonants are retroflex (ḷ etc.). Aspiration is represented by *h* following the consonant: *ḳ-ḳh*, *t-th*, as in "anthill," not as in "that" or "then"; *ph* represents the aspirated *p*, as in "uphill," in Skt., but in modern Indian languages it is generally pronounced as in "phial."

Rules for stress are difficult to give so as to apply to all languages quoted; for Skt. the rule is: stress the penultimate when long, the antepenultimate when the penultimate is short: Mahābhā́rata, Rāmā́yaṇa, Mahāyā́na, never Mahábharáta, Rámayána.

J. A. B. VAN B.

University of Chicago
Chicago, Illinois

I. THE SOCIAL ORGANIZATION OF TRADITION

THE BRAHMAN TRADITION

By Daniel Ingalls

TO give an intelligible account of the Brahman tradition of India in the space of a few pages, the writer must simplify his facts drastically. He must also limit himself to what is most peculiarly associated with the Brahmans, for there is a wide area where it is impossible to set a boundary between Brahman culture and the general culture of India. Finally, he must keep his eye more to the past than to the present, for the Brahman tradition is now changing at different rates and in different directions in various parts of India in such a way as to make general statements meaningless.

I shall try to abide by these restrictions, and to speak to you of the Brahman tradition under two headings: first, the content of this tradition and the method of its transmission; second, the humans who have been its carriers.

From the viewpoint of content, the heart and origin of the Brahman tradition is the Veda. Actually, the study of the Veda is enjoined by the lawbooks on all the twice-born, that is, all members of the upper classes,[1] but for the past two thousand years at least, this study has been usually limited to Brahmans. The Lawbook of Manu says that a Brahman who knows not the Vedic verses receives no more profit from this world and the next than a eunuch receives from women.[2] In fact, as the eunuch is not properly a man, so he who knows not the Veda is not properly a Brahman. He is a *brahmabandhu*, a Brahman in name only.

What is meant by knowing the Veda is primarily the memorizing of Vedic verses, especially those verses which are necessary to a Brahman for the performance of his personal ritual. He may go on to memorize more, to memorize the whole of one of the four great Vedic collections. Something close to this is necessary if he is to perform the ritual for other persons, that is to say, if he is to earn his living according to the traditional manner prescribed for his class. For, according to the lawbooks, a Brahman except in times of calamity, should earn his living as a priest, as a teacher, or as a minister of state.

Each of the four Vedas contains at least three parts: the *mantras*, that is, the sacred or magical words; the *brāhmaṇa* or explanation, which tells one how to employ the *mantras* and furnishes the mythological and religious explanation of the ritual; and finally, the *sūtras* or practical rules of procedure. To indicate the amount of memorizing necessary to master all this, one may take an example. The White Yajur Veda according to the Mādhyaṃdina school, as it stands printed in the edition of Albrecht Weber, comes to somewhat over 3,000 quarto pages of Sanskrit text. And this does not exhaust the Indian power of memory. Brahman families are still found with the names Dube, Tiware, Chaube, words which derive from the Sanskrit *Dvivedī*, *Trivedī*, *Caturvedī*, meaning that some remote ancestor of the family once memorized two, three or four Vedas respectively.

The memorizing of a Veda was expected to take eight years, and the traditional time for beginning this study was when a Brahman boy was eight years old. In that year would be held the *upanayana*, the ceremony of investing the boy with the sacred thread. Directly after the investiture he would be taught the Gāyatrī, a three-line verse from the Rig-veda which he would prefix to his morning and evening prayers for the rest of his life.

A Veda knower with whom I have spoken has told me that he already knew a good many verses before he was eight years old. He had older brothers whom his father had taught before him, so he had overheard the Veda lesson every day since he could first remember. There is very little privacy in an Indian house. After his investiture, by repeating the verses for two or three hours a day word for word as his teacher recites them, a boy can soon memorize a vast amount. Sometimes he is made to recite the words backwards or in other elaborate arrangements so as to be sure that no syllable is omitted, no accent misplaced. In all this period of learning the boy is seldom told anything of the meaning of the verses, and he often passes his life in complete ignorance on this score. He is told simply how to use the verses, which verses to use in which rituals. And if he is studying what is specifically the ritual Veda, he will be given instruction in the complicated acts of his trade.

Until the last twenty or thirty years there was always a wide market for the services of these Vedic memorizers. They were needed at weddings and funerals; they were needed at the hundred and one apotropaic ceremonies that middle and upper class Hindus used to find necessary. A wife had had a nightmare, her son was sick of a fever, the husband had taken impure food on his trip to the city—for all these things there was a ceremony to ward off the evil. And even when business was bad there were still eclipses and holidays. I know of a Yajurveda priest who always used to walk with his sons to the neighboring village the day before new moon and full moon. He would call at the house of each of his patrons and tell them that the next day was a holiday. "Otherwise," his son told me, "they might not have known, for you see they were not Brahmans." And the families would give him vegetables and rice which the boys would carry home.

But from ancient times there were other Brahmans who followed different paths of learning. Instead of emphasizing memory, they emphasized analysis and an intellectual approach. The earliest forms of this learning were exegesis and grammar. I have not time to trace the gradual development of the Brahman intellectual tradition. Surendranath Dasgupta devoted five volumes to it and was still far from having covered the whole of its history.[3] But let me try to make clear at least the present nature of this intellectual tradition.

The word *śāstrī* is applied in modern times to the man trained by this analytical or intellectual method, and the chief branches of sastric tradition as still preserved are grammar, rhetoric, poetry, logic, and philosophy. The *śāstrī*'s method of learning, as also his place of learning, differs considerably from that of the Vedic student. Whereas the repeater of the Vedas is trained by a single teacher usually in a village, the *śāstrī* is usually trained in a school or *ṭol*, and the school is usually in a town or city. There are exceptions to this statement, but it is worth emphasizing that the sastric tradition is essentially an urban tradition and has flourished chiefly at the capital cities of Hindu dynasties and at important places of pilgrimage: at Poona, Dharbhanga, Mysore, Banaras, or going back to earlier times: at Vijayanagar, Pratiṣṭhāna, Ujjain, Pataliputra. The golden age of this tradition was between the ancient period of invasions and the advent of the Moslems in the thirteenth century. But it continued after the thirteenth century in the south and has held out in a few corners of India into our own time.

The *śāstrī*, it is true, is subjected in his youth to what we should consider a formidable amount of memorizing, but it is considerably less than is expected of the Vedic student, and it is much less important that he remember it exactly word for word. There are various ways in which a child may begin in this tradition. A favorite way is to start him out with Sanskrit grammar, usually with the *Siddhāntakaumudī* for textbook. He will be expected to memorize the rules and to learn to apply them. To watch children applying these rules is something utterly fascinating. They will be given a Sanskrit inflectional form, say the form *vijigīṣavaḥ* and told to construct it from the beginning. They then take the simple root, reduplicate for the desiderative, add the sigmatic suffix, retroflex it after the high vowel, append the participial suffix and so forth and so on. Often there are ten or twelve steps. At each step the child justifies what he has done by quoting the pertinent grammatical rule, running through these rules as fast as the auctioneer on the Lucky Strike Program. Often there are conflicting rules or a choice of various methods of explanation. The constructions then are like the problems of geometry. They require not only memory but imagination and ingenuity. If a child can stand this training for the first year, he usually comes to enjoy it, and one can see these young grammarians testing each other after the teacher has turned away from his class. The teacher of the beginners is usually an older student of the school, and if the children have not understood what he taught or if it seems wrong to them, they will go to the master and say, "Joshī Śāstrī has told us so-and-so, but surely he must be wrong," and the master will reexplain the problem in the presence of the older student. There is more honesty, more patience, and more true teaching in these antiquated *ṭols* than there is in the Westernized colleges of India, at least to the extent that I have been able to observe them.

The teaching of logic and philosophy proceeds in much the same way. The basic texts offer as it were a map of the universe. All the categories and the major types of relations are there precisely defined. The student is then tested with various sets of circumstances which he is asked, as one might say, to fit into the map. One student will take one point of view, another another, and at each step justification is given by reference to the rules of the game. A senior student acts as umpire with occasional reference to the master. On special occasions, that is, on holidays or on the visit of some great *śāstrī* from another city, there will be a more formal debate with advanced students and even the masters taking part.

There is a third sort of Brahman tradition beyond the Vedic and the sastric, what one might call the esoteric tradition. The tantras and much of the Vedānta fall within this category, although the Vedānta originally was firmly attached to a ritual base. The esoteric tradition consists of dogma, symbolism, and poetry concerning the ultimate truths, the nature of reality, the afterlife, and *mokṣa* 'freedom' or 'release.' Bits of this tradition are known very widely, but the tradition as an organized whole is passed down within special sects or orders of ascetics. It is imparted as a whole to a student only after he has passed through a fairly long period of service and training.

Finally, with a good many Brahmans the traditions of their class run a good bit thinner than anything I have indicated. There have always been Brahmans who took their Vedic study very lightly, learning little more than the Gāyatrī, and who possessed no intellectual or esoteric education either. In the same way, there are professors' children in America who spend the day looking at television or reading comics.

Now to consider the Brahman tradition from the viewpoint of the tradition bearers. The heart or center of the tradition bearers has always been what one might call the respectable Brahman family, that is to say, a family which earned its livelihood, married, and was burned according to the memorized, and since the time of Christ or so, according to the written traditions. The head of the family would serve as a priest for Kṣatriyas and the well-to-do, or would be a householder in an *agrahāra*, that is, a tract of tax-free land given to Brahmans. An enormous number of land grants to Brahmans are revealed to us by the inscriptions. And it is interesting to note that in some instances, for example in the inscriptions of the kings of Vallabhī, the recipients of the grants bear precisely the same caste names as the Brahmans who still live on this land 1300 years later.[4]

The training in such a family emphasized time and again the supreme position of the Brahman. A Brahman was a god on earth. The earth actually belonged to the Brahmans, but Kṣatriyas were allowed to rule it so that Brahmans could avoid the necessity of taking life and could devote themselves to their ritual. There was an enormous amount of this ritual, of which you may find a faithful record in the essays of Colebrooke or in Mrs. Sinclair Stevenson's *Rites of the Twiceborn.*[5] The head of the family might spend five hours or more of the day in ritual performances, in the *saṃdhyā* or crepuscular ceremony, in the bathing, the offerings, the fire ceremony, the Vedic recitations. The Brahman's wife or some other female member of his family would devote an hour of the day to the worship of the household idols.

This family life minimized the importance of wealth without, however, inculcating asceticism. The important thing was not to grow rich but to lead a decent, harmonious life. Perhaps the most pleasing pictures of this traditionalism come from the pen of Kālidāsa, although his name indicates that he himself was not a Brahman. Constantly he is attracted by the peaceful smoke of sacrificial fires. He writes lovingly of the dignified matrons going about their religious rites in the rooms of a great house.[6] And it is Kālidāsa who sums up the ideal of ultratraditionalism in his praise of King Dilipa. Under the good King Dilipa, "the people swerved not a rut's breadth from the path traveled by the ancients, no more than the tire swerves under a skillful driver."[7]

Even the intellectuals among the Brahmans always gave lip service to this traditionalism. The logicians, for example, completely transformed the doctrines of the sage who compiled the *Nyāya-sūtra*. Indeed they had to do this if they were to compete in argument with the Buddhists. But only seldom did they write professedly original works. What they would do is comment on an older text, claiming that although the sage was silent on a given point, what he had meant to say was such and such. The school of Prācīna Nyāya, extending over a thousand years, consists essentially of a single work six layers deep: *sūtra*, commentary, supercommentary, super-super commentary and so on to the sixth degree.

There is no question but that traditionalism has been a steady ideal in Brahman culture. But this does not explain the immense influence of Brahmanism on Indian culture as a whole. This influence, I think, derives largely from Brahman minorities who broke with traditionalism either covertly or overtly. I shall mention two such minorities.

There were in the first place those Brahmans who sought wealth. The pathway to wealth was education, a Sanskrit education, specifically the education of what is now called a *śāstrī*. It is hard for us few Sanskritists nowadays to realize what material pleasures could once be attained by our discipline. The *Sāhityadarpaṇa*, a standard textbook of the fourteenth century on literature, states that Sanskrit literature is the primary means to all the ends of man. The reason it gives is instructive. In the first place, excellence in Sanskrit procures wealth, and with wealth one can buy sensual enjoyments. It goes on to say that by attention to the content of traditional literature one will also gain religious goals and final release, but the first and obvious reason for this exacting training was that it was profitable.[8] The argument of the *Sāhityadarpaṇa* is not an uncommon one. In classical Sanskrit poetry, in the works of the literary critics and in the anecdotes that were told of ancient writers, one is reminded time and again that the ability to turn a good Sanskrit verse, especially a good panegyric of the king, was a passport to a lucrative position at court. The inscriptions furnish evidence that the argument is sound. Thus, we know Umapatidhara as an author of elegant verses in the anthologies.[9] The inscriptions show that he was a great minister of the Sena dynasty of Bengal. He composed verses for royal land grants himself, of which an example has been recovered, showing in its preamble the sort of exaggerated but delicate praise of the ruling house which had probably earned the minister his post.[10] The author of the *Sāhityadarpaṇa*, from which I have just quoted, was a Brahman minister of the kings of Orissa.[11] One could give a hundred other instances. The ministers of King Bhoja of Dhar, the ministers of a whole line of kings of Kashmir, the great Sayaṇācārya of Vijayanagar in the south—all these were Brahman scholars who owed much of their wealth and prestige to their intellectual accomplishments in the sastric tradition.

These successful scholars in the position of temporal rulers were able to influence Indian institutions and mores far more than could the stay-at-home traditionalists. In some places they even attempted to carry out the letter of the old Brahman lawbooks. In all places they established the prestige of a Brahman code of behavior. Even if not followed, it was recognized as an ideal. It is also worth noting that these mighty Brahmans seem also to have been the cause of whatever anti-Brahman sentiment there was in the India of the past. And it is no accident that the only areas of modern India where there is an active anti-Brahman political movement are those areas where the Brahmans recently occupied this position of power and wealth.

A second group who broke with traditionalism were of very different character. These men gave up the leisurely life of the respectable householder, but they renounced wealth instead of seeking it. Toward the end of the Vedic period, there appear traces of ascetic orders recruiting members from the Brahman class. There is evidence that such orders had existed among the non-Brahman indigenous population from a much earlier period. The Brahman ascetics become more numerous as one passes into the Christian era. Some of their orders were bound together by worship of a particular god, others were atheistic. An interesting chapter could be written on the battle between these new ascetics and the orthodox. For many centuries the Brahmans of respectable families regarded them as renegades. The orthodox of the orthodox, represented by the Mīmāṃsā, or school of ritualists, held out against the movement the longest, and perhaps have never been entirely reconciled to it.

The man who made asceticism and mysticism respectable in the eyes of most of the orthodox was the great Śaṃkara, who lived in the eighth century A.D. He accepted orthodox views as tentatively valid. That is, they were the correct views up to the point where one sought for absolute truth. This could be found only by a life of thorough asceticism, a life which he admitted was to be recommended to very few persons.

Śaṃkara founded an order of monks from which ten sects of the present day trace their descent.[12] A scholarly history of the movement has yet to be written, but it is abundantly clear that Saṃkara's monks exerted an immediate influence not only on the orthodox but on Indian culture at large. From Śaṃkara's time forward the popular admiration that had been directed toward Buddhist monks and teachers shifted to this new Brahman minority.

These Vedānta monks had certain qualities that were immediately appealing and evocative of admiration. Śaṃkara insisted that they give up everything, not simply family and wealth; they must give up even their Brahman pride. He was the first Vedānti to insist that his pupils give up the sacred thread. To the man who would see truth all things must be pure. In modern works on Śaṃkara such points are often forgotten in a maze of philosophical speculation. But for explaining the popularity of his movement they are important. Equally important are the nonphilosophical hymns which he or his followers taught to the wandering monks, hymns which sing with glowing passion of freedom and the unity of mankind.[13] The word for 'freedom' is *mokṣa*. The philosophers sometimes forget its basic meaning and spend all their effort speculating on what sort of metaphysical entity is left when you are ultimately free. But *mokṣa* to the monks who sang the Vedānta hymns meant first of all freedom from the ritual, freedom from social bonds; then it meant freedom from desire, and finally freedom from personality, a state in which there would no longer be any mine and yours, any I and you.

The effect of Śaṃkara and his followers on the Brahman majority was profound. Not that many were actually converted to the new asceticism and mysticism, but for the most part they respected it, and this respect somehow broadened their outlook on the world. Asceticism and mysticism have been, for many centuries now, to the respectable Indian classes what art has been for the last century and a half to the bourgeoisie of Western Europe: something for which most of the majority has no talent, or dares not try, but which many of them feel somehow justifies their own dull and unimportant lives.

I have run to the end of my space, and yet have left much unsaid. I have not mentioned temple priests, nor *paurāṇikas*, nor astrologers, nor those Brahmans who emigrated to southeast Asia, introducing into those lands the learned language and the learned notions of India. And, finally, I have said nothing of the many Brahmans who simply do not fit into any category one can construct. For while Brahmans have their traditions, they are also human beings, and the range of variation among human beings, while not infinite, is certainly greater than any one human being can conceive.

NOTES

[1] *Manusmṛti* [The Laws of Manu] *śrīmat-Kullūkabhaṭṭa-viracitayā Manvarthamuktāvalyā sametā* (Bombay, 1902), II, 165.

[2] *Manusmṛti*, II, 158.

[3] Surendranath Dasgupta, *A History of Indian Philosophy* (Cambridge, Eng., 1932-1955).

[4] Sylvain Lévi, "Les donations religieuses des rois de Vallabhī," *Bibliothèque de l'École des Hautes-Études, Sciences religieuses,* 7 (1896), 75-100, reprinted in *Mémorial Sylvain Lévi,* ed. Paul Hartmann (Paris, 1937), p. 228.

[5] H. T. Colebrooke, "On the Religious Ceremonies of the Hindus, and of the Brahmans Especially," *Miscellaneous Essays* (London, 1837), I, 123-226. Mrs. Sinclair Stevenson, *The Rites of the Twiceborn* (Oxford, 1920).

[6] Kālidāsa, *Vikramorvaśīyam,* (Bombay, 1942), III, 2.

[7] Kālidāsa, *Raghuvaṃśa with the Commentary of Mallinātha* (Bombay, 1892), I, 17.

[8] *Sāhityadarpaṇa,* Kashi Sanskrit Series 145 (Benares, 1947), I, 2ff (p. 5ff.).

[9] See *Saduktakarṇāmrta,* Punjab Oriental Series 15 (Lahore, 1933), pp. 40-42.

[10] *Epigraphia Indica,* I, pp. 305-315.

[11] In the colophon to Chapter I of the *Sāhityadarpaṇa,* he signs himself "Viśvanātha, Poet Laureate, First Minister of Peace and War. . . ."

[12] G. S. Ghurye, *Indian Sadhus,* The Popular Book Depot (Bombay, 1953), p. 92ff.

[13] Such verses may be found in *Minor Works of Śrī Śaṅkarācārya,* 2nd ed., Poona Oriental Series 8 (1952). A few are translated in a little book by V. Raghavan, *Prayers, Praises and Psalms,* (Madras, s.d.). See, for example, the verse "Worship Govinda, worship Govinda," p. 228ff. Many such hymns are certainly not by the great Saṃkaracarya, but they spring from the movement which he initiated.

Harvard University
Cambridge, Massachusetts

THE IDEA OF THE MARTIAL RĀJPŪT

By John T. Hitchcock

A FOCAL aspect of the ethos of a group of Rājpūt landholders in northwestern India[1] is an idea which may be called "the idea of the martial Rājpūt."[2] The idea of the martial Rājpūt may be thought of as a type of person, and I will often speak of the idea as if it were a person. But since actually it is a construct, a putting together of impressions received from many different persons in many different contexts during the course of my fieldwork, it describes no one particular Rājpūt. The idea is reflected more fully in the behavior of some men than it is in the behavior of others; it also may be reflected in the behavior of the same man at one time and not at another. What I think of as the martial Rājpūt can be and often is something fleeting and impressionistic, a matter of accent and stance, a matter of what is meant by "form" when speaking of the performance of an athlete.

The existence of the idea of the martial Rājpūt was suggested in many ways. Sometimes, for example, when I asked one of the Rājpūts why he had done something, or why he had expressed a certain sentiment, he would reply simply, "I am a Rājpūt." On other occasions, in answer to other questions of the same type, either this man or another informant would reply by using exactly the same words, but the meaning would be quite different. Before answering the question he would draw himself up and expand his chest. Then he would make the statement forcefully, with pride and even a touch of defiance: "I am a Rājpūt." The second way of making the statement, with its different stance and posture, its different emotion, and different implied self-image, points to the general area of ideas and values from which the concept of the martial Rājpūt is derived.

The Rājpūts themselves recognized this aspect of their subculture. The idea of the martial Rājpūt embodied what they thought of as peculiarly and uniquely Rājpūt. It was this idea, they felt, which especially distinguished them from other caste groups in the village. The Rājpūts often explicitly noted qualities and forms of behavior which expressed the idea, and it is understanding derived from these explicit statements which has made it possible to sort out with some confidence qualities and forms of behavior in which the idea is implicit.

The idea of the martial Rājpūt as an ideal of conduct was never accepted by every Rājpūt,[3] and during the past century and a half its power in this respect has been very much weakened by the establishment of more peaceful, orderly, and prosperous conditions in this section of North India. Like the eighteenth century fortress in the center of the village, a structure now crumbling in ruins, the qualities and forms of behavior embodied in the idea are now much less useful as guides to conduct than they were during former periods of intermittent warfare and social disruption. The martial Rājpūt as an ideal of behavior has also been weakened by the Ārya Samāj movement of socio-religious reform and more recently by the example of such national leaders as Gandhi. There are many of the educated younger men in the village who regard the martial Rājpūt as something of an anachronism. They see his long mustaches, high turban, and heavy wire-bound staff—what Steed so aptly calls "an insistent, self-styled physical appearance and dress symbolically denoting strength"[4]—as symbols of a passing day. These young men express their allegiance to different values by closely cropping their mustaches, and by wearing *khaddar* and Gandhi caps—the latter symbol causing the more martial of the older Rājpūts, privately at least, to speak of them somewhat derisively as *topī-wālās*. It must be remembered, in short, that I am illustrating a concept which is only more or less, and now and then, descriptive of any one of the 2,000 or so members of the Rājpūt population of the village of Khalapur.

I will first note and illustrate some of the more salient features of the idea of the martial Rājpūt; then I will describe some of its sources and supports. In conclusion, I will very briefly consider the status of this idea as an aid to research.

The idea of the martial Rājpūt. The Rājpūt caste as a whole is divided into three major divisions, according to whether claims to divinity of origin are traced through the Sun, the Moon, or Fire. The Rājpūts of Khalapur are Surajbaṃsī, or descendants of the Sun. Rām Candra, the epic hero of the *Rāmāyaṇa*, whose reign is a synonym for justice, harmony, and prosperity, is also a Sun Rājpūt. All the Rājpūts of Khalapur are, of course, proud to claim direct descent from this godlike king, the foremost figure among the Kṣatriya ruler and warrior class of ancient India. They are also proud to claim a connection with the less closely related Rājpūt heroes of the medieval period, and especially they mention Pṛthvī Rāj, who met and defeated the Afghans of Ghor at the end of the twelfth century. They also mention the brave garrisons of the fortress of Chitor, and tell how men, women, and children preferred to die rather than fall into the hands of the enemy.

What differentiates the martial Rājpūt from other Rājpūts is the great stress he lays upon his connection with these illustrious ancestors. When discussing his caste one elderly man began by throwing out his chest and striking it with his palm. "We are the descendants of Rām Candra," he said. Largely because of this stress upon the blood relationship between themselves and the kings and heroes of the past, one of the most basic attributes of the martial Rājpūt is the strongly held belief that he himself, at least by tradition and innate capacity, is a warrior and ruler. During the course of a conversation in the field, it was remarked that a certain highly placed official was a good administrator. A Rājpūt who was present replied, "And why not? He is a Rājpūt, he belongs to a ruling race, and they have been doing this work since time immemorial."

There are a number of things which follow from the emphasis placed by the martial Rājpūt upon an image of himself as ruler and warrior by birthright and natural endowment. The martial Rājpūt, for example, regards it as his duty to see that the proper social relationships between all castes are maintained, and that the hierarchical order of society is preserved. As a prerogative of his status, he expects both deference and obedience from members of the lower castes. He also feels that only Rājpūts have qualities which make competent rulers, and regards other groups who do not share this heritage as fundamentally incompetent to meet the demands of such a role. When I asked an elderly Rājpūt whether he thought Pandit Nehru was a good ruler, he snuffed with disdain. "He is a Brahman," he said.

Belief in his capacity and right to rule makes the martial Rājpūt ambitious to attain political power. As one of the means to this end he stresses physical prowess.

When discussing the new universal adult franchise, a Rājpūt said, "These are critical times because now we have to fight the Camārs with the vote. Formerly it meant something that we were bigger and stronger men." It is stress upon physical prowess which is often implicit in many of the martial Rājpūt's expressive gestures and mannerisms.

Power for the martial Rājpūt is also represented by numbers of male supporting kinsmen. To him one of the most important aspects of his family or lineage is its utility in the political arena. He describes the loyal and cohesive kin group as being "like a wall," and symbolizes such a family in expressive gesture by a tightly clenched fist.

The martial Rājpūt tends to steer his course in village politics according to the number of staffs he can muster in comparison to his rivals. When contending with another Rājpūt, he may take his supporting kin group and go and stand before his rival's men's house, shouting abuses at him and challenging him and his kinsmen to come out and fight.

Besides the loyal male kin group, there are two other aspects of family life which reflect the martial idea, though the martial idea alone is not sufficient to explain them. The seclusion of wives makes the family a more effective political instrument. Wives come from other villages. They are comparative newcomers to the family. They have not been steeped, as the men have, in its own special values and the intricacies of its political relations. By secluding the wives, the chance that they may adversely effect the family interests is minimized. The building arrangements of the Rājpūt household symbolize the stress upon males as the proper representatives of the family in village affairs. The women's houses consist of enclosed courtyards, and the women are hidden from view. The men's houses consist of a room which is open on one side, and these rooms are fronted by raised, unwalled platforms, on which the males of the family spend much of their time. The males, as a group, are conspicuous, are raised up, as it were, to be seen and counted. Though it cannot be said that only the martial Rājpūts have men's houses with raised platforms, it does seem to be those with the more martial value-orientation who are the strictest and the most sensitive about the observance of purdah.

Another form of family organization which reflects the martial idea is the custom of freeing one son from all responsibility for running the farm. This son, who is often a younger son and who now is usually given an education, acts as family representative. He moves about in the village keeping track of what is going on. One of his major tasks is to attend marriage celebrations, a function which takes him out of the village and keeps him informed of developments in a large number of other Rājpūt villages. One of the Rājpūts described the function of such a son as similar to that of the C.I.D. (Criminal Investigation Department).[5]

The martial Rājpūt is brave, mettlesome, and very quick to perceive and resent an insult. It is part of his code that a slight to his prestige should be avenged. The preferred method of taking revenge is to wait and plan until just the right moment has come. As one Rājpūt said, "We like to wait until we get our enemy to the edge of the pond and then push him in." The following account describes a revenge which was typical of the martial Rājpūt in its careful planning and achievement of a maximum blow to the enemy's prestige:

One night Prahlad Singh was returning [to his home] after attending a feast in the village. Dharam Singh and some others were sitting with Bharat Singh. When Prahlad Singh passed they called him up to the men's house platform and gave him a beating. Six months later when Bharat Singh was in [town], Prahlad Singh attacked him and gave him four or five good blows with his staff. Prahlad Singh then sent a message to the men's house of Bharat Singh. "Your Singh [this may also mean 'your lion'] is lying in the market place. Come and fetch him." They had to bring Bharat Singh back to the village in a bullock cart.

Question: Didn't the police take any notice?

Answer: Prahlad Singh had already made contact with them and had bribed them. This made it possible for him to take revenge in a public place, which is even more insulting.

One of the most characteristic qualities of the martial Rājpūt is the tendency to carry his warrior and regal virtues to extremes. His ambition tends to become overweening; his concern for his reputation tends to become immoderate pride; and his bravery often borders on the rash. One Khalapur Rājpūt of the martial type, when he had been drinking, sometimes used to come alone from his side of the village to a side where several large families of his enemies lived. He would walk up and down before the platforms of their men's houses and challenge any or all of them to come down and fight him.

The tendency to overweening ambition, extreme pride, and rashness, plus the code of revenge and the tendency to rely on force as an instrument of policy, has led to turbulence in village affairs. During the past three decades in one subdivision of the village for which I have accurate data, there have been three deaths as a result of stick fights in a Rājpūt population of about six hundred.

The tendencies which lead to political turbulence are also expressed in a type of biography which is recognized as being characteristic of the martial Rājpūt. Ambitious Rājpūts of ability who are supported by a large kin group and have good sized holdings almost automatically become influential in village affairs. If they follow the martial pattern, such men are proud and are eager to extend their power. These sentiments often lead them to violate customary rights of other members of the village caste brotherhood. Such acts bring counter-alliances into existence, alliances which are held together mainly by a desire to bring down the overreaching member of the brotherhood. Resentment and fear of the powerful individual often flares into violence, and he is either killed or else he incurs such a severe blow to his prestige that he is very much weakened as a political force.

The tendency to rely on force, which characterizes the martial Rājpūt in his dealings with his own caste, also colors his relations with lower castes. If supported by custom, the martial Rājpūt is angered by disobedience or a failure to show proper deference, and he will often slap the offender or strike him with his staff. He sometimes justifies this act by comparing himself to a schoolmaster. Just as he considers it to be the duty of the teacher to strike his son, if necessary in order to make him behave and learn his lessons, so he considers it to be a part of his duty as guardian of the social order to strike a member of the lower castes in order to teach him what to do.

His warrior and ruler heritage also leads the martial Rājpūt to regard other ways of life as inappropriate. He feels that the life of a mendicant in search of spiritual enlightment is not really suitable for a Rājpūt. In illustration, a story is told of a Rājpūt now living in the village who was so disappointed at having no sons that he went to Banaras in order to join a religious order and become a wandering holy man. But he soon returned to the village, saying that as a Rājpūt he had found he was too proud to beg for a living. His decision is cited with approval.

The martial Rājpūt also regards shopkeeping as unsuitable and speaks with some scorn of those Rājpūts who have turned to this occupation. He calls them "*baniyā*-types." He also regards manual labor and field work as unsuitable. One Rājpūt expressed his feelings in this way: "The life I want is the life of a soldier. This is the life I want for all Rājpūts. Let the Camārs come and occupy the land. . . . Rājpūts should be given their own work, and that work isn't beating the hind end of a bullock."

Formerly it was possible for many of the Rājpūts to depend upon members of other castes to work their farms. But in recent years, as a result of land reforms, many more of the Rājpūts have had to begin working in the fields. Some of them, at the age of forty or more, have had to learn to plow, a form of field labor which was especially objectionable.

The martial Rājpūt is one who is more keenly aware than others of the incongruity between his regal heritage and his present status as village agriculturalist, particularly if he is one who must work the land himself. He feels that he must justify his present condition, and the form the justification sometimes takes is a mythico-historical tale such as the following:

> The Rājpūts are a very superior race who have been reduced to this level that they have to do farm work themselves. During the reign of Akbar, they were the only caste that rebelled against the Muslim conquerors and they kept on giving them endless trouble. So Akbar consulted his Vizir, Birbul, who decided that some of the land which had been taken from them should be given back. They were given the land and were told to carry on their pursuits, the idea being that the regular contact with the cows and bullocks would make them patient and calm, and that they would become like the earth they plowed, all broken and scattered.

The ideal of the martial Rājpūt is to have no field work, and those who are able to afford hired labor, may be said to exhibit a conspicuous abstention from agriculture. They sit on their elevated men's house platforms during the day, talking with friends and smoking the hookah.

The martial Rājpūt regards it as a kind of warrior's dispensation that he is permitted to hunt, eat meat (except of course for beef), drink liquor and eat opium. Both drinking and opium eating seem to be related in two ways to abstention from agriculture. For those Rājpūts who are wealthy enough not to have to work in the fields, indulgence becomes one of the symbols of their freedom and their martial Rājpūt status. For the Rājpūts with martial proclivities who are poor and find it necessary to work in the fields, indulgence serves a different function. Dissatisfied with their present lot because of what they believe themselves to have been, opium and alcohol help them to soften the present and to support fantasies about the past. The martial Rājpūt is something of a romatic and a Miniver Cheevy.

The martial Rājpūt not only has a tendency to dream about the past, he also sometimes attempts to relive the past in the present. A good example of this tendency occurred in the village about three decades ago. One of the wealthy young Rājpūts of Khalapur had become very fond of a Muslim prostitute in a nearby town. The girl eventually married a rich merchant. When the merchant failed to fulfill a number of promises he had made, she decided to leave him and informed her Rājpūt friend by messenger that she needed help. One night the young man, with a large group of companions, all of them on horseback, rode into the town where she was living and abducted her. The significant thing about this episode is that when it is recounted in the village, the resemblance between this abduction and the way in which Pṛthvī Rāj obtained his wife is always pointed out. To use Singer's phrase, the episode is seen as a kind of "cultural performance"[6]—a way of making evident to one's self and others some aspect of a tradition.

The idea of the martial Rājpūt may be summarized as follows: All the village Rājpūts are proud of the blood tie between themselves and the Kṣatriya and medieval warrior kings. What differentiates the martial Rājpūt from other Rājpūts is the great stress he lays upon his connection with these illustrious ancestors. Because of this heritage, one of the most basic attributes of the martial Rājpūt is the strongly held belief that he himself, at least by tradition and innate capacity, is a warrior and ruler. The martial Rājpūt is very highly motivated to attain political power. The means to political power which is stressed is force. The martial Rājpūt's use of force as an instrument of policy, his extreme pride and sensitivity to personal slight, his tendency to overweening ambition, his mettlesome nature and his code of revenge have led to turbulence in village affairs.

The tendency to rely on force which characterizes the martial Rājpūt in his dealings with his own caste also colors his relations with lower castes. This is justified by his belief that it is his duty to maintain the proper order and hierarchy in social relations.

His warrior and ruler heritage leads him to regard other ways of life as inappropriate. In his dissatisfaction with his present lot, he uses opium and alcohol, indulgence in both of which he claims as part of his warrior's dispensation, to help him to soften the present and support his fantasies about the past. His strong orientation to the past sometimes leads the martial Rājpūt quixotically to attempt to relive the past in the present.

Sources and supports of the idea. There are two strands in the local oral village tradition which support the idea of the martial Rājpūt: the folktale and the historical tale. There are many folktales which illustrate qualities of behavior of the martial Rājpūt. One, for example, relates how a Rājpūt who is old, weak, and hungry considers becoming a sneak thief in order to provide for his needs. But he decides instead to act like a Rājpūt and go out onto the high road and take what he wants by force. He attacks a strong, young merchant, who easily overpowers the old man and falls to the ground on top of him. As he lies there, the old man says to himself, "Why here I am, a Rājpūt, lying on the ground with a merchant on top of me." The very thought fills him with such anger and vigor that he easily throws the merchant from him, snatches his golden necklace, and makes off with it.

In the historical type of tale, the exploits of martial village ancestors are recounted. It is often told how one Rājpūt, the man who built the fortress in the center of the village, once shot and killed a young bridegroom who rode by him at a gallop without reining in and offering him the proper deferential salute. Other stories tell how the villagers stood off the raids of Sikhs and Marathas. The Rājpūts of Khalapur themselves have had a history of marauding and cattle theft. There are tales of happenings which occurred on these expeditions. Some of them relate how the police were hoodwinked; others emphasize the physical prowess of various participants.

The portion of the Great Tradition[7] which is best known to the Rājpūts consists of the epic poems, the *Rāmāyaṇa* and the *Mahābhārata*. Their role in forming the self-image of the martial Rājpūt has already been noted.

Another literary source of the martial idea is *The Annals and Antiquities of Rajast'han.*[8] Two of the Khalapur Rājpūts claim to have read portions of this book in an Urdu translation. In recommending it to me one of them called it "the best history of the Rājpūts ever written." In Khalapur, therefore, a work by one of the New Kṣatriyas, as Srinivas calls the British,[9] is playing at least a minor role in shaping the concept of the martial Rājpūt.

The martial idea also reaches the village through the medium of professional entertainers. Traveling singers recite the deeds of the Rājpūt heroes, and episodes in which they appear are acted out by traveling players. The singers and players adapt their offerings to the tastes of their patrons; and in a Rājpūt dominated village they realize that it is tales of Rājpūt glory which are most likely to please their listeners and bring them the highest rewards.

One of the most important sources and supports of the martial idea is the professional genealogist (*jāgabhaṭ*) who serves the Khalapur Rājpūts and their caste subdivision (*gotra*). This man comes to the village about every six years and goes from family to family recording births and deaths. Besides reinforcing the martial Rājpūt's claim to blood relationship with the great warrior kings of the past, the genealogist is the carrier of the myth and history related to the *gotra*. One of the tales he most often recounts emphasizes the bravery of the mother of a *gotra* ancestor. Since he comes from Rajputana (to which he returns for a part of every year), the genealogist forms a link with an area which for centuries has been a focus of the Rājpūt tradition.

The idea of the martial Rājpūt as an aid to research. Although the aspect of Rājpūt ethos which I have illustrated would benefit greatly from a more systematic and thorough attempt to discover its dimensions in the village of Khalapur, it has proved useful to me in three areas. First, as suggested earlier when the different value-orientations of many, young, educated Rājpūts and older and more martial Rājpūts were pointed out, the concept has been useful in understanding and describing one significant dimension of change among the Rājpūts of this village. This change, which might be called a kind of "demilitarization" of the martial Rājpūt, has had significant consequences for social relations both within the caste itself and between the caste and other caste groups in the village Second, I have also found the concept useful in understanding some of the dynamic aspects of village politics. This is especially true of the cyclic rise and fall of Rājpūt families, including the characteristic biography of the family leader, and the tendency for Rājpūt interpersonal relations to flare into violence from time to time. Third, the concept has been helpful in understanding the regal and martial, as well as the romantic and quixotic streak in the Rājpūt ethos.

When viewed in a wider context, the idea of the martial Rājpūt raises a number of questions. Although many of its sources are local and are related to local history, perhaps the greater part of the idea is derived from sources which are part of the Great Tradition. Is the selection from these ideals of conduct and the way they are accented actually unique for more Rājpūts than the Rājpūts of a single village? Presuming that the Rājpūts in a given region do share a similar idea, does it have similar implications for the behavior of each village group? And does the idea give the Rājpūts of a region their unique tone and coloring, effectively distinguishing them from other high caste landowning groups of North India, such as Jāṭs, Gujars, and Brahmans? More research is needed before questions of this kind can be answered with assurance.

NOTES

[1] Material on which this article is based was obtained while working from October 1953 to July 1955 as Station Director of the Cornell University India Program station in the village of Khalapur, District Saharanpur, U. P. I am especially indebted to the Ford Foundation, Board of Overseas Training and Research, for funds which made the research possible; to Shyam Narain Singh, whose knowledge of the language and practical understanding of the culture was of immense value in collecting information and establishing friendly relations with the people of Khalapur; and to Milton Singer, for stimulus leading to the preparation of this article, which was conceived as part of a lecture for the course in the Introduction to the Civilization of India at the University of Chicago. The article was read at the Annual Meeting of The Association for Asian Studies, Boston, 2 April 1957.

[2] A more correct label would be "The Martial and Regal Rājpūt," but since this is unwieldy I am omitting the second adjective.

[3] John T. Hitchcock, "Leadership in a North Indian Village: Two Case Studies" (in press).

[4] Gitel Steed, "Personality Formation in a Hindu Village in Gujerat," *Village India,* ed. McKim Marriott, Comparative Studies in Cultures and Civilizations, The American Anthropological Association, Vol. 57, No. 3, Part 2, Memoir No. 83 (June 1955), 114.

[5] The C.I.D. is similar to the F.B.I.

[6] Milton Singer, "The Cultural Pattern of Indian Civilization, A Preliminary Report of a Methodological Field Study," *The Far Eastern Quarterly,* XV (November, 1955), 27.

[7] Robert Redfield, *Peasant Society and Culture* (Chicago, Ill., 1956), pp. 70 ff.

[8] James Tod, *The Annals and Antiquities of Rajast'han,* 2 vols. (London, 1829-32).

[9] Srinivas, M. N., "A Note on Sanskritization and Westernization," *The Far Eastern Quarterly,* XV (August 1956), 488.

University of California
Berkeley, California

TRADITIONS OF THE INDIAN CRAFTSMAN

BY STELLA KRAMRISCH

THE traditions of the Indian craftsman are the means and ways by which his professional activity puts into form and practice his knowledge of the Principle. His particular craft is the sphere in which he is competent to apply this knowledge. The knowledge of the Principle is imparted to him through the Tradition. The Principle is the source and origin of his calling, and is known by the name of Brahmā or Viśvarkarmā, the sum total of creative consciousness. The Indian craftsman conceives of his art not as his own, nor as the accumulated skill of ages, but as originating in the divine skill of Viśvakarmā and revealed by him. This is how the sacred texts, the Āgamas, Purāṇas, and Vāstuśāstras trace back the traditions of the craftsman to the fountainhead. As practitioner of the Tradition, the craftsman fulfills a double obligation. In a straight line he is linked with the fountainhead, sum total of Consciousness, of Knowledge and inspiration. Its immediate presence in the actual moment of his work is guaranteed by the unbroken line of sages and craftsmen who have transmitted to him his particular craft. He carries and forms it and makes it available to the community which shares in the Tradition, each according to his particular place and station in life. The Tradition embraces the life of the whole community. Thus, the craftsman is involved with his own people more deeply than by common interests or a sphere of cooperative living. Tradition thus is not only an oral transmission of information and beliefs from ancestors to posterity but also an inherited culture. It is a body of doctrine and discipline, put forth and revealed in the word of the Veda.

The name for any art or craft is *śilpa*. The meanings for this word are "multicolored," and comprise art, skill, craft, labor, ingenuity, rite and ritual, form, and creation. Neither the word "artist," nor "artisan," nor "craftsman" are adequate translations of *śilpin*; for the arts and crafts in India partake in the nature of rites whose technical performance had magic power. "*Śilpāni*, works of art of man," says the Aitareya Brāhmaṇa (VI 5.27) "are an imitation of divine forms; by employing their rhythms, a metrical reconstitution is effected of the limited human personality." The range of the crafts extends over the entire culture and comprises the work of the wheelwright and the sculptor, of potter and perfumer, weaver and architect. The number of the arts is unlimited, but they are summed up under sixty-four major headings. These are viewed in twofold respect inasmuch as they belong either to Tantra, and master nature in its magic, or to the arts of Love.[1] In addition to these sixty-four techniques (*kalā*) are the thirty-two sciences (*vidyā*) whose teaching is mainly verbal.

All these subjects are related to the Veda, Revelation, the sum total of all Knowledge. Architecture, for example, the foremost and comprehensive visual art, is part of the fifth appendix (Vedāṅga) to the Veda, inasmuch as architecture is applied astrology; inasmuch as it is a ritual, it is part of Kalpa, the sixth appendix to the Veda. As an applied knowledge, moreover, it belongs to Tantra (an Upaveda) and, therewith, to the Atharvaveda.[2]

The crafts were hereditary, or the succession was by apprenticeship and adoption, for skill is not inherited. The crafts did not form the prerogative of any caste. The members of a craft share their traditional occupation and the belief in a common origin or mythical ancestor. This is also characteristic of caste, although all members of a caste do not necessarily have the same occupation, and caste remains hereditary even if a man leaves the special occupation which is the traditional work of his caste. According to Parāśara, all the four orders, Brahmans, Kṣatriyas, Vaiśyas and Śūdras, may practice crafts. Against this liberal pursuit of the arts, however, we have the Arthaśāstra,[3] qualifying the Śūdras as artisans, and the Viṣṇusmṛti [3rd cent.],[4] which makes all branches of art the duties of the Śūdras.

These conflicting views have India's ethnic past as their background. That Brahmans lived by handicrafts is documented in the Jātakas where Brahman carpenters are mentioned. Baudhāyana[5] (4th cent. B.C.), describing the preparations for the horse sacrifice, enumerates the artisans who establish themselves near the king, the sacrificer, the carpenters, wheelwrights, brickworkers, potters and metalworkers. The Rathakāra, the chariot-builder, is, according to Baudhāyana, a son of a Vaiśya father and a Śūdra woman; whereas the Suttavibhaṅga enumerates wheelwrights and builders amongst the untouchables as they are the issue of a Śūdra father and a Brahman mother.

A double set of considerations thus operated in assessing the status of a craft. As far as a craft ministered to the Vedic sacrifice, it had prestige. When the selfsame craft, however, was practiced outside the Vedic pale, it did not carry the same dignity; it was not considered hallowed. Mixed marriages, on the other hand, of the Aryan with the other Indian populations, in *anuloma* and *pratiloma* relations, determined the higher or lower status of the practitioner of an occupation.

While the subdivision of the hereditary crafts is on the basis of difference in methods employed, ethnic considerations and social ambitions produced improvement or deterioration in the caste status of the craftsman. The goldsmiths of Maharashtra, for instance, admitted Āhirs who were cattleherders, to start with, and rated as Śūdras. They formed a sub-caste of the Sonārs, the Āhir-Sonārs; the word "Āhir" denoting first the subdivision and later on being no more than a surname.[6] Lately the goldsmiths of Maharashtra have started asserting their dignity by refusing to take food at the hands of castes other than Brahman.

The upward trend within a craft, however, has also a deeper cause than social ambition. This was implicitly recognized in the law books. Manu says that the hand of a craftsman engaged in his work is always ritually pure.[7] The Gautama Dharmaśāstra[8] postulates that a Brahman may not accept food from an artisan. The law books thus distinguish the craftsman in his social position on the one hand, and in his state of grace on the other—when he is engaged in his work, when he creates and, thereby, gives effect to his being an embodiment of Viśvakarmā.

It is from the latter point of view that the Kammālar, or artisans of South India, dispute the supremacy of the Brahmans. They hold themselves equal in rank with them, claim to be of Aryan descent and have their own priests. They know themselves descended from Viśvakarmā and his five sons, Manu, Maya, Tvaṣṭar, Śilpaka and

Viśvajña,[9] who are the archetypeal ironsmith, worker in wood, brass and stone, and the goldsmith. The son of anyone of these may follow any of the five crafts.

In Kerala, however, the same classes of craftsmen, the Kammalan, who are Śūdras, look to their fellow workers in Tamilland, change their tuft of hair from the front to the back of the head, wear the sacred thread and call themselves Brahmans. A variation of this theme is illustrated by a forged deed of adoption from Golconda, dated in 1294,[10] but actually belonging to the seventeenth century as proved by V. Raghavan. The deed establishes the adoption of a Seth of the Komadi class, a Vaiśya, by the Kammālar Deva Brahmās, or Pañca Brahmās, but he remains a Vaiśya by caste.

The myth—a form of awareness—of the descent of the craftsmen from the Principle, has its counterpart in the myth of the fall of the craftsmen from the Principle. This is told in the Brahmavaivarta Purāṇa.[11] Viśvakarmā, cursed by an Apsaras descended to earth, was born by a Brahman woman, and became an unparalleled architect. He had nine illegitimate sons, by a Śūdra woman, the garlandmaker, blacksmith, potter, metalworker, conch-shell carver, weaver, architect (Sūtradhāra), painter (Citrakāra) and goldsmith. All were expert in their crafts, but the last three became incompetent to offer sacrifices and unholy because one had stolen gold from a Brahman, the other had failed to carry out the order of a Brahman, and in the painter's case a pictorial composition was defective and not according to the rules.

In this account of the Fall, two categories of the lowering of level are taken into consideration. The first accounts for the descent of the Principle to the order of the Śūdras. This is accepted; for the Śūdras were expert in their art. The second category, however, applies to the moral and artistic defection from the Principle. This defection is limited to architect, painter-sculptor and goldsmith, the arts which demand the highest intellectual, imaginative and technical skills. The fall, therefore, is the deeper, for the artistic defection goes hand in hand with a betrayal of the Tradition.

The awareness of the Tradition is active on all the levels of the craftsman's being. If he infringes on the Tradition, if the composition of a painting has no wholeness, the painter shows himself not only as a poor artist but he becomes, thereby, an unholy person. Creative work has the sanctions of a sacrament. In many parts of India to this day, the craftsmen worship their tools at the Daśahrā festival on the day of Viśvakarmā Pūjā. From the day of the Sūtras on, both the materials and the tools of a craft are known to be sacred, for they are the seat of particular powers. The tree which is to be felled by the carpenter or sculptor is propitiated with offerings; he lays his hand on it with a mantra, asking pardon of the spirits residing in the tree (Bṛhat Saṃhitā 57.10-11). The axe which is to fell the tree is anointed with honey and butter so that the tree is not hurt when the transformation is begun by the craftsman by which a shape of nature becomes a work of art.

Before a craftsman takes up his tools for any particular assignment, the axe, the line, the hammer, and all the other instruments are worshipped with incense, flowers and unhusked rice,[12] for they are that extension of the craftsman's hand by which he reaches beyond the ranges of his limited human person. All the work is done in a secluded place, with self-control and concentration (Matsya Purāṇa). The bricks being invoked as goddesses, the material itself is deified prior to the consecration of the building.

The craftsman was trained from childhood in the workshop of the master, whose son, or younger brother, or apprentice he was. There he learned technique and the *dharma*, the culture to which he belonged and which he was to become an active part of. From the beginning, he shared in real work and real problems; there was no division of school from life. He learned the trade secrets. With devoted receptiveness, he prepared colors and tools and learned the form and theory of his branch of the Tradition. He was initiated into his craft. The initiation was bound up with the particular craft and took it for its basis. His craft will be the field of application of the initiatory knowledge, which is the knowledge of the Tradition.

We are acquainted with the rite of initiation of one major and comprehensive art, that of architecture. The initiation of the architect consisted in the drawing and knowledge of a symbolic diagram which is a site-plan and ground-plan, the Vāstupuruṣa-maṇḍala.[13] It is the diagram of existence here on earth. In its symmetry and proportions are stationed all the powers that are active in the cosmos and in man. Their hierarchy is conveyed by their definite allocation on the plan. The plan is a kind of module which has to be applied to any architectural enterprise. Moreover, its meaning is made explicit by its myth, the myth of the Vāstupuruṣa. The myth tells of the condition of man here on earth, of existence itself—of which the plan is a symbol—the cause of his state which is a fall from heaven, and the dangers of this state which are turned into opportunities for the aspirations and ascent of man. The aim of initiation in general, and the architect's initiation in particular, is a waking up of the latent possibilities of the being so that he rises above individual concerns and takes part in the plan of the Great Architect of the Universe.

Each craft has an initiation imparted through the idiom of that craft. For the painter, the free hand drawing of certain abstract curves and curvilineal configurations serves this purpose. These curves are the root form of any design, whether abstract, symbolic or making use of the shapes of nature. Such curvilineal configurations were the essentials of art teaching in Sinhalese art into the nineteenth century. They are nearly identical with configurations carved in Rajasthan, on a temple of the fifteenth century (Ranakpur).

At all times, and in villages to this day, the craftsman was an organic element of society. He was either a member of a village community or, if he lived in a city, he was a member of a guild of merchant craftsmen living in their own streets and quarters, or else he was a feudal servant of a king, nobleman or head of a religious order.

In the village, already at the time of the compilation of the Jātakas, the craftsman was either the only one of his calling in the community, or else craftsmen of one kind associated in villages of their own; for instance, in a village of 1500 carpenters or 1000 smiths. If he was the only one of his calling in a village, he made his living by an exchange of his service for those of villagers of an equal occupational standing, whereas fixed allotments were made to him from the higher groups, grants of land and other concessions such as free residence, food, and clothing. Perquisites were given on special occasions, but cash payments were rare. Part of the profits of the villager was the share of the king. According to Manu, the king took a five percent tax on objects sold. Security and contentment would, on the whole, have ruled in the village community whereas in the professional villages, competition was keen and rewards uneven. In a twelfth century inscription from Chingleput,[14] a carpenter refers to himself as owner of the better half of the land of the carpenters in the village. Every craftsman was a cultivator. The state craftsmen, who worked and stayed within the fort at the palace, had land settled on them which was looked after by their family. Other craftsmen came to the palace, or to a religious order, for definite assignments, but worked generally from their own home for local demand. Inscriptions like one of Tanjore, of Rājarāja, the Coḷa King (985-1018) register the lands assigned to a master carpenter, to other carpenters, goldsmiths and jewel stitchers.

The craftsmen, other than those of the village community which was self-sufficient, were organized in guilds (*śreṇi*). These were powerful bodies, particularly in the great cities, some of which were world markets. Although according to Manu, VIII.41, the king establishes the laws of the guilds, and according to one Jātaka (Nigrodha), the king's treasurer was the judge of all the guilds, an office established at the time of the redaction of the Jātakas—still, according to another Jātaka (VI.427), the guild of painters laid down its own laws to be respected by the king.

Hereditary officers governed the guilds; membership of a guild was also hereditary. When the son had mastered his father's craft, he took his place in the guild. Each guild comprised all the practitioners of one craft, irrespective of their caste. The income of the guild came from the fees which newcomers had to pay and from fines in case of infringements of rules. The guild laid down the hours and amount of work; they maintained standards of living and of quality, both of material and of design. These, and all contracts were supervised by them, and they negotiated with other guilds. They had standing provisions for helping their members when in need, and sometimes increased their funds by levying contributions on looms or anvils. They collected, also, a certain percentage of sales or profits, or levied a cess on their members' work at a particular temple, for the maintenance of the temple. The guilds, sometimes also contributed the work of their members as a gift to a sacred monument, as did the ivory workers of the town of Vidiśā, in Sanchi of the first century A.D. In that particular case, their work was superlative and by far exceeded the work of the foreman of the artisans of the royal workshop of the Āndhra King Śatakarṇī, on the same monument. Collective monuments, the work of guilds from various regions, and of individual craftsmen irrespective of caste and creed, and subscribed to by all possible strata of the people, were dedicated to God, whatever his name. This is how the craftsmen were able to give back to Viśvakarmā what he had given them. On the social level, the guilds were represented at public functions when they appeared, for instance, in the amphitheatre of Mathurā, as described in the Harivaṃśa, at the performance of a mythical play. Their pavilions were decorated with flags bearing the implements and emblems of the various crafts.

The king was the foremost patron of the arts. Under Emperor Aśoka (275-231 B.C.), capital punishment was inflicted on any person who impaired the efficiency of a craftsman by causing the loss of a hand or an eye.

There were artists amongst the kings: Mahendravarman, the Pallava King (seventh century), who called himself a tiger amongst painters; Akbar, the Great, who was the spiritus rector of his imperial workshops; and other lesser ones, kings who "girt up their loins" carrying out decoration work set as tasks by the sovereign at the marriage of a princess to which companies of skilled artists had been summoned from every country, as described in the Harṣacarita[15] (seventh century). Although royalty was not necessarily confined to the Kṣatriya caste, it is enjoined in the Samarāṅgaṇa-Sūtradhāra that Meru, the loftiest of all temples, must have a Kṣatriya for its patron, while the architect should be a Vaiśya or Brahman. A Kṣatriya, however, though versed in the science of architecture, must by no means be the architect (SS. LVI.35-43).

This injunction is magically motivated. The virtue, or merit, that is in the work of art is communicated to the patron. Without the artist, who works for the patron, that merit would not be there. The magic transfer of merit, the acquisition of a spiritual value, is ritually transmitted to the patron when the work of art becomes his own. The bond of the work with the maker is severed when he receives his remuneration in gold, clothes, and ornaments from the patron. Were they both of the same caste, the transfer would not be complete—a common bond would remain.

The patron who wants to build a village, palace, temple, or bathing pond should select a guru (according to Śilparatna) and a Śilpin. The name for the patron is Yajamāna, the Sacrificer, as it has been in Vedic times. The guru who is the architect-priest, the Sthāpaka, or Ācārya, performs the sacrificial rites for him. It is he who conceives the building to be and who directs the designing architect, the Sthapati, or Kartṛ, the actual "maker" of the building. With him are associated three other craftsmen: the surveyor, Sūtragrahin; the sculptor, Takṣaka; and the overseer-plasterer-painter, the Vardhakin. The surveyor is the son or disciple of the designing architect, and works under his orders; the sculptor, it is said, should work on his own initiative and in obedience to the designing architect. Here, as throughout all the work, stress is laid on the superlative work, the quality of inspiration which transmutes skill and competence into a formal statement of the Principle. This ultimate quality cannot be taught. It is released by the rite of the craftsman's initiation and supported by his entire training. Flawless execution of the rules is one of the conditions, but it does not make the true work of art. The Vardhakin, the fourth in the team of craftsmen, consults with the surveyor. All these artists should be honored, for by their creative work and during its execution their status is sacerdotal.

Apart from technical competence, the qualifications of the designing architect are: knowledge of the architectural scripture and of the principles of the other traditional sciences. He should be perfect in body, righteous, kind, free from jealousy, and well-born. He should know mathematics and the purāṇas, painting, the various countries, be of a happy disposition, his senses under control, clad in a dhoti and scarf. He should have firm friends. The guru should be a Brahman of high birth, he should know the essence of Vedas and Āgamas, be an initiate, ardent in his work and well versed in Śilpa Śāstra. Their collaboration begins with the ploughing of the ground on which the building is to be. The plough is consecrated by the touch of the guru, the chief architect ploughs the first three rounds. They both perform the rites of ploughing, and Śūdras complete the work (Mānasāra V.25). The distinction is made between the craftsmen and the laborers, though unskilled manual labor itself, when it was for a sacred purpose, was performed by members of all castes from the highest downward. Citizens and villagers collected earth from riverbanks and fields (according to Hayaśīrṣa Pañcarātra) or they conveyed stone beams for the construction (as for the temple of Sucīndram).

The prestige of the chief architect was high; princes of distant countries came to consult him. They put on splendid garments for their visit and brought presents in their own hands (Kathākośa). The anonymity of the Indian craftsman is relative to his task. He has left his ego behind and gives his creative powers to his work. The anonymous builder of the stupendous Kailāsanātha Temple of the eighth century in Elura exclaimed in wonder when he had completed his work: "O, how did I make it?";[16] whereas some craftsmen inscribed their names as a challenge to others to do it better, for they had done their best.

Families of architects are known to us by their work over the centuries. The Bhangora family went from Gujerat to Rajasthan to build for the royal patrons in Mewār, from the fourteenth to the seventeenth century.[17] Maṇḍana was their outstanding member. He built the Kīrtistambha in Chitor (1440-80) and is the author of textbooks (Rūpamaṇḍana, Vāstu-Rājavallabhā, etc.) which are still in use by the traditional architects of Western India. We also know of patrons and gurus, successive heads of a monastic order, the Saiddhāntikas of Mattamayūra, who, from the ninth to eleventh centuries, built monasteries and temples still in existence all over central India from the west coast to Magadha and laid down their teaching in a detailed textbook of the craft, the Īśānaśivagurudevapaddhati.[18] In this book the sustaining power of the Tradition and its meaning are expressed by the rites when the Sthāpaka, the guru, installs the temple. He places in it the seed (*bīja*) of the temple. While the temple was built, the seed, the causal creative image of the temple, dwelt in the heart-lotus of the guru. On completion of the building, the seed is ritually brought from the heart of the guru and placed in the temple. This seed is Consciousness (*cit*) itself. It is then that the Sthapati, the architect, gives the entire merit to the patron, for says the same text, "Brahmā himself is the Architect."

NOTES

[1] The sixty-four arts (*kalā*) are listed in *Vātsyāyana, Kāmasūtra I.3.* Cf. *Yaśodhara's* commentary, *Jayamaṅgalā.*

[2] Stella Kramrisch, *The Hindu Temple* (Calcutta 1946), p. 11.

[3] Arthaśāstra, 1.3.7.

[4] Viṣṇusmṛti, 2.10-14.

[5] Baudhāyana, 15.13-22.

[6] D. R. Bhandarkar, "Foreign Elements in Hindu Population," *Indian Antiquary* (1901), p. 16f.

[7] Manu 5.129; cf. Viṣṇu 23, 48.

[8] Gautama, 17.17; cf. Manu 4.214-221.

[9] Mānasāra, II. 1-20.

[10] *Journal of the Indian Society of Oriental Art,* 13 (1945), Pl. 15.

[11] Brahmavaivarta Purāṇa, I.10.20-23f.

[12] Viṣṇudharmottara, III.90.29; Samarāṅgaṇasūtradhāra, 32.28.

[13] Kramrisch, pp. 18-85.

[14] "South Indian Inscriptions," *Epigraphia Indica,* III, 82.

[15] Bāna, Harṣacarita, ch. IV, ed., P. V. Kane, p. 14 (trans. Cowell-Thomas [1897], p. 123).

[16] *Epigraphia Indica,* I, 159.

[17] *Epigraphia Indica,* 24, 56.

[18] *Īśānaśivagurudevapaddhati,* Trivandrum Sanskrit Series, Trivandrum, 1920-24, Introduction to Vol. II. See also *Epigraphia Indica* I, 251, 354; III, 297; XXI, 149; XXII, 127; XXIV, 241, and Memoir, Archaeological Survey of India, No. 23, pp. 110-115.

University of Pennsylvania
Philadelphia, Pennsylvania

THE INDIAN MERCHANT

By Helen B. Lamb

INDIA has long been famous for its cities; from the times of the Greeks on, foreign travelers have commented on the many towns and cities of great size and wealth. Yet the traders who sparked this urban development have constantly had to contend with numerous hostile forces, among them successive waves of tribal invaders from the northwest. The culture which these tribes brought with them, while eventually modified by contact with the Indian environment, was initially antithetic to trade, business, even settled industry and agriculture. There have also been many invasions from the sea by foreign merchants who came in peacefully to trade, but ended up playing the role of Trojan horses; as conquerors they favored themselves over Indian businessmen. Even the great empires which in the past ruled India were sometimes inimical to business interests. Although these empires established peace and a stable government over wide areas—factors conducive to trade expansion—they were jealous of the merchant's wealth and throttled his activities by arrogating lucrative trade monopolies to the state, and by taxation, regulation, and outright confiscation. The insecurity of property during the Great Mogul era is a case in point. Similarly, the chaos which accompanied the disintegration of the great empires also threatened Indian traders, though a few of the wealthiest were able to profit from the petty wars and intrigues which occupied the rival chieftains. Finally, the status of Indian business has been depressed by the ancient and persistent Brahman tradition which disparaged those who engaged in trade and accorded them a subordinate position in the caste hierarchy. In view of these grave handicaps the vitality exhibited by Indian traders has been remarkable. Not only did they survive—and thrive—in their own land, but they expanded their operations beyond the shores of India to Africa and the Middle East, to Ceylon, Malaya, Indonesia, Indochina and elsewhere. We do not know too much about how this great expansion took place, but we can see the fruits of these adventurous traders' efforts in the many ancient relics of Hindu culture in distant places.

One is puzzled by the apparent contradiction between the hierarchical view of society as contained in Indian caste and the obvious vigor of Indian trading communities. Can this be explained by the gulf between the theory and the practice of caste? Is the rationale of caste as freezing the positions of different elements of society nothing more than a myth which masks the reality of social mobility? In actual fact, the position of many castes has altered over time, and wealth and prosperity have been of crucial importance in achieving an improved status. Or does the contradiction merely provide another case of the permissive all-inclusiveness of India with the men of business having their own traditions, mores and goals, a distinct group existing side by side with other groups possessing different goals and mores? This view would appear at first glance to have much validity, but it raises certain questions. Is there no interaction between leading groups and the kinds of power they wield, the power of the priest in a priest-ridden society, the power of the temporal ruler, and the power of wealth? Such a lack of interplay and struggle for position stretches one's credulity.

It is also puzzling that within the realm of business itself there are marked contrasts in the position of the merchant in different parts of India and during different historical epochs. Why these differences? Why are some business families and some business communities more highly regarded than others? Can one accept the facile explanation that some groups have been able to concoct more illustrious ancestors or closer affinities with mythical godheads than others? What underlying factors make for an improved status for the trader? My speculations have run something like this: originally there was some kind of equilibrium when traders were both economically weak and looked down upon. This balance was subsequently destroyed by the growth of trade and wealth, which have always been explosive solvents of a hierarchical, theocratic and materially poor society. The importance of the trader's function is, of course, an overriding consideration in the determination of the position of Indian business. This new situation set in motion forces which tended further to improve the status of business. Certain of these forces will be discussed, namely the rise of the new religions, the development of banking, and the emergence of the guild form of organization. Another key factor, which appears to be a necessary, though not sufficient, cause of business power and prestige, should be mentioned: control by Indians of the state apparatus as opposed to foreign rule. This paper deals primarily with two high points of business status.

Before plunging into this chronicle let us digress briefly on caste. We are dealing both with trading communities and with trading castes. The chief trading caste names, Cheṭṭiārs in south India, Vaniyās and Baniyās elsewhere, are derived from Indian words meaning trade. The function and the caste are definitely related but they are not identical. Most men born into the old trading castes remained in these profitable traditional occupations, but many groups without this background also took to trade—the Parsis for example, who are Zoroastrian in religion and outside the Hindu caste structure. Hindu groups like the Bhātiyās and Lohārs also entered the trading fields. Though they have been in trade for centuries, they have apparently not yet been identified with the trading function for a sufficiently long time to be ranked as Vaniyā castes.[1] Although confusing, this is mentioned only to demonstrate that there have been trading communities which are not strictly speaking trading castes.

According to folklore, caste grew out of the fourfold division of society in early Vedic times. Indian business castes, which had to belong somewhere, have been assigned to the Vaiśya caste (class or estate) below Brahman priests and Kṣatriya rulers but above Śūdra menials. The Vaiśya was entitled to wear the sacred thread of the twice-born, but he was the lowest high caste, the lower-middle class in the typology of modern social anthropology. This is an ambiguous position and may help explain why the Baniyā is sometimes referred to as an upper casteman and sometimes as a man of humble caste. The borderline position is precarious and some Baniyā groups have lost their status as twice-born castes, especially in parts of India which have tended to polarize around the two extremes.

So much for caste. To return to the narrative, perhaps the lowest point of business kudos occurred in ancient times. Business and trade were least important in the early Vedic period (2000-1000 B.C.), from which the cultural values of Indian social structure have, in theory, been derived. The Aryan invaders were a wandering pastoral people organized on a tribal basis. Their chief property was cattle which were herded in common. The cow was, in fact, the medium of exchange. Aryan military heroes were called *puraṃdaras*, that is, destroyers of cities.[2] They apparently wiped out the settled agriculture of the pre-Aryan Harappa civilization of the Indus valley by breaking up the system of river irrigation and demolished the cities which this settled agriculture had made possible. Among the victorious Aryan tribes, trade had little function and was, in fact, identified with the hated and despised enemy.[3]

With time there was a fusion of Aryan and pre-Aryan peoples and cultures. Kingdoms emerged embracing several tribes and centered in the rich Gangetic plain. Settled agriculture, trade, cities, the concept of private property—all came into being, and one can assume that in this whole transformation traders played a crucial role.[4] By 600 B.C. Indian traders had scattered far and wide throughout India and abroad. The laws of Manu, codified somewhat later, give us a description of the necessary attributes of the trader.[5] He must have knowledge of the prices and qualities of precious stones, metals, and woven goods; the rules for weighing articles; information about the wages of artisans, about soils, and sowing of seeds; about measurement of land; about the profits and losses from the sale of different articles; he must have ability to forecast price fluctuations; he must be skilled in methods of buying and selling; he must be conversant with the good and evil traits of nations; he must speak the languages of different peoples, know how to multiply his riches by honest means. In brief, he needed a knowledge of economic realities, of people and of foreign countries, and he needed the profit motive.

The period from roughly 600 B.C. to well into the first millenium A.D. witnessed a great flowering of intellectual and material culture centering in the Gangetic plain where great cities grew up and leading businessmen came to hold important positions. Three factors which contributed to the improvement of business status and which are particularly impressive are the development of banking, the emergence of the guild form of organization, and the coming into being of new religions, of which Buddhism (550 B.C.) was the most important.

Let us mention the religions first. One way for the rising traders to emancipate themselves from the social disabilities to which traditional Brahmanism subjected them was to espouse new religions which denied Brahman pretensions and were imbued with a somewhat different ethic. This the new religious movements did, and traders and city dwellers embraced them in large numbers.[6] Both Buddhism and Jainism struck a blow at the priestly domination of society. They preached against the sanctity of the Vedas, against the notion that Brahmans were the indispensable intermediaries with the gods, against Brahman exclusiveness (anyone so inclined could join the new religious orders), against the rivalry and hereditary power of Brahmans (the monks in these new religions had to be celibates), and against the costly animal sacrifices which Brahman ritual exacted. The new religions moved away from the social, economic, and political concomitants of a tribal society and moved toward the proclaimed virtues of a private property environment with considerable stress on individual effort and responsibility, nonstealing and nonencroachment on the possessions of others, honesty of word, and frugality.

The emergence of banking, which was likewise associated with the new urban society and the expansion of trade, tended to bifurcate the Indian merchant class: the few highly placed influential business families connected with large scale merchant banking operations, who financed trade caravans and whole fleets of trading ships, and the many humble retail traders and village moneylenders. Henceforth merchants do not form a functionally homogenous body but rather these two quite distinct elements. The status of these two groups has also differed, reflecting differences in their wealth, power, the nature of their business and the status of their clientele. Bankers, unlike moneylenders, not only lend but also take deposits. They have rich customers looking for a safe haven for their wealth. Even in the lending business there are important distinctions between the banker and the moneylender. While the typical rural moneylender does a small amount of business at usurious rates and is universally condemned, the city banker ordinarily does a larger amount of business at lower interest rates. This is the consequence of the greater competition in cities, as well as the fact that bankers are at the apex of the business pyramid; they finance other businessmen. This kind of loan operation is more economically productive and less personal than the moneylenders' distress loans to the poor, borrowed for consumption purposes and frequently defaulted. There was a recognized scale of business interest rates in these early days, the rates increasing with the distance the merchandise had to travel.[7] Long distance transportation was apparently very risky and commanded high interest rates, which bear testimony to the large speculative profits to be made in such ventures. Also the biggest bankers have from early times financed the state itself and received great honors in recompense. The Laws of Manu—and here the Laws are not invoking normative precepts from an ancient religious tradition, but merely registering current practices in the work-a-day world—advise people to pick their banker with great care and to make deposits only with bankers of good repute, good family, and good conduct, who possess truthfulness, a knowledge of the law, many relatives and great wealth.[8] Heirs are important because in Hindu tradition the payment of a debt is a sacred obligation which sons are supposed to assume on their fathers' death. In contrast to the trader, the banker was clearly far more a man of substance, wealth, social position, and sound reputation. Banking, perhaps because it requires greater capital, expertise and public confidence, has been a much more exclusive occupation than moneylending which, at least in recent times, has proved easy of access by any and all groups.[9] Banking also requires greater organization, since it presupposes a network of reliable correspondents throughout India and even abroad to honor the banker's *huṃḍī*, a kind of promissory note or bill of exchange which is backed by the reputation and the word of the individuals singing it. Banking expertise and capital were passed on from one generation to the next. The title used in addressing a reputable merchant banker has long been *śreṣṭhī* or *seṭh* 'descendant of a banker.'

Merchant bankers and traders in this pre-Christian era developed their own organizations to give themselves greater security and strength. It is hard to reconstruct the details of business organization in early times, but traders and bankers apparently had their respective guilds as did other groups. These guilds were subject to considerable state regulation. The leaders of the guilds, described as men of great wealth, were important functionaries who served as intermediaries between the state and the guilds, and as peacemakers in regulating the relationships among guilds.[10]

An interesting sidelight on the vitality of business in classical times comes from the development of the science of arithmetic with the invention of the concept of zero and the decimal place value system of numerology—this new discovery being the basic building block of subsequent mathematics and science. Why were the

Hindus able to make this new formulation, while the Greeks with their capacity for abstraction were not.[11] Perhaps because the social impetus and need for these new tools came from expanding business and trade, which were held in higher esteem in ancient India than they were in Greece. Early Sanskrit works on mathematics are full of the problems of trade, taxation, interest and debt calculation. Indian businessmen at this time also developed double entry bookkeeping.[12] They are famous even today for their ability to figure difficult compound interest calculations without benefit of pen, paper or abacus.

This early period has been dealt with at length because it was one of great commercial wealth and activity and appears to have been a high point in the approximation of business prestige to business power. This development is reflected in the emergence of a certain degree of social freedom and mobility, emancipation from the tyranny of Brahman superiority, growth of banking and guild organization, and the control of extensive kingdoms by Indian rulers. The Brahmans naturally attempted to resist these encroachments on their monopoly preserve, and the Laws of Manu, which reflect their efforts in this regard, contain endless regulations for keeping people in their places. But these rules and more particularly the fulminations against infractions, which had apparently become myriad in this pre-Christian era, echo the futility of the Brahmans' attempt to freeze the world in their own image.[13] But the first millenium A.D. saw a long, slow, almost imperceptible decline of trade, punctuated by new invasions and a Brahman revival in the Gangetic plain area. Why this upsurge and why this decline? Perhaps this transformation was a consequence of the emergence and solidification of a highly developed rural economy centering on the self-sufficient village and eventually supplying the chief source of state revenue—thereby relieving rulers of any necessity to rely on and favor traders and town dwellers. The Gangetic plain cities became, in effect, inundated by village India.[14]

To find another epoch and region offering circumstances which favored the fulfillment of business power and prestige, one has to turn to the mediaeval period, 1000 A.D. and thereafter, and to the Bay of Cambay. This area, which we will call for convenience the Gujarati area, really includes the states of Kutch, Kathiawar, Saurashtra and Gujarat, as well as the directly adjacent area of Rajputana, whence come the Maṛwārī businessmen. Business still has a higher status in this region than elsewhere in India.

This section had long been an important trading area. It had several good ports—Broach, Cambay, and later Surat. The city of Ahmedabad is located here, and important trade routes from the Gangetic plain area passed through Rajputana to the western ports. Here Indians retained the tradition of seafaring. Located at the center of important land and sea trade routes, this region attracted foreign traders from many areas, and the ports acquired a cosmopolitan atmosphere. The area developed some commerical agriculture, chiefly cotton for export. Here the cities were not lost in a sea of self-sufficient villages. In fact, the cities, at least by Mogul times, had to import food from considerable distances.[15]

In religion this region had already moved a long way from Brahman domination. It had become the chief home of Jainism, an austere religion which developed contemporaneously with Buddhism, was similarly opposed to Brahman pretensions, and also established a similar type of religious order of celibate monks.[16] But while Buddhism with its universal appeal succumbed to a revived Brahmanism, Jainism, which had a much smaller following, migrated to western India and survived. Its appeal was limited to a small number of devoted adherents, largely merchants and town dwellers; Jain laymen have been businessmen—so overwhelmingly so that they are equated with Baniyās. Some scholars attribute the survival of Jainism to the greater organization and participation by the laity in the support and regulation of the Jain religion than was the case with Buddhism. In the Gujarat area, the Brahmans had no monopoly of learning and access to sacred literature, since Jainism had its own learned monks and sacred texts. The Jain faith prescribes an extraordinarily high and exacting moral code for each individual believer. Jainism has been lauded by a western scholar as "one of the most emphatic protests the world has ever known against accounting luxury, wealth, and comfort the main things in life."[17] It has been defended by an Indian scholar as a practical religion "essentially fitted to give the state good subjects and the country successful businessmen."[18]

Most businessmen in the area, however, are not Jains but Vaiṣṇavas, the numerically dominant religious group there. This manifestation of Hinduism was also originally, some hundreds of years ago, a protest movement against the narrowness and exclusiveness of ancient Brahmanism. Vaiṣṇavism introduced new gods not associated with the Vedas and emphasized the exuberant affirmation of life and good works rather than escape from existence, but it retained an hereditary priesthood.[19]

There are some important similarities between Jainism and Vaiṣṇavism: both practice *ahiṃsā*, the injunction against killing. It is frequently averred that the Jains had to become businessmen because they were kept out of farming, which involved the killing of insects. Perhaps the belief in *ahiṃsā* merely reinforced their already existing remoteness from manual agricultural labor and thereby contributed to the further degradation of these occupations. There are many more Vaiṣṇava than Jain businessmen, but the epicurean Vaiṣṇavas have not made as much money as the puritanical Jains. The Jains have produced most of India's biggest bankers, that is, merchant bankers or shroffs. According to an English author writing in 1829, "more than half of the mercantile wealth of India passes through the hands of the Jain laity. . . . The officers of the state and revenue are chiefly of the Jain laity, as are the majority of the bankers from Lahore to the ocean."[20] Akbar's treasurer was a Jain from Rajputana. The greatest banking family of them all, which received the hereditary title Jagatsāth 'banker of the world' in the late Mogul empire, likewise were Jains from this area. Merchant banking has tended to be monopolized by the professional business communities, especially Gujarat and Rajputana Baniyās and Jains, and in south India the Nattukotai Cheṭṭiārs.[21] The Cheṭṭiārs, however, have had considerable competition from Gujarati bankers and even local Brahmans.[22] It is significant that in south India, an area of powerful Brahman domination, Brahmans have apparently been more successful in breaking through this banking monopoly by professional business communities than elsewhere.

The Gujarat area is a region where trade and craft guilds flourished, and there are still some vestiges of them there. Gujarati traders have been known on occasion to demonstrate considerable solidarity and concerted action—the closing down of their shops—when some violence was done one of their members by a Mogul revenue officer.[23] The top guild organization, coordinating and arbitrating between the many lesser guilds, has been dominated by leading bankers. Apparently city government revolved around these guilds. The Nagarsāth 'city banker,' a kind of mayor, probably was neither elected nor appointed, but held his office because of his family's hereditary position in the banking hierarchy.[24] Many of the rulers of these small mediaeval states in western India came under Jain influence and employed Jain businessmen in their administration. Jaipur in Rajputana was called the Baniyā Rāj because of business influence at court.[25] These states succumbed to a succession of Muslim raids, but Rajputana states held out for a long time, protected by the desert of Sind and the rugged terrain. When Rajputana was absorbed in the Mogul empire, it was treated more as a tributary fief than as directly occupied territory and apparently still provided a haven for businessmen, who migrated to the cities of the Ganges for business purposes but kept their families and fortune in Rajputana, safe from the depredations and fickle favor of Mogul rulers.[26] Thus this area was less subjugated than the rest of India, and even later, during British times, many states in the Gujarati area and all the Rajputana states remained outside that part of India directly administered by the British. A good number of Indian businessmen coming to Bombay to trade have had their roots in nearby princely states.

To describe the impact of British rule on the position of Indian business is a complex task, as it has varied from period to period and from region to region. One of the paradoxes of British rule was that it apparently both strengthened the position of the Brahman in Hindu society and set in motion forces which ultimately undermined Brahman supremacy. Only two aspects of British rule will be touched upon: its impact on the moneylender and the banker. Eventually, British investment in transport, communication and irrigation as well as the removal of internal customs barriers encouraged a great expansion of trade in agricultural products. The ruralization of India provided great opportunities for one segment of Indian business—the moneylenders and financiers of agricultural production at the local level. Freed from customary restraints, Maṛwārī moneylenders swarmed all over northern and central India in pursuit of profits.[27] The alienability of land, which the British introduced, and rising land values made it possible and profitable for moneylenders to foreclose on mortgages and become landlords. In brief, British rule brought the expansion of that type of business activity which has the lowest possible prestige rating in India or elsewhere.

Under British rule, Indian merchant bankers, though they were initially relied on and used by the East India Company, eventually lost their positions of power and influence and many of their functions as well.[28] They were no longer bankers for the state since British banks were set up to take over this role. They were no longer needed as moneychangers since the imposition of a uniform currency obviated this function. They were no longer revenue collectors. And they were no longer at the apex of trade since the British exchange banks pretty much monopolized the financing of foreign trade. Indigenous banking had to face competition from western-style joint stock banking, which for a long time was monopolized by Britons. Indigenous bankers still continued to do business in the same old way in the declining cities of the hinterland where western bankers did not penetrate. But they were relegated to a subordinate position in the new, growing ports of Calcutta, Madras and Bombay. They usually financed trade only up to the export level, or they became actual middlemen, brokers and factotums for British firms.[29] As middlemen, of course, they did not enjoy the same prestige as principals. They suffered this fate much less in Bombay and western India where merchant-bankers had a higher status in their own society.

It was in this area that members of Indian merchant-banking families were able later on to move from being middlemen to being principals, engaging more and more in foreign trade on their own, constructing modern textile mills and ultimately setting up western joint stock banks.

With the growth of Indian nationalism and its emphasis on economic as well as political independence and on the need to expand industry, a new dimension of business prestige emerged, that of industrial performance. Those merchant bankers like J. N. Tata, a Parsi, and Walchand Hirachand, a Jain, who made a contribution to India's basic industrialization and to her economic independence of British business and British shipping, became national heroes. A good many Indians were able to make the transition from merchant banking to light industry—more particularly, cotton textiles. Indian textile manufacturers until World War I belonged to the leading business communities of Bombay and Ahmedabad: Parsis, Bhātiyās, Gujarati Baniyās and Jains, and Khojās, i.e., a trading community which had been converted to Islam. The implications for business prestige of this new focus on the urgent need for industrial development can be seen clearly in the evidence introduced before the Indian Industrial Commission 1916-18.[30] There the point was repeatedly made that, outside the Bombay-Gujarat area, the much needed industrial expansion had failed to materialize in large part because the professional business communities refused to venture their capital in industry, whereas the Brahmans and intelligentsia, who had a patriotic concern for India's industrial development and freedom, had generally failed in their efforts to establish successful industrial undertakings because they lacked the capital and business know-how. Indian business communities were berated for their failure to emulate the Bombay and Gujarati business achievement. This situation has since changed; leading business communities like the Maṛwārīs and Cheṭṭiārs and others have in the last thirty-five years begun to finance industrial operations.

Before concluding this paper we should add a brief note on the impact of growing wealth and power on communities which have taken to trade and more recently to modern industry. What happens to their image of themselves and to their social mores?[31] Certainly the most successful and distinguished of them come to regard themselves as members of the elite and to act accordingly—like the elect of early Calvinism who substantiated their claim to election by a strenuous dedication to acts and articles of faith. Historically, trading communities have tended to adopt customs of the higher castes, such as early marriage, taboo on widow remarriage, seclusion of women, strict vegetarianism, and rigid rules concerning the question of those with whom one eats and intermarries; and often a fractionalization of the group itself has taken place in the quest for greater purity. But as the community becomes more affluent and sophisticated, there appear to be tendencies operating in the reverse direction. The hallmarks of orthodoxy are less rigidly adhered to, the age of marriage is extended, widows are allowed to remarry, women are not so secluded, intercaste dining is allowed and even some intercaste marriages, higher education and even the education of women are encouraged, and various social and religious reform movements are advocated. This shift has long been noticeable among the leading Bombay business communities and the Ahmedabad Jains, but recently has become evident among business groups in other parts of India. And with these changes laymen seem to be better able to cope with their hereditary priests, to bring them more in touch with modern life and to reduce their hold over the population. This has occurred both among the Parsis, whose religion is remote from Hinduism, and among the Hindu Vaiṣṇavas. There was a fascinating controversy in the mid-nineteenth century between Gujarati businessmen and their priests, the upshot of which was that businessmen established the principle of the dispensability of their priests by their successful assertion that household worship without benefit of priest was on a par with temple worship; the priest's power to deny temple worship had been his main weapon against recalcitrants. An author on Vaiṣṇavism comments on this episode as follows: "This shows to what extent Brahmin supremacy has been losing its hitherto unchallenged position in an environment of trade, commerce, industry and increasing education. Thus some rich Bhatias and Vanias have proved themselves a remarkably efficient social force to deal with the evils in their 'church.' "[32]

In the twentieth century, Indian trading communities helped to achieve the long sought goal of a free India and the establishment of a government favorable to the development of Indian business over foreign interests and dedicated to a rapid industrialization program. These basic changes are likely to enhance the position of Indian business. We have seen how the status of the merchant has fluctuated with the importance of his function to society and the relative degree of urbanization. While, to be sure, the state is today increasingly assuming responsibility for the building of a heavy industry base, the very fulfillment of this goal should create expanding opportunities for Indian business in the light industry sector. The Brahman view of life which places Brahmans firmly on the pinnacle of the social hierarchy has been losing ground in modern India and thereby the gulf between Gujarat and the rest of India has been lessened. Nationalism, economic development and urbanization, as well as specific movements of social protest, have all contributed to this development. In the field of business organization there has been a steady growth during the past fifty years not of guilds, but of modern Chambers of Commerce and specialized trade and industrial associations. With the advent of economic planning in the framework of a mixed economy, these organizations assume a new importance. And in the new India, certain leading industrialists of wealth and enterprise, like the merchant bankers of long ago, have a prestige and influence out of all proportion to their numbers. It would appear, then, that India may be entering a new phase in which business plays a significant role in an expanding economy—provided, that is, that the Indian formula for a mixed economy turns out to be viable and that business is able to adjust to the mildly socialistic overtones of a welfare state.

NOTES

1 R. E. Enthoven, *Tribes and Castes of Bombay* (Bombay, 1922).

2 H. D. Malaviya, *Village Panchayats in India* (New Delhi, 1956), p. 41.

3 D. D. Kosambi, *An Introduction to the Study of Indian History* (Bombay 1956), pp. 67-72.

4 C. A. F. Rhys Davids, "Economic Conditions According to Early Buddhist Literature," *Cambridge Ancient History of India,* ed. E. J. Rapson (New York, 1923), Chapter VIII.

5 S. Bhargava, *Indigenous Banking in Ancient and Mediaeval India* (Bombay, 1935), p. 9.

6 Kosambi, pp. 156-162.

7 Kosambi, p. 140.

8 L. C. Jain, *Indigenous Banking in India* (London, 1929), p. 9.

9 Jain, p. 28.

10 R. C. Majumdar, *Corporate Life in Ancient India* (Poona, 1922).

11 See discussion of this question in Jawaharlal Nehru, *The Discovery of India* (New York, 1946), pp. 211-214.

[12] Bhargava, p. 165.

[13] The Laws of Manu also asserted the principle that interest rates should hinge not on the nature of the business and the element of risk but on the caste of the borrower. Kosambi, p. 240.

[14] S. N. Roy, "Bengal Traditions of Trade and Commerce," *Bombay Anthropological Society Journal*, XIV (1929), 431; K. S. Shelvankar, *The Problem of India* (New York, 1940); Kosambi.

[15] W. V. Moreland, *India at the Death of Akbar* (London, 1920), pp. 240-244.

[16] Joel Carpenter, "The Jains," *Cambridge Ancient History of India*, pp. 150-171.

[17] Mrs. Sinclair Stevenson, *Heart of Jainism* (London, 1915), p. 22.

[18] Jagmanderlal Jaini, *Outlines of Jainism* (Cambridge, England, 1940), p. 73.

[19] N. A. Toothi, *The Vaishnavas of Gujerat* (London, 1935).

[20] Quoted from J. Tod, *Annals and Antiquities of Rajast'han*, I, 518-19, in L. C. Jain, p. 146.

[21] Indigenous banking as contrasted with joint stock banking is still organized on a business community basis. See Benegal Rao, "Indigenous Banking in India," address before the All India Shroffs Conference, 21 July, 1951, published in Reserve Bank of India *Bulletin* (October 1951), pp. 743-44. In one community, that of the Nattukotai Chettiārs, there exists something approaching joint responsibility of the community as a whole for the liabilities of individual members. See M. S. Gubay, *Indigenous Indian Banking* (Bombay, 1928), p. 11.

[22] S. K. Muranjan, "The Indigenous Banking System," *Modern Banking in India* (Bombay, 1952), pp. 8-24, especially p. 10.

[23] Moreland, p. 37.

[24] A. Appadorai, *Economic Conditions in Southern India, 1000-1500 A.D.* (Madras, 1936), p. 386.

[25] Bhargava, pp. 212-33.

[26] Bhargava, pp. 212-16.

[27] N. V. Sovani, "British Impact on India before 1850-57," *Cahiers d'histoire mondiale* I (April 1954), 862, 870.

[28] H. Sinha, *Early European Banking in India* (London, 1927), pp. 36-38, 163-71.

[29] R. P. Masani, "The Banking Castes and Guilds of India and the Position Occupied by Them in the Economic Organization of Society from the Earliest Times," *Bombay Anthropological Society Journal* XIV, No. 50 (February 1930), 22-26.

[30] Indian Industrial Commission, *Report* 1916-18, pp. 64-66, and *Minutes of Evidence*, IV, p. 288.

[31] Enthoven; R. V. Russell, *Tribes and Castes of Central Provinces* (London, 1916); Edgar Thurston, *Castes and Tribes of Southern India* (Madras, 1909).

[32] Toothi, p. 98.

Cambridge, Massachusetts

CLASS AND CULTURAL TRADITIONS IN INDIA

BY W. NORMAN BROWN

THE four preceding papers in this section deal with Indian tradition and civilization from two contrasting viewpoints. One is that of the authoritarian, theological, or religious tradition. According to it, the rules by which society should live were decreed by a deity or are enshrined in some cosmic impersonal system, operating mechanically and automatically, and transcending even the lofty deity who supervises its administration. This viewpoint is explicitly presented in two papers: first, that by Daniel Ingalls on the Brahman, that respository, custodian, and expounder of Hindu tradition; and second, that by Stella Kramrisch on the craftsman, whose task is to provide, under indicated specifications or standards, objects of worship and daily living with which man is to fulfill his heaven-decreed duty.

The other viewpoint is that of social institutions as man-made products, ever changing and evolving into new forms, each of which may or may not constitute a more stately mansion than the last, but in any case is meant to serve man in his ever expanding universe. Helen Lamb's paper on the merchant views him and his social function in such an evolutionary setting. She takes relatively little account of Hindu traditional theory of the merchant class and instead views the merchant with considerable detachment, somewhat as an experimenter observes animals in a maze learning new ways to circumvent the ever varying complications interposed between them and the apples which are their goals.

John Hitchcock, in treating the warriors, describes the plight of one living in modern India who would like to deal with life from the first point of view, but alas, decayed gentleman that he is, must needs let the eternal verities go and clutch at any new ad hoc means he can discover merely to maintain his existence.

What do these papers, taken as a group, teach us about class and cultural traditions in India? To what degree are the authors' remarks valid in the light of evidence in the literature? Can we fuse these papers and give them a setting and a generalized interpretation that will be suggestive today?

The earliest picture we can draw of society in India is based upon the Rig-veda—unfortunately, we can do little or nothing in describing the still earlier society of the Indus Valley. In the Rig-veda, as everyone knows, society was sharply divided between Aryan and non-Aryan. Aryan society is presented there as composed of three classes—the priest or Brahman, the warrior or nobility, and the commons or folk—just the three classes that have been treated in our papers. There was also a non-Aryan segment of Vedic society, the serfs, which has not been treated here, though their post-Vedic descendants have been mentioned often.

In the Rig-veda, which is a collection of hymns composed chiefly by professional priests for use in ceremonies conducted by them, there is preserved a myth (Rig-veda 10.90) about these four classes, which, as might be expected of the priestly author, affirms the supremacy of the priests. All four classes came into existence at the time of creation, when the gods dealt with the primeval world substance which was then only a conglomerate mass. This was conceived as having the form of a human being, and this the gods sacrificed and divided. From that being's mouth came the priest; from his arms came the warrior; from his loins the commons; and from his feet the serfs.

It is not just a hierarchical coincidence that the Brahman or priest as the highest class—in the Brahmans' own estimation—came from the cosmic being's mouth, and that the next highest class, the warrior, was born on the next lower physical level, that is, sprang from his arms. The mouth and the arms are symbolic of the functions of these two groups in Vedic man's view of society. The mouth as the organ of speech has a special power. For sound has in itself a metaphysical power. The hymns of the Rig-veda as recited by the trained priest have such power, because they consist of the right sounds in the right combinations (words—and, of course, these are Sanskrit words) uttered in the right sequence and with the right intonation; and when they are so recited and accompanied by the right manual acts, they are irresistible. They are sure to accomplish the reciter's purpose. Demons and gods are subject to their power. Still more, at the time of creation, which is several times represented as having been effected by the gods or a supreme god at the first sacrifice, the prototype of all sacrifices, the gods or the supreme god formulated the idea and then uttered the names of creatures, whereupon those creatures came into existence (Rig-veda 10.82; 10.125). Sound is personified as Vāc 'speech,' a goddess, to whom in some Rigvedic hymns all power is ascribed (10.125; 10.71). The Brahman, as custodian and user of potent sound, that is, the sound of the Veda, is, by his own claim, the most powerful class of society. I think I may add that, to the Brahman of all periods, the idea of the cosmic power of sound was not just a theory. He has acted, or at least written, throughout Hindu history as though he believed it to be a fact. The tradition of which Kramrisch and Ingalls speak was put into literary form by the Brahman, and when it was so put, it was regarded as sacred, valid and binding, to be honored and observed by men, especially when the Brahman, or his fellows or successors, felt that the utterances were inspired, that is, reproduced the eternally potent collection and arrangement of sounds that constitute an authoritative text.

The Brahman was then the final authority on earth, or so he would have had us believe, and his whole point of view was authoritarian and traditional. Even when a Brahman expressed a new philosophical concept, he tried to convince himself and his hearers that it really was nothing new, that the old texts, properly understood, meant just what he was teaching, and that he had not broken with tradition but rather was voicing or fulfilling it.

Not all of Hindu society, even in Vedic times, acted as though it accepted the Brahman's view of himself. The warrior, we may infer, was not always submissive to Brahman pretensions. He had the temporal power, the army, and he owned the land. As king, he was in control; as nobility, he shared control with the king, supported the king, or possibly sought rulership for himself by usurpation. A good deal has been written on the subject of rivalry between priest and warrior in ancient India. Little direct data exist on it in Vedic texts themselves, but much is expressed there by allusion or implication.

As for the commons, the people, the Vedic texts treat them with only bare civility, having little to say about them, being devoted instead to the affairs of the aristocracy, which consisted of the warrior class and the priesthood. And the non-Aryan serfs are, of course, denied the privileges accorded even to the Aryan commons.

In the Rig-veda the relations of the classes of society to one another are not defined, but in the later Vedic texts, there is at least one passage where the relations and functions of priest, commons, and serf to the warrior, this time as king, are described. This is in the Aitareya Brāhmaṇa vii.29. There it is said that the Brahman, or priest, is a receiver of gifts (*ādāyī*), a drinker of the sacrificial soma (*āpāyī*), and a seeker of food (*āvasāyī*), and liable to removal at will (*yathākāmaprayāpyaḥ*). That is, he performs the sacrifice for the king, in return for which he is to receive a fee, and if his services do not produce results satisfactory to the king, his employer, he may be discharged. The commoner (Vaiśya), the text goes on to say, is tributary to another (*anyasya balīkṛt*), that is, to the king; is to be lived on by another (*anyasyādyaḥ*); and is to be oppressed at will (*yathakāmajyeyaḥ*). This means that the king may assess taxes against him at his pleasure. The serf (Śūdra) is the servant of another (*anyasya preṣyaḥ*), to be expelled at will (*kāmotthāpyaḥ*), and to be slain at pleasure (*yathākāmavadhyaḥ*). The free classes of priest and commoner must submit to the warrior and serve him, the one by giving him advice, the other in return for the protection that lets him make money. The case for unlimited and arbitrary levies upon the merchant, high taxation of business in modern terms, can be illustrated abundantly in post-Vedic literature such as the epic[1] and others, down to the conduct of Indian princes in modern times. Princes regarded this as their prerogative, and some years back one such ruler complained rather bitterly to me that under British overlordship he could not exercise this traditional right on a wealthy merchant subject.

It is the traditional Hindu view of class and caste that each caste has its own function and should keep to it. In this way the cosmos operates most smoothly. The warrior's duty is to protect, the priest's to advise, the commons' to pay the bill. But it is just as certainly a fact that at no period was there ever any such sharp differentiation. All four papers have in one way or another illustrated that fact. In a world where most people must get a living by their labor, it has been inevitable in India, as elsewhere, that a son should often undertake a profession or craft different from his father's. Further, a member of one group, impressed with the importance of his own profession, may view it not as just a member of a team of professions of equal importance, all cooperating for the public good, but rather as the dominant profession, with an importance beyond that of any other—a sort of monarch among the professions. Thus in a Vedic text (Aitareya Brāhmaṇa viii.25) the king's priest, who is the king's adviser and his representative at the great sacrifices and the director of the whole sacrificial performance, is called outright *rāṣṭragopa* 'protector of the realm' because he preserves both the king and the kingdom by means of his spells and rites. He appears there not merely as exercising the priestly duty of interpreting the divine will and advising the king, but also as arrogating to himself the warrior's prime duty of giving protection. So, too, the Arthaśāstra in one of its early sections (II.7) makes the point that the most important of the three ends of worldly life is not religion (*dharma*), or pleasure (*kāma*), but wealth, the public economy (*artha*), for all the others depend upon it—a sentiment which sounds very modern.

Even in the performance of his class function, a member of one group may seem to have the motivation of another. The Vedic priest seeking his fee is, as Maurice Bloomfield pointed out,[2] responsible for a pretty substantial section of Vedic poetic composition. His fees are represented as very large; for example, the sage Yājñavalkya, after his conversations with King Janaka, as reported in the *Bṛhad Āraṇyaka Upaniṣad*, must have gone home with tens of thousands of cows. And the Brahman was very jealous of his property rights; there are hymns in the Atharva Veda (5.18; 5.19; 12.4; 12.5) invoking the direst of curses upon anyone trepassing upon those rights. If the literature is at all to be relied upon in this area, there must have been a good many successful Brahmans who had to manage large landed estates, like warrior landholders and prosperous Vaiśya cultivators. Assumption of temporal power and acquisition of material wealth by Brahmans may well have been part of the complex of reasons for the popularity which Buddhism and Jainism, which were anti-Brahmanic, won among noble landholders and wealthy urban merchants in Magadha, a development which Ingalls and Lamb have mentioned.

The phenomenon of the old aristocracy in decay, which Hitchcock describes, is probably age-old. It is an aspect of the constant shifting in class composition and caste hierarchy. As far back as the late Vedic period, it is possible to observe assimilation of Vaiśya and Śūdra, Aryan commonalty and non-Aryan serf. The overlapping of crafts is also an ancient phenomenon. We can see in successive strata of literature the shift in position of the chariot makers, for example, and Kramrisch has told us of craftsmen whose hands were always considered pure when they were assisting in the ceremonies, but who were in other circumstances not to be touched by Brahmans.

As classes shift in occupation, they must incur new responsibilities. When a Brahman or a warrior becomes an agriculturist, he has to start paying taxes, like the Vaiśya, for whom the term "taxpayer" (*karada*) is a standing epithet. The new obligation is one of the marks of the decayed aristocrat's degradation.

In a society like that of India today, where the Vaiśya is supreme, the Brahman and the Kṣatriya seem likely to lose more and more of their old status, to be increasingly assimilated to the Vaiśya and the Śūdra, and to live more and more by their wits rather than by their position. This is not a happy thought for some of them, who see in this degenerate Kali age the prospect of even further degeneration, when the Śūdra, largely ignored in our review, will dominate society, and the traditional three upper classes will be downgraded to his level. The still further decline of society to the level of the Fifths is an appalling prospect which no traditionally minded Brahman has yet mentioned to me.

There is another point which I wish to suggest. Kramrisch has indicated the noble origin of the crafts in the Hindu view. Viśvakarman, celebrated in various Vedic hymns (Rig-veda 10.81; 10.82) as the great artificer who created the material world, the gods, and man, who is himself the Absolute, invented these crafts. In Jainism, the first Savior of our era invented them, billions of billions of years ago, when the world in the progressive decline from the primordial golden age needed these crafts to make men's lives more tolerable, just as he became the first king and invented laws.

It is a general Indian view that all the crafts, as Kramrisch has pointed out, are part of the pattern of life, just as are religious rites and the functions of rulership. Nothing known to man or practiced by him exists, in the Hindu view, without necessity. Even the thief operates under divine sanction and the prostitute too has a duty to perform, to make a complete world, though there is also a need for police and judges to keep the thief and the prostitute within bounds. All the many groups of society are viewed as parts of a vast and complicated machine in which all parts are interdependent and must mesh for perfect operation. How much will such a view influence the creation of India's new society? Does it show itself, for example, in the field of commerce and banking, with which Lamb has been dealing? I have no information with which to answer my question.

But I do have a comment, a kind of caution. Back at the beginning of the nineteenth century, when India was learning about our Western world, there were Europeans, like Macaulay, and Indians, like Ram Mohan Roy (1774-1833) who expected the traditional order to disappear before a Western order. It did not disappear, though it changed a good deal. I would think it possible that the old order still has a good deal of life in it. Just as in the past it has always been changing, showing dynamic qualities, proving its adaptability, so today it may still be letting down new airroots from sound old branches.

In all the new developments of that rapidly changing nation, I suspect that there are vital elements, subtly present, influencing the character of the new nation. I should like to see us discover, by some process of investigation, just what is the central and unchanging element in the ancient, shining civilization of India that is being projected into new forms today. It does not, I think, consist of religious rites, for these are altering. Nor does it lie in art forms; a modern, yet still Indian, art is now flourishing. Neither is it a specific social structure, for many features of caste and family are disappearing. All these things change. Yet one—or at least I—cannot help feeling that India is still characteristically Indian and not anything else. Perhaps the enduring element, which has animated that civilization for so long, is tolerance, a tolerance of the new, the unusual, and the different, a capacity to reshape itself in changing conditions, a quickness of comprehension and a willingness to seek for new solutions to new problems. Certainly her history from period to period has revealed this kind of flexibility. She can keep the old, if it is useful, because she can also uncomplainingly give up the old, when it is no longer useful. She does not have to experience a violent conversion, get rid of all her past at once, and suddenly become something different. She can instead progress by successive steps, even by steps taken in quick succession, as at present. She can always be adapting herself, without experiencing a devastating feeling of guilt in doing so. Or so, at least, I surmise.

NOTES

[1] E. W. Hopkins, *Position of the Ruling Caste.*
[2] *Religion of the Veda* (New York, 1908).

University of Pennsylvania
Philadelphia, Pennsylvania

THE VAHĪVANCĀ BĀROṬS OF GUJARAT: A CASTE OF GENEALOGISTS AND MYTHOGRAPHERS

By A. M. Shah and R. G. Shroff

FOREWORD

By

M. N. Srinivas

It is well-known that during the last twenty years much progress has been made in the structural analysis of "segmentary" societies in Africa and elsewhere. A significant conclusion which has emerged from this research is that genealogies, as remembered by the people who are being investigated by the field anthropologist, do not always provide accurate accounts of actual descent. More specifically, in those segmentary societies which are non-literate, genealogies have been known to respond to the dynamics of clan and of lineage structure; there is, for instance, the process of "telescoping" by which generations drop out regularly to give fixity of form to the genealogical structure. It enables the various segments of the lineage or clan to maintain the required structural distance between each other, and this, in turn, regulates their mutual relations. "Telescoping" occurs at the remoter generation levels, beyond the reach of the memory of even the old people.[1]

The question then arises, "What happens in segmentary societies in which written records of genealogies are kept?" Prima facie, *it would appear that the existence of such genealogies would make alterations difficult if not impossible.*

The existence of a caste of genealogists and mythographers variously known as Bhāṭs, Cāraṇs, Vahīvancā Bāroṭs etc., over the whole of north India provides us with a crucial situation in which this problem can be studied. Shri Shah and Shroff make it clear that the genealogies recorded by the Bāroṭs of central Gujarat are accurate up to a particular genealogical level, and beyond it they are unclear. This lack of clarity at particular levels makes it possible to forge links between a lineage and the clan of which it claims to be a part, and between the clan and the caste to which it claims to belong. The Bāroṭs, in their role as recorders of genealogies and of other data, are acting as historians. They are also something else—they provide a lineage or caste with written material which enables it to raise itself in the hierarchy as well as symbolizes the fact that it has arrived in the world. The Bāroṭs, however, seem to be able to help only those castes which want to pass for Rājpūts. They do not seem to be able to help castes which aspire to become Baniyās (Vaiśyas) or Brahmans. These two castes, which are literate as well as highly Sanskritized in their way of life, do not patronize Bāroṭs. It is usual for a Brahman or Baniyā caste in Gujarat to have a myth about its origin recorded in a caste purāṇa. *The caste* purāṇas *have not been studied as yet. Shri Shah and Shroff indicate that there is a connection between the existence of a written* purāṇa *for a caste and its failure to patronize Bāroṭs. This matter needs to be investigated further.*

It is interesting to note in this connection that the Pāṭidārs of central Gujarat, who until recently claimed to be Rājpūts (Kṣatriyas), now claim to be Baniyās (Vaiśyas), and this change in their collective ambition is accompanied by an increasing disinclination to patronize Bāroṭs. In Gujarat the Baniyā caste enjoys prestige, and this is the reason why Pāṭidārs want to pass for Baniyās even though according to the Varṇa-scheme, Kṣatriyas are higher than Vaiśyas.

The Bāroṭs, in the course of their work, bring local lineages and clans into contact with regional if not all-India myths and history. The lineages and clans concerned desire to raise themselves in the local hierarchy, and the history and myths recorded in the books of the Bāroṭs help them in their ascent. This results in linking the myth and history intimately with the people concerned. The Bāroṭs thus bring the Little and Great Tradition together. They also stimulate the Sanskritization of the way of life of the people they minister to.

It is essential to realize that the Bāroṭ who enables members of other castes to push themselves up in the hierarchy, is himself part of the caste system. And he has modelled himself on his most important patron, the Rājpūt.

The bardic castes of north India cover a vast stretch of territory, and an immense quantity of information about genealogies and other matters are to be found in their books. One of the Bāroṭs of Baroda has literally a roomful of books with him. It was not our aim, however, to bring the data recorded by Bāroṭs to light. We went to the Bāroṭs only in order to secure data having historical depth to supplement the data which the field anthropologist usually gathered, in the hope that this would enable us to pose a new set of problems, synchronic as well as diachronic. It was decided, therefore, to carry out a field study of a multicaste village in central Gujarat after ascertaining that some, at least, of these castes patronized Bāroṭs. The investigators assiduously cultivated the Bāroṭs, and they were gradually drawn into a study of the Bāroṭs themselves. They became deeply interested in the Bāroṭ's attitude to his books and patrons, and in his mode of working. The present paper is concerned only with this aspect of the total study.

The authors of the paper point out that the Bāroṭs are extremely secretive about their books, and that they are suspicious of people who want to know what is in them. The Bāroṭs are used to parting with information recorded in their books only to their patrons, and not to outsiders. They fear that they may be driven out of business by unscrupulous rivals, and the books are still an important source of a Bāroṭ's income. In recent years they have been approached by a few scholars, and this has led some Bāroṭs to think that their books are worth even more than they thought they were.

The understandable doubts and hesitations of the Bāroṭs slowed down the progress of our inquiry. But gradually Shri Shah and Shroff were able to win the confidence of a few Bāroṭs who gave them much valuable help—they showed a few of their books, and also introduced Shri Shah and Shroff to other Bāroṭs. It may be mentioned here that the work of the inquiry was divided in such a way that Shri Shroff concentrated on the Bāroṭs while Shri Shah conducted the field study of the village. Shri Shah also planned the inquiry at at every stage, and it is he who drafted this paper.

It is indeed surprising that though the existence of castes of genealogists and mythographers has been known since the publication of James Tod's famous Annals and Antiquities of Rajast'han *(1829-1832), statements have been made ad nauseum by European observers of Indian life that Indians do not have any sense of history. This myth has obtained such wide currency that even Indian intellectuals subscribe to it. It is hoped that the publication of this paper will help in destroying it though myths die hard.*

I would like to thank Robert Redfield and Milton Singer, of the Department of Anthropology of the University of Chicago, for a generous grant which enabled the Department of Sociology of the M. S. *University, Baroda, to undertake the inquiry. I would also like to thank Shrimati Hansa Mehta, Vice-Chancellor of the M. S. University of Baroda, for advice and help at every stage, and my colleague and friend, I. P. Desai, for supervising the inquiry during my absence from Baroda in 1956-57.*

A special word of thanks is due to the Bāroṭs who, once they were convinced of our bona fides, *allowed us to copy from their books, gave us much other information, and also put us on to other helpful Bāroṭs. Foremost among them was Shri Banusinh F. Barot without whose help and cooperation we would not have made headway with the Bāroṭs. Other Bāroṭs who have helped us in various ways are Shri Maheschandra M. Barot, B.A., M.S.U.; Shri Jaswantsinh K. Barot, B.A., LL.B.; and Shri Mahipatsinh M. Barot, and Sabursinh J. Barot. We are indebted to every one of them.*

THE Vahīvancā Bāroṭs are one of eighteen or more bardic castes in Gujarat. The *Bombay Gazetteer*[2] mentions the following: Bhāṭs, Cāraṇs, Vahīvancās, Atits, Devaḷvakiyās, Bhāṇḍs, Kāpḍīs, Lāvaṇiyās, Māgaṇs, Nagārīs, Pālimagās, Rāṇimagās, Tūrīs and Ḍhāḍhīs. Zazerchand Meghani[3] mentions a few more: Udiyās, Mīrs, Motisarās and Rāvaḷs. These castes may be classified into those who keep records and those who do not. Only the Vahīvancās and Rāvaḷs, from the eighteen castes listed above, keep records. Among those who do not keep records, all, except Bhāṭs and Cāraṇs, are regarded as mendicants of a sort. This paper will be concerned mainly with the four nonmendicant castes, Vahīvancās, Rāvaḷs, Bhāṭs and Cāraṇs.

We shall begin by considering the Bhāṭs and Cāraṇs, who do not keep records. The main themes of bardic ballads are battles, warriors and kings. These ballads have to conform to a prosody, meter, and rhyme which are peculiar to themselves. To be fully appreciated, the ballads have to be heard as sung by a Bhāṭ or Cāraṇ with suitable gestures and modulations of voice. The ballad which is sung for a regular patron gives the history of his lineage and traces its genealogy. Hindu Rājās and chieftains used to have a bard in their courts, who attended them on public occasions and ceremonies; he loudly sounded the Rājā's praises and proclaimed his many high sounding titles. Bhāṭs and Cāraṇs were also used to cheer the troops with their songs, and to compose verses defaming or chastising the enemy. Besides these, they have also composed poems about love and death, about gods and goddesses, and about nature. Some Bhāṭs and Cāraṇs have written long poems called *rāsos*, and some have rendered the *purāṇas* and epics into ballads. The *duhās* or couplets are considered a speciality of bardic poetry. The Bhāṭs and Cāraṇs are also professional story tellers. Several of their stories have been printed, but they lose much of their charm when reduced to writing. The plot of the story may be simple and brief, but the bard in telling it stretches it out to last two or three nights.

Although Bhāṭs and Cāraṇs follow the same occupation, they follow two different traditions in their poetry. Cāraṇs compose their poetry in a dialect known as Ḍingaḷ.[4] This is a poetic dialect of Western Rājasthānī evolved by Cāraṇs, and not used for ordinary purposes. On the other hand, Bhāṭs compose their poetry in a well-known dialect of Hindi called Braj Bhāṣā. There has always been rivalry between the two traditions, and the poetry of the Bhāṭs is regarded as a higher form than that of the Cāraṇs.[5]

Formerly, a Bhāṭ or Cāraṇ was called a Devīputra, i.e., the son of a goddess. This term needs to be understood in the context of the cult of the *mātā* or mother-goddess in Gujarat. The cult has two levels, the Sanskritic and non-Sanskritic. It is known as the Śakti cult at the Sanskritic level, which is elaborated in many Sanskrit works beginning with the sixth and seventh centuries A.D.[6] The mode of worship at the Sanskritic level corresponds more or less to those texts. The two modes of worship are, however, not mutually exclusive. The proportion of the two modes in the worship of *mātās* by a group of devotees varies with the level of Sanskritization achieved by them.

The names of *mātās* worshipped by the Sanskritic mode are usually Sanskritic. The names of so-called non-Sanskritic *mātās* are, however, often corrupt forms of Sanskritic names. And sometimes a *mātā* who has not only a non-Sanskritic name but is also worshipped in the non-Sanskritic mode, comes to be worshipped in the Sanskritic mode, and also acquires a Sanskritic name in the course of time. While the Sanskritic *mātās* have a Gujarat-wide spread, and some of them have an all-India spread, only a small number of non-Sanskritic *mātās*, such as Khoḍiyār, Śikotār, Meladī and Haḍakvāi, have a Gujarat-wide spread. A large number of non-Sanskritic *mātās* are named after villages, towns, streets and castes, and after women who commited self-sacrifice. Some *mātās* perform specific functions. For instance, Śitalā is the *mātā* of smallpox; Randel, the *mātā* of fertility; and Haḍakvāi, the *mātā* of hydrophobia. But to a large number of *mātās*, Sanskritic as well as non-Sanskritic, no specific function is attributed, and such a *mātā* may be a patron deity of several castes, clans, lineages, *gotras*, families, villages, fields, towns, and streets.

Although a Hindu worships several gods and goddesses, he tends to extol one deity above all the others. One who extols *mātās* above all other gods and goddesses may be called a *mātā* worshipper. Several castes in Gujarat are *mātā* worshippers. They are also called Devī or Śakti worshippers. Among them, the deity not only of the caste but also of almost every clan, *gotra*, lineage and family, is a *mātā*. Besides these, they also worship the *mātās* performing specific functions, and the patron *mātās* of their village, field, town and street. Bhāṭs and Cāraṇs were called Devīputras because they were *mātā* or Devī worshippers, the former at the Sanskritic, and the latter at the non-Sanskritic level. At the Sanskritic level, a *mātā* worshipper looks upon the different *mātās* as different manifestations of Śakti 'energy,' which is the personification of the female principle in the creation of the universe.[7] The same idea is expressed in different words at the non-Sanskritic level: "The different *mātās* are manifestations of a single *Mātā*, the mother of all creation." The term "Devīputra" is used in this sense, and not in reference to any specific *mātā*.

A distinction is made between the "clean" and the "unclean" mode in the worship of *mātās*. The non-Sanskritic mode is "unclean" because it usually includes the practice of animal sacrifice and the use of liquor. There is also an "unclean" element in the

Sanskritic mode because of the influence of the five m's, namely, *māṃsa* 'flesh,' *matsya* 'fish,' *madya* 'wine,' *maithuna* 'copulation' and *mudrā* 'mystical finger signs,' advocated by the Left-hand Path (*Vāmācārī*) of the Śakti cult.[8] Animal sacrifice was common about fifty years ago at Ambāji, Bahucarājī and Pāvāgaḍh, principal seats of the three most widely worshipped Sanskritic *mātās* in Gujarat, viz., Ambā, Bahucarā, and Kālikā, respectively. On account of the influence of Vaiṣṇavism and Jainism in Gujarat, however, only a few individuals nowadays use wine or flesh in *mātā* worship at the Sanskritic level, and more and more people are avoiding them at the non-Sanskritic level. Orthodox Vaiṣṇavas and Jains consider the entire cult of *mātā* or Śakti as "unclean," because there are "unclean" elements in the latter at both the Sanskritic and the non-Sanskritic levels, and also because, in the Śakti cult, *mātās* are considered to be manifestations of Śiva's wife, Pārvatī. The Vaiṣṇavas have no objection, however, to the worship of several consorts of Viṣṇu and Kṛṣṇa. Several Bhāṭs and Cāraṇs have come under the influence of Vaiṣṇavism, and have ceased to be *mātā* worshippers.

The person of a Bhāṭ or Cāraṇ was considered sacred because of his position as a Devīputra. This belief was the basis of several sanctions at the disposal of Bhāṭs and Cāraṇs. The Bhāṭs and Cāraṇs practiced *trāgu*. This practice consisted in shedding one's own blood or the blood of some member of one's family, and in calling down the vengeance of heaven upon the offender whose obstinacy necessitated the sacrifice. A Bhāṭ or Cāraṇ always carried a dagger with him. There was a widespread belief that the shedding of the blood of a Bhāṭ or Cāraṇ brought ruin on the person responsible for it. If he was murdered, or if he died as a result of *trāgu*, his ghost was greatly feared. It was believed about Cāraṇ women that those who sacrified themselves became *mātās*. There are a number of such non-Sanskritic *mātās* in North Gujarat and Saurashtra. There is also a widespread belief that Bahucarā, one of the three most important Sanskritic *mātās* in Gujarat, was a Cāraṇ woman who cut off her breasts when attacked by members of the Koḷī caste. Moreover, a Bhāṭ's or Cāraṇ's wrath was held to be as destructive as the wrath of a *mātā*. His curse and satire were also greatly feared.

The sanctions at their disposal enabled Bhāṭs and Cāraṇs to perform several important functions. They used to stand as surety (*jamān*). When two parties entered into an agreement, one would ask the other to offer a Bhāṭ or a Cāraṇ as surety. Each party feared that if he did not carry out the agreement, he would incur the wrath of his Bhāṭ or Cāraṇ and lead him to commit *trāgu*. The Bhāṭ or Cāraṇ was paid by the party for whom he stood as surety. The Bhāṭs and Cāraṇs used to stand as sureties in transactions referring to the transfer of property, rent, trade and money. They offered themselves as sureties for the good behavior of feudatories, zamindars and village headmen. They also became sureties for treaties between chiefs, and the British accepted Bhāṭs and Cāraṇs as sureties in some of their early treaties with the chiefs of Saurashtra.[9] Since the sixteenth century, if not earlier, governments have recognized Bhāṭs as sureties for the collection of land revenue.[10] From the later Mogul to the early British period, land revenue was collected from cultivators through intermediaries. The intermediaries entered into an agreement with the government to remit a particular sum of revenue irrespective of what they collected from the cultivators. The system of Bhāṭ and Cāraṇ surety was prevalent in such agreements until 1816.[11]

Bhāṭs and Cāraṇs also acted as guides for travellers and carriers of goods. A Bhāṭ or

Cāraṇ would commit *trāgu* if anyone tried to rob him or his party. In Rajputana, Cāraṇs were themselves professional carriers of goods.[12] Near the entrance of almost every village in Saurashtra stand guardian stones, or *pāḷiyās*, which were set up to perpetuate the memory of Cāraṇ men and women who performed *trāgu* to prevent robbers from carrying off the cattle of the village.[13] Thus even robbers came under the religious sanctions of Bhāṭs and Cāraṇs.

Bhāṭs and Cāraṇs had great influence with Rājpūts. Tod tells us that the Rājpūts had more respect for bards than for Brahmans. He remarks, "These chroniclers dare utter truths, sometimes most unpalatable to their masters. Many a resolution has sunk under the lash of their satire. The *viṣ* or poison of the bard is more dreaded by the Rājpūt than the steel of the foe."[14]

As mentioned above, the system of Bhāṭ or Cāraṇ surety in revenue collection was discontinued by the British in 1816. The safer means of travel and the British system of courts also made it useless to have a Bhāṭ's or Cāraṇ's surety in travel or in transactions referring to the transfer of property, rent, trade or money. The British, in addition, began trying cases of *trāgu* as cases of murder from 1808, although the full punishment for murder was not awarded until 1872.[15] At the same time, several Bhāṭs and Cāraṇs ceased to be *mātā* worshippers, and therefore lost their position as Devīputras. Thus the Bhāṭs and Cāraṇs lost the sanctions at their disposal, and their power consequently weakened. The power of their most important patrons, the Rājpūt and Koḷī chiefs, was also greatly reduced under British rule. In the Westernized sections of society new forms of entertainment further reduced the appeal of ballads and stories. The Vahīvancās have maintained the bardic tradition of reciting ballads and telling stories, but the Bhāṭs and Cāraṇs themselves, except a few Cāraṇs of Saurashtra, have left their traditional occupation. They consider the bardic occupation as a sort of begging, to be followed by the mendicant castes mentioned earlier. The Bhāṭs and Cāraṇs have now taken to other occupations. There is, however, a difference between Bhāṭs and Cāraṇs. Bhāṭs are more urbanized, and on the whole, richer than Cāraṇs. They are also more Sanskritized than the Cāraṇs. Recently, they adopted some customs of the Brahmans, and a Brahmanic caste appellation, Brahmabhaṭṭ.

The genealogical and historical records kept by bardic castes have been studied by several scholars. L. P. Tessitori, an Italian philologist, described a few bardic records of Rajasthan in the *Descriptive Catalogues of Bardic and Historical Manuscripts* published in the 1920s.[16] James Tod, the author of *Annals and Antiquities of Rajast'han* (1829)[17] and Alexander Kinloch Forbes, the author of *Rāsmālā or Hindu Annals of the Province of Goozerat* (1856)[18] used the bardic records as a source of regional history. A descriptive catalogue of bardic manuscripts collected by Forbes has also been published.[19] In recent years, D. K. Shastri has tried to evaluate the bardic traditions as historical sources in his *Medieval Rājput History of Gujarat*.[20] Our main aim is to make a study of Vahīvancās from the sociological point of view, and in this task we accept the help of the historian, the linguist, and the student of bardic literature.

The Vahīvancās of Gujarat are divided into three endogamous groups, those of central Gujarat, of north Gujarat, and of Saurashtra. South Gujarat has no Vahīvancās. We have limited ourselves to Vahīvancās of central Gujarat, most of whom live in three towns, Baroda, Ahmedabad, and Dholka. We do not have much information about the Rāvaḷs, who live in Saurashtra. Recently, the Turīs, the bards of the Untouchables, have also started keeping records, but we do not have any information about them. We shall, however, have to refer to the Vahīvancās of other regions occasionally. Although the Vahīvancās of one region have most of their patrons (*yajmāns*) in the same region, they have also some patrons in other regions. In other words, each region is served not only by its own Vahīvancās but also by those of other regions. Some Vahīvancās of Gujarat also have patrons in Madhya Bharat, Rajasthan, and Khāndesh. Similarly, some Vahīvancās of Rajasthan have patrons in Gujarat. Moreover, a Vahīvancā of one group may serve as a clerk with a Vahīvancā of another group. There is also rivalry between Vahīvancās of different regions.

Literally, a Vahīvancā is one who reads a *vahī*. The word *vahī* has three meanings: a book of genealogy, an account book, and a book in general.[21] It is, however, mostly used in the first two senses. The reason seems to be that a book of a particular size and binding is used almost exclusively by Vahīvancās for writing genealogies, and by the merchants of Gujarat for the traditional system of bookkeeping. This book is from two to three feet long, and six to twelve inches broad. It is bound by piercing the pages at one end. The book is folded in the middle, and tied together by a cord. It is significant that in a manuscript dated *Saṃvat* 1466 (A.D. 1410), the word *vahī* is mentioned along with *pothī*, a book of loose and long leaves, and *pāṭi*, a slate, in a list of the tools of learning (*jñānopakaraṇas*).[22] Therefore, it seems that the word *vahī* formerly meant a book of a special size and binding, and the word acquired the other two meanings because of its use for writing accounts and genealogies. A man whose occupation was to read such a book of genealogy came to be known as a Vahīvancā.

Like Bhāṭs and Cāraṇs, the Vahīvancās also tell stories and recite bardic poetry. A few of them occasionally compose bardic poems. The Vahīvancās are also *mātā* worshippers, and are therefore called Devīputras. Although no Vahīvancā seems to have stood as surety, the Vahīvancās talk about a few ancestors who performed *trāgu*. A Vahīvancā's curse was also considered to be effective. A Vahīvancā woman of Ahmedabad is believed to have become a *mātā*. There is a strong tradition among both Bhāṭs and Vahīvancās that the Vahīvancās were formerly included among the Bhāṭs, and that, as is frequently the case in caste, they left the main group to form a separate caste on the basis of their occupation. Some facts support this tradition. The Vahīvancās follow the same tradition as the Bhāṭs in composing and singing poetry. The names of the streets in which the Vahīvancās live are still called Bhāṭ Wāḍās. The term "Bāroṭ" is used both for Bhāṭs and Vahīvancās. It seems that "Bāroṭ" was originally an honorific title used for both these castes, and was later adopted by them as a caste appellation. The honorific title used for a Cāraṇ is different—it is "Gaḍhvi." It is significant that no clear distinction is made between Bhāṭs and Vahīvancās in early ethnographic accounts.[23] These works convey the impression that there was no clear distinction between the literate and nonliterate Bhāṭs. Even today the Bhāṭs of some villages are becoming genealogists and historians. They start by working as clerks with Vahīvancās, and thanks to the institution of hypergamy, become incorporated into the latter caste. Even though they change their occupation, they do not change the caste appellation, Brahmabhaṭṭ, for some time. Just as Bhāṭs have become Vahīvancās, Cāraṇs have become Rāvaḷs.

The Vahīvancās' genealogical records are built up by a process of periodical recording. The process starts when a Vahīvancā decides to accept a lineage group in a village as his patron. He goes to the latter's village and takes down the genealogy as known by the members of the lineage. He also takes information from other villagers having special genealogical knowledge. The older informants are more useful than the young. The Vahīvancā enters as many of the following details as are remembered about each man, from the first known ancestor to the present generation: 1) the name of the man and his wife, and of father, clan, lineage and village; 2) if the man has two wives it is mentioned who is the senior, and who the junior; 3) the names of sons and daughters in chronological order; 4) if the man has two wives, the offspring by each are mentioned separately and in chronological order; 5) all the above details are mentioned for married sons; 6) if the daughters are married, the names of the husband of each daughter and of his father, clan, lineage and village, are mentioned. The memory about these details becomes hazy as an informant goes back in time. Only the names of male ancestors are remembered for the first few generations. A Vahīvancā is able to take down a genealogy of at least five to seven generations in this way. We have not yet come across a person who remembers his genealogy beyond the seventh generation, among the literate or nonliterate, the landowning or nonlandowning groups. Persons remembering a genealogy beyond the fifth generation are also rare. If the members of the lineage remember facts about the immigration of their ancestors into the village, the Vahīvancā also records them. When the work of recording is over, the head of each family in the lineage gives a gift in cash and kind to the Vahīvancā, and the Vahīvancā mentions it against the patron's name in the book. He also mentions the date of his visit. The Vahīvancās use different symbols for different types of entries, and sometimes symbols of one Vahīvancā differ from those of another.

This is how the Vahīvancā's work as a recordist starts. Afterwards, he goes periodically to the members of the lineage, and each time he records births and marriages which have occurred during the period between two visits. He also records gifts and the date of each visit. His sons inherit his books after his death, and they follow their father's procedure. A Vahīvancā's book thus becomes a record of genealogy of many generations.

A Vahīvancā has in his possession several books, and the living persons in the genealogies in these books at any point of time are his patrons at that time. When a Vahīvancā's son inherits books from his father, he also inherits a particular number of patrons from him. The number of books and patrons, however, does not remain the same. At every generation, each Vahīvancā recruits some patrons and starts a few books, and thus he adds to his collection of books. The old and new books are both then passed on to the next generation. The number of books has thus progressively increased since the Vahīvancās began their occupation, and this process is still going on. Each Vahīvancā has in his possession books started at several different dates.

The depth of a genealogy in a Vahīvancā's book would therefore depend upon the time when a Vahīvancā started recording it. There are, however, two qualifications to this statement: first, the earlier statement that only a few persons remember their genealogy beyond the seventh generation is made on the basis of observation of present behavior. It is probable that formerly many people remembered their genealogies beyond the seventh generation. Second, it has been argued that the Vahīvancās' caste has developed from that of the Bhāṭs. Therefore, in the past, if a lineage patronized a Bhāṭ regularly, the Vahīvancā could record a long genealogy orally preserved by him.

How far back in time does a Vahīvancā's genealogy take us? So far we have not found any genealogy on palm leaves. It is known that paper came to be used for writing books in Gujarat and Rajasthan in the thirteenth century.[24] The huge quantities of paper required for Vahīvancā's books must have been available at a still later date. No Vahīvancā book is written in Sanskrit or Prakrit. The oldest book we have seen so far is dated *Saṃvat* 1796, i.e., A.D. 1740. It is written in Devanāgarī script, and the language is Old Gujarati.

We have, however, come across a genealogy that takes us back to A.D. 1234, although the book in which the genealogy is found is of a later date. It is the genealogy of Rāthoḍ Rājpūts of village Radhvāṇaj, Tālukā Mātar, District Kaira. We have not been able to discover the date of starting the book, but it is clear from the language that the book is not so old as 1234. The genealogy does not seem to be fictitious, because it can be corroborated by an epigraph we have discovered in the village mentioned above. The epigraph was found in the ruins of a small shrine on the outskirts of the village. It is inscribed at the foot of an image, which is so broken and mutilated that it cannot be identified. The epigraph is also broken, but the following words can be read clearly: *Śrī Saṃvat 1290 Śrāvaṇ . . . Rājā Jagdev*. (*Saṃvat* 1290 = A.D. 1234.) The Rāthoḍ Rājpūts of the village are the dominant caste in the village. Until recently they held a large part of the land in this village as well as in a neighboring one, under the Wāṇṭā tenure, which is, as we shall show, an old Rājpūt tenure. The name Jagdev occurs in the Vahīvancā's genealogy at about the same date as in the epigraph, and this Jagdev seems to have assumed the title of Rājā, because, as the book mentions, he was the chief of Radhvāṇaj and a few neighboring villages. We should like to mention that we have not analyzed the book throughly, and our observations should be considered tentative.

If after the starting of a book by a Vahīvancā, a member of the lineage leaves his original village and settles elsewhere, the Vahīvancā goes to his new place of residence for periodical recording. The Vahīvancā also records this change in his book. After migration, the man starts a lineage in his new place of residence. In course of time, such lineages develop in several villages, and the original Vahīvancā's descendants serve them from generation to generation. If the members of a lineage migrate to another region, the Vahīvancā also goes there. This is the reason why some people of a region are served by Vahīvancās of another region. For instance, the Pāṭaṇwāḍiyā Koḷīs of central Gujarat are served by Vahīvancās of north Gujarat, because they migrated from that region. There is a caste of Maṛwārī carpenters in central Gujarat who came from Marwar about one hundred and fifty years ago. They are served by Maṛwārī Vahīvancās. Similarly, a large number of Pāṭidārs of Gujarat have gone and settled in Khandesh. They are served by Vahīvancās of Gujarat. The Vahīvancās also go to their patrons settled in cities such as Bombay, Madras and Nagpur. Recently a few Vahīvancās went to their patrons settled in East Africa.

A large scale migration of patrons from one region to another leads also to the migration of their Vahīvancā. For instance, the Vahīvancā of the Kapoḷ Baniyās has gone to settle in Bombay city along with his patrons. Similarly, a Vahīvancā of Baroda has settled in Surat city. About half a dozen Vahīvancās of Gujarat have settled in Khandesh. There is a widespread tradition that the Vahīvancās of Gujarat themselves came from Rajputana along with their patrons during the great population drift in the Solankī period (942-1245 A.D.).[25]

The Vahīvancā also records how the lineage property has been divided among his present patrons if they so request. Sometimes the documents of sale of land and houses are also recorded by him. He may be asked, besides, to record some outstanding events in the patron's life. Thus some books contain references to men who took part in the Mutiny of 1857. Other events which are thought worthy of record are the death of an ancestor in a skirmish with armed dacoits, the giving of a big feast to one's caste or village, or the conferment of a distinction by a Rājā on an ancestor, or the assumption of *Saṃnyāsa*. There are many references to conversion to Islam. There is a whole caste of Molesalāms, who were converted to Islam during the reign of Mahmūd Begdā (1458-1511). The genealogy clearly shows which ancestor became a Muslim, and which remained a Hindu. The Vahīvancās' books thus supply information about the social institutions and values of the patrons.

To ensure the truth of entries, the Vahīvancā makes them in the presence of all the members of the lineage and a few respectable men of the patron's village. The latter's names are entered as witnesses. An attempt at a false entry by one member of the lineage is usually opposed by all other members and by the witnesses. The Vahīvancā's records therefore have documentary value. The courts give due weight to these records. We find seals of courts and signatures of judges and princes in several books. When a villager wants to present evidence from his Vahīvancā's book, he goes to the Vahīvancā's house and requests him to come to court with his book. The Vahīvancā is suitably rewarded for his troubles. Sometimes a dispute may not be taken to court at all, or if already taken to court, it may be withdrawn, if the parties to the dispute find the Vahīvancā's evidence overwhelming. The Vahīvancā might also advise the disputants to make a compromise on the basis of his book.

The Vahīvancā's genealogy is particularly useful in disputes about the inheritance of property and the succession to hereditary offices or titles. It is frequently used in disputes regarding succession to village headmanship, and, in the former princely states, succession to the throne. If a lineage group owns common property, the income from it is divided according to the genealogy supplied by the Vahīvancā. There were until recently several tenures, such as the Tālukdāri, Wānṭā, Grās, Mewāsi, Narvādārī and Bhāgdārī, under which a large part of the land of a village, and sometimes a whole village, was held jointly by a lineage group. If the members of such a lineage decide to break the joint property into individual shares among the coparceners, the Vahīvancā might record them by request.

Many patrons get a genealogical chart made by their Vahīvancā for ready reference. They are so used to relying on the Vahīvancā's genealogy that they do not care to remember their own genealogy beyond four or five generations. Beyond this, they remember names of the founder of the lineage and a few outstanding ancestors, but they rarely remember the entire genealogy. The Vahīvancā makes the genealogical chart in the same way as anthropologists do, except for the fact he does not have symbols for men, women and marriage. Another peculiarity is that he records only the male members of the lineage. Some people have the chart painted in the form of a tree, the lineage segments being shown by branches stemming from one another. Such a chart may be framed and hung on the wall. In some castes, a person's status is strongly determined by his place in the genealogy of his lineage. This status system plays such a great part in the marriage system of Pāṭidārs that the Pāṭidārs of "high status villages" have their genealogies printed, so that everybody in the caste can refer to them. Some others have also had their genealogies printed.

Until recently, a Vahīvancā willingly gave a genealogical chart when requested by his patrons, because he received some more money. But the abuse of the genealogical chart by some patrons has led to the Vahīvancā's increased sense of secrecy about his tools. Some patrons printed the genealogies which they wheedled out of their Vahīvancā, and subsequently ignored him. This, however, only diminished his importance; it did not destroy it. He mentions in the chart only the names of the male members of the lineage. People have to approach him if they want his help in a law suit or in a marriage dispute. On such an occasion the Vahīvancā not only demands more money, but extracts a promise that he will be properly received in the patron's village. Besides, he is useful to his patrons not merely as a record keeper but also in several other capacities. The worst blow to the Vahīvancā, however, would be for his genealogical chart to fall into the hands of a rival who used it to start a book for the unscrupulous patron. All this has made the Vahīvancās highly suspicious, and our task very difficult.

The Vahīvancā's records are not above suspicion. It is assumed that the presence of all the members of a lineage, and of a few respectable men of the village, at the time of recording, ensures the truth of entries. But this assumption is not always true. Sometimes all of them agree to supress a fact, and the Vahīvancā may have no knowledge of this collusion. For instance, the entire lineage may decide to ask the Vahīvancā to enter false clan names of their wives, or of their daughters' husbands, in order to raise the status of the lineage. Allegations are also made that the Vahīvancās take bribes, and forge the records. It is difficult to inquire into such allegations and give a definite opinion about them. Some of them may be true. But such cases cannot be many, otherwise people would stop patronizing Vahīvancās. Some people also make such allegations because the recorded facts go against their interests.

That part of a Vahīvancā's book which is recorded from time to time may be called factual. There is also another part, which may be called mythical. In the latter, the Vahīvancā records a genealogy beginning with the creator of the universe and going to the first ancestor of the factual genealogy. The factual part has been discussed prior to the mythical, for the sake of analysis. In a Vahīvancā's book, however, the factual part comes after the mythical. In the mythical part, the Vahīvancā's aim is to give the "history" of a lineage, and of its caste and clan, in such a way that the "history" validates the claims of his patrons for a proper status in society.

The mythical part may be divided into two subdivisions. For the first subdivision, the Vahīvancā draws material mainly from the Hindu Epics, the *Rāmāyaṇa* and the *Mahābhārata*, and from the *purāṇas*. In this part are to be found accounts of the origin of the universe, of the four *varṇas*, and of the caste, clan, and *gotra* of the lineage in question. The Vahīvancā tries to show that the structural groups within the caste have their origin in the epics and *purāṇas*. He borrows long genealogies from the epics and *purāṇas* for this purpose. Although the epic and puranic genealogies are not historical genealogies according to modern historical research,[26] they are real genealogies for the Vahīvancās and their patrons. The Vahīvancās claim that the Sūtas, the authors of the epic and puranic genealogies, are none other than Vahīvancās with a different name. Recently, a Vahīvancā published a book of genealogies, in which he quoted passages from the epics and *purāṇas* to show that the Sūtas were Vahīvancās. According to the *Vāyu Purāṇa*, the Sūta was to preserve the genealogies of kings and great men and the traditions about learning or books. The narrator of most of the *purāṇas* is the Sūta. The Sūta is also mentioned in the *Atharvaveda* and *Taittirīya Brāhmaṇa*. In the *Taittirīya Saṃhitā*, he is mentioned among the *ratnas* 'jewels' of the kingdom. There were also Māgadhas and Bandins, who, according to *Anuśāsana*, made a living from speech.[27]

The second subdivision of the mythical part of the genealogy may be called mythico-historical. In this part, the Vahīvancā tries to boost the status of his patrons by associating them fictitiously with some historical figures and events. It has been argued that the Vahīvancās' caste has developed from that of the Bhāṭs, and that the oral genealogies of Bhāṭs might have been recorded by the Vahīvancās in their older books. In the same way, the material for the mythico-historical part of older books seems to have been drawn from the historical traditions preserved orally by the Bhāṭs. This observation is corroborated by a preliminary comparison of the mythico-historical parts of Vahīvancās' books with the specimens of Bhāṭ literature printed in the catalogues of Forbes's and Tessitori's collections.[28] The Vahīvancā draws the material for the mythico-historical part of a new book from the mythico-historical as well as the factual parts of the older books. Sometimes the factual genealogy of a new book is fictitiously joined to the factual genealogy of an old book, and the latter thus becomes a mythico-historical genealogy for the former. In the same way, the factual genealogy of an old book might have been fictitiously joined to an orally remembered factual genealogy. In forging links between the factual genealogies of older books and those of the new, the Vahīvancā makes suitable changes in the former in order to boost the status of his patrons. The Vahīvancā is thus both the preserver and the creator of myths. It is necessary to realize that the Vahīvancā has to make his book acceptable to his patrons as well as to the members of his occupation. He is born a Vahīvancā, heir to the traditions of the caste, and shares their values, and is sensitive to what other Vahīvancās think of him. He therefore preserves the myths. At the same time, he has to satisfy his patrons, and therefore creates myths.

The factual and mythical parts of a book are written in two different ways. When the Vahīvancā starts a book, the manner of writing the mythical part is continuous, one line following the other. In the factual part, the genealogies of the different lineage segments are written on different pages of the book, and space is left on each page for the Vahīvancā to make new entries periodically. The mythical part is also less detailed than the factual. The mythical part may be comprised of any number of generations from a hundred to two hundred. In almost the entire epic or puranic genealogy, and for several generations in the mythico-historical genealogy, the name of only one male heir is mentioned at each generation. Only when we approach the end of the mythico-historical part are the names of all the sons of a man mentioned at each generation, but the genealogy is carried to the next generation only through one son, usually the eldest. The clan and village of the wife of only the descendant in the main line are mentioned. The gifts given to the Vahīvancā by the main heir and his wife, and the date of the Vahīvancā's visit, are also mentioned. Sometimes it is mentioned that the other sons have gone to settle in other villages.

It has been shown how the process of periodical recording of the factual part goes on from generation to generation. In the course of time, the population of some lineage segments grows more than that of others, and some do not leave any descendant at all. As a result, some pages of the book are filled and some remain partly blank. The lineage segments grow into lineages, and new lineages also have their segments.

Each new segment requires a page for periodical recording. The handwriting of some Vahīvancās doing periodical recording may also be clumsy. Therefore, after a few generations, the Vahīvancā begins a new book. While the mythical part of the original book is copied into the new book without any change, the factual part is summarized. Moreover, the summary of the factual part is written along with the mythical part in the new book in a continuous manner, one line following the other. The pages of the new book are reallocated according to the new lineage segments. Thus the mythical and factual parts, which are distinguishable from the manner of their writing in the original book, become indistinguishable in the new book. The date of copying, and the names of the copyist and of the owner of the book, are mentioned in the beginning of the new book.

When the copy has been made, the Vahīvancā does not bother to preserve the old book. Insects devour it, or it is immersed in a river or tank. The precious information is destroyed in order to ensure that it does not fall into a rival's hands. The Vahīvancās have thus a vested interest not only in recording but also in destroying valuable historical data.

The Vahīvancās state that their ancestors periodically transferred the material to new books, and in this process the earlier material became increasingly scanty. But for such summarizing, the books would have become unmanageable. The Vahīvancās argue that the epic and puranic genealogies in their books are also less detailed because of this process.

The nature of the factual as well as the mythical parts of a Vahīvancā's book is different for different castes. For instance, there would be no clan names in the factual part, and no clan history in the mythical part, if there are no clans in a caste. The Vahīvancā's genealogy and history also play different parts in the social life of different castes. It is not possible for us to deal with all the castes served by Vahīvancās, as they are many and spread out over a wide area. We shall deal with three castes, namely, Rājpūts, Koḷīs and Pāṭidārs. We shall begin by considering the Rājpūts, a caste for which we have fuller data than for any other.

Rājpūts are divided into a number of patrilineal clans, some of which are the Jāḍejā, Jhālā, Vāghelā, Solankī, Mahiḍā, Rāṭhoḍ, Parmār, Paḍhiyār, Chāuhāṇ and Gohil. Each clan is exogamous. It is believed that all Rājpūts bearing the same clan name, wherever they live, are ultimately the descendants of the same ancestor. The Vahīvancā's book invariably shows a single ancestor for all the members of a clan. They therefore believe that they are all brothers and sisters, and therefore should not intermarry.

The name Rājpūt became current some time after the tenth century A.D. However, there were several tribes or clans in the seventh century A.D., such as the Pratihār, Guhiloṭ, Chāvoṭaka and Chāhamāna, which came to be known as Rājpūt clans at a later date. Each of these clans had established a dynasty in the seventh century A.D.[29] Afterwards, several other clans rose to power, and established dynasties. Some clans, such as the Jādejā, emerged as Rājpūt clans as late as the fourteenth century.[30] A few clans, such as Pratihāra, Rāṣṭrakuṭa, Parmār, and Caulukya, had established powerful empires. A clan was called Rājpūt only when it had established a dynasty, and the founder of the dynasty was called the founder of the clan.

Some clans are considered to be original, and some to be the offshoots from them. Definite historical evidence is available for only a few. Thus the Vāghelā clan branched off from the Solankī. The Solankī king Kumārpāla's (1144-1174) mother's sister was married to an agnate of Kumārpāla. The latter had a son, Arṇorāja. He was Kumārpāla's vassal, holding a village named Vyāghrapalli (*vyāghra* 'tiger,' *palli* 'village'). His descendents grew powerful and occupied the throne of Pāṭaṇ. They came to be called Vāghelās after the name of their original village.[31] After the formation of a new clan, marriages are allowed between the new and the parent clan.

There were several Rājpūt princely states during the British period. The ruling families of these states claim to be the scions of the old ruling dynasties. Besides, there is a large population of lesser Rājpūts, usually known as Grāsiyās. They also claim genealogical connection with the ancient Rājpūt rulers. A Grāsiyā wears the dress which is worn by the warrior and king, and he wants to be called "Darbār" or princeling. The present Rājpūts' claim to descent from ancient Rājpūt dynasties is to be understood in the context of the Rājpūt political system.

Tod was the first to study the Rājpūt political system.[32] Later, A.C. Lyall wrote an essay on the political institutions of Rājpūt states.[33] Recently, Daniel Thorner has drawn a sketch of the feudal system of Rājpūt states, on the basis of the data of Tod and Lyall.[34] While Tod and Lyall were concerned mostly with Rajasthan, their picture is in many essentials similar to what we learn about Gujarat from *Rāsmālā*[35] and the volumes of the *Bombay Gazetteer*.[36] Finally, Steed's study of a Rājpūt village[37] shows that a Rājpūt village is a Rājpūt state in miniature.

In each Rājpūt state the governing authority rested in the hands of the hereditary chief of the dominant clan. He was at the top of a hierarchy of vassals of higher or lower rank. A vassal was called a Grāsiyā. The word Grāsiyā is derived from *grās* 'mouthful,' which means an estate for subsistence. Every vassal received a *grās* estate from the chief. The position of a vassal in the hierarchy depended upon the size of his *grās* estate. Each *grās* estate was subdivided among its holder's sons at every generation. This process of subdivision extended to an estate of lowest denomination. Hereditary heads of the branches of the ruling clan acted like chiefs in miniature. All vassals were bound to the chief, each through the one above him, by several customary obligations, military, economic and social. Disobedience to a lawful summons, or refusal to pay homage, involved sequestration of the lands.

Most of the vassals were kinsmen of the chief. If a vassal belonged to a different Rājpūt clan, the estate of the latter was of inferior title. Though in all the states there was a mixture of Rājpūts of several clans, the clan of the chief used to predominate. Some of the vassals belonging to other clans were affinally related to the chief's clan. Moreover, only those of pure blood in both lines could hold a *grās* estate. A Rājpūt was considered to be of pure blood if both of his parents were Rājpūts. The greatest prince among Rājpūts could wed the daughter of a Rājpūt father so poor that he possessed a small plot of land, and not be degraded at all by such a marriage. Though there was an administrative system in every Rājpūt state for tax collection and such other purposes, the Rājpūt chief's hold over his chiefdom rested largely on this system of Grāsiyā estates.

The principle of seniority ran through the entire hierarchical structure. The chief was the eldest son of the senior branch of the senior lineage of the dominant clan. At each succession to the chieftainship, the younger brothers of the new chief received *grās* estates as their patrimony. In cases of adoption the nearest of kin had the first claim. The same principle was followed by the vassals.

It has been assumed above that a Rājpūt state was an unchanging entity. If this were so, a rapid breaking up of estates would take place according to the law of dividing the estates at each generation. However, a constant struggle for increasing one's territory and power went on throughout Rājpūt society. It is remarked above that the vassals acted like chiefs in miniature. Although they were bound to the chief by several obligations, to use Lyall's phrase, "their jealousy of his power never sleeps."[38] An enterprising younger branch might enlarge its borders, not only at the expense of its feudal lord and brethren, but also at the expense of neighboring clans. It would exercise, or threaten to exercise, physical force. The weak and timid either lost, or took refuge under some powerful neighbor, keeping enough land for subsistence. Separate independent states came into existence in this way. Sometimes an enterprising Rājpūt might also establish a separate state by subjugating the tribesmen in hills and jungles. The less enterprising would seek employment where obtainable, in some other Rājā's court or army, and receive an estate as remuneration. A new clan might also emerge as a result of this process. As soon as the new state was established or a new estate acquired, however, the same principles of political system were followed. It was the establishment of *Pax Britannica* that put an end to the Rājpūts' struggle to increase their territory, and converted a dynamic system into a stable one.

Even during the British period, the Rājpūt princely states followed the old system. A large number of villages in a princely state were held as *grās* estates by the members of the prince's lineage. The prince and these Grāsiyās together formed a ruling lineage. The only difference between a modern Rājpūt state and an old one was that the struggle for power and authority had assumed new forms. It is well known that machinations for power and authority went on among the members of the ruling lineages in Rājpūt states. They were a constant source of trouble to British administrators supervising the affairs of the Rājpūt states.

In British Gujarat, a *grās* estate was known as Tālukdārī and Wānṭā. These terms became current during the Muslim period. The Muslim rulers did not grant *grās* estates, but they did not remove the estates which were already in possession of Rājpūts. The more powerful *grās* estates were retained as they were. The Rājpūts holding these estates were called Tālukdārs during the later Mogul period.[39] The minor *grās* estates were completely removed by Ahmed I, the Muslim ruler of Gujarat during 1410-1442. As a consequence, these Grāsiyās turned dacoits, preying on the roads and villages. To reconcile them, three-fourths of each estate held by them was acknowledged, under the denomination of Taḷpad, as the property of the king, and one-fourth was given to the Grāsiyās under the denomination of Wānṭā. While full assessment was levied on Taḷpad lands, the Wānṭā holders paid only a quit-rent or *salāmī* to the king. In 1645 the Wānṭā lands were resumed forcibly by Sultan Mahmud III, but were reversed by the Emperor Akbar in 1653.[40] The Marāṭha rulers as well as the British retained the Tālukdārī and Wānṭā estates.

There were nearly five hundred Tālukdārī villages in British Gujarat.[41] The dominant Rājpūt lineage in each Tālukdārī village was the full proprietor of the village, and it was exempted from several rules and regulations applied to ordinary villages. Under the Wānṭā tenure, it was rarely that an entire village was owned by Rājpūts. Usually a part of the land of a village was held jointly by a Rājpūt lineage. Although the Wānṭā holders were given certain concessions in land revenue, they were not independent like the Tālukdārs. There were, however, several villages in which the proportion of Wānṭā lands in comparison to lands held by other castes was so high that the Rājpūts were the virtual rulers in these villages. In some villages, not only the fields around the village but also the village site was divided into Wānṭā and Taḷpad. The Wānṭā part was the joint property of the Rājpūts, and the other castes were under their authority. It was also considered a separate village for revenue administration. In such villages, the Wānṭā holders were almost as powerful as the Tālukdārs.

The Tālukdārī and Wānṭā villages were Rājpūt states in miniature. They followed the same principles of political system as in a Rājpūt state. The Rājpūts of these villages were also well known for their habit of intrigue. The British Government had a Tālukdārī Department to look after the affairs of the Tālukdārī and Wānṭā estates. These tenures were removed after Independence by land reform legislation.

The foregoing sketch of the Rājpūt political system shows that a Rājpūt's status in society depends on his position in the genealogy of his lineage, whether he is a member of a ruling lineage in a state, or of a lineage holding a Tālukdārī or Wānṭā estate. The genealogist is consulted at every succession dispute. No adoption can take place without consulting the genealogy. The Vahīvancā is very particular about the principle of seniority. He records the names of sons in order of their age. The genealogist is thus a necessity for the preservation of the Rājpūt political system. It is noteworthy that the British administrators kept detailed genealogical and historical records of Rājpūt states and estates.[42] This strengthened the position of the Vahīvancā's caste.

It is, however, necessary to ask, "How far back in time does the factual genealogy of a Rājpūt lineage take us?" The answer to this question varies according to whether all Rājpūts kept a Vahīvancā in the past, or only a few. It is not possible to say anything definite about this, for lack of data. It is probable that the earlier genealogies have been lost because they were not reduced to writing. It is also not possible to say whether only a few or all Rājpūt lineages had their genealogy recorded. Besides, in times of armed struggle between one prince and another and the resultant political uncertainty, genealogical records were not very useful. Such struggles were not infrequent, and it would indeed be a matter for surprise, if not suspicion, if we were to find unbroken genealogies stretching over several centuries for the ruling lineages of princely states. The principle of seniority is also an important factor. When a Rājpūt establishes himself as an independent prince, he tries to show that he belongs to the senior line, beginning from the founder of the clan. It is only in this way that he can claim equality with other independent princes of his own clan, and consequently with those of all other clans. For him to continue to belong to a junior branch of the lineage of another prince, is to accept the latter's vassalage. It is the Vahīvancā who is believed to be able to "prove" authoritatively the new chief's claim. Even if the chief's real ancestors are known, the Vahīvancā would forge a link between the chief and the ancient dynasty of his clan. The Vahīvancā provides, in the Malinowskian sense,[43] a mythical "charter" to the new chief.

The genealogy is not likely to be fictitious when the political system is established. In this area, where rights and duties are clear and frequent, there is no room for fiction, although forgery cannot be ruled out. But outside this area, there is room for imagination. The factual part of the genealogy of a ruling lineage in a state usually begins from the date of the founding of the state. As the date of foundation varies, the depth of the genealogy varies.

The genealogies of Grāsiyās of some Tālukdārī and Wānṭā estates also begin from the date of founding of their estates, as if they were independent states. The Grāsiyās in British territories, unlike those in princely states, did not have to recognize any chief as their head. However, sometimes a group of Tālukdārī and Wānṭā lineages not only trace a common ancestor but also acknowledge one of the kinsmen as their nominal liege. For instance, there is a group of about thirty-four Tālukdārī villages owned by Vāghelā Rājpūts in Ahmedabad District. They have administrative ties with the District Collector, but all the Tālukdārs of the group have an emotional allegiance to one of their Vāghelā Rājpūt kinsmen, the *Ṭhākor Sāheb* of Sanand. Steed has noted how a Tālukdār expressed his allegiance to the *Ṭhākor Sāheb* of Sanand, "In him, we believe as in our God. He in Sanand is our King. If he called ten thousand Rājpūts, we would go and give our heads to him."[44] The position of such a nominal liege is analogous to that of a chief at the head of a hierarchy of vassals. The former, like the latter, claims descent from the ancient dynasty of his clan. Other Tālukdārs and Wānṭā holders may not recognize a liege at present, but a careful analysis of the Vahīvancās' books about all the Tālukdārī and Wānṭā estates in Gujarat is likely to reveal a hierarchy of vassals in the past.

The Rājpūt states and estates not only follow a common political system, but also claim that their present position is a result of that system. They have been following this system at least since the eleventh century.[45] Rarely, however, does an ordinary Rājpūt know the detailed genealogy of his lineage. This is left to the Vahīvancā to record and recite. But every Rājpūt believes that the Rājpūts have followed the same political institutions everywhere and at all times that they follow today. The estate holders believe that their estates were gained by their forefathers as *grās*, or were founded by their own valor. They say, "Either way, our forefathers were Rājās." The system also provides them with an argument for clan exogamy. As every Rājpūt lineage claims descent from the dynasty which founded the clan, the members of all the lineages in the clan are agnates, and cannot therefore intermarry. A Rājpūt clan is actually a very amorphous social unit. A Rājpūt of Gujarat would claim that a Rājpūt of Rajasthan belonging to his clan is his agnate, even though there may be no social intercourse whatever between them. Having a common clan name is enough for two Rājpūts to say, "After all, we are brothers." The basis of this claim is their common ideas about their past, and these are supported, if not substantiated, by the Vahīvancās.

How does a Vahīvancā reconstruct the genealogy prior to the founding of a chiefdom? As stated earlier, a Vahīvancā has to make his book acceptable not only to his patrons but also to the members of his occupation. He makes use of a number of stories about Rājpūt heroes from different clans, which have come down to him from his ancestors. The works of Tod[46] and Forbes[47] give some indication of the richness of this lore, and they do not exhaust it. The Vahīvancā knows which city and fort was built by which Rājpūt. He knows the details of crucial battles in the history of a clan. He knows the crucial dates. He remains faithful to his heritage in recording the genealogy and history of the old dynasty of his patron's clan. The same history is therefore found in all the books of the same clan.

But in drawing up the link which he forges between the old dynasty and the factual genealogy of his patron's lineage, the Vahīvancā manufactures names, events, and dates. He tries to make the link look real by inventing myths which are consistent with the traditions of Rājpūts. He needs to show that the lineage belongs to a martial and royal clan. Only then can it claim an honorable status among Rājpūts.

Let us now consider the puranic and epic portion of Rājpūt genealogies. The origin of the Rājpūts—who they were and where they come from—is a subject of dispute among historians.[48] One school argues that the Rājpūts were tribal folk, the bulk of whom were foreigners who came to India during the decline of the Gupta Empire in the sixth century A.D. or earlier. Their emergence as Hindus is said to be the result of their successful absorption into Hindu society—a familiar process which has been going on since Vedic times. Their claim to descent from the puranic and epic Kṣaṭriya heroes is also part of a familiar process—the desire of local castes to belong to a particular *varṇa* and to "substantiate" such a claim by "establishing" links with suitable characters and events in the epics and *purāṇas*. There is another school of historians, equally powerful, who think that the Rājpūts are the descendants of the Kṣatriyas of the Vedas.

It is not our province to discuss these theories. It is, however, noteworthy that the Vahīvancās have recorded in their books the same theories of origin as found in the medieval historical literature.[49] For example, they describe a Rājpūt clan as belonging to the *Sūrya Vaṃśa* (Solar Lineage), the *Candra Vaṃśa* (Lunar Lineage), or the *Agni Kula* (Fire Lineage) in the same way as a Rājpūt dynasty of the same clan was described in the past. The Vahīvancās also give the *gotra*, *pravara*, *veda*, and *purohita* of a Rājpūt lineage. These social categories have, however, no more than nominal importance in present Rājpūt society. There is no attachment whatever to *gotra* exogamy among Rājpūts. The name of the *gotra* is required to be uttered during the wedding ritual. If it is found that the bride and groom belong to the same *gotra*, the Brahman priest calmly chants the name of some *gotra* other than that assigned by the Vahīvancā. The specifically Kṣatriya categories *Sūrya Vaṃsa*, *Candra Vaṃsa* and *Agni Kula* also have no importance today. It is doubtful if these social categories had any importance even in the past. The Vahīvancās employ them only to show that the Rājpūts are descendants of the Vedic Kṣatriyas, and it appears that the medieval authors also invented their theories to establish the Rājpūts in the *varṇa* system. Every Rājpūt boasts before other castes that Rāma, Kṛṣṇa, and the Pāṇḍavas belonged to his caste. The puranic and epic parts of the Vahīvancās' books validate the Rājpūts' claim to belong to the Kṣatriya *varṇa*, the warrior and ruler caste since time immemorial, whereas the mythico-historical parts validate the claim of a Rājpūt lineage to belong to a warrior and ruler clan within the caste.

While it is doubtful whether all Rājpūts had Vahīvancās in the past, nowadays hardly any Rājpūt is without one. Among other castes, it is rare that the entire caste patronizes Vahīvancās. The Vahīvancā is important to the Rājpūt not only as genealogist but also as mythographer. Anyone who wants to call himself a Rājpūt should show that he is descended from an ancient Rājpūt dynasty, and it is only the Vahīvancā who is believed to be able to show this authoritatively. A Rājpūt's existence as a member of his caste depends upon the Vahīvancā. Moreover, some of the most vital social and political institutions of the Rājpūts are based on the belief that these have existed since time immemorial. The Vahīvancā's records are, to the Rājpūt, proof of the antiquity of the institutions. It does not matter if a particular genealogy is fictitious, but the belief in the past social system, as both Rājpūts and Vahīvancās see it, is so strong that evidence from this system is sought to support each particular case. The Vahīvancā supports the general beliefs which prevail among Rājpūts about the past history of Rājpūts. By providing evidence for their past, he strengthens their present social institutions. These in turn impinge upon the Rājpūt individual. Steed has shown how this happens.[50]

The Rājpūts recognize the Vahīvancā's importance in their lives. They have a great veneration for him. The Rājpūt princes used to invite their Vahīvancās to weddings and coronations, when Vahīvancās would be allotted prominent places to sit, and given gifts. When the Vahīvancā goes to his Rājpūt patrons' village, he is treated like a prince. Sometimes he is brought from the village entrance to the lineage hall (*deli*) in procession. He stays in the *deli*. He is seated on a cot while others sit on the ground. A servant attends him. The Vahīvancā is addressed as Rāojī, which is a title used for a king. He is also given rich food.

The Rājpūts are generous in giving gifts to the Vahīvancā, and the latter, knowing the Rājpūt's weakness, tells him what a glorious past he had, and then asks for bigger gifts. He will also show from his books that his patrons' forefathers gave big gifts, and tell the descendants that they should keep up the tradition. Sometimes he flatters a patron by singing a couplet in his honor. If a patron refuses to give a suitable gift, the Vahīvancā threatens to record a derogatory sentence about him in his book. In a bigger lineage, the different segments vie with each other in giving gifts, and the Vahīvancā exploits such rivalry to his own benefit.

The Vahīvancās have imitated Rājpūts in many ways. Like Rājpūts, the Vahīvancās also consider themselves Kṣatriyas, as distinct from Brahmabhaṭṭs. Several Vahīvancās attach the suffix *singh* to their name like a Rājpūt. In the old days when opium was freely bought and sold, the Vahīvancās, like Rājpūts, were very fond of opium. When the Vahīvancā went to his Rājpūt patrons' village, he brought opium from the town. In the evening everyone first took opium, and then the Vahīvancā would recite bardic poetry and tell stories.

The recent dissolution of the princely states and of the Tālukdārī and Wānṭā tenures has begun to affect the Rājpūts and their relations with Vahīvancās. They pay less to Vahīvancās nowadays. The big Rājpūt estates, held jointly until recently, are now being partitioned among the coparceners. This fact has reduced the importance of the factual genealogy in the inheritance of property, office, and title. With the disappearance of princely status, the claim to belong to the ruling caste has lost its charm, if not its rationale. Rājpūts are not a great force in modern politics in Gujarat. Educated Rājpūt youths do not find much to interest them in either opium or bardic songs. But still a feeling prevails that "the Vahīvancās are after all our *gors* (priests). They are Devīputras. We should honor them as we honor the Brahmans."

The next important caste after the Rājpūts are the Koḷīs. "Koḷī" is a blanket term covering a number of widely divergent groups found all over Western India. In Gujarat, the Koḷīs form about one-fourth of the total Hindu population. The first mention of Koḷīs in the history of Gujarat occurs during the reign of the Solankī King Karṇa I (1064-1094), who is said to have subjugated a chieftain of 600,000 Koḷī and Bhil tribesmen.[51] The Koḷīs were a wild tribe noted for piracy at sea and pillage on land. They had plundered the camp of the Mogul Emperor Humayun at Cambay in 1535.[52] During the political confusion in the later Mogul and Marāṭhā periods, the Koḷīs plundered not only villages, but also the towns of Ahmedabad, Cambay, and Baroda.[53] By the time the British came, the Koḷīs had established a number of small principalities and independent estates in different parts of Gujarat. The Koḷī estates were known by the term Mewāsī. The British retained the Koḷī states and estates. They were abolished after Independence. At present, the bulk of the Koḷīs are petty landholders and agricultural laborers.

The Koḷīs of Central Gujarat are divided into two groups, Taḷpadās and Pāṭaṇwāḍiyās. Pāṭaṇwāḍiyās are so called because they have migrated from the Pāṭaṇ region in north Gujarat. They are called Pardeśīs 'foreigners' as against Taḷpadās 'indigenous.' The people of other castes refer to Taḷpadās as Dhārāḷās, but the Taḷpadās consider it a derogatory term. "Dhārāḷā" means a person who carries a weapon called *dhāriyā*.

The Taḷpadās and Pāṭaṇwāḍiyās neither intermarry nor interdine. Within each endogamous group, there are two exogamous units, village and lineage. A Taḷpadā or Pāṭaṇwāḍiyā lineage is comprised of as many generations as its members can remember. The Koḷīs in general do not remember their genealogies beyond the fourth or fifth generation. Sometimes two lineage segments may have forgotten the name of their common ancestor but they may continue to regard themselves as belonging to a single lineage. We have, however, not come across a lineage tracing a traditional common ancestor beyond the seventh or eight generation.

Among Pāṭaṇwāḍiyās, a lineage is known by the village from which its first ancestor migrated and settled in central Gujarat. Among Taloadās, a lineage is known by any of the following names: Bāriyā, Khānṭ, Paṭeliyā, Koṭwāl and Pagi. Each name is believed to denote the status of a lineage. For instance, Bāriyās are considered to have the highest status, so much so that the Taḷpadās have adopted Bāriyā as a caste appellation. Pagīs are considered to have the lowest status. Lineages of several different names are found in every village, however, and the lineages bearing the same name have different status in different villages. These names denote neither exogamous nor endogamous groups. Outside the village, a Taḷpadā or Pāṭaṇwāḍiyā lineage may take wives from another lineage bearing the same name, or from a lineage bearing any other name. It is noteworthy that there are no widespread exogamous groups among the Koḷīs like the clans among the Rājpūts or the *gotras* among the Brahmans.

It is necessary to refer briefly to Rājpūt hypergamy in order to understand the role of the Vahīvancās among the Koḷīs. Rājpūts are stratified into several groups, and the low Rājpūts give their daughters to high Rājpūts, but the latter do not give their daughters to the former. For instance, the Wānṭā holders of central Gujarat give their daughters to, but do not receive from, the Tālukdārs of Ahmedabad District. The latter give their daughters to, but do not receive from, the princely families of Saurashtra.

Nearly a hundred years ago the Jāḍejā chiefs of Saurashtra and Cutch, the highest group in the hypergamic order in Gujarat, practiced female infanticide, because there were no Rājpūts above them to whom they could give their daughters. The British suppressed female infanticide, and this led eventually to the Jāḍejā chiefs' giving their daughters to Rājpūt chiefs of equal rank.[54] Thus at the top levels, a certain fluidity has come about, but the middle levels continue to be as rigid as before. No Tālukdār of Ahmedabad District, for instance, has given his daughter to a Wānṭā holder of central Gujarat. At the lowest levels, Rājpūts find wives among non-Rājpūts. In Gujarat, they take wives from the Koḷīs. This tendency to take wives from the tribes seems to be an India-wide custom for Rājpūts.[55]

In Central Gujarat, the Rājpūts take wives from the Taḷpadā chiefs and their kinsmen. These chiefs have generally Rajputized their way of life and their political institutions. The economic and social status of the chiefs, plus a certain cultural homogeneity, helped in establishing hypergamous relations between Taḷpadā chiefs and Rājpūts, and this led the chiefs to claim Rājpūt descent. Rājpūt hypergamy has thus provided a rope by which Koḷīs can pull themselves up. Secondly, the chiefs had political power, as did the Rājpūts. And as Rājpūts were considered to be Kṣatriyas by everyone, the Koḷī chiefs, when they claimed to be Rājpūts, were also claiming to be Kṣatriyas. Although other Koḷīs do not have political power as the Taḷpadā chiefs do, and have not given their daughters to Rājpūts in marriage, Rājpūt customs and manners, as well as the claim to be Rājpūts and Kṣatriyas, have spread among all Koḷīs. Each Taḷpadā and Pāṭaṇwāḍiyā wants to be addressed as *Ṭhākor* 'princeling.'

A Taḷpadā lineage adopts a Rājpūt clan name in order to claim to be a Rājpūt lineage. No Taḷpadā now likes to call himself by the old caste and lineage names. For the last fifteen to twenty years, the new names have been used in government records, schools and correspondence. We do not have enough data about the system followed by the Vahīvancās in giving new names to Taḷpadā lineages. However, it is found that the adoption of Rājpūt clan names by the Koḷīs, has not led to the adoption of the clan exogamy of the Rājpūts. Two lineages bearing two different older names might adopt a single Rājpūt clan name, and yet one may take wives from the other. Similarly, two groups bearing the same old name might take over two different names. However, periodical recording of the Koḷīs' genealogies by the Vahīvancās has led to an important change in the lineage system of the Koḷīs—the generation span of their genealogies, and consequently, the size of the exogamous group, have increased. Except for the Vahīvancās, the usual tendency among Koḷīs to forget the remoter ancestors would have persisted. The Koḷī chiefs were the first Koḷīs to be served by the Vahīvancās, and they therefore have the longest recorded genealogies among the Koḷīs.

The Vahīvancās have provided a mythical charter to Koḷī mobility. The Vahīvancās describe in their books how the Koḷīs were originally Rājpūts, but lost their caste and were degraded because they took water and food from the Koḷīs, or took their girls as wives.[56] The mythical part of every Koḷī genealogy follows the pattern of Rājpūt genealogy in the beginning. The Vahīvancā records an epic or puranic genealogy, and shows the origin of the Rājpūt clan adopted by the Koḷī lineage, in the same way as he does in the case of a Rājpūt lineage. He also shows the different branches of the Rājpūt clan, and the heroes, forts, and battles associated with each of them. Towards the end of the mythico-historical part, however, the Vahīvancā describes the circumstances under which a member of the Rājpūt clan had to accept water, food or wife from a Koḷī. Here the Vahīvancā makes use of a tradition. Historians do not say anything definite as to what happened to the Rājpūts of Gujarat after the fall of the Rājpūt kingdom of Pāṭaṇ in 1299, and of Pāvāgaḍh in 1484. The Vahīvancās have a tradition that a number of Rājpūts fled after the fall of these Rājpūt kingdoms, and being pursued by the Muslims, took refuge among the tribesmen of Gujarat. The Vahīvancā also assigns a *gotra*, *pravara*, *veda* and *purohita* to a Koḷī lineage as he does to a Rājpūt one.

This theory of the Vahīvancās presupposes a time when the Rājpūts did not take wives from Koḷīs. There is no evidence to prove or disprove this argument. It is, however, certain that no Rājpūt has lost his caste by marriage with an acceptable lower caste. A Rājpūt might take a Koḷī wife, but his son may raise his politico-economic status and be able to marry a girl born of a Rājpūt father. It is the Koḷī girl who loses her caste by marriage with a Rājpūt, but her husband remains a Rājpūt and her father remains a Koḷī. The Rājpūts do not take food from Koḷīs with whom they are not related by marriage. The Vahīvancās also accept food and water from Rājpūts but not from Koḷīs. The Koḷīs say, "If your history says that we are Rājpūts in origin, you must take food with us." The Vahīvancā replies, "It is true that you were Rājpūts in the past, but you are not Rājpūts now. You are also not Rājpūts in your behavior. You practice *nātaruṃ* (i.e., remarriage of widows and divorced women). You are not as cultured as Rājpūts. And you are not considered as equals by Rājpūts themselves." The Koḷīs who have never given their daughters to Rājpūts in marriage have no further argument to offer. But it does not silence the Koḷīs who have thoroughly Rajputized themselves and have given their daughters to Rājpūts. To those Koḷīs the Vahīvancā says, "You are cultured, but not your brethren." This argument does not satisfy them. They refuse to patronize a Vahīvancā who does not accept food from them. The Vahīvancās refused to yield, and did not visit their patrons, for several years. As a result they lost income from them. But now, under the pretext of general relaxation of the rules regarding pollution, some Vahīvancās have started taking food from these Koḷīs. The Koḷīs who have not given their daughters to Rājpūts are not as adamant as other Koḷīs.

The Vahīvancās have invented a theory that satisfies the Koḷīs without offending the Rājpūts. It establishes homogeneity, but not identity among the Koḷīs and the Rājpūts. If the Vahīvancās identified them with Rājpūts, they would be giving offence to the Rājpūts. This theory has satisfied the Koḷīs because it has given them a status in the *varṇa* scheme. The association of Koḷīs with Rājpūt heroes of the past encourages the Rajputization of Koḷīs; and having Rājpūt-like political power and Rājpūt customs and manners means belonging to a martial and ruling caste, and, therefore, to the Kṣatriya *varṇa*. Neither the Vahīvancās nor the Koḷīs doubt the identity of Rājpūts with Kṣatriyas. To put the matter in simple words, Rājpūts are the visible Kṣatriyas. Therefore, any Koḷī who wants to call himself a Kṣatriya, should adopt Rājpūt customs, and link himself with Rājpūt heroes. It is only the Vahīvancā who is believed to be able to link the Koḷīs with Rājpūt heroes authoritatively. Moreover, the Vahīvancās are themselves an institution intimately associated with Rājpūts. A Koḷī who wants to claim to be a Rājpūt should therefore patronize a Vahīvancā.

The imitation of Rājpūts means the adoption not only of specifically Rājpūt customs but also of the Hindu sacraments allowed to the Rājpūts. It is known that the Brahman priests did not minister to Koḷīs in the past, and there are still many Koḷīs who have to go without a Brahman priest at the wedding ritual. It is usual for the Vahīvancā to follow the Brahman in recruiting a Koḷī as patron. The necessity of uttering the *gotra*, etc. during the Brahmanic rituals has contributed a great deal to the Koḷīs' demand for the Vahīvancā's services.

The Koḷīs are a rising caste in Gujarat. They are fast Sanskritizing as well as Rajputizing themselves. Just as a Koḷī is considered low if he does not have a Brahman priest at wedding and funerary rituals, he is considered low if he does not have a Vahīvancā. Recruitment of Koḷīs as the Vahīvancās' patrons is still going on. While the Vahīvancās' income from Rājpūts has begun to decline, their income from Koḷīs has increased. The Vahīvancās say, "An average Koḷī still pays less than an average

Rājpūt, and they do not know the niceties of Rājpūt hospitality, but they have great reverence for us."

The Pāṭidārs are next to the Koḷīs in population in central Gujarat. They are traditionally known as the real cultivators of Gujarat. Their former caste name was Kaṇbī. There are three groups among them—Levā, Kadvā and Ānjaṇā. We shall confine ourselves here to the Levās, who are found mostly in central Gujarat. Formerly, the term Pāṭidār denoted only those Kaṇbīs who held land under the Narvādārī tenure. The others were called simply Kaṇbīs. This distinction does not, however, exist today. The term "Kaṇbī" has no prestige and is used only in a derogatory sense.

Under the Narvādārī tenure, the Pāṭidārs of a village were joint proprietors of all the land of the village, just as the Rājpūts were the rulers of Tālukdārī and Wānṭā villages. During the later Mogul and Marāṭha periods, many Pāṭidārs were collectors of revenue called Desāis and Amins.[57] This gave them much power, and a few of them even established small principalities. British rule resulted in spectacular economic change for the Pāṭidārs. Though the bulk of them are still landowners, many Pāṭidārs are to be found following modern occupations—they are civil servants, doctors, engineers and pleaders. They have settled in large numbers in East Africa and several other countries abroad. They are an important force in regional and state politics. They have Sanskritized their way of life.

According to the theory of castes laid down in the Hindu scriptures, agriculture, trade, and pastoral pursuits are to be exploited by the Vaiśya.[58] In Dalpatram's *Jñāti Nibandh* or *Essay on Caste* (1851)[59] and Forbes's *Rāsmālā* (1887),[60] the Pāṭidārs are classed among Vaiśyas according to the scriptures, because they practiced agriculture. Another prominent writer of that time, Narmadashanker (1873)[61] described them as Sūdras. The Vahīvancās, however, faithfully recorded the Pāṭidārs' own claim of being Kṣatriyas. Dalpatram also referred to this claim, but he obviously did not accept it. The Pāṭidārs claimed that the Levās and Kadvās were the descendants of Lava and Kusha respectively, the two sons of the epic hero Rāma. The Vahīvancās' books explain the Pāṭidārs' descent from a warrior to a cultivator caste by the myth that Lava and Kusha were cursed by their mother Sītā to become cultivators. The books then describe a long account of the migration of Pāṭidārs from Ayodhyā to central Gujarat. The Vahīvancās have also credited the Pāṭidārs with *gotras*. This is another instance of the Vahīvancās giving a "historical" sanction to a caste's claim to a status in the *varṇa* scheme.

It should be noted, however, that the Rājpūt pattern is not found in the history of the Pāṭidārs as it is found in that of the Koḷīs. The Pāṭidārs claimed to belong to the Kṣatriya *varṇa* without claiming to be Rājpūts. Nevertheless, they could not ignore the fact that Rājpūts were the only caste whose claim to the Kṣatriya *varṇa* was long established. The Pāṭidārs argued that they were Kṣatriyas because they had political power like the Rājpūts. They had also adopted several Rājpūt customs, and love of opium and bardic literature had also spread among them. The Vahīvancā's genealogy was as important to Pāṭidārs as it was to Rājpūts—the shares in the Narvādārī lands were divided according to the Vahīvancā's genealogy. The Pāṭidār lineages and lineage segments were arranged, as among Rājpūts, in a hierarchy which provided a basis for hypergamy. The Pāṭidārs held their Vahīvancā in as high esteem as the Rājpūts did.

The Pāṭidārs' respect for Vahīvancās has declined nowadays, however. Pāṭidārs now claim to be not Kṣatriyas but Vaiśyas. Why have the Pāṭidārs changed their *varṇa*, in spite of the fact that, according to the classical *varṇa* theory, Vaiśyas are lower than Kṣatriyas? The Pāṭidārs now assert the scriptural dictum that agriculture and trade are the occupations of Vaiśyas, and try to establish their claim to the Vaiśya *varṇa* by claiming the same status as the Baniyās, the traditional merchant caste of Gujarat, because the latter are known to be Vaiśyas by everybody. The Pāṭidārs once claimed to be Kṣatriyas because the kingly model was dominant in society at that time, and they tried to establish their claim by imitating the Rājpūts because the latter were known to be Kṣatriyas. But now neither is the kingly model dominant nor are the Rājpūts in power. Business is one of the most highly preferred occupations in Gujarat, so much so that Gujarat is popularly known as a region of businessmen. It may be said that the business model is dominant in Gujarat.[62] Baniyās are the traditional businessmen, and the Pāṭidārs have taken to business. Baniyās, along with Brahmans, were also the first to take to English education and modern professions, and the Pāṭidārs soon followed them. The Baniyās are also one of the most Sanskritized castes in Gujarat. They rank next to Brahmans in a ritual context. The Rājpūts, who are known to be Kṣatriyas, are in this context lower than Baniyās, who are known to be Vaiśyas—the direct reverse of the *varṇa* hierarchy. The Pāṭidārs are almost as Sanskritized as Baniyās, and are higher than Rājpūts in a ritual context. Thus the politico-economic changes during the last one hundred and fifty years has brought about changes in the relative position of different castes in the local hierarchy, and this has in turn, brought about a change in the Pāṭidārs' position in the *varṇa* hierarchy. But the Vahīvancās cannot change the theory of Pāṭidār origin recorded in their books. This is one of the main reasons why Pāṭidārs have not much interest in the Vahīvancās.

The Pāṭidārs of "high status villages" ignore the Vahīvancās because they have printed their genealogies. Two of them have brought their genealogies up to date and published the second edition. The "high status" Pāṭidārs are also the most urbanized and Westernized. They have no love for bardic literature. Finally, during the process of economic change there has been a reshuffle in the economic status of many Pāṭidār lineages and lineage segments. A cleaner past, or as the Pāṭidārs say, the absence of "a black spot" (*kalaṅk*) in the lineage, is itself one of the criteria of higher status among them. Many Pāṭidārs who have become wealthy in recent years feel annoyed when the Vahīvancā excavates the "black spots" in their past. They therefore do not like the Vahīvancā to read the past at all. At one time the Pāṭidārs were a rich source of income for the Vahīvancās, but nowadays the number of Pāṭidār patrons has fallen sharply, and patrons have also lost respect for the Vahīvancās.

The above analysis of the Vahīvancās' role in the social life of Rājpūts, Koḷīs and Pāṭidārs, shows that the Vahīvancās link up the local caste (*jāti*) with the all-India scheme of *varṇa*,[63] and they mostly follow the Rājpūt or Kṣatriya model. A few facts about other castes served by Vahīvancās also support this statement. It is noteworthy that the Vahīvancās have many more patrons among castes claiming to be Kṣatriyas, than among those claiming to be Brahmans or Vaiśyas. Two Brahman castes, the Bāj Khedāvāḷs and the Anāvils, formerly patronized the Vahīvancās, but the Bāj Khedāvāḷs stopped patronizing them about forty years ago, and the Anāvils are not now warm towards Vahīvancās. We have come across only one Baniyā caste, the Kapoḷs, who are considered to be staunch patrons of the Vahīvancās. A group of Nāgar Baniyās began patronizing the Vahīvancās about a century ago, but has now stopped. Among the important reasons why the Brahmans and Baniyās do not patronize Vahīvancās are the facts that they have a literate tradition, and that they do not own land, like Rājpūts, on a lineage basis. But it is also possible that many Brahman and Baniyās castes do not patronize Vahīvancās because they have *purāṇas* dealing with their caste origins—*purāṇas* which are different from the traditional eighteen *purāṇas*. It is noteworthy that a group of Jain Baniyās claim to be Kṣatriyas, and not Vaiśyas like other Baniyās. These Jain Baniyās patronize the Vahīvancās. The reason behind their claim to be Kṣatriyas is the fact that all the Jain *Tīrthaṃkaras*, including Mahavīra, the founder of Jainism, were born in Kṣatriya families.[64] The Vahīvancās also describe several artisan and servicing castes as Kṣatriyas. Even the Molesalāms, already referred to as a caste converted to Islam during the fifteenth century, patronize the Vahīvancās, because they were formerly Rājpūts and still retain a number of Rājpūt institutions. Recently, several Molesalāms have discarded even the few Muslim institutions they had retained, and the Vahīvancās have contributed a great deal to this change.

There is a tradition among the Vahīvancās themselves that they served only the Rājpūts to begin with. They started serving other castes subsequently. In the Vahīvancās' books we have seen so far, we have also found that the books about Rājpūts are older than those about other castes. And it has also been pointed out that the Vahīvancās are Rajputized, and consider themselves to be Kṣatriyas. The Vahīvancās were thus a Rājpūt institution to begin with, and they came to be considered a Kṣatriya institution because Rājpūts were considered to be Kṣatriyas by all. Though it is not possible to establish a definite relationship between the Vahīvancās and the Sūtas of the Vedic and puranic literature, it is signficant that the latter are mostly associated with kings.[65] There are no Vahīvancās in south Gujarat because the Rājpūt influence is negligible there. The caste of Bhāṭs, from whom the Vahīvancās' caste has developed, is also "a distinctively Rājpūt institution, and, except for the colonies in Telingana and eastern Bengal, is only found where Rājpūt influence is supreme."[66]

The Vahīvancā's position in society is vulnerable precisely because he follows mostly the Rājpūt or Kṣatriya model. As soon as his patrons cease to follow that model, they cease to patronize him. This is clearly shown by the changes in his relations with the Pāṭidārs, and even with Rājpūts themselves. The patrons may change, but it is difficult for the Vahīvancā to change because of the written tradition of his occupation. Not only the mythical part but also the factual part of his book may become inconsistent with the present social life of his patrons. It has been shown that the Pāṭidārs do not want the Vahīvancā to excavate "black spots" in their past. Some Koḷīs also do not wish the Vahīvancā to read from his book that their ancestors were dacoits. The Vahīvancā is successful in his occupation as long as the myths and facts recorded in his book are consistent with the social life of his patrons. However, it cannot be said that the Vahīvancās will never change their records. Recently, a Vahīvancā has changed the entire mythico-historical part of his book, cleverly introducing pieces from up-to-date historical research.

Some of the success of the Vahīvancā in his occupation is due to a widespread belief that he is a Devīputra. Though all the patrons of the Vahīvancās are not exclusively *mātā* worshippers, the worship of *mātās* forms a significant part of the religious life of most patrons. On the other hand, it has an insignificant place in the religious life of most Brahman and Baniyā castes, who do not patronize the Vahīvancās. These castes are predominantly Vaiṣṇavite, Jain, or Śaivite. They do not have much faith in the idea that the Vahīvancā is a Deviputra. Changes have, however, taken place in the religious life of the Vahīvancās themselves. Until recently, all the Vahīvancās were *mātā* worshippers. But nowadays there are also a few Śaivite and Vaiṣṇavite Vahīvancās. A few Vahīvancās have also become members of the Swāminārāyaṇ sect, because their Pāṭidār patrons belong to it—and this is a sect which was started as a reform movement within Vaiṣṇavism.

Let us now consider the organizational aspect of the Vahīvancās' occupation.

The Vahīvancā's books are the chief source of his income. Generally speaking, the more books he has, the higher is his income. But some castes pay more than others. Thus an average Rājpūt pays more than an average Koḷī, and an average Pāṭidār pays more than an average Rājpūt. Within the caste, again, patrons belong to different economic levels. For instance, the ruling lineage of a Rājpūt state are likely to pay more than a lineage of Tālukdārs, and the latter more than the Wānṭā holders. Similarly, the lineage of a Koḷī chief would pay more than the ordinary Koḷī cultivators. Futhermore, the Vahīvancā has to consider the economic composition of a lineage. In one lineage almost all the members may be rich, and in another, one or two members may be rich and the others poor. He cannot hope to extract from his patron a gift beyond his means. He has to take less from the poor and more from the rich for performing the same service. For instance, he might take more than a hundred rupees for entering the name of a rich patron's son but only five or even two rupees for a poor patron's son. The Vahīvancā has an estimate of income he is likely to get from each book. It may be called its potential income. The actual income depends upon how effectively he exploits the patrons.

The potential income of a book can be effectively exploited if a particular amount of effort is spent on it. The Vahīvancā makes an estimate of the aggregate amount of effort needed in his occupation. When either he or the members of his joint family are not able to look after all his patrons, he employs a poorer Vahīvancā (with fewer books) as his clerk (*gumāstā*). Similarly, a disabled Vahīvancā or a minor Vahīvancā or a widow appoints a clerk. The employer allots some of his patrons to the clerk every year. The clerk does all the work, including the collection of gifts, on behalf of his master. He gets one-third of the income as his remuneration, and the rest goes to the employer. The clerk goes out to the villages between the end of one monsoon and the beginning of the next. But some of his time must be given to his own patrons. His employer does not, however, usually delegate the duties of receiving a patron in the town, and of going to court with him.

It has been mentioned earlier that the Vahīvancās of central and north Gujarat form separate groups. The former group is smaller than the latter. A Vahīvancā of central Gujarat has on the average a larger number of books and a greater potential income than a Vahīvancā of north Gujarat. The Vahīvancās of north Gujarat provide clerks for the Vahīvancās of central Gujarat. Some Bhāts or Brahmbhaṭṭs also work as clerks.

It is also possible for a Vahīvancā to take up some other occupation besides his traditional one, delegating the latter largely to clerks. The number of such Vahīvancās is growing in central Gujarat, as more and more of them are taking to higher education, and seeking employment in modern professions. But even they have a working knowledge of their traditional occupation. The secondary employment should provide enough time to receive patrons in town, to go to the courts to give evidence on behalf of patrons, and to visit the villages occasionally to supervise the clerk's work, solve disputes, and meet important patrons. In a joint family, one member may devote himself entirely to the traditional occupation while the others look after their own jobs. The Vahīvancās of north Gujarat are still uneducated and most of them carry on the traditional occupation, supplementing the income from their own books by working as clerks with the Vahīvancās of central Gujarat.

Employing a clerk creates certain problems. The employer has to see that the clerk mentions in the book all the gifts given to him by patrons. The clerk might conceal some gifts from his master. The master has also to see that the clerks behave properly with the patrons. Most serious of all, the clerk may doublecross the employer by passing on information in the books to a rival Vahīvancā, who would be enabled to poach on the employer's custom.

The Vahīvancā has to deal with problems created not only by the size of the patron group, but also its composition. Every Vahīvancā makes a catalogue of his books, classifying the patrons according to caste and village. There are some Vahīvancās who have books about only one caste. Usually, however, the patrons of a Vahīvancā belong to several different castes. Each caste needs special treatment in almost the entire behavior of the Vahīvancā with his patrons, in knowledge of history and mythology, in story-telling and poetry, in the technique of extracting gifts, and in ceremonial dress. The Vahīvancā with patrons of only one caste has therefore an advantage over the Vahīvancā with patrons belonging to several castes. The latter might be able to learn the skills required for two or three castes, but it is impossible to acquire skills required for all the castes. He has therefore to give some of his books to the specialist Vahīvancās, and the income is shared between the two. Some clerks also specialize in dealing with particular castes. Only a Vahīvancā with a large number of books can afford to give some of his books to others in this way. A Vahīvancā with fewer books has to choose between giving up some money by taking a specialist's help, and risking the loss of patronage of the groups he cannot cope with. A Vahīvancā who specializes on one caste puts all his eggs in one basket. If his patrons should, for some reason, lose their interest in the Vahīvancā, he is lost. A Vahīvancā with patrons from several castes would be distributing the risk.

Each book has an index which shows the spatial distribution of the patrons. It has been shown that frequently the members of a lineage contained in a book live in several villages due to intervillage migrations which took place during the period covered by the book. If all the books of a Vahīvancā are consulted, his patrons will be found to be scattered over a number of villages. It is impossible for him to cover all the villages in a year. It is not in his interest, however, to cover all his patrons in a year. Frequent visits to a patron mean less money each year. They also mean more expense for the Vahīvancā. Besides, there is very little to record after the lapse of a year. The Vahīvancā so spaces his visits that his troubles are recompensed adequately. Some Vahīvancās visit their patrons after an interval of fifteen to twenty years, and if there is a protracted dispute between the patrons and the Vahīvancā, a larger period might elapse between two visits. The Vahīvancā stresses the fact that he does not visit every year and so he is the loser. Usually he goes only after ascertaining whether the patrons are willing to welcome him. He does not go if they are hit by a calamity such as drought or flood. His visit is expensive for the villagers. A Vahīvancā with a large number of patrons can afford to visit them at longer intervals, while another with a smaller number of patrons has to go at shorter intervals. The latter is also more dependent on his patrons than the Vahīvancā with a larger number of patrons. He has to be more particular about pleasing his patrons and he cannot afford to have a protracted dispute with them.

Formerly the Vahīvancā used to travel in a bullock cart. He would set out with his books and servant as soon as the roads were free for travel after the monsoon. He would select some one direction and visit patrons in all the villages on the way. He would travel in another direction the following year. If he had clerks, he sent them in different directions. Nowadays, however, he travels by rail and bus. He is able to cover a large number of patrons in a year, and he can choose to visit any village he likes, irrespective of direction. He must, however, go only after the harvest, when the villagers have money as well as leisure. He visits his urban patrons any time during the year.

The books are an important item in the property of a Vahīvancā, and they are inherited by his sons along with other property. They are divided not according to number but by their potential income. The books are so divided that each son gets roughly the same income, and this may mean one son getting more books than another. The inheritance of books at each generation tends to make the Vahīvancās progressively poorer. This tendency may be arrested or accentuated by three main factors. The first is the number of shares at each generation. It is said that the Vahīvancās of north Gujarat are poorer than those of central Gujarat because of excessive subdivisions among the former. It appears that the population of the Vahīvancās of central Gujarat has decreased and this has made them rich. Secondly, the books may be mortgaged or sold. Such cases are, however, very few. This is the last resort in a financial difficulty. Thirdly, a Vahīvancā may recruit new patrons. He can do this in only a few castes, and the process of recruitment is long drawn out. For instance, he can recruit one or two lineage groups in a period of five or seven years. There is not much scope for enlarging one's patron-group by poaching on a fellow Vahīvancā's field. Such a practice leads to disputes within the caste, with serious repercussions on kinship relations. Moreover, every Vahīvancā is extremely secretive about his books. He rarely opens his book before another Vahīvancā. He does not allow his clerks to mix with other Vahīvancās. While rivalry within Gujarat is restrained by prevalent kinship relations, no such restriction obtains between the Vahīvancās of Gujarat and those of Rajasthan. Several Rājpūt lineages have tried to raise their status by getting "nobler" genealogies manufactured by the Vahīvancās of Rajasthan. The latter also recruit patrons among lower castes whom the Gujarati Vahīvancās refuse to serve.

The substitution of one Vahīvancā for another, or of one Vahīvancā group for another, does not affect the occupation as such. It has been shown that the occupation is adversely affected if a whole group of patrons ceases to patronize the Vahīvancās due to a change in their attitude. On the other hand, the profession is adversely affected by a change in the Vahīvancās' own attitude towards their traditional occupation. The Vahīvancās of central Gujarat are increasingly taking to modern professions. Ahmedabad and Baroda are big cities, and Dholka is a sizeable town. The Vahīvancās of north Gujarat live in towns which are only overgrown villages. Formerly, the Vahīvancā used to take his sons with him to villages. Nowadays, the sons of the Vahīvancās in central Gujarat go to schools. They do not learn bardic stories and poems. They find that their profession has no prestige in the town. They do not like going to villages. They are ashamed of putting on ceremonial dress. They are annoyed at the element of begging involved in the practice of the traditional occupation. They feel they are backward. They like to take up modern occupations. They delegate their work to clerks, but as was seen earlier, only some of the work can be so delegated. As a result, the Vahīvancā tends to visit his patrons at longer intervals. There are many patrons who are prepared to welcome the Vahīvancās, but the Vahīvancās do not visit them.[67]

NOTES

[1] I now find that the first mention of "telescoping" of genealogies is in E. E. Evans-Pritchard, *Nuer* (Oxford, 1940), pp. 199-200.

[2] Vol. IX, Part I (1901), 207-227.

[3] *Chārano anē Chārani Sāhitya* (Guj) (Ahmedabad, 1943), pp. 183-184. Though we have done some fieldwork among bardic castes other than Vahīvancās, our chief sources of information about them are the *Bombay Gazetteer* and Zaverchand Meghani.

[4] Meghani, 1943, pp. 42-45.

[5] Meghani, 1943, p. 49; also C. V. Raval, "Chāraṇ anē Chāraṇi Bhāshā (Guj), *Buddhiprakāsh Lēkhasangraha* (Ahmedabad, 1941), I, pp. 160-168.

[6] J. M. Farquhar, *An Outline of the Religious Literature of India* (London, 1920), pp. 167, 199-204.

[7] John Woodroffe, *Shakti and Shākta* (Madras and London, 1920), pp. 8, 95.

[8] Woodroffe, 1920, p. 337.

[9] C. U. Aitchison, *A Collection of Treaties, Engagements and Sanads* (Calcutta, 1932), VI, pp. 2, 165, 167.

[10] *Bombay Gazetteer,* Vol. IX, Part I, p. 209.

[11] *Bombay Gazetteer,* Vol. III (1879), p. 92.

[12] James Tod, *Annals and Antiquities of Rajast'han* (first published 1829-32), edition used: two volumes in one, with a Preface by Douglas Sladen, (London, 1950), II, 500.

[13] *Bombay Gazetteer,* Vol. IX, Part I, p. 218.

[14] James Tod, 1950, I, xvi, 25.

[15] *Bombay Gazetteer,* Vol. IX, Part I, p. 212.

[16] (Calcutta, 1917-18), Section I, Parts I and II.

[17] Tod, 1950.

[18] New Edition, with an Introduction by J. W. Watson (London, 1878). Forbes gave the title *Rāsmālā* 'a garland of *rāso* chronicles' because, as he himself states (pp. xii-xiv), he used bardic legends as the sources of his work.

[19] A. B. Jani, ed., *Hastalikhit Pustakoni Savistar Nāmāvali* (Guj) (Bombay, 1923).

[20] *Gujarātno Madhyakālin Rājput Itihās* (Guj) (Ahmedabad, 1953).

[21] *Sārth Gujarāti Jodnikosh* (Ahmedabad, 1949), p. 1028.

[22] Muni Sri Punyavijayji, "Bhārtiya Jain Shramaṇ-Sanskṛti anē Lēkhankalā," (Guj), in S. M. Nawab, ed., *Jainchitrakalpadrum* (Ahmedabad, 1936), *Lekhankala* Section, p. 111, footnote 130.

[23] See quotations in *Bombay Gazetteer,* Vol. IX, Part I, pp. 207-209; also *Walker's Reports* (1804-5), Selections from the Records of Bombay Government, No. XXXVII, pp. 184-86; A. K. Forbes, 1878., pp. 558-59.

[24] Muni Sri Punyavijayji, *Jñābhandāroñ par ek Drshṭipāt* (Hindi) (Ahmedabad, 1953), p. 8.

[25] D. K. Shastri, 1949, pp. 5-13.

[26] R. C. Majumdar and A. D. Pusalker, eds., *The Vedic Age* (London, 1951), pp. 304-11.

[27] P. V. Kane, *History of Dharmaśāstra* (Poona, 1944), Vol. II, Part I, pp. 43, 98-99; P. L. Bhargava, *India in the Vedic Age* (Lucknow, 1956), p. 12. Kane and Bhargava cite detailed references to texts.

[28] A. B. Jani, 1923; L. P. Tessitori, 1917-18.

[29] R. C. Majumdar and A. D. Pusalker, eds., *The Classical Age* (Bombay, 1954), p. 153.

[30] *Bombay Gazetteer,* Vol. VIII, pp. 111-12; R. B. Jote, *Gujarātno Sanskṛtic Itihās* (Guj), (Ahmedabad, 1945), I, p. 259; *Ruling Princes, Chiefs and Leading Personages in the Western India States Agency* (Delhi, 1955), pp. 17-18.

[31] K. M. Munshi, *Glory that was Gūrjara Deśa* (Bombay, 1955), Part II, p. 379.

[32] This is contained in a section on "Sketch of Feudal System in Rajasthan," *Annals and Antiquities of Rajast'han* (1950), I, pp. 107-171.

[33] "The Rājpūt States of India," *Asiatic Studies: Religious and Social,* 2nd Edition, Part I (London, 1907), pp. 203-64, quoted by Daniel Thorner in "Feudalism in India," *Feudalism in History,* Rushton Coulborn, ed (Princeton, 1956), pp. 133-43.

[34] Daniel Thorner, 1956, pp. 133-43.

[35] A. K. Forbes, 1878.

[36] Chapters on "Population," "History," and "Land Administration," Vols. I-VIII.

[37] Gitel P. Steed, "Personality Formation in a Hindu Village in Gujarat," *Village India,* McKim Marriott, ed., (1955), pp. 102-144.

[38] Quoted by Daniel Thorner, 1956, p. 142.

[39] W. H. Moreland, *The Agrarian System of Moslem India* (Cambridge, 1929), pp. 150-56; *Bombay Gazetteer,* Vol. IV (1879), 179-85.

[40] M. S. Commissariat, *History of Gujarat* (Bombay, 1938), pp. 118-19, 430.

[41] M. B. Desai, *Rural Economy of Gujarat* (Bombay, 1948), p. 99.

[42] The genealogies and history of the Rājpūt princes are printed in *Ruling Princes, Chiefs and Leading Personages in the Western India States Agency* (Delhi, 1955). F. G. H. Anderson's *Manual of Revenue Accounts of the Bombay State* mentions that the Deputy District Collector has the Watan Registers (*waṭan* 'estate') giving genealogies and history (Bombay, 1951), p. 34. The genealogies and history of Tālukdars and Wāṇṭā holders are found in these bulky registers. Besides, the Village Accountant in every village in the former British territories keeps a Register of Heirship Inquiries.

[43] "Myth in Primitive Psychology," in *Magic, Science, and Religion, and Other Essays* (Boston, 1948), p. 120.

[44] Gitel Steed, 1955, p. 114.

[45] Daniel Thorner, 1956, p. 134. The earliest references are found in the tenth century; see R. C. Majumdar and A. D. Pusalker, eds., *The Struggle for Empire* (Bombay, 1957), pp. 275, 277.

[46] Tod, 1950.

[47] Forbes, 1878, and A. B. Jani, 1923.

[48] C. V. Vaidya, *History of Medieval Hindu India* (1924), II, 1-69, 259-300; K. M. Munshi, 1955, Part I, pp. xii-xv, 18-28; R. C. Majumdar and A. D. Pusalker, *The Classical Age,* pp. 64-65.

[49] For the discussion of the theories in the medieval literature, see D. K. Shastri, 1949, pp. 126-35; K. M. Munshi, 1955, Part I, pp. 18-20.

[50] Steed, 1955.

[51] D. K. Shastri, 1949, pp. 231-46; M. S. Commissariat, 1938, p. 60.

[52] M. S. Commissariat, 1938, pp. 356-57.

[53] *Bombay Gazetteer,* VII (1883), 167, 337; Ali Muhammad Khan, *Mirāt-e-Ahmadi,* Vol. II in four parts, translated into Gujarati from Persian by K. M. Zaveri (Ahmedabad, 1933-36), Part III, pp. 526-28, 573-80; Part IV, pp. 613-16.

[54] The proceedings adopted by various British officers to suppress female infanticide in Saurashtra are recorded in *Suppression of Female Infanticide in Kattywar* (1805-1855), Selections from the Records of the Bombay Government, No. XXXIX (New Series), Part II (1856), pp. 318-721.

[55] Irawati Karve, *Kinship Organisation in India* (Poona, 1953), pp. 143-4.

[56] For a similar myth about the origin of the Coorgs of South India, see M. N. Srinivas, *Religion and Society Among the Coorgs of South India* (Oxford, 1952), pp. 34, 219-20.

[57] *Bombay Gazetteer,* III, p. 90.

[58] G. S. Ghurye, *Caste and Class in India* (New York, 1952), p. 84.

[59] (Ahmedabad, 1857), p. 46.

[60] Forbes, 1887, p. 537.

[61] *Narmakosh* (Surat, 1873), p. 107.

[62] For a discussion of the dominance of the business model in Gujarat, see D. P. Pandit, "Creative Response in Indian Economy—A Regional Analysis," *The Economic Weekly,* 23 February and 2 March, 1957.

[63] For a discussion of the relation between *jāti* and *varṇa,* see Srinivas's essay, "Varna and

Caste," in *A. R. Wadia: Essays in Philosophy Presented in his Honour* (Bangalore, 1954), particularly pp. 363-64.

[64] G. S. Ghurye, 1952, p. 71.

[65] Ghurye, 1952, p. 19.

[66] Athelstane Baines, *Ethnography: Castes and Tribes,* Verlag von Karl J. Trübner (Strassburg, 1912), p. 86. He writes about the Bhatrāzu of the Telugu country, "This branch of the caste is an exotic, introduced, under the name of Māgadha, through Orissa and probably from Bihar, in the course of invasions of the Andhra region from the north, and has not kept up either its traditions or its occupation amongst the ònce military Dravidian castes to which it was attached" (p. 86).

[67] This article has much improved by the comments of Srinivas. We are grateful to him for his guidance. We also thank I. P. Desai for his remarks. We are thankful to Milton Singer for helpful criticism in the preparation of the manuscript.

University of Baroda
Baroda, India

II. CULTURAL PERFORMANCES AND CULTURE MEDIA

THE RĀM LĪLĀ

By Norvin Hein

"RĀM LĪLĀ" means, literally, Rāma's sport. The uninitiated English reader may think "sport" a trivial term to apply to dramas which rehearse the deeds of a deity as told in an epic regarded as sacred scripture. The word *līlā* must necessarily be translated thus, but the reader should understand that "sport" represents a technical term of Hindu theology which is full of special meaning. A major tradition of Hindu thought describes as "sports" the whole of the divine acts in space and time. Confronted with the problem of how the Supreme Being, while axiomatically perfect and self-sufficient, could yet have had reason to produce the cosmos, Hindu thinkers have long taught that the creation, preservation, and dissolution of worlds spring from no lack or need on the part of God, but are the manifestations of his spontaneous joyful disinterested creativity—are his "sports."[1] Though the doctrine of *līlā* is not the whole of Vaiṣṇava thinking on this problem, it is an accepted Vaiṣṇava teaching. Not only Viṣṇu's creation of the cosmos is viewed as *līlā*, but also his actions within the cosmos when he enters into his creation in the form of his various incarnations. Thus the myths of all of Viṣṇu's *avatāras* relate his sports, and Tulsī Dās in the introduction to his *Rāmāyaṇa* can refer to the entire content of his *Rāmcaritmānas* as "Harilīlā," sports of Hari (i.e., of Viṣṇu), in his Rāma-incarnation.[2] When dramas which systematically enact the story of the *Rāmāyaṇa* are called the Rām Līlā, they are being identified by reference to their subject matter.

Dramas called Rām Līlā are produced by several different kinds of troupes, but the performances which go by this name are always based upon the *Rāmāyaṇa* of Tulsī Dās. They cover the main incidents narrated in his *Rāmcaritmānas* in a series of performances lasting many days, and they employ an unusual stage technique which combines recitation of the sacred text with simultaneous acting and dialogue. Dramas which Hindī usage consents to call Rām Līlā are sometimes produced by travelling companies of professional actors. Two such professional Rām Līlā *maṇḍalīs* were at work in Vrindaban in August 1949, when the troupe of one Paṇḍit Dīp Cand held forth nightly on a platform erected in the fruit bazaar, while another party was enacting the same sort of plays in the nearby grain market. In November of 1949 and again in February of 1950 a group of Caube Brahman actors came from Mathura and put on a month-long series of *Rāmāyaṇa* dramas. The season of Rāma's birthday in March (Caitra śukla 9th) is a time of year when troupes capable of performing on *Rāmāyaṇa* themes are likely to be active. These professional performances are called Rām Līlā, but they are not *the* Rām Līlā, and it is not these which come to mind when the words are used without qualification. The great Rām Līlā of North India is a distinct social institution, an annual feature of the *daśahrā* holidays which begin in the latter part of September. Unlike the other traditional forms of drama found in Mathura District, the *daśahrā* Rām Līlā is a strictly local production. It is organized, financed, and staged in each town under the supervision of a committee selected for this duty in a roughly democratic manner by the local Hindu community. This is the Rām Līlā which touches the experience of the average person who grows up in North India. It is this autumnal series of *Rāmāyaṇa* dramas which this essay describes.

The account which follows is based largely on personal observation and enquiry in Mathura and Vrindaban. The writer attended ten Rām Līlā performances in those towns and nearby Hathras in the *daśahrā* season of 1949 and obtained the publicity materials of the actors of the town of Aligarh. Friends from more distant cities contributed personal descriptions of the observances of their respective localities,[3] and actors and members of managing committees in Mathura and Vrindaban obligingly answered questions and supplied financial reports and other printed literature of their societies. Finally, the author is indebted to half a dozen writers of various generations of the past who have left descriptions of worth.[4] To be mentioned especially is an account of the Rām Līlā in Ghazipur written by H. Niehus in 1905, and James Prinsep's description of the festival in Banaras in the year 1825. The oral and written sources of information on practices of communities outside Mathura District were of special value in distinguishing local peculiarities from practices which are general throughout North India.

Deferring the question of how communities organize to produce these plays, we shall deal first with the persons who act in them, and the unique stage methods which they employ. The actors are recruited from the community in which they perform. The minor parts in the plays are open to all boys and men who belong to one of the four castes and whose age is regarded as proper for the particular role. Opportunities to act in the Rām Līlā tend to be sought after particularly by certain families, who provide a disproportionate number of the community's performers. There are special eligibility requirements for the roles of Rāma, his wife, and his brothers. The actors who represent these divine persons must be of Brahman caste, because, when they appear in costume and crown as the very embodiments (*svarūps*) of the divinities, even Brahmans will bow down to them and worship them. A Brahman boy may begin acting at the age of about ten years, when he may take the role of one of King Daśaratha's children—Rāma, Bharata, Lakṣmaṇa or Śatrughna—in the childhood scenes of the early books of the *Rāmāyaṇa*. On attaining the age of eleven or twelve, such a boy may be selected for the role of Sītā. At thirteen or fourteen, if talented and fortunate, he may be entrusted with the part of the grown-up Rāma. He holds this position for three or four years at most. When hair appears on his upper lip, an inexorable law of the Vaiṣṇava stage demands that his career as a *svarūp* come to an end. A younger actor must be found to take his place.

Rām Līlā actors are essentially amateurs even though they receive small cash payments and other favors. Out of the considerable treasuries raised to support the plays, Rs. 555 was divided at the end of the season among the actors and workers in Mathura in a recent year, and Rs. 161 among those in Vrindaban. In view of the large number of persons included in the distributions and in view of their month-long labors, the small individual shares were tokens of appreciation rather than pay. Free meals are provided for actors who remain on duty over meal hours. On the occasion of the enactment of Rāma's marriage, benevolent spectators give wedding presents as in real life to the actor playing the part of Rāma, and he is allowed to keep them. On the night of the enactment of Rāma's coronation, special admirers of any actor may come forward and place personal gifts in his hands. But the actors' chief gains are pleasure and prestige. Nothing of the ancient disrepute with which India has traditionally rewarded her actors attaches to the performers of the Rām Līlā. The boys who are selected for this work are highly respected and widely envied.

The *Rāmcaritmānas* of Tulsī Dās is the subject matter of the Rām Līlā. Its function is to mediate the words and meaning of this *Rāmāyaṇa* to the Hindu public through musical recitation of the text and through acting which makes the meaning of the recited text clear and vivid. In technique, the Rām Līlā harmonizes the requirements of cantillation with those of drama. *Rāmāyaṇa* recitation has the priority and determines the structure of the play. The central person in all the stage proceedings is the chanting *paṇḍit*. From a prominent vantage point on or near the stage, he sings out to audience and actors the lines of the sacred text. One who wishes to follow the progress of the drama can do no better than to take a seat beside the *paṇḍit* and follow his recitation down the pages of his large *Rāmāyaṇa* from marked verse to marked verse. Sometimes he sings all the verses without omission for several pages together; then he may skip over many pages, pick out a verse or two here and there to serve as a bridge for the narrative, and pass on to a distant episode that has been selected for intensive dramatization.

In some communities it is considered praiseworthy or even obligatory to read the entire *Rāmāyaṇa* on the stage during the days of the Rām Līlā celebration. Prinsep noted that in Banaras under the patronage of the maharaja of that place ". . . nearly the whole of the Ramayana is read through in the course of twenty or thirty days, and whatever incidents are capable of being acted, or displayed, are simultaneously exhibited."[5] But in Banaras nowadays, according to Alexandra David-Neel, the entire epic is covered only in certain extraordinary years.[6] In Satna twenty years ago the reading of every word of Tulsī Dās was considered a rigid duty. This sense of obligation involved the people of Satna in occasional trying situations. The *Rāmcaritmānas* contains numerous descriptive passages which cannot possibly be cast into lively stage action. The majority of the local people no longer understood the archaic language of Tulsī Dās well enough to enjoy it as mere literary recitation. Therefore ingenious devices were employed to lighten the burden of the audience, yet fulfill the letter of the law. The book was so divided for the stage that a night's performance ended just at the point in the book where such a wearisome passage began. The next day the *paṇḍits* would arrive early and dutifully sing the passage through to an almost empty house, finishing just as the crowds began to arrive. If an undramatic passage of some length fell unavoidably in the middle of an evening's program, the singers proceeded through it in subdued voice while the audience was kept pleasantly amused by a dance or farcial interlude.

The Rām Līlā players of the Mathura area feel free to make whatever selection from the *Rāmāyaṇa* they wish. Some incidents of the epic are omitted entirely; others are presented in abstract, so to speak; and others are produced in full with great pomp and emphasis. The selection of passages is made to be of such length that the aggregate can be acted out in the time allotted to the local dramatic festival. The chosen episodes are grouped into units of such size that each can be covered at one sitting. The resulting schedule of performances is organized into a calendar and is published before the start of the season in the form of a large handbill or poster (*līlāpatra*). A comparison of the handbills of a number of towns showed that each community's selection is uniquely its own. However, each town's way of editing the *Rāmāyaṇa* for the stage tended to be traditional, the same selection of incidents being repeated year after year.

The statement that the *Rāmcaritmānas* is the substance of the Rām Līlā requires two qualifications. The first is that some use is made of a *Rāmāyaṇa* composed by a recent poet named Radhesyam. Its modern Hindī verse is much more easily intelligible to present-day audiences than the now difficult poetry of Tulsī. In keeping with the general Indian literary custom of resorting to poetic expression in emotional situations, the actors of Vrindaban in intense scenes often abandon their usual prose dialogue for the verses of Radhesyam. This *Rāmāyaṇa* has a limited use in Satna as well. In neither town does it replace the *Rāmcaritmānas* as the text of basic recitation.

Secondly, the bulky editions of the *Rāmcaritmānas* used by the *paṇḍits* contain a good deal of material which was not written by Tulsī Dās. Printed for pious rather than scholarly use, they include a number of interpolated stories (*kṣepak*) which one cannot find in critically edited editions. One such interpolation elaborates into an episode the incident of Śabarī, the jungle woman who offered Rāma her best hospitality though it was only an offering of wild fruits. Another is the story of the *satī* of Sulocanā, the wife of Meghnād, and the extended episode of Ahirāvaṇa's carrying off of Rāma and Lakṣmaṇa into Pātāla, and the beloved passages in which Hanumān proves by tearing open his chest that the name of Rāma is written on his heart. These interpolations provide several of the most popular episodes of the Rām Līlā performances.[7]

There is no need to retell here the familiar narratives which the Rām Līlā dramatizes. With a few exceptions of the kind just mentioned, they are the stories told by Tulsī Dās, and may be read in the pleasant translations of F. S. Growse or of W. Douglas P. Hill.[8] An impression of the scope and content of the whole of a city's observances may be gained from the translation of Mathura's day-by-day calendar contained in the appendix to this chapter. It will be noted there that the presentations do not consist of dramas only. On the opening day and on the final day important rituals are performed. On numerous occasions throughout the season pageants and processions—spectacles rather than dramas—are held in the streets and other public places. The gods, for instance, go in procession to plead with Brahmā for help against the evil power of Rāvaṇa. Rāma and the demoness Tārakā lead their respective adherents through the streets, meet, and lock forces in decisive combat. When Rāma is to be married to Sītā, he travels to her parental home in a colorful wedding procession like that of mortal bridegrooms.[9] Later, Rāma with Sītā and Lakṣmaṇa walks barefoot to the edge of the city on the sad road to exile, amidst the genuine tears of many who line the streets. The citizens pour forth in a body to visit them at Citrakūṭ, which is identified for the time being with a certain spot in the suburbs. And when all the trials of the heroic family are finished, the victorious Rāma returns to meet his brother Bharata, travelling in triumphal procession with his monkey friends and allies.[10] Last and greatest of these vast open-air spectacles is the *Rāvaṇvadh*, the great outdoor pageant of the slaying of Rāma's demon enemy. In the Mathura festivities this episode was to be given serious dramatic rendering on a stage during the hours of evening, but in the afternoon it was massively and crudely represented under the open sky before a crowd equal in number to the entire population of the city. The arena was a sunken field at the edge of town, surrounded by banks and hillocks from which a hundred thousand people looked on. At one end of the field, colossal paper effigies of Rāvaṇa and his brother Kumbhakarṇa (Kumbhkaraṇ) manned the flimsy walls of a paper "fortress" of Laṅkā. There was some semblance of mute drama as Rāma and his monkey cohorts swarmed on the scene and prepared to attack. Two carriages bearing impersonators of Rāma and Rāvaṇa circled round and round in lively imitation of the tactical gyrations of the chariots of the two champions in combat. A great shout went up as Rāvaṇa was struck down. The ebullient crowd swarmed through the lines of police, the walls of Laṅkā were torn to tatters, and the images of the demons went up in flames.

These commemorative spectacles involve no dialogue nor any but the most rudimentary of pantomime. Yet these are the conspicuous public events which have time and again caught the eye of the foreign visitor and have often been photographed and described as the Rām Līlā in occidental memoirs.[11] The majority of writers have persistently reported the Rām Līlā to be a dumb show, devoid of dialogue. H. H. Wilson in *Selected Specimens of the Theatre of the Hindus* mentions it as "a mere spectacle," and Sylvain Lévi says, "The dialogue is entirely omitted. ... The action is cut up into a series of striking tableaux. ..."[12] These statements can be dismissed because their only foundation is the account of Jacquemont, who himself saw nothing of the Rām Līlā save the *Rāvaṇvadh* pageant. But writers who knew their local Rām Līlās more intimately have also reported them to be pantomime. Niehus says of the dramas in Ghazipur: "The performance consists entirely of pantomimes, to which the text is read out from the Ramayana." And Prinsep's report from Ramnagar in Banaras says, "The whole of the acting is necessarily in dumb show, and the *dramatis personae* are so numerous, and in general so unskilled in their duty, that the leaders... have great difficulty in making the performance keep pace with the oral declamation of the choir, or band of priests, who chaunt the sacred legend." In face of such testimony this writer must concede that in some places and at certain times the Rām Līlā has evidently been staged as a dumb show. But he must insist that in none of the contemporary observances that he has either seen or heard of, is this the case.

The Rām Līlā of today, at least, is full drama. Its dialogue is subordinated to textual recitation, it is true, but the subordination does not mean that dialogue is minor in quantity. Its dependence is functional, and lies in the fact that the recitation carries the thread of the story and regulates what the speech and action of the performers shall be. The *paṇḍit*, ever the key man in the proceedings, sings out the *dohās*, *caupāīs*, and *sorathās* of the printed page in the ever recurring tunes appropriate to their meters.[13] If the acting is being done on a proper stage, the *paṇḍit*'s lectern is usually seen at its right-hand border. Sometimes he and his accompanists sit on a small detached platform which projects into the audience slightly in advance of the main stage and to its right. He is often equipped with microphone and amplifier to enable him to make himself heard above the sometimes boisterous chatter of the crowd. In Vrindaban, where most of the acting is done in the out-of-doors, the *paṇḍit* seated himself on a table placed at the edge of the rectangle of dusty lawn which served as stage. In swift moving action scenes he sometimes descended to the sidelines and strode up and down with the tides of battle, holding his book before him and singing out the verses in a stentorian voice. As these *paṇḍits* begin their scriptural chant from one of these vantage points, the performers on the stage begin to display in bodily motions the action being narrated, and when the verses of the *Rāmāyaṇa* have reported the words of this or that personality, the *paṇḍit* pauses while, on the stage, the appropriate actor repeats the substance of the speech in modern Hindī prose. Sometimes the actor's utterance is a fairly literal translation and sometimes a paraphrase of the *Rāmāyaṇa*, and sometimes it is a fanciful elaboration along lines which the text merely suggests or provides with a reasonable occasion.

How cantillation and dialogue are interwoven may be seen in the transcription below of a sound recording made at an actual performance. The recording was made on the Rām Līlā stage in Mathura. The occasion was the enactment of the *Rājgaddī* or coronation of Rāma. After fourteen years of exile, Rāma is seated at last upon his rightful throne, amidst the rejoicing people of Ayodhyā. The devout of Mathura, acting nominally in the role of Rāma's loyal Ayodhyan subjects, press upward to the stage to salute their king and present gifts. Brahmans chant the Vedas before their sovereign and depart with rich rewards. Brahmā and Śiva pay their respects and take their leave. Farewells are being exchanged, and Rāma is thanking his helpers and allies of the late war and dismissing them with gifts. Here our recording begins.[14]

Chant 1

Umā's Lord[15] praised Rām's virtues,
and, happy, he went to Kailāś.
Then the Lord arranged for the monkeys
all sorts of easeful abodes.

That beauty, that pleasure in meeting
speech cannot tell, Lord of Birds![16]
Śāradā, Śeṣ, Veda[17] describe it;
such charm is known to Maheś.

Vibhīṣaṇ, contented, arose then—[18]
took up in his hand a necklace of gems.

Vibhīṣaṇ

O see! When my brother Rāvaṅ conquered the Ocean, the Ocean gave my brother at that time this necklace of gems.

Chant 2

What the Treasury of Waters gave to Rāvaṅ
Vibhīṣaṇ received in turn.
That same pleasing necklace of gems
he dropped upon Jānakī's neck.

Vibhīṣaṇ: Now I make a presentation of this necklace to the revered queen!
Bystander: Cry out, "Victory to King Rām!"

Chant 3

Its brilliance became so great
the rulers could not gaze on it directly.
It was more glorious there than the concourse of kings;
the hearts of all were charmed to see it.
At that moment Janak's daughter the queen
looked at Rām and then smiled.
The gracious Rām said, "Please listen, dear.
Give whatsoever you wish to whomsoever you please."

Rām: O Darling, please give this necklace to whomsoever you wish.

Chant 4

Then the beloved daughter of Janak, hearing the speech,
took the string of jewels from her neck.
"To whom shall I give this?" she thought in her heart.
She looked in the direction of the Son of the Wind.[19]

Sītā: To whom shall I give this necklace?

Chant 5

Noting her merciful glance, the Son of the Wind,
pleased, made a prostration.
That necklace of jewels the daughter of Janak
dropped around his throat.[20]

Bystander: Cry out, "Victory to Queen Sītā!"

Chant 6

Mahāvīr reflected in his mind,
"There is some great excellence in the necklace."

Hanumān

In the necklace which the revered Mother has graciously given me there must surely be some special excellence. Only for this reason has my Mother shown me the favor.

Chant 7

Soaked in the syrup of love for the Supremely Blissful One,
he began to look at all the gems.
"Save light, there's nothing else in it
to appeal to the hearts of devotees!"

Hanumān

The revered Mother has doubtless given this out of kindness. But in it, apart from light, no other thing is visible to which the minds of devotees should be attracted.

Chant 8

"Within the gem there must be some kernel."
Then he broke one pearl.

Hanumān

But a thing given by Mother cannot be without importance. Therefore there surely must be some kernel inside these gems. I am going to break one bead first, and see. (The actor crushes one bead between his teeth. Since the "gems" are grapes, this is not difficult.)

Chant 9

He began to scrutinize the inside of it.
Seeing this, people were soaked in astonishment.

Hanumān

Inside this, nothing is visible but lustre. Just as there is lustre outside, there is lustre inside too, but far more than that.

Chant 10

Then stout Hanumān broke another.
Seeing it to be without kernel, he discarded it.

Hanumān: There's nothing in this either!

Chant 11

In this way he breaks one pearl after another.
It gives great pain to the multitude of bystanders.

Bystander: O look! Why is Hanumān here breaking this necklace of gems in this way?

Chant 12

They began to say, each in his own mind,
"To one who has no fitness
Please do not give such a thing,
or see the same sad state of affairs!"
Then some king cried out,
"What are you doing, Hanumān?
Why are you breaking the necklace—
the beautiful jewels—O Wise One?"

Bystander

O Hanumān, why are you breaking up and throwing away a necklace of such beautiful and priceless jewels?

Chant 13

Hearing the speech, the Son of the Wind said,
"I am looking for the joy-giving name of Rām.
The Name is not to be seen in this;
that is why I am breaking it, O brother."

Hanumān

Brother, I am looking in it for the name of the joy-giving Rām. The name of my Lord is not visible in it, brother. That's why I'm breaking it.

Chant 14

Someone said, "One does not hear anywhere
that the name of Rām is in all things!"

Bystander

O Hanumān, the name of Rām is not inside everything; and we, with our ears, have never heard anything to that effect anywhere!

Chant 15

Said the Son of the Wind, "What hasn't the Name in it,
isn't of any use at all."

Hanumān

O brother, that thing is not of any use in which there is not the name of my Lord!

Chant 16

The same person said, "Listen, O Abode of Strength!
does the name of Rām exist in your body?"

The Same Bystander

O Hanumān, you abode of strength, is the name of the Lord Rām written even in your heart?

Chant 17

Hearing the speech, the Son of the Wind said,
"Certainly Hari's noble name is in my body!"

Hanumān: Yes, the name of the supremely noble Lord must surely be in my body!

Chant 18

Having spoken thus, the ape tore open his own heart.
On every hair's breadth were the infinite names of the Lord.
Seeing the name of Rām stamped everywhere,
all became astonished at heart.
There was a rain of flowers, shouts of "Victory!" in the sky.
Raghunāth[21] gazed with gracious glance.
Hanumān's body became as hard as the thunderbolt[22] again.
At once the Lord rose up;
With his body a-tingle and tears in his eyes
he took Hanumān to his heart.

In costuming, each North Indian community follows its own fancies, guided by only a few generally shared conceptions.[23] One such accepted notion is that murky colors are appropriate for demonic beings. Everywhere, Rāvaṇa and his henchmen are seen in blue or black clothing; the faces of the lesser demons are blackened with soot. Rāvaṇa's ten-headedness is always somehow represented, but in headgear of patterns differing greatly from community to community. The general intention in designing the dress of Rāma is that he should be made to look a king. But since the conceptions of royalty in the popular mind are vague, the results are various. In some towns Rāma wears a *cogā*. The costume worn in Mathura is a richly embroidered, red velvet coat reminiscent of an old style of western court dress. Sītā wears her distinctive coronet, called a *candrikā*, and a nose pendant of pearl (*bulāk*). The headdress of Rāma, here as everywhere, is a high cylindrical crown of a type peculiar to himself. A white feather (*turrā*) is fixed at its forward peak, and at the very top there rises a spade shaped crest called *kirīṭ*. Major protrusions from the right and left sides of the headgear are said to represent earrings (*kuṇḍal*). A tassel of strung pearls (*jhūṃkā*) dangles from each of these ear ornaments. A halo (*tej*) is attached to the rear of the crown. The lower border of the crown is fringed with a string of pearls (*baṃdanī*). The dots and lines of sandalwood paste which often ornament the face of the actor are without special meaning. The *tilak* worn in the middle of the forehead by Mathura actors is of the pattern peculiar to members of the Śrīvaiṣṇava or Rāmānuja Saṃpradāya.

There is great local variation in stage design. No single structure or layout can be called the Rām Līlā stage. Since audiences sit upon mats on the ground, actors remain passably visible even when the stage is only a rectangle of earth under the open sky.

Therefore, communities can be found which do not trouble to put up any kind of erected stage. When elevated and covered platforms are built for the Rām Līlā, their function is not always to provide a central floor for the action. They may represent specific fortresses, palaces, or other buildings, serving only occasionally as the scene of some part of the panoramic action. It is a widely acknowledged principle of staging that, whenever a change of geographical setting occurs in the story of the *Rāmāyaṇa*, the scene of acting must undergo a complete shift to indicate the change of place. A move is made at such times to a new arena, usually in another part of the town. The Mathura players perform during their season in six different localities within their city. The events set in Ayodhya and Janakpur are enacted on a stage erected in a large open air grain market in the heart of the Mathura business district. The heaven of Viṣṇu to which the gods go to plead for help against Rāvaṇa is set up in a nearby bazaar. Viśvāmitra's hermitage is identified with the grounds of a local temple. A landing place on the banks of the Jamna River becomes Prayag, where Rāma's famous dialogue with Kevaṭa the ferryman takes place. Citrakūṭ has yet another location, and the jungle scenes another. At most of these places a good deal of labor is expended in preparing special facilities for players and spectators. A group of young men who gained control of the Rām Līlā in Vrindaban some years ago were convinced that their audiences had no real need of such costly literal representation of the various localities of the Rāmāyaṇa. Defying the convention of the shifting stage, they began a tradition of holding preformances night after night in a single arena on the grounds of the Temple of Raṅgjī. They give token recognition to the older principle, however, by enacting their various scenes now on one side, now on another, of the extensive strip of lawn that is their stage.

In building whole new theaters, so to speak, for each major change in scene, the Rām Līlā is lavish. But it is economical in use of scenery and stage properties. Save for a solitary throne in palace scenes, the stages are practically bare. Therefore they can be conceived as elastic, like the fields on which occidental pageants are enacted. If the plays are currently running in the spot designated as Ayodhya, the stage set up in that place can, with trifling shifts or none in stage equipment, represent any and every part of Ayodhyā. When later another stage is used for the jungle scenes, it serves as setting for every action said to have taken place in a thousand miles of jungle; one of its borders represents the site of Rāma's military headquarters on the Indian mainland, and the other side, twenty feet away, is Rāvaṇa's throne room in Ceylon.

This nonliteral way of conceiving and using the stage area manifested itself in facilities of quite different appearance in the three cities of the writer's experience.

In the town of Hathras a great pavilion had been erected, accommodating on its broad earthen floor not only the contending actors involved in the battle for Laṅkā, but most of the audience as well. A low platform under the center of this canopy served as the field headquarters of Rāma. A smaller platform in a distant corner represented the fortress of Laṅkā. Throughout the performance it was the place of Sītā's imprisonment and the roosting place of Rāvaṇa and his demon henchmen. A corridor between these two centers was kept clear of spectators, and up and down its length the war between the factions raged to and fro.

In Mathura the spectators sat upon mats under the open sky, but, for the protection of the actors, raised stages with roof and sidewalls of cloth were built on a framework of heavy bamboo poles. The floor-space was divided by partitions into three fairly equal sections. At the rear was a large dressing room, sufficient to contain the great number of actors required by the dramas. The forestage was open, without curtains of any kind. The middle section was separated from the forestage by a filmy gauze curtain. When unlighted, its reaches were invisible to the audience, and were used as a waiting room by actors about to go on stage. But when illuminated, its interior was fully visible and served as a stage-within-a-stage for the representation of visions, dreams, or reveries. The forward section of the stage was the scene of the principal action of the plays. Though the space available for acting there was vast, it always shrank steadily during an evening's performance through the creeping encroachment upon it of children and the deferential seating of dignitaries along its borders. On this stage, too, particular sides or corners were made to represent particular *Rāmāyaṇa* localities. Rāvaṇa's stronghold was at center rear, and there he usually squatted with his sooty crew around him, even when not participating in the current action of the play. Rāma and his chiefs formed a continuing cluster likewise, just off the center of the forestage. Throughout the Laṅkā scenes the two parties confronted each other thus across a stage floor on which envoys went hither and thither, and across which the respective champions made their raids and fought their personal combats.

The staging arrangements in Vrindaban were analogous, but not at all similar superficially. The field of action was an avenue of beaten grass and earth some forty yards long and twenty broad. On one side of it sat and stood the adult male spectators; on the other the women and children. There was a roofed platform at the north end of this strip, but it did not serve the purposes of a true stage. The deities sat formally in its shelter to receive worship at the beginning and at the close of each evening's performance. During the conflicts of Rāma with Rāvaṇa it served as headquarters and rallying place for Rāma's forces. A low and roofless platform at the south end of the avenue was Rāvaṇa's citadel and the principal hangout of his demons. The action of the play moved up and down on the no man's land between. To present the story of an embassage or a foray, there was no need to replace painted jungle scenery with canvas battlements, for all localities involved in the epic narrative were continuously before the eyes of the spectators.

Let us describe how this outdoor stage was used on the evening of 11 October 1949. The portions of the *Rāmcaritmānas* which were to be enacted included the accounts of Rām's battle with Kumbhkaraṇ, and of Lakṣmaṇ's victory over Meghnād. These episodes were cast into tumultuous action. No recording machine could have caught all the dialogue, nor would the dialogue if recorded provide an adequate account of the happenings. Some scenes were made up of almost pure motion, few words being heard save the occasional narrative chant of the *paṇḍit*. But if a recording had been possible, it would usually show a mixture of recited verses and prose dialogue as in the text already presented.

The first stirrings of activity on this Rām Līlā stage begin at nine o'clock in the evening. Paṇḍit Kundanlāl arrives on the stroke of the hour, deposits his harmonium on the reader's table at the margin of the reserved area, and confers with the accompanists who are to handle the cymbals and drums. Rām and Lakṣmaṇ in full regalia now enter the stage at north and seat themselves with quiet dignity on a dais. An *āratī* tray with flaming wicks is brought and moved gently up and down in a circular pattern before them. A second attendant unwraps a large copy of the *Rāmcaritmānas* ceremoniously, rotates it over the flame of the lamp, and carries it to the *paṇḍit*'s reading stand. Hanumān, who has been attending on the deities, now bounds down from the stage and leads the spectators in a shout of *Rāmcandra jī kī jay* 'Victory to Rāmcandra!' At 9:20 the *paṇḍit* raises his voice in chant, and with this act the drama proper begins.

The previous night's performance had ended with Lakṣmaṇ's recovery from a grievous wound inflicted by Meghnād's magic weapon, the *śakti*. Now Lakṣmaṇ's renewed fighting power again threatens the demons. Rāvaṇ, worried, is seen leaving his dark southern fortress to call to his aid his monstrous brother Kumbhkaraṇ 'Pot-ears.' That massive demon has been sleeping—a shapeless heap—on a rope bed in the middle of the field. We can hear as well as see his slumbers. Kumbhkaraṇ has eaten such a gluttonous meal six months past that for half a year he has been sunk in sleep. The counterpane pitches and quivers with each inhalation of his mountainous paunch. The blare of his hoarse snores reaches the farthest spectator.

Rāvaṇ prods him. Rāvaṇ pleads his desperate need of help. Pot-ears hears nothing. The demon king calls from his capital a host of minor imps and orders them to wake his brother. The average age of these apprentice demons is perhaps nine or ten. Their whole equipment is a soot smeared face, a blue-black shirt well fouled with dust, and an exuberant willingness to attempt any mischievous assignment. The clowning spirit in which the demons carry out their diabolic responsibilities is striking. In this day and age the goblins of old are taken lightly and even take themselves lightly. The imps swarm upon Kumbhkaraṇ—sit on his neck, clamber to the top of his abdominal hump, jump up and down on his paunch and shriek. Kumbhkaraṇ belches, shrugs them off. They climb on again. His belches become awakening grunts. He sits up and roars. Rāvaṇ tries to explain to him the current peril to the demon cause. Kumbhkaraṇ's mind is preoccupied with ordering breakfast: a herd of roasted buffalo, and a million bottles of wine. The imps lug in huge baskets of victuals. Like stokers, they throw food with shovels into the minister's greedy maw—all the while stuffing themselves as well. His mouth is too full to speak clearly, but Kumbhkaraṇ keeps bellowing for more. In his greedy appetites and loud voice, Kumbhkaraṇ incarnates the qualities which Hindu feeling looks upon as the nadir of breeding and virtue.

Finally, bloated with food and heated with wine, Kumbhkaraṇ picks up his ungainly body and lurches off toward the wars. As demon general, he musters an untidy army from among the imps. He drills his disorderly squads by bawling in corrupt English, "*rāīṭ, leyafṭ, rāīṭ, leyafṭ . . . hālṭ!*" To salute, the demons assume a squatting posture and hold their noses. They prostrate themselves in the dust before their commander. Now the whole body rises and charges off in the direction of Rām's camp in a formation as military as the snake dance at a high school football rally.

In mid-field, Kumbhkaraṇ meets his brother Vibhīṣaṇ, who has abandoned his evil kin to espouse the cause of Rām. The fate driven brothers pause to take final leave of each other. Vibhīṣaṇ then breaks away to warn Rām of Kumbhkaraṇ's impending attack. Rām gives the alarm to a host of juveniles who have been swarming about him in the red jackets of his monkey allies. The signal stirs them up even beyond their usual agitation. They pour down upon the field. Ununiformed irregulars join in from nearby rows of young spectators. Rām's motley host rolls out, collides with the horde of Kumbhkaraṇ, and both dissolve in dust: the rival groups of little boys catch hold of each other's shirttails and pull and push each other down into the dirt in the best of spirits. A group of agile "monkeys" begins to tease Kumbhkaraṇ. He lunges vainly at them again and again, with threatening roars. Finally he pulls up a "tree" (a branch planted upright in the ground for the purpose), and with menacing sweeps he drives the young apes back before him to their camp.

Twanging the string of his bow, Rām leaps down from the platform to succor his fleeing allies. The soldiers of the demon army see him and turn tail, leaving Kumbhkaraṇ to face Rām alone. A protracted duel begins between the two champions. To the measured rhythm of the *paṇḍit*'s continuous scriptural recitation, the combatants circle each other. The whirling steps and the stylized brandishing of weapons give the battle almost the appearance of a dance. Rām discharges light reed arrows which drop at his opponent's feet or flutter in the air above. At last the two close in. Kumbhkaraṇ goes down heavily. Wails go up from the demon camp, and from the crowd a shout of "*Rāmcandra jī kī jay!*"

Meghnād, son of Rāvaṇ, rises from among the demon cluster now, a picture of vengeful wrath. Standing on the edge of the platform and waving a scimitar, he makes a vaunting speech in a *rākṣasa* tongue that sounds very much like Urdu. Then he rushes forth and falls upon the dark gowned actor who plays the role of Rām's ally, the bear Jāmbavān. They grapple. The bear throws Meghnād down and pins him to the earth for a moment, but he breaks free and returns, shaken, to his base. Next Meghnād tries to gain supernatural power by performing a Vedic-type sacrifice. He and his urchins fix their black pennant in the ground, build a fire, and seat themselves around it. A ritual chant goes up from them in the cadence of Vedic recitation, but their language is a jabberwocky, a demon's pseudo-Sanskrit which brings a roar of laughter from the audience. At the other end of the field Vibhīṣaṇ warns Rām that the sacrifice, if completed, will make Meghnād almost invincible. Rām sends forth his monkeys to interrupt the rite. The monkeys swirl around the group of sacrificers, at first keeping a respectful distance. The busy demons take no notice of them. The monkeys grow bold; they swarm in, kick the demons' backs and pull their hair. They badger Meghnād to such a fury that he breaks away from the fire. Thereby his sacrifice is spoiled. Rām requests Lakṣmaṇ now to put an end to Meghnād altogether. As Meghnād is pursuing the monkeys up and down the field, Lakṣmaṇ stops him short. The two join in the dance-like combat, and Meghnād falls under Lakṣmaṇ's arrows.

The last scene of the evening showed the *satī* of Meghnād's faithful wife Sulocanā. The day's events ended at midnight with the usual flame worship of the impersonated deities.

The Rām Līlā is produced under the supervision of a committee elected by an annual meeting of all the Rām Līlā enthusiasts of a locality. The committee raises and spends the budget, marshalls the public processions, and exercises a power of final decision in every matter connected with the observances. The supervisory bodies of all communities are much alike in structure and function, but they bear a variety of names. The promoting body in Satna was known by the English title, The Ram Lila Committee. The dramas in Hathras are publicized as the activities of the *Sārvajanik Dhārmik Sabhā*, The Public Religious Society, and in Vrindaban the publications of the association appear under the name of the *Śrī Pañcāyatī Rāmlīlā Kameṭī*, the Public Rām Līlā Committee. The general public and even the officials of the organizations use these names casually, substituting equivalents freely in speech and in print.

The idea is an established one that a town ought to have one Rām Līlā celebration, conducted under the auspices of a group representing the united Hindu community.

Though this ideal is recognized, it is often honored in the breach. Banaras has long had at least three bands of performers at work during the *daśahrā* season. Any group of malcontents or enthusiasts are conceded a right to organize an independent performance in their own ward of a town and to compete for the preeminence. If they prove clever in assembling talent and funds they may eventually win the position of the recognized Rām Līlā of the place. The memory of the older residents of Vrindaban is long enough to record the decline of several Rām Līlā organizations and the rise of others to supremacy. Though a rivalry of this kind is found to be going on frequently enough, the normal situation in any town is that one group of players either has the field entirely to itself or surpasses all others so decisively that it is recognized without question as *the* Rām Līlā society of the city.

In Vrindaban at the present time such preeminence belongs to the performers who meet at the Temple of Raṅgjī, the city's one large shrine dedicated to Rāma. The *Śrī Pañcāyatī Rāmlīlā Kameṭī* of Vrindaban was organized about forty years ago when the Temple of Raṅgjī (Rāma), then still relatively new, first attracted to itself a group of Rām Līlā players. The temple authorities provide a room for the committee's meetings and for the storage of its equipment, but neither the priests nor the temple manager exert any special influence in the society's affairs. The managing committee has a membership of about twelve, half of whom are businessmen and the other half Brahmans engaged in professional religious duties of one kind or another. Several members have college degrees.

This committee, like others of its kind elsewhere, is responsible eventually to the subscribers who provide the funds. In August of each year, about thirty days before the performances are to begin, the committee of the previous season sends messengers through the city to announce by beat of drum the annual meeting of the full society. The voting membership at this gathering consists of those present who made contributions toward the expenses of the Rām Līlā of the year before. The informal proceedings are governed by no written constitution or rules of order. The agenda seldom includes decisions on the detailed manner of performing the dramas, because such matters are rather completely fixed by local custom. The most important work of the evening is the election of new members to fill vacancies in the managing committee, and the launching of the financial campaign. The old committee proposes for the meeting's approval a list of new co-workers. One consideration in the selection of new members is enthusiasm and capacity for organizational work. But a second qualification, at least as important, is ability to help in one way or another in raising funds, for the most essential function of the managing committee is to meet the expenses of producing the plays and spectacles. The meeting also draws up a list of authorized solicitors. The committee members themselves form the core of the money raising staff.

During the month's interval between this general meeting and the beginning of the performances, the committee's canvassers scour the city, receipt book in hand, asking contributions from the head of every family of any substance. The extent to which the Rām Līlā is a folk affair is indicated by the published financial reports of the committees of Vrindaban and Mathura.[24] The Vrindaban committee raised Rs. 891 in 1946. Rs. 727 of this came from 613 contributors, most of whom gave one rupee. The largest single sum was a grant of forty rupees from the municipal government. The names of 183 of the donors were plainly Brahman, 164 were recognizable as those of persons of the merchant class, three were Muslim names. The remaining twenty percent of the budget was obtained from the public largely through offerings given on certain ritual occasions connected with the spectacles themselves. When the *Bharatmilāp* procession is making its leisurely passage through the city, shopkeepers along the way invite the impersonators of the deities into their shops and offer refreshments and small gifts of money. And when each night's drama comes to a close with the *ārati* worship of the enthroned deities, many devout onlookers press up to the stage, pass their fingers over the flame of the lamp, and drop a coin into the tray on which it rests. The final evening of the series, the night of the coronation of Rāma, is an occasion when it is the duty of all those who have attended throughout the season to come forward at the time of the *ārati* and present a special gift. This is an obligation recognized and felt by all. The finance drive is the opportunity for those affluent enough to give in rupees; the *āratis* are occasions for those who can give only in coppers.

The report of the Mathura committee for the same year was signed by twelve members, seven of whom were merchants, three *paṇḍits*, one a teacher, and one a doctor. The total budget of Rs. 4151 reflected Mathura's greater population and wealth, but the sources of income were much the same. A total of Rs. 3572 was contributed by 740 donors. More than a hundred subscribers gave ten rupees each or more, but once again the treasury was filled mainly through contributions of one or two rupees. The municipal government made no direct cash grant, but paid a bill for special street lighting amounting to ninety-four rupees. In addition, the public works department of the city made available the services of a gang of its laborers to move equipment about and keep the grounds clean. A corps of boy volunteers contributed personal service in maintaining order and directing the crowds at the performances. A club of *Rāmāyaṇa* enthusiasts called the *Rāmāyāṇ Pracāriṇī Sabhā* usually assumes some special responsibility for the costumes of the actors. Generally speaking it is the middle classes of these cities which furnish most support to the Rām Līlā and fill the ranks of its managing committees. Nevertheless, our study shows that its financial burden is widely distributed among hundreds of people. No individual or clique is in a position to control it through financial patronage. So broad is the popular support of the Rām Līlā that it would be hard to find any activity which expresses more directly the ideals and tastes of the Hindu public of a North Indian town.

One of the responsibilities of a Rām Līlā committee is to decide when the series of dramas shall begin, and for how many days it shall continue. To try to discern the principles by which the committees are guided is a puzzling study. It has been possible to collate information on the calendars of sixty-three communities: the four small cities of Braj mentioned before, and fifty-nine places whose usual calendar for the *daśahrā* season as listed in the *District Gazetteers of the United Provinces of Agra and Oudh*[25] makes clear reference to the existence of a local Rām Līlā, and specifies the dates on which it customarily started and ended. The data of the gazetteers is fifty years old, but because it includes information on the observances of a great many small towns and villages it is probably still needed as a corrective for the impression made by the elaborate celebrations of the cities. The duration of the Rām Līlā in these sixty-three places ranges all the way from nine to twenty-six days. In our four cities of Braj, long runs of eighteen to twenty-six days prevailed, but the places large and small listed in the gazetteers showed an average run of only ten or eleven. Our conclusion is that a nine day series of dramas is evidently considered a minimum, and that a Rām Līlā committee may lengthen the season beyond nine days according to its financial means, the talent and interest of the people of the community, and the established custom of the place.

After deciding how many nights the dramas shall continue, the Rām Līlā committee must set the dates on which they shall begin and end. In the sixty-three calendars studied, the one common factor was that all included the nine days leading up to and including the tenth day of the light fortnight of the month of Āśvin, the *vijayā daśamī* day or "Triumphant Tenth" on which Rāma is said to have slain Rāvaṇa and stormed his citadel. Futhermore, there seems to be an almost universal sense that the final defeat of Rāvaṇa should actually be staged on that day. Only the Vrindaban players—ever unconventional—disregarded this rule by enacting Rāvaṇa's defeat eleven days later. In places where only a short series of nine or ten nights' performances is being put on, the story of victorious Rāma's happy return and ascension of the throne is abbreviated and included in the performance on *vijayā daśamī*, and with that day the whole project terminates. Many towns which can afford to be more leisurely continue for two more days—not by shifting the *Rāvaṇvadh* from its customary date, but by devoting a separate evening to Rāma's reunion with his brother (the *Bharatmilāp*) and another to the coronation scenes. A few even add two futher sessions, featuring first Rāma's farewell to the monkeys, and then a concluding benedictory ritual. The generalizations about the Rām Līlā calendar which will stand are as follows: the dramas are held on dates which are sure to include Āśvin śukla 2nd through 10th; the killing of Rāvaṇa is almost universally enacted on the 10th; and communities may, with perfect conventionality, add three or four days of drama after the 10th, and begin as many days before the 2nd as they like.

The managing committee does not usually take direct responsibility for rehearsals and stage management. They take an active part in recruiting actors, but find it wise to delegate their training and supervision to persons having special practical skill. These directors are usually men who, in their younger days, acted in the Rām Līlā themselves. In Vrindaban one *paṇḍit* Puruṣottam, the priest of a local temple, coaches the young actors in the dialogues which are traditional in that town. Allowing them some liberty in formulating their prose speeches, he drills them with strictness in the exact recitation of the occasional verse components of their parts. The teaching function is carried out in Mathura by a trio which includes a *sādhu* named Bhadra Babaji, a professional *paṇḍit* named Govindji Caube, and a jeweler named Girrajmal who knows the entire series of plays by heart and whose specialized task it is to sit beside the stage during rehearsals and call to account any actor who departs verbally from the dialogue sanctified by custom. The town of Satna followed the unusual practice of bringing in from Ayodhya for the season a professional director of the Rām Līlā.

Considering the immensity of the material of the plays, rehearsal is taken rather lightly. Vrindaban's director tutors his actors individually in their recitations, but holds hardly any group rehearsals at all. Consequently the finished pageantry shows an awkwardness arising from constant physical improvisation. Rehearsals begin in Mathura two or three weeks before the opening night. Every third year or so, when new actors must be trained for the major roles, practice begins a little earlier. There, training in bodily movement is not entirely neglected, but the generalization still holds that the Rām Līlā emphasizes facility of verbal expression and views stage deportment as a matter of minor importance.

To undertake an aesthetic evaluation of the Rām Līlā is to attempt to judge the standards and tastes of the North Indian masses. Not many of the performances are filled with such heroics and buffoonery as the farcical struggle with Pot-ears which we have just seen, nor is the intense emotional piety of our earlier recorded text to be taken as representing the single mood of the Rām Līlā. The mixture of piety and light heartedness, together, gives it its tone. It grips its audience of thousands because, the community as a whole being its producers and to some extent its playwrights, it is the mirror of traditional folk interests and ideals. Seasoning the episodes with humor and feeling, the actors go through the old stories playing upon one popular emotion after another; the delight in children, the love of weddings, the sympathy for separated lovers; admiration for the obedient son and loyal wife, delight in the grotesque, feeling for animals, adoration of the fearless hero. The affectionate piety of Tulsī Dās suffuses play and audience; one sees it in the raptness of many an eye in the audience which seems to expect at any moment an actual appearance of its god. Through Tulsī's influence also, vulgarity is not among the Rām Līlā's concessions to the popular mind. Nothing indecent is so much as hinted at. It is as true of the dramas as of the scripture on which they are based, ". . . here are no prurient and seductive stories like snails, frogs and scum on the water, and therefore the lustful crow and greedy crane, if they do come, are disappointed."[26] From Tulsī, too, comes the ethereal but earnest moral idealism of the Rām Līlā's ingenuous tale of a clear-cut struggle between good and evil.

Regarding the Rām Līlā's technical sophistication, Niehus calls it "the theatre in its baby-shoes"—and with some cause. It moves on amidst a degree of confusion which many outsiders would regard as intolerable. Spectators are allowed to invade the dressing room and even the stage. Onlookers when momentarily tired of the play chatter among themselves without inhibition. The paintings daubed on the cloth partitions of the stages are far less effective than pictures of the pure imagination. By foreign standards, the emotion of pathos is often indulged excessively. Since the project is too massive to be brought to perfection in the time allowed for rehearsal, the stage action lumbers on jerkily. The physical movements of the actors are usually somewhat stiff and under-expressed, showing little of the Indian dancer's facility in translating meaning into felicitous motion. The performers themselves measure their accomplishment in terms of quality of declamation, and this, as the writer has heard it, has been very well done indeed. With only the slightest trace of a sing-song, the actors spoke with a clarity, volume, poise and feeling that would be highly creditable anywhere, especially in teenage actors. The artistic level of the Rām Līlā as a whole reflects the fact that it is an amateur and popular institution, but sometimes at least it rises to excellence. Visitors who have pronounced it a primitive exhibition have done so on the basis of too slight acquaintance, usually limited to attendance at one of the crude outdoor pageants.

We turn now from aesthetic to social appraisal. How important is the Rām Līlā as an instrument of Hindu cultural education? A mere summary opinion on so general a question would not be instructive nor convincing. Let us break the inquiry down, therefore, into specific questions which can be answered more or less objectively. How deep an impression do the dramas make upon those who attend them? How large a part of the population of a given community do they reach? How thickly distributed are the centers in which the Rām Līlā is performed? How wide is the geographical area in which the Rām Līlā prevails? How long has this dramatic tradition been going on?

Of all these matters only the question of the power of the Rām Līlā to hold and impress its audience will have to be dealt with on the basis of personal impression. The performances observed by this writer were obviously highly successful in communicating the mythology and moral teachings of Hinduism. Their effectiveness could be perceived directly, in the intent faces of row on row of wide-eyed children who nightly packed its theater. Night after night for several weeks boys and girls of every age absorbed through eye and ear at the Rām Līlā a précis of the *Rāmāyaṇa* with a most vivid and intelligible commentary. A considerable body of lore is necessarily fixed upon the memory of any Hindī knowing person who has sat through the Rām Līlā even two or three times during the course of his life. The high degree of familiarity with the mythology of the *Rāmāyaṇa* which one finds among the common people of North India is hard to explain without assuming the existence of an effective means of oral education. Reading alone cannot explain it, because the majority cannot read. The Rām Līlā, if proved to be widespread in North India, may be regarded as an important contributor to this result. To my own judgment that the Rām Līlā is a powerful influence I can only add the testimony of the beloved poet Hariścandra of Banaras, "the Father of Hindī Literature," who about eighty years ago composed the following tribute: "Hari's play is a giver of happiness in every way./It enters the heart through speaking, hearing, and seeing and increases devotion./Love grows, sin flees, love of virtue springs up in the heart./That is why Haricand daily listens and applauds the deeds of Hari."[27]

Pending demonstration that the Rām Līlā is an institution of some age, we may credit it with having helped to preserve the continuity of Hindu political aspiration also. In the region where the Rām Līlā goes on, it is the most universally accepted and the most widely attended of Hindu festivals, having an appeal as nonsectarian as that of the *Rāmāyaṇa*. While all eyes focus upon the great culminating spectacles of the Rām Līlā—the return of victorious Rāma to his kingdom, his ascension of the throne, his acceptance of the fealty of his rejoicing subjects, and his making of arrangements for a utopian reign—the attention of the Hindu community is united as at no other time. Though the participants have not generally felt any conflict between their devotion to King Rāma and their allegiance to Mogul or British monarch, there was political significance, nevertheless, in the rare unity shown on these occasions, and in the specific content of certain of the pageants, and in the intense self-identification of the Hindu onlooker with them. When the Hindu citizens of a town at the time of the *Bharatmilāp* flocked in thousands to the edge of their city to join with Bharata in welcoming the returning Rāma, they were not turning out as mere spectators to see actors perform in a play. According to a prime doctrinal assumption of the Vaiṣṇava stage, they were thronging to welcome the god-king himself, incarnated temporarily in the body of an actor. And they themselves who hailed him as he passed in procession had a role to play: for the moment they were part of no Muslim nor Britannic empire, but subjects of King Rāma and citizens of his capital, Ayodhyā the Unassaultable. Robert Needham Cust perceived the subtle relation between Rām Līlā and national feeling in a striking comment on the excitements of the pageantry in Banaras more than a century ago: "More wondrous is it, when we consider, that it is a people, who have naught of real nationality, who know not even the name of patriotism, who have bowed for centuries abjectly to any conqueror whom chance might place over them; who are incapable of unity for their own advantage; yet on this one occasion they raise the cry of victory, though defeated; display unity of action, though hopelessly dissevered; and might pass for patriots, did we not know they were not so."[28] From the vantage ground of today we may add that the appearance of patriotism was not entirely an illusion. A seed of patriotic feeling was being guarded in this institution like a spark in ashes. As a mere spark it had no political force, but it was a spark which Mahatma Gandhi would blow into open flame one day by speaking to the simple folk of restoring *Rāmrāj*, the happy rule of Rāma. They could respond to this ideal because they had long responded to it. It was one of the few vital indigenous political ideas remaining in the vastly unpolitical mind of the oldtime Indian peasant. Through centuries of foreign rule the Rām Līlā helped preserve a basis for civic resurrection. It is a thing to be considered in the history of Indian nationalism.

We have ventured to speak of a possible widespread effect of the Rām Līlā before ascertaining how wide its outreach really is. What fraction of a community's population may be supposed to be touched by its Rām Līlā? Very high percentages could be given here if one wished to speak of the great crowds of twenty to a hundred thousand which in Mathura turned out to witness the processions and pageants. But the deep influence is that of the daily recitation-dramas, and we shall take account of the attendance at them only. By the rough estimate of this writer and others, the evening performances at Mathura drew crowds which averaged not less than 2500 people. About three percent of the population of Mathura and Vrindaban turned out nightly to see the plays at their respective centers. The provincial gazetteers include estimates of the Rām Līlā attendance of three hundred and eight towns, the average of which is 3525 persons. Since some of the attendance figures which are listed for certain towns run as high as 150,000 persons, it is clear that some local officials reported to the editor of the gazetteers the attendance at the great Rām Līlā pageants. The average of 3525 has been inflated considerably thereby, and we must discount the figure a great deal if we would get a true notion of the attendance at the plays. But if we suppose that the average crowd throughout the province actually numbered nearer one thousand than three, we are still reminded that we must not compare the audiences of the Rām Līlā with the relatively small groups of people attending western stage plays. The percentage of the population which turns out in Mathura and Vrindaban is probably not unrepresentative. Though these places are great centers of pilgrimage and might be supposed to have an exceptional number of residents interested in religious dramas, this fact is balanced by the smallness of the number of Rāma shrines and the high preference of the people of the area for the worship of Kṛṣṇa.

How intensively the Rām Līlā covers the Uttar Pradesh or United Provinces can be judged with some objectivity from the data on festivals given in the district gazetteers. Three hundred and twenty-one towns are named as celebrating the *daśahrā* holiday with a Rām Līlā. In addition, a vast number are said merely to celebrate "*daśahrā*," with no indication of whether Rāma or Durgā is honored. Fifty years ago, many more than 321 towns staged some kind of Rām Līlā—how many more we cannot tell. We venture the opinion that there must be few villagers in the North Indian plains who are not within an evening's walking distance of a Rām Līlā during the *daśahrā* season.

The boundaries of the territory in which the Rām Līlā prevails can be traced out roughly by examining a sea of literature on the holiday customs of many places.[29] As we have just mentioned, Uttar Pradesh (with the exception of the Himalayan districts) is thoroughly devoted to the Rām Līlā. The Rām Līlā extends into Bihar and East Panjab, and deep into Madhya Pradesh. It has been reported as far south as Nagpur, but our material indicates that in Berar's Marathi speaking country, the enactment of Rāma's deeds takes place during ten days of April, uses a different technique, and no doubt has a different literary basis. Rām Līlā is not reported in descriptions of the *daśahrā* observances of Nepal, Bengal, Mysore, nor even Maharashtra and Rajputana; instead we read of Durgāpūjā, animal sacrifice, and worship of weapons. Performances have been noted in such distant places as Calcutta, Lahore, and Srinagar, but the plays there seem to be put on by groups of émigrés from North India. During September and October the Rām Līlā country is like a great central island in a sea of Devī worship. In general, its geographical home is that area in which Hindī is an everyday language and the *Rāmcaritmānas* can be made intelligible without great difficulty.

How old is the Rām Līlā tradition? The more remotely it can be traced, the more justice there is in attributing to it a significant role in the transmission of Hindu culture in North India. When Niehus asked how long it had gone on in Ghazipur, he was told only, "Since very ancient times," i.e., since time out of mind. Neither have the Rām Līlā societies of Mathura and Vrindaban any records or traditions about the beginnings of the Rām Līlā in those towns. Jacquemont, Prinsep, and Heber have left solid witness to the fact that the festival was a well-established institution in Barrackpore, Banaras and Allahabad in the 1820's.

A probe for evidence of the Rām Līlā in earlier times involves careful and critical examination of references to *Rāmāyaṇa* dramas in various Indian literatures. To introduce and examine the relevant texts is a complicated and space consuming project which would almost double the length of this article. Since the earlier history of the Rām Līlā will be dealt with thoroughly in a book soon to be published by the Oxford University Press, the matter can be handled in a summary fashion here.

North India has one well-established tradition, known in Banaras and Ayodhya, according to which a personal disciple of Tulsī Dās called Meghā Bhagat first staged the *Rāmcaritmānas* of his master at Nāṭī Imlī in Banaras about 1625 A.D.[30] Certain details in the printed version of this tale are definitely fabulous, but its basic assertion about the time and circumstances of the first dramatic use of Tulsī's *Rāmāyaṇa* is credible. It is especially plausible in view of independent evidence that serial *Rāmāyaṇa* dramas having characteristics of the Rām Līlā were already known in the sixteenth century, before the *Rāmcaritmānas* was written.

In the *Uttarakāṇḍ* of the *Rāmcaritmānas* itself, Kāka Bhuśundi reminisces in these words on his childhood activities in a previous birth: "At last I obtained the body of a twice-born man (*dvij*)/which Veda and Purāna declare difficult to attain./Meeting and playing with the children then,/I used to perform all the *līlās* of the Hero of the Raghus."[31] The Hindī words translated "playing" and "perform" have the same ambiguity which troubles the interpretation of the English words. They do not, in themselves, prove that the playing of formal dramas is meant. But the reference in the last line to performing all the *līlās* of Rāma suggests a systematic and comprehensive "playing" which is hardly children's momentary imitative make-believe. Also, being born as a *dvij* (which in the *Rāmcaritmānas* means a Brahman) is regarded here as being in some special way a preparation for performing these *līlās*. Here we remember that in the Rām Līlā all impersonators of deities must be children who are

Brahman by caste. All in all, we believe this passage to show that Tulsī had known—probably in his own childhood—a dramatic tradition in which high-caste children enacted the *Rāmāyaṇa* in a manner akin to that of the present Rām Līlā.

Additional evidence to the same effect and coming from about the same time is found in the *madhyalīlā* of Kṛṣṇadāsa Kavirāja's *Caitanyacaritāmṛta*, a life of the great Bengali religious leader Caitanya who died in 1533 A.D. Describing Caitanya's autumnal stay in Puri, this biography has the following to say of one of his pastimes: "On the 'Bijaya dasmi', the day of the storming of Lankā, the Master with His followers played the part of the monkey army (of Rama). Transported by the spirit of Hanumān, He seized a branch and broke it off as if it were the citadel of Lankā, shouting in a rage, 'Where art thou, Rāvana! Thou hast kidnapped the mother of the world, wretch! I shall destroy thee with thy kith and kin!' The people marvelled at His passion and exclaimed 'Glory! Glory!' "[32] We note that this drama at Puri was enacted by amateurs; that it dealt with a *Rāmāyaṇa* episode that is still enacted with great spirit, and that it presented the assault on Laṅkā on the very *vijayā daśamī* day that is still considered the proper day for staging that event. Mention of the *vijayā daśamī* as "the day of the storming of Laṅkā" implies that other episodes were acted on other days and hence that a series was being presented as in the Rām Līlā. Lastly, this was a popular festival drama rather than an aristocratic spectacle for a few: the audience was "the people." The description of these plays of Orissa was necessarily written before 1615 A.D., the latest possible date for the writing of the *Caitanyacaritāmṛta*.[33] But Kṛṣṇadāsa was referring to events in the life of Caitanya in the first decades of the sixteenth century. He could, of course, have connected these dramas wrongly with the time of Caitanya, but he could not well have deceived his readers about their existence in his own time, because religious persons of Bengal were accustomed in those days to go on pilgrimage to Puri in great numbers. This reference is taken as satisfactory proof that a *Rāmāyaṇa* festival drama quite similar to the Rām Līlā was in vogue in Puri before the time of Meghā Bhagat's activity (c. 1625) and probably before the writing of Tulsī's *Rāmāyaṇa* (c. 1575).

Taking this evidence together with Tulsī's reference to the plays of his childhood, we conclude that the work attributed to Meghā Bhagat was only a new application of a stage tradition existing in the sixteenth century. Sometime in the seventeenth century performers of this style of epic dramatization began to use the *Rāmāyaṇa* of Tulsī Dās as their text. The combination of the effective older dramatic technique with the forceful new literary creation gave the Rām Līlā power to become the universal North Indian festival which it is in the present day.

The search for traces of the Rām Līlā before the sixteenth century has not been fruitful. Neither the Sanskrit dramaturgists nor general classical literature has provided information on older *Rāmāyaṇa* dramas having its peculiar features. The literature of the learned is of course silent about a great many aspects of the life of the common people, and such a folk institution could have been current for generations without being mentioned in belles-lettres. But the cumulative silence of century upon century amounts eventually to a prohibition. The Rām Līlā could not have been ancient, and is not likely to have originated much before 1500 A.D.

Historical search beyond this point has been more profitable when seeking the predecessor from which the Rām Līlā developed. Ancient and medieval literatures do provide descriptions of a type of epic dance drama, quite different from the Rām Līlā in external appearance, from which the present institution was probably derived. Though the tracing of the connection must await another occasion, it may be permissible to say here that the Rām Līlā represents one of the readjustments toward simpler art forms made necessary by the intrusion into Hindustan of a powerful Muslim culture. In modifying and revitalizing an older method of staging the *Rāmāyaṇa*, the creators of the Rām Līlā did much to preserve the influence of that epic in North Indian life.

Enough has been said in the foregoing pages to indicate that the influence of the Rām Līlā in its modern form has been operative for at least three hundred years, and that for most or all of that time it has touched the lives of a significant proportion of the population of a large area. It has carried traditional Hindu ideals to the youngest and simplest of many generations and has helped preserve the continuity of Hindu culture in North India during periods of unusual stress and change.[34]

APPENDIX

A Partial Translation of Mathura's Rām Līlā Calendar for 1949

Reverence to Śrī Rāmcandra!
"Without association with the good
There's no telling of the story of Hari;
Without that, no flight of delusion,
And without delusion's departure,
No firm love of Rāma's feet."

Līlāpatra of the Mathura Rām Līlā for 1949 A.D., Saṁvat 2006

September 16: With the impersonators of Jānakī, Bharat, Lakṣmaṇ and Śatrughna present in full dress, the wrist-cords will be tied [solemnly binding all to fulfill their respective duties until the end of the season]. After this, all the actors go from the front of the mosque into Paṇḍit Kavalisingh's temple. They turn back and go into Durgacand Lane via the Central Bazaar. The drama of the wedding of Śiv with Pārvatī. The reducing of Kāmdev to ashes, etc.

September 17: The terrible austerities of Nārad. Sent by Indra, Kāmdev comes with Apsarases. Nārad goes to Śiv. Nārad's conceit and his going to the Lord Viṣṇu. The Lord's creation of an illusory city to rid Nārad of his conceit. Nārad's falling in love with Viśvamohanī and his going to the Lord and asking for a handsome appearance, and the Lord's giving him the shape of a monkey and destroying Nārad's pride. Nārad's cursing the Lord. Svāyambhuvamanu's going to do austerities; his vision of the Lord. The birth of Rāvaṇ and his doing of austerities; his asking a boon of Brahmā and achieving universal victory.

September 18: The procession moves from Ray Bahadur Paṇḍit Kavalisingh's temple and goes to the Asakunda Bazaar by way of Bharatpur Gate and Tilak Gate. The going of the gods to Brahmā. Then Brahmā and all the hosts of gods and the Earth in the form of a cow are fearful and recite the praises of Nārāyaṇ. The voice from the heavens. Thereafter the procession will pass the Svamighat Mosque and end at Ray Bahadur Paṇḍit Kavalisingh's temple.

September 19: The celebration of the birth of Rām and his brothers will be held. The christening, the childhood play, and Rām's exhibition of his vastness. King Janak's ploughing because of a famine, and Jānakī's appearing from the earth.

September 20: The sage Viśvāmitra asks Daśarath, the Lord of Avadh, for Raghunāth and Lakṣmaṇ to protect a sacrifice, takes them, goes onward, and rests on the way in the ancient ashram of the Ṛṣis. (This drama will take place in front of the Temple of Vaidya ratna Paṇḍit Sohanlal Paṭhak.) The killing of Tārakā and the demons on the road. Viśvāmitra's performing the sacrifice, and the attack of the innumerable army of demons on the assembly of sages in order to interrupt the sacrifice. Raghunāth's killing of Mārīc, Tārakā, and Subāhu with a headless arrow. The destruction of all the demons by the arrows of Lakṣmaṇ. Rāmcandra's going to Janakpur with Lakṣmaṇ and Viśvāmitra. The deliverance on the way of Ahilyā by the dust of Rām's feet. The bathing and worshipping in the Ganges. Arrival at Janakpur. (This drama will be held at night at the Kaṭrā also.) Tārakā's procession will start from Ray Bahadur Paṇḍit Kavalisingh's temple, and that of Rāmcandra and Viśvāmitra will move from the Temple of Mahādev Mathurānāth at Dig Gate.

September 21: The arrival of Rāmcandra with Lakṣmaṇ to see the splendor of Janakpur, and the Janakpur ladies' talk among themselves. Janak's daughter goes with her companions to worship Pārvatī. At the sage Viśvāmitra's order Raghunāth with Lakṣmaṇ arrives in the flower garden. Rāmcandra and Jānakī's sight of each other, their falling in love, and exchanging of glances.

September 22: The presence of many kings at Sītā's *svayambar*, and Raghunāth's breaking the bow with his lotus hands. Paraśurām's sudden coming in great wrath into the hall of sacrifice. The dialogue between Paraśurām and Lakṣmaṇ. Paraśurām's going to the forest after testing and praising Rām. King Janak inquires of Viśvāmitra and sends a messenger to Ayodhyā. The messenger's arrival in Ayodhyā, the delivery of the letter, and the joy after it is read.

September 23: The wedding procession of King Daśarath from Ayodhyā to Janakpur (from Baṭivali Grove via the Central Bazaar, Kaserat Bazaar, Svamighat, Tilak Gate, Bharatpur Gate, and the front of the mosque, into the enclosed market). Enactment of the wedding of Rāmcandra.

September 24: King Daśarath's preparation to anoint Rāmcandra to the kingship. Mother Kaikeyī's going into the sulking chamber on the instigation of the slave woman Mantharā. The dialogue between King Daśarath and Kaikeyī. Rām is ordered to the forest.

September 25: Rām, Jānakī, and Lakṣmaṇ have hermit's clothing made and go in procession on foot from the enclosed market of Janakidas into the new Svamighat Bazaar in front of the shop of Lālā Lallomal. The interview with the king of the Niṣāds. The leave taking of Sumant. Their dialogue with Kevaṭ at Vishramghat, their sitting in the boat and disembarkation across the Ganges at Bengalighat. The farewell to Kevaṭ. The Lord's going to the ashram of the Ṛishi Bharadvāj (in the Jairamdas Temple in the Biharidas Compound). The carriage procession and the performance done by the inhabitants in Javaharganj. The arrival, via Bharatpur Gate, at Valmiki's ashram at the Ghee Market in Kishoriramanganj. The affectionate interview. The going from there to Citrakūṭ via the Shahganj Gate.

September 26: The procession of the host of Bhīls will begin from the temple of Ray Bahadur Paṇḍit Kavalisingh and will go to the Red Gate via Svamighat, Chatta Bazaar, Tilak Gate, the police station and the Central Bazaar. Bharat will start with the inhabitants of Avadh from Govindganj. Accompanied by the procession of Bhīls, Bharat will arrive at Citrakūṭ via Chatta Bazaar, Dori Bazaar, the central square and the Red Gate. The meeting and conversation between Rām and Bharat at Citrakūṭ.

September 27: Jayant goes in the form of a crow and pecks at the feet of Jānakī. Bhagavān pierces his eye. Bhagavān goes into the ashram of the Ṛiṣis and grants interview to all. His arrival at Paṇcavaṭī. Sūrpnakhā's ribaldry with Rāmcandra. Lakṣmaṇ cuts off Sūrpnakhā's nose and ears. Khardūṣaṇ makes war on Rāmcandra and Rāmcandra and his army kill all three demons. Rāmcandra pursues Mārīc in the disguise of a golden deer; Rāvaṇ comes in the dress of a holy man, steals Sītā and takes her away. Rāvaṇ's fight with Jaṭāyu. Jaṭāyu is wounded by Rāvaṇ. Rām's wandering in search of Sītā. He meets Jatāyu and performs his cremation.

September 28: Rāmcandra goes to the hermitage of Śabarī. Śabarī's hospitality. Kabandh's death at the hands of Bhagavān. Bhagavān meets Nārad, Hanumān, and Sugrīv and makes friends with them. The fight of Bālī with Sugrīv and the killing of Bālī. Tārā's mourning. The coronation of Sugrīv. Lakṣmaṇ goes in a rage to Kishkindhā. Sugrīv sends the monkeys. Hanumān goes to Laṅkā with a ring and tells Sītā of the welfare of Rāmcandra. His battle with the demons after the conversation, and his return with a bracelet.

September 29: Rāmcandra meets Vibhīṣaṇ and inquires about the secret. The placing of the image of Rāmeśvar on the seashore and the construction of the bridge. Aṅgad goes into the court of Rāvaṇ. The firm planting of his foot. The controversy. The attack on Laṅkā. Meghnād's terrible battle with Lakṣmaṇ. The *śakti* weapon strikes Lakṣmaṇ. Rāmcandra's lament. Hanumān brings the physician Suṣeṇ and the medicine. Lakṣmaṇ wakes from unconsciousness. After a battle, Kumbhkaraṇ is killed.

September 30: Lakṣmaṇ's terrible battle with Meghnād. Meghnād is killed. Sulocanā goes to Rāmcandra asking for Meghnād's head, and performs *satī*.

October 1: Ahirāvaṇ kidnaps Rāmcandra and takes him to Pātāl. Hanumān brings him back after killing that rascal. Rāvaṇ's grim fight with Rāmcandra. The killing of Rāvaṇ. Jānakī's meeting with the King. Vibhīṣaṇ's enthronement.

October 2: The procession of Rāmcandra will start from Citrakūṭ and will come to the Central Bazaar via Shahganj Gate and the Red Gate. The procession of Bharat will start from Govindganj and the meeting with Bharat will take place in the central square. They will then go to the compound of Lala Janakidas by way of Svamighaṭ, the Chatta Bazaar, Tilak Gate, and the Ghee Market.

October 3: The coronation of Rām. The reciting of praises by the (personified) Vedas. The farewell to Sugrīv and the other monkeys. Rām's sermon on the duty of a king to his subjects.

October 4: The Rām Līlā's benediction and oblation ceremonies, etc.

NOTES

[1] See *Vedāntasūtra* II.1.33 with Rāmānuja's commentary, tr. George Thibaut, *Sacred Books of the East*, XLVIII, Part III, p. 477; also Girindra Narayan Mallik, *The Philosophy of Vaiṣṇava Religion* (Lahore, 1927), I, 550-557; and Sushil Kumar De, *Early History of the Vaiṣṇava Faith and Movement in Bengal* (Calcutta, 1942), pp. 260-262.

[2] Tulsīdās, *Śrīrāmcaritmānas* (Gorakhpur, *saṃvat* 2004), p. 34 *caupāī* 3.

[3] Particular thanks are due Radha Krishna Misra for data on the Rām Līlā in Aligarh, and to Kishori Mohan Nigam for a detailed account of the Rām Līlās of his childhood in Satna, U. P.

[4] H. Niehus, "Das Ram-festspiel Nordindiens," *Globus*, LXXXVII (1905), 58-61; James Prinsep, *Benares Illustrated in a Series of Drawings* (Calcutta, 1833; London, 1834), 4 unnumbered pages, il.; also in *Selections from the Asiatic Journal* (Madras, 1875); Reginald Heber, *Narrative of a Journey through the Upper Provinces of India from Calcutta to Bombay, 1824-25* (London, 1849), I, 190ff; Victor Jacquemont, *Voyage dans l'Inde* (Paris, 1841), I, 213-215; John Campbell Oman, *The Great Indian Epics* (London, 1912), pp. 75-86; Alexandra David-Neel, *L'Inde, Hier-Aujourd'hui-Demaine* (Paris, 1951), pp. 67-73; Mischa Titiev, "A Dashehra Celebration in Delhi," *American Anthropologist* N. S. XLVIII (1946), 676-680; "Hindu Passion Play," *Life* (12 February 1951), pp. 90-97. The foregoing are partial and sometimes casual eyewitness accounts of the Rām Līlā. Documentary information of a different kind was obtained from the published annual reports of several Rām Līlā committees, including: Radhagovind Tentivāla, pradhān-mantrī, *San 1946 ke āy vyāy kā vivaran, śrī pañcāyatī rām-līlā* (Vrindavan, n.d.); Keśavdev, secretary, *Hisāb śrī rāmlīlā āy-vyāy sthān Mathurā san 1949 ī.* (Mathura, *saṃvat* 2003).

[5] Prinsep, 1833, first page.

[6] David-Neel, 1951, p. 67.

[7] The interpolations mentioned are included in Vidyāvāridhi Paṇḍit Jvalaprasad Mishra's edition of the *Rāmcaritmānas*, 20th edition (Bombay, *saṃvat* 1992).

[8] F. S. Growse, tr., *The Rāmāyaṇa of Tulsī Dās* 7th edition (Allahabad, 1937); W. Douglas

P. Hill, tr., *The Holy Lake of the Acts of Rāma* (Indian Branch, Oxford University Press, 1952).

[9] The wedding procession (*barāt*) took four hours to make its round of the city of Mathura. As in any wedding procession a corps of drummers (*tāśāvāle*) headed the column. In this case they were bearded Muslims. The royal brothers and their relatives brought up the rear. In between rolled the floats and exhibits of every person, seemingly, who possessed any kind of animate or inanimate conveyance, and something which he wished to bring to the notice of the public. On one float the Rāmāyaṇ Pracāriṇī Sabhā, a religious organization, conducted a mobile *kathā* or public reading of the *Rāmāyaṇa*. Merchants rolled by on carts piled with their choicest merchandise, exhibiting their wares and passing out advertisements to the massed bystanders. The slow procession brought the goddess Kālī into view, seated upon a moving throne. On the petition of a walking attendant, she leaped down to the street to manifest her destructive powers. In a ferocious charge down the pavement and back she swept the narrow street with terrifying circles of her flashing sword. The crowd scattered pell-mell. Śiva and Pārvatī, on tinseled jeep, came by in the role of special friends and clients of the Vaiṣṇava deities—the status usually granted them in this overwhelmingly Vaiṣṇava area. The seething crowd soon closed in tightly around all the floats save that of a snake charmer who, with insistent generosity, kept trying to bestow handfuls of serpents on all bystanders within his reach.

[10] The number and nature of the processions vary greatly from town to town according to local desires and the funds available for these costly affairs. In Aligarh, judging by the printed calendar of that place, some sort of procession is held every day. The Hathras program mentions five only; and in Vrindaban only the procession of Rāma's wedding and that of his final reunion with Bharata are held. In 1944 a group of young men gained control of the Vrindaban festival on a platform of eliminating the multiplicity of processions, holding that they conferred no aesthetic or educational benefit proportionate to their extraordinary expense. Even now almost half of the Vrindaban budget goes to the support of the two processions which are still maintained.

[11] The best descriptions of the *Rāvaṇvadh* pageantry are those by Titiev, Prinsep, and *Life* magazine, mentioned above. See also Fig. 39 in William Ridgeway, *Dramas and Dramatic Dances of Non-European Races* (Cambridge, Eng., 1915), p. 152.

[12] Horace Hyman Wilson, *Selected Specimens of the Theatre of the Hindus* (London, 1871), I, xxix; Sylvain Lévi, *Le théatre indien* (Paris, 1890), p. 317; likewise A. B. Keith, *The Sanskrit Drama* (Oxford, 1924), p. 42.

[13] Some of the melodies used currently in the Rām Līlā in Banaras are recorded in Ethnic Folkways Library P431, "Religious Music of India," Folkways Records and Service Corp., 117 W. 46th St., New York City. The chief musician is Paṇḍit Amarnāth Miśra, *mahant* of the Sankat Mocan Temple, Banaras.

[14] Obtained by sound recording as far as chant 13 and transcribed by Govind Das Gupta, M.A. The remainder of the verses were taken from the stage copy of the *Rāmāyaṇa,* and the speeches were dictated by the actors privately.

[15] Epithet of Śiva, whose special abode is Mount Kailāsa.

[16] Garuda, to whom the story is being narrated.

[17] Great fluency of utterance is ascribed here to Sarasvatī, the goddess of speech, to Ādiśesha, the primeval serpent, and to the personified Vedas.

[18] This and all subsequent lines are an interploation in Tulsī Das' text.

[19] Hanumān.

[20] The story to this point is found in Valmiki's *Rāmāyaṇa,* VI.128:78-83, ed., Kasinath Pandurang Parab (Bombay, 1902), p. 767, and the *Adhyātmarāmāyaṇa,* Lankākhaṇd 16:5-8, Calcutta Sanskrit Series No. XI (Calcutta, 1935), p. 895. The source of the episodes which follow is doubtful or unknown to this writer. Hanuman's cracking the jewels between his teeth may have been suggested by *Rāmcaritmānas* (See Note 2.), p. 831f, wherein Vibhīṣan at Rām's bidding showers raiment and jewels down upon the monkeys, who stuff the precious things into their mouths.

[21] Rāma.

[22] Hindi simile regards the thunderbolt as the model of adamantine hardness, rather than of speed and force.

[23] Pictures of actors in costume may be seen particularly in Ridgeway, 1915, pp. 135, 137, 193, 195f.

[24] Reports by Radhagovind Tentivala and Keśavdev, detailed in Note 4 above.

[25] D. L. Drake-Brockman, ed., *District Gazetteers of the United Provinces of Agra and Oudh*, vols. 1-2, 6-11, 14-36, 40, 42-44, 47-48 (Allahabad, 1904ff).

[26] Growse, 1937, p. 31.

[27] Bharatendu Hariscandra, *Bharatendu granthāvalī*, ed., Brajratna Dās (Banaras, *saṃvat* 1991), No. 61. "śrī rām lilā," p. 770.

[28] Robert Needham Cust, *Pictures of Indian Life, Sketched with the Pen, from 1852 to 1881* (London, 1881), p. 36f.

[29] The geographical limits of the Rām Līlā have been defined mainly on the basis of information from the following literature. General: M. M. Underhill, *The Hindu Religious Year* (Calcutta, 1929), pp. 53-57; William C. Crooke, "The Dasahra: an Autumn Festival of the Hindus," *Folk-Lore*, XXVI (1915), 28-59; E. Denison Ross, *An Alphabetical List of the Feasts and Holidays of the Hindus and Muhammadans* (Calcutta, 1914), pp. 16, 66. Nepal: Sylvain Lévi, *Le Népal* (Paris, 1905), II, 54ff.; Henry Ambrose Oldfield, *Sketches from Nipāl* (London, 1880), p. 342ff., "The Dassera." Panjab: Oman, 1912; Richard Carnac Temple in *Indian Antiquary*, X (1881), 289f. The literary basis of Rām Līlā in the Panjab is not clear. Kashmir: Florence H. Morden, "House-boat Days in the Vale of Kashmir," *National Geographic Magazine*, LVI (Oct. 1929), 451, il. Rajputana: Louis Rousselet, *India and Its Native Princes* (London, 1882), pp. 268-271; B. A. Gupte, *Hindu Holidays and Ceremonials*, 2nd ed., Calcutta, 1919), pp. 185-188. Gujarat: Rousselet, 1882, pp. 119-122; N. A. Thoothi, *The Vaishṇavas of Gujarāt* (Calcutta, 1935), pp. 286-289—a superior sketch without clear place reference. Bombay: Lucia C. G. Grieve, "The Dasara Festival at Satara, India," *Journal of the American Oriental Society*, XXX (1910), 72-76; Ridgeway, 1915, quoting D. R. Bhandarkar, p. 184, 190; Byramjee Jeejeebhoy, *The Bombay Calendar and General Directory for 1849* (Bombay, n.d.), p. 56f. Mysore: L. N. Gubil, "The Dasara at Mysore," *Modern Review* (Oct. 1942), pp. 314-316. Berar: *Panjab Notes and Queries*, III (1886), sec. 674; Śrī Purohit Swāmī, *An Indian Monk* (London, 1930), p. 17f. Nagpur: Ridgeway, 1915, quoting Paṇḍit Hira Lal, p. 204. Bengal: Oman, 1912, p. 85, ". . . the Bengalees do not perform the Ram Lila;" Jacquemont, 1841, I, 220, notes participants ". . . come almost all from the Upper Provinces . . . ;" Padmina Sen Gupta, "Puja in the Bustees," *The Statesman*, Calcutta, Puja Supplement, Sept. 25, 1949, p. 2. Fiji: C. F. Andrews, "Indian Labour in Fiji," *Modern Review*, XXII (1918), p. 587. Ceylon has a *Rāmāyaṇa* festival drama in Tamil which is similar to Rām Līlā in some ways: Hugh Neville, "The Ramayana as a Play," *The Taprobanian*, II (1887), 150-160, 170-172; Carl Hagemann, *Spiele der Voelker* (Berlin, 1919), pp. 50-57.

[30] Sarju Dasji Ayodhyanivasi, *Rāmkrishṇalīlānukaraṇ Siddhānt* (Lucknow, *saṃvat* 1976). pp. 3-20.

[31] Tulsī Dās, *saṃvat* 2004, p. 944: *"caram deh dvij kai maiṇ pāī, / sur durlabh purān śruti gāī. / khelaun tahūn bālkanh mīlā, / karaun sakal raghunāyak līlā."*

[32] J. N. Sarkar, tr., *Chaitanya's Pilgrimages and Teachings. From his contemporary biography, the Chaitanya-charitamrita: Madhyalila* (London, 1913), p. 169.

[33] Sushil Kumar De, "A Note on Kṛṣṇadāsa Kavirāja's Caitanya-Caritāmṛta," *Journal of the United Provinces Historical Society*, IX (1925), p. 98ff.

[34] The support of the American Council of Learned Societies in this study is gratefully acknowledged.

Yale University
New Haven, Connecticut

THE INDIAN HERO AS VIDYĀDHARA

By Hans van Buitenen

TO a large extent it is true that we are better informed about the religious doctrines and practices, moral ideals, and metaphysical speculations of pre-Muslim India than about any other aspect of the Indian civilization. The authors whose works have come down to us, whether Hindu or Buddhist, largely belonged to a class which was preoccupied with its sacerdotal prerogatives, its pedagogic duties, and its functions as the guardian of a sacred tradition. But, although we must recognize the great significance of their articulate eschatology in our valuation of the Indian Weltanschauung, the mere mass of evidence for one set of values should not tempt us to overlook the actual importance of different outlooks. While the increasingly prevailing note of quietistic world despair may have set the key, other notes were sounded. Nor should we forget that the Indian looked upon anything that fell short of a conceivable ideal state of being as an occasion for sorrow, and that accordingly the intention of the very notion of sorrow was inflated. In spite of an undeniable plaintiveness about life in general, the Indian's attitude was essentially melioristic; and though the moralists in unison complain about the misery of man's fate to live, there are few indications that the average person's life was more than ordinarily unpleasant. To a point, sorrow was a theological presupposition, comparable to original sin, and one cannot help feeling that it was more dogma than reality. Meanwhile, the stereotype of the miserable life has passed into the cultural history, and now, corroborated by some distressing facts of contemporary Indian economics, has become the most widely known item about the Indian civilization—the teeming millions of suffering humanity.

If one reads those texts least afflicted by moralists—the poetry, especially lyrical poetry, and the vast literature of tales and romances—one gets a different picture of civilized Indian life. There was a delight in living, an artistic sensitiveness, a cool headed drive to make good in the world, and an air of cultured sophistication in the enjoyment of the rewards of prosperity, as far removed from the stern disenchantment of the sages as is the spirit of a rustic Brahman freehold from the urban wit of the ocean-port Tāmraliptī.

Yet, if one comes down to essentials, the ideals and aspirations—the "daydreams"—which find expression in the stories and romances, remain, in spite of vast difference in temper and spirit, close to those that have guided higher Indian thought. Or perhaps we must change the order; for it is an enduring characteristic of Indian thinking, even of the highest order, that it never loses contact with popular conceptions and beliefs, but returns time and time again to find new inspiration in the immediate experiences of everyday life. When we inquire into the salient features with which the people who enjoyed stories have endowed the character of their heroes, we find the same features that characterize the Indian culture ideal of the saint. Even a cold blooded adventurer like Apahāravarman of the *Tales of the Ten Princes* has more of the virtues that go into the making of a saint than his cynical behavior would make us suspect. It is the purposes to which he applies his virtues, and not his qualities themselves, which distinguish him.

The ideal type of man in the stories, the composite of many heroes who display the same characteristics in varying degrees, is endowed with a particular quality of spirit which we can perhaps best paraphrase as presence of mind. He is consistent and persevering in his endeavors, dedicated to his goal, and more often than not he is so because he has given his word for it. Although his actions are primarily self-centered, this very constancy in the pursuit of his purposes renders him dependable for others when his self-interest happens to coincide with theirs. If he is in a subordinate position, which of course does not happen often, this makes for an unstraying loyalty. The latter is also the function of the last basic characteristic, the capacity for relinquishing anything that is his or due to him, a capacity that is only imperfectly rendered as generosity, but when actuated by compassion, a quality often adorning his character, is close to it.

The quality which we paraphrase as presence of mind is not so much a function of worldly wit or cleverness, as its condition. It is the articulation of a constant cagy awareness of what is going on, the refusal to permit oneself to be distracted momentarily, the preparedness and collectedness of one's faculty of discrimination and decision. It is what the philosophic psychology calls *buddhi*, which comprises both this wide-awake vigilance and the capacity for immediately acting upon what comes within its purview. This faculty is the hero's principal weapon in the struggle for survival. When Gomukha, one of the most appealingly human personalities of Indian literature, finds himself unexpectedly in the presence of a very beautiful girl and is caught unawares, his first exasperated thought is, when he has collected his senses, "Damned be my presence of mind and my voice which were surprised off guard and praised be my hands which went through the motions of greeting! I am nothing but my hands—mind and tongue have perished on me. For only the vigilant live, and he who is found off guard is already dead!" Seldom does the hero allow his mind to be distracted; when he does, and danger, always lurking, assails him, it is his own distraction he blames, not the forces that beset him. Apahāravarman, the master burglar, has been drinking with his wife, and in his drunkenness decides to empty the city of its wealth and fill his wife's house with the loot. "I burst loose, like a rutting elephant from his chain, and with no other weapon than my sword, set out in a fury of violence. When I fell in with a patrol of the town-guard I fought them without thinking: crying 'thief,' they attacked, but hardly angry, playful rather, I killed off two or three of them before the sword slipped from my drunken hand and I collapsed with rolling bloodshot eyes. The emergency sobered me up and my head cleared at once. In a moment I collected my senses and thought: 'Aho! I am in dire trouble, and only because of my own lunacy!' " The heightened awareness, the undistracted concentration on what is going on which characterizes the hero, is exactly the same faculty the aspirant to release employs in the pursuit of man's highest purpose. It is this same mental discipline which does not allow a moment of distraction, the same concentration which, intensified to the apogee of consciousness that changes its essence, breaks through to the beyond.

A corollary of the hero's supreme presence of mind and resolution is his ruthlessness in taking advantage of his adversary's lack of control. The hero is one of the perils perpetually lying in wait for anyone who lowers his defences. Apahārvarman mercilessly ruins the wealthy and greedy merchant Arthapati; but the moral is not primarily that the merchant should have been less greedy but that he should have been better prepared. In a world where only the vigilant survive, he had the misfortune to be a short-sighted fool.

The hero's perseverance, sometimes against heavy odds, is the quality by which he is able not only to bring out the latent potential of his personal destiny, but even to overcome its limitations and progress farther on his road to perfection. The story of the gambler Śaktideva, who finds and eventually possesses the City of Gold, is an excellent case in point. The perseverance which the hero exhibits in his exploits is frequently forced upon him by his word, for to be true to his word, as Somadeva says somewhere, is the true greatness of the great. In the Śaktideva story it is the gambler's promise, made in a moment of frustrated anger, that is his main motivation to continue in his apparently vain pursuits to find the City of Gold. Thus a hero's given word may become his destiny. And it is not necessarily his own word which is binding. Budhasvāmin's version of the Bṛhatkathā includes an interesting dispute between a disillusioned mendicant and an eager Brahman student about the relative importance of fate and a person's own agency. The mendicant, upholding the automatic fulfilment of destiny, tells the story of a young man of whom it is predicted that he will marry an evil wife just before the woman is actually born. The man flees from Sindh to the Doāb, unknowingly marries there the girl who had been evacuated by her parents from Sindh, flees again to Indonesia, and on his return to the mainland, meets her again in Banaras. In this tale of the blind workings of fate there is no clear indication whether it was the fate predicted by the seer which pursued him, or rather that the prediction itself had become fate. But in the counter-tale of the student, describing a solemnly sworn alliance between two merchants who predestine the marriage of their yet unborn children, it is perfectly clear that it was their word which was the actual fate, circumvented only with the greatest of efforts. It is, obviously, the old idea of the inherent efficacy of the solemnly or ritually uttered word; though in a gradually lesser degree, the man who has given his word has subjected himself to the power of his word, which, once spoken, is irrevocable because it is no longer within his control, just as the discomfited sage who has too rashly cursed an offender must confess himself unable to change the autonomous operation of the power thus let loose, though by a new word he may be able to decree how this power will be spent and the curse terminated. This notion of the inherent efficacy of the solemn word, however unfamiliar to us (in spite of the invariably quoted, and misquoted, passage *John* I: 1), is of fundamental importance at the beginning of Indian philosophy.

Perseverence and constancy have as their function dependability. The word is *dhīra*, describing the poise and mental equilibrium which is the condition of constancy and reliability, frequently likened to the repose of the ocean deeps which, in spite of minor disturbances at the surface, remain largely unperturbed. Thus it is synonymous with wisdom as expressed in action, and the qualification of *gambhīra* 'deep' denotes less the penetration of a man's intelligence than the profundity of his imperturbability.

This profundity is also articulated as the hero's capacity of relinquishment. This renunciation is celebrated in many stories. It may be a brigand's relinquishment of a stray girl (lost property which, when found, will not be claimed by the owner) as in one of the Vampire's Tales and in Apahāravarman's story; it may also be the ultimate relinquishment of the Bodhisattva who renounces the Buddahood, which is within his grasp, to do good to his fellow beings by acts of great sacrifice. Compassion often inspires this renunciation in favor of others, but this compassion is not a momentary emotion aroused by incidental encounters. It is the corollary of the saint's own sense of relinquishment and not rarely it has an admixture of contempt for the beneficiaries of his renunciation. In one of the Vampire's Tales a little boy sacrifices himself for the king of his country; for the author and his audience the nobility of the gesture does not lie in the other-directed emotions that inspire it, but in the self-directed merit of the action: it is primarily to add this merit to the balance that is carried forward from life to life, and the boy is quite explicit in his contempt for the motivations of those who are involved in his self-sacrifice. To the maniacal self-renunciation of the great sages of the epic, Buddhism may have added an element of compassion, but one feels that it is this renunciation itself as the means to a person's higher purposes which is fundamental, not the benefit of others.

As sketched, the hero's character seems designed for purposeful action; naturally, one would say, for a story lives by its action. Still in the Indian hero there is an instinct deliberation and a pinpointed concentration of purpose not easily matched by the stories of other cultures. Moreover, the range of his action is unlimited. And it is in the infinite capacity of the persevering man that we find the most characteristic theme both of Indian thought on its highest levels and of the Indian tale on a more worldly plane. What I should like to note as the most characteristically Indian type of tales of the Indian culture is the Vidyādhara story. This is not just a subjective selection from a wide choice of story types which the literature offers; it is proved to be characteristically, and therefore inalienably, Indian by its peculiar failure to migrate. A stupendous amount of work and erudition has been bestowed by scholars on the study of tales migrating from India to other cultures, but rarely, if at all, has the question been raised why certain tales, popular and widely distributed in the homeland, either were not exported or failed to make good elsewhere. The Vidyādhara tale tried to migrate, we have evidence for that, into Muslin territory, but failed signally. And it is clear why.

The Vidyādhara is one of the most interesting of the twenty-odd different kinds of supernatural beings that occur in the story literature. For unlike any other god, deity, vampire or hobgoblin, the Vidyādhara is originally a man. Though his affinity with other celestial beings, like the Gandharvas, has occasioned a similar mythology of a race of Vidyādharas created by Śiva, with a king in control, definitely localized cities, etc., there can be no real doubt that the Vidyādhara represents man become superman by virtue of his knowledge. By his own efforts and through the proper science man can become a Vidyādhara, not through the usual promotion from life to life through which an occasional human soul may aspire to become a god for a while, but instantaneously, during this very life.

The word means 'possessor of science,' science being virtually synonymous with magic. For the science that makes a man a superman is the knowledge of the appropriate formulae and spells that give him entire control over his destiny and allow him to transcend his human limitations. There is no doubt that the figure of the Vidyādhara has been patterned on the aspirant to liberation; for the common man in any case and, we may presume, for many practitioners, the main requirement to gain entrance to that yonder world of liberation which, transcending the old heaven, immediately assumed the attributes of the old heaven in the popular mind, was the mere knowledge of the secret formulae upon which the Brahmans of old had based their ascendancy over world and afterworld. It is related as much to the mysticism of a higher order, yoga in its different applications (which itself has many magical trappings), as to the black arts of the necromancer. In the Vampire's Tales an aspirant to the state of Vidyādhara arranged an elaborate black *pūjā* and ritual offering terminating in a human sacrifice meant to gain control of the corpse-spirit Vetāla. Elsewhere the preliminaries involve the ripping out of an unborn child. The character of the Vidyādhara shares the dual characteristics of its origination: it is a benevolent, artistic and amorous spirit, but also a boon companion of demons and goblins and a bogy with which small children are frightened.

The Vidyādhara as the apotheosis of the ideal hero is largely confined to the popular domain where a complete literature has sprung up around him which has been styled bourgeois. His great vehicle is the famous Bṛhatkathā, the "Great Storybook," a dialectic composition from the first half of the first millennium A.D., ascribed to a Guṇāḍhya, now lost in the original but surviving in several Sanskrit reproductions from which Lacôte[1] in an excellent study has authoritatively attempted to describe and, to some extent, reconstruct the original. Later literature shows that this book was considered the book of the Vidyādhara par excellence, but there were many other Vidyādhara tales which were incorporated in the Kaśmīrian recension of the Bṛhatkathā, best known from Somadeva's eleventh century work *Kathāsaritsāgara*, the 'Ocean of Story.'

Man's attaining the position of a Vidyādhara is, in most tales, the reward of great and persistent efforts. The idea very evidently is that man can work himself up to that celestial status, though it remains reserved for the very few, just as the attainment of release, by its severe demands upon capacity and effort, remains closed to the many. The pleasures of his high status are hardly novel and reflect disarmingly the common ambitions of the average person: an infinite capacity of gratifying an amorous nature; the ability to escape gloriously and take to the air as an aerial spirit, fast as thought, snatching occasionally an unsuspecting princess; a regal residence in vast terraced palaces with golden and gem studded walls where hosts of attendants wait on the hero, recumbent on a gem encrusted couch, with the choicest banquets; a talent for music and song; and lastly a celestial bride of unsurpassed beauty and accomplishments.

The very human aspirations of which the Vidyādhara is the incarnate fulfilment should, however, not make us forget that the man who has attained this position has transcended his human limitations in a very real sense; and it is this very same belief in man's capacity to overcome his human condition which is at the foundation of Indian thinking, however the pleasures attendant upon the transcension may be described. The extent to which this type of tale, of a human being passing to a higher superhuman state of being through his own efforts, is culturally determined is illustrated by the reception it found in Islamic culture.

In the Kathāsaritsāgara we find a small cycle of Vidyādhara stories built around the narrative of Śaktideva and the City of Gold. The story is that a certain princess announces that she will marry only a man (Brahman or nobleman, adds the class conscious compiler) who has seen or visited the City of Gold. Proclamations are made but nobody puts forward his claim, until a bankrupt gambler, who has nothing to lose, Śaktideva, tries to risk it and claims falsely that he knows the city. His ignorance is exposed and the hero vows that he will prove his word and find the city. He sets out on a veritable odyssey which leads him from hermitage to remote hermitage, those traditional clearing houses of travelers' reports, and is directed to the ocean. He sets sail with a merchant, but the ship founders, and the hero is swallowed by a fish which is caught off a distant island, and set free. The king promises his help and takes him in a small craft to a festival where pilgrims from all corners of the archipelago assemble: someone may know the city. In the middle of the ocean the hero sees a divine tree rise from the surface and the craft is pulled to a maelstrom at the foot of the tree. While ship and skipper are dragged to the Mare's Head fire at the bottom of the maelstrom, the hero saves himself in the tree. A swarm of giant birds comes home to roost, and when one of them announces that it will fly to the City of Gold on the next day, the hero hides between its feathers and is thus transported to his goal. He is welcomed and entertained by a Vidyādhara girl with whom he lives in anticipated wedlock, until the girl tells him that she will be absent for a short while and warns him not to enter the middle story of the palace. Curious, the hero cannot help himself and entering the middle story finds in a room the dead body of the princess of his home town. In adjacent rooms two more bodies of beautiful damsels are found. Wonderingly, the hero walks out to the balcony, and looks down on a pond in a garden where a riderless saddled horse stands waiting. The hero descends to mount the horse but is kicked into the pond from which he emerges in his home town. He makes good his claim to the princess that he knows the City of Gold, only to see the girl drop dead after a reassuring promise of eventual reunion. The hero starts once more and finally, after many adventures, reaches the City of Gold, marries the princess and the other girl as well as the meanwhile revivified bodies, and at last is transformed into a Vidyādhara.

There are other stories which clearly derive from a common basis. The seventh Vampire's Tale has a hero who, sailing to Ceylon, sees a flagpole rise from the surface of the ocean. His ship founders but he dives after the sinking flagpole to find himself in a temple of the goddess in a submarine city. He meets a celestial girl who, while pretending to welcome him, has him bathe in a pond from which he emerges in his home town. The king, indebted to him, lends his assistance and together they repeat the journey to the submarine city and the girl, where the hero finally marries her.

In the twelfth Vampire's Tale, a king's councillor, on his way to Sumatra, sees a celestial tree rise from the surface of the ocean. A beautiful girl in the tree sings a song of fate. Back home the councillor tells the king his adventure and the king falls in love with the idea of the girl, repeats the same journey, dives after the sinking tree, finds, and marries the girl. Then his bride tells him that she must go away for a few days and warns him not to enter the Crystal Pavillion, where is a magic pond which transports a man back to his homeland. The king embraces his bride, jumps in the pond with her, to emerge in his kingdom. The woman, really a Vidyādharī, appears now to have lost her knowledge, and remains.

It is clear that the last story is built on (the originals of) the other two, of which the principal characteristic is that a man finds a celestial woman in an only magically accessible city, loses her through a horse and/or a magic pond, but returns, and on his return becomes a Vidyādhara, wedding the girl and reigning in her city. This story, with numerous elements that are unmistakably identical both in content and sequence with those in the Indian stories, has migrated to Muslim territory. We find it in at least three related forms, twice in the *Arabian Nights*, that is, in the Third Qalander's Tale (16th night) and the fourteenth tale of the Sindibādnāma (588th-591st nights),[2] and once in a Persian tale, the first story of the Three Dervishes.[3]

The third Qalander, 'Ajīb ibn Khasīb, after many other adventures, arrives at a palace with curious residents: an old *shaikh* and ten youths all blind in one eye. At a set hour the youths cover their heads with ashes and begin mourning. 'Ajīb is urged not to inquire into their curious behavior, but at last he persuades them to tell him. Reluctantly they sew him in a ram's skin, the lump is snatched up by a giant bird who leaves him on a mountain near a beautiful palace where forty damsels welcome him. He lives there for a year in great joy, but at the end of the year the girls announce that they have to absent themselves for forty days. He is urged to make himself at home in the meantime, to enter forty doors that open on entertaining scenes, but under no condition to open one golden door. He cannot help himself, and enters the forbidden chamber where he finds a black horse with a golden saddle. He mounts the horse, but it does not stir until he kicks it with his heel and finally strikes it with a dagger. Then the horse opens its wings, soars up in the skies and finally alights on the roof of another palace. When the hero dismounts, the horse flicks its tail and strikes out his eye. Tumbling into the palace 'Ajīb finds the *shaikh* and the ten one-eyed youths, who expel him. He spends his life mourning.

The other Arabian story has a similar unhappy ending, and so has the Persian one. In the latter, a jeweler's son, who sings entrancingly on his roof, is kidnapped by a giant bird who brings him to a palace inhabited by birds. At a set hour the birds are transformed into a fairy princess and her attendants. The hero falls in love, but after having been entertained for several days, receives on a certain day a resounding blow from his beloved, which transports him back to the roof of his dwelling.

It is clear what has happened to the original from which the three related Muslim stories have descended. Crossing from one culture granting the ability of man to rise from the limitations of his manhood to a higher condition described in the secular stories as semi-divine, into another culture with a religion whose first article of faith is that there is no other god than God, that human beings can never transcend their humanity, and are able to reach salvation not through their own efforts but only by destiny, the original tale was so adjusted to the new environment in which it ventured so as to lose its entire point. The point of the Indian story is that after an initial failure which sets the hero back to his starting point, because as yet he has not earned the position that would permit his success, the hero once again sets out on the same journey and now succeeds by transforming himself, or earning an automatic transformation, into a being of higher order. At the exact point where the Indian story describes the return of the hero, Islam made a cut.[4] There is no god but God, and the Muslim hero who never tires of extolling the deity spends his life mourning over a lost paradise which he is forbidden to regain.

NOTES

[1] Félix Lacôte, *Essai sur Guṇāḍhya et la Bṛhatkathā* (Paris, 1908).

[2] "Alf Laila wa Laila" in the Macnaghten edition.

[3] Reuben Levy, *The Three Dervishes* (Oxford, 1923).

[4] We must add that in Kathāsaritsāgara 108, 52-56, elements of the Śaktideva story are used in a story of a hero who lives some time with a witch and loses her through the kick of a horse in a forbidden "middle storey." There is no return, the hero attaining *siddhi* in a different manner. However, it is out of the question that it was this abbreviated and incomplete episode which originated the Muslim versions.

University of Chicago
Chicago, Illinois

ORAL POETS OF SOUTH INDIA—THE TODAS

M. B. Emeneau

A CRITIC of English literature[1] once wrote that literature, "simply defined, is memorable speech placed on record." Much discussion and expansion would be required to make this a really serviceable definition—e.g. what are to be the criteria of "memorability." But, for our purpose, the critic Quiller-Couch has said something useful in his identification of two factors: the speech, which is primary, and the placing on record, which is secondary, but which has provided literature with its name.

The student of the earliest literary works of our Western culture, those of Greece, soon learns that not all of them are literature in the strict sense. The Homeric poems are not works that were composed with the aid of writing materials. They bear within themselves very patently the marks of oral composition and recitation, and the Greek traditions about them are hardly intelligible on any other interpretation. European poetry, however, soon exchanged oral composition for that based on the use of writing materials, and our literatures in the Western world are to the present day predicated in an extraordinarily intimate fashion on this newer technique and its consequences. So much is this so, that for many scholars over many centuries the implications of oral composition for the understanding of Homer were forgotten. Not all had been oblivious, to be sure—one need mention only Gilbert Murray and the Chadwicks to refute that—but there was a need for some new impulse to make the matter vivid enough to be vital in Homeric studies. This new impulse was external and analogous, as it turned out. An American classical scholar originally of the University of California, Milman Parry, knew well enough the method of composition of the Homeric poems and knew too that there existed in the modern world and in a geographical area not far removed from Greece an oral epic. In the comparatively peaceful period between the two World Wars he went to Yugoslavia and in the mountains of the southern part of that country and of Albania he recorded and investigated the South Slav epic. He and his collaborators and pupils found there a technique remarkably similar in many details to that which had been postulated for Homer. It was possible to go on and to apply profitably to Homeric interpretation other details of the technique of the South Slav epic singers. Much of the needed reexamining of several of these literatures based on oral composition has been done by Maurice Bowra in his masterly and suggestive book *Heroic Poetry*, which was published in 1952. His title shows how he has restricted himself to one of the genres that he persuasively distinguishes, namely the heroic epic, whether Homeric Greek, Mesopotamian and Hittite, Old Germanic and Old Romance, or South Slav, East European, Uzbek, Yakut, or Ainu. Other genres still require detailed treatment of the same kind; several of these will be referred to in what follows. But we must gratefully say that very much of Bowra's treatment of the oral technique applies just as well, *mutatis mutandis*, to some other genres as it does to the heroic epic.

Other oral literatures have long been known. In fact, it has been clearly recognized that, in the long millennia of human life before the comparatively recent times when writing became commonplace, all memorable speech, or literature, if it may be called such for lack of a better term, was composed orally and transmitted orally, without benefit of writing. When writing was beginning, some of this oral literature was recorded, as we believe happened with Homer. The problem for literary scholars has been to distinguish in the oldest records what was written down from the mouths of oral composers and what was composed on paper (or cuneiform bricks, or palmleaves, or birchbark, or whatnot) in imitation of oral composition. That the latter happened we know—witness the Hellenistic Greek epic and its Latin successor. This must certainly be a problem in dealing with such Hebrew literature as the Psalms of David and the prophetic books of the Old Testament. It is likewise a problem in dealing with the old Germanic literatures—those of Iceland, the earliest Anglo-Saxons, the speakers of Old High German—or with the poetic literatures in the oldest stages of the Romance languages, e.g., that of Provence and that centering around the song of Roland.

To mention a literary corpus which is closer to the subject of this symposium than is Homer—the problem of oral composition arises in Sanskrit literature at more than one point. Old as is writing in the history of the culture of India in its classical form, there is literature there that is even older than writing. The Vedas, the oldest religious texts of Hinduism, contain in their earliest layers hymns and other ritual utterances, the beginning of which can be conservatively placed in the second millennium B.C. These texts present clear evidence that they are oral compositions. Perhaps the most striking kind of evidence is the extensive repeated use, in the verses, of traditional poetic units. Maurice Bloomfield in his intensive study of the phenomenon in the two volumes called *Rig-Veda Repetitions* found that in the Rigvedic collection of over 1000 hymns, approximately one-fifth of the lines are involved in this repetitive use. He and his pupil, Franklin Edgerton, who was my teacher, carried on further studies of this repeated material in the whole of the Vedic literature, with profit for the interpretation of these texts. The result was the three volumes of *Vedic Variants*, in the third of which I had the honor of collaborating in 1931-32.

More important than the details is the tradition that the whole immense corpus of Vedic literature was both composed and transmitted without any recourse to writing. Oral transmission down to the present day by memorization is undoubted—but at the same time suspect, since it is clear that there has at times been recourse to good old manuscripts to correct corrupted oral tradition. This only illustrates the tenacious hold of traditional ways of doing things in India. It does not invalidate the necessity of treating the oldest Vedic texts as examples of oral composition before writing was usual in India, since this in effect is what the tenaciously held tradition means for us in this connection. Our suspicions must lead us to close examination of each text to determine, as was said before, what is the record of oral composition and what the imitation. The safeguards which the Hindus invented very early against change in their holy texts make this determination on the whole easy for the earliest Vedic texts and not too difficult even for the latest.

Another Sanskrit literary corpus that traditionally was both composed and transmitted orally is the epic, consisting of two enormous works, the *Mahābhārata* and the *Rāmāyaṇa*. The marks of oral composition and of a very early synthesis of numerous oral recitations into one unified text are clearly evident in both these epics (as they are in Homer). The tradition of the transmittal of the *Mahābhārata* (and of the *Rāmāyaṇa* too) even illustrates the postulate that in a living oral tradition and barring special conditions, no two oral recitations of what purports to be the same work are identical, but each recitation is a fresh composition. For we are told in the *Mahābhārata* itself that its length is not always the same (Book 1, adhyāya 1) and that the text as we have it is the third recitation in a succession of famous recitations of different lengths. This oral characteristic (which we know very well from Bowra's work) did not come to an end even after the *Mahābhārata* was written down, perhaps in the fourth century A.D., perhaps somewhat earlier. The copyists have never ceased to add more good, bad, or indifferent passages or stories to their versions when they could do so. It is only recognition of the oral technique of composition and its implications that makes it possible to deal with the Sanskrit epic in any but the most fumbling way. Bowra excluded this enormous corpus from his study as being not strictly heroic epic; he said (p. v): "a truly heroic foundation is overlaid with much literary and theological matter." But the truth is that the *Mahābhārata* at least, is an amalgam of several different genres of oral poetry. One is truly heroic in Bowra's sense. Another is the theological or moralistic oral genre, for which there is much evidence outside the epic—in the latest Vedic texts, in the early law books, in the early texts of Buddhism, and in many works of later date which draw much from the oral traditions of Hinduism. Still another genre, closely related to the last, is that which states in verse form the laws, the manners and customs, of Hinduism. Again there is much evidence for an oral tradition, probably even a tradition of free oral composition, in this genre. There may also be other types of oral composition to be identified as part of the epic combination. And in all probability we must recognize that the same composers worked in all or most of the techniques. Bowra was really defeated by the complexities of the Hindu epic, rather than justified logically in excluding it from his work.

In 1935, after undergraduate and graduate training that had included study of Homer and the Sanskrit epics and Vedas, as well as study of linguistics, I went to India to apply my linguistics to several of the non-literary languages of South India. I worked first on the Todas of the Nilgiris. They were already very well known to anthropologists through a lengthy account published by W. H. R. Rivers in 1906. Their language, however, though known to be one member of the Dravidian family, was a problem, for the solution of which there was only poor and scanty evidence, and indeed it turned out to be the most aberrant of the languages of the family and very difficult to analyze, both descriptively and comparatively.

The culture of the Todas is just as divergent from its Indian roots as is their language, because of their long isolation (since the beginning of the Christian era, as I think I have now proved) from the general streams of Hindu culture. This isolation was produced both by their geographical situation on a lofty, 8000-foot-high plateau and by the general framework of the Hindu caste system within which they and their few neighbors live. This social framework favors diversity within unity, and on the Nilgiri plateau, an area of forty by twenty miles, has allowed four communities to live symbiotically, but with four remarkably different cultures and four mutually unintelligible languages.

The linguistic scholar working in the field has perforce to be or become something of an anthropologist, so that he may understand what his informants are talking about in the language he is studying. It was no different in my own case. I soon learned much about the life of the Todas, some, though very little of it, not already known to Rivers. They are a remarkably attractive looking people—even if one makes all allowance for a field investigator's personal preference for his first tribe. They are aware of it—they sing that "in the Nilgiris live a black-headed people," referring to their distinctive and attractive coiffures; they spend much time over these with the aid of butter, which is, alas, all too often rancid and evil smelling. And their neighbors, the Kotas, admit that "the Todas are useless, but so beautiful." In the local caste system of the Nilgiris, the Todas rank highest. Small as the community is, numbering approximately 600 people, it has a most complex social structure. It is usual within Hindu endogamous castes to find subcastes which are also endogamous, i.e., which do not intermarry. So with the Todas, who have two nonintermarrying subcastes, one ranked higher than the other. Within each subcaste there are a number of exogamous clans; members of a clan may not marry each other but must marry members of other clans within the endogamous subcaste. The Todas complicate matters by having the members of each subcaste completely divided into two different systems of clans, one system on a patrilineal basis, the other on a matrilineal basis; each Toda, therefore, belongs to a patrilineal clan and to a matrilineal clan and must avoid marriage with two different sets of kin—the matrilineal clans were not known to Rivers.[2]

This is by no means the end. There are subdivisions of clans, right down to the individual family, and all the divisions and subdivisions are identifiable and definable in terms of specific functions apart from those connected with marriage. When we reach the family, it is prevailingly polyandrous, several brothers having a common wife. Paternity of children within a polyandrous family is determined by a ceremony during which the pregnant wife is given a toy bow and arrow by one of her husbands; he is the socially accepted father of all children born to the woman until the occasion arises sometime to change the paternity by having another brother give the bow and arrow. The economic side of marriage arrangements is complex. Divorce and regularized wife-stealing are possible and even common. Alongside of marriage within the subcaste, there are also socially approved and regularized arrangements between individuals of the two subcastes; in theory, each man has a regular sexual partner in the subcaste not his own, and so has each woman. It is considered bad manners to mention it if a woman's child looks like her partner in the other subcaste. And besides all these regularized arrangements, there are also more casual love affairs.

The Todas are a community of buffalo herders. All their economic life is based on the dairy products of the herds and consequently on the pasture lands. The herds and pastures are inherited within the patrilineal clans. Even in the social structure, the number of the polyandrous husbands in a family depends on the relation between the size of the family's herd and the number of buffaloes that can be sustained by any one clan pasture location; if the herd becomes too large, the brothers must split up to utilize two different locations, and each group of brothers then needs a separate wife to do the housework.

The care of the buffaloes has been made the basis of religion. Every item of dairy practice is ritualized, from the twice daily milking and churning of butter to the great seasonal shifting of pastures, the burning over of the dry pastures, and the giving of salt to the herds. Periodical rebuilding of dairies and the ordination of dairymen are all occasions for ritual. The holy entities of the religion are the pasture locations with their necessary dairy buildings, pens, calf sheds, streams, and herds. The ritualization has been carried to extreme lengths, in the sanctification of locations and the avoidance of ceremonial impurity, in ritual practices, and in the accompanying ritual utterances. In general the sacred herds (they are not the only herds) belong to the clans of the higher subcaste, and the sacred dairymen are drawn from the lower subcaste (it is general Hindu practice that Brahmans who are officiant priests of temples are lower in rank than those who are not).

One other conspicuous feature of Toda culture can be mentioned—the funerals. Regulations and practices are complicated, and center about the dispatch of the dead person to the afterworld with a proper complement of buffaloes, which are slaughtered so that they may accompany him on his path. The chase and capture of the buffaloes is an opportunity for men to show prowess, and the funeral in general is an opportunity for a great gathering in best clothes and for festivity and dancing.

In this sketch we have not exhausted all the themes of Toda life; we have not even attempted to clothe the themes in the elaborate detail that fills so much of Rivers' book. The total impression given by the Todas is that in the course of centuries they have produced a culture marked by extreme elaboration of a smallish number of basic themes, and that little of the detailed elaboration is not obligatory. There is variation possible, to be sure; there are choices and alternatives; but once one theme is chosen rather than another, there is little freedom of choice in the way in which the theme is carried out in actions and even in utterances. This is a culture of the kind that has been called "closed."[3] It is so nearly closed, so little open to option or conscious choice ("open-ended" is the fashionable word) that it has proved difficult in the last century for the Todas to acculturate or to admit any but the most inconsequential changes. Once any major theme should go awry because of pressure from outside the group or because of a novel preference that is pushed by a strong personality within the group, the whole fabric of embroidered detail would disintegrate. This is especially true of the economic basis on which so much of Toda culture is founded. The pasture lands on which their herds depend are coveted by surrounding agriculturalists and have been alienated to a small extent to one or another pressure group, the Badaga farmers or the English town builders or tea growers. In spite of this, alienation has on the whole been sparingly allowed by the local government. But it is instructive that when one of the clans (*ïṇḳity*) lost its nuclear dairy locations, it lost its ritual, its single-minded emphasis on pastoralism, and its desire to follow through all the obligations and rights that tied it to the unchanged remainder of the tribe. A funeral of a member of this clan that I attended was marked by more pugnacious, ill-natured quarreling than any other in my experience, and the Todas of this clan hardly seemed in their preoccupations or even in their appearance to be Todas any longer.

It was not long after my work started on the Toda language that I found that the utterances of greatest interest to the Todas themselves were their songs, and that here was a new example of oral poetry. If I have reverted to study of the Toda songs again and again in the last twenty years, it is not only because, as I said before, one has a preference for his first tribe, but also because of the intrinsic interest of the songs and because there seems always to be something new to say about them.[4]

Part of my current research is the preparation of over 250 song texts for publication. These were recorded from dictation as part of linguistic research that covered a period totaling about eight months made up of shorter intervals within a total of three years spent in India. I would leave the Nilgiris at times to work elsewhere, and when I returned, the accumulation of notable songs composed during my absence would be dictated; or, while I worked on another Nilgiri language, Todas would come to me once a week or so and would dictate new songs or songs that they remembered. Unfortunately, this was in the times before tape recorders, or in fact before any reasonably good recording apparatus of a portable character, and no records of this kind are in my possession, although I hope that tape recordings can be made in the near future. It will be only when such recordings are available that work can be done on the music of the songs, and I hope that the Todas and their song art will not become extinct before this happy event. I am not trained in the requisite type of musicology, much to my regret; there are very few who are. My work, then, consisted only in taking down at dictation, as if it were prose, the words of the songs. There is perhaps the less regret for this, since the singing of songs is only one of two manifestations of the Toda art. Identically the same types of words are used also as a shouted accompaniment to the men's dancing, and although samples of this also should be recorded on tape, little would result from it of musicological interest apart from the metrical distribution of the words with reference to the dance rhythm. The words on these dance occasions are all important, and my records suffice.

I shall describe the essentials of the verbal structure of the Toda songs, a structure that is, as I have said, identical for both the songs as sung and the dance songs. The metrical structure is the simplest that I know of in any elaborate poetic art. Each sung unit consists of three syllables, which may comprise one or two or three words. This is all—no rules of accent, quantity, alliteration, rhyme, or the like, are discoverable. It is a syllable-counting meter and nothing more. From this simple beginning, however, there is built up a complicated structure on principles other than metrical. Sentences consist of from one sung unit to as many as five or six or even seven, with a possibility of quite complicated syntax. But, one very striking feature of the structure, no such sentence may be uttered without being paired with another sentence exactly parallel to it in syntactic structure and in number of units. And the second characteristic feature: all the paired units are rigorously dictated within the technique (with only the most minor of qualifications, which I shall present later). For example, if a man is to be identified by mention of his patrilineal clan, each clan of the higher subcaste has a pair of three-syllable names for use in the songs—similarly for many other entities that are mentioned in song. On the other hand, many entities are sung of only in pairs, e.g. in describing a wife-stealing affair that is settled by discussion before the assembly of chief men, there is a song-pair formed by the words for wife (*mox*) and the compensation that is paid to a husband by a man who has stolen his wife (*teɽ*): *teɽ wïḍ o·ŧķ öšṭyïθşiķ* 'you (pl.) settled compensation for each man'/*mox wïḍ o·ŧķ ķïsïθşiķ* 'you (pl.) made a wife for each man.' Thorn bushes and fallen stones mark the disrepair of a neglected dairy, and are mentioned as a pair: *u·ɽyïθ muṭ po·ṇyïθşiķ* 'you (pl.) cleared the thorns that had grown up'/*pïḍθïθ xaş tu·ķyïθşiķ* 'you (pl.) lifted the stones that had fallen.' Pen bars (*tošt*) and pen posts (*tüṭy*) are always mentioned together, as are the dairy bell (*moṇy*) and ax (*mošt*), the dairyman-priest's garment (*tüṇy*) and the cane (*peṭ*) that he uses to drive the buffaloes. Children and buffalo calves are mentioned together, either as the crying child (*oɽyïθ mox*) and the bellowing calf (*ķarθïθ xoɽ*), or as the child on the lap (*moɽyïš mox*) and the calf in the calf pen (*ķaɽïş xoɽ*). The technique also dictates all the syntactic constructions that may occur on the basis of the paired words and units. There is, in effect, a stereotyped two dimensional poetic language—the syntactic construction is one dimension, the required paired construction the other. One occasional complication is the interweaving of two such structures; the two first halves are sung, and then the two second halves.

The subjects of the songs are a close match for the Toda culture and the interests of the Todas. Every event in their lives is likely to be sung about on the spot or immediately afterwards, either by the participants or bystanders, or by specialists in the song technique. A really notable event will become the subject for more than one song. Some songs will be remembered for weeks or years or generations, usually because the events they commemorate are of sufficient note to come to mind again and again; and this, of course, includes the small number of songs that deal with the lives of the legendary culture heroes. We do not know much about the history of the song technique, but it became clear after a large number of songs had been recorded, that in the course of the presumably long development of the technique, every theme in Toda culture and every detail of the working out of every theme have been provided with one or several set patterns of words and turns of phrase for use in song. We have seen that though Toda life is complicated in its patterns, these are limited and rather tightly closed. The song technique provides a rich verbification of all Toda life, but rich as it is, the basic features that characterize it and that I have sketched out, ensure that it also is a limited and tightly closed technique. Its themes, its set pieces, are in part covered by the sketch of Toda culture that I have given. Funerals and their accompanying dance-songs and sung laments bulk largest in the record. These rehearse in outline the life of the deceased—a man's marriages and children, his prosperity through the increase of his herds, a career as a dairyman-priest who starts as a poor servant boy and ends as the owner of many buffaloes after service in many dairies, or a man's repute as a person of wisdom in settling disputes, or whatever else he may have been notable for in his lifetime; a woman's beauty and many husbands, or her careful attention to her family's needs, or her brood of children may be celebrated. The provision of the buffaloes to accompany the dead is a matter of emulation as well as of dispute, many quarrels occur over them, and the buffaloes figure prominently in the funeral songs. Weddings and the wife-stealing or the negotiations that precede them are sung about at length. So are other domestic ceremonials, like the giving of the bow and arrow to legitimize children, or the ceremonial piercing of the ears if it should by chance be delayed until adulthood. The dairy ceremonials of a seasonal nature are accompanied by dance-songs, as are the rebuilding and reconsecration of a dairy. Love songs are common. There is a popular song that details all the important places of the Nilgiris—hills, valleys, streams, villages, etc. Fragments from it, as well as many other geographical phrases, are found in most songs. All this geographical nomenclature is a verbification of the love for familiar places that is not unknown as a subject for poetry in the literatures well-known to us. That this is the Toda emotion is clear from the song composed by two homesick small girls whose father, because of drought, had to pasture his buffaloes away from the familiar places among people and places strange to them.

Given the technique and the interest in the songs, a corollary but perhaps unexpected consequence is that every Toda can and does compose songs. The two little girls who were homesick did not do it very well, since their knowledge of the technique was imperfect. Many adults too have an imperfect mastery of the art. It is surprising, however, how many are competent and how many different names occur in my records as composers. The best, of course, are those who work hard at it, and the impression that I got was that there were a few men and women who had made a high reputation for themselves as singing composers, and that the best composers were those who officiated during the dances, since they had to work hardest to acquire a technique that would carry them through the fast moving dance without stumbling over what to sing.

Solo composition is only one of the manners of delivery, and perhaps not the commonest. It must be obvious that with all details of composition closely dictated by the technique, duet and choral delivery is always possible. All the performers will have a good knowledge of the technique and will know what is being sung about. The first unit, even the first syllable of the first unit that is uttered by the chief performer almost always gives a certain clue to the limited possibilities of the two dimensional structures that he intends to use; a quick intelligence on the part of his accompanists does the rest. In the dances there is usually a chief composer assisted by one companion; they shout in unison. If a song is being sung, the composer whistles the tune first, and those who sing with him can then accompany him in unison, or he may sing the first half of each two dimensional structure and a single accompanist may sing the other half antiphonally, or a large group may likewise split up to perform antiphonally. My impression is that group performances are preferred to solo work.

A striking feature of all Toda singing is its enigmatic and allusive character. Traditionally, no person is identified in song by his or her name. When the song is addressed to a person, alive or dead, a buffalo name is used in a vocative form instead of a personal name. All the identification that is provided consists of allusion to the patrilineal clan membership by means of the paired units that I have mentioned earlier. When the song is composed on a public occasion, a funeral, a wedding, or the like, this is sufficient for the Todas. They all know exactly who and what is being sung about. If the song is sung again on a later occasion, a minimum of explanation is needed. This indirection of reference is compounded for the outside observer by the set phraseology. Even in a tightly closed culture like that of the Todas, no two events are identical, and the fixed song units are not really closely fitted to any actual event, but only to the generalized themes of the culture. They are, in fact, counterparts of the ethnologist's abstractions from a number of similar but not identical events within a culture. The Toda verbalizations then, like the ethnologist's generalized descriptions, need much comment to point out their relevance to particular manifestations of the cultural themes. The relevance, I must emphasize, is not overtly provided in the song words. It must be recognized by the audience of the songs, and life-long practice in hearing and in composing makes them expert at this. It is this recognition of the relevance of old words to the slightly differing recurrence of old themes that in all probability stimulates the Todas' esthetic pleasure in their songs. I should suppose that the greater the range of relevances a composer can bring to bear on a particular situation, the more he is appreciated as a composer. However, even though the external observer finds that all Toda singing is an exercise in the enigmatic, the Todas themselves recognize a sub-class of their songs as being particularly enigmatic. These are the love songs. The occasions of these are, in general, not a matter of public knowledge, the personae are not identified even by mention of their clan membership, and in the outcome no one but the composer, his or her beloved, and perhaps their most intimate friends who assist in furthering the affair, know what it is all about. These songs are identified by a pair of song units: *warịty xe·ṭf*, *warịty foṇt*, as "riddling words." This distinction is for the Todas, of course, a valid one. For us it is only a matter of degree, and the technique as a whole must be characterized as enigmatic and allusive.

This then is oral poetry, with all the marks that we have learned to recognize as characteristic of oral poetry.

One such mark is that every performance, even of what purports to be the same song, is a free composition and that there cannot be two identical performances. This has been amply demonstrated in all accounts of modern living oral literatures, it is clear within the Vedic corpus, and I have already alluded to it as a tradition about the transmission of the *Mahābhārata* that is contained within the frame material of that epic itself. The time available for performance will dictate the length of the song, as will the interest of the singer or of the audience; or, if one singer's song is repeated by another singer, their differing tastes and capabilities will determine different handling of the phraseology. Setpieces will be expanded or cut down, alternative possibilities in the choice of formulaic phrases will be adopted, and so on. The subject matter will, however, be the same, and usually the overall organization of the song—and the song can be said to be the same. And yet the differences between two renditions of the same song by the same singer at a long interval may be enormous, as I found when in a number of instances I took down the same song twice with an interval between. This happened even when very old traditional songs were concerned. The most patent instance was that of the song of the homesick girls. A practiced composer overheard them, liked the tune, and expanded the words until they satisfied him as a worthy effort. I did not record the girls' version, but I am sure the two versions would hardly have been recognizable as the same song, and yet within the Toda rules of the game they were the same.

Another alleged characteristic of oral poetry is concerned with the language. The poetical language is often (it has been said, always) different, and often markedly so, from the vernacular of the singer. This needs no demonstration to be evident to the student of Homer. The dialect of the Homeric poems is not merely different from the everyday dialect of all Homeric singers, no matter what their vernacular; it is clear that it could never, in the form in which we see it, have been the vernacular of anyone at all, because of historical accidents in the transmission of the technique. Bowra was content to mention this, and to add a little about similar situations in some of the other poetries that he treated. It might have been discussed by him at greater length, but he probably was justified in his sketchy treatment, first by the limitations of his linguistic training (no one is well enough at home in twenty-five or more languages to produce a comparative treatment of the desired detailed kind), and secondly, by the danger of exhausting the interest of his audience. I shall take my cue from him, and merely say that the Toda poetic language is different from the everyday language. I cannot go into details, nor do I know the answers to all questions that arise. The syntax of the songs is looser than in the colloquial, perhaps as a function of the formulaic nature and the metrically defined shortness of the song units. The morphology, especially of the verb, is different, whether more archaic or merely a contrived difference I cannot yet say. In a few points, by comparison with related languages, it has been possible to identify archaisms of morphology or of vocabulary. But at the same time, by the same method it is possible to identify very numerous borrowings from the language of the neighboring Badagas, who have been in the Nilgiris for roughly five centuries, and whose song technique, if they have one, is quite unknown for purposes of comparison. Much detailed study is still necessary before it will be possible to make useful generalizations about this matter of language. It suffices to note that Toda poetry does agree with other oral poetries in using a language that has features differentiating it from the language of everyday life. But I should add the proviso that this is true of all poetry, oral or written; it is part of the definition (or rather of some definitions) of poetry that something of the sort should be so. We do not yet really know all the criteria that distinguish the two varieties of poetry.

The last mark of oral poetry that I shall mention is the use of fixed phraseology that has been studied so extensively and profitably in Homer, the Vedas and Sanskrit epics, and the South Slav epics. I have met it also in the songs which the Coorgs compose at harvest festivals and on other religious occasions. They also live in South India, in the mountains between the Malabar coast and Mysore state. Their technique is very different from that of the Todas, and if there is a historical connection between the two, it can be only of the most remote nature. I must say no more about their songs, interesting as they are. The Toda technique is of extreme interest in this matter of fixed phraseology, since it seems to and actually does operate almost completely with formulaic language, as does no other oral composition that we know of so far. The corpus that I am operating with consists of roughly 10,000 or 11,000 couplets, i.e., two dimensional structures, and I doubt whether in this sizeable body of material there is found any paired song unit which does not recur at least once. Most paired units recur again and again. Certainly this almost complete failure to use unique units is not characteristic of any other of the oral poetries that I have mentioned. Each of them, moreover, except the Coorg material, exceeds my Toda corpus in volume by anything from two to ten or a great many more times. The unique repetitiousness of the Toda songs is not to be explained away by the relative proportions of the material examined. The Toda technique is really virtually a closed one, as none of the others is. Bowra, in examining various heroic poetries, found (p. 233) that the Homeric language comes closest to this. I quote a small part of what he has to say:

> In the first twenty-five lines of the *Iliad* there are at least twenty-five formulae of one kind or another, and in the first twenty-five lines of the *Odyssey* there are about thirty-three. Nor are these passages exceptional; they give a fair sample of how the poems are composed. There is hardly a passage in either poem in which there are not many small formulae, while about a third of each poem consists of lines and blocks of lines repeated elsewhere . . . . It is clear that the formula plays a more important part in ancient Greek heroic poetry than in any oral poetry which we have examined . . . . It is present equally in the machinery of narrative and in the highest flights of poetry, though here it is managed with uncommon tact and seldom makes itself noticeable. Homer clearly derives his art from a powerful tradition which has worked out formulae for almost every occasion, and his task was to make good use of them.

So Bowra on Homer. If my findings for Toda poetry are correct in this respect, as I feel sure they are, it exceeds even Homer.

Can there be no broadening of the Toda technique in this matter? The answer is certainly yes. One of the composers, during the period that I was observing, boasted repeatedly that he was innovating by introducing the names of persons into his songs, and lamented that it was not catching on. If he was correct in claiming this as his own invention, it was certainly being used by others also in imitation of him, in spite of his lament. If he was incorrect in his claim, at least the use of personal names must have been so infrequent before him that this was for all practical purposes an innovation.

For our present purpose it means of course an expansion of the permissible phraseology. Occasionally the provision of a paired unit for a name was clever, e.g. the name of the boy, Piɫyfo·to·w, has *piɫy* 'silver' as its first element; the paired unit in a song was Pïnfo·to·w, in which the first element is *pïn* 'gold.'

I repeatedly inquired whether there were any new song units in songs that were being dictated to me, and seldom was told that there were. Those few that were identified as such were usually not impressive. They are indications, however, that the formulaic language is still being added to, if only very slowly. I must admit, however, that this impression of slowness is only to be expected from inspection of a selection of the songs composed over the short period of three years. Innovation must have gone on steadily in the past, but at what rate or rates we cannot hope to know. When the English first came to the Nilgiris, new phraseology was certainly added so that they and some of their innovations in Nilgiri life could be sung about. And the total of the poetical language could only have been achieved by such a process. But it still remains true, I think, that this technique is, of all that have been examined carefully so far, the one most formulaic in character.

Having treated Toda poetry as typically oral composition, it remains to ask whether it fits into the typology of oral poetry offered by the Chadwicks in their voluminous work *The Origin of Literature*. They have set up a category of personal or occasional poetry, which, as they exemplify it, is certainly the one into which Toda poetry fits. They find it, as they say, "probably everywhere," and they cite notable examples of extempore topical poetry among the Kirghiz Tatars, the Polynesians, and various East African communities, including Yoruba, Galla, and the Amhara of Abyssinia. Unfortunately, the Chadwick book does not discuss this type at sufficient length, probably because there is not on record a sufficient body of authentic material. Perhaps when the Toda corpus is published and a few others similar in content, it will be possible for some scholar to give us a treatment of this type parallel to Bowra's book on the heroic epic, and to show fully its role as a type of lyric poetry.

I cannot close without a slight discussion of values. What part does their poetry play in the life of the Todas, and what are their attitudes towards it? Can we justly and fruitfully examine it in a wider, more universal frame of reference?

I have already said something about the occasions for songs, and need only repeat that all the events of Toda life seem to be the subjects of song and that there is a tendency for every event of note to be celebrated on the spot. This is in truth an occasional poetry. It is so intimately connected, however, with all Toda life that its character is very different from that of the verses written by a poet laureate to celebrate a coronation or whatever other state occasion is so celebrated. Every Toda can be his own poet laureate. No event is complete without its accompanying song or shower of songs. No action is perfect without its highly stylized verbal accompaniment in the traditional terms that praise, blame, or merely comment. Few past actions of note are remembered without a notable comment in song being remembered and recomposed. Most cultures are given to discussion of events after they have happened. Few can be so given to highly formalized statements about past events, or can have the directions of discussion so tightly controlled as they would seem to be among the Todas, for whom the judgments on events are so rigorously channeled into traditional phraseology. If the culture is as nearly closed as I have said earlier, one of the factors making for this situation, perhaps only a minor one but still worth identifying as such, is, in all probability, the role that the songs fill as a censor. This is the judgment of an external observer, and I have nothing in my record of Toda utterances to back it up. It is a matter worth futher investigation.

Certainly the songs are an esthetic factor of importance in the Todas' lives. They draw from them tremendous pleasure. Bowra commented on the heroic singers (p. 29): "The poet wishes not to instruct but to delight his audience." And this is true too of the Toda lyricists, with the corollary that they delight themselves as well. No one can watch the dance song composers without recognizing this: the rapidly circling, shouting ring of dancers, the flashing teeth and thrown back heads of the composer and his accompanists, their eyes gleaming with the excitement of the words they are uttering, are warrants for this conclusion. On occasion my interpreter came to me in the morning still excited by the virtuosity of the composers at the funeral dances of the previous day, and all agog to dictate the dance songs to me. And I have found them equally exciting, though this is perhaps not fair evidence, since I was affected also by my own scholarly excitement as an observer.

I should add that when songs are sung, another æsthetic factor is involved, that of the music, with which I could not deal. I was told, however, that ideally every new song that is sung should have a new tune. One composer went so far as to tell me that only the tunes matter; anyone can compose the words. This is a statement that must be taken into account in judging the total æsthetic effect. But he was being very one-sided. The verbal utterances that are common to the sung compositions and the dances are unquestionably an important element in both. They add an æsthetic moment to the tunes of the one and the dance movement of the other. This moment is surely the combined effect in the song words of the social comment and the noncolloquial language in which it is phrased.

Can we find in these songs poetical values which make them worth notice in a world survey of literatures? I am no expert in these matters, but I should attempt what I can, since no one else is likely to examine Toda poetry very intensively for a while.

It is especially difficult to discuss the matter, since there have been so many differing definitions of poetry. Leaving aside all others, it is perhaps useful, with some of the Hindu poets and critics, and occasionally with Western critics, to think of poetry as marked by "suggestion," which is fitted "to move by words unspoken,"[5] by implications. Toda poetry, with its enigmatic-allusive technique, might seem to possess this characteristic. And in a way, I think, it does. As the Hindu critics developed the theory, the suggestion is one of an emotion which is to be communicated to an audience, not by a bald statement of the emotion, but by suitable statement of all the factors and the accompanying situations that produce the emotion. This the Toda words are fitted to do, if the emotion is taken to be one of a range that includes social values as well as the individual's private emotions. The panegyric for a dead man suggests, by stereotyped, but noncolloquial statements about his buffaloes and the disputes that he settled, that he was a person of consequence in the community. This, I think, is poetical suggestion. But the Toda range is limited, and its suggestion is, as we have seen, so imprecise and so stereotyped and inflexible, that this poetry cannot with any justice be ranked high in a universal scale.

Toda poetry, with its insistence on the single situation spoken of in terms of a generalization of Toda cultural themes, hardly allows of generalization into universal human terms. But can we expect more than a minimum of this in any nationally or geographically delimited culture, even if it is carried by millions rather than by a few hundreds of people? European literature at times attempts to generalize for all

European experience, but does not always succeed. And its results are seldom applicable to the Chinese, or to the Australian tribesman, except in the most minimal way. Toda poetry does not attempt it. If the Englishman or the visiting anthropological linguist has to be sung about, he is treated in Toda terms—he is living away from his familiar places, as were the homesick girls; he knows the clan buffaloes, as does the Toda clansman; and so on. Occasionally something better may be achieved, by reuse of those traditional phrases that allow it. The breakers of the ocean, seen by two Todas at a distant place of pilgrimage, were poetically sung about by a transfer of the language applicable to the rapids of the Nilgiri rivers and to the driving monsoon: *ï xömo·ṣ pa·we θwïḷg pïsxwïθïn* 'one wave beats like the rapids of the river' *ï fiṭymo·ṣ ḳwa·ṛe θo·š̌t pïsxwïθïn* 'one wave beats like gusts of monsoon rain and wind.' One Christian Toda composer succeeded in adapting the old song units to the theme of the Benedicte in his prayerbook ("O all ye works of the Lord, bless ye the Lord; praise him and magnify him forever"); the result had values which I venture to think approached universality. But these values were won by acculturation, and could hardly have emerged unprompted from Toda culture as such.

We must come to the conclusion that the Todas in their poetry aim neither at universality nor at the poet's individual expression of his own psyche. The technique, as it has been evolved, has as its aim a generalization of all that makes the Todas Todas. They are a peculiar, even a self-consciously peculiar, people, as befits a segment at the top of a local caste system of the Hindu type. There is in their world view no urge to universalize the themes of their culture and the verbal expression of them. At the same time there is no urge towards self-expression; it is, in fact, an urge that would be out of place and might even be divisive in the closed culture of a small community. Their poetry then is strictly a miniature and provincial, even parochial, art with many limitations. But it has no obnoxious features and has numerous esthetically pleasing ones both for its practitioners and for the external observer. For the Todas it is an enrichment of every facet of their experience, and an art that produces such abundant achievement deserves respect and admiration. As an expression of the values and emotions of a culture in memorable speech, it is poetry.[6]

NOTES

[1] A. Quiller-Couch, *Studies in Literature,* Third Series (New York, 1930), p. 188.

[2] *American Anthropologist,* XXXIX (1937), 103-112; *Language, Culture, and Personality; Essays in memory of Edward Sapir* (Menasha, 1941), pp. 158-179.

[3] See, e.g., E. R. Dodds, *The Greeks and the Irrational* (Berkeley, 1951), esp. pp. 237, 255 (note 1), and the bibliography contained in the latter reference.

[4] A preliminary account was given in "The Songs of the Todas," *Proceedings of the American Philosophical Society,* LXXVII (1937), 543-560.

[5] Terence Rattigan on the theater in *The Collected Plays of Terence Rattigan* (1953), I, xx. See Franklin Edgerton, "Indirect Suggestion in Poetry: A Hindu Theory of Literary Aesthetics," *Proceedings of the American Philosophical Society,* LXXVI (1936), 687-706, and the work of Lascelles Abercrombie referred to by him. See also Daniel H. H. Ingalls, "Sanskrit Poetry and Sanskrit Poetics," *Indiana University Conference on Oriental-Western Literary Relations,* 3-24.

[6] This paper was delivered as the Faculty Research Lecture on the Berkeley campus of the University of California in 1955-56.

University of California
Berkeley, California

THE FORMS OF COMMUNICATION IN VĪRAŚAIVA RELIGION

By William McCormack

THE goal of this paper is to describe the means by which the religious ideas of the Vīraśaivas are transmitted and to use a classification in this description which can be reproduced for all Vīraśaivas and for other sectarian religions in South India. The classification to be used allows a two-fold categorization of the forms of communication as "old" or "new." The dividing line between old and new in this classification is the year 1900 plus or minus twenty years. A type of religious communication in vogue before 1880 will fall into the old or traditional category, while the fashions for communicating the Vīraśaiva creed which have become important after 1920 are included in the modern category. The traditional forms of communication to be discussed here will be the following: life cycle rites, folksong, *purāṇa* and similar recitations, and religious fair. The modern forms will include the following: printed publications, drama-radio-cinema, and cultural development including boys' and women's clubs, free boarding for students, and the singing of preachings (*vacana*) of Vīraśaiva saints in the style of classical Indian music. The modern and traditional media will be compared briefly in the concluding section in order to illustrate the possible use of the classification to establish trends in the communication of the Vīraśaiva religion.

The Vīraśaiva or Liṅgāyat sect constitutes the majority of the Kannada speaking class of peasants and traders, Vīraśaivas forming something more than twenty percent of the nineteen million-odd speakers of this Dravidian language. Liṅgāyats are concentrated in their greatest strength in Dharwar, Belgaum, and Bijapur districts, where they account for about thirty-five and a half percent of the population. The two principal castes of the Liṅgāyat sect are everywhere the Jaṅgams, or priests, and the Banajigas, or traders. They are thus one of the largest of the groups which have a distinctive *bhakti* religion in India. Their philosophy of devotion to a single God, Śiva, whom the Vīraśaivas link with the driving force of the universe, and the significance of Vīraśaiva life cycle rites for the symbolic expression of this religious conception has been unusually difficult for non-Vīraśaivas to grasp. One reason for the failure of outsiders to understand this religion may be that the important literature of the sect was written in the Kannada language, rather than in the traditional medium which was created for religious thought in India, the Sanskrit language.

Life cycle rites. The life cycle rites of the Vīraśaivas are religious performances which serve the principal function of marking changes in the status of individuals, but they also serve to dramatize the three cornerstones of the Vīraśaiva faith. These are the worship of the guru, or religious preceptor, of the *liṅgam*, the visible symbol of Śiva, and of the Jaṅgam, the visible human incarnation of Śiva. During worship, the guru and the Jaṅgam, that is, respectively, the family religious advisor and a man who has the hereditary right to be worshipped as an earthly embodiment of Śiva, are represented by one and the same person. *Liṅgam*, which is the symbol of Śiva's supremacy and of the potentiality of the Vīraśaiva's soul to attain fusion (*aikya*) with Śiva, is represented at the time of worship by the personal *liṅgams* of the guru and of the Vīraśaiva devotees. The wearing of the *liṅgam* (*liṅgadhāraṇe*) is the external sign of membership in the Vīraśaiva or Liṅgāyat sect, and it is worn by men, women, and children. The personal *liṅgam* is a small replica in soft stone of the familiar Śivliṅg in temples, and it is covered over with a black substance which hardens so that the whole resembles a robin's egg in shape and size. There are styles of wearing the *liṅgam*, but commonly it is placed in a silver case which is suspended from the neck by a cord (Śivadhara) to slightly above belt level.

It is common for Vīraśaivas to perform ten ceremonies to mark the changes in a woman's life, while eight ceremonies suffice for men. The tenet of the sect that these ceremonies should be conducted by a Jaṅgam and not by a Brahman is followed. The following are the life cycle ceremonies which are observed for men: birth, naming, initiation to adult religious status, marriage, first consummation of marriage, death, and first memorial day. These ceremonies are also performed for women, and added to these are the ritual observances of first menstruation and first pregnancy. The family guru, or Jaṅgam, is not called to the house for the ceremony which marks the first consummation of marriage, but he is consulted for astrological advice at this time.

Worshipping the feet of the guru, or Jaṅgam, with water is a prominent feature in Vīraśaiva rituals, and this worship symbolizes both the fusion of guru and devotee, and the fusion, or oneness, of the guru-Jaṅgam with Śiva. The water which is used in this worship is believed to have been consecrated through contact with Śiva, as in the more familiar case when water which has been poured over a temple *liṅgam* is believed to have been consecrated by God. When the devotee uses the water that is consecrated by contact with the guru in worshipping his personal *liṅgam*, it is believed that during the time of worshipping his *liṅgam* the devotee attains the status of guru, or of oneness with Śiva. At marriages the feet of the officiating Jaṅgam are not worshipped as part of the wedding ritual; rather the feet of the bridal couple, who are regarded at that time to be embodiments of Pārvatī and Śiva, are worshipped. The guru-Jaṅgam is not invited to the first consummation of marriage rite, and so worship of his feet is also omitted by this ceremony. With these exceptions, it can be said that the remaining life cycle rites of the Vīraśaivas are occasions for the worship of the feet of the guru-Jaṅgam. There is a practical difficulty during funerals, which the Jaṅgam solves by placing his foot on the head of the corpse, and he sprinkles consecrated water on it so that the dead body's worship of Jaṅgam can be complete. Some families worship a Jaṅgam's feet daily, others on Mondays, and some make a point of inviting the Jaṅgam on new and full moon days. The Jaṅgam is invited and is worshipped as often as possible in Vīraśaiva households during the holy month of Śrāvaṇa (July-August), and he must visit houses on the festival occasions of the New Year (*Ugadi*), the birthday of the most famous Vīraśaiva saint (Bāsava), and on Śiva's fast day (Śivarātrī).

The most significant life cycle rite for the indoctrination of the Vīraśaiva is the ceremony for attaining adult religious status, or the initiation (*ayyācār*) ceremony. The guru who officiates at initiation cannot be the usual family guru, except in the very rare case when the family guru is a *pattadsvāmi*, that is, a celibate Jaṅgam with the right to conduct initiations because of his official association with a religious establishment (*maṭh*). It is a rare and costly affair to celebrate an initiation individually, and so this is the only life cycle rite which is regularly performed in the religious establishments (*maṭhs*) which are headed by the red-robed, celibate, Jaṅgam saints. Initiation is open to both sexes, but with the difference that women commonly undertake this *saṃskāra* after marriage, while boys are initiated between the ages of five and twelve. This is also the ceremony of conversion for persons who want to join the Vīraśaiva religion. The ritual requires about six to seven hours for its performance and can be discussed under three main headings. First the thrones of the five founders of the religion, which survive today as five large monasteries, are worshipped in the form of five pots. If Jaṅgam boys are among the initiates, a representative of the monastery to which each boy is affiliated through his patrilineal ancestors is present, and the Jaṅgam's connection to one of the thrones is symbolized by a string which he holds. The second step in the rituals dramatizes the importance of the *liṅgam*, with which the initiates are soon to be invested. In this stage the guru who is officiating holds his *liṅgam* above the *liṅgams* of the initiates, and worship to the accompaniment of Sanskrit mantras goes on for four to five hours. The *liṅgam* worship is climaxed by the guru's tying of the initiates' *liṅgams* to their bodies, whispering of sacred syllables in the initiates' ears, and exacting from them an oath to perform their religious duties. The third and final part of initiation consists of about two hours of advice on religious and social conduct which the officiating guru delivers.

The audience for all life cycle rites, except initiation, is recruited from among relatives, friends, and neighbors, so that no new social relationships are established by the performance of these rituals. Even in the case of marriages, the establishment of new relationships is avoided as far as possible by the practice of marrying close relatives, sister's daughters and cross cousins, and by caste and territorial endogamy. The rituals of the life cycle do not establish new social bonds which might bring together in greater unity the competing castes and social classes; and there is nothing to be found which parallels the founding of a *compadre* relationship in these ceremonies. Initiation continues the theme of close confinement of social ties, for it is the nearest religious establishment that can perform this ceremony which people visit to observe this rite.

Folksongs. The folksongs of women are not to be disassociated, in the first instance, from the life cycle rites of which they form a prominent feature. Women sing traditional songs at all stages of the marriage, that is, on the day of betrothal, on the wedding day, on Wednesdays and Saturdays in the respective houses of the bridal couple for one to five weeks after the marriage, and on the day the marriage is consummated. Women do not usually sing at funerals, but they do perform at the death ceremonies of the celibate saints. The death of these Vīraśaivas particularly symbolizes the happy occasion of fusion of the devotee with Śiva, and mourning for the death of saints is not permitted. The women's songs during life cycle ceremonies cover a variety of subjects, but the outstanding themes are praise of the religious and social conduct of Vīraśaiva women saints and praise of the mother-goddess Devī (or Ādiśakti), who is identified both with Śiva's wife Pārvatī and his mother Śakti, who was the first cause of the universe and the mother of Ṣaṇmukha, who destroyed the demons in the world. These same songs are performed when women work in the house or in the fields, when they carry a coconut offering to the temples or to the grave of a Vīraśaiva saint, when they worship the mother goddess, and during their evening leisure hours. The singing groups are composed of relatives, neighbors and other friends of the same village. Women only rarely visit other villages or towns in order to perform their songs. The language of folksongs is the colloquial dialect of the region in which they are sung. Three popular folksongs with religious themes, which are identified as the folksongs of women, are given below in translation:

Can people give you anything which will satisfy your mind? If you pray to Lord Śiva, he will give his incomparable riches and so your house will be blessed and your mind will be fully satisfied.

I had too much faith in people, and they left me in the middle of difficulties. O Lord Śiva, I ask you to protect me always.

You must have the companionship of your son when you go as a pilgrim to Sangam [the place where Bāsava worshipped], and your daughter-in-law must be by your side to serve you, and you must have full faith in Lord Śiva.

The folksong performances of men present a greater degree of formal organization than the performances of women, and the purpose of the singing is more specialized. The songs which men sing are called *bhajana*, and the theme of the songs is most often the praising of a particular male god, Śiva, Bāsava, or Hanumān, for example. *Bhajana* is celebrated outside of a house where death has occurred, and the singers take part in the procession to the graveyard. The main occasions for *bhajana* are the public religious functions, that is fairs, festivals, and processions, but *bhajana* is usually performed at least once a week on a day that is sacred to a particular deity such as Monday, Tuesday, or Saturday. These singing groups may also perform on full moon days, and some perform once or twice a day in temples or in prayer houses. Membership in a *bhajana* group provides opportunity for travel, and one of the attractions of the religious fair are the famed *bhajana* groups which have come or have been invited to perform. The funerals of saints, of famous persons, and of persons whose relatives or friends can bear the expense of bringing men singers give more opportunities for travel and tour. *Bhajana* is sung in unison or by solo and chorus to the accompaniment of small cymbals, a small drum, a triangle, and a one or two-stringed lute. Frequently the harmonium provides background chords, and there is a type of instrumental *bhajana* in which the human voice and the harmonium are not heard. Folk singing can be learned by anyone and is performed by groups of mixed caste composition under leaders who may be of any of the castes represented in the group.

Vacanas are the concise preachings of Vīraśaiva saints, especially of those who are believed to have lived in the twelfth century, and many *vacanas* are included in the repertoire of the folksingers of both sexes. The final line of each *vacana* praises the tutelary male god of the saint to whom the *vacana* is attributed, and so the form of the *vacanas* is suited to the purpose of folksingers who wish to show their devotion by praising God. Each *vacana* is composed in the form of one to thirty lines of simple metered prose. Although the language of *vacana* literature is relatively simple, the graphic form of the *vacana* is sometimes reformed into colloquial forms in the dialect of the singers. The structure of the longer sentences is sometimes broken by the requirements of melodic line and repetition by the *bhajana* singer, so that elisions and substitutions are especially likely to occur. Thus a line of a *vacana* attributed to the Vīraśaiva saint Bāsava, "As the nightingale longs for the brilliance of the moon," is transformed in *bhajana* into three wholly new segments as follows: "Nightingale and moon; good-mind; wish for color." The graphic form in Kannada is as follows: *caḳōrange candramāna belagina cinte.* In the song the forms become: *ceḳōrange cendramā; cendramāna; rangīna cinte.* Three popular *vacanas* in which the graphic forms are not changed by the singers are given below:

If we sow a *neem* seed, make a platform of sugar in which it will grow, and water it with milk and honey, the *neem* fruit will still be bitter. I know this, O Lord of Saṅgam, and so keep me apart from persons with sweet external appearance who do not worship our Lord Śiva. (Bāsava)

There is no religion without mercy. Be merciful to living things, for mercy is the root of religion (*dharma*). Our Lord of Saṅgam says we must keep to this rule above all others. (Bāsava)

Why does a fisher who takes pleasure in killing his catch not mourn their deaths as he mourns the death of his own child? So, Lord Śiva, I call persons butchers who are not merciful. (Akkamadevī)

Bhajana performers commonly sing *vacanas* attributed to the following saints of the twelfth century: Bāsava, who was the principal saint; Akkamadevī, a nun who is fabled for devotion and intelligence; Cenbāsava, the son-in-law of Bāsava; Allama Prabhu or Prabhudeva, Bāsava's guru; and Mogi Mallaya, a king who joined Bāsava's followers and maintained himself by woodcutting. The *vacanas* of Bāsava, Cenbāsava, Akkamadevī, and of Nilamma (Bāsava's wife) are popular among women singers. The popular *vacanas* show a variety of themes, but they most commonly preach disapproval of the externals of religion, superiority of the method of devotion for attaining salvation, equality of all Vīraśaivas, and the primacy of Śiva in everything.

Purāṇa. Purāṇas, stories of the miracles of saints and deities, are read every night in the month of Śrāvaṇa (July-August) to the audiences which assemble in the Vīraśaiva religious establishments (*maṭhs*). The size of the audience depends upon the skill of the expositor, and upon the popularity of the *purāṇa* which is read. The performers are paid from the funds of the *maṭh* where they read, or in some cases the *purāṇa* is performed by the head of the *maṭh* or by some other person who is associated with the *maṭh.* Each public performance lasts for about two hours, and only the highlights of the text can be read and explained in one month. In some instances the entire *purāṇa* is read, from six to twelve thousand lines, so that three or four months is required to complete the book, but usually only one-fourth to one-third of the text is read and the book is completed in about a month. Most *purāṇas* are written in six-line stanza form, and one stanza, or perhaps two to four lines, is read out, explained, and then another stanza is taken up in the same way. The specialized skill, which must be learned from a teacher, is not in reading the *purāṇa,* which an assistant often does, but rather in explaining the significance of the text by means of *vacanas,* authoritative Vīraśaiva books and anecdotes. A mixed dialect of colloquial forms and of forms approved by literary convention is used for the exposition of the text. Jaṅgams are usually the practitioners of the art, although it is not considered to be a hereditary profession.

The *purāṇas* of modern Vīraśaiva saints are publicly performed in the vicinities where the saints passed their lives, so that local patriotism accounts for the popularity of many *purāṇas.* Twenty-five *purāṇas* have been found to be popular everywhere among Vīraśaivas, and they are as follows: Akkamadevī (*purāṇa*), Akkamadevī (*vacana*), Anadanīśvar, Athaniśivayogi, Balalīlmahanśivayogi, Bāsava (*purāṇa*), Bāsava (*vacana*),

Cenbāsava, Corbāsava, Devī, Fakirīśvar, Falaisvar, Hanagalkumārsvāmi, Hemareddimallamma, Seranabāsveśvar, Kotturbāsveśvar, Mahāliṅgalīlā, Nalwatwadśivaserana, Prabhuliṅgalīle, Reṇukācārya, Revanasiddeśvar, Sidramiśvar, 63 Puratanru, Tontadarya, and Virbhadra. The *vacanas* of Bāsava and of Akkamadevī are performed as *purāṇas*, and the *purāṇas* which relate the lives of these saints are also popularly performed. The Prabhuliṅgalīle, which narrates the life of Bāsava's guru, Allama Prabhu, is said to be the most difficult of the *purāṇas* to perform because the guru's metaphysical (*māyā*) and cosmological (*sṛṣṭi*) ideas are to be explained to the audience.

Purāṇas may be read to the family by Vīraśaiva householders during the Śrāvaṇa month, and many middle-class men begin to read *purāṇas* daily to their families when their period of retirement begins. *Bāsava Purāṇa*, *Anadanīśvar Purāṇa*, *Akkamadevī Purāṇa*, and especially the *Devī Purāṇa* are favored for family reading. *Devī Purāṇa* is also read widely in villages where trained specialists in the puranic art are not available. This book is read every Tuesday and Friday in many *maṭhs* and houses throughout the year, while some householders prefer to read *Devī Purāṇa* only on new and full moon days. The *Purāṇa* itself is regarded as a form of *Devī*, the Mother of the universe and its principal driving force (Ādiśakti). Thus, more ritual attention is accorded this book a propos of its status as the embodiment of religion and religious force than is given to any other puranic text. It is forbidden to handle the book without a preparatory bath, and immediately after reading from the book it is obligatory to offer special *nevidya* sweets to it and to bow down before it. A cycle of reading *Devī Purāṇa* can begin only at certain auspicious times, as for example during Śrāvaṇa or Kārtik months, or on the occasion of celebration of spectacularly successful undertakings. Sickness and family disaster are believed to fall upon those who do not handle the *Devī Purāṇa* in this prescribed way. These directions for use can be found printed at the beginning of the popular editions of the *purāṇa*, along with the prose commentary on the story.

Devī Purāṇa, which consists of 796 stanzas of six lines each, tells the story of Devī conquering the demons and is allegorically interpreted as the struggle between the forces of good and of evil in everything. Śiva, Viṣṇu, and Brahmā are depicted as the three sons of Devī, who instructs the world that all three are equally deserving of religious devotion. Śiva is also the narrator of the *Purāṇa*. The person for whose benefit the story was first narrated is Bāsava, and he is the only Vīraśaiva saint who appears in the text. The *Purāṇa* promises the reader and listeners salvation (*mukti*) and freedom from the cycle of births and deaths which is preached by modern Hinduism. The final chapter of the *Purāṇa* describes a worshipper who has attained fusion (*aikya*) with Devī by the recommended path of devotion (*bhakti*). This chapter may be summarized as follows:

The devotee who has reached the last stage is both teacher (guru) and taught (*bhakta*), and so he has attained the highest pleasure in fusion with Śiva. He sees Devī as the world and the world as Devī. He has given up the companionship of bad people. His words are Brahmā's words, and whoever acts by them gains salvation. To face him is to go to heaven, to remember him is to gain blessings, and to say he's man is damnation. Where he stands is Kāśī, the most holy of places. The externals of religion are nothing to him. Only his voice is manlike, the rest is God. When Śiva calls him to his side, there is merging like fluids in a glass, milk with milk, water with water.

Prabacan is a much simpler form of sacred public performance, which may be substituted for the reading of the *purāṇa* in Śrāvaṇa month. The narrative sequence of the *purāṇa* is replaced by topical organization in *prabacan*, and the discussion of religious subjects is almost entirely in the colloquial dialect of the region. The discussions proceed daily on a particular religious or moral topic from one to as many as twenty days, depending on the depth of the subject. Subjects may be drawn from puranic texts for presentation in *prabacan* style. As in *purāṇa* recitations, the preachings of Vīraśaiva saints and the authoritative books for the sect provide the basic material for the performer's exposition. Questions from the audience are, however, permitted during *prabacan*. A *prabacan* performance closes every day, in the same way as a *purāṇa* reading, with distribution of consecrated food which symbolizes the benefits that God will bestow on the listener, namely, material prosperity and spiritual salvation. Some popular *prabacan* topics are the following: life of a twelfth century Vīraśaiva saint, anger, truth, guru, *liṅgam*, any or all of the six stages in the progress of a Vīraśaiva toward fusion with Śiva, and the *vacanas* of Bāsava.

Kīrtan is a more complex public performance than *purāṇa*, and *kīrtan* may also be substituted for the reading of *purāṇa* during Śrāvaṇa month. A *kīrtan* performer should be trained from childhood in the art in order to satisfy a critical audience, but many Vīraśaiva *kīrtan* artists have not had the advantage of such long training. There is no book or text in a *kīrtan* performance; everything depends upon the memory and organizing skill of the performer, who is expected to explain in a cadenzalike style any religious or moral subject. The language of these expositions is a mixture of stage dialects, including female impersonations, of colloquial forms, and of spoken graphic forms. The *kīrtan* artist has freedom in choosing his subject, so that it sometimes happens that Liṅgāyat *maṭhs* sponsor Rāmāyaṇ or Bhārat *kīrtan*, which have Vaiṣṇavite themes and could not be said to advance the sectarian plea for Śiva's devotees. *Kīrtan* attracts large audiences even when the artist is considered by some discriminating listeners to be deficient in skill. *Kīrtan* artists frequently choose from among the following subjects for their lectures: story of Gaṇapati, Śiva and Pārvatī, the idea of God, female chastity, the life of Akkamadevī, and the place of *vacana* literature in Hinduism. Each *purāṇa* or *prabacan* recitation continues for about two hours, but it is understood that no *kīrtan* performance will have less than three hours' duration.

Fairs. Religious fairs are held under Vīraśaiva sponsorship during the slack seasons for agriculture, from January to March and in August (Śrāvaṇa). There are fairs which are celebrated on a large scale at half a dozen places which are held to be sacred because of events in the lives of the twelfth century Vīraśaiva saints, at the numerous *maṭhs* of living celibate saints, and at temples in district and subdistrict towns. Every village celebrates, in addition to these, the fair of one or more of the deities which have temples in the village. The famous large fairs which are associated with the twelfth century saints are held at Ulivi, Sri Saila, Sholapur, Kalyan, Godaci, and Sangam. Ulivi and Sri Salila are situated in remote forested areas, Sholapur is a district town; Sangam, Kalyan, and Godaci are situated on the Deccan plateau. Sri Saila is also the center of Sūryasiṃhāsan, one of the five thrones of religious authority for the Vīraśaivas which are associated with the founding of the religion.

The main business in fairs is the chariot drawing function, in which the chariot of the god of a particular temple or of the deceased saint who established the particular *maṭh* which may be sponsoring the fair is pulled in a religious procession. The procession symbolizes the descent of Śiva's horde from their heavenly home on Mount Kailās, and it is preceded by Śiva's banner affixed to a tall pole (Nandīkol). The pole symbolizes

Śiva's vehicle, the bull (Nandī or Bāsava), and the pole is believed to have power to protect those who follow behind. There is a conception that spirits draw the chariot, and so astrology is resorted to in fixing the exact time and place for beginning the procession. The palanquin of Bāsava, or of any deity, with accompanying *bhajana* groups to sing the praises of the deity in the palanquin, is included in the procession. There are drummers and dancers who precede the chariot, and water is poured before the god, or saint, who is transported in the chariot. Women worship the chariot with lighted lamps and betel tray at least once during the procession. Consecrated food is distributed from the chariot, in the sense that onlookers hurl fruit at the vehicle which is consecrated by this contact with the god or saint.

Fairs provide excellent opportunities for *bhajana* performers, and the bigger fairs attract the best *bhajana* groups of the district. *Kīrtan*, *prabacan*, *vacana* singing, and the life cycle rite of initiation commonly are held during the fairs which *maṭhs* sponsor.

There are management committees which direct the big fairs, and if there is a managing committee of a *maṭh*, it will function in organizing the annual fair of the *maṭh*. Village fairs are executed more informally and are financed by subscriptions from each household. Guests are fed without charge at the fairs which *maṭhs* and villages sponsor, but the other fairs charge entrance fees, rent rooms, and sell stall space to shopkeepers so that the whole takes on the aspect of a commercial venture.

The celebration of the Śivarātrī festival at many *maṭhs* is the occasion for a fair, with the difference that the chariot dragging procession may be optional under these circumstances. Public fairs are not usually held in villages on this festival day, but Jaṅgams are called to houses, just as they are also called at the time of village fairs, so that guru-*liṅgam*-Jaṅgam may be worshipped.

Printed publications. The most frequently used modern medium for communicating Vīraśaiva sectarian ideas has been the printed publication. This category includes newspapers, weekly and monthly magazines, pamphlets, popular books, and scholarly books. There is no daily newspaper which is devoted to Vīraśaiva propaganda, but the activities of *maṭhs* and religious clubs, fairs, and the speeches of the celibate Liṅgāyat saints and literary men are given full coverage by newspapers. The magazines of the sect, now six in number, devote all or most of their space to religious news and feature articles about the religion. Religious pamphlets, of from ten to seventy pages each, are separately composed and printed every year by about twenty-five booksellers. The material of these pamphlets includes short collections of *vacanas*, folksongs, and life stories of Vīraśaiva saints, and there are about one hundred and thirty separate titles which may be purchased, each for less than a rupee. The category of popular books includes collections of *vacanas*, the most popular *purāṇas*, dramas, and explanations of Vīraśaiva philosophy and religious practice. About two hundred titles fall within this category. The scholarly publications consist of about twenty-five critical editions of *purāṇas* and *vacanas*, in which a number of manuscripts have been compared and an authoritative text prepared.

Pamphlets are sold in book stalls by street peddlers on market days, and by touring booksellers at the larger fairs. The same, or similar, pamphlets may be published by two or three different makers, and so the purchaser rarely finds difficulty in locating a desired item. Popular books are available at the fairs and in book stalls, and some *maṭhs* maintain a stock of these books. The scholarly books are sometimes available in the largest book stalls in district towns, but the usual way to obtain these books is by placing an order with the publisher. This does not mean that scholarly books are not read, since libraries make them available to the interested public. Some of the larger *maṭhs* maintain good libraries and there are Vīraśaiva libraries in twenty district and subdistrict towns. These libraries also supply their readers with newspapers and the less frequent serial publications of the sect.

A few of the popular books and the pamphlets are written for an audience with the minimum standard of literacy, such as can be gained in the four years of primary school education. According to the 1951 census, 20.6 percent of the population of Dharwar, Bijapur, and Belgaum districts, the three districts in which about half of all Vīraśaivas live, had acquired literacy. Scholarly books, popular editions of *vacanas*, and *purāṇas*, dramas, newspapers, and magazines are written for persons who have had at least seven years of formal schooling. The 1951 census figures for these three districts show that 1.25 percent of the people had been educated to this seventh standard.

Cultural development. The category of cultural development is used here to include students' free boarding institutions, boys' and women's clubs, and singing of *vacanas* by classical musicians. There is a common element in these three kinds of activities which may be called social upgrading, or cultural improvement, or even increased participation in the national culture of India. The point is perhaps most strained in the abstract with respect to the classical performance of *vacana* songs, but to witness such a performance before an audience which is not accustomed to listen patiently to a classical performer is a strong argument for its inclusion in this category. Like the *bhajana* singer, the classical artist does not always follow closely the written form of the *vacana* he is singing.

Students' free boarding clubs are managed by the *maṭhs* in the district and subdistrict towns and in other places where there are high schools or colleges. The subscriptions which finance these charitable arrangements are under the management of special committees, and these funds are not merged with the general *maṭh* funds. The clubs allow villagers to continue their education in towns and cities, and they provide opportunities for close association between members of the different constituent caste groups which are included in the Vīraśaiva sect; some clubs admit non-Vīraśaivas as well. The club in Dharwar was founded in 1920, and work is proceeding on the plan to convene the three thousand or so alumni of this club in 1957 for an organizational meeting so that there can be an annual convention and other activities of the alumni group.

The Vīraśaiva boys' clubs, which have now spread to nearly every town and many villages where Liṅgāyats live, have the main purpose of preparing boys for yearly examinations in philosophy and religious practices of the sect. Certificates are issued on the basis of the examination scores which provide an objective standard of the boy's knowledge of Vīraśaiva philosophy and religion. Thus, the clubs appear to porvide motivation for learning and rewards for merit, as well as training in examination procedures which will be valuable if the boy is to continue his education. The funds for these groups are provided by charitable subscriptions and the examination fees.

The women's clubs of Vīraśaivas are largely an urban phenomena; they are known as Akkanna Balaga after their patroness, Akkamadevī. Many of these clubs meet daily for discussions of *vacana* literature or other religious, moral, or national topics. There may be more than one club in a particular town, and in these cases the membership of the different clubs is drawn from different social classes. Some clubs teach Hindī or handiwork, and a few manage free boarding clubs for girl students. These societies regularly conduct public celebrations of Akkamadevī's birthday, participate in Gandhi's birthday function, and for the new local holidays (*nadhabba*) which symbolize Indian independence, the clubs sponsor lectures, plays and stick dances. Some women are given opportunities for travel to the annual convention of Akkanna Balagas. There are no caste restrictions against attendance at the club meetings, but the membership is limited to Vīraśaiva women. Charitable subscriptions, membership dues, and a tax levied on Vīraśaiva marriages provide funds for the clubs.

Drama, radio, and cinema. Of the three modern media of radio, drama, and cinema, it is drama which makes the most concerted appeal to the religious emotions of the Vīraśaivas. Leaders of some drama companies have been celibate saints, and in other companies the leader may perform *kīrtan*, *prabacan*, *vacana* songs, or *bhajana* on special occasions, or when the company is not performing any play. Thus with respect to stage drama there is no strong division between sacred and secular interests. "The Life of Bāsava" has been the most successful Vīraśaiva drama, and its success has been helped by the fact that the role of Bāsava was taken by a celibate saint in one of the productions. Vīraśaivas who have the opportunity attend the play five or six times, and one of the two current productions of this play is in its second year of daily performances.

Dharwar radio station began broadcasting in 1949, and though hardly a sectarian institution, the station does present many programs of religious interest to Vīraśaivas. The birthday of Bāsava was celebrated by a special program in 1957, which occupied most of the evening broadcasting time. Villagers with access to radio sets try not to miss the *bhajana* programs, which are labelled simply "For Villagers" in the station program guides. *Vacanas* sung in the style of classical music are the most common of the sectarian broadcasts. The Dharwar and Bangalore stations have many *vacana* records, and *vacana* programs occur on the average once in two days from each of these two Kannada broadcasting stations. Radio dramas are occasionally produced which narrate the lives of Vīraśaiva saints, as, for example, Akkamadevī. The language of these dramatic presentations is literary Kannada, which is written for an audience with about seven years of formal schooling.

The costs of cinema production, upwards of seventy thousand rupees, place severe limitations on this medium as a form of religious communication. Two movies have depicted the lives of Vīraśaiva saints, and a third is now in production. One of these two films was released in 1957 and has not been enthusiastically received. The comedy, the appeal to sex, and the imitation of Hindī screen songs and dances disturbs many people, Liṅgāyats and others, who are interested in the sacred elements of the screen performance. Kannada and Telugu pictures with more general Śaiva, rather than Vīraśaiva, themes attract Liṅgāyats in large numbers and particularly appeal to villagers. A popular release in 1953 was made by a Vīraśaiva producer-actor and tells the story of the Tamil Śaiva saint, Kannappa. This picture would be classified as of the more general Śaiva type. Another Śaiva picture played for a year in one subdistrict town and ran for six months in Dharwar and other towns during the year of its release, 1941. This movie still plays to large audiences at Liṅgāyat religious fairs where touring talkies are frequently set up. The movie tells the legend of the installation of the *liṅgam* in the temple at Gokarna in Karwar District, and its principal appeal to villagers, who formed the majority of its audiences, was the pictorial representation of Śiva throughout the performance. Many villagers broke coconuts in the theatres as Śiva appeared on the screen, and they distributed money offerings to the theatre attendents, treating the theatre as if it were a temple. There was less than the usual amount of comedy in this screenplay. There was less dancing, and only religious songs were sung. The language of the serious characters in the cinema is literary and is written for persons with about seven years of formal education. Those in the audience with no more than four years of schooling may be able to understand ten to twenty percent of the spoken literary forms of their own language, and so they often miss the point of a particular speech or sequence.

Trends. Four old forms of religious propaganda—life cycle rites, folksongs, *purāṇa*, and fairs—have been briefly considered along with three new forms—printed publications, radio-drama-cinema, and cultural development. The classification of these forms of communication into new and old is a simple one and has been confirmed by expert and authoritative judgment in the Vīraśaiva sect. It remains to be seen, however, how far the classification is a useful one for comparative study, that is, for comparing Vīraśaivas of one region with Vīraśaivas in other districts and for comparing Vīraśaiva with non-Vīraśaiva religions.

If the old and new forms of communication are compared, the tendency for the new modes to produce greater integration between different social classes and castes may be seen. This trend of the newer media in the direction of greater social integration is not to be confused with judgments about the effectiveness of the forms of propaganda, because today the old forms both collectively and individually outweigh the effectiveness of the new forms. It is apparent, however, that the tendency of the new media, particularly printed publications, is to simplify the communication structure within the sect and so to bridge the gap between competing social classes and castes. Anyone can purchase from a book stall or browse through a peddler's assortment of religious pamphlets, and Vīraśaiva libraries do not exclude or differentiate among readers according to their caste. In the *purāṇa* form there are always two levels of competence in the mastery of Vīraśaiva philosophy and religion—that of the performer, and the lower level of the audience. The examinations of the boys' clubs establish, on the other hand, different standards for competence, and the examinations break down the expert-layman dichotomy into several levels. The trend for greater integration is illustrated by the students' free boarding clubs, where members recruited from several castes are brought together in the closer fellowship of group living and common educational goals. The programs of the women's societies give moral sanction for contact with national activities in which there are opportunities for cooperation with non-Vīraśaivas. The cinema and newspapers are modern mass media which strive for universal appeal, since it is less profitable for even a majority of their audiences to be drawn from only one sect. Thus, when the modern forms of communication of the Vīraśaiva religion are compared with the old, the new forms appear to show a trend in the direction of social unification which is not found among the traditional modes of propaganda of the sect.[1]

NOTE

[1] A longer account of the rituals, philosophy, and literature of the Lingāyats, written by a member of the sect, may be found in the following work, which is soon to be made available in the United States: S. C. Nandimath, *A Handbook of Vīraśaivism* (Dharwar, 1941).

Karnatak College
Mysore State, India

METHODS OF POPULAR RELIGIOUS INSTRUCTION IN SOUTH INDIA

BY V. RAGHAVAN

IN no country of such vast dimensions could the countryside be found to be so imbued with the teachings of the religion of the land as in India, and it is remarkable how, in the past, when the modern means of communication and the mechanical aids for the dissemination of information were lacking, the *ācāryas* could spread their teachings from one end of the country to the other. In this ancient land, the teeming millions were no doubt illiterate, but they were never uninformed or uncultured. The ancient teachers, concentrating on the direct communication of essential knowledge, helped people to be imbued with effective culture without scholastic education. It is significant that knowledge is called in Sanskrit *śruta* and in Tamil *keḷvi*, which mean 'that which is heard.' In fact, the high level of the moral and spiritual attainment of the unlettered, like the shopkeeper and the hunter, and the so-called repositories of learning, like the Brahmans, taking a lesson or two from them, is a recurring theme in the epics, e.g. the Tulādhāra and Dharmavyādha stories in the *Mahābhārata*. That our religious history has thrown up saints from among weavers, cobblers, potters, shepherds, and Harijans shows how widely the soil has been irrigated and fertilized by the country's spiritual engineers.[1]

Recitation and exposition of Itihāsas and purāṇas. The Himalayan waters of Vedic faith and Upaniṣadic philosophy were brought to the plains of the people through several projects, the biggest of which were the *itihāsas* and the *purāṇas*. Vyāsa says that the *Mahābhārata* was specially composed to broadcast the Vedic lore to the people at large, and that the four Vedas became complete with the fifth, namely, the *ākhyāna* or epic. Vālmīki composed his musical epic to reinforce the Vedic teachings. Illustrating the teachings of the Vedas through the stories of *rājarṣis* 'sage-kings,' who upheld truth and right, and those of the sports of God, who became incarnate to salvage the reign of *dharma*, and by giving, incidently, an epitome of the knowledge of cosmogony, periods of time, and the like, the *itihāsas* and the *purāṇas* proved themselves to be the most efficient means of popular instruction in religion and philosophy. As the rhetoricians put it, the commands of the lordlike Vedas (*prabhusammita*) were put to the people by the *itihāsa* and *purāṇa* in the persuasive manner of the friend (*suhṛt-sammita*). According to the preface of all the *itihāsas* and the *purāṇas*, they were recited to vast congregations of people gathered at sacrificial sessions (*sattras*) by a class of reciters called *sūta-paurāṇikas*. The evidence of numerous inscriptions establishes the fact of continuity of this practice of exposition all through the course of Indian history; the wide provenance of these records shows that this machinery of popular religious education was active not only in every part of the mother country, but in Greater India too.

If, without flame and sword, Hinduism spread over the whole of the Far East, it was possible because the *Rāmāyaṇa* and the *Mahābhārata*, through the oral expounder, the sculptor, and the dancer, went forth in advance clearing the way and conquering the peoples' imagination. As early as A.D. 600, one Somaśarman is found to present to a temple in Cambodia the *Mahābhārata*, the *Rāmāyaṇa*, and the *purāṇas*, and provide for their daily exposition; a regular temple to Vālmīki was raised in Campā by King Prakāśadharman, and, in the tenth century, the kings of Cambodia had a *kavi-paṇḍita* attached to them to expound the *Rāmāyaṇa* and the *Mahābhārata*. In North India, we have epigraphic evidence to show that endowments were made for the popular recital of the epics and the *purāṇas*.[2] From Bāṇa's *Kādambarī* we know that the *Mahābhārata* was recited in the Mahākāla temple, and, from his *Harṣacarita*, that *Vāyu Purāṇa* was recited in his own village house.

The South Indian rulers, the Pallavas, the Coḷas, and the Pāṇḍyas, knew the value of the *itihāsa* and *purāṇa*, and epigraphs found all over the peninsula show how these kings helped these works to fulfil their mission of disseminating country-wide religious education. In the Kūram and Taṇḍantoṭṭam plates of the Pallavas, provisions are specified for the reading and exposition of the *Mahābhārata* (*Bhāratākhyāna*).[3] A portion of the endowment was specified for the *Bhārata*-expounder (*Bhāratappaṅgu*), and a stage (*ambalam*) was assigned for his discourse in the temple at Śendalai in Tanjore District (No. 63 of 1897).[4] In A.D. 1048, in the time of the Coḷa Rājādhirāja I, the college at Tribhuvani was required by the endowment to expound for the people the *Bhārata* and the *Rāmāyaṇa*. The *Mahābhārata-vṛtti* in the form of land was given to two brothers by Māravarman Sundara Pāṇḍya for the exposition of the *Mahābhārata*, the *Rāmāyaṇa*, and the *purāṇas* (No. 546 of 1922 found at Tiruttāṅgal), and Māravarman Kulaśekhara (A.D. 1268) conferred a privilege on a Brāhmaṇa at Āḻvār-tirunagari (No. 467 of 1909), who expounded the *purāṇa* and *itihāsa*. Besides the epics and the *purāṇas*, other religious books were also expounded under these endowments: the *Manu Saṃhitā* and *Vaikhānasa-Sūtra* at Tribhuvani; the *Śivadharma* in the assembly hall in the Tirunāgeśvaram temple (A.D. 1054; No. 214 of 1911) and at Tiruvalīśvaram (No. 327 of 1916). Even the more difficult works of philosophy were studied: the *Rāmānuja-bhāṣya* at Kāñcī (No. 493 of 1919) and the Vedānta by a follower of Śaṅkara at the same place (A.D. 1293).[5] The Śaiva hagiological text, *Śrī purāṇa* of Āḷuḍaiyanambi (Sundaramūrti), and the *Somasiddhānta* form the subjects of exposition provided for according to some other records (Nos. 241 of 1911, 321 of 1917, and 403 of 1896). In the times of the Vijayanagara empire, a grant of Acyutadevarāya does the same thing for the exposition of a Vaiṣṇava scripture called *Bhaktisañjīvinī* (A.D. 1534-35).

Thus the practice of popular exposition of the epics and the *purāṇas* has been handed down to the present day in an unbroken tradition. Today such expositions, though to a lesser extent, constitute one of the leading forms of popular religious instruction all over South India, especially in the Tamil country. The *purāṇas* are only rarely taken up; even the *Bhārata*, which, as inscriptions prove, was originally more popular, is not so frequently handled; the epic that holds the people enthralled is the *Rāmāyaṇa*. Whether it be Vālmīki's Sanskrit original, as is more often the case, or Kamban's Tamil version, hardly a day passes without some sweet-voiced, gifted expounder sitting in a temple, *maṭha* (centre of religious preaching), public hall, or house-front and expounding to hundreds and thousands the story of the *dharma* that Rāma upheld and the *adharma* by which Rāvaṇa fell. Sometimes the Paurāṇic accounts relating to particular shrines and holy waters, *kṣetra* and *tīrtha*, become themes of such popular expositions at certain pilgrim centers or during certain seasons, e.g. the *Tulākāverī-māhātmya* during the holy bathing season of Māgha. This *purāṇa-pravacana* (exposition of *purāṇa*) is in vogue in Keraḷa also, where it is called *pāṭhakam.*

Translations and compositions of religious works. If the *purāṇas* and the *itihāsas* were created to put the Vedic teachings in a popular form, it soon became obvious that to bring them still closer to the masses, it was necessary that, along with their oral exposition, the original Sanskrit texts themselves should be given to the people in their own languages. A more masterly epitome of the teachings of the Śrutis and Smṛtis than the *Tirukkuraḷ* of Tiruvaḷḷuvar, revered as a Tamil Veda, cannot be produced. A host of authors brought, through poems and didactic writings, the entire wisdom of the *ṛṣis* to the Tamils. Under royal patronage, the epics and the *purāṇas* began to appear in Tamil, Telugu, Kannada, and Malayalam translations. The *Mahābhārata* was rendered into Tamil by the Pāṇḍya king Pūḷiyan himself,[6] and about A.D. 1210 a Śaiva named Aranilaiviśākhan Trailokyamallan Vatsarājan composed the *Bhārata* again in elegant Tamil (Tiruvālaṅgāḍu, No. 482 of 1905). In the eleventh century, the Telugus also got their *Bhārata* from Nannaya Bhaṭṭa; in the next century, under the Coḷas, Kamban sang his famous Tamil *Rāmāyaṇa;* two later Pāṇḍya kings, Ativīra and Varatuṅga, in the sixteenth century, rendered into Tamil the *Kūrma Purāṇa*, the *Liṅga Purāṇa*, the *Kāśī-khaṇḍa*, and the *Brahmottara-khaṇḍa;* from two earlier records at Cuddalore (A.D. 1111-19), it appears that two persons, named Parasamaya Koḷari Mahāmuni and Kamalālaya Bhaṭṭa, had not only written in Tamil the local *Kannivana Purāṇa*, but also had rendered into it all the eighteen well-known *purāṇas.*[7]

Royal patronage to devotional singing. The Pallavas and the Coḷas extended munificent patronage to men of learning through educational institutions call *ghaṭikās*, temples, and foundations of *agrahāra*-settlements, from where they carried on their educational activities. If the Tamil country had been acclaimed in the *Bhāgavata-māhātmya* as the birth-place of *bhakti*, the credit of spreading that devotion all over the South belongs not only to the saints and teachers, but to the great Pallava and Coḷa monarchs themselves, who, besides giving encouragement to these teachers, were themselves great devotees; Mahendra Vikrama and Rājasiṃha Pallavas are referred to as *paramamāheśvara*, *śivacūḍāmaṇi*, and *āgamapriya;* and Kocceṅgaṇān and Gaṇḍarāditya Coḷas are counted among Śaiva saints and canonical hymnists. By far the most important of the religious activities inaugurated and carried forward in the Pallava times are those of the groups of Śaiva and Vaiṣṇava saints, the Nāyanārs and Āḻvārs. Patronized by the Pallava kings, these saints went from place to place, sang their devotional hymns to the deities at the several shrines they visited, disputed with and put down their religious opponents, and spread among the people the gospel of devotion to Śiva and Viṣṇu.

Moving in their appeal, by virtue of both their devotion and music, the Tamil hymns of these Śaiva and Vaiṣṇava saints, called *Devāram* and *Tiruvāimoḻi*, respectively embodied the truths of the Vedas and the Vedānta, and came to be revered truly as as the Tamil Veda. Although they were collected and codified only during the reign of Rājarāja Coḷa (tenth century), in the Later Pallava age itself attempts were made for popularizing these sacred hymns, *Tiruppadiyam*, by instituting special endowments for their recital in Śiva and Viṣṇu temples. In the time of Nandivarman III Pallava, an endowment was made for the recital of *Tiruppadiyam* at Tirumallam;[8] in Parāntaka Coḷa's time, their recital by Brāhmaṇas was arranged for at Lālguḍi and Āttūr (Nos.

373 of 1903 and 99 of 1929); in the times of Rājarāja I, Rājendra I, and Rājādhirāja, endowments were made for the singing of the *Tiruvāimoḷi* at Uttaramerūr, Śrīraṅgam, Eṇṇāyiram, and Tribhuvani (Nos. 181 of 1923, 61 of 1892, 176 of 1923, 194 of 1923, 333 of 1917, and 557 of 1919); a fifteenth century record (No. 70 of 1909) in the former Pudukottai State makes a gift of a village to a reciter of the hymns of Śaṭhagopa.

A similar series of inscriptions recording the practice of singing the Śaiva canon, *Devāram*, is found throughout the Coḷa times (No. 349 of 1918, issued in Rājakeasrī's time, and No 99 of 1929, in Parāntaka's time); a large number of epigraphs show that in the great Rājarāja's time this arrangement was in full swing (Nos. 333 of 1906, 275 of 1917, 40 of 1918, 423 of 1908, and 624 of 1909), no less than forty of the 212 servants at the big temple at Tanjore having been engaged in the recital of these hymns with musical accompaniments. Realizing the appeal of music and the power of that art to aid spiritual exaltation, the authors of the *Devāram* hymns sang them as musical compositions in different melodies; in a Tiruvorriyūr record of Vīrarājendra Coḷa (No. 128 of 1912), sixteen gifted songstresses of the temple dancers' class (*devar-aḍiyār*) were commissioned to sing these hymns in classic style (*aha-mārga*). This institution is still alive in South Indian temples; a special class of temple singers called *oduvārs* recite them every evening in a hall in the temple, and, during festivals accompany the deity in procession, singing the *Devāram* in a party.

Maṭhas as centers of religious preaching. Corresponding to the *āśramas* and *tapovanas* of *ṛṣis* mentioned in ancient Sanskrit literature, there developed, in later historical periods, centers of spiritual endeavor and headquarters of different kinds of saints and their religious activities called *maṭhas*, which were originally natural habitations in the form of mountain caves, *guhais* (*guhās*), but were later enlarged into structural buildings. The rich epigraphic records of South India, again, reveal a continuous succession of these *maṭhas* and the part they played in the religious life of the people. In the Later Pallava times, we had at Tiruvorriyūr a *maṭha* presided over by Nirañjanaguru and Caturānana Paṇḍita, who were both looking after the temple affairs and services. Attached to the same shrine, there arose several other *maṭhas*, called after Tiru-jñānasambandar, Rājendra Coḷa, Nandikeśvara, and Aṅgarāya. It is from such beginnings that there developed the Tamil *maṭhas* now functioning at places like Dharmapuram, Tiruvāvaḍuturai, and Tiruppanandāl, which are centers of Śaiva teachers having the charge of temple management. The Liṅgāyata *maṭhas* of the Telugu and Kannada areas also had a similar course of evolution; other religious sects of Advaitic, Viśiṣṭādvaitic, and Dvaitic persuasions developed their own *maṭha*-organizations for keeping up their religious propaganda among the people. Besides teaching texts of higher philosophy to select sets of qualified students, the heads of these *maṭhas*, who are constantly on the move, accompanied by disciples and scholars, come into close contact with the people, to whom they give popular discourses. That the imparting of such popular discourses forms a regular and time-honored function of these *maṭhas* is attested by an inscription of Vijayagaṇḍa Gopāla (A.D. 1293), which records a grant to a Śaṅkara Maṭha at Kāñcī for the exposition of the Vedānta.

Temples as centers of religious and cultural education. The temple, as seen above, was the place where the *itihāsa* and *purāṇa* were expounded, sacred hymns recited, and *maṭhas* developed. It is to the great work of the Pallavas and the Coḷas that South India owes the temple—its most glorious achievement, its primary and all-comprehensive religious institution, and, in fact, the very center of all its cultural activity.

Starting as excavations on mountain sides in the Early Pallava times, and gradually becoming stone structures, the South Indian temples grew in the golden age of the Coḷas into huge establishments, dominating the entire locality and coordinating all the aspects of local life, religious, social, and economic. Āditya I Coḷa is said to have covered the banks of the Kāverī with them; king after king vied with his predecessor, and one dynasty excelled the other, till throughout South India no village or town was left without its visible symbol of the spread of *bhakti*. Not only through worship and daily service of the images of the deities, but through the grand celebrations of their annual festivals, when the deities were taken out in procession, these temples created religious fervor among huge crowds of people drawn from far and near. The car-festival, especially, drew together the entire population of the locality. That such festivals in temples served as suitable occasions for religious discourses is also known from a reference in the Tamil poem *Peruṅkathai* (*Bṛhatkathā*).

The temple was also an art gallery, even as it was a hall for concert, lecture, or transaction of local affairs. The masterpieces of sculpture in the temples taught the entire mythology and the deeds of gods to the mass of people gathering there. All temples had paintings of similar religious themes, and even now, once a year, during festival time, the walls of temples are painted over with divine pictures. In the Pallava Kailāsanātha temple at Kāñcī, in the Jaina cave temple at Śittannavāśal, and in the Bṛhadīśvara temple at Tanjore, we have the exquisite paintings of olden times still preserved. All these show how the art of painting also was harnessed for religious teaching in ancient India.

A class of mendicants known as Maṅkhas went about exhibiting religious pictures.[9] We see from the *Mudrārākṣasa* that a class of mendicants went about showing scrolls painted with the horrors of hell (*yamapaṭa*) and exhorting people to observe *dharma*. In Saṅgam literature in Tamil, we find the *Paripāḍal* mentioned pilgrims edified by the religious paintings in the Tirupparankunram temple.

Dance and drama. The appeal of the arts of dance and drama was not ignored by the ancient teachers. The educative, didactic, and religious usefulness of the play was emphasized by Bharata himself in his *Nāṭya-śāstra*; rhetoricians also said that drama and poetry taught the same lessons as the Vedas and the *purāṇas*, but in the winning manner of the beloved (*kāntā-sammita*). All through its history, we find that the drama was, for the most part, enacted in temples during festivals. In the Tamil poems, *Jīvakacintāmaṇi* (2573) and *Peruṅkathai*, we find references to dramatic presentations in temples. Ample light on the systematic use of religious drama in temples, especially during festival times, is thrown by the Coḷa inscriptions. The greatness of the shrine of Rājarājeśvara at Tanjore was depicted in the form of a *nāṭaka* by one Śāntikkūttan at Tanjore (No. 55 of 1893, issued in Rājendra's time). At Cuddalore, the *māhātmya* of the shrine was presented by Kamalālaya Bhaṭṭa through his *Pūmpuliyūr-nāṭaka*.[10] *Śākkai* or *kūttaccākkayan* was a dancer, and an endowment made for his art in a temple was called *śākkakkaṇi* or *nṛtyabhoga*. One Alayūrccākkai was given a grant for enacting three scenes of *śākkaikkūttu* at Tiruvālandurainallūr (No. 250 of 1926). In Rājarāja's time, at Tiruvāvaḍuturai and Tiruviḍaimarudūr, two *śākkais*, named Kumāran Srīkaṇṭan and Kittimaraikkāḍan, were engaged to do the seven acts of *āriyakkūttu* in the temple (Nos. 120 of 1925 and 154 of 1895). Similarly, in Rājendra's time, Śākkai Mārāyan Vikramacoḷan performed the *śākkaikkūttu* at Kāmarasavalli (No. 65 of 1914) thrice during the Mārgaśīrṣa or Vaiśākha festival. That the *śākkai* and the dance he performed on a mythological theme were old institutions is known from the Tamil epic, *Śilappadikāram* (XXVIII. 65-80), in which we find the king Śeran Seṅkuṭṭuvan and his queen witnessing at the *nāṭakaraṅga* (theatre) the *koṭṭiccheda* dance of Śiva (the *ḍima* of Tripuradāha) by a *śākkai* of Paraiyūr.

As a vehicle of popular religious instruction, this dramatic recital has persisted to this day in the *śākkaikkūttu* or *prabandhamkūttu* of Keraḷa, where it has exercised a wholesome influence on the life of the people. This dance recital, as it now obtains in Keraḷa, is done by a *cākyār* on a stage in the temple, *kūttambalam*, to the accompaniment of a drum played by a *nambiyār* and time kept with cymbals by a lady, *naṅgiyar*. The *cākyār* recites his theme, dances, gesticulates, and, with a gift of wit, brings under his review, during his exposition, the whole course of contemporary affairs, not excepting, in the freedom of speech sanctioned to his office, even the king from the scope of his criticism. Born out of this *cākyārkūttu* is the *tuḷḷal*, which Kunjan Nambiyar fashioned as a further popularized form. During festivals, one finds these performances taking place in the corridors of Keraḷa temples, and Koṭiliṅga Yuvarāja gives a fine picture of these in the description of the Bhagavatī temple at Cranganore in his *Rasasadanabhāṇa*.[11]

Besides these, plays in local languages on Paurāṇic themes were developed in all the linguistic regions of South India, their aim and inspiration being as much religious as literary or artistic. In Andhra arose the *yakṣagāna*[12] and the Kūcipūḍi *Bhāgavatamu*; *yakṣagānas* are operatic plays on mythological themes, and cognate with them are the *bayal-āṭa* (open air play) of the Kannada area and the *teruk ūttu* (street play) of Tamilnāḍ. There is a manuscript in the *Mackenzie Collection* which informs us that Akkaṇṇa and Mādaṇṇa, the Hindu ministers of the Qutb Shāhi rulers of Golconda, maintained their own troupe of *yakṣagāna* players and made them tour the entire Qutb Shāhi dominion every year.

Kūcipūḍi is an *agrahāra* in the Krishna District where Bhāgavatas, the Brahman devotees of the Lord, took to the art of dance for the propitiation of the Lord, and enacted, with music and gesticulation, dramas on the sports of Kṛṣṇa. From this tradition, the *Bhāgavata-melā-nāṭaka*[13] of some villages in the Tanjore District, like Meraṭṭūr, Ūttukkāḍu, Nallūr, Śūlamaṅgalam, etc., took its birth. Even today, Brahmans of these villages stage plays like *Prahlādavijaya*, *Uṣāpariṇaya*, *Rukmāṅgada*, and *Mārkaṇḍeyacarita*, before the temple deity, during the springtime festivals. The plays are part of the worship, some of the actors playing the divine parts, even observing fast; and the entire population for five miles around gather and sit through the night watching the devout Brahman Bhāgavatas present their *nāṭakas* with song and gesticulation. Their ideal, best set forth in the text which they quote, is that it is the sacred duty of the Bhāgavatas to adore the Lord with song and dance, with as much devotion to it as they have to statutory rites prescribed by the Vedas (*Viṣṇorgānaṃ ca nṛttaṃ ca . . . kartavyaṃ nityakarmavat*).

Corresponding to this, the Malayalam country has its own religious plays. Taking its inspiration originally from the singing and gesticulation of the *Gīta-Govinda* of Jayadeva, the religious drama of Keraḷa developed into the Sanskrit *Kṛṣṇāṭṭam*, and from that evolved into the Malayalam *kathakaḷi*, the last having been fashioned by the chief of Koṭṭūrakkara in the latter half of the seventeenth century for the sake of a wider popular appeal. With elaborate make-up, song, and very detailed gesticulation, the *kathakaḷi* presented, through several nights cycles of epic and Paurāṇic stories to large audiences, which sat all through the night in the open to watch them. All these forms of dance drama, as well as the puppet shows, *bommalāṭṭa*, and the shadow-plays, *tolpāvai* prevalent all over the South, had the same religious setting and promoted the same religious purpose.

Devotional music. If the greatest contribution of Tamilnāḍ to the sphere of devotional music is the body of hymns called *Devāram* and *Tiruvāimoḷi*, the outstanding contribution of the Kannada speaking area to the same sphere is represented by the large body of musical composition, *padas*, *devaranāmas*, and *kīrtanas*, sung by the members of the Dāsa Kūṭa tradition. Couched in popular language, enlivened by homely wit, and glowing with the truths of spiritual realization, the compositions of the Dāsa Kūṭa saints, forming a triple heritage of literature, music, and philosophy, and sung by them in their pilgrimages from shrine to shrine, served to create among the masses a spiritual awakening and religious enthusiasm. The Dāsa Kūṭa, the origins of which are traced to a line of Smārta devotees beginning with Acalānandadāsa (ninth century) of the Rāṣṭrakūṭa times, was later represented by a line of Mādhva saints—Narahari Tīrtha (A.D. 1281), Śrīpādarāja who sang the whole of the Tenth Book of the *Bhāgavata*, Vyāsarāya (fifteenth century), Purandaradāsa (1480-1564), his shepherd contemporary Kanakadāsa, Vijayadāsa, Jagannāthadāsa, and others. The greatest of these is Purandaradāsa, and if ancient South Indian music is indebted to the *Devāram* and *Tiruvāimoḷi* of the saints of Pallava times, modern South Indian music (Karnatic) owes its evolution to this Karṇāṭaka saint-musician, Purandaradāsa. Side by side with these Haridāsas, who fostered the growth of *Viṣṇu-bhakti*, the Vīraśaiva saints, Bāsava and Allama of the twelfth century and the Śivaśaraṇas who followed them, spread *Śiva-bhakti* with their *vacanas* among the Kannaḍigas (Kannada-speaking people).

The mission of evoking devotion among the people through songs was then taken over by Telugu, which gave from Tirupati the large corpus of *saṅkīrtanas* composed by a family of devotees called the Tālappākkam poets, Annamācārya, Tiruveṅkaṭa and others, who flourished in the fifteenth and sixteenth centuries; their numberless lyrics addressed to the 'Lord of the Seven Hills,' preserved in heaps of copperplates at the hill temple, form a substantial contribution to Telugu music and to the path of adoring the Lord through song, the *bhajana-paddhati*. Next in importance are the *kīrtanas* which Rāmadāsa of Bhadrācala (seventeenth century), a devotee of Rāma who was imprisoned by Tani Shāh of Golconda, sang from his prison and which are current all over the Telugu country. While, on the side of actual practice and literary propaganda, these devoted souls popularized this cult among the learned and the lay by writing hymns and treatises and by organizing congregational singing of divine praise and founding *bhajana-maṭhas* for this purpose, the renowned saint-musician, Tyāgarāja (1757-1847), made an outstanding contribution with his songs and provided a rich musical medium for this method of worship. This school infused a new life into the old path of devotion. *Bhajana* now developed on a large scale, and the visit, to Tanjore and other centers, of performers of *saṅkīrtana* from the north, especially from Mahārāṣṭra, perfected the *bhajana-paddhati* which came to be maintained by a chain of *maṭhas* in places both big and small.

The climax of this movement of singing the name and glory of the Lord was reached in the Kāverī delta, in the heart of Tamilnāḍ, where the cult of *nāma-siddhānta*, recital of God's name as the most potent means of salvation, was developed by saint-authors of the eighteenth century, like Śrīdhara Veṅkaṭeśa and Bodhendra.

From very ancient times, the month of Mārgaśīrṣa (November-December) was considered especially sacred and appropriate for adoring the Lord, and both the Śaivas and the Vaiṣṇavas had their own devotional recitals for this month, the *Tiruvempāvai* and the *Tiruppāvai*; and even special temple-endowments were made for the latter in Coḷa times (Nos. 12 of 1905, 421 of 1912, and 128 of 1912). This special adoration of the Lord through devotional singing in Mārgaśīrṣa has continued to the present day. Parties of devotees get up early in the Mārgaśīrṣa mornings, bathe despite the chill, and go round the local temple and the tank singing devotional songs. This practice, popularly called *bhajana*, is also referred to as *giripradakṣiṇa* 'going round a sacred hill,' pointing perhaps to its origin in the circumambulation of the early mountain-cave temples, which the Nāyanārs did with hymns on their lips. While a few gifted singers, who led these *bhajana* parties, stopped at particular places to sing elaborate songs, there were *nāmāvalis* or simple strings of God's names and epithets which they uttered as they moved on and which the accompanying congregation took up in chorus. As each song or *nāmāvali* was finished, the leader pronounced what is called a *puṇḍarīka*, an expression of devotion to God like '*Namaḥ Pārvatīpataye*' or '*Sītākāntasmaraṇam*', to which the whole party responded with formulas like '*Hara Hara Mahādeva*' and '*Jaya Jaya Rāma*'. This *bhajana* was conducted in a more organized manner, within the precincts of *bhajana-maṭhas*, every day or on special weekdays or on holy days like the *ekādaśī* (the eleventh lunar day).

In a far more elaborate manner, a whole *bhajana*-session was conducted for several days once or twice a year, when the Bhāgavatas would celebrate festivals, *utsavas*, of the marriage of Sītā-Rāma or of Rādhā-Kṛṣṇa. In the manner of an *upakarman* (a ceremony for the reading of the Vedas during the rains) during the *cāturmāsya*, the Bhāgavatas go through, during these days, their entire repertoire, *gopikāgītā*, Jayadeva's *aṣṭapadīs*, the *devaranāmas* of Purandara, the *kīrtanas* of Rāmadāsa, the *Kṛṣṇalīlātaraṅgiṇī* of Nārāyaṇa Tīrtha, a Sanskrit operatic composition on the whole story of Kṛṣṇa, and similar devotional songs. Besides these, the Bhāgavatas sing, during these festivals, special series of songs called *utsava-sampradāya kīrtanas* and songs invoking the Lord with simple addresses and epithets called *divyanāma-saṅkīrtanas*, to both of which Tyāgarāja made his contribution. Some of these are sung with a simple dance movement around a brass lampstand or a *tulasī* pot, in imitation of the circular *rāsa*-dance. Some *utsava*-specialists among these execute more difficult dances, carrying the lampstand or circumambulating it with their prostrate bodies. Large numbers of devout people of either sex take part in these *bhajanas*.

Harikathā or religious story recital. An exposition of a mythological story with music and dance is defined by Bhoja in his work on *alaṅkāra* under the name *ākhyāna*; Bhoja's remarks in another context show that this refers to the art of the *kathaka*. It is to this ancient form of the *kathaka's* art that we have to relate the *kathākālakṣepa* or *harikathā*, as it evolved later in Tamilnāḍ, and is now widely prevalent in South India. The exposition of a religious story took the present *kālakṣepa* form at Tanjore, as a result of the impact of the *kīrtana* style of some Mahārāṣṭra *buvas* (religious preachers), chiefly Ramachandra Buva Morgaunkar (1864), who visited Tanjore. Before this time, *kālakṣepa*, which was an old way of spending time listening to a holy discourse, was not perfected as an art form with the addition of music and dramatic touches. Krishna Bhagavatar (1847-1903), who refashioned it after listening to the Mahārāṣṭrian style, even introduced some dancing in his performances.

The main Bhāgavata (*harikathā* reciter) stands in front, usually supported by a musician assistant standing behind him, and the minimum instrumental accompaniment is a *mṛdaṅga* (a kind of drum). The Tamil Bhāgavatas who took this up handled the art with their emphasis shifting between music and exposition, according to their individual gifts.[14] The themes are from the *Rāmāyaṇa*, the *Mahābhārata*, the *purāṇas*, lives of saints, not only of the Tamilnāḍ, but of the other parts of the country also, like Rāmadāsa, Kabīr, and the Mahārāṣṭra saints. After some preliminary invocatory singing on Gaṇeśa, Sarasvatī, Hanumat, and the *guru*, the Bhāgavata sings a song which is the text of his sermon. This song emphasizes that devotion to the Lord, or a particular mode of His worship, is the only means of salvation, or that the Lord is the only refuge of man. To illustrate this, the Bhāgavata takes up a story which forms the main part of the performance. It is called the *harikathā*. In the end the story is wound up by harking back to the burden of the first song, to illustrate which the story was expounded. During the exposition of the story, the Bhāgavata's wide learning in sacred literature is to be brought into display. He has to elevate the listeners with his knowledge, drive home with wit moral and ethical principles, and move the hearts of his audience with his dramatic and devoted narration. In fact, as an art form, the *Harikathā* is almost a mono-drama. Undoubtedly this, along with the *purāṇa-paṭhana*, forms the most effective vehicle of popular religious instruction in South India.[15]

NOTES

[1] See V. Raghavan, "Adult Education in Ancient India," *Memoirs of the Madras Library Association* (1944), pp. 57-65.

[2] See Bhandarkar, *Summary of Inscriptions of North India*, Nos. 623, 1639.

[3] *South Indian Inscriptions*, I, 150-51.

[4] *South Indian Inscriptions*, VI, 12.

[5] *Epigraphia Indica*, XIII, 196.

[6] Larger Śinnamanūr Plates, *South Indian Inscriptions*, III, 454.

[7] *South Indian Inscriptions*, VII, 752-53.

[8] *South Indian Inscriptions*, III, 93.

[9] See V. Raghavan, "Picture-Showmen: Mankha," *Indian Historical Quarterly*, XII, 524.

[10] *South Indian Inscriptions*, VII, 752-53.

[11] Kāvyamālā, XXXVII, 56-57.

[12] See V. Raghavan, "*Yakṣagana*," *Triveni*, VII, 2.

[13] See V. Raghavan, "*Bhāgavata-melā-nāṭaka*," *Journal of the Indian Society of Oriental Art*, V.

[14] For further details on this form, see V. Raghavan, *Commemoration Volume* in honor of the leading lady *kathā* artiste of Madras, Srimati C. Saraswati Bai (1939), pp. 57-58.

[15] This article is reprinted from *The Cultural Heritage of India* (Calcutta, 1956), IV, 503-14, with permission of The Rama Krishna Missions Institute of Culture.

Madras University
Madras, India

III. SOME PROBLEMS AND PROCESSES OF CULTURE CHANGE

THE GREAT TRADITION IN A METROPOLITAN CENTER: MADRAS

By Milton Singer

To readers of "The Cultural Role of Cities" by Robert Redfield and myself, the linkage of a great cultural tradition with a modern metropolitan center may appear puzzling if not incongruous.[1] For in that earlier study it was suggested that Great Traditions get fashioned out of local folk cultures, or Little Traditions, through a process of continuous development by professional literati centered in orthogenetic towns and cities. And we also said there that in metropolitan centers, ancient and modern, another process—heterogenetic transformation—operates to destroy or supersede the great cultural traditions of an indigenous civilization. This transformation is carried on with the help of a new social type of professional intellectuals—the intelligentsia—who stand astride the boundaries of the cultural encounter, mediating the alien cultural influences to the natives and interpreting the indigenous culture to the foreigners.

We also suggested in that article, however, that the two processes—that of primary urbanization leading to the growth of a Great Tradition in orthogenetic centers, and that of secondary urbanization leading to a heterogenetic transformation of that tradition—are not always discontinuous. There seem to be civilizations, or at least particular historical phases of some civilizations when they undergo imperial and colonial expansion, in which we can almost see how one process is succeeded by the other and how a new social type, the intelligentsia, takes over from the old, the literati. Indic civilization appeared to us to be particularly well characterized by such lines of continuity, and the communities of western Guatemala with their well-established institutions of trade and travel may even represent a simpler pre-urban phase of the process.

The details of the subsequent fate of a Great Tradition as it undergoes secondary urbanization have, we must confess, remained shadowy because there are few intensive case studies to give a detailed picture. In the general literature on cultural and civilizational history, this kind of change is usually presented as a sharp one and a change for the worse, representing a decadence, fossilization, or secularization of the great cultural traditions. Because I suspected that this common view of the matter is, in part, influenced by a particular kind of cultural analysis—the textual study of the outstanding products of art and learning, abstracted from social and cultural context and the matrix of little and popular cultural traditions—I undertook in a preliminary way a functional and contextual study of what happens to a Great Tradition and its literati in a metropolitan urban center in South India.[2]

1. *Madras as a heterogenetic and as a colonial city.* Because Madras is an heterogenetic and was a colonial city it is a good place to investigate the effects of urbanization on cultural traditions.

The urban characteristics that usually go with large metropolitan centers are found in Madras city, the capital of Madras State—a large population, rapid growth, predominance of males over females, a high proportion of immigrants, high literacy rates, a highly specialized nonagricultural occupational structure, an abundance of social and cultural facilities and organizations, and a heterogeneity of linguistic, religious, and ethnic and social groups. These characteristics do not always have the same high absolute values in Madras that they have in other metropolitan centers of the world, but the degree of urbanization is high if compared with the city's hinterland in Madras State or with India's present degree of urbanization. The city's hinterland is about eighty percent agricultural villages and small towns. It includes a predominantly Telugu speaking North as well as a predominantly Tamil speaking South.[3]

Located on the coastal plains of the Bay of Bengal in Southeast India, Madras is India's third largest city with a population at the 1951 census of 1,416,056. This is exceeded only by Bombay with a population of over 2,800,000, and by Calcutta, whose population is over 2,500,000. The year 1921 marks an important change in Madras' population growth. For at least thirty years before that date the rate of growth is fairly steady; after that there are a series of spurts probably induced by immigration to escape famine, or to take advantage of opportunities in employment or of the city's medical and educational services and cultural amenities. The population figures in round numbers for these periods are: 1891, 450,000; 1901, 500,000; 1911, 518,000; 1921, 526,000; 1931, 645,000; 1941, 776,000; 1951, 1,416,000.

Before 1891, the population figures are less reliable and the earliest accurate figure is probably that of the 1871 census, which gives 399,552 as the population of the city.

The steady and slow growth of Madras until very recent years has permitted the survival of many parts of the villages and small towns which have become incorporated into its limits as it has expanded. As late as 1908, the Imperial Gazetteer describes Madras as "a collection of villages." And even today many of the pre-urban characteristics are visible: large tracts of unused land with palms growing on them, paddy fields and irrigation tanks, buffalo and washermen in the city's rivers and lagoons, fishermen's thatched huts and catamarans on the beach. The accelerated growth of the last twenty years is, however, quickly filling up the vacant land and sending an increasing number of daily commuters farther and farther out of the city on the electric trains.

In its origin Madras city resembles many other pre-European towns in India and some mediaeval European towns: it began in 1640 as a settlement of traders around a fort and several villages. But because the fort was one of the trading factories of the English East India Company, the settlement soon developed a character and career distinctive of the British colonial city in Asia. These cities, like Madras, Surat, Bombay, Calcutta, at first entrepôts for European trade with Asia, later became bases for the spread of European political and military control over the entire country. The history of these cities is the story of the encounter of differing civilizations and of their mutual transformations.

As early as 1688, the East India Company's Directors in London were so impressed with the prosperity and growth of Madras that they decided to call it a city rather than a town. In 1752 it became the seat of Madras Presidency and from 1774 it was subject, through the Bengal government, to the control of the British parliament.

The city's importance as an administrative center has continued to the present, with a concentration of state and union government offices. It is, however, also a foremost commercial, transportation, and cultural center. With ninety-eight percent of its population depending on nonagricultural employments—production other than cultivation, (twenty-five percent), commerce (twenty-two percent), transport (nine percent), government and professional services (forty-two percent)—and only two percent on agriculture, Madras is a highly urbanized metropolitan center.

2. *Localization of the Great Tradition in sacred geography and in social structure.* Where in a metropolitan center shall we find the Great Tradition of Hinduism? It is natural for a Westerner to assume that a large modern city is not a very likely place to look for it, but in India this assumption does not hold. It is true that the full blown "classic" version of the tradition as it might be constructed from selected texts is not evident in the city today. In fact there is not a single unequivocal version of the Great Tradition in Madras, but several overlapping and competing versions with varying degrees of admixture of regional and local traditions. This is not surprising in a study which begins with a functional analysis in a limited region. Only as the accumulation of studies in different regions and in different historical periods permits an extension of comparisons will we be able to say with some confidence what is common and pervasive and what is local and episodic in Indian civilization as a whole.

There are three general methods for localizing a Great Tradition within a limited area: through a study of its sacred geography, of its professional representatives and their social organization, and of its cultural performances (including religious rites and ceremonies). Since in this paper I shall be dealing chiefly with the third method, let me comment briefly on the first two.

Although modern Madras is not a major temple city or pilgrimage center, its relation to the sacred geography of Hinduism is not insignificant. For the modern city grew up around historic temple villages like Mylapore and Triplicane whose large Śiva and Viṣṇu temples, respectively, continue to be actively patronized today. And even as the city developed under the East India Company, the local merchants and landlords continued to build new temples and to patronize Sanskrit scholars, traditional poets, musicians, and dancers.[4] It would be interesting to trace the continuity of the historical cultural associations of the city with the neighboring religious and cultural centers like Kanchipuram, (the present residence of the head of the Śaṅkara *maṭh*), Sriperumbudur, and Tirupati, and with the many other temples and *maṭhs* in South India, as well as with the modern temples and religious seats which have located in the city, e.g., the Ramakṛṣna Mission, the Divine Life Society, a Śiva-Viṣṇu temple, and a Sai Baba temple in honor of a Hindu-Muslim saint, among others.

Contemporary Madrasis not only visit the major and minor temples (of which there are hundreds) within the city but also make frequent pilgrimages to other shrine centers in South India and in North India. This practice has been helped by modern improvements in transportation. Automobiles and buses, planes, and trains now take large numbers of pilgrims on organized tours of the major temple and shrine centers. These pilgrimages now tend to merge with patriotic sightseeing which has become popular even with the secular-minded.

The 1951 census tells us that 81.62 percent of Madrasis declared themselves as Hindus, 9.91 percent as Muslims, and 7.72 percent as Christians. But we cannot assume without further evidence that every Hindu is a representative of the Great Tradition, even an active participant in it, or that there is a single system of Hinduism.

Hindus in Madras city are subdivided into a number of sect-like groups. The most important of these are the Smārta Brahmans, followers of Śaṅkara (?788-820), believers in monistic or Advaita vedānta who are supposed to conform to Smṛti traditions; the Śrivaiṣṇava Brahmans and non-Brahmans, followers of Rāmānuja (1017-1137), and believers in a qualified monism; the Madhvas, predominantly Brahman followers of a dualistic Vaiṣṇavite system developed by Madhva, a Canarese theologian of the thirteenth century; and the predominantly non-Brahman Śaivasiddhantins, followers of a dualistic and monotheistic system of Tamil Śaivism. Each of these groups has its distinctive theology and philosophy, canonical scriptures, ritual practices, shrines, and centers of religious teaching and leadership known as *maṭhs* in different parts of the South. They do not generally intermarry.

In addition to these major Hindu groups, there are also in Madras city small numbers of Sikhs, Jains, Buddhists, and Zoroastrians. Of these only the Jains exceed 1000, numbering about 6000 in 1951. The 1951 census returned 1267 self-declared atheists for Madras city and very few members of the Ārya Samāj, the Brāhmo Samāj, and the Rationalists. The increase in atheism in Madras city and state (the 1921 census listed four for the state as a whole) is generally attributed to the active anti-religious propaganda of two non-Brahman organizations, the Dravidian Federation and the Dravidian Progressive Federation.

The second method which I used to identify the Great Tradition in Madras city was essentially an application of Robert Redfield's suggestion that a great tradition is cultivated and transmitted by a class of learned specialists, the literati, who have a definite social structure and organization.[5] This idea is very apt for India, where for thousands of years a special learned and priestly class, the Brahmans, have had almost a monopoly as officiants, teachers, and scholars of Hinduism. And in Madras city I was able to locate many different kinds of these Brahman literati: temple priests, domestic priests, gurus, *paṇḍits* specializing in sacred law, in logic, in poetics, in Vedic exegesis; astrologers, ayurvedic doctors, and others. But I also found that not all Brahmans are literati; they are also lawyers and high court judges, businessmen, physicians, movie producers, authors and journalists, professors and architects, cooks and chauffeurs. Many of those in the higher professions have been trained abroad and have been agents of Westernization and modernization in India. Some of the literati, on the other hand, are non-Brahmans.

These findings raise the question whether the Brahman literati in Madras are changing their social role, giving up their traditional role as cultivators of the Great Tradition (and agents of Sanskritization, as M. N. Srinivas would say)[6] to become intelligentsia, i.e., agents of Westernization and modernization. To some extent I believe this is occurring, but it is difficult to give a clear cut answer to this question because there have always been important social and status differences between priestly Brahmans (*vaidikas*) and worldly Brahmans (*laukikas*), because some Brahmans are traditionalizing and Westernizing at the same time, and because new forms of Sanskritization have been developing under urban conditions. A detailed study of how the worldly Brahmans have been recruited into modern professions, of their family histories, of the statistics of changes in traditional occupations, of how they relate themselves to Hinduism, and of the ancient parallels and precedents is necessary before definite answers can be given.

These sociological studies are just beginning to be made in different parts of India, and I shall not report them at this time. There is some evidence, however, from Madras, which suggests that the Brahmans are relating themselves in new and constructive ways to the changes affecting Indian traditions and are not schizophrenically split down the middle into traditional Indian and modern Western halves. This evidence is indirect and comes chiefly from observation of cultural changes. I should like to present some of it because it is intrinsically interesting and also because it illustrates a third method of approach to the problem of urbanization and culture change.

3. *Localization of the Great Tradition in cultural structure: comparative analysis of cultural performances.* This third method emerged naturally in the application of the second method. Whenever Madrasi Brahmans (and non-Brahmans, too, for that matter) wished to exhibit to me some feature of Hinduism, they always referred to, or invited me to see, a particular rite or ceremony in the life cycle, in a temple festival, or in the general sphere of religious and cultural performances. Reflecting on this in the course of my interviews and observations, I found that the more abstract generalizations about Hinduism (my own as well as those I heard) could generally be checked, directly or indirectly, against these observable performances. The idea then occurred to me that these performances could be regarded as the most concrete observable units of Indian culture, the analysis of which might lead to more abstract structures within a comprehensive cultural system. Looking at performances from this point of view, it soon became evident that the rites and ceremonies performed as ritual obligations, usually by domestic or temple priests, had many elements in common with the more secular cultural performances in the theatre, concert hall, radio programs and films, and that these linkages revealed not only the outlines of a cultural structure but many indications of trend and process of change in that structure.

Through an analysis and comparison of these cultural performances and their constituents, e.g., the media and themes, the place and occasion of performance, the performers, the audience, it is possible to construct the structure and organization of particular kinds of performances. Then by tracing the linkages among these structures and organizations it is possible to arrive at the more comprehensive and abstract constructs of cultural structure, cultural value system, and a Great Tradition. To the extent that exact dates or relative temporal orderings are available for the different performances or their constituents, it is also possible to analyze continuities, trends, and processes of change in these structures and organizations. Given such data about the persistences and transformations of cultural traditions, it is then possible to relate these persistences and changes to urbanization and other relevant causal conditions.

This method is an operational one: it begins with concrete units which can be directly observed, the cultural performances, and proceeds, through analysis and abstraction, to constructions which are not directly observable at all or only indirectly so. It thus makes up two methodological deficiencies in holistic concepts of culture—directly observable units of observation and a "ladder of abstraction" that leads from these units to the holistic constructs. In studies of the relations of urbanization to culture change it is more usual to begin at the societal end—with particular social groupings, their structure, organization, interrelationships; the impingement on them of economic, demographic, geographical, and other changes. This, too, is a legitimate procedure and is required in a complete analysis of the problem to complement the procedure which begins with cultural traditions.

I shall now present some examples of the method of comparative analysis of cultural performances. The generalizations to be considered concern the changes in religious orientation adopted by Madrasi Brahmans under the influence of the urban environment. These changes are verbalized by some of the Brahmans as involving a change in preference among the ancient paths to religious salvation within Hinduism.

4.1. *The widening path of devotion in urban culture. An easier path to salvation: Bhakti.* The path of ritual observance (*karma-mārga* or *karma-yoga*) and the path of devotion (*bhakti-mārga* or *bhakti-yoga*) are two of the three standard paths within Hinduism that lead to eternal bliss and salvation. The third path is that of knowledge (*jñāna-mārga* or *jñāna-yoga*). The three paths have been interpreted as providing a variety of roads open to an individual depending on his degree of spiritual evolution and type of personality:

> . . . to those intent on work, there is Karma-yoga, the path of fulfilling the ordained duties and performing such meritorious acts as have been perscribed by scriptures. To those who are of an emotional nature, whose heart is not satisfied with impersonal acts or principles of ethical conduct and in whom there is an inner cry for hugging a supreme personality to whom it could pour forth its love and homage, there is the path of devotion, Bhakti-yoga. And to those of the highest class who can revel only in the Abstract, there is the path of knowledge, Jnāna-yoga, and the goal of realising the one impersonal Absolute Brahman, which is of the essence of Being, Light, and Bliss, *Sat*, *Chit*, and *Ananda*. Truly cultivated, these are not mutually conflicting, but different paths to the one ultimate goal.[6]

What is particularly significant about these paths in Madras city today is that orthodox Brahmans traditionally committed to the paths of ritual observance and of knowledge are turning to the path of devotion, that they seem to be doing this as a result of moving to the city, and, finally, that the paths themselves are acquiring some new content and form in an urban setting.

There is a very general consensus among the Brahmans of Madras city that they have neglected the paths of knowledge (*jñāna mārga*) and the path of ritual observance (*karma mārga*). It is the path of devotion (*bhakti mārga*) which is now most popular and considered to be a last defense against atheism. As one public speaker put it: "We modern men and women who have learnt, or are being taught, that we need not follow the *Śāstras* but can follow our own inclinations, are sure to derive very great spiritual profit and mental comfort by studying the hymns of the popular saints." This is a constant refrain in the speeches of cultural leaders, who never tire of extolling devotional puranic recitations, plays, films, music and dance concerts as an accessible path to salvation open to "modern" man. Even Svāmī Śaṅkarācārya, the spiritual leader of *advaitins* in Madras state, who does not regard *bhakti* as a very deep or lasting form of Hinduism, has sponsored conferences of Tamil hymn singing for "inculcating the spirit of *bhakti* among the people at a time when atheists were doing their best to poison the minds of youngsters through propaganda."

This turning to devotional religion is, in part, a response to anti-religious movements and trends, and, in part, represents a distinctive development of religious and popular culture in an urban enviroment. To some extent, this development is a continuation or revival of traditional devotional movements in which Brahmans have always played a leading part, but it has also entered into modern cultural and mass media and serves new needs.

Bhakti movements are very old in India and have been traced all the way back to Vedas.[8] Most generally, however, they have been associated with the post-Vedic and post-Buddhist sectarian movements: Vaiṣṇaivite primarily in North India, Śaivite and Vaiṣṇaivite in South India. In Tamil tradition there are sixty-three Śaivite singing poet saints (called *mayanars*) whose canon of hymns (*devāram*) was collected in the tenth century A.D., and twelve Vaiṣṇaivite singing poet saints (called *Āḷvārs*), whose canon of hymns (*divyaprabandham*) was collected in the eleventh century. These hymns, together with the *Bhāgavata purāṇa*, particularly the story of Kṛṣṇa's life, are part of the scriptures of Tamil Śaivism and Vaiṣṇavism, and have been placed on a par with the Vedic and Āgamic scriptures.

Traditionally the doctrine of *bhakti* taught that religious merit and even salvation could be acquired by those deficient in sastric learning, ritual observance, and ascetic penances if they would but love the Lord and sing His name and praises in the presence of other devotees (called *bhāgavatas*). This doctrine gave the movement a mildly anti-caste and anti-intellectual tone. The following verses illustrate this mood of many of the Tamil hymns:

> Though they give me the jewels from Indra's abode,
> Though they grant me dominion o'er earth, yea o'er heaven,
> If they be not the friends of our lord Mahādev,
> What care I for wealth by such ruined hands giv'n?
>
> But if they love Śiva, who hides in His hair
> The river of Gaṅga, then whoe'er they be,
> Foul lepers, or outcastes, yea slayers of kine,
> To them is my homage, gods are they to me.
>
> Why bathe in Gaṅga's stream, or Kāviri?
> Why go to Comorin in Koṅgu's land?
> Why seek the waters of the sounding sea?
> Release is theirs, and theirs alone, who call
> In every place upon the Lord of all.
>
> Why chant the Vedas, hear the Śāstras' lore?
> Why daily teach the books of righteousness?
> Why the Vedāṅgas six say o'er and o'er?
> Release is theirs, and theirs alone, whose heart
> From thinking of its Lord shall ne'er depart.
>
> Why roam the jungle, wander cities through?
> Why plague life with unstinting penance hard?
> Why eat no flesh, and gaze into the blue?
> Release is theirs, and theirs alone, who cry
> Unceasing to the Lord of wisdom high.
>
> Why fast and starve, why suffer pains austere?
> Why climb the mountains, doing penance harsh?
> Why go to bathe in waters far and near?
> Release is theirs, and theirs alone, who call
> At every time upon the Lord of all.[9]

These sentiments of an easier path to salvation have naturally been popular among non-Brahmans and lower castes. They have given devotional groups the distinctive emotional tone of a brotherhood of mystical devotees of Kṛṣṇa or of Śiva. Among some devotional groups in contemporary Madras, this emotional tone persists, but the brotherhood is now conceived in terms of modern democratic and equalitarian ideology. And Brahmans from orthodox families have become active participants and leaders of the devotional movement. The devotional movement in Madras city has become ecumenical, an expression of democratic aspirations within Hinduism. It links village and town, traditional and modern, the folk and classical, the sacred and secular spheres of culture. It brings together, at least within the religious and cultural sphere, different castes and sects, different linguistic and religious communities. Historically, devotional movements have had similar tendencies but have usually resulted in the formation of exclusive sects. The contemporary movement does not so much inspire sectarian and denominational formations as a diffuse emotion of brotherhood which softens the rough edges of group differences.

4.2. *Urban pastoral: bhajans.* The kind of cultural performance which is closest in form and spirit to the older *bhakti* movements is a form of group hymn singing called *bhajans*. These are very informally organized as part of temple processions around the streets of the city, or in private homes and halls. Older men distinguished for their devotion and knowledge of the songs (and known as *bhāgavatars*) act as *bhajan* leaders, but many *bhajan* groups meet without special leaders. Some of the leading singers, of whom there are about 100 in Madras city, come from families who have been devotees for four or five generations. Every Saturday night it is usual for these groups to hold a *bhajan* at home with friends. These usually last three or four hours from 7 to 10:30 at night and consist chiefly in chanting of the Lord's name and singing of devotional songs. A larger all-night *bhajan* is held about once a month. For these, it is usual to have a leader who knows the technique and also some musicians. The more elaborate of these long *bhajans* include not only chanting of the Lord's name, but a greater variety of songs and an acting out by the devotees of the story of Kṛṣṇa and his beloved milkmaids or *gopīs*, as well as of the wedding of Rādhā and Kṛṣṇa.

A full *bhajan* program, several of which I attended, includes a complete *pūjā* to Kṛṣṇa, who is invoked with songs, in lithographs on the walls, and in a lamp placed on the floor in the center of a circle of devotees. All of the "attentions" (*upacāras*) offered to a temple image by a priest are offered to the lamp by the singing devotees. The offerings are chiefly in the songs, although some articles like fans, garlands, and sandal paste are also used.

One leading devotee, a well educated *bhāgavatar* who very kindly gave me running comments on the *bhajan* in which he was participating, explained that these "attentions" represent "services of all kinds." My devotee friend declared: "We let the Lord enjoy all kinds of happiness, comforts, conveniences and so forth. We offer all these to Him as servants or Devotees who always think in this way, 'What shall I do to the Lord next? What service shall I offer? Shall I hold an umbrella for Him? Shall I fan Him? Shall I do this thing for Him? Shall I do that thing for Him?' and so forth. We do all imaginable kinds of service to Him."

As they sit singing in a circle around the lamp, the devotees imagine themselves to be milkmaids or *gopīs* playing with Kṛṣṇa. "The philosophy here," the *bhāgavatar* explained, "is that all men and women in the world are spiritually women, and the Lord alone is male, because the woman's love for her lord or husband is the only greatest possible love, and we can acquire such great love only by imagining ourselves as women—as the *gopīs*—and love the Lord, calling after him."

The marriage of Rādhā and Kṛṣṇa in a complete *bhajan* is a replica of an orthodox

Hindu marriage. The form of it, according to the *bhāgavatar*, was supposed to have originated in Sītā's marriage to Rām. In *bhajans* the Vedic part is usually left out, but all the rest is included, with the pictures of Rādhā and Kṛṣṇa, and the devotees, playing the roles of bride and bridegroom. A marriage string (*tali*) is put on Rādhā's neck in the picture; the devotees' feet and those on the pictures are painted with sandal paste or turmeric powder; the pictures are taken in procession, flowers are thrown, *pān supārī* is offered, a miniature swing is used, etc. Some of the Radhā-Kṛṣṇa love songs for this part of the *bhajan* are taken from Jayadeva's *Gīta-Govinda* and sung in Sanskrit.

The songs and dances of the *bhajan* follow a definite sequence which is known to experienced devotees and can also be learned from printed books. The songs come from various traditional sources—the *Bhāgavata Purāṇa*, and from the regional devotional songs. Some are in Sanskrit, others in Tamil, Telugu, Hindi, Marathi. There are many songs in praise of the ten incarnations of Viṣṇu and also some in praise of Śiva, "to show that we do not dislike Śiva though we have been praising Kṛṣṇa all along."

The dances include the *Ras Krīḍā*, a Kṛṣṇa dance, and the *Kummi* and *Kolaṭṭam*, both folk dances, the former usually performed by women at work. These dances were called "sports" by my *bhāgavatar* informant, a translation of *līlā*. They represent the *gopīs*' expression of joy at being with Kṛṣṇa. "There may be several other sports as well—all imagined to be resorted to by the *gopīs* as they are now most happy, having got back Kṛṣṇa and enjoying His company once again. Happy people will sport in a variety of ways."

In the eyes of the devotees the climax of the *bhajan* comes when they embrace one another and roll on the floor to take the dust of each other's feet. A young devotee, a college instructor and the *bhāgavatar's* son, explained that this part of the *bhajan* expresses "the spirit of equality without respect to young or old, caste or creed. Each devotee shows that he considers the others as his equals and is willing to worship them as the Lord." One of the verses which they sing at this point says: "Let us purify ourselves with the dust that has fallen from the feet of the devotees. Let us praise the two glorious feet of our guru. Let us enjoy the bliss by mutual embraces and attain ecstacy."

Local interest in *bhajans* has greatly increased in the last twenty years. Non-Brahmans as well as Brahmans hold *bhajans*, although Brahmans predominated at the ones I attended. There are *bhajans* of the "sitting type" where only Tamil songs—usually from the *Devāram*[10]—are sung and where Brahmans do not give the lead. Non-Brahman Vaiṣṇaiva *bhajan* halls and *bhajan* parties are also common.

The group of about fifteen to twenty devotees I had seen at two *bhajans* are mostly Brahmans and have been doing these *bhajans* together for about six or seven years. They are all personal friends and have generally developed their friendship from meeting at the *bhajans*. "That is why the *bhajans* are so good; they make us friends. We accept all, we accept even foreigners."

Women who attend the *bhajans* may also join the singing, although they usually sit silently on the side. In the last ten years there have been efforts to organize all-female *bhajans* where women do the singing and the men are silent. In fact, there are now probably as many of these *bhajans* of women as there are *bhajans* of men.

4.3. *Bhakti in the storytelling media*. A less dramatic kind of devotional performance consists of readings and recitations from the epics and *purāṇas*. India is a story-telling civilization. Stories from the *Rāmāyaṇa*, the *Mahābhārata*, and the *Bhāgavata Purāṇa* are a staple upon which the Indian imagination feeds in all parts of the country. While I was in Madras I saw hundreds of people daily sitting in public halls avidly listening to the recitation of these familiar stories. The reciters were usually professionals (called *paurāṇikas*); some were Brahmans, some non-Brahmans, some were Śaivite, some Vaiṣṇavite, and there were women as well as men among them. One woman I heard usually had an audience chiefly of women, while the male reciters drew mixed audiences but with the men sitting on one side of the hall and the women and children on the other. The style of recitation varied from the austere erudite manner of the *paṇḍit* who would not depart from the Sanskrit texts he knew well, to the folksy, humorous, and anecdotal manner of the reciter who traded on his histrionic and comic talents rather than on his learning. An individual recitation lasts about two or three hours, although it is customary to arrange a sequence lasting seven or fifteen days.

Not all the reciters were professionals. In the home, parents and grandparents will tell the stories to the children. And if the householder is orthodox, he will also read, or have read, a canto from the *Rāmāyaṇa* (or *Mahābhārata*, or a *purāṇa*) every day as part of his morning prayers. Because the section on the discovery of Sītā (*sundara kanda*) has greater merit, it will be read at the rate of seven cantos a day. This ritual type of reading is usually done in the Sanskrit text, and is carried on over a period of about a year and a half until the entire epic is completed. Then a new cycle of reading is begun either in the same text or in another one like the *Mahābhārata*.

Recitation of stories from the epics and *purāṇas*, whether done by amateurs or professionals, in ritual Sanskrit, or in the vernacular, is only one of the media through which these themes are presented. The same stories may also be sung in ballads, danced, dramatized, painted in pictures, carved on temple towers, and written in books. Each medium has its own special development and combines in many ways with several of the others. This variety of storytelling media is reflected in the numerous Sanskrit words for "story"—*kathā*, *harikathā*, *kālakshepa*, *pravacana*.

Historically all of these media have been used to communicate and transmit the traditional religious culture. Professional specialists in these media are known from remote times, performing in the temples of village and town and in palace courts on the occasion of religious festivals, weddings, and royal celebrations. These media came to have a special "popular" function because the masses of the people were not ritually excluded from them as they were from Vedic ceremonies and recitations. For the orthodox, this distinction persists today, the Vedic culture being reserved to the Brahmans and "twice-born," the epic and puranic literature being the vehicle of dissemination for the "masses."[11] Yet many changes have occurred and are occurring to blur and shift the distinction. Non-Brahmans, Śūdras, and untouchables, are being given direct access, not only to temples, but to Vedic rites, artificially revived, and to discourses on the Upaniṣads. Brahmans participate not only as performers, patrons, and organizers of the popular cultural media, but have become an eager audience for them. The development of the newer mass media of print, radio, and movies has not eliminated the older cultural media and these traditional themes, but has transformed and incorporated them. The increasing concentration of population in urban centers has also brought with it changes in cultural media, specialists, and places and occasions of performance. How far all these changes have produced a mass, secular culture different in values and in organization from the traditional religious culture is a question which I shall now consider.

4.4. *Cultural effects of mass media.* Mass media like the movies, the radio, the daily newspaper, and the printed book tend to reinforce the trend towards greater popularization. Whether privately or governmentally controlled, they cannot afford to cater to a limited caste, sect, or linguistic group but must seek to maximize the audiences for continuous performances of their media. Popular entertainment is for them a more important value than religious merit and salvation. The technology and organization of the mass media make these shifts possible and introduce, as well, new characteristics in the cultural transmission which are quite different from the traditional cultural media.

Most important of these characteristics is that the mass medium produces an impersonal record—on paper, wax, wire, tape, or film—which exists separately from both performer and audience and can be mechanically reproduced. This makes it possible to send the program to mass audiences quickly and in practically any location.

There is a further difference in quality as well as in quantity. The mass media develop their own times, places, and occasions of performance on a principle of continuous daily "showings." This cuts them off from the ceremonial calendar geared to the important events of the life cycle and of the agricultural cycle which were the major occasions for the cultural media. On these new occasions and cultural stages it becomes possible to by-pass the distinctions of caste, sect, language, and sponsorship that were important in the traditional performances. Another difference is that the cultural media were equally at home in village and in town, and travelling performers used to spread a living cultural network over the countryside. The mass media, on the other hand, are centered in the large city, and require elaborate mechanical equipment and personnel to operate. Although their programs are sent to towns and villages, it is the impersonal record and not the performers who travel. They remain in the urban centers.

These distinctions tend to place the mass media in a relation to the traditional culture, its social structure, and its religious values, which is very different from the relation of the cultural media to those traditional elements. A constant repetition of themes in the mass media is no longer regarded, at least by the producers, as "eternally new," but is merely a source of dependable income or an obstacle to novelty. The cultural tradition which in India is thought of as being transmitted from what has been revealed to the seers (*śruti*) and through that which is remembered (*smṛti*), by *paṇḍits* and storytellers, undergoes a transformation when it is transmitted impersonally over the mass media without the benefit of seers, gurus, or reciters.

4.5. *Bhakti in the films.* But even these changes introduced by the mass media have not yet resulted in a secularization of religious culture. Print, radio, and film are used to disseminate puranic stories and devotional music, and *bhakti*-inspired audiences have their own ways of personalizing the impersonal mass media. In Tirupati, in some of the bigger temples of the Tamil country, and in Annamalai University, the loudspeaker and gramophone record are used to broadcast devotional music, hymns and prayers. Recently, the availability of tape recorders at about Rs. 1,000/ has led to a number of people keeping recordings of such devotional recitals at home and listening to them regularly. The hymns recited at the Tirupati shrine in the small hours of the morning to wake up the Lord have been tape recorded and kept by some devotees.

The example of the "mythological" and "devotional" films is instructive. During our stay in Madras, a non-Brahman and practically illiterate chauffeur kept urging us to see the film "Avvayyār," which was then very popular and which he characterized only in an enthusiastic murmur as "*bhakti, bhakti.*" We did eventually get to see this film and also to interview its producers. The story is about the female saint and poet, Avvayyār, of the Tamil country who goes about performing miracles with her devotional songs. Usually each song is connected with an incident teaching a moral lesson, and as it is sung, the incident is dramatized on the screen. A giant image of Gaṇeśa was kept in the theater lobby.

This technique of narrative song sequence in the "Avvayyār" film has also been used in other devotional and historical films as well as in radio dramas and in epiclike narratives about Ghandi and the Congress Party struggle for independence. It is an adaptation of a village ballad form called "bow song" (*viḷḷu pāṭṭu*) to urban mass media.[12] One person responsible for these adaptations was the producer and director of the "Avvayyār" film. He is a folk poet by avocation and is known as "the Bobby Burns of Tamil," and has a nickname which means "soaked in the soil." He has composed over 1000 folksongs in village meter on harvest festivals, weddings, war, and modern themes. The village background of folk plays, folksongs, ballads, and puranic recitations to which he was exposed as a child have provided him, he believes, with great literary wealth. His was the only Brahman family in the village and their relation to the non-Brahmans was very good. He came to Madras in 1935 at the age of twenty-five, but mentally he still lives, he says, in the village. He goes back at least once each year. And in town he tries to live as in the village with some thirty-five to forty relatives under one roof—including four different generations.

The "Avvayyār" picture is expected by its producers to run five years and make a large profit for the company. Its great success has encouraged Indian film producers to turn once more to "devotionals" and "mythologicals" as dependable sources of investment. One film producer stated that about eighty percent of the stories in Indian movies are now traditional, reflecting the desire of the movie companies to play for safety by relying on the familiar. Many of these traditional stories are drawn from the epics and *purāṇas* or from stories about the lives of regional saints like Avvayyār or Caitanya.

This trend, which represents a return to the mythological themes of the early Indian films, is considered regressive by some of the modern producers. They do not feel that this traditional subject matter is as "educational" as "social" or "landscape" films. The educational value of the "mythological," according to one producer, is restricted to "what has already happened." This comment sounds paradoxical to a Westerner, but probably reflects the Indian's realistic acceptance of his mythology. This same producer also worries a good deal about whether a medium like the films is not too powerful in a country like India, "where people are so ready to believe." He seemed particularly impressed by the case of an actor who played the role of a saint in one devotional film and was for several years afterwards followed around and worshipped by large crowds as if he were really a saint.

On the other hand, this producer is convinced that the filmmaker must think of the Indian "man in the street," the rickshaw puller in the city, and the villager, as his audience, and suit the film to their taste and understanding. Film music and dancing cannot be classical or even authentically Indian. Film music is a mixture of Spanish, Hawaiian, and Indian, and the dancing is a mixture of streamlined classical Indian dances and European styles like the waltz.

Not all Indian films have traditional or devotional themes. As in the United States, comedy and variety films are also very popular. There is an Indian "Costello" who is in such great demand at the studios in Calcutta, Bombay, and Madras that he spends much of his time flying from one studio to another. This emphasis, too, needs no special justification in the filmmakers' minds: "The cinema is often all the rickshaw puller or the villager has. It has to combine everything in an evening's entertainment—dancing, comedy, fighting, romance, and lots of songs." The villagers see the films in the nearest towns or in the village at the mobile theaters sent out by the film companies or the government. The government films are documentaries, shorts, and information films, and must also be shown in urban theaters.

4.6. *The folk-urban continuum in dramatic cultural media.* Comedy, variety, social, and educational films belong to an international urban culture and are not especially associated with the devotional outlook, as the mythological, devotional, and historical films are. Yet even these purer "international" films retain many distinctive Indian features—traditional song and dance forms, the combining of many different media in one program, the long and rambling sequences, the use of regional languages. The mass media have brought in new urban forms of devotional and nondevotional story telling, but they are also still linked in themes and techniques to the folk and traditional storytelling media.

A very similar continuum can be traced in popular urban drama. The village folk play (*terukkūttu*) has migrated with the low caste communities and thrives on city lots as vigorously as it once did around village temples. As in the village, these are all-night performances, given about four times a year during festivals and important occasions. The actors are all amateurs, young men of the community who are rehearsed for several months by an older man who happens to know the plays. The most popular of these are based on incidents from the *Mahābhārata* and *Rāmāyaṇa* and from Tamil epics and legends all familiar to the audience. Comic interludes and farce, usually having no relation to the play, help to sustain interest through the night. There are also presentations of garlands and gifts to the leading actors on first appearance because they are the important people who organize the plays and raise the money for city license fees. This little ceremony and the colorful costumes of the leads gives a touch of glamor to the kerosene lighted, roped off lot on which Arjuna and Draupadī, Rāma and Sītā, Kōvalan and Kaṇṇakī act and sing their roles.

While the folk play persists unchanged in the city, there has also developed within the last fifty years a form of popular devotional drama that corresponds to the devotional films and the urbanized forms of puranic recitation. Specializing as these other media do in mythological, devotional, and historical themes, the devotional play incorporates with its bright costumes, professional lighting, and stage effects some elements of the court theater and of the modern stage. To a Western observer, the action in these devotional plays seems predominantly of a tableau form, with occasional songs and dances and numerous sound and trick stage effects. This serves to highlight the mythological incidents and personages and to present each in as luminous a manner as might be desired from a chromolithograph.

These devotional plays are probably the most popular dramatic performances in Madras, with all classes of the population paying to see them at a commercial theater. They have been developed by a professional actor and producer, "Nawab" Raja-Manickam, who has a reputation for *bhakti*. Before the curtain goes up on one of his plays, puffs of smoke roll out under it and from the sides indicating that he is performing a *pūjā* to Gaṇeś. He has produced plays based on Rāmdās and the life of Christ, as well as on south Indian deities like Murugan, to teach the message of devotion and national unity. The first scene in the Murugan play, "Kumāra Vijayam," opens with a singing tableau representing Indian unity. Various figures, all young boys, appear with papier-maché heads of Gandhi, Nehru, and other Indian leaders, as well as regional types, against a backdrop showing a temple, a mosque, and a Christian church.

This devotional drama is a more colorful and urbanized form of the folk play. It is performed by professionals on a commercial stage for mixed audiences and uses modern stage techniques. Its themes remain devotional and its tableaus are more akin to the painted scenes on temple towers than to the modern theater.

Within the last fifty years, however, there has been rapidly developing in the city a modern theater which cuts across caste and sect and has some resemblances to western theater. Sponsored at first by amateur dramatic societies, particularly of male college students, this movement is now in the hands of professional companies, performing in permanent theater halls. The amateurs, particularly the Suguṇa Vilāsa Sabhā, undertook to stage a great variety of plays in a variety of languages, Kālidāsa in Sanskrit, Shakespeare in English, and plays in Tamil, Telugu, Kanarese, and Hindi. They also occasionally took them to the country and to Ceylon. The professionals are more limited in scope. As in the cinema, which is the chief medium now for popular drama, the aim is to reach a wide audience, so Tamil is the major language. Types of plays are categorized, again as in the film, into devotionals, mythologicals, and historicals on the one hand and socials and comedies on the other. The first group is regarded as representing the indigenous Indian theater, and the latter as being largely Western influenced. The Sanskrit drama is virtually neglected by the professionals, although a recent Sanskrit revival may bring it back into popular esteem. In the National Drama Festival organized in 1955 in New Delhi by the newly formed National Academy of Drama, a performance of Kālidāsa's *Śakuntalā* started the program. In the regional competition for this festival in Madras, of the six plays presented, all were in Tamil and one had the English title, "Oh, What a Girl." The play finally selected for presentation in New Delhi, after some controversy among several local drama groups, was a Tamil historical play.

The social play replaces the traditional puranic stories and the traditional media of presentation with modern problems and prose dialogues. It corresponds to the novel, the short story, and modern poetry, and tends in the main to be cultivated by a similar group of people, those with modern education and in the middle and upper classes. The urban theater prefers to use Tamil and the other Indian vernaculars or even English. It is also more secular than the traditional drama in being less determined by caste and sect. Performances are in public halls open to all who can pay the price of admission. The times and occasions of performance are not geared to temple festivals or other religious occasions; they are brief and are set in accordance with the commercial and cultural exigencies as perceived by the owners of the theater halls, the performers, and their organizers and sponsors. In these respects, dramatic media resemble the cinema and the radio and tend to develop their own "festival" calendar.

The involvement of drama in the political arena is reminiscent of the storytelling media. Both the state government and the national government have shown active interest in dramatic activities. In addition to the officially sponsored academies and drama festivals, there has also been use of dramatic media to tell villagers the story of independence, of the five-year plan, and of specific projects for village improvement. Both the traditional and modern dramatic forms have been employed for this purpose. And not only the government has made this political use of drama. Private voluntary groups, opposition political parties and movements have also made similar use of this medium. An attempt by some followers of the Dravidian Progressive Federation to enact a dramatic parody of the *Rāmāyaṇa* has recently led in Madras State to riots and to highly restrictive legislation regulating dramatic performances.

5. *The Classicists.* Pervading almost all cultural media and mass media and appealing to all classes of the population, the path of devotion has become a main highway. It is nothing exceptional that Brahmans, too, should find themselves on it as performers, patrons, and audience. Those belonging to Bhāgavata sects of course find this situation congenial to their traditions, despite the novel elements that have appeared in it. Many Smārtas, too, have been drawn into it, although their tradition has stressed the paths of knowledge and ritual more than that of devotion.

Not everyone, however, has taken this path of *bhakti*. Beside it and overlapping it, another path, far smaller, is clearly discernible. This is the path of classical art cultivated by a very distinctive class of patrons, critics and connoisseurs, among whom Brahmans predominate.

The classicists are not regular or frequent participants in *bhajans*, which they regard as too emotional and uncontrolled a form of religious expression, suitable perhaps for less cultivated people. If they go to puranic recitations, they prefer the austere *Paurāṇika* who knows the Sanskrit texts well and adheres faithfully to them, to the reciter who caters to popular tastes and humor. They may not themselves always have sufficient Sanskrit to follow, but they nevertheless insist on purity of standards.

The musical form of puranic recitation known as *harikathā* they consider as an art form superior both to *bhajans* and to traditional recitation without music. In the field of the drama, they fail to see how the modern social play has improved on the classical play and they prefer the devotional and folk play to the "social." Highest in their esteem are the classical South Indian dance, the *bhārata nāṭyam*, and the classical South Indian or Carnatic music, vocal and instrumental, which they regard as the very peak of asthetic achievement.

For the classical critics there is, in other words, a definite hierarchy of cultural media and performances. This hierarchy does not only depend on the general character of the media, but on the degree of sophistication, knowledge of the art tradition, and cultivation of taste with which they are rendered. As one ascends the hierarchy, the values of popular entertainment as well as of *bhakti* become less and less, and the values of "pure art" become more important. The "pure art" at the top is to some extent an "art for art's sake," but it is not completely secularized. It represents a fourth and distinctive path to release and the absolute, and a kind of sublimation of the paths of ritual observance and of knowledge.

5.1. *Story and song: harikathā.* The distinctive technique of reciting, called *harikathā kālakṣepam*, uses songs in several languages, Sanskrit, Tamil, Telugu, Kannada, Marathi, and Hindi; dramatic exposition in Tamil, and musical accompaniment, and is considered an art form since it demands a knowledge of music, languages, and dramatic technique. This form of *harikathā* was developed in the Tanjore Court about 100 years ago through adaptation of a Maharashtrian form. The Senior Madras performer in this technique is Saraswati Bai, a lady Brahman noted for her knowledge of music, both North Indian as well as South Indian, a gifted voice, excellent pronunciation of a wide range of Indian languages, and for erudition and good taste in the selection of song and story material. Her style of *harikathā* is regarded as unique because it combines the best styles of her predecessors.

Krishna Bhagavatar of Tanjore is credited with the creation of the distinctive Tamil *harikathā* from the Maharashtrian model. Saraswati Bai, who claims descent from him through her guru or teacher, believes that this form began in the South in the nineteenth century. In a personal interview she gave the following account:

> Before that there were just long recitations of stories from the *Rāmāyaṇa* and other Puranas. During the reign of the Maharatta Court, a *harikathā* artist from the North, Ramachandra Morgar Bhava, came on a pilgrimage to Tanjore. He came during the four sacred months—July-October—when he was not supposed to travel. So he stayed at the court and gave *harikathā* performances. The princess heard him and was very much impressed because this was very different from the *paurāṇika's* way of telling stories. She had a protege, Krishna Bhagavatar, at the court who was then 14 years old and was learning the violin. She and the minister wanted him to learn *harikathā* and simply from watching R. M. Bhava, he learned the art in one year.
>
> The princess then arranged for performances on successive days, the old man performing the first day, and the boy the second. After it was over she said that Bhava's performance must be heard but the boy's performance must be heard *and seen.* She meant that the boy's acting and dancing were improvements over the singing of Bhava. Krishna Bhagavatar also introduced Tamil as the language of the narration. Bhava had used Maharatti. He was a Maharashtrian Brahmin. My guru knew and admired Krishna Bhagavatar.

Her guru, Pandit K. Krishnachar, was a Sanskrit *paṇḍit* in the Christian College of Madras, and although himself not a *bhāgavatar*, was a thorough student of the art and of South Indian music. He gave up his teaching duties at the College when he decided to train S.B. as a *harikathā* performer. He taught Saraswati Bai Sanskrit as well as *harikathā* and was always present at his pupil's performances even when she toured.

Saraswati Bai has been awarded several titles, including that of "expert musician" (*Gāyan Paṭu*) and "expert in *harikathā* performance" (*Kīrtan Paṭu*) and several others.

She considers herself as equally a storyteller, a singer, and religious teacher. "All three must be present in equal proportion; no one is primary." She does not restrict her moral teaching to one special lesson or sect but teaches about Hinduism. She performs before both Vaiṣṇavite and Śaivite sects. She herself comes from a Madhva Brahman family. Her repertoire includes stories about Śiva, Viṣṇu, Subrahmanya, and many other gods. These are usually taken from the *Rāmāyaṇa*, *Mahābhārata*, minor *purāṇas*, and the hagiology of the saints. When I asked whether she repeated the same story many times, she said that she did but insisted that there is no such thing as "repetition." People love to hear the same story over and over and will call for it in advance. A popular favorite is the story of Nandanar, the Tamil Śaivite Harijan saint, which she thinks she has told at least 10,000 times.

The occasions on which she performs include festivals and festivities, usually of special castes; marriages; temple festivals; before institutes and *sabhās* associations and before Maharajas. She has performed before the Maharajas of Mysore, Travancore, Cochin, and others. "Three generations have heard me; I have been doing it for forty-eight years." Marriages are the most frequent occasions, festivities next, temple festivals next, performances for *sabhās* and Maharajas least. Temple festivals are now slightly less frequent occasions probably, she thinks, because of the spread of atheism. To some extent, too, musical associations and concerts are taking the place of temple festivals.

She is willing "to tell any kind of story everywhere, provided it is about God. But the essence must be devotion (*bhakti*) and I would not sacrifice this anywhere." *Harikathā* she thinks is the most appropriate medium for the expression of *bhakti*. In a public speech she said: "Music is not only a medium of entertainment in this world but also the means of realizing the Godhead."

She has given *harikathā* performances all over India, as well as abroad, in Calcutta, Bombay, Banaras, Rangoon, and Ceylon. Before foreign audiences who do not understand her Tamil narration, she always selects songs in the language of the region, and with these and her "mono-acting" she can hold them. The audiences are, of course, already familiar with the stories and have shown great enthusiasm wherever she went.

She has also travelled to the villages. "I have not spared a single village and not a single village has spared me." Whenever she travelled by cart, crowds of villagers would come out to greet her and would follow her from one village to another. The arrangements for village performances are usually made by a landlord who invites her for a marriage or a temple festival. The landlord gives a fee for her, her musicians, and her guru; the villagers will also give her shawls and other presents. The musicians include a drummer who has been with her for nearly forty years, a harmonium player who has been with her for nearly as long, and a supporting singer who also plays cymbals. The harmonium is used instead of the *tambura* for a drone because the *tambura* is big and difficult to transport. The travelling party also includes her cook and servants.

The trips used to last two or three months, but now she goes only for a week or ten days. A manager makes the arrangements for the distant trips; for the near ones she makes them herself. Local arrangements are usually made by the inviter, who pays all the expenses of the party, and, in addition, pays her a fee. When she was in Bombay she received a fee of about 2,000 rupees. For performances close to Madras she usually receives about 600 rupees. No written contracts are drawn but "it is all written in letters, so it is like a legal contract."

Village audiences and town audiences are not too different, she said, but she has found village audiences more appreciative of both her stories and music. This is not because, as I suggested, they are more religious, but because "they just respond better." Thousands of villagers will come to hear her from neighboring villages. Southerners show more interest in art and music than Northerners, and when they settle outside of South India they always organize music and art activities. In Rangoon, Burma, where there are many "overseas Tamils," 10,000 people came to hear her at one performance.

The epic and puranic stories are also still recited in the villages in the old style by *paurāṇikas* but now not as much as in the cities, where the *paurāṇikas* receive more recognition and are paid more. In her opinion, the *harikathā* performances are probably more popular than the regular readings which go on for periods of six months to a year, because they are for special occasions and distill the essence of the teaching in a short time—in about four hours.

There are many *harikathā* performers now, both women and men, and she knows them all. When they are in town they come to her for advice and she has helped many of them to get started.

The most difficult thing in *harikathā*, she thinks, is to take the many different parts in a single story. She has been highly praised just on this score. One admirer has written: "I have seen her, in her Kalakshepams, put great actors in the histrionic field to shame, by her masterly impersonation of the characters of a Rāvaṇa, a Hanumān or a Garuḍa, a giant or a cooing bird, a Bhakta or a scoffer, a lover or a libertine, a god or a goddess, a saint or a sinner, a man or woman, King or peasant, with equal ease and yet remain in her decorous Sari—"rich but not gaudy"—the sweet, simple, generous and loving Lady Bhāgavathar she has been and is today."[13]

These varied roles require knowledge, too, of the appropriate dialects, of some Urdu for the story of Ramdas, and of Tamil slang for that of Nandanar. As one scholar has written, *harikathā* is a kind of concentrated drama, a "monodrama," in which one gifted actor enters swiftly a whole series of characters, moods and manners.

The day before my interview, one of the local newspapers carried an announcement that the Union of India government was going to use *harikathā* to publicize the five-year plan. In reply to a question about this program, Saraswati Bai said she hoped that the government would set up a national academy for *harikathā*, as it has set up an academy for letters and the dance; otherwise the art would be lost. I asked her whether *harikathā* could be used to get people to dig pits and clean wells, whether devotional songs were not inappropriate for this purpose. This question aroused much laughter from her and the members of her family who were present. But then she said, seriously; "No, the devotional songs would not be appropriate. But I would be willing to compose new songs if I were asked. This is a matter of patriotism and I would be willing to sing about pits and wells, too."

Several *harikathās* about Gandhi's life have been written and performed. One of these was recorded by another lady *bhāgavatar* who comes from a Brahman Vaiṣṇava family in Mysore. In her version the story of Gandhi's life is told after the fashion of the lives of the saints. In fact, Gandhi is treated as an incarnation (*avatāra*) of God who has come to deliver India from foreign domination. Gandhi's death is also effectively told as the death of a martyr. Gandhi Bhagavatar (Rajaram), a Tamil Smārta Brahman and a Tamil poet was a pioneer in this line.

To tell Gandhi's story the reciter uses all the songs and Sanskrit verses that are used in the traditional *harikathā*. She begins with the famous song of the Gujarāti saint Narasimha Mehta, which starts with the words, "Vaiṣṇava janato," and declares that "he is a true devotee of Lord Viṣṇu who knows the suffering of others." This was Gandhi's favorite song. The reciter emphasizes the great faith which Gandhi had in devotion (*bhakti*) and in the recital of Rāma's name. Gandhi's doctrine of help and uplift for the poor and his belief in equality are also stressed.[14]

5.2. *Classical South Indian dance and music.* In *harikathā bhakti* is still an important element, although considerations of artistic and dramatic technique and learning also loom large. In the classical south Indian dance called *bhārata nāṭyam*, and in classical south Indian or "Carnatic" music, esthetic standards and the rules of art predominate. In fact, it is primarily these two media that are most frequently associated with the ideas of classical art. They are almost never referred to without the prefix "classical." Their more active revival is dated from two political events, the Madras meeting of the Indian National Congress in 1927, and the All-India Khadi and Swadeshi Exhibition organized by the Tamil Nadu Provincial Congress Committee in Madras in 1935.

On the occasion of these meetings local cultural leaders organized an All-India

Music Conference in 1927 and a Music Festival in 1935. Before this, voluntary organizations called *sabhās* arranged periodic public performances of music and *harikathā*. Apart from the publicity given at these times to dancing and music, one of the most important results of the early meeting was the organization of the Music Academy of Madras. Funds remaining after the expenses of the All-India Music Conference of 1927 were met were donated by the Reception Committee of the Congress for establishing a Music Academy. This institution soon became an important center for the promotion of Indian dance and music. It has sponsored regular performances of leading artists, holds annual conferences at which both scholars and artists come together to exchange knowledge, encourages new talent, sponsors music and dance schools, and tries to set high standards of public taste. The *Journal of the Music Academy* has become an all-India forum for learned discussions of the technicalities of Indian music and dance, and enjoys an international circulation as well. The success of the Music Academy stimulated the organization of other voluntary associations and now there are about twenty "cultural *sabhās*" in Madras carrying on similar programs. During the Christmas season, which also usually falls in the Hindu holy month of Mārgaśīrṣa, these different cultural associations vie with one another to bring the best artists to Madras and to put on the most interesting programs. The most elaborately planned among these programs is that of the Music Academy and usually consists of expert demonstrations and discussions in the morning, popular auditions and programs in the afternoons, and classical concerts in the evenings. Two of the halls most frequently used for these programs are the Museum Theater in Egmore and the *Rāsika Rañjanī Sabhā* of Mylapore ("Association Which Pleases Connoisseurs").

These cultural associations, or their leaders, also organize special local programs for visiting dignitaries, foreign cultural delegations, and for the national drama, music, and dance festivals which are now held in New Delhi on Republic Day. These programs are not always the same, although there is usually a common core of classical south Indian dance and music in them. In 1955 on the occasion of the Congress meetings at Avadi near Madras, free cultural programs for the delegates and visitors included in addition to classical music and dance, several varieties of folk dances, a puppet show, a dummy horse dance, a folk play, a devotional drama, a social drama, and devotional singing or *bhajans*.

The Music Academy and the other local cultural associations, while tolerant of "folk" and "popular" culture, regard the promotion of classical music and dance as their own primary responsibility. It has been the influence of these associations that has secured a hearing for the "classics" on the radio, to a lesser extent in the films, and has prompted the organization of state and national academies of music, dance, drama, and letters. They are the institutional representatives of the classic revival and although Brahmans have played an active part in their formation, they are not restricted with respect to caste or sect.

5.3. *The revival of classical dancing: bhārata nāṭyam.* The "revival," strictly speaking, was not only a revival but brought in major innovations. This is particularly true of the dance. Before it was revived it was known as the *nautch* or *sadir nautch* and was performed by hereditary families of dancing girls. These were called *devadāsīs* 'servants of God' because they were usually "dedicated" or given to particular temples where they sang and danced at the temple processions. Their "dedication" involved a "marriage" to one of the deities in the temple so they could not become widows. If they had children, these would take the mother's father's name and could inherit his property as well as the mother's. The dancing girls were trained to sing and dance by professional teachers known as *naṭṭuvanārs*. These were men who came from hereditary families of teachers and musicians and were also attached to the temples. Some of them were the male members of the *devadāsī* community while others came from a different community. The dancing girls, their teachers and musicians performed not only on the occasion of temple festivals and ceremonies, but also for private parties, particularly at weddings, and at palace parties. Special troupes of dancing girls and musicians were sometimes permanently attached to the courts.

Because of the association of some of the dancing girls with prostitution, an "anti-nautch" campaign was waged at the turn of the century by British and Indian reformers to stop temple dancing and "dedication" of girls to temples. In 1905, the Executive Committee of the Prince and Princess of Wales' Reception Fund unanimously decided that there should be no performance by *nautch* girls at the entertainment to be given to Their Royal Highnesses at Madras. In 1947, Madras State forbade the "dedication" and temple dancing.

After the revival, the name of the dance came to be called *bhārata nāṭyam*;[15] daughters of respectable families, including Brahmans, now take it up; it is taught in high schools, and in diluted form has become one of the most popular items in cultural programs in the films, on the stage, and at private gatherings. Although in the recent past it was developed in South India, especially around Tanjore, it is now popular all over India and has also been performed abroad by Uday Shankar, Ram Gopal, Shanta Rao and other dancers.

The major agents of the change are, as usually happens, transitional figures. Three kinds of transitional figures have played an important part in transforming the *sadir nautch* into *bhārata nāṭyam*—dance critics, the traditional dancing teachers, and some dancing girls.

5.4. *Dance critic.* One influential critic highly respected by friends of the art and by professionals was K. V. R. His perspective was gained from a wide academic background since he was a keen student of ancient Indian art, sculpture and painting and of all aspects of traditional culture. He was a technically well informed critic of classical dance and music and a sharp tongued enemy of mass culture and everything he considered counterfeit.[16]

K. V. R. wrote one of the first technical appreciations of *bhārata nāṭyam* in a series of articles published in 1935 in the magazine *Triveni, Journal of Indian Renaissance.* This journal, founded in Madras in 1928, became a major organ of the cultural revival in the South, in form and format like the old *Dial.* The articles are highly detailed analyses of the dance movements of the *nautch*, still so called at this time and of its affiliations with the Brahman dance drama, the Tamil folk play, and Bharata's *Nāṭya Śāstra.* The article is illustrated with photographs of many of the movements posed by R. and his wife.

Since 1942 K.V.R. has lived in Coimbatore where he does a flourishing business making and selling a very popular hair tonic. The formula for this scalp treatment he discovered himself about 1929 when his wife began to lose her hair after the birth of their first child. They were living in Madras at the time where he ran a small druggist shop. The success of the tonic made the problem of living much easier and enabled him to devote more of his time to the study of classical Indian dance and music. He has also studied Western music because he regards himself as a "citizen of the world whose antennae spread all over the world." He knows Mozart, Beethoven, Wagner, and Handel and is especially fond of Debussy, in whose music he finds Javanese influence.

K.V.R. comes from a Smārta Brahman family learned in music and Sanskrit. Four of his uncles were musicians and some of his cousins were paṇḍits. He himself studied music and Sanskritic tradition. He first became seriously interested in the classical dance when he was in college in Madras from 1915 to 1919. The stimulus was his reading of Coomeraswamy, Otto Rothfeld, and Havell. But even as a boy he had been attracted by the aesthetic charm of the dance and used to watch the *devadāsīs* and their dancing teachers at marriages and temples as often as he could, both in the city and when he went to the villages during vacations. At that time there were at least 500 professional dancing teachers in Madras and many *devadāsīs.* This was before the anti-nautch movement came to a head and before public concerts were popular. He thinks that the first public dance concert was held in Madras in 1933 and that Chokkalingam Pillai was the teacher.

His reading of the secondary works on the dance stimulated him to go to some of the original sources like Bhārata's *Nāṭya Śāstra* and to the temple dance sculptures at Chidambaram and Tanjore to reconstruct the orginal forms of the classical art. The dance poses on the temple sculptures, while valuable, have to be reconstructed with caution, since they represent only a single "frozen section" within a moving sequence. However, he believes that through a careful study of these literary and temple sources and of the "authentic living traditions of the art," in Java and Bali as well as in India, it is possible to recover the true classical dance.

When he was married in 1925 he encouraged his wife to learn dancing from a professional temple dancer in Mylapore and from a Brahman dancing teacher who taught her the art of interpretation (*abhinaya*). He often corrected his wife's poses as well as those of professional dancers who came to him for advice. He has also encouraged his daughters to take up dancing and singing.

K.V.R. believes that Brahmans have always played an important role in transmitting the classical dance. Because of their knowledge of Sanskrit and rhetoric they were especially qualified to teach *abhinaya*. This tradition has almost died out, although remnants of it can still be found in the dance-dramas (*bhāgavata melā nāṭaka*) performed by male Brahmans in a few Tamil and Telugu villages. At some point the Brahmans taught the art to the guilds of non-Brahman teachers or *nattuvanars* who have jealously guarded it since.

The *devadāsīs*, too, have played an important part in keeping the dance traditions alive, R. believes. The dancing girls themselves rarely married, but were kept as concubines by well-to-do patrons. The children were raised by the mother and her relatives without any stigma. The male members of the community were usually dancing teachers and musicians and married within the community. Whatever faults moral reformers may have found with their social life, R. thinks their mode of life did not prevent these professional dancers from achieving very high standards of proficiency, taste, and judgment in the art and general culture as well.

K.V.R.'s sympathies have always been with the Congress movement although he did not belong to the party. He ran classes for Harijans when Gandhi was in jail and has always been a nationalist at heart. When he was a child he used to have his hands caned for singing the *Vande Mātaram*. His elder brother was very active in the movement and went to jail and later became a leading journalist. He does not, however, believe that Congress has been very sympathetic to cultural pursuits. Its claims to extend the Swaraj to Indian culture he cannot take seriously. The founding of the Music Academy in 1927 on the occasion of the Congress Party meeting in Madras that year, he regards as merely a coincidence, and the Madras 1935 Music Festival sponsored by the Tamilnad Congress Committee, in which he himself participated, was of the same character. "The political movement just makes a show of patronage but has really very little influence and never picks the right people. The politicians are like flies on the wheel of culture."

His attitude to present trends is highly critical. Dance performances have been commercialized, "the mob calls the tune"; the art has lost refinement and the artists are interested only in revenue. The emphasis on translating all songs into Tamil so that everyone can understand them has not increased the number of people who can understand the music. And "acoustical cranks" who are themselves quite unmusical have become music critics.

But he is not without hope for the future: "We will die before these things die." With a long-range view and a "better class of people," the classical arts can be kept alive. The proper approach would be first to understand what you have, then to clear up misconceptions and only after this to undertake to develop new forms within the frame of the old. He thinks even temple dancing could be restored if political conditions were favorable, since people at large are not bothered by "morality."

In Indian villages today little survives of the classic forms. They have more of the folk arts which, he supposes, may be "the soul of the classics, like a child lisping," but these do not become important until they have been influenced by classical forms.

The renaissance of Indian culture which started with great hopes in the twenties and thirties he thinks has, in its contemporary sequel, proved a failure. The "cinema people" have taken it over and now "the monkey has got it." Indian culture has become more and more attenuated in every generation and "like a child with an enlarged liver lives on in an enfeebled way." The development of modern dance and music schools have "merely increased the scope for fraud."

The reason it was possible for a classic culture to flourish in the past was that performances were regularly held in temples and palaces, that the patrons were themselves musicians and connoisseurs, that the audiences were highly critical, and that the artists were responsive to this atmosphere. Now the audiences are very uncritical and the "artists play down, not up to the audience." In the past too, the artists considered it a privilege to perform before the deity, and there was no stress on personality and the ego; the compositions were impersonal and anonymous. The cultivation of the art through family tradition was also a factor.

Himself a student of Tamil before he studied Sanskrit, K.V.R. believes the present effort to Tamilize the arts by "the left-wingers" is culturally suicidal. Although *bhārata nāṭyam* developed in Tamil country, its life source has been its connection with Sanskrit. Without this connection it will dry up or have a lopsided development.

K.V.R. regards the classical dance as an expression of a spiritual reality. In his presidential address in 1956 before the Indian Institute of Fine Arts in Madras he refers to some of the religious elements in the dance, especially to its connections with temple worship. He speaks of the first item on a *bhārata nāṭyam* program, the *Alarippu*, as "a divine adoration." "While the main root connects Naṭya with the Vedas, others connect it with the Agamas which govern and regulate temple worship and tantric rituals."

Secularizing trends in the dance he regards as unfortunate: "By secularizing it, we have converted it into an affair of the drawing room; and imported the spirit of the market place into the tabernacle . . . all our arts were auxiliary to our religion; a restoration of faith in that religion might help to restore the arts."

5.5. *Traditional dance teacher.* The image of the classical dance constructed by the dance critics needs to be supplemented by the reports of the surviving traditional teachers and dancers. One of these dancing teachers is now conducting a *bhārata nāṭyam* dancing school in Madras. We had an opportunity to visit his school and to interview him twice and also to learn from him something of the traditional ways of teaching and dancing as practiced in the villages.

The city dance class was held in a small school hall during the hours when school was not in session, about two hours early in the morning and another two hours in the late afternoon. We visited it one afternoon and watched teacher and students communicate perfectly without the use of language. The teacher sat cross-legged at one end of the room. He vigorously tapped the time with a small round stick and chanted it in nonsense syllables. With his free left hand, he would describe the positions that the hands or feet should assume in the different steps. Occasionally he would put down the stick and use both hands to describe these positions. These movements of his hands were intermittent and highly abbreviated, like the sketchiest line drawings. But the pupils followed them intently and were guided by them and by the beats of the stick through the complex intricacies of *bhārata nāṭyam.*

There were eight students in the class, a young girl from Orissa, an older Parsī girl from Bombay on a government scholarship, an American woman from New York, and five little girls from eight to ten, most of whom came from Brahman families in the city. They were all learning *bhārata nāṭyam.* Only the small girls knew the teacher's language, Tamil; the others communicated with him through the medium of the dance's gestures and rhythms.

The class and teacher were sponsored by the Indian Institute of Fine Arts, a cultural association devoted to the promotion of classical Indian dance and music. "We teach only the purest classical type of dancing," said the wife of the Institute's secretary who had received us at the class. She and another official of the Institute were proud that Chokkalingam Pillai, the dancing teacher, attracted students from all over India and from abroad. The Institute had given diplomas, representing usually the completion of three years training, to at least twenty dancers. Some of these graduates have become professional dancers, but many are interested in the art only for its own sake, and the families of the younger students are not interested in having their daughters become professional dancers, but in learning a social accomplishment.

Chokkalingam Pillai himself is a traditional dancing teacher, a *nattuvanar,* who once taught *devadāsīs.* He is the son-in-law of Meenakshisundarum Pillai of Pandanallur Village, a famous *nattuvanar* who, before he died, attracted some of India's best dancers to come to study with him in his village. There are three different families of dancing teachers in Pandanallur village: Chokkalingam's family, Meenakshisundarum's family, and a third family. These families are all interrelated and directly descended from a famous "Tanjore quartet" of *nattuvanars.* They have been historically attached to the two temples in the village, one Śiva temple and one Viṣṇu, to some temples in surrounding villages, and to the Big Temple in Tanjore, about fifty miles away. Chokkalingam Pillai believes that the families of dancing teachers in the village can trace their affiliation to the Tanjore temple back to the Cola kings who founded it in 900 A.D.

Chokkalingam was very insistent that the community of dancing teachers were in no way related to the community of dancing girls (*devadāsīs*) whom they taught, contrary to the opinion that the women of the *nattuvanar* community were sometimes dancing girls and that the men of the *devadāsī* community were dancing teachers and musicians. The two communities do not intermarry or interdine. No dancing girl would be allowed to sit in front of a *nattuvanar*; she only came to the house to learn.

Meenakshisundaram Pillai, who taught the art to Chokkalingam, came from a distinguished family of musicians and dancing teachers. His mother was the daughter of Ponniah, one of the famous Tanjore quartet. Meenakshisundaram first studied in the village and was then sent to Tanjore city for further study. He learned Tamil, Telugu and Sanskrit well enough to compose songs in all of these languages. Some of these songs were in praise of the deities in his village temple. He also learned singing, violin, dancing in practice, and the theory from digests of Bharata's *Nāṭya Śāstra*. In Tanjore he married the daughter of his guru who was himself a son of another of the four Tanjore brothers, Sivananda. When he returned to the village he taught music, dancing, and singing. Among the famous dancers who studied with him are Shanta Rao, Mrinalini Sarabai and Ram Gopal. He died in 1954 at the age of eighty-six in his village. One son and several sons-in-law carry on his tradition.

Chokkalingam's early memories are of young girls from *devadāsī* families and boys from the whole community coming to learn dancing and music from his father-in-law. The children would begin their training from their fifth year. Some came to live with his father-in-law, others returned home daily. The routine of the house was very strict and severe. It began at 5 A.M. with music lessons for all. The first meal of the day, cold rice and curry, would be served by 7:30. From 8:30 to twelve the girls practiced dance steps under his father-in-law's supervision and the boys sat on the side following with sticks of their own. Mistakes, whether made by the girls or by the boys, were punished by slaps or rappings with the stick. Shaming insults with the help of the other children were also used.

Between one and four o'clock in the afternoon, after the noon meal, the children went to a modern school to learn languages. In the training, Tamil was the medium of instruction but Telugu songs were also learned. On their return, there was dance practice again from four to six, music lessons from six to 8:30, lessons in *abhinaya* (interpreting songs through dance gestures) from 8:30 to ten, another rice and curry meal at 10:30 and to bed at eleven. They did not find this routine exhausting, Chokkalingam Pillai said, because "the food was right".[17]

Serious lessons would begin when a child was about ten, and continue until about the thirteenth year. This meant that a total period of training would usually last from seven to eight years. The completion of the training was marked by the giving of a first performance—*Aragentram*—by the pupil. This was usually given in a temple and only for the girls; there was no special ceremony for the boys who always assisted their teacher and never performed independently of him.

At the *Aragentram* ceremony, the teacher usually received presents from the mother of the pupil as well as from others. Thereafter, if the pupil performed in public and received any compensation, she would give half to the teacher, who assisted at such performances by keeping time with small cymbals.

This system continued until seven or eight years ago, when temple dancing girls were abolished by law. Chokkalingam and his father-in-law were brought to Madras by Rukmini Devi who, although herself a Brahman, learned to dance, and organized a dancing school at *Kalakeshetra*. He does not think, however, that the old methods of instruction can be followed now or that the same type of dancers can be produced. The pupils do not have so much time to give to training and the traditions are not in their families.

Chokkalingam's family was attached to a temple in a village several miles from their home village of Pandanallur. To this village some members of the family went every day to participate in the *pūjās* held at the temple. Dancing by the dancing girls was involved in these *pūjās* in the form of *mudrās* (hand gestures) to the nine deities of the nine directions. In these *pūjās* the *nattuvanar* kept the time with cymbals and drums, and the *pūjāri*, or temple priest, gave the orders. Sometimes there was singing and pipes.

But the biggest performances came at the *Brahmotsavam* or the chief annual temple festival, which comes in April and lasts for ten days. The festival begins with a hoisting of the temple flag and a propitiation of the nine gods of the directions. Once the flag is hoisted no villager can leave the village until it is lowered at the end of the festival. During the festival, the *devadāsīs* would dance for about an hour and a half each day accompanying the processions of the gods and dancing at the street corners. The *nattuvanars* assisted at these dances and also helped with the morning and evening *pūjās* each day.

The ninety minute festival dance program was quite similar, Chokkalingam Pillai said, to the present *bhārata nāṭyam* programs, both in arrangement and in types of songs used. The songs were mostly devotional about Kṛṣṇa and the Gopis and other gods. In a dance program one of his pupils performed in 1954 in Madras, we found only one song out of ten which could not have been used at the temple festival. This was a song which praised a human being, the only type that was prohibited at the temple.

The song is given below in English translation and immediately after another song addressed to Śiva which was included on the same program and which would have been allowed in temple dances. The dancer does not sing these songs but acts them out with a standardized gesture language (*abhinaya*) as they are sung in Tamil or Telugu by specialized singers.

> Oh my friend! I am deeply in love with Him
> Take Him quickly and secretly
> He Ramalinga endowed with all good qualities and a generous mind.
> I feel the cool moonlight very hot.
> Manmatha [God of Love] is tormenting me with his arrows
> Do take him here at once.

This song was written by Ponniah Pillai, one of the famous *nattuvanars* of Tanjore, and a relative of Chokkalingam's. The second song was written by Marimuttu Pillai, a devotional singer.

> Will He not come down the street
> Oh! if only He could favor me with a fleeting glance

That Lord Nataraja, who burnt Manmatha and Tripura
Oh! if only He would tarry in front of my door and have a word with me
That I may conquer the God of Love whose arrows are tormenting me?
Time does not move
I have none to carry my message of love.
I am blameless:
He whose dancing feet are worshipped by Lord Brahma and Vishnu, the three thousand holy Brahmans of Chidambaram and all the celestials
Will he not come down the street and favour me with a fleeting glance?

Even to this prohibition there is an exception. At the Tanjore temple, e.g., on the eighth day of the festival, a dance-drama called *Kuravanji* is performed by the dancing girls in honor of King Serfoji. There was no *Kuravanji* at his village, but they are also performed at other temples in honor of the elephant-headed deity, Ganes.

For their participation in these festivals and the performance of their other temple duties, the *nattuvanar* family usually received two or three rupees a month and a portion of the cooked rice offerings from the temple. The *devadāsīs* received less than this. They could also augment their income by taking pupils and by performing at marriages, private parties for a "big man," and other festivities. The structure of the dance programs was the same on all of these occasions although the songs were usually "lighter." Thinking that "lighter" meant secular I asked about these "lighter" songs. No, they too were devotional. Even Maharajas at their parties insisted on hearing the songs in honor of their deities. Some of the temple songs were in honor of local temple deities and could not be used outside, but in general all the songs were similar.

In the old days the village audiences knew as much as the town audiences. They knew who the best dancers and teachers were and would go for miles to other villages to see them and to appreciate the science of the art. Now the audiences in the city *sabhās* and in the villages do not know very much about the art, but the audiences in the towns are beginning to learn.

Chokkalingam compared some of the local dance forms in relation to *bhārata nāṭyam:* the Brahman dance-drama (*bhāgvata melā nāṭaka*) is restricted to just a few villages. Its technique has some similarities in the pure dance steps (*nṛtta*) and uses the same interpretative gestures (*abhinaya*) but because it is performed by males it does not have the "soft" movements of the *bhārata nāṭyam*. So far as he knows the *nattuvanars* did not teach the Brahman *bhagavatars*, although each group may have learned from the other.

The folk play—*terrukūttu*—has very little of the dance in it—no *nṛtta* and a bit of *abhinaya*. It is all devotional, based on puranic themes, and depends on narration.

Some of the folk dances have steps corresponding to those of *bhārata nāṭyam*, although they do not use much *abhinaya*. The *Kollatam*, or stick dance, has been done in temples, in October and November, in praise of Lord Kṛṣṇa, by villagers. Ch. Pillai, who knew it from his village, has introduced a form of it, the *Pinnal ḳollatam*, to the Institute school.

Before we left I asked the *nattuvanar* whether he thought Americans could learn *bhārata nāṭyam*. He said he has had some good students and went out of his way to praise the American woman student then studying with him. But whether they really could learn it if they didn't begin young and "believe," he doubted. He had similar doubts about the younger generation of Indian students, for they too lacked dedication.

5.6. *Dancing Girls.* The *devadāsīs* and their dancing teachers were not attached to temples exclusively. Royal courts also made claims on their time. There is a record of a troupe of Tanjore dancing girls, dancing teachers, and musicians which was in the service of the Maharaja Sayajirao III of Baroda until Baroda was merged with Bombay.[18] Two of the dancing girls, who were retired with pensions in 1941, came from *devadāsī* families attached to the Kamakshi Temple at Tanjore and two of the dancing teachers were grandsons of the same Tanjore dancing teacher whose granddaughter married Chokkalingam's father-in-law. The entire group had come to Baroda from Tanjore as the wedding dowry of the Tanjore princess who married the Maharaja in 1879.

At the Baroda palace, the troupe was subject to the supervision of a State Department of Artists which fixed the regulations and recorded them in print. The two dancing girls were paid together 433 rupees per month, and their musicians a total of 272 rupees per month. A dearness allowance was later added. The dancers had to provide their own costumes.

Leaves and discipline were governed by strict rules. The women were given a regular monthly leave of four consecutive days and three months leave with pay when in pregnancy. All the artists had to register every Saturday at the State Department in a special book. If Saturday was a holiday they had to go the following working day.

The dance team had to perform for the Maharaja every Wednesday and Saturday after dinner. Dance performances also had to be given in Durbar for ceremonies and for distinguished visitors. No performances were required when the Maharaja was away. The Superintendent had to give the dance team at least two hours notice before a performance. Gifts in cash and presents from the audience had to be surrendered to the Superintendent who divided some of it among the artists and put the rest into the State treasury.

The dance repertoire included the standard *bhārata nāṭyam* program (it was called the "Tanjori Nautch" at this time) and some "light" dances at the end. The five "light" dances, which were performed by the two dancing girls as a team, were called the Radha Kṛṣṇa Dance, the Kite Dance, the Scorpion Dance, the Drunkard's Dance, and the Snake Charmer's Dance. Although these included some of the *bhārata nāṭyam* movements and gestures, they were, in general, more free and frivolous than the regular nautch and very popular with the Court audience. As was the custom, the ruler's name was included in some of the dance songs. A Tanjore song in honor of Shivaji, coming in the Varnam part of the program, was slightly changed to honor the Maharaja of Baroda.

When the original dancing girl, Gowri, retired fifty-two years after she was brought to the Baroda court at the age of ten, the Maharaja had a metal statue made of her in one of her dance poses at a cost of 50,000 rupees. This is still in the Lakshmivilas palace in Baroda.

In 1949, when Baroda merged with Bombay, the State Department of Artists was abolished. A dance department was, however, organized in the M.S. University of Baroda with the son of one of the Tanjore dancing girls as a dancing teacher. *Bhārata nāṭyam* and *kathak* dancing are taught and both the B.A. and M.A. degrees are awarded.

The National Academy of Song, Dance, and Drama (Sangeet Natak Acadami) selected for the first time in 1955 outstanding Indian artists in music, dance, and drama for "Akadami awards." The award for the outstanding *bhārata nāṭyam* dancer was presented by the President, Rajendra Prasad, to Balasaraswati of Madras. Balasaraswati's great-great grandmother was a famous *vina* player and her mother is a famous singer. Yet she is a transitional figure belonging neither wholly to the family tradition of *devadāsīs* nor to the modern trends which she is helping to bring in. She is the only one of four daughters who took up dancing, and that against her family's wishes. Because of the anti-nautch movement she did not have too many opportunities for seeing the old style dancing during her childhood. And she was not "dedicated" to a temple. She was trained by a *devadāsī* who was once attached to the Mylapore temple and by a *nattuvanar* from Tanjore. Her own dancing, usually to be seen at public concerts, is distinguished for its expressive *abhinaya*. Because of her artistic proficiency and because she is now considered a representative of the authentic classical tradition, the Music Academy of Madras sponsors her dancing school where, with the help of her teacher's son, she teaches *bhārata nāṭyam* to the young girls coming from different classes and families of Madras.

When we interviewed her at the Music Academy, her mother, brother, and young daughter were present, as well as several other visitors, including some friends and supporters of her school.

Her family is one of twenty-five *devadāsī* families who have preserved the traditions of the community in Madras. Among them are singers, instrumentalists, dancers, and dance teachers. There is no settled division of labor, but taste determines the choice of occupation, except that the men of the community are usually the dance teachers.

She has heard of Brahman dancers and thinks that they have contributed to the development of *abhinaya*. She herself had known one, Ganapathi Sastri. However, she did not show a great deal of interest in the theory of the dance, in temple dance sculptures, or in Bharata's *Nāṭya Śāstra*.

She has performed *Kuravanjis*, the *devadāsī* dance dramas, and told us the story of the play about Serfoji as well as the occasions on which it used to be performed in the villages.

She regards her training as the secret of her success and her ability to act the different roles called for in the dance songs. She found it embarrasing to say which is her favorite role.

The methods of dance training are now changing and, in her opinion, for the worse. She does not think a restoration possible and the present products are "too inferior to offer to God." Future prospects for the dance she does not consider very encouraging although "it depends on providence."

In her school she makes no distinction between amateurs and professionals and will take anyone that she can get. The usual course in other schools is six months, but she considers five years a minimum for talented youngsters who begin from the age of six. She adapts her methods of instruction to the age of her pupils in order to take account of the growth in stature, body control, etc. Non-Indian students, she thinks, can learn the pure dance steps (*nṛtta*) but do not easily master the proper gestures and expressions for the interpretative parts or *abhinaya*.

She does not go to movies of dancing because she does "not want to spoil the art." However, she would consider making a movie on her own conditions.

She has danced before leading members of the present Indian government but does not enjoy doing it because it is obvious from their faces that they do not understand the art or follow the songs. A far more knowing and appreciative spectator was the Sardar-i-Rasat of Kashmir (son and heir of the disposed Maharajah) who recently came to see her dance, and who followed every step and every song along with her.

5.7. *Carnatic music.* The classic revival in music has had a smoother, if less spectacular, course than in dance. Music has not been so closely associated with the controversial dancing girls. Although many famous musicians have come from the *devadāsī* community, this is an art which Brahmans and other castes have also cultivated for a long time. Technical development in music has a long continuous history in the south, and has reached greater specialization and refinement than the dance. Technical virtuosity with instruments like the *vīṇā* (a kind of lute), the *flute*, the *mṛdaṅgam* (South Indian drum) and the *nāgasvara* (or long pipe) has been so highly developed that it is not at all uncommon to hear musical concerts devoted exclusively to performances on these instruments. Vocal music is similarly highly developed and the large number of "modes" (*rāgas*) gives the individual singer, who is as often a female as male, great opportunity for virtuosity. While some of these instruments still have a ritual use, particularly the long pipe and the drum which are played at weddings and other functions to frighten away evil spirits, their purely musical development began very early. The ancient Tamil epic of the second century A.D., "The Lay of the Anklet," mentions four kinds of Vīna, five kinds of flute, thirty-one kinds of percussion instruments, and lays down the technical qualifications for a singer, male and female, a drummer, a flutist, and vīna player. There are other discussions on music and the system is based as it is today on melody and rhythm and a basic scale of seven notes.[19]

Many features of this southern musical system are also described in the Sanskrit treatises, in the *Nāṭya Śāstra* of Bharata, where it is directly derived from Vedic chanting, and in later treatises like the *Saṇgīta Ratnākāra* of Śārṅgadeva in the thirteenth century. From the sixteenth century, when the Carnatic composer saint, Purandara Dās, flourished southern music, "Carnatic Music," developed in distinction from northern or "Hindustani music." The present classical form of the Carnatic system is usually attributed to three Tanjore composers, all Brahmans, of the early nineteenth century: Tyāgarāja, a Telugu living near Tanjore, Mathusvāmī Dīkṣitar, and Śyāma Śāstri, both Tamils. They are often referred to as occupying the same position in the recent history of classical southern music as is occupied in the nineteenth century by the Tanjore "quartet" of dancing teachers. After them, musical development is seen in decline because of an over-emphasis on rhythm, a failure to coordinate theory and practice, loss of princely and patrician patronage, and weakening of the gurukal system of training. The revival aims at restoring the Carnatic classical traditional to its historic path.

5.8. *Definitions of "folk," "popular," and "classical."* The distinction between "classical" and "folk" music is frequently invoked by music critics who regard it as equivalent to the ancient Sanskrit contrast between *mārga* and *deśī* respectively. In a recent paper on "Popular Music and Classical Music"[20] V. Raghavan of Madras University undertakes a systematic definition of the folk-classical distinction as it applies to music, and also traces some of the historical interaction of the two types. He includes in "popular music" folk music as well as popularized classical and "light" music. The main difference between "popular" and "classical" he finds in the rendering:

"when the rendering is sophisticated, it is art or classical music; when it is plain and simple, it is the popular or folk variety." Sophistication depends on rules and principles into which an art is codified and systematized. Just as "to evolve a principle and to conduct oneself in conformity to it is the mark of culture" so it is in art where the standard of judgment is based on "artistic criteria" that have evolved. This is what connoisseurs care for and enjoy, whereas the layman likes other things. "That is art-music in which artistic considerations alone prevail; the moment one sings down to the populace, one relaxes the high austerity of his art."

Folk or popular music then, Raghavan finds, is not bound by strict rules and principles and is characterized by features likely to appeal to popular tastes: simple rendering; accentuated and obvious rhythm; group singing; stereotyped, monotonous form; emphasis on words; basis in a festival, a season or an event; emotional and dramatic tone.

These elements are present in art-music but must be "duly proportioned" and made subservient to "expression." Melody (*rāga*), rhythm (*tāla*), and idea and feeling (*bhāva*) must be "evenly integrated" into a "fine synthesis."

Even the classical pieces of the great musicians who have been mostly saints and teachers are often overloaded with thought and words and "when they are rendered as vehicles of teaching or as a means of devotional transport, they depart from the concert and take the turn towards *harikathā* and *bhajan*."

Art music should evoke its *rasa* 'mood' by the actual music and not by importing extraneous elements. "To evoke Rasa with the words alone is to surrender music to poetry; to evoke it through overloading one's rendering with pure feeling is to surrender it to drama; to evoke it by pure music is really pure music, and the Rasa which this pure music evokes leaves far behind that realm in which the mundane sentiments of Śringāra (love), Vīra (heroism), etc. have their meaning; it is that ineffable bliss in which one gets absorbed as in Samādhi (Yogic concentration). Thus does *Nāda* (sound) become the nearest portal to the *Brahman* (world spirit)."

Raghavan's summarizing characterization of "art-music" is that it is music in which "the canons and requirements of art, the rules of balance, harmony, proportion, propriety, concentration on pure artistic resources to the exclusion of adventitious circumstances are to hold sway or absolute sway." To dilute these strict standards and to make concessions in any direction to please a lay audience is to make the music popular "or if it is purposely done for subserving another art or other purpose it is applied music."

5.9. *Influence of folk and popular music on classical music.* In this same paper Raghavan describes how "folk" and "classical" have interacted on each other. This is a futher development of the view which he has stated more comprehensively elsewhere that the historic formation of the major Indian cultural tradition has involved a two-way give-and-take interaction with local and regional traditions. "Almost always, the major cultural tradition spreads out and consolidates itself over new regions by absorbing, incorporating within itself and adjusting to its own scheme such of the local elements as are valuable and attractive. So do all major traditions become national cultures, of signficance to every region and group of people."[21]

This give-and-take cultural process is particularly clear in music and dance, although it may also be traced in language, social organization, and in other departments of human activity. Many of the musical "scales" (*rāgas*) have regional and tribal names and probably represent sophistications of tribal melodies. The association of the *Rājamātaṅgī rāga* with the *vīṇa* as the goddess of music may be connected, he suggests, with a tribe called Mātaṅgas who were once numerous and artistically endowed but later were degraded socially as Cāṇḍālas and untouchables. Numerous musical technical terms, names of instruments, of varieties of voice are still in the local language of western India and reflect the movements of the cultural tradition across India. *Deśī* terminology not only occurs in the classical music, but the treatises stipulate that a musician is not entitled to the foremost status of *Gandharva* unless he is proficient in both the *mārga* and the *deśī* styles.

In the classical dance, too, there are *deśī* strands. The treatises on music and dance include descriptions of local and folk dances. Jayasenāpati's *Nṛttarattnāvalī* devotes its last three chapters to the varieties of folk dances. Someśvara, the author of another treatise, "was captivated by the dance of the hunters, the *Goṇḍalīs*, and systematized it in a set scheme and described it in his work from which it passed into the regular repertoire of dancers elsewhere also."

Raghavan finds these folk influences beneficial; they contribute "a frequent invigoration and enrichment of the main tradition by local forms which are fitted into the basic technique and higher ideology of the classical tradition. The *deśī* supplied the material, the *mārga* refined it and assigned it to a place and wove it into the larger and richer scheme. The popular and the classical were the two currents, so as to say, of the energy of our culture. Our art and culture thus soared forth like the image of Pārvatī and Śiva in one, the Ardhanārīśvara, a synthesis of the two into an inseparable unity."

6.1. *Summary and implications for a theory of culture change. Little and Great Traditions in village and city.* In India, Little and Great Traditions are not neatly differentiated along a village-urban axis. Both kinds of tradition are found in villages and in the city in different forms. Folk and ritual kinds of performances survive in fragments in the city, but they are very old forms and are common in villages and towns. The popular devotional and the classical forms are essentially urban developments of the last hundred years, although they have more ancient precedents. The modern urban forms are the most recent of all, and are essentially urban in origin. These five different kinds of performances are but points on a single continuum when we compare their media, performers, language, place and occasion of performance, and themes. In such folk forms as the folk play, folksongs, folk dances, and ballads, the performers are generally non-Brahman men in the case of the plays and ballads, women in the case of dances and songs. There is some hereditary cultivation of skill within certain families, particularly in ballad making, but in general the performers are amateurs who "pick it up" or are trained by some teacher. The language of the folk forms is usually a regional dialect of Tamil or Telugu and is rarely written or printed. Non-Brahman village temples have been the place for the performance of the folk plays on the occasion of seasonal festivals, while the songs, dances, and ballads may be performed at almost any place and time. The audiences at these performances are generally members of the non-Brahman community. Puranic themes are mixed with themes from local legend and history and from the commonplaces of daily life. These folk performances are close to the little traditional pole of cultural performances, but not completely cut off from great traditional influences.

At the opposite pole, but still found in villages as well as in towns, are the ritual kinds of performances, the life cycle rites and ceremonies, temple festivals, chanting and recitation of scriptures, and until about 1947, temple dances and religious dance dramas. These belong to the sacred sphere of the culture and are closely associated with Brahman priests and *paṇḍits* as performers, teachers, and patrons. The performers are men, except for the community of temple dancers, and belong to families who have cultivated the special media for many generations. The verbal texts used are generally Vedic and classical Sanskrit and have been transmitted through an oral tradition, although books are used as aids to memory. In some Vaiṣṇavite and Śaivite rites, Tamil hymns and scriptures have been incorporated into the ceremonies. The themes are mainly Vedic and puranic. Some ritual performances differ in one other respect from other kinds of cultural performance: the daily rites performed by householder or temple priest do not require an audience, they are addressed only to a deity.

The popular devotional and classical types of cultural performances which have developed in an urban environment differ from the village forms in a number of important respects. The duration of the performance is much shorter in the city; a puranic recitation usually lasted from six months to a year in the village; in the city it has been condensed into seven or fifteen-day sequences. The devotional films and plays, as well as the *harikathā* performance, do not exceed three or four hours, whereas a village folk play or temple festival play went on through the night, and at the major festivals for ten days. The performers at these urban performances are nonhereditary professionals who have usually been trained in modern schools. They come from all communities, Brahman and non-Brahman, and include women as well as men. Since the place of performance is a public hall or theater and the occasion is the performance itself, there are no caste or sectarian restrictions on the audience. The language of the popular devotional performances is predominantly the urban colloquial vernacular of the region, with some verbal texts in Sanskrit and other Indian languages, used by the more erudite performers in *harikathā*, in classical concerts, and of course in Sanskrit plays. Stories from the epics and *purāṇas* and from the lives of the regional saints continue to provide thematic material for the urban forms, but these are increasingly mixed with secular and political themes.

The greatest transcendence of local folk and ritual forms is reached in the strictly modern urban forms—the social play, the social film, the short story and the novel. In these the language is predominantly a regional vernacular or English and the themes are the social, economic and political problems of the day. The language and the distinctive cultural content of some of these problems—inter-marriage of castes, the plight of the villager, a foreign trained graduate's qualms about an arranged marriage—add a distinctive flavor to this younger branch of a world-wide urban culture.

6.2. *Two rhythms in culture change.* The differentiation of folk, ritual, popular devotional, classical, and modern urban cultural performances in relation to urbanization suggests the operation of more general processes of culture change operating in different spheres of culture. The differentiation between classical (*mārga*) and folk (*deśī*) in art styles is paralleled, as Raghavan has pointed out, in the field of language by the differentiation between *Samskṛta* (perfected, refined, civilized) and *prākṛta* (unrefined, vernacular), and in the field of social customs by the distinction between customs sanctioned either by *śruti* (revealed scripture) and *smṛti* (remembered scripture), or customs sanctioned by local usages (*deśācāras*) and family usage (*kuladharmas*).[22]

Each sphere of culture seems to be subject to opposing directions of change, one type of change tending to push a given cultural sphere in the direction of greater refinement and strict codification, the other in the direction of maximum popularity and practicality. At any given time, the outcome within a given cultural sphere is something of a compromise between the two extremes, a range of intergrading cultural forms. The prevalence of the refining tendencies sustained in several departments of culture over a long period will result in a level of aesthetic and intellectual achievement deservedly called a "Great Tradition."

The question now arises whether the operation of these opposing rhythms of change within differing spheres of culture is merely formal and structural or whether there is some direct and organic relationship among changes in the different spheres. And is there, in particular, a distinctive pattern of change which a Great Tradition undergoes in a metropolitan environment? Perhaps a process of secularization?

Culturally, the effect of urbanization, so far as the Madras case is concerned, has been to shift attention and activity away from ritual observances and sacred learning and to the fields of popular culture and the arts. This shift carries with it a shift in values from those predominantly connected with religious merit to those of mass entertainment and aesthetics. There are also associated changes from cultural media to mass media and from sacred centers and occasions of performance to cultural centers and secular occasions. Movie actors and concert artists compete with priests and *paṇḍits* as performers. "First nights" succeed "first fruits."

It would be inaccurate, however, to apply the Western concepts of secular urban mass culture and of "art for art's sake" in interpreting these changes. There are, indeed, secularizing tendencies, but they have not yet cut off urban culture from the traditional matrix of sacred culture. There is no sharp dividing line between religion and culture, and the traditional cultural media not only continue to survive in the city but have also been incorporated in novel ways into an emerging popular and classical culture. Much of the urban popular culture is seen as an extension of the path of devotion (*bhakti mārga*), more easily accessible to modern man than the paths of strict ritual observance (*karma mārga*) or the path of sacred knowledge (*jñāna mārga*). The classical arts, as well, are viewed as offering a special path and discipline for those able to cultivate it that is akin to yogic concentration.

Nor are these religious interpretations of popular and classical culture limited to the verbalizations of religious leaders. They are interpretations which are borne out by the many continuities in themes, media, audience reaction, that link the urban culture to the traditional sacred culture. The films and other mass media, e.g., although disposed by technical and economic organization to cater to a mass market without respect to caste, creed, or language, have nevertheless found it profitable to draw on the old mythological and devotional themes and to adapt freely the media of folk and classical culture. The newer political themes introduced with the struggle for independence, and now with economic development, are also effectively communicated when joined to the traditional themes and media. The effect of the mass media, in other words, has not so much secularized the sacred traditional culture as it has democratized it.

In the revival of classical south Indian dancing and music, the strands connecting these arts with the sacred culture are evident. The revival, to be sure, has its creative aspects, particularly in having introduced new classes of people as teachers, performers, audience. It also tends to make the concert stage and the social recital, rather than the wedding of the temple procession, the normative cultural forum for the performance of these arts. It is still the hereditary teachers and performers, however, or those directly trained under them, who are in greatest demand and have the highest prestige. And a program of authentic classical dancing or music is still pretty much what it was when part of a ritual calendar. The *pūjās* of invocation, the devotional songs, the hand gestures (or *mudrās*), many of the dance movements, and the musical instruments used for village festivals fifty to one hundred years ago are now used by modern artists in city concerts. In judging these performances, the critics and connoisseurs will apply standards of technical virtuosity and aesthetic refinement, but they take for granted the puranic themes and also judge whether the performance is a "worthy offering to the deity."

Many of these very same media, or elements of them, enter into the performances of more popular culture—puranic recitations, devotional plays, *bhajans*—since the difference between popular and classical culture rests not on a sharp difference in kind of media or theme, but depends rather on the degree of sophistication, technical refinement, and balance between aesthetic, devotional, and entertainment values which characterize the performance.

The continuum implied here of media and themes extends right into the sphere of ritual observance. The *pūjās* and *mudrās* of the temple and domestic priests are clearly similar to the *pūjās* performed in *bhajans*, devotional plays and films, and in classical dancing. And it is not too far-fetched to suggest that the modern classicists' doctrine of pure music with its insistence on preserving fixed rules of art and its deemphasis of the meaning of the words may be analogous to the ritual necessities of Vedic chanting. In the Sāma Veda chanting, e.g., there is a highly developed technique of vocal and instrumental music with specialized singers and instrumentalists. The singing was part of mystic sacrifices and highly esoteric. The Sāman singers are still reluctant to disclose their special techniques. The verses of the *Rig-veda* furnish the libretto for this singing, but there are also many syllables without particular meaning (*stobhas*) which are used as aids in the singing. The mystic efficacy of the singing depends on the correct enunciation of the sounds and it thus became all important to repeat the sounds each time without any change.[23]

Classicism in art may be a sublimation, if not an actual derivation, of ritual singing and dancing. And popular mass culture, to which it is opposed, is itself an extension of the devotional reaction to ritualism. The dialectic of the two rhythms of culture change continues on a new plane with some new, some old, media and themes.

The new plane on which this dialectic of cultural rhythms is operating is an urban one. Although several of the older ritual and village folk forms survive in the urban environment of Madras, the distinctive cultural developments in the city have been the revival and modernization of classical forms and the creation of popular devotional forms in each of the major media—literature, puranic recitation, drama, music, and dance.

These classical and devotional forms are not without ancient precedents, but their immediate and contemporary sources are urbanized ritual forms and urbanized folk forms. Urbanization has adapted the traditional forms to create modern versions of class and mass culture. It is also beginning to produce a form of urban culture that derives neither from the sacred culture or from the local folk culture. This is either an importation from another urbanized culture—as in the novel, the social play, the symphony—or represents a creative synthesis of indigenous and foreign sources.

6.3. *A profile of urbanized literati.* To this point the discussion has been primarily cultural, basing itself on a comparative analysis of cultural performances. Can such a method throw any light on the sociological question raised at the outset: Are the Brahman literati turning into intelligentsia in the urban environment? The results of the cultural analysis suggest one natural inference, that urbanization differentiates the literati into social types corresponding to the cultural types of performances. There would then be ritualists who follow the path of ritual observances (e.g., domestic and temple priests, and strictly orthodox householders); sages who follow the path of sacred knowledge (e.g., *paṇḍits*, yogis, swamis); popularizers who follow the path of popular devotionalism (e.g., the puranic reciters, *bhajan* leaders, dramatists); and classicists who follow the disciplines of the classical arts. All of these are literati in the sense that they seek through their activities to continue the Great Tradition. But the last two types, the popularizers and the classicists, represent new urban types who seek to restore, revive, or adapt elements of traditional culture under modern urban conditions. The ritualists and the sages are old literati types who are found in a metropolitan center but do not feel at home in it.

On this scheme of classification only the modernists, who seek to introduce modern and western cultural forms even where they conflict with the traditional culture, would be classed as intelligentsia. These are the novelists, short story writers, playwrights of modern plays, producers of films, artists and composers in western music, scientists.

The folk performer (bard, reciter actor) ia a proto-*literatus* who cultivates the cultural forms of the Little Tradition. In India, however, where Little, Great, and urban traditions interact so freely, he also performs some of the functions of the literati and of the intelligentsia, bringing the local traditions into the culture of the city and taking the city's cultural products back to the countryside.

This typology of intellectual types suggested by a typology of cultural performances deserves to be checked against direct sociological studies of the groups concerned. Such studies, I think, will find a good deal of overlap among the different types because there is a continuity of social types, as there is of cultural forms. The modernist film producer who attends *bhajans* regularly is not an unusual person, and the new literati are also responsible for introducing some novel forms within the frame of traditionalizing change.

Rather than scan the cultural data for additional indications of social typology, I should prefer, in these closing pages, to sketch a composite profile of the urbanized Brahman literati in Madras city and then attempt some explicit generalizations about types of culture change.

Madras city would not appear to be a very good place to study the Great Tradition of Indian culture. It is a large metropolitan center and a major cultural, political, and commercial center of South India. Nevertheless, it presents an unusually good situation in which to trace the heterogenetic transformation of a Great Tradition that results from secondary urbanization, because the leading professional representatives of that tradition, the Brahmans, and the non-Brahman merchant patrons, have been closely associated with the city from its very beginnings in 1640. They have come to the city from adjoining villages and towns to help build up its educational, cultural, administrative, and economic services and themselves to take advantage of these services.

For these tasks they were particularly well qualified by their relatively high literacy, linguistic abilities, and long association with learning and literary activities. As they exercised these abilities within an expanding urban center and passed through the modern educational system into modern professions, they came to perform in increasing numbers the role of intelligentsia, or agents of culture change, and less and less that of traditional literati. That is to say, they found in their new preoccupations less time for the cultivation of Sanskrit learning and the performance of the scripturally prescribed ritual observances, the two activities for which as Brahmans they have had an ancient and professional responsibility. They have not, however, completely abandoned these activities and to some extent they have developed compensatory activities which have kept them from becoming completely de-Sanskritized and cut off from traditional culture.

They continue, e.g., to make pilgrimages to Banaras and the Ganges as well as to many of the shrine centers in South India, albeit with modern means of transportation and new motives of patriotic and cultural sightseeing added to the old religious ones. They employ family priests (*purohitas*) to help them conduct domestic rites, and those who can afford it are very lavish on the occasion of a sacred thread or wedding ceremony in observance and expenditure. They go to the temple for the big festivals several times a year and visit their *jagadguru* and their *maṭh* at least once a year. Legislative restrictions against these sacred institutions are actively resisted and organizations to finance ritual activities and to promote Vedic learning have been formed by them. While they deplore the passing of the old *gurukula* system of education and the decline in the number of sastric *paṇḍits*, they are interested in keeping Sanskrit learning alive and support moves to incorporate more of it into high schools, colleges and universities. Their ritual status as Brahmans may have been somewhat lowered through increasing violations of some of the pollution taboos, and a generally more careless attitude towards them, but the taboos against intercaste marriages are still very strong and pollution from death or birth in the family and from many other sources is still carefully expiated.

Above all, these urban Brahmans have taken an increasing interest in popular religious culture, traditionally designed for the lower castes, women and children. They form *bhajan* groups, listen to recitations of the hymns of Tamil saints, organize and attend puranic recitations, devotional plays and movies, and discourses in English or Tamil on the Upanishads delivered by non-Brahmans, contrary to sastric sanction. These cultural performances are increasingly held at public halls and theaters rather than in temples or at domestic ceremonies and are open to all without respect to caste or sect. They are considered an extension of the devotional form of religion of the older *bhakti* cults and sects to a democratic mass culture. Brahmans not only make up part of the audience, but are also some of the leading performers, producers, directors, and writers for these programs.

A relatively small group among the more educated and sophisticated Brahmans (and non-Brahmans too) have kept aloof from these mass religious cultural activities. To their taste, these activities are too emotional, unrefined and unauthentic. They are classicists, and insist on greater fidelity to the ancient Sanskrit texts in readings and recitations, and on the predominance of purely artistic values (as articulated in the ancient *śāstras* and exemplified in temple sculpture and cultivated by hereditary performers) over the values of popular entertainment or even religious devotion. This group is responsible, both as leading critics and as an audience of connoisseurs, for the revival of classical south Indian dancing and music. The revival, as some of the more percipient classicists have observed, is not entirely backward looking. It contains creative innovations linking it to the modern urban scene and to its popular culture. These include a change in the methods of instruction from the apprentice system to the modern school, a change from hereditary families of teachers and of performers to nonhereditary teachers and pupils drawn from all quarters, including the most respectable families, and the substitution of the social accomplishment or a commercial career for a ritually defined role. Some of the classicists deplore these innovations and call for a total restoration of the traditional pattern—temple dancing, the apprentice method of teaching, a practically hereditary professionalization of performers and teachers. Others are content to seek a wider hearing for classical culture in the mass media and to raise the levels of popular taste. Most of them look upon their classicism not as a secular doctrine of "art for art's sake" but as offering a distinctive path of release and religious salvation, akin to yogic concentration, to the sophisticated and cultivated individual.

6.4. *Cultural structure and social organization of cultural traditions.* The above summary combines social and cultural description and makes no attempt to set out the special concepts and hypothetical processes involved. These have been implicit throughout the paper and only occasionally discussed in direct fashion. In this concluding section it may be useful to make the theoretical implications of the case study explicit.

A cultural tradition needs to be conceived both culturally as a cultural structure and societally as a social organization. Looked at as a structure of culture content, it is made up of sequences of cultural performances combining various cultural media, verbal and nonverbal, performed at cultural centers by professional and semi-professional performers. These performances, media, centers, and performers have each of them a complex and differentiated structure of their own. It is possible to place each of these structures along a two-dimensional line of variation between two poles—an uncultivated Little Tradition of folk culture at one end and a cultivated and learned Great Tradition at the other. The line, however, is a continuum, and there seems to be constant interaction between the extremes, whether one looks at performances, texts and media, cultural centers, or cultural performers. In India the Great Tradition is still closely tied to a sacred culture, so that the performances are frequently religious rites and ceremonies, the centers are temples and shrines, performers are priests and spiritual teachers, and the media are linked to a canon of sacred scripture and myth. Urbanization has secularized this sacred culture in some degree, but the line between the sacred and the secular spheres is never a very sharp or constant one.

It is natural to look beyond the concept of a Great Tradition as an aspect of several differentiated cultural structures and to regard it as something of a governing pattern and principle of an integrated culture. Or at least we are tempted to look for the total culture pattern of a civilization in its Great Tradition, which is usually highly articulated, sophisticated, and comprehensive. Can we, however, identify this integrating pattern of the Great Tradition through a comparison of the similarities and differences among the cultural forms to be found in each of the parts of the cultural structure?

This procedure may with unusal virtuosity and good luck discover such an over-all pattern, but more frequently it seems to result in a highly fictive construct. I do not mean to say that civilizations (or simpler cultures for that matter) do not have overall integrating patterns, only that it is necessary to supplement the cultural analysis by a societal one to discover them as actually operative in a concrete situation. There are a great many different ways in which the elements and part-structures of a cultural tradition could be organized into unifying patterns. The problem is to discover those ways in which they have actually been organized. And to do that requires a knowledge of the social organization of tradition, of how particular communities of people are related to particular cultural performances, centers, media, and performers.

In India these communities are overlapping: communities of tribes, castes and subcastes, of villages and towns, of religious and linguistic groups. And each kind of community has its distinctive organization of the common cultural traditions. The social organization of Indian traditions may, of course, be studied in any of these kinds of communities, although it would take a great many different studies of the different groups in different parts of the country to establish a solid basis for generalization about India as a whole. In South India, one particularly useful kind of group to study are the sectlike denominational groups within Hinduism. Each of these has a comprehensive version of what it takes the tradition to be, and by comparing in detail the social organization, personnel, and institutions, particualrly the *maṭh*, of the major sects, Vaiṣṇavite and Śaivite, it is possible to arrive at a general picture of the overall structure of Hinduism within the region where the constituency of these sects are to to be found. This procedure will not, to be sure, yield a single authoritative version of the Hindu Great Tradition, but rather a structure of related and overlapping versions. An outside observer cannot say which of these is most authoritative without assuming the vantage point of a particular sect or group.

6.5. *Types of culture change and culture process.* Neither the cultural structure nor the social organization of a tradition remains fixed and unchanging over time. One of the main interests of the Madras study has been to determine the kinds of change in Hindu traditions related to urbanization. Some of these processes are primarily cultural, and some are societal as well as cultural. Let us now attempt a more explicit and precise analysis of these processes in terms of their dimensions and agencies.

Culture change, like any other kind of change, has a temporal dimension which it is useful to distinguish into linear and cyclical varieties. Linear types of culture change imply a specification of a date or approximate date which allows us to fix a "before" and "after" division. Modernization of a cultural tradition is a linear type of change in this sense. It implies that the tradition has been transformed into a form which it did not have before a certain date. For purposes of the Madras study we have taken the early seventeenth century as such a dividing line between modern and traditional. Pre-British India is taken as traditional India. Not all changes which the tradition undergoes in the modern period, however, result in modernization. Pilgrimage, e.g., although it has incorporated modern means of transportation, still seems to conform to its traditional pattern. It is useful, in other words, to consider whether the result of any particular change in tradition is continuous with the structure prevailing before a certain date, or whether that structure has been replaced by a new one. In the former case we might speak of the change as a traditionalizing type, in the latter as a modernizing type. The changes in the pilgrimage pattern have been traditionalizing, but the changes in the educational system have been modernizing. If the change results in a structure which is neither quite like the traditional one nor a predominantly new one, we might speak of a compromise formation.

The Madras College of Indigenous Medicine, for example, was a deliberate attempt to construct a compromise formation between traditional Indian medicine and modern medicine, but it seems to be going in the direction of modernization. A more stable case of compromise formation is in the field of popular culture where the traditional cultural media and puranic themes have been adapted to the mass media of print, radio, and film and linked to a democratic interpretation of the traditional devotional (*bhakti*) movements and ideologies.

Cyclical cultural processes do not require reference to a "before" and "after" dividing line. They are recurrent processes which, of course, take time, but the temporal duration of the process is a cycle which may recur within the traditional or within the modern period. Sanskritization and de-Sanskritization are cyclical processes in this sense. And while, in general, we should expect modernizing changes to be de-Sanskritizing and traditionalizing changes to be Sanskritizing this need not always be the case. The Sanskritization of the Camārs described by Cohn is for them a modernizing process, since it has changed their traditions into novel forms. The Westernization of some Brahmans, on the other hand, who approve of alcoholic drinks, nonvegetarian diets, and widow remarriage, may be both a de-Sanskritizing and a modernizing process if considered in relation to their previous traditions, but may be traditionalizing if considered in relation to the traditions of lower castes who drink alcohol and eat meat, or even if considered in relation to the earliest Vedic traditions when such customs seem to have been sanctioned for Brahmans.

The processes of Sanskritization and de-Sanskritization involve, in other words, an essential reference to a particular set of cultural norms or values, which takes us beyond the temporal dimension, linear or cyclical. Since these norms will vary for different groups and change over time for the same group, it is necessary in analyzing such processes to specify both the group and the time during which the norms in question prevail. The time reference is not necessarily introduced here as a baseline for judging linear change, but as a way of locating the cultural content which is being transformed. The transformation may be either cyclical or linear. Whether the changes in cultural norms will change the total structure of the tradition will depend on many things—the balance between traditionalizing and modernizing changes, the speed of the change, the degree of looseness or flexibility built into the tradition, and, ultimately, upon the judgment and actions of those considered the "authorities" among the literati. Many of these changes they regard as continuous with their Great Tradition and are incorporating them within a redefined orthodoxy. A few of the changes they regard as fundamental threats to the tradition and have actively organized resistance and defense against them.

There is a kind of built-in flexibility within the orthodox Vedānta position which permits an easy incorporation of a wide variety of changes. The *paṇḍits* who are called upon to decide difficult cases say they follow a fixed hierarchy of authorities and standards in their deliberations and decisions. At the top of the hierarchy are the revealed scriptures (the *śruti*, including the Vedas and Upanishads). Next come the remembered scriptures (the *smṛti*), including the treatises on religious law, the epics and *purāṇas*, and the auxiliary sciences. In case of a conflict among scriptures, the opinion of a wise man should be consulted. Local customs and usages, and individual concience, finally, may be followed if the scriptures are not available.

This hierarchy gives the wise man—the *paṇḍit*, the guru, the head of the *maṭh*—a comfortable scope for interpretation and reconciliation of scriptural sanctions. He quite freely invokes considerations of logic, experience, the convenience or inconvenience of a particular circumstance, and local usages in coming to his decision. In this process the wise men and particularly the learned literati are an institutionalized agency for changing tradition, so long as they regard the change as primarily preservative of the tradition's essentials.

The long run result of this process has been consolidative and selective. Some elements of language, learning, and the arts, as well as of ritual custom, drop out (.eg., Vedic sacrifice); new ones are added (e.g., temples and monastic organizations). Aspects of heterodox sectarian movements and of tribal and regional custom are assimilated to orthodoxy. Fragments of Little Traditions have been absorbed into the Great Tradition and the culture of the villages and tribes has, in the long run, also been responsive to the authoritative teachings of literati. And just as a large and famous temple will contain numerous shrines to stones, snakes, trees, and the planets, as well as to the pantheon of major deities, so a learned and sophisticated Brahman will make offerings to these shrines and follow many local and family usages, as well as adhere to a very abstract *advaita* philosophy. As one of them said, describing just this kind of situation, "I suppose I am a museum."

Some limits are recognized, however, to what can be assimilated by the orthodox tradition. The anti-Brahman, anti-Sanskrit, anti-Hindu movement now popular with some Tamil groups is certainly looked upon as an attack against the essentials of Hinduism. And the weakening of the caste system, particularly as a ritual structure, is viewed in the same light by the more orthodox. Svāmī Śaṅkarācārya, the most authoritative spokesman for Madrasi Smārtas, thinks that what is distinctive and essential in the nature of Hinduism is the caste system considered as a set of hereditary family disciplines. If these decline, he thinks Hinduism will not be very different from other religions, many of which have similar systems of ethics, theology, and philosophy, but lack the hereditary sociological foundation for them. The Brahman community, he believes, has become lax, for one reason and another, in the observance of these disciplines of diet, marriage, social intercourse, ritual observance, and sacred learning. He is inclined himself to appeal to devout non-Brahmans to preserve the essentials of Hinduism in these difficult times, since the Śāstras make less sever demands on them and they are able to conform.[24]

Even in the face of this uncertain future, the Svāmī and his Brahman followers remain detached and resilient. Their long run cosmic perspective gives them a hopeful serenity in the face of disturbing changes. Discussing the recent restrictive legislation against temples and *maṭhs*, one of these Brahmans said cheerfully: "Well, many of these temples and maths are only 700 or 800 years old. They have been destroyed before and revived. New values must be admitted. Life will grow, if old values are not destroyed. Life is one huge, infinite ocean in movement."

NOTES

[1] Robert Redfield and Milton B. Singer, "The Cultural Role of Cities," *Economic Development and Cultural Change,* III, No. 1 (1954) pp. 53-73; reprinted in *Man in India,* 36 (July-Sept. 1956), 161-94.

[2] A preliminary report of this study was published by the author under the title "The Cultural Pattern of Indian Civilization" in the *Far Eastern Quarterly,* XV, No. 1 (Nov. 1955) 23-36.

The six months period my wife and I spent in India during the autumn and winter of 1954-55 (and only about two and a half months in Madras city) was not sufficient for an intensive field study. It was a sufficient period, however, to establish the relevance of a method of analyzing cultural traditions for a study of urbanization and culture change, and also for exploring some of the problems involved in applying the method. In this sense the study was a "methodological field study" and not a descriptive sociological or ethnological study. If, in the summary of a part of this study which follows, there are many more positive statements than seem to be warranted by the evidence presented, this is not because I regard these statements as proved. On another occasion I shall publish what detailed evidence I do have. In the meantime, the apodictic formulations will serve as a greater stimulus to discussion and further research than statements properly qualified with a "perhaps" or "maybe."

I am grateful to Robert Redfield and the Cultural Studies Fund, directed by him at the University of Chicago, financed by the Ford Foundation, for making my trip to India possible; to V. Raghavan of Madras University for generously putting at my disposal his profound knowledge of Indian culture; and to David Mandelbaum for an opportunity to do further research at the Institute of East Asiatic Studies at the University of California. To the three of them and to M. N. Srinivas, McKim Marriott, and Hans van Buitenen I am also indebted for helpful comments on an earlier draft of this paper. Free time for travel and research was granted by the University of Chicago.

[3] Statistical data are available in *Census of India 1951,* III. Madras and Coorg, Part I, Report; Part II-B, Tables, by S. Venkateswaran, I.C.S. (Madras, 1953). George Kuriyan, "The Distribution of Population in the City of Madras," *Indian Geographical Journal,* XVI, No. 1 (1941), 58-70, and N. Subrahmanyam, "Regional Distribution and Relative Growth of the Cities of Tamil Nad," *Indian Geographical Journal,* pp. 71-83, contain useful material on growth and topography. H. D. Love, *Vestiges of Old Madras, 1640-1800,* 4 vols. (London, 1913), is very valuable for early maps and records.

[4] V. Raghavan, "Some Musicians and Their Patrons about 1800 A.D. in Madras City," *Journal of the Music Academy,* Madras, XVI (1945), 127-136.

[5] Robert Redfield, "The Social Organization of Tradition," *Far Eastern Quarterly,* XV (1955), 13-21; *Peasant Society and Culture* (Chicago, 1956).

[6] M. N. Srinivas, "A Note on Sanskritization and Westernization," *Far Eastern Quarterly,* XV, No. 4 (Aug., 1956).

[7] V. Raghavan, "Some Leading Ideas of Indian Thought," *The Vedanta Kesari,* (Madras, February 1955).

[8] V. Raghavan, "The Vedas and Bhakti," *The Vedanta Kesari,* Madras (December, 1955).

[9] Tirunavukkarasu Swami (more commonly referred to as Apparswami), in F. Kingsbury and G. E. Phillips, *Hymns of the Tamil Saivite Saints,* (Calcutta and London, 1921).

[10] The hymns of Tiru Jnana Sambandamurti Swami, seventh Century, A.D., Sundaramurti Swami, ninth Century A.D., and Tirunavukkarasu Swami (Apparswami).

[11] V. Raghavan, "Methods of Popular Religious Instruction in South India," in this volume.

[12] For an account of the "Bow Song" outside of Madras, see K. P. S. Hameed, "Bow Song: A Folk Art from South Travancore," *Tamil Culture,* V, (July 1956).

[13] *Commemoration Volume,* in honor of Srimati C. Saraswati Bai (Madras, 1939). See also Y. B. Damle, "A Note on Harikatha," *Bulletin of The Deccan College,* XVII (Poona).

[14] I am indebted to V. Raghavan for information about this Gandhi Kathā.

[15] *Bhārata nāṭyam* means dance based on the technique originally laid down by the sage Bharata, author of the oldest surviving text on the art, the *Nāṭya Sastra.* This name was introduced and came to be regularly used for the first time by V. Raghavan who played a significant part, on the learned and academic side, in the renaissance of the art. Before this the dance was called the art of *bhāratam* as well as *sadir* and *nautch. Bhāratam* or *bhārata Śāstram* is still in use and it was also independently known as *nāṭyam.*

[16] I have recently learned that K. V. R. has unfortunately passed away. Since the following account of his views and activities is largely based on personal conversation with him, I shall leave it in the historical present.

[17] Compare the account of her training by the dancer Shanta Rao in B. Zoete, *The Other Mind,* pp. 200-203.

[18] Moban Khobar, "Bharata Natya in Baroda," *Indian Institute of Fine Arts, Proceedings* (1954). The author is head of the Department of Dance, Maharaja Sayajira, University of Baroda.

[19] *The Śilapparikāram,* translated with notes by V. R. Ramachandra Dikshitar (Oxford, 1939), pp. 57-62.

[20] Presented at the Symposium held by the Bharatiya Kala Kendra, Delhi, 5-7 February, 1956.

[21] V. Raghavan, "Variety and Integration in the Pattern of Indian Culture," *Far Eastern Quarterly,* XV, No. 4 (Aug. 1956).

[22] Raghavan, "Popular and Classical Music," *Journal of the Music Academy,* XXVIII.

[23] Raghavan, "An Outline Literary History of Indian Music," *Journal of the Music Academy,* Madras, XXIII (1952), 64-74. For a musical analysis of the Sāma Veda in relation to classical Indian music, see Strangways, The *Music of Hindustan.*

[24] Personal interviews. See also *The Call of the Jagadgurn,* a discourse delivered by Śrī Śankarācārya during his stay in Madras in the autumn of 1957, compiled by P. Sankaranarayanan (Madras, 1958).

University of Chicago
Chicago, Illinois

RELIGION OF THE ANĀVILS OF SURAT

By T. B. Naik

THE Anāvils, a Brahman caste of Gujarat living compactly in the Surat District, Bombay State, have a total population of about sixty thousand persons. Many of them are agriculturists in villages, where a few have taken to shopkeeping, teaching, and other professions. Though most of them are village dwellers, some of them (about twenty percent) have migrated to towns like Ahmedabad, Bombay, Calcutta, Surat and also to such foreign countries as East Africa, Fiji, Madagascar, New Zealand, Rhodesia and the United Kingdom.

The Anāvils were the first settlers of South Gujarat, clearing the land for rice and garden cultivation. In Surat District, they possess the best land and the largest acreage holdings of land per family as compared with all other castes. The social economy of the area is thus organized around the Anāvil land owners, almost all other castes being in functional dependence on them.

The Anāvils are divided into two sections: *bhāṭhelās* 'spoilt,' the lower; and *desais*, the higher. The superiority of the *desais* is derived from larger land holdings, former political power, and "purity" of marriage. Though Brahmans, the whole body of Anāvils are laymen who never carry out priestly duties or accept alms from others. As accepting the priesthood is unthinkable for them and considered below their dignity, even in Surat they are all laymen. There are no Sanskrit *paṇḍits* among them.

An attempt is made here to study the changes that take place in the ritual and religious forms of the Anāvils living in Surat town. The town is the headquarters of the district of the same name in Bombay State, and lies on the southern bank of the river Tapi, fourteen miles distant from the sea by water and ten miles by land. Surat was once the chief commercial city of India; while it is still an important mercantile place today, the greater portion of its export and import trade has long since been transferred to Bombay. It is also a station on the Western Railway, 167 miles north of Bombay. The Anāvil population is six to seven thousand persons in the total town population of 223,182.

Two historical facts have much to do with the Anāvil culture in Surat. During the seventeenth and eighteenth centuries, Surat ranked as the chief export and import center of India. As late as 1797, its inhabitants were estimated at 800,000 persons and the town boundaries continued growing outside the city walls, encompassing nearby villages like Khalwa, Umarwadi, Bhatar and Angara, the Anāvil residents of which built their own streets on the periphery of the town. These streets are known as Sagram Paṛā, Vadi Phaliyā, Store Śerī (*paṛā*, *phaliyā* and *śerī* all being Gujarati words that mean a street). These Anāvils still own and cultivate their lands in the villages from their town homes.

Early travellers describe the city of Surat as populous and wealthy, with handsome houses and a busy trade. The fifty years between the establishment of the English and the Dutch and the accession of Aurangzeb were remarkable for increasing prosperity.

With the access of wealth the city greatly improved in appearance. During the busy winter months, lodgings could hardly be obtained, so great was the influx of people. Caravans passed between Surat and Golconda, Agra, Delhi and Lahore. Ships arrived from the Konkan, and from the Malabar coast, while outside merchants came from Arabia, the Persian Gulf, Ceylon, and Sumatra. It was called the Blessed Port by the Moguls who travelled to Mecca from there. In 1695, it is described as the "prime mart of India, all nations of the world trading there, no ship trading in the Indian ocean but what puts into Surat to buy, sell or load." After the death of Aurangzeb in 1707, however, the authority of the Delhi court gradually declined, and the Marathas extended their power up to the very walls of Surat. It was during these times that one Sagram Vashi, an Anāvil of the Desai division, was politically very powerful in the town and in the neighboring country. He settled that part of the town now called Sagram Paṛā. Other Anāvils, in turn, settled other parts known after their names as Hari Paṛā, Inder Paṛā, Mahidhar Paṛā, Rām Paṛā and Rudar Paṛā.

Sagram Vashi was a strict religious believer, and he brought and settled a number of Brahman families in his street. He also ordained that no Anāvil of the town should have his meal without bathing and repeating the name of God; and also that each Anāvil should contribute twenty pounds of clarified butter to be burned in earthen lamps before a town god. A story goes that a delinquent began to repeat the name of God while easing himself. When he was asked the reason, he said: "One has to obey his orders. What does place matter?"

The early Desais also built a temple dedicated to Hanumān, the monkey god, with a separate entrance and a place for standing before the deity for their woman folk. Even today this temple, called the Rokadia Hanumān *mandir*, is a very popular place of worship in the Sagram Paṛā area of Surat. The Anāvils thus have a strong orthodox religious history and background in the town.

The Anāvils in the rural areas are almost all followers of the Śiva sect of Hinduism, their chief god being Śankar, one of the forms of the *parabrahma* (the absolute), as they call him. He is variously known as Īśvar, Rudra, Sadāśiva, Mahādeva, Hara, and by a host of other names. His principal attribute is the power of destruction. His *liṅgam* is worshipped by pouring water over it or by hanging a water-dripping pot over it. In some places a *liṅgam* of clarified butter, a small architectural curio, is made and worshipped for a month ending on the Mahāśivarātrī day, on the last day of the Hindu month of Maha. Every Anāvil village has a temple dedicated to Mahādev, where lamps are lighted, water poured, flowers and gifts offered, worship sung, and obeisance made daily and also on special occasions. Śukleśwar or Sakaleśvar, the Śiva deity at Anāvil, thirty-eight miles southeast of Surat, is the mythological chief god of the Anāvils, whom they worship even today with great devotion. There are five local cultic capitals, their names all beginning with "K," devoted to the territorial forms of Śiva—Koteśvara, Kāntāreśvara, Kapileśvara, Kaṅkeśvara and Kunteśvara—where many devotees go every day or at least once a year when a fair is held there. Andhareśvara (near Amalsad, thirty miles south of Surat) and Gaṅgeśvara (three miles from Amalsad) are household words with the Anāvils of Navsari and Gandevi *taluḳas*, where, in many homes, boards declaring "Gaṅgeśvara is my only asylum" are prominently hung.

This means that generally one will not expect any Anāvil to follow any other Hindu sect than the Śaivite but, surprisingly enough, a few families in Surat town, especially the Mehta lineage, were and even now are devout believers in the Svāmī Nārāyaṇ, most modern of the Vaiṣṇava sects, the founder of which, Sahajānand Svāmī, was born in 1780 A.D. in Uttar Pradesh. At the age of twenty, he began to preach the tenets of his new faith. In 1804 he came to Ahmedabad and spread his creed. The tenets of the Svāmīnārāyaṇ faith are embodied in a Book of Precepts, Śikṣāpatrī, which is a treatise on practical ethics, and in the Vacanāmṛta (Nectar of Sayings), which forms an exhaustive treatise on all branches of religious philosophy. The Book of Precepts strictly prohibits the destruction of animal life, promiscuous intercourse with the other sex, use of animal food and of intoxicating liquors and drugs, suicide, theft and robbery, false accusations against a fellowman, blasphemy, partaking of food with low caste people, caste pollution, frequenting the company of atheists and heretics, and other practices which might counteract the effect of the founder's teachings.

The Mehta lineage has personal names ending in Prasād. Ordinarily an Anāvil personal name would never end in Prasād or Dās (the author of this paper, for example, would be called Thakor Lal or Thakor Bhai but never Thakor Prasad) but such first names as Thakor Prasad and Naran Prasad are common among the Mehtas of Surat. One of their ancestors was called Nīcabhāī Svāmīnārāyaṇ. They still give contributions, *lāgā*, and presents, *bheṭ*, (as all lay followers have to do), to their cultic seat at Vadtal (Kaira district).

In Surat town there has been, on the other hand, very little influence of another religious movement, the Ārya Samāj, while in some villages—Kachholi, Amalsad, Chikhli, etc.—it was quite strong. This sect was founded by Paṇḍit Dayanand Saraswati, born in 1824. He was attracted by the practice of Yoga or ascetic philosophy and studied it with great ardor. The Ārya Samāj was founded in Lahore in 1877. The sect furnished a haven for educated Hindus who could no longer credit Hindu mythology but who did not wish to break away entirely from their religion, which would mean cutting their caste and kinship ties. In theory, members of any religion were welcome to the sect. Intercaste marriages were allowed and lavish expenditure on weddings was discouraged. Probably the reasons why the *samāj* was acceptable to the Anāvils in villages are that, being set in a hypergamous social structure, some of them have always been "left out" for marriage and have turned to other castes for mates, and the fact that conspicuous ceremonial exhibitionism is a great but compulsory burden on an indebted agricultural economy. The sect also reduced the swollen body of Hindu ritual, and recommended worship of only a few gods without their theistic encumbrances. The *samāj* does not believe in any literal heaven and hell, and its members do not perform the *śrāddh* ceremony nor offer oblations to the dead. The principal aim of the *samāj* tends mainly to be the social improvement of its members and their fellows. It is against child marriage and encourages the remarriage of widows. It busies itself with female education, with orphanages and schools, dispensaries, public libraries, and philanthropic institutions. In Surat town these were founded by secular bodies, which is another reason, perhaps, why the influence of the Ārya Samāj was very slight there.

Still other observations point to the strengthening or reinforcing of the religious sphere in the lives of the Anāvils of Surat. The town has a very famous temple dedicated to the goddess Ambājī, who is a favorite and almost universally worshipped deity of Gujarat, together with two other goddesses, Kālikā and Aśapurī. This temple is visited by hundreds of devotees every day, and on the eighth of the bright half of the month of Āso (Āśvina), thousands of them go to the temple and offer coconuts, lamps, incense, flowers, and some presents. The Anāvils have also taken to this cultic center. In the villages, belief in and the worship of the goddess by Anāvils, though they existed, were more diffused. Here in Surat, their belief in the goddess has become concretized and centralized around the idol in the temple, and the ritual has been patterned on the general town mould.

Printed literature about the goddess is abundantly available in the town, and I have seen this literature passing into the Anāvil devotees' homes also. I have come across a few books with poems in praise of the goddess of very little poetic value but showing the immense faith of the composers, who were unsophisticated devotees. There are also *garba*[1] thus composed to eulogize the goddesses. Blank notebooks are sold, too, each page of which is full of small squares; in each square a god's name has to be written. There are books for fifty-one thousand names, 125 thousand names and so on, sold on a nonprofit basis by an organization called the *Rāmnām Bank* (the bank specializing in Rāma's name), c/o Paṇḍit Sevashram, Mani Nagar, Amedabad. This body also publishes a religio-literary magazine widely read by the Anāvils and others. These examples show how the printed word and the printing press have helped to strengthen the religious actions of the people.

Mention must also be made of another small but enlightening fact, namely that while the rural Anāvils (especially men) are not very observant about fasts—which are generally kept on all Saturdays and/or Mondays and/or Thursdays, on the eleventh and fifteenth days of a month, and also on special festivals like the eight bright day of Āso—and about the daily purificatory ablutions (so much so that a proverb alleges that the *bhāṭhelā* Anāvil bathes to eat his meal only) the Anāvils in Surat observe many fasts, and "not a single Anāvil can be found who has not fasted on the eighth of Āso, *mātā nī āṭhem*," said an informant.

Another change in the same direction is that some of the Anāvils' religious activities have become more "decorative" in the town. While in the villages there may or may not be a separate corner in the house for displaying and worshipping the gods, in Surat it has been observed that in many houses the gods are displayed in a small cupboard placed in an improvised corner, perhaps in the storeroom or under the staircase, the corner being well decorated and the gods worshipped and honored with flowers and lighted ghee lamps there every morning. In one of my informant's homes I saw images of Lāljī (brought from his original village), Gaṇpati and Ambājī (an heirloom). In the front rooms of the Surat Anāvil houses, one can see a large number of framed pictures of a variety of gods and goddesses. Although this is seen in the villages as well, the facilities for displaying the pictures being greater in Surat, they are found in larger numbers there. In one house I counted as many as fifty such pictures.

As for the cycle of festivals, the Holī bonfire is burnt on the full moon day of Fāgun (Phālguṇa, March-April) by all the Anāvils of a village at a particular place and they worship it with new fruits and coconuts. Newlyweds go around it. The moon is also worshipped before dinner, which generally consists among other things of *śikhaṇḍ* (a sweet made from curds). In Surat, though this bonfire is burnt with equal joy, there is no separate Holī-spot for all the Anāvils of the town. Inhabitants of a street, including Kāyasthas, Baniyās, Sutārs, etc., along with the Anāvils who live there, would have it burned in their street. The usual offerings and the special menu of the dinner are also found in Surat.

Aluṇāṃ is an unmarried girls' holiday in the villages, on which these girls worship the goddess Pārvatī, the consort of Śiva. They prepare a clay elephant, worship it every day, sing songs, dance, eat no salt, and on the final day immerse the elephant in a pond or a well. In Surat the festival is also observed in the same way. All the girls, mostly Anāvils of Sagrapaṛā, for example, have their elephant and go through the festival together. A couple of other caste girls accompany them.

Nāgpaṃchem, on the bright fifth of Śrāvaṇ, is also known as Khichdi Pañcam, and its presiding deity is the cobra, which is represented in villages by drawing a picture of it on the wall; the picture is then worshipped by the ladies of the house. *Khicḍī* (rice and *dāl* cooked together) is the menu prescribed for the day. In Surat also I have seen the cobra represented on the walls of many Anāvil houses. *Khicḍī* is eaten by the Surat Anāvils also on this day. On Śerī Sātem, the bright seventh of Śrāvaṇ, Śītalā, the goddess of smallpox, is worshipped. The hearth is also worshipped and cold food eaten on this day in the villages. The Surat Anāvils also observe the day with the same details. On the bright ninth of the same month, called Norī Nem, the rural Anāvils worship the mongoose and eat *juwār* bread and sprouted pulses. In Surat also the festival is celebrated in the same way. The full moon day of Śrāvaṇ is important for the Anāvils because on this day they change their old sacred threads for new ones and tie on their wrists the *rakhdī*, the wrist band of variegated colors and designs (supposed to be a protection against evil). In the villages as well as in Surat, this is an individual affair, each one changing the thread in his house, the officiant being the family priest. Unlike Bombay, where there are castewise collective thread changing ceremonies, Surat on this day follows the rural practice, probably because of the availability of the priests who have time enough to go around to their *yajamāns* 'clients.'

A word on the protective wrist bands will not be out of place here. In Surat there are artisans who make these of innumerable designs, permuting the colored threads and materials. These are bought by the Anāvils as well as by others, and sent by sisters—real, classificatory and pseudo—to brothers and their children. The wives of brothers also send them to their husbands' sisters and their children. The material culture aspect of this festival shows a distinct urban influence which soon spreads to the rural areas.

In the first nine days of Āso, the last Hindu month, the mother goddesses are worshipped and *garba* songs are sung in their praise every night in the rural areas, by men as well as women. In Surat it is only women who sing these songs (in company with other caste women) and the men just look on. In Surat there are competitive and exhibition *garba* singing fests which are not found in the rural areas. As in the case of religious literature sold at temples and book stalls (mentioned above), *garbāvalis*, collections of *garba* songs, are also sold at various places and these are readily bought by women. Many Gujarati poets also write new style poems which can be sung as *garba*, and because of the exhibition value and the competitive aspects, these are at once taken up by the urban women. These compositions come to the rural areas also, but comparatively late. The radio stations of Bombay (in its Gujarati programs), Rajkot, Ahmedabad, and Baroda relay *garba* sung by their station artists or by expert parties. This has two effects: first, these new-style *garbas* are in no time picked up by the listeners and sung in their own programs, and second, some men and women, instead of going to see the *garba* in the town, listen to them on the radio.

The full moon day of the same month is called Pauva Pūṇem or Manek Thari

Pūṇem; on this day the moon is offered *pūjā*, and puffed rice with milk is eaten. The next day is *candanī padvo*, the moon-lit first, which is not celebrated by the rural Anāvils; in Surat, however, following the general town behavior, the Anāvils go on late-night picnics and eat sweets and snacks in the moonlight.

Dīvālī, the last day of the month of Āso, which also marks the end of the year, is devoted to the worship of lights, both in the rural and urban areas. Lamps fed with sweet oil and clarified butter are lighted on this and the preceding two days. Festival food is eaten on all these days. Ornamental designs, *śanthia*,[2] are drawn by ladies in front of the house. In villages these designs are simple; but in the urban Anāvil houses, the *śanthias* are in various figures, more complicated, better colored, and more ornate. There are *śanthia* competitions also, which help the development of this art towards more refinement and complexity of design. Innumerable guide books now appear every year which also bring a kind of sophistication to this folk art.

On the first day of the new year, the rural Anāvils worship Lakṣmi and set up a miniature dung hill, Govardhan.[3] In Surat, the Anāvils who have been settled in the town for less than a hundred years, especially for service, etc., do not set up this dung hill.

The agriculturist Anāvils who have lived on the periphery of the town for the last two or three centuries still practice the old Anāvil agricultural festivals. On the third day of the bright half of Vaiśākh, which is the farmer's New Year Day, they mark their bullocks' foreheads with *kaṃkuṃ* (a red powder) and worship their ploughs. On the bright eleventh of Posh, they profusely give grass and dried *javār* stalks to all cattle that pass through their street, and, as the rural Anāvils do, they bury small earthen pots filled with pounded rice in their fields on the second day of the first month.

The Anāvils in villages observe a festival called Divāso on the last day of Ākhāḍ (Āṣāḍha, June-July). In the main, this is the festival of the Dublās, a tribe which has worked for centuries as hereditary field servants with the Anāvils, who are a substantial and dominant agricultural caste of the district. The Anāvils cook festival food on this day, which is called the harbinger of a hundred festivals, as all the important festivals begin from that day. They also give food to their Dublā servants. The agriculturist Anāvils in Surat observe the festival with the same earnestness and details as found in the villages, but others in the town do not.

Among religious books usually read by the Anāvils, mention must be made of *Satyanārāyaṇ nī Kathā* 'The Story of God in the Form of Truth,' which is read as a matter of ritual both in the villages and in Surat. No difference exists in this between the town and the village practice. An Anāvil family takes a vow to have the story read if some wish of theirs—a boy passing an examination, a girl recovering from an illness, a marriage function ending happily, or a family member who has gone abroad returning home after a long time—is fulfilled. The family priest, or, in Surat, the caste priest, *nāt gor*, is called, and through him all the Anāvils are invited. In Surat others may also come. The priest then sets up a small wooden stool, *bājat*, on which is laid a white cloth, rice, and in its midst a copper vessel, over which hangs a flower decked thread. To the four corners of the stool are tied banana and sugar cane leaves. Gods Gaṇpati and Viṣṇu are set there; incense is burnt and a ghee lamp is lighted there. The headman of the family, washed and dressed in a silken cloth, sits on a wooden plank before the stool and the invitees sit around him. Then the priest leader gets the headman to worship the water containers, god Gaṇpati with his wives Ṛddhi and Siddhi, the mother Earth, and the lamp, and then he repeats the thousand names of Viṣṇu, with each name the *yajamān* offering flowers and *tulsī* to god Viṣṇu, placed in a plate kept on the water vessel. The *Satyanārāyaṇ nī Kathā* is then read; at the end of each one of its five chapters, the reader asks the spectators to call: "*Satyanārāyaṇ dev kī je*" 'Victory be to God Satya Nārāyaṇ,' which they all do with one voice. Ultimately there is the singing of a prayer in unison; this is followed by the distribution of some *prasād* (sweets, fruits, etc.). The story mentions mythological events showing the importance of the *Satyanārāyan nī Kathā* and the potency of Truth.

As far as the religious functionaries of the Surat Anāvils are concerned, two important developments have taken place. The Surat Anāvils, especially those of Gopīpaṛā and Sagram Paṛā, which are their strongholds (to whatever village they originally belonged), formed themselves into a body called *panc*, the membership being open to all the caste men who paid an entrance fee of one rupee (this was called *ekdo nodhavu*, crediting one's one). This *panc* had its own cooking and serving utensil sets and mattresses, which were given to members whenever they needed them for a marriage or an initiation ceremony. The *panc* could outcaste any of its members who did not obey its rules. The *panc* had a priest who was called *nāt gor*, whose main duty was to carry invitations to Anāvil invitees to a function. He also goes around on the first day of Śrāvaṇ to his Anāvil *yajamāns* and takes a betel nut from each of the devotees desiring him to do *saṃkalpa* (worshipping the God and repeating his name for all the thirty days of the month, this being considered very pious) and returns the nuts to them at the end of the month after completing his mission. This priest gets from his *yajamāns* uncooked food on all the festivals and on both the elevenths of the month of Śrāvaṇ.

On the other hand, some of the Anāvils also have their family priests, who officiate at almost everything religious in their homes. Some of the families have taken up the priests of their kinfolk who formerly lived in Surat. One of my informants told me that he had the priest who formerly worked with his father's sister's family, who do not now live in Surat.

In Surat quite substantial donations have been given by a few Anāvils; this is supposed to be meritorious, giving in charity being considered very religious and bestowing other worldly benefits. One of the Anāvils had the Anāvil Vāḍī constructed. A *Vāḍī*, though the word literally means a garden, is a community center where caste members (and others also by paying a fee) can celebrate their socio-ritual functions, enough space and plenty of the requisites being supplied there as part of the activities of the Vāḍī. (Vāḍīs of various castes are found in urban areas but not in villages.) A rural Anāvil who wants to curtail marriage expenses may celebrate the function in the Anāvil Vāḍī, inviting only a few persons, which he cannot do in his village.

Some Anāvils have donated scholarships to the local high and middle schools. One Anāvil "charity" (the institutions thus created are known as "charities") includes the construction of a room for members of the bar and provision of a library in the district judge's office. One donated a gymnasium building for a women's college in Surat; and one has had a Prārthnā Mandir (Hall of Prayer) constructed in the hostel formerly meant for Anāvil students only. This hostel itself has various halls constructed from money given in *dān* 'gift, charity' by many Anāvils.

In other religious spheres, the Anāvils of Surat seem to have taken part, not as leaders but cooperatively in the middle ranks. There is an Āśram called Śrī Bhadra

Āśram, whose main object is to hold prayer meetings, in which three or four Anāvils take quite an active interest. Some Anāvils also go to hear the discourses of sectarian leaders in the local Vaiṣṇava temples. Although they do not have their own *bhajan maṇḍals*, the Anāvils of Nanavat and Sagram Paṛā areas join prayer singing parties composed of several castes. Similarly they also do not have any dramatic club association of their own, though a few do take part in amateur performances staged by companies not organized along caste lines.

NOTES

[1] *Garba* are a form of folksong sung in Gujarat during the first Nine Nights in the bright half of the month of Āso. They are generally about one or the other of the goddesses (Ambā, Bahucarā, Kālikā, and Khodiyar).

[2] *Śanthias* are folk drawings done by hand. The pattern is easily made by first filling a required sized rectangle (in points, the distance between two consecutive points being about an inch) with an equal number of points length and breadthwise, and then connecting these points to form the designs—flowers, butterflies, swastikas. All these points and designs are drawn with rice flour or stone powder dropped with the help of the thumb and the index finger. Necessary dry powder colors are also then filled in.

[3] Śrī Kṛṣṇa, one of the ten incarnations of God, saved the village of Gokul from incessant rains under a hill named Govardhan which he held high supporting it on his little finger. This miniature is perhaps in the memory of that feat, the Anāvils say.

Tribal Research Institute
Chhindwara, M. P., India

SOME ASPECTS OF CASTE IN BENGAL[1]

By Nirmal Kumar Bose

CASTE has always been of interest to students of Indian history and civilization. While the interest was formerly more in the direction of origin, the emphasis has apparently shifted in modern times to a study of its contemporary functions. In the Presidential Address to the Section on Anthropology and Archaeology of the Indian Science Congress in 1957, M. N. Srinivas showed how caste has not only not been weakened by forces of modernization in India, but has, on the contrary, been fortified, so that it plays a significant role even in the determination of the character of democratic institutions in the country.[2]

Whether one should limit one's field of observation to one particular field or allow comparisons to be made in other fields also, is a question which can be legitimately raised in this connection. For, it is well known that caste derives its strength not merely from the power structure of society, but also from its association with a particular form of organization in the economic as well as the religious life of the country. Occupations are ranked into high and low, and so are various forms of religious beliefs and practices. And thus various shades of philosophy and ways of life have been allowed to coexist in apparent avoidance of conflict with one another. The question may legitimately be raised as to what is happening in the other aspects of caste's many sided organization.

With this end in view, it may be profitable for us to examine the case of a state like Bengal where the ancient ways of life have been subjected to more profound alteration than in many other parts of India. The causes which have led to this special development have been both accidental and intentional. British commerce found a favorable roosting place in Bengal at the end of the seventeenth century, while about a century or more afterwards, awakened and indigenous Indian leadership recognized the imperative necessity of "modernization"; as a result, wave after wave of social reform arose and brought about significant changes in the cultural as well as the social life of the province. If the forces of change have affected Bengal's life in one particular manner, or have also set up contrary forces of diminishing strength in their train, it may not be unreasonable to expect that similar forces may bring about comparable results in other linguistic or cultural provinces of India, if the forces happen to be similar to those encountered in the case chosen for our present study.

Birbhum is a district in West Bengal which has retained its predominantly rural character. In the heart of this rice growing country lies the village of Jajigram with a population of 2160 individuals. The name of the village is derived from *yājana*, *yajña*, Vedic 'fire sacrifice,' and *grām*, 'village'; and the fact that the place has a large Brahman population is probably the result of its ancient historical origin when a colony of Brahmans took up residence in this place. There are, altogether, twenty-eight castes in residence here, and the following table presents the number, traditional occupation, as well as actual occupation followed by each of these castes. It may be pointed out that the census presented below was the result of a local social worker's survey undertaken in the year 1947.[3]

GROUP A: CASTES FROM WHOM WATER IS NOT ACCEPTED BY BRAHMANS

Name	No. of Families	Individuals	Traditional Occupation	Actual Occupation
Muci	65	325	Tanning, shoemaking	Landless labor
Bhuĩmāli	40	150	Sweeping, cleaning	T.O.;[4] landless labor; 2 peasant proprietors
Phulmāli	7	25	Gardening, supplying flowers for religious offering	Landless labor
Rājbamśi	10	35	Boatmen and agricultural labor	Landless labor
Bhaṛ	12	35	Mfg. of chapped rice, labor	T.O.
Māl	80	400	Agricultural labor	T.O.
Konāi	15	350	do.	T.O.
Bāuri	1	5	do.	T.O.
Ḍom	5	20	Working in bamboo (basket weaving)	T.O.
Koṛā Sāntāl	25	65	Digging earth, labor	T.O.
Jele	11	55	Fishing	T.O., 2 peasant proprietors
Dhobā	2	10	Washing clothes	T.O.

GROUP B: CASTES FROM WHOM WATER IS ACCEPTED BY BRAHMANS

Name	No. of Families	Individuals	Traditional Occupation	Actual Occupation
Goālā	8	25	Milk trade and cow-keeping	T.O. and farming
Sadgop	5	10	Farming	Landless labor
Kumor	4	10	Mfg. Pottery	T.O.
Kāmār	6	20	Blacksmithery	T.O.
Chutār	1	5	Carpentry	T.O.
Nāpit	7	50	Shaving and hair-cutting	T.O.
Bene	2	5	Trading in spices	Trade and farming
Bārai	40	200	Cultivation of betel vine	T.O.; 2 grocers, 3 unskilled physicians
Bhāt	2	10	?	Clerical jobs
Kāyastha	28	120	Clerical work	Farming, clerical job, 2 physicians, some unemployed

GROUP C: HIGH CASTES

Name	No. of Families	Individuals	Traditional Occupation	Actual Occupation
Rājpūt	4	15	Soldiers	Landless labor
Chatri	6	15	Soldiers	Farming, clerical work
Brahman	30	150	Priestcraft, teaching, etc.	Farming, clerical job, 1 physician, some unemployed
Grahācārya (Brahman)	1	5	Astrology	T.O.
Vaidya	12	50	Physician	Farming, physicians, clerical job, also unemployed
Bairāgī (Vaiṣṇava mendicant)	5	15	Religious mendicancy	T.O., 1 in farming

It is observed in the table that sixty-eight percent of the population belongs to the section from whom water is found unacceptable by "upper" castes like Brahman or Vaidya. Leather workers have mostly lost their hereditary occupation, because hides and skins have, for many years past, formed an important collection from the villages of India for purposes of export. They have gradually drifted towards agriculture, and form a fair proportion of the landless labor corps of the village. Bamboo workers, i.e., basket-weavers, and fishermen alone have been able to retain their own profession; among the last, two have become peasants owning land.

Among the "clean Śūdras," i.e., those farming and artisan castes from whom water is acceptable to Brahmans, the change from traditional occupation has been less marked in character. These Śūdras constitute altogether 22.6 percent of the total population. We find that milkmen have also taken to agriculture, while one member of the blacksmith caste has joined clerical service. The comparatively more prosperous cultivators of betel vine, namely Bārai, are, by and large, farmers; while two of them trade in grocery, three are physicians, and some are unemployed. The Kāyasthas form, in this group, an educated and professional class; while there is also some dependence among them upon cultivation through hired laborers. The Brahman (including Grahācārya, astrologer) and Vaidya, who claim equal status with the Brahman in society, are both dependent on farming through hired laborers, or earn their livelihood through professions like clerical service, teaching etc., or are unemployed. They altogether constitute about nine percent of the total.

The inhabitants of the village, therefore, depend largely on agriculture, even though the more favored ones educationally may supplement their income through one or other of the higher professions.

Although the village has succeeded in retaining its predominantly rural character, yet there has taken place a considerable alteration in the economic relationship which binds together its permanent and floating population. At one time, part of the payment due for the annual services of artisans like carpenters, potters, etc. used to be in terms of a share of the annual harvest, while services like those of barbers or washermen were recompensed by the grant of small areas of service land. These have now been largely replaced in the village by cash payments. One of the reasons is that the village offers today an open market for artisans from other villages, just as it does, during the harvest season, to a large number of Santal laborers from the neighboring district of Santal Parganās.

It is also significant that although many of the castes are in the same profession, yet there is no intermarriage between them, whether they belong to the landless or the land owning section of the population. Ranking has remained the same; except for the fact that due to reform movements in recent times, the untouchables have straightened their back, and adult franchise has also made it imperative upon all castes to court the favor of the latter for purposes of patronage during elections.

In Bengal, there have always been several kinds of villages. Some have been predominantly agricultural, with or without a fair proportion of artisan and upper castes, while others have owed their origin to trade or industry, or been centers of administration or learning. A village like Jhalakathi in East Bengal is essentially a center of trade and commerce. In West Bengal, too, villages like Katwa, lying at the junction of two rivers, or like Ilambazar, which was once a river port from which roads radiated into the surrounding country, have been villages of the same character. In addition, they have sometimes attracted industries to their neighborhood. Weavers, in particular, find such market villages suitable for buying yarn and also for disposing of their manufactures to wholesale dealers. There have been, besides villages of the above kind, also centers of religious pilgrimage, or seats of Sanskrit learning, or perhaps a place which served as the administrative headquarters of some local dignitary, which in consequence succeeded in attracting people of various interests round the neighborhood.

Santipur is a town in West Bengal which bears many of these characteristics. Its description, as presented below, is based entirely on the research conducted by Ilika Chatterjee, a student of the Geography Department of the University of Calcutta in 1956-57.

The town has been an important center of learning and a focal point of Vaiṣṇava revival since the late fifteenth century. It was also the headquarters of Muslim conquerors in Bengal at an earlier date, when perhaps two small forts were established on its eastern and western flanks. Textile weaving, and also the indigo industry, were so important at one time that the East India Company established one of their trading posts at this point; while another was founded at Kalna on the other side of the river Ganges. It is interesting that as the weavers, Tānti, of Santipur grew in prosperity, some of them built temples at great expense in the quarter of the town where they principally resided.

As the town thus progressively added one function to another, it also increased proportionately in size. Small villages or *mauzas* which lay in the neighborhood became so overgrown that eventually several of them became fused to give rise to the municipal town which bears its present name. Yet, in spite of this fusion, the original preponderance of various castes in different localities has remained a distinct feature of the municipal town. Although a very strict delimitation is not possible, many areas bear distinctive caste names, and are inhabited by a preponderance of one particular caste, except where poverty or migration for better prospects elsewhere has altered the character of the population.

The eastern and western flanks of the town, near its southern border bounded by the river, are predominantly inhabited by Mohammedans. Perhaps two forts were situated here at one time, for they have given the names Sutragaṛ 'fort in the beginning' and Sārāgaṛ 'fort at the end' to the respective localities. The southern low-lying land, which actually forms a part of the river bed, is inhabited by the Kurmi, a caste of sturdy cultivators who originally migrated from Bihar and until recently still retained some of their distinctive social customs. At one point in the west, contiguous to the area inhabited by the Mohammedans, there is a small settlement of Rājpūts and also of Pathāns, the latter being, naturally, Muslim by religion. The last two claim to have arrived here in company with the Muslim conqueror, Bakhtiar Khalji. Both these groups have likewise preserved their separateness in ways of life from the neighboring people.

Within the most congested part of the town, there are several localities bearing the names of the commercial Tili, weaving Tānti, and priestly Brahman castes. There is also a locality which bears the name of the Kāṃsāri, or brass and bell-metal working artisan caste. The fishing Jele, pottery making Kumor, banking Subarṇabaṇik, and the Goālā who deal in milk, are concentrated in some areas, although they have not succeeded, perhaps because of paucity of numbers, in adding their names to particular localities.

A map indicating the distribution of occupations can be superimposed on the previous one relating to caste, and then a series of interesting facts begins to reveal itself. The Brahman locality shows a predominance of occupations connected with clerical jobs, education, law, medicine, etc. Pathāns and Rājpūts have been converted into small traders or laborers; while Muslims residing in the neighborhood of the forts which have disappeared are, by and large, laborers or drivers of bullock carts and horse drawn carriages. Potters have retained their profession to a large extent, while the brass and bell-metal working Kāṃsāri have lost it considerably. This might be due to the increasing use of aluminum ware made by machine, which is cheaper than brass or bell-metal ware. The Moirā, sweet meat and sugar manufacturers, and many of the Goālā, milkmen, have taken to weaving. Coarse, country made sugar is no longer as popular as cheap cane sugar made in factories. Much of the *guṛ* which was refined in Santipur used to be imported from districts which are now in East Pakistan. That supply has been virtually cut off; and may account for part of the change in the occupation of the Moirā. The Goālā have, on the other hand, been affected by the importation of powdered milk from abroad. The Moirā of Santipur supply this type of dried milk to the Goālā, who take it home and bring it back in the form of curds used in the preparation of sweet meats, so that the Goālā earns no more than by mere processing. He has, like many of the Moirā, taken to weaving, as that industry still retains a high standard of reputation in the rest of Bengal. It is noteworthy that Brahmans have completely avoided the profession of weaving, but have shifted from their former Sanskrit learning and priestcraft to professions which have arisen in the wake of English education.

One might enter into a statistical analysis of the number of persons within each caste who have shifted from their hereditary, traditional occupation, and thus try to discover if there are any avoidances or preferences in the choice of new occupations evinced by castes occupying varying ranks. That would be unnecessary for our present purpose, which is no more than to show that even when people do not leave their ancient homes, and retain territorial or geographical separateness to an appreciable extent, changes in occupation may be proportionately more extensive than the physical movements involved. In the case of Santipur, such changes have not been due to the growth of industries; but due to an alteration in the character of occupations arising from small economic or administrative and political changes, so that the latter have not been attended by wide-spread demographic alterations.

Perhaps this may account for the fact that, as the old society with its established code of conduct thus remained intact, the rules of caste also largely persisted. Although the Moirā, Goālā, and some others have adopted the same profession as that of the Tānti (weaver), yet each of these castes continues to remain as strictly endogamous as before. There are cooperative societies which bring all weavers living in one neighborhood under the fold of one marketing organization; yet identity of interest in trade has not succeeded in breaking through the barriers of caste endogamy.

A study of occupational changes along somewhat different lines was undertaken by Priti Mitra, a research student in the Department of Anthropology, Calcutta University in 1941-43. She carefully compared the number of those in West Bengal who still retained their traditional occupation in different census years and those who had forsaken it for other profitable occupations. Some of the results of her inquiry were published by the present author in 1949,[5] and a part of this is presented below. The census reports of 1901, 1911, 1921 and 1931 yielded necessary figures in regard to fourteen castes only, while in the case of others, figures were available in some censuses, but not in all. Figures after 1931 become very unreliable as caste was not often recorded by informants, and this condition was aggravated in the censuses of 1941 and 1951.

KUMOR: MFG. OF POTTERY

	1901	1911	1921	1931
Population	195,533	278,206	284,514	289,654
Earning members		92,659	75,326	53,506
Percentage of literates	6.56	8.04	10.18	9.66
Percentage in:				
traditional occupation	75.16	73.80	61.69	58.87
agriculture	16.60	13.40	19.76	19.89
industries		78.14	64.50	65.66
higher professions		0.857	1.288	4.257

KĀMĀR: BLACKSMITHERY

	1901	1911	1921	1931
Population	176,873	238,595	256,853	256,526
Earning members		86,902	89,633	81,710
Percentage of literates	10.34	14.98	17.88	14.91
Percentage in:				
traditional occupation	47.35	57.48	34.11	43.76
agriculture		19.30	26.02	21.81
industries		67.53	52.04	56.11
higher professions		1.745	1.290	5.321

CAMĀR AND MUCI: LEATHER WORKING

	1901	1911	1921	1931
Population	96,391 (only Camār)	533,131	564,879	564,682
Earning members		238,058	244,145	217,366
Percentage of literates	3.19	2.97	3.11	4.52
Percentage in:				
traditional occupation	23.26	33.77	23.94	24.59
agriculture	33.47	32.33	28.60	32.88
industries		37.06	42.84	43.93
higher professions		0.254	0.449	1.071

BĀGDI OR BYAGRA KṢATRIYA: AGRICULTURE AND FISHING

	1901	1911	1921	1931
Population	703,147	847,228	886,821	987,315
Earning members		392,472	371,477	366,455
Percentage of literacy	1.57	1.91	2.13	1.92
Percentage in:				
traditional occupation	70.13	71.28	42.28(?)	69.79
agriculture		73.41	68.66	81.74
industries		10.05	9.23	5.03
higher professions		0.247	0.355	1.171

GOĀLĀ: COW KEEPING AND MILK TRADE

	1901	1911	1921	1931
Population	494,699	583,790	582,597	599,281
Earning members		251,829	239,429	217,438
Percentage of literacy	6.33	7.68	10.57	10.17
Percentage in:				
traditional occupation	41.45	31.39	21.30	24.77
agriculture		41.00	42.21	37.49
industries		6.47	7.43	7.28
higher professions		1.650	1.873	5.421

VAIDYA: MEDICINE

	1901	1911	1921	1931
Population	31,357	88,298	102,870	110,739
Earning members		21,133	24,114	26,292
Percentage of literacy	45.62	53.21	57.52	51.79
Percentage in:				
traditional occupation	36.10	20.11	15.02	18.80
agriculture		7.163	12.418	6.04
industries		2.13	1.22	1.85
higher professions		54.663	46.811	49.40

BRAHMAN: PRIESTCRAFT, TEACHING ETC.

	1901	1911	1921	1931
Population	1,019,348	1,191,867	1,314,430	1,456,180
Earning members		400,064	425,173	417,157
Percentage of literacy	35.84	39.85	43.15	37.28
Percentage in:				
traditional occupation	33.54	21.79	14.57	16.57
agriculture		19.39	22.63	15.38
industries		2.92	3.57	4.50
higher professions		43.71	34.96	30.76

A comparison of the tables will indicate that, on the whole, changes have taken place in two directions among various castes. Artisan castes like Kumor (potter), Kāmār (blacksmith), or Camār-Muci (tanner and leather worker) have drifted either towards agricultural labor, or skilled labor in industries other than their traditional one. The percentage of literacy among them has tended to remain low, at a lower level than the average for all castes in Bengal. Castes like the Byagra Kṣatriya (formerly recorded as Bāgdi), whose traditional occupation was labor in the fields, have retained it to an appreciable extent; and their percentage of literacy has also tended to remain at a considerably low level, lower than that of the average for artisan castes, for example. In the case of castes like Brahman or Vaidya, the departure from traditional occupation has been very high indeed; while there has been a corresponding concentration, not in agriculture or industries, but in "higher professions," like medicine, law, office work of various kinds, or landowning or land management. Percentages of literacy are naturally higher in comparison with the country's average.

Furthermore, it is of interest to note that figures for employment in traditional occupations have been steadily reduced in the case of those castes referred to in the last portion of the above paragraph. Thus, the decline has been as follows:

Percentage of earning members engaged in traditional occupations	1901	1911	1921	1931
Brahman	33.54	21.79	14.57	16.57
Vaidya	36.10	20.11	15.02	18.80

It is interesting that here, too, castes have remained endogamous; or, in other words, sameness of occupation, whether in the learned professions or agriculture, has not tended in any way to break down the barriers of endogamy. Some investigation along this line has recently been conducted among two "upper" and two "lower" castes in West Bengal under the direction of Iravati Karve, which tends to show that rules of marriage have remained practically unaltered in the course of at least three generations. One will naturally await with interest the publication of the results of this very significant piece of investigation.

There is thus some amount of evidence to indicate that changes in occupation have been widespread in the state of West Bengal, but this has not been attended by an alteration of the rules of endogamy to any appreciable extent. Should that be taken to mean that there has been no change in the internal affairs of caste at all?

For this purpose, let us turn once more to the work of Priti Mitra referred to above. After an analysis of census figures, Mitra proceeded to investigate some of the caste organizations separately. It appears that from about the beginning of the present century, when castes and their ranks began to be recorded in census returns, many organizations along modern lines have also been established in India to take charge of a few of the interests associated with caste. Srinivas noted in his presidential address referred to above that some of these go back to about the middle of the last century; but, by and large, many were established, or became particularly active, from the census of 1901 onwards.

At least, this has been so in the case of West Bengal, where associations were formed at or near the latter event by castes like the Yogī, Sadgop, Gandhabaṇik, Subarṇabaṇik, Namaḥśūdra, Kāyastha, Vaidya or Brahman. These organizations appear to possess very few functions in the ordinary life of their members. But when there is some question of rank involved, popular enthusiasm can be raised high, and even made to serve some purposes of internal social reform. In the case of castes enjoying a high rank, like the Brahman, Vaidya, or Kāyastha, the specific organizations do not ever seem to have reached any high point of activity.

The organizations of the Yogī, a "clean" caste of weavers, and of the Namaḥśūdras, who are considered very low in the social scale, and whose traditional occupation happens to be agriculture and the plying of boats, can be taken up for consideration, on the basis of Priti Mitra's work.[6]

An author named Radhagovinda Nath presented a newly published book entitled *Baṅgīyā Yogī Jāti* 'The Yogi Caste of Bengal' to the Census Commissioner before the census of 1911. In the journal founded by the caste organization, entitled *Yogī Sakhā* 'Friend of the Yogi,' some of the articles published were as follows: "[Our] Historical Past," "The Historical Position of the Yogī Caste," "Ray of Light," "Who Are We?", and "Downfall and its Prevention."

During the census of 1921, a claim was made by members of the priestly section of the Yogī that they should be enumerated as Brahmans. It should be noted that the Yogīs had priests belonging to their own caste. In 1931, the entire Yogī caste claimed the status of Brahmanhood. At an annual conference, a resolution was adopted that the Yogī should wear the sacred thread characteristic of Brahmans in Bengal. Articles on the subject were published in the *Yogī Sakhā* of 1318, 1320, 1321, 1328 B.S., corresponding to 1911 onwards. These bore titles like "The Ritual of Wearing the Sacred Thread," "Popularity of the Sacred Thread," etc. It was also suggested in one of these articles that the priestly section of the caste should educate themselves in the proper manner, so that they could be truly worthy of their profession.

It is significant that some articles published in the same journal advocated the liquidation of endogamous subdivisions within the caste. Child marriage was condemned, and articles were published in order to promote women's interests; for, in the matter of literacy, women lagged far behind men belonging to the caste. Such articles bore titles like the following: "Our Duty Towards Women," "Female Education," "An Appeal to Our Sisters," "Will Not Women Grow Up?" and "Women's Problems." The caste seems to have been divided in its mind on the question of the marriage of widows; a few widow remarriages were performed in spite of the opposition of the older, more conservative section.

The question of occupation was also important. The Yogī are, by tradition, weavers; and the handloom industry has received fitful encouragement in Bengal, as a result of the boycott of British piecegoods since the Swadeshi movement of 1905. The caste has consequently not suffered very much from lack of employment. Yet questions like the following were raised and discussed in the *Yogī Sakhā* of 1321 B.S. (1914 A.D.). Can Yogīs who have worn the sacred thread employ themselves in agriculture? The answer was yes. It was also recommended that the Yogī should adopt any industry which was likely to yield profit.

In contrast to the Yogī, who tried no more than to gain recognition as equal to Brahmans, and this without much bitterness, or to effect certain internal reforms, the organization of the Namaḥśūdra appears to be charged with a more urgent demand for recognition to a socially elevated rank. This populous and hard working agricultural caste has suffered from a social stigma whose origin is difficult to ascertain; and it is justifiable, therefore, that there should be a considerable element of bitterness displayed by the educated members of the caste against the "upper" castes in general.

This caste has its own organizations which publish journals like the *Patākā* 'Banner' or the *Namaḥśūdra Suhṛd* 'Friend of the Namaḥśūdra.' In an article published in 1908, a writer named Raicharan Biswas stated: "We are Brahmins by caste. Prompted by envy or anger, people may dislike us; but if one observes our clean Brahmanical way of life as practiced generation after generation, they will have to admit unanimously that the Namashudra caste is descended from the ancient sages and *Rishis*, i.e., from pure Brahmins. Secondly, our occupation is the *ārya* or noble one of agriculture; and this has always been considered a very lofty profession indeed." A book was also published in order to substantiate the claim thus made. It was entitled *Jātitattva O Namahsya Kuladarpaṇa* 'The History of Caste and a Mirror of the Lineage of the Namahsyas.'

Widow remarriage was in vogue among the Namaḥśūdra community. But as the claim to recognition of Brahmanhood became more insistent, widow remarriage was correspondingly discouraged.

In 1916, an editorial was published in the *Patākā*, in which it was stated:

It has been due to education received through the favours of the British government that we have now realized what we are, and how great is our strength. A caste with a population of 25 lacs cannot remain asleep for ever. We had been put to sleep by the blind Hindu kings who ruled over Hindu society. Today we have woken up from that slumber through the grace of the mighty British, who believe in the equality of men and not in caste. Laws framed by narrow Brahmins prevented us from reaching within the boundaries of the temple of learning. But why should we worry any longer? The British government itself has now come to the aid of the uneducated; they have ever been the help of the poor, and the hope of the downtrodden castes.

The gazetteer of the Dacca district records that, by and large, the Namaḥśūdra caste abstained from participation in the anti-partition agitation of Bengal in 1905. Nagarbashi Majumdar and Raghunath Sarkar, two prominent Namaḥśūdra citizens of Vikrampur in Dacca, fervently expressed their loyalty to the Lieutenant Governor of Bengal and claimed special favors from the government in matters affecting education and employment. In 1907, when the Swadeshi movement was at its height, a deputation of representative Namaḥśūdra citizens waited upon the Lieutenant Governor and prayed for the perpetuation of British rule.

The pattern of production associated with caste seems to have been so successful at one time that some Muslims of rural India followed the rule of ranking of occupations, and even of endogamy, in clear contravention of the dictates of Islam. As late as 1927 A.D., Mohammed Yaqub Ali, Headmaster of Rajarampur High School, published a book in Bengali entitled *Mushalmāner Jātibhed* 'Caste Among the Mussalmans,' in which he bitterly complained that ignorant Muslims had been corrupted by contact with Hindus, and looked upon the professions of fishing, oil pressing, etc. as lowly. The so-called upper class Muslims even hesitated to intermarry with groups of Muslims following these professions along the family line; and this was clearly against the tenets of Islam.[7]

When it became impossible to earn one's living in Bengal by means of the traditional, hereditary occupation, and a more or less urbanized middle class began to emerge from among all castes of Hindus, as well as Muslims, one of the roots which held caste firmly received a rude shock. Changes in occupation have not, however, become completely free and universal. Movements of people from and into the villages have also been slow, so that, altogether, the impact of changed occupation, and of the rise of an urbanized, educated, professional class, has not, up till now, resulted in liquidating the bonds which gave permanence to caste. Yet, it cannot be questioned that the bonds of the latter have been considerably weakened in so far as choice of occupations is concerned. A Brahman today might own a shoemaking factory, and yet not arouse social disapprobation in express form. The backbone of orthodoxy seems to have been broken, at least on this plane, in Bengal. Among the former "lower" castes, again, the claim to higher rank does not today evoke the same amount of resistance as it perhaps did fifty years ago. Moreover, the claim, i.e., the revolt against relegation to a suppressed rank, has been accompanied by a conscious endeavor of approximation to the social practices of the upper castes. This has been both in the direction of orthodoxy and of reformed practices. In any case, caste has not remained unchanged, but shows some amount of alteration in regard to features connected with economic pursuits as well as ranking in society, on the basis of occupations.

There is another direction in which caste continues to receive a strong, though perhaps milder and less perceived shock, than the one noted above. But that promises to have more far reaching effects as the process becomes more consolidated. Hindu religion has always believed in a pluralism of faiths, each suited to the particular spiritual requirements of the community or the individual in question. Provided there is common agreement on a very limited number of points, faiths of widely divergent character have passed as lying well within the federation of faiths known as Hinduism. According to Marxian historians, such a religious organization would be considered to be the logical superstructure of a productive system in which castes were graded into high and low, and occupations fixed in perpetuity along hereditary lines, so that they formed an interlocking mesh, with privileges permanently guaranteed to some and service perpetually to others. Whether such a view is justified or not is beyond our present concern. What is important in the present context is that in the caste system, different elements are encouraged to persist in their local, communal culture, so that cultural pluralism happens to be stabilized so long as various castes are bound to one another in mutual interdependence by traditionally fixed exchanges of goods and services.

Not only Marxians, but political thinkers of various schools have long looked upon this aspect of caste with varying degrees of misgiving. Many have described the system of hereditary occupations and of the pluralism of faiths as a bar to the growth of national unity in India, and to progress. Great reformers, who have, however, favored the pluralistic character of faiths encouraged by Hinduism, have occasionally tried to distinguish the grain from the chaff; and they have recommended that while there should be no bar to a man's choice of occupations, there should be no ranking if all such occupations are necessary for the existence of society. One need not discourage pluralism in faiths, for that might turn out to be one of India's great gifts to human civilization. Vivekananda and Gandhi were both ardent social reformers; and while both subscribed to the highest faiths of Hinduism, they did not see any reason why unity should only be achievable through uniformity.

Others in India have been less clear on the subject. Every urgency of demand for national integration, when political unity has been threatened, has been attended by demands of uniformity. There can be a natural, as well as a forced growth of uniformity. It may be hard to distinguish between the two, yet it is not an impossible task.

If the threat to national integration in India becomes more urgent through the growth of sectional interests, as during the reorganization of the provinces, or if India is threatened by involvement in war, it is more than likely that the exigencies of political organization may encourage a standardization of culture much sooner than slow, conscious, educative endeavor may succeed in bringing about. But the question may well be raised whether we may not, in that very process, when the needs of war become more clamorous than those of peace, do away in our haste with an element of Indian culture which may have an abiding value for mankind? Historically, one need not forget that nationalism arose in Europe partly as a result of the needs of war, whether that was waged in the political or the commercial field. Its contribution to progress need not be minimized; it liquidated smaller barriers which divided man from man within the nation states. But nationalism can also become a danger when it usurps to itself a superiority that every narrow minded individual can also assign to himself or his small tribe.

In any case, let us at the moment do no more than draw attention to the fact that just as caste has been changing undoubtedly in Bengal in the field of men's economic activity, there is an indication that, on the level of its cultural superstructure, there are forces at work which tend to weaken its hold upon the mind of urbanized, politically conscious people, eager for change along the lines of the West. It is not enough to say that much is left over from the past, much remains to be done; it is also necessary to observe how much has been achieved even within the last fifty years in an organization which served India economically and culturally for many centuries in the past.

A possible and perhaps significant line of inquiry might be to investigate what proportion of marriages among politically active persons follow the traditional and the reformed patterns; and if, again, there is any significant difference between parties belonging to different age groups. How again do parties fare if they are committed to programs of social reform or otherwise?

Srinivas has indicated in his presidential address that the success of candidates in election was often due to the support which was given to them on considerations of caste. Caste rivalries also had their due share in determining the fate of candidates. While there is some reason to share the fear raised by Srinivas in his address, there is no reason to believe that, at least, in the sphere of politics, one need give way to despair. In West Bengal, at least, caste has played a more negligible role than in the neighboring state of Bihar. One has to remember that, in Bengal as well as in Bihar, political parties bearing an all-India character, like the Congress, the Socialist and the Communist parties, or the Jan Sangh and the Hindu Mahasabha have been guided by considerations other than caste in the choice of the majority of their representatives. Personal qualifications have been counted to be of more importance, even where caste has shaped choices to a certain extent. The steady growth of socially revolutionary ideology in India, which has been carried farther in the field of ideas than in the plane of action, has tended more to welcome change than to create further resistance to its advance.

Attention should be drawn here to a significant fact which also tends to prove that the social climate has been subject to serious alteration in recent times. If we pursue the history of nonconformist reformatory sects of the past, like those associated with the names of Caitanya-Nityānanda, or of Kabīr or Nānak (and this may even be stretched back to the time of the Buddha and the Jaina Tīrthankaras), whenever there was a revolt against caste, and men were drawn into a new brotherhood on the basis of individual merits instead of birth, such groups slowly became converted, first into a sect, and eventually into a caste in which marriage was restricted to people of the same faith. So that, instead of weakening the bonds of caste, such revolts only succeeded in the end in adding one more to the number of castes which already existed.

This phenomenon has its parallel in the economic field also. Brahmans in southern Orissa, near Berhampore, are popularly divided into Dānuā, Sāruā, and Haluā sections. The first word comes from *dāna* 'gift'; and those Brahmans who live purely on the gift of others, because they are scholars or priests, belong to this group, and are considered highest in rank. *Sāru* in Oriya stands for 'taro.' Many Brahmans have taken to its cultivation, do all the farm labor personally, with the hoe and other implements, but do not actually set their hand to the plough; they belong to this class. The ploughing is done by hired labor. Sāruā Brahmans raise large crops of taro in irrigated fields and are prosperous farmers; they are, however, considered to be a kind of degraded group. Yet, there is a third class who use the plough with their own hand, and are known as Haluā; the word being derived from *hala* 'plough.' As far as is known, these groups, separated by occupation and rank, do not intermarry.

The difference that we notice in the present century and a half is that deviations do not give rise now to an endogamous division as in the past. In the field of religious reformation, the Brāhmo Samāj very nearly did; but it was saved from that fate because, as some state, the urbanized Hindu in Bengal has to all intents and purposes become like a Brāhmo, while there has been no bar to intermarriage between the reformed and orthodox sections. Economically, adaptations to modern conditions are now so much on a personal, individual basis, that this does not lead to the formation of a new caste as in former times, when adjustments were quite often on a group basis.

It may be claimed that the speed with which demographic movements take place today, or the fact that those accused of deviation from standard caste practices may easily find refuge by migration to cities or plantations in distant states has been chiefly responsible for preventing the growth of new castes as in the case of mediaeval or ancient India. But a different explanation can also be suggested.

Buddhism, in its later developments, took the shape of a revolt against caste. So did the reform movements of the fifteenth and sixteenth centuries. But none of them had an alternative plan for the economic reorganization of the country. The hereditary guild organization of caste continued to function as before; so that its prestige and success in everyday life led to its perpetuation elsewhere also. Any deviation in the superstructure was trapped by being made to contribute an additional member to the already elaborate panel.

It is here suggested that, precisely because the impact of the modern world came to India chiefly in the form of an alternative system of production (no matter that it was colonial in character and subject to the dominant interests of British imperialism), the chief basis of loyalty to the caste system was demolished very nearly to completeness. In an atmosphere where caste assemblies, or the village communities formed of members of many castes, have lost all power to regulate the economic life of its members, and when movements have become freer and easier on account of modern means of transportation, deviant practices do not lead today to the formation of new castes, i.e., of endogamous groups marked by commonnesses of social and ceremonial practice. This fact alone, of all others, may tend to prove that caste is not just the same as before; and that economic associations did form a significant and vital part of the system as a whole.

Some have suggested that the weakening of caste has been due to the spread of Western education. This seems to be a wrong reading of the case. Islam operated in India for nearly a thousand years with its message of human equality, both in the cities as well as the villages. But the success of caste's economic substructure was so marked that even Muslim converts in rural India continued to pay homage to it by a virtual allegiance to the hereditary pattern of endogamous guilds. It might be argued that Western education alone would not have succeeded in weakening the sytem if it were not accompanied by a nearly total reorganization of the economic life of the country. It has been the success of the alternative form in the productive field, even though it was bolstered up by political power, that has helped in dealing a fatal blow to caste; and the consequent narrowing down of its field of operation, as in the state of West Bengal.

The situation is undoubtedly unequal in other states of India; but if things have changed in ample measure even in rural Bengal, then with parallel technological and educational processes affecting other states, the social situation may reveal parallel favorable trends in the future. And here we come to the sociologists' responsibility in regard to questions of vital interest in the society in which he himself lives. When one is assailed by the urgency of desirable reform, the apparent slowness of change may reasonably give rise to a feeling of despair. But a sociologist may test against the objective character of observed facts how far his despairs, or even his hopes are justified. And it is exactly in this field that the need of caution and of scientific rigor should be recognized to be of more value than any other qualification.

In West Bengal, as in every other state in India, the extension of Community Development schemes and of National Extension services has been throwing up newer and newer challenges to students of social science. India has been passing through unplanned and planned economic changes across all the time of which we have any dependable record. Some of these have been induced by growth of population and consequent fragmentation of land under existing laws of proprietorship; some by the extension of modern means of transport; some by movements of population under the attraction of gain elsewhere; and some lastly have been the result of consciously directed processes of education and purposeful changes in the fields of technology and of law. Claims have been made by the sponsors of the last, planned processes that the accompanying results have been, more or less, satisfactory. It is in this field that social scientists can bring their technique of investigation into operation, and help planners, whether official or non-official, in an assessment of the results of their undertakings.

Of late, studies of villages, or of the interlacing pattern into which India's rural inhabitants are tied to groups outside the village through the operation of markets or of caste organizations, have been increasing in frequency. These have often attained high levels of objectivity, and yielded valuable pictures of structural relationship in various fields of life. But the field of operation can be, and also needs to be, extended a little further.

Some villages lie within the operational area of Community Development Projects or of National Extension Services. If pairs of villages are chosen in which population, facilities of transport, and occupational structure are more or less the same, and if one of them lies within the Community Development block, and another near enough, but outside, and if records are kept of various social, economic, and even land-use data in both, so that the two villages can be resurveyed after the lapse of, say, five years, then we will have at our disposal a better means of assessment of the achievements of planned organized endeavor. For the difference in change between the results obtained from comparable pairs of villages may be assigned to the credit of the planned operation.

It is necessary to exercise an element of caution in the choice of villages for control. For a village inhabited by hitherto socially neglected untouchable castes, or of aboriginal tribes, may show a much more favorable response to governmental attention, or to a social reformer's zeal, than a village with a more sophisticated population. The ideal conditions of comparison and control may be hard to attain. Within certain reasonable limits, however, it may be possible to obtain favorable sets of the above kind. The use of scientific method in the assessment of social change, whether in the field of economic life in India, or of social reform connected with the ranking of occupations or of intermarriage even, may provide opportunities to our anthropologists and sociologists when they can be of real use and service to the society from which they draw their sustenance.

Even social sciences are operated by men who may be moved by strong emotions of sympathy or of antipathy towards particular values. But it is the gift of science that even while one may burn with the desire for reform, one can be objective, and make objective knowledge, gained through a growing perfection of observational technique, to serve the ends of hope rather than despair. A skilled physician may have an intense desire to help his sinking patient to recovery. Yet it is his scientific training which prevents him from being either elated or depressed by the temporary character of his patient's response, so that the results of his strictly scientific investigation may give him the courage and ability to achieve the result on which his mind is set. It is this mental attitude of the skilled physician which can help us in raising the level of the social sciences in India so that eventually they begin to shape national policies, as well as help education, so that those policies, whether official or nonofficial, may, in the end, raise the nation from the miserable condition under which we are all living today.

NOTES

[1] This paper is appearing simultaneously in *Man in India.*

[2] M. N. Srinivas, "Caste in Modern India," *Journal of Asian Studies,* XVI (August, 1957).

[3] Nirmal Kumar Bose, *Hindu Samajer Gaṛan* [Structure of Hindu Society] (Calcutta, 1949), p. 129.

[4] T.O. stands for "traditional occupation."

[5] Bose, 1949, p. 125ff.

[6] Bose, 1949, p. 135ff.

[7] Bose, 1949, p. 142ff.

University of Chicago
Chicago, Illinois

CHANGING TRADITIONS OF A LOW CASTE

By Bernard S. Cohn

THE Camārs are a widespread and numerically important part of the population of North India. Their traditional occupation is skinning, tanning, and working in leather; however, only a small number of this extensive caste derives its income from the traditional occupation, and the great majority make their living as agricultural laborers and, increasingly in the twentieth century, as urban laborers.[1]

Socially the Camārs are untouchable. In North India this is not a literal untouchability, but rather a situation where high caste men will not take water or cooked food from the Camārs. In the villages of Uttar Pradesh the low status of the Camār is symbolized by the fact that frequently the Camārs of the village have a separate hamlet or quarter on the outskirts of the village. In an agricultural village the Camār will be found doing most of the heavy agricultural labor, as traditional employee of a landlord, as a day laborer, or as a tenant. Only in rare instances are Camārs economically well enough off to be proprietary cultivators.

As with the majority of lower castes, Camār religious life differs markedly from that of the upper castes. Brahmanical Hinduism, as seen from the viewpoint of a village of India, is differentially diffused among the hierarchically ranked castes. Very roughly, involvement in and knowledge of the content of the great tradition follow caste lines, with those at the top—Brahmans, Rājpūts, and Baniyās—having the greatest involvement and knowledge and those at the bottom—Camārs, Dhobīs, and Āhirs—having the least.

In the past, the Camārs of Senapur have centered their main religious activity in rituals to propitiate godlings of disease such as Bhāgautī, Sītalā, and local ghosts and spirits. These spirits and godlings may be propitiated by offerings of water and food on an individual or family basis, or on more important occasions by the offering of *ghī* and spices by a *darsanīyā* (a devotee of one of these godlings) for a whole hamlet, whose members will assemble to observe the offering and participate in it by singing and praying. Other rituals include magical practices to revenge slights, cure diseases, and to recover stolen or lost property.

Camārs appear to lack many of the values and concepts which are associated with Hinduism of the Great Tradition. When I discussed matters of the afterlife with Camārs, I invariably heard the statement that they do not know what happens after death. They do not have any ideas about rebirth. When asked the reason for their very low status, they replied that it was fate that had assigned them to this low position. The more verbal often answered by relating myths which depicted a period when the Camārs were not the despised untouchables of today. Rather they were Brahmans or Rājpūts, but through an act of omission or through trickery of others they became associated with dead animals and the practice of midwifery. Their low status was not, however, rationalized in terms of *ḳarma* and *dharma*.

The stories, myths, and legends that Camārs tell deal with matters of status, history, diseases, and ghosts. Some Camārs do know stories from the *Rāmāyaṇa* and of legendary Camār saints, but, as will be discussed below, this is largely due to recent changes in the life of the village and the Camārs.

The reason for the minimal effect of the orthodox Hindu traditions on the Camārs is not difficult to understand. The Camārs as *achūts* (untouchables) are forbidden to hear the Vedas. Respectable Brahmans did not and do not officiate at Camār ceremonies. Camārs do not have Brahmans as *purohits* or gurus. Some of the local Brahmans, however, do cast and interpret horoscopes for Camārs, and will recite *satyanārāyaṇ kathās*, and advise Camārs on religious matters. Brahmans do not officiate at Camār wedding or death ceremonies. Theoretically, Camārs were barred temple entry until the Constitution of 1949. These prohibitions, coupled with Camār illiteracy and poor economic position, effectively barred Camārs from participation in or knowledge of even village upper caste Hinduism.

Camārs do participate in the celebration, in their own hamlets, of Dīvalī, Holī, Makar Saṃkrānti, Daśahrā, and other festivals. Generally the festival is celebrated, as one Camār described it, "by putting on clean clothes and eating good food." With few exceptions, Camārs could not give any explanation for the celebrations of these festivals, and had little or no knowledge of the mythology that surrounds these celebrations.

The Camārs also celebrate some of the life cycle rites which are basic rituals in Hinduism. Camārs have ceremonies at birth, marriage, and death. The form in recent years is that of traditional, Hindu life cycle rites, but apart from minor services, Brahmans play no part in these ceremonies, the sacrifices and offerings are pale reflections of what upper castes do, and the duration of these ceremonies is considerably shorter than those of the upper castes. Birth ceremonies, instead of being carried out for twelve days, are usually completed in five or six days. The marriage ceremony, instead of lasting three days as it does with the upper castes, is over in one day. Mourning is observed for ten rather than thirteen days.

The dominant caste of the village from which I will draw my materials are Ṭhākurs (Rājpūts).[2] The Ṭhākurs of Senapur are not especially sophisticated or active in religious activities; however, the Rājpūts are served by Brahmans, their life cycle rites more approximate the rituals as described in the sacred literature, and one can hear discussions of philosophical-religious points among the Rājpūts. Several of the older Rājpūts have an extensive knowledge of the sacred literature. Minimally, every Rājpūt is well acquainted with the *Rāmcaritmānas* of Tulsī Dās, and every year during the six days before the Daśahrā festival (September and October) the Rām Līlā is performed by the Ṭhākurs of the village. The Camārs as well as all other castes of the village attend this dramatic presentation of the life of Rām. The Camārs do participate in some upper caste religious activities, primarily in those parts of life cycle rites which symbolize the ties among the Ṭhākurs, their dependents (*prajā*) and traditional workers (*parjūniyā*). In the welcoming of the Ṭhakūr bride to her husband's village, it is the Camārin (female Camār) who guides the bride to the village shrines. Food, money, and other presents which are distributed at Ṭhākur life cycle ceremonies and by Thākurs at festivals such as *Makar Saṃkrānti* are given to Camārs along with other dependants and traditional workers.

The people of Senapur are changing their way of life in response to changing social and economic conditions. The Camārs as well as the Ṭhākurs are affected by these changes. In a previous paper I described the attempts of the Camārs of village Senapur to raise their social status, principally through attempting to organize themselves to achieve a better power position in the village and trying to Sanskritize their behavior to make themselves more like the upper castes in their social and ritual activities.[3] In the remainder of this paper I will describe the relation between urban employment, education, and this movement towards Sanskritization, and the attempts of the Camārs to relate to the great traditions of India.

Urban employment and education in relation to the Great Traditions of India. In 1948, out of the 1852 people enumerated in a census conducted by the village accountant there were 636 Camārs, 436 Ṭhākurs, 239 Noniyās, 116 Āhirs, and 67 Lohārs in village Senapur. There were less than fifty members of the other eighteen castes which live in the village.

The Camārs derive the principal part of their livelihood through farming small plots of land as tenants, and hiring themselves out as agricultural workers to work on the land of the Ṭhākur landlords. In December 1952, when I conducted a census of the Camārs, thirty-six were employed out of the village. Ten of these were in or around Calcutta, working largely as unskilled laborers in the jute mills, and eight were in Kanpur working in cotton mills. Others were in the coal fields of Western Bengal or in Delhi, Banaras, Bombay, and Cuttack as mill hands, rickshaw drivers, or tonga drivers. With the exception of two primary school teachers who teach in Jaunpur District and a compounder who works in Kanpur, all the Camārs who are employed out of the village have unskilled laboring jobs, and with the exception of the compounder all have left their families behind in the village.

Extra-village employment is not a new phenomenon with Camārs. In the middle of the nineteenth century they were often found as grooms working in British households. Sherring described their relations to the British thusly:

> Many of its members are menial servants, expecially those of the first or Jaiswara sub-division. They are willing, obedient, patient, and capable of great endurance; yet are apt to be light fingered and deceitful. It is a singular phenomenon, and hard to be explained, that, although they come so much in contact with foreign residents in India, they should, nevertheless, have been so little improved by such intercourse. I believe that of all the Hindus who have been brought extensively under European influence, they have profited the least.[4]

Several of the older Camārs still recall the days that they or their fathers or uncles worked for the Sāhibs.

The figure of thirty-six Camārs working out of the village does not give an adequate picture of their experiences out of the village. The majority of adult male Camārs have at one time or another worked away from the village in a city. Urban employment is not, however, a way of life for these people; rather they turn to it only in dire necessity, to raise money to pay for a wedding or funeral, to pay off a debt, or to buy livestock. A few younger men work in the cities through choice, and some even say they like it, but the older men, i.e., those over thirty, seem to prefer the village.

The Camār is a sojourner in the city, but the city provides a very different social, physical, and psychological environment than he is used to in his rural home. The Camār is not cut completely adrift from his home ties as he lives in a room with Camārs from his own village, or, if no Camārs from his own village are in that particular city, he will live with acquaintances or relatives from nearby villages. The Camār is usually found in a building that houses other Camārs of his subcaste in an area of the city where other low caste men live.

In the city the Camār engages in activities which for caste or economic reasons essentially are barred to him in the village. Camārs and other low castes have their own temples in the cities.[5] Camārs also sponsor and participate in *bhajans* in the city. Singing of religious and of political songs seems to be a major recreational activity and the few Camārs who were pointed out to me as being good singers, usually of *bīṛhā* (a type of song associated with Āhirs, having a characteristic rhythm and form with a religious or historical theme), learned these in cities or from men who were trained in the form in cities.

It should be noted that urban employment not only affords the Camār an opportunity for learning the Great Traditions of India, but several of the *ojhās* 'exorcists' and *darsanīyās* 'devotees' (specialists associated with aspects of India's Little Traditions) among the Camārs learned their skills while employed in cities.

Calcutta, Lucknow, Kanpur, and Bombay have Śiva Nārāyaṇ temples. The Śiva Nārāyaṇ sect is a Sanskritic religious movement among the Camārs. The present leader of the Śiva Nārāyaṇ sect in Senapur received his training as a *mahanth* in Bombay and his father, who was *mahanth* before him, was trained in Calcutta.

I am suggesting that the experience that Camārs have in the Indian urban setting may provide them with a chance to participate in activities which enable the Camār to relate to the practices and beliefs associated with the Great Traditions of India. It is usually thought by observers of Indian life that urbanization and industrialization will be the main contributors to the Westernization of Indian life; however, there are a few indications that urban employment might be an influence in the Camārs' taking over a more traditional Hindu ritual pattern.

Education similarly has a somewhat mixed effect upon Camār beliefs and practices. First, let me describe what education is for the Camārs of Senapur. There has been a primary school which taught up through grade four in village Senapur since the 1880's, but the students were largely drawn from the Ṭhākurs and the low but clean castes like the Lohārs (carpenters and blacksmiths). It is not too clear if Camārs were actually forbidden to attend the village school. Most informants agreed that in 1952 a Camār twenty-seven years old was the first to graduate from the village school; he had entered the primary school about 1936. Camār attendance at school has steadily risen since this time. The rise in Camār attendance has been helped by the fact that during the war, because of the rise in agricultural prices, many Camārs could afford to send their children to school. Camār families could forego the labor of their children and could afford the costs of sending a child to school. Since Independence, Camārs have not had to pay tuition in district schools; however, they still have to buy books and writing materials.

In 1952 there were seventy-two Camārs who were literate, seventy-one males and one female. This is out of a population of 583 who were above five years of age (287 males and 296 females). Of these seventy-two, only eight were above thirty years of age. One of these men learned to read from his son who is a school teacher. One learned in Bombay during his training as a *mahanth*. Another was taught by a relation, and several learned while working in mills or mines, but none of the literates over thirty went to the Senapur school.

In 1952 there were over thirty Camār children registered in the village and about twenty of them attended regularly. There were 168 Camārs, eighty-three males, eighty-five females, between the ages of six and twelve. There are no Camār girls in the village school, and out of the eighty-three boys of school age, thirty-three were in or had been enrolled in the school. The school was taught by four teachers, three of them Ṭhākur and one Kahār. In the past there have been Camārs, Āhirs, and men of other castes as teachers. Some Camārs believe that their children are badly treated in the school, they tell stories of Camārs being kicked and beaten with shoes; none of these stories could be substantiated, and in talking to Camār children about their experience in school, none expressed any feeling of being badly treated because of his low status.

The principal skill that a child learns in the first four years of school is to read and write Hindi. The villagers themselves speak a dialect of Bhojpurī, one of the dialects of Bihārī. At one time there was an extensive literature in Bhojpurī; however, this seems to have been largely replaced by Hindi. Only two Camārs that I knew had books other than school texts, and excepting the *Guru Anyas* (the holy books of the Śiva Nārāyaṇ sect), these were copies of stories from the *Rāmcaritmānas* of Tulsī Dās.

As of September 1953, only three Camārs had more than four years of education; one had gone through grade eight, including the successful completion of teachers training school in a nearby town. He was a school teacher. Another had eight years' education, but had failed to obtain a fully qualified teaching certificate. He also taught school, but was not as secure in his position as the first Camār teacher. The third had seven years of education and was trained as a tailor. In 1953 he was trying to obtain enough capital to open a tailor shop in the nearby bazaar.

The fully qualified school teacher had taught for a while in the village school, but a land dispute with a village Ṭhākur led to his transfer. He now teaches in a school four miles from the village. He seems to be accepted by the students and teachers of this school as a teacher and not a Camār. I have seen him at his school, sitting on the same *cārpāī* 'string bed' with high caste teachers, something he could not do in his own village.

This Camār teacher speaks Hindi well, dresses very well, and upper caste villagers commented to me that he spoke, dressed, and acted like a Ṭhākur.

I gathered a considerable amount of stories and folklore from this teacher, principally about Rāi Dās, a Camār saint. All of these stories, he told me, he had learned by reading. He also knew a great deal about the mythology of Hinduism and frequently in his conversation made illusions to the tradition. This teacher was a vegetarian and often commented unfavorably on Camār customs which deviated from what he thought to be good Hindu behavior.

It would appear that some of the Camārs who become literate do read, and the literature which they seemingly read are versions and accounts of the life of Rām, this being reinforced by the annual presentation of the *Rām Līlā*, and a few at least read tales of saintly Camārs. Being literate enables them to learn aspects of the Great Tradition which formerly had been closed to them because of their low status and their illiteracy.

The Ṭhākurs of Senapur are relatively speaking much better educated than the Camārs. There is one man with a Ph.D. from an American university; at least two with M.A.'s, one of whom teaches in a college, and the other is a specialist in dairy farming; and several holders of B.A.'s. Many Ṭhākurs have had high school educations, and at least a dozen of the Ṭhākur young men were attending a local intermediate college. The Ṭhākurs with college educations speak and read English, and are exposed to the ideas and values of Western civilization through their education; in addition, many of them go into "Western style" occupations, college teaching, police administration, and Western style businesses, and they tend to live in more "Westernized" parts of the Indian urban centers. Their education gives them the tools with which to begin to relate to the Western way of life. The Camārs who become educated are equipped, for the first time, to relate to the high tradition of India through their ability to read Hindi, and through urban employment which brings them closer to religious and social activities that to some extent draw their content from the Great Traditions of India.

The transmission of the Great Traditions. The principal agent of traditionalization among the Camārs is the Śiva Nārāyaṇ sect. The Śiva Nārāyaṇ sect was founded in the eighteenth century by a Rājpūt follower of Rāmānanda, a fifteenth century religious reformer. Śiva Nārāyaṇ established a sect, the principal tenets of which were the worship of one god who is Truth, vegetarianism, and the eschewing of the worship of idols. Four *maṭhs* (monasteries) were established: one in Ghazipur and three in Ballia. As of 1917, these *maṭhs* were still active, but the census of 1911 enumerated only seventy followers in Ghazipur.[6]

There have been followers of the Śiva Nārāyaṇ sect in Senapur among the Camārs for three generations. It should be noted, however, that the present Camār followers of the sect, do not adhere closely to the tenets of the sect, in particular in relation to diet and the prohibition of idol worship. At present they total fifty active members, and these members belong to a larger group which includes several hundred Camārs from seven villages in the area. They are led by a *mahanth*. The present *mahanth* lives in Senapur, but he was trained for his position in a Śiva Nārāyan temple in Bombay, where he was a *celā* 'pupil' for several years to learn to read the *Guru Anyas*, the sixteen volume holy book of the sect. The holy books are made up of sayings of Śiva Nārāyaṇ and incidents from his life. The sect in Senapur has four handwritten volumes all in an archaic form of the dialect of Ghazipur. The main activity of the sect is the holding of *gādīs* (rituals for the worship of Śiva Nārāyaṇ and the *Guru Anyas*). *Gādīs* are held at least twice a year, on Kṛṣṇa's birthday and on Basant Pañcamī, in the *mahanth's baiṭhak* 'men's house.' Upwards of one hundred Camārs, males and females, attend.

At the *gādī* the *Guru Anyas* is placed on a low table which is covered with a red cloth and is decorated with a garland, and has two silver rupees, a string of beads, and some *pān* on it. At *gādīs* that I have attended the table also had vases, a rose water dispenser, and a small statue of Gaṇeś. The devotees explained to me that they did not worship *Gaṇeś*, but since one of the members of the sect owned the statue, they put it on the table for decorative purposes.

The ceremony starts a little after nightfall, when the devotees begin to drift in; usually there is group singing to the accompaniment of a harmonium for several hours. The songs which are sung are usually devotional songs, but not necessarily particularly associated with the sect. I have also heard current movie and political "folksongs" being sung. During this singing the *mahanth* and other members of the governing council of the local sect, and perhaps a visiting *mahanth*, sit by the table and join in the singing. After several hours of singing, the *mahanth* signals for the *gādī* to begin. Everyone assembled bows his head up and down and then to the east as a sign of respect to the God who is Truth. After singing of songs from the *Guru Anyas*, the *mahanth* leads the group in the chanting of verses from the book and then reads a portion of the book to the group. After the reading the book is worshipped with a small *havan*, a small fire is kindled in a clay dish and *ghī*, *daśang* (a sacred mixture of ten substances), camphor, flower, and betel are offered to the flames of the fire. After offering these items, the *mahanth* moves the plate with the smouldering ashes around the book. (This is called *āratī*.) A conch shell is blown and bells are rung. The *gādī* closes with the passing of a large tray with the plate in which the offering was made and the *Guru Anyas*. Everyone inhales the fragrance of the smouldering ashes and makes a monetary contribution. The ritual part of the *gādī* is then followed by several hours more of singing.

The ritual itself is an attempt to copy a Brahmanical *pūjā*. And although many Camār rituals of propitiation or life cycle ceremonies include offerings of *ghī*, water, or other substances to the accompaniment of the chanting of the names of gods and goddesses, this is the only Camār ceremony I observed in which *āratī* was performed or where there was an extensive and formal saying of Sanskrit *mantras*. Other ceremonies performed by Camār religious leaders tend to be individualistic, reflecting bits and pieces of ceremonies observed. Two educated high caste men who accompanied me to a *gādī* remarked on the completeness of the ceremony and on its obvious and close approximation to the Brahmanical *havan*.

The *mahanth* is a part time priest, the rest of the time he acts as a day laborer, but he derives part of this income from his position. Unlike the majority of the Camārs, the *mahanth* is a vegetarian. The activities and beliefs of the sect stand in contrast to other Camār religious activity, in that they consciously attempt to copy Brahmanical Hinduism, and the source of imitation in the form of the training of the leaders is urban.

The dance party. As a part of a Camār wedding ceremony, a party of dancers is hired for the entertainment of the guests. These parties are usually made up of five or six males, one or two of whom are dressed as female dancers. The rest are musicians, usually drummers and singers. There were several Camārs in Senapur who were members of dancing parties.

There was one group, headed by the son of the *mahanth* of the Śiva Nārāyaṇ sect, that put on a drama instead of a dance as entertainment. The story they enacted was the life of Hariścandra.

Hariścandra, according to the version put on by these Camārs, was a Rājpūt king who gave all of his kingdom to Viśvāmitra, a Brahman, as charity. Viśvāmitra then demanded an additional 10,000 mohars (a coin). In order to satisfy this request Hariścandra sold himself in slavery to a Ḍom, and his wife and child to a Brahman. Hariścandra worked for the Ḍom in Banaras. One day his wife came to him and begged for fire to cremate their son. Hariścandra refused and said, "I am no longer king and you are no longer queen. I work for the Dom." At this point the gods intervened and the couple and the child were carried away and restored to their position by the gods.

The leader of the dance party, a young man of twenty-five and son of the *mahanth*, read the story, which is based on a Sanskrit play, in a book. The play emphasizes values, such as charity for Brahmans, sacrifice, and divine intervention, which are as yet quite different than are usually operative in Camār life.

Although dancing parties among the Camārs appear to be of considerable age, the putting on of a formal drama is of recent origin, and, in this presentation, we find a conjunction of the Śiva Nārāyaṇ sect in the person of the *mahanth's* son, a Sanskrit drama, and the fact that the story was read in a book.

The celebration of Rāi Dās's birthday. Rāi Dās was a Camār shoemaker who was a follower of Rāmānanda. The Camārs revere him as their great saint, and tell stories of his supernatural ability. In many of these stories, Brahmans are held up to ridicule and are bested by Rāi Dās, through Rāi Dās's superior spiritual qualities. Some Camārs when asked their caste reply "RāiDāsī," taking the name of their great saint as their caste name.

In January or February in recent years, the Camārs of the local region join together to celebrate the birthday of Rāi Dās by a procession, during which a *gādī* is performed on bullock carts, and by speeches.

In January 1953, the celebration was organized by a group of Camār young men who were students at the local intermediate college, and prominent participants were a Camār school principal and a Camār member of the Legislative Assembly of Uttar Pradesh. The M.L.A. was elected to a seat in the Assembly reserved for untouchables. There was a procession from the local bazaar, led by two elephants borrowed for the occasion from local landlords. There were also three bullock carts in the procession. On one there was a large picture of Rāi Dās, on another a band, and on a third several Śiva Nārāyan *mahanths* performing a *gādī*. There were approximately 500 Camārs in the procession, shouting Rāi Dās's name.

The procession stopped in the orchard adjacent to the local Intermediate College. The M.L.A. chaired the meeting, and the Camār school principal delivered the welcoming address. The first speaker was a Camār teacher from the local teachers college who spoke of the life of Rāi Dās. He was followed by a Camār student at Banaras Hindu University who told many of the same stories, but urged the Camārs to give up all connection with working in leather because it was this degrading occupation that was responsible for their low status. He was followed by another college student who spoke of Ambedkar and his success as a lawyer and politician. He also urged the Camārs to raise themselves up.

One of the Rājpūt teachers from the Intermediate College also spoke. He said that equality of men was a necessity in the new India, and that all caste distinctions should be ended, and that the Camārs, by following the example of their saint Rāi Dās in living a clean and saintly life, could make themselves the equals of anyone.

Several young men then spoke of incidents in Rāi Dās's life where through his saintliness he was able to best Brahmans.

The celebration was attended by between 600 and 700 people, the bulk of whom were Camārs, but there was a sprinkling of members of other castes in attendance. The principal part in the celebration in organization, speech making, and cheer leading, was played by young educated Camārs. The official sponsor of the meeting was the Harijan Student League of Dobhi, who looked upon this as an occasion to instruct their fellow Camārs on the life of Rāi Dās, and the significance of living a Sanskritized life as a means of raising their status. All the speeches were delivered in "City Hindi," not the local dialect which the Camārs use in their daily life.

Summary. In this paper I have suggested that there are a number of new social and economic situations which are affecting the traditions of a group of Camārs in an Uttar Pradesh Village.[7] Literacy has enabled the Camārs to relate to aspects of the Hindu Great Tradition through reading stories available in vernacular books. Urban employment has enabled Camārs to participate in rituals, derived from the Hindu Great Tradition, at low caste temples in the cities. Simultaneously there continues an earlier movement, the Śiva Nārāyaṇ sect, whose goal was Sanskritization.[8] Another strand is represented by the celebration of Rāi Dās' birthday, which now is in the hands of Camār college students, who are, among other things, urging political action. The stories about Rāi Dās have an anti-Brahman tint to them and they stress right action and right principles rather than the more orthodox activities of worship and ritual. These four strands found in the changing Camār traditions are not completely compatible, but they all aim at raising the Camārs' low social status. Sanskritization in the form of the Śiva Nārāyaṇ sect, the neo-Hinduism learned from vernacular literature and from contact with urban temples and religious activity, directs the Camārs to a traditional form of caste mobility of taking on the style of life and symbols of the upper castes. The Rāi Dās stories and the speeches accompanying the celebration of Rāi Dās's birthday point to a turning away from traditional mobility to a use of modern political methods. The ambivalence is a reflection of the situation the Camārs and other low castes are in as they strive to improve their social lot.

NOTES

1 The field work on which this paper is based was done in 1952-1953, while the writer held a Social Science Research Council Area Research Training Fellowship and a scholarship grant from the United States Educational Foundation in India under the Fulbright Act. The writing was done while the author was supported by the Cultural Studies Fund at the University of Chicago. I would like to express my appreciation to Morris E. Opler, Robert Redfield, Milton Singer, and Rudra Datt Singh for providing support and direction during the field work and in the subsequent writing.

2 For a description of the village, its caste composition, and its economic and political structure, see M. E. Opler and R. D. Singh, "The Division of Labor in a North Indian Village," in Carlton Coon, ed., *A Reader in General Anthropology* (New York, 1948), pp. 464-496; "Economic, Political and Social Change in a Village of North Central India," *Human Organization,* XI (Summer 1952), 5-12; "Two Villages of Eastern Uttar Pradesh (U. P.). An Analysis of Similarities and Differences," *American Anthropologist,* 54 (1952), 179-190; Rudra Datt Singh, "The Unity of an Indian Village," *The Journal of Asian Studies,* XVI (November 1956), 10-19; Morris E. Opler, "The Extension of an Indian Village," *The Journal of Asian Studies,* XVI (November, 1956), 5-10.

3 Bernard S. Cohn, "The Changing Status of a Depressed Caste," in McKim Marriott, ed., *Village India* (Chicago, 1955), pp. 53-77.

4 M. A. Sherring, *Hindu Tribes and Castes as Represented in Benares* (London, 1872), I, 39.

5 Radhakamal Mukerjee, "Caste Proximity and Attitude Change in the City," *Inter-Caste Tensions* (Lucknow, 1951), p. 26; and G. S. Bhatt, "The Chamar of Lucknow," *The Eastern Anthropologist,* VIII, (September, 1954), 38.

6 George A. Grierson, "Siva Narayanis," *Encyclopedia of Religion and Ethics,* XI (New York, 1921), 579.

7 I am indebted to discussions with McKim Marriott for clarifying some of the aspects of these often conflicting movements.

8 For a full discussion of Sanskritization, see M. N. Srinivas, *Religion and Society Among the Coorgs* (Oxford, 1952), and "A Note on Sanskritization and Westernization," *Far Eastern Quarterly,* XV (1956), 481.

London, England

A TRIBAL PEOPLE IN AN INDUSTRIAL SETTING

BY MARTIN ORANS

THIS is a report from fieldwork in progress on an Indian tribe, the Santal, in the industrial setting of Jamshedpur, site of the largest and earliest industrial producer of iron and steel in India, as well as of a number of associated industries. What my wife and I are attempting to observe are the effects of Jamshedpur's urban and industrial milieu on traditional Santal culture. In the widest theoretical sense, our study is meant to be at least a contribution of data toward the solution of the general problem of the relation between economic activity on the one hand, and noneconomic social and cultural patterns on the other. I also hope that the study might prove applicable in providing for the welfare of the Santals and other closely related Mundari speaking tribals, and forward the development of industry in this area, so rich in natural resources.

This study, of which the report presented here is a fragment, may also be viewed as an attempt, in traditional anthropological fashion, to study an entire culture from a particular point of view—in this case, an entire culture in process of change. I am convinced that this holistic approach leads to sounder interpretations than any other method. It should be admitted, however, that in situations like the one I am studying, which depart so radically from the traditional anthropological unit of study—the approximate primitive isolate—the quantity of data one feels obliged to collect becomes overwhelming. If the advantages of the holistic approach are to survive the decline of the primitive isolate, the days of the lone anthropological investigator must perhaps come to an end.

The main body of this report is divided into three sections, concerned respectively with the recruitment and commitment of the Santal portion of Jamshedpur's labor force, with changing beliefs and practices concerning witchcraft, and with quantitative variations in marriage forms. These sections are intended as samples of the methods employed and the results obtained. Since the method of investigation followed depends on special circumstances prevailing in the area under investigation, the remainder of this introduction describes the necessary background for understanding these circumstances.

The Santals are a very large tribe, numbering today close to three million. They are primarily located in the Chotanagpur plateau of Bihar, in parts of West Bengal, and in northern Orissa. The Santals who have come to work in Jamshedpur are mainly from the territory adjacent to Jamshedpur, that is, from Dhalbhum subdivision of Sighbhum district in Bihar, the Mayurbhanj district of Orissa, and the former princely state of Seraikela now also in Singhbhum. A few Santals have come from Manbhum district of Bihar north of Jamshedpur, and from Midnapur district of Bengal on the east. Almost all the Santals who have come have settled outside Jamshedpur in what were, before the existence of the city, strictly agricultural Santal or other aboriginal (*ādibāsī*) villages. From these villages, which will be referred to by the generally used Hindi and Bengali word *bustee*, the Santals commute daily to Jamshedpur. These *bustees* lie three to ten miles from the edge of the city. Almost none of these workers have acquired land in the *bustees*. The traditional mud houses built in the *bustees* are on land bought or rented from the original inhabitants. The appearance of the settlement is something like that of a true agricultural village with the same material provisions. The one pronounced difference is the great crowding together of houses on what has become scarce land due to the influx of workers. In these *bustees* the relatively few descendants of the original farmers may still practice agriculture, but most of them hire servants to help with farming and take up industrial employment themselves.

A few Santals have come to live in town *bustees*, i.e., village-like communities within the town. Although these are, for comparative purposes, important to the general plan of research, they must be excluded from consideration in this report for lack of space. The city dwelling Santals who will be considered in this report live in houses provided by the Tata Iron and Steel Company. Some of these twenty-five families now living in Jamshedpur, have been there for as long as thirty years, and a few Santals have even grown up and been educated in the town. There is one important cultural distinction among these city Santals which must be taken into account. About half these families, all coming from a part of Seraikela within ten miles from the city, have come to live within one small area just within the town and nearest to their native villages. Most of these form a tight Santal community within this area. Furthermore, living so close to their villages, they make weekly trips back and forth. As a result of these factors and others, they tend to differ sharply from the other city Santals, among whom none of these conditions exist. Like the city *bustee* dwellers, they are, for comparative purposes, important to the general study but will not be dealt with in this essay. There are, then, Santals from two kinds of industrial communities to be discussed in this report, i.e., those living in *bustees* lying outside the town, and those non-Seraikela city Santals who live scattered in various sections of Jamshedpur.

The method of investigation and interpretation followed seeks to take advantage of the built-in differences between these communities in assessing the relative contributions of industrialization or urbanization to changes in traditional Santal culture. The procedure of interpretation followed is to attempt to explain the social and cultural continuity and variation between these differing communities and the parent traditional agricultural village. The problem is much complicated by the fact that the village, the baseline for comparison, has itself been considerably altered during the fifty years of the existence of Jamshedpur. The village has been changed by India's revolutionary political changes during this period. Village economic life has been altered by the development of Jamshedpur and the mines supplying Jamshedpur. Most important for this study, the village has been changed by the periodic visits of emigrant workers back to their native village, carrying with them all the changes that they have themselves undergone. What must be reckoned with is the continuous interaction of the industrial Santal communities with the rural communities, as well as the historical changes that each has undergone. Finally, it is necessary to take into account the differing non-Santal cultures which surround these varied communities and to determine in what manner they interact with Santal communities.

A brief characterization of traditional Santal culture in this area and the dominant cultural trends of Jamshedpur will now be given.

The social organization of the Santals is primarily organized on the basis of real and fictitious kinship. Named patrilineal clans and subclans regulate marriage and serve as guides to the establishment of fictitious kinship relations which structure social interaction among non-kin. Weak corporate lineages of varying depth carry out periodic and special religious functions. The strongest social unit not bounded by kinship is the village with its headman and other patrilineally inherited and appointed offices. It is the primary judicial unit and has in addition important religious functions. Villages are weakly joined together in varying numbers into a kind of super-village judicial unit much like the new governmental *grām pancāyats* and under the authority of a kind of multi-village headman. In some cases these organizations have been absorbed into the *grām pancāyat* organization, especially where the multi-village headman became head of the *grām pancāyat*.

The typical landholding units are either the patrilineal extended family or its nuclear components. The extended family in the traditional village seldom survives the marriage of all of its sons. The Santals have been settled rice cultivators for at least one hundred years, though they have a tradition of once having been shifting cultivators and hunters and gatherers. Even at the beginning of the fifty year period here under consideration, hunting had become only a sport and the occasion for certain festivities, and gathering is virtually nonexistent. The Santals' techniques of cultivation are not different from those of their Hindu neighbors from whom they almost certainly acquired settled agricultural practices. Although they are primarily subsistence farmers, they have long become accustomed to money transactions through the necessity of paying taxes to the rulers of the country and through attendance at weekly markets.

Like most tribal religions, the Santal religion tends to express itself more directly in rites and less in doctrine or dogma than is characteristic of religions as systematized in a Great Tradition. Again unlike the great traditional religions, Santal religion has only weak connections with morality, and the gods of the Santal tend to be amoral. The Santals do not make images of their gods as the Hindus do, but ordinarily represent them with simple unworked stones.

Almost all the several thousand Santals working in Jamshedpur were born and raised in strictly agricultural villages. In most of these villages, the majority of residents are Santals; in many there are some caste Hindus, particularly *tāntīs* 'weavers' and *ḳamārs* 'blacksmiths.' The Santals once obtained most of their cloth and metal implements from these fellow villagers, but in recent years have increasingly obtained these goods from regional country markets or even in nearby towns, where the choice, quality, and prices are more to their liking. In a few of these villages one may also find other tribals, particularly Ho, Munda, and Bhumij, three related Mundari speaking tribes. A few Santals come from predominantly Hindu or non-Santal tribal villages.

Jamshedpur was carved out of the jungle of Singhbhum district, Bihar, just over fifty years ago. It is one of the fastest growing cities in India, having a population today of over 218,000. Within any classification of Indian cities, it is of an extremely atypical variety. Some of this atypicality stems from it being a company town of unprecedented size. The Tata Iron and Steel Company has from the beginning completely controlled the government of the town, provided housing for most of its workers, operated a school system, etc. The physical facilities provided by the Company have made Jamshedpur perhaps the cleanest and healthiest city in India.

Broadly speaking, one may divide the traits and institutions characteristic of Indian cities today into three categories differing both in their nature and in their origin. The first two categories, which are primary, would be "great traditional," dominantly of Hindu origin; and "modern," of Western origin. The third would be "modern Indian," a self-conscious attempt to fuse the best elements of the primary available traditions into a new coherent whole. This latter development appears to be the one most favored by India's leading modern thinkers and it is much in evidence in, for example, a city like New Delhi, where many of India's intellectual elite are congregated. In any Indian city most of the inhabitants will be carriers of at least some traits from both primary traditions.

If Jamshedpur is characterized in terms of these coexisting and intermingled traditions, it will be found to be one of the most modernized and least "great traditional" of India's major cities. It is a city as much dominated by modern industry as a medieval city was by its cathedral. Traditional institutions such as temples and organizations for the propagation of the Great Tradition exist but are relatively weakly developed. The Tata Company, the Tata Workers Union, and the town's competing regional and national political parties are the dominant corporate groups. Caste persists as an institution for regulating marriage, for regulating employment in certain traditionally degrading occupations, and to a certain extent in structuring social interaction. But class in the traditional Western sense is increasingly displacing caste as the organizing principle of membership in social groups and in social interaction. Jamshedpur is again extreme in the proportion of leisure time spent in modern Westernized forms of diversion as compared to devotional or entertainment forms characteristic of the Great Tradition. It should be noted that modernism is more pronounced among the upper classes, but even the lower classes have absorbed more of it than people of similar status in other more typical Indian cities. This modernism which trickles down with increasing distortion through the social order, is partly the result of the relatively extreme modernism of the Parsi community which fills the top positions in the company and hence in the community. It also happens to be the dominant tendency among the highly skilled engineers and technicians, whatever their community.

In Jamshedpur the traits of the two primary traditions tend to remain clearly discrete and there is little self-conscious effort to shape new patterns by fusion even among the city's elite.

Some aspects of recruitment and commitment. The aim of this section is to establish the factors that push or pull the Santal toward industrial employment in Jamshedpur, and the factors tending to hold him to such employment or drive him away from it.

In the early days of Jamshedpur, unskilled labor was not so superabundant as it is today, and the early employment policy of the Tata Company was extremely lax and haphazard. Many Santals and others with farms nearby therefore deserted industrial work during the farm season and were able to return to their old industrial jobs or even better ones when the farm work was completed. In the 1930's employment policy tightened and it became impossible to return to an industrial job after a long absence. If one could not make a living on the farm alone, it became necessary to stick to industrial labor to keep alive. With this superabundance of labor still prevailing, the question of recruitment and commitment is somewhat academic as far as maintaining a stable work force is concerned. However, because such a study is necessarily concerned with what a worker likes and dislikes about his job and industrial environment, it has some applicability in the realm of industrial relations. It is offered here as a contribution toward the growing data on the recruitment and commitment of tribal and peasant people to industrial labor and as an example of an anthropological approach to the problem.[1]

If one asks a Santal why he came to work in Jamshedpur, he will in almost every case give an exclusively economic reason. Generally he will say something like, "I came for the sake of my stomach"; somewhat less frequently he will say, "I came to improve myself." By this latter response he means to indicate not only that he was not driven by dire necessity, but that he is a man not content with the ordinary low socio-economic status of a Santal. If one makes detailed enquiries concerning his precise economic condition at the moment he decided to seek industrial employment, it may be found that though he was not destitute, there were more than enough people on his land to harvest the entire crop. If one had no other techniques of investigation than asking the Santal laborer why he came and what his economic condition was, as in a questionnaire, this is about all that one could learn. Let us see what an anthropological approach can add to this meager data.

The Santals are a singing people who have channeled almost their entire artistic talents into song and dance. As they express their covert feelings more readily and effectively in the poetry of song than in conversation, this source may be tapped for evidence on almost any topic. Three songs concerned with work have been collected which might be relevant. In the first, presented here in translation, will be found some expression of the Santal sentiment toward traditional agricultural labor: "My parents from whom I was born held me to their bosom; / With cot and umbrella they raised me while they worked in the fields. / In the monsoon season, *halae halae*[2] with the wind comes the rain. / Dripping wet we work in the fields. / As I remember all this I become sad and tears fall."

Evidently the Santals regard agricultural labor as a process which takes up a great part of their life, and which is fraught with discomfort during the monsoon. If a Santal is asked directly how he regards the work of agriculture or industry, or why he prefers one to the other, he will not say anything about the work itself. He will say that farm work is better than industrial work because it involves only six months labor, while industrial labor offers him much less time for pleasure (*ṛaskạ*). He will also say that industrial labor has the advantage of paying more. He may add that with this greater income he will be able to improve himself by buying more land, or help his children to improve themselves by sending them to school. One might conclude, if this were all the evidence, that the Santals were impervious to pleasures derived from work.

It has already been indicated that the Santal is aware of certain things that he does not like about agricultural work in itself; it would be easy to compile a list of things that he does not like about industrial work by watching him on the job. The important point is that if you simply ask him he will tell you little about the unpleasantness of different types of work and virtually nothing about rewarding work activity. There are two reasons for this. If the question is put to him in the form of a choice between the two kinds of work, he cannot conceive of the possibility that one could ever make a choice between two jobs for other reasons than simple economic ones. He has certainly never had much of a chance to do so. If, instead, he is asked separately about his attitude toward the work, there is a different reason why he says nothing about the pleasure and little about the discomfort associated with it. This reason one learns by observing Santal ridicule directed toward those who regard work frivolously, or who, on the contrary, are always complaining about it. The proper attitude toward work is that it is a serious business carried on to earn a living. It is not to be taken lightly but to be borne with patience.

By watching a Santal at work one will also see that he does occasionally get pleasure from the work itself. This is particularly the case when the nature of the labor is such that it can be performed in company with others. On such occasions the demeanor of the men and the enthusiasm with which the work is performed convince one that the Santal can indeed derive pleasure from work. To be sure he may also be seen with a grim determined look driving a rather intractable bullock before him, particularly, as in the song, during the rainy monsoon, or in the hot summer season. The industrial worker, if observed, for example, while explaining his job to another or while performing a job which gives him some scope for skill or involves some mastery of impressive machinery, may be seen to derive pleasure from his work. Nevertheless, the Santal, though he takes work seriously and does it with a will, is essentially a pleasure loving man. Typically, pleasures mean to him dancing and singing, love making and drinking, and the pleasure that he derives from work is hardly on a par with these. The dominant feeling among the Santal toward work is the not uncommon one that work is what deprives one of the leisure necessary to engage in purely pleasurable activities. A number of city Santals and a few *bustee* Santals, however, eager to raise their status, have sharply curtailed their own and their children's commitment to pleasure. These Santals are sharply critical of their more pleasure oriented fellows, whose pleasure seeking activities detract from their economic well-being and make them appear unrefined before the non-Santal world. Their own status is threatened by the behavior of their rude fellows.

TABLE 1

Income categories

	0-5	6-10	11-15	16-20	21+	Total
Farmers who emigrated:	24(48%)	20(40%)	3(6%)	2(4%)	1(2%)	50(100%)
Farmers who remained:	22(44%)	16(32%)	7(14%)	1(2%)	4(8%)	50(100%)

The second song with relevance to the problem at hand expresses the dire need motive for taking up industrial work. It is offered here for this reason, in spite of the fact that it actually refers to work in the mines of the Tata Company rather than in the works of Jamshedpur: "Come with me, my queen (*rānī*), come to work in the mines of Tata Company./For the sake of our little stomachs and the little life left within us. / We will work in the mines of the Tata Company."

With respect to economic motivation for coming to Jamshedpur it is, of course, possible to make some relevant economic calculations. For example, one can compare per capita farm income at time of emigration for those who became workers with those who did not. One can also make an estimate from these figures of what percentage were forced off their farms by sheer economic necessity and what percentage must have been attracted by something more than bare subsistence. The figures given above are for maunds (about 80 lbs) of husked paddy per person and after taxation.[3] A comparison of these two sets of figures indicates that those who became industrial employees were not at the time of emigration significantly poorer than those who remained on the farm. I have calculated that the Santals, with their extreme dietary reliance on rice, require a minimum of about one pound per day. On the basis of this minimum figure a Santal then requires at least 360 lbs per year or four and one half maunds. Since forty-eight percent of those who become industrial workers fall in the 0-5 maund category, it is clear that nearly half fall in the "dire need" category and were virtually pushed out of their villages. Recognizing the vagaries of agricultural production, it is probable that a sizeable proportion of the forty percent in the 6-10 maund category may also be assigned to the group who were forced out of agriculture. That leaves, then, at least 10 percent to be assigned to the "improve themselves" category, or those who were perhaps significantly attracted by noneconomic lures. What of the forty-four percent of the farmers who have not taken up industrial employment but who fall in the 0-5 maund category? Some of these simply do not make ends meet and are continually in debt. Some help out on other's farms and get enough rice in this manner to survive. This kind of employment on other Santals' farms is limited by two factors. The most important is that very few Santals have much surplus. The second is that only a few have more land than they can cultivate. It should be mentioned, with respect to the surplus factor, that a Santal will eat up to two pounds of rice per day, or nine maunds per year if he has this much. It can be seen from the per capita income table of the farmers that only about twenty-four percent have any surplus over nine maunds per capita per year.

The final song to be offered serves as an introduction to the subject of Jamshedpur and its environs as a factor in commitment.

Kalka and Manpur are dark
While Holy (*holi*) Bistupur (main section
of Jamshedpur) is light.
The train moves, the whistle sounds,
Tata coolies are dressed to go

By day the bus, by night the train
ḳhoḳoḳ' the big train has arrived.
O my friend, my old friend, bundle your
things, let's go to Tata,
ḳhoḳoḳ' let's climb aboard the big train.

Like poets everywhere, those of the Santals see the city's lights as symbols of its drawing power. The city is contrasted with Kalka and Manpur, two small towns in Dhalbhum which, before the development of Jamshedpur, were thought by the Santals of the region to be quite urbane. Kalka receives mention perhaps because it has a liquor distillery of which the Santals make use. The phrase "dressed to go" is also significant because the Santal industrial workers have special work costumes including Western long pants, shirt, and shoes. These clothes are admired by the rural folk since they are associated with the status and affluence of the *sāhib*.

To the Santals, Jamshedpur offers an alluring spectacle of complex industrial machinery and gigantic industrial structures; it has superior markets where a comparatively wide range of merchandise can be seen or bought. Perhaps most important for the young Santal man is the fact that its atmosphere is free from many of the strictures of the rural village.

Those who live in company houses have become attached to the unusual amenities provided with these houses, for example, water from a tap, electricity, special sanitation facilities, and a house that doesn't leak and doesn't have to be repaired. When these city dwellers (the non-Seraikela Santals) visit their villages, they find life somewhat uncomfortable and their children find it even more trying. Those who live in the *bustees*, on the contrary, live under the same conditions as they did in the village. A few of these *bustee* Santals would like to move into company houses in town. The attraction seems not so much the physical facilities provided but rather the cultural climate of the city. It is the urbanity of the city folk that they prize, and it is the vulgarity of their fellow *bustee* Santals that they wish to escape from. This vulgarity manifests itself, as they see it, particularly in the rather violent quarrels which break out in the *bustee* especially after considerable drinking, and in the sexual display indulged in, for example, by men during the dance. Such Santals who disdain the life of the *bustee* are a small minority, but it is they who are most desirous of moving into town. Generally the *bustee* dweller prefers his position to that of the city dweller. He pays virtually no rent, he may have enough land for a respectable garden, and above all he is surrounded by congenial Santals rather than treacherous and hostile non-Santals (*diku*, particularly Hindus).[4] With these Santals, he may enjoy all the traditional forms of behavior that he desires, while comparatively little notice will be taken of him if he chooses not to enter into these forms. The *bustee* is congenial, familiar, and at the same time relatively permissive.

The city dwellers tend to be more firmly attached to their jobs, which are generally better paid, require more skill, and are, in a few cases, of the white collar variety, and they are deeply committed also to their new physical environment. Both groups have become more committed to their jobs through a number of special inducements offered in recent years by the various companies. One of the most effective of these inducements to the Santal is the right to name one of his sons to a job after he has served at least thirty years. As the Santals say, "Having a job at Tata is like having land, you can pass it on to your son."

Changing beliefs and practices concerning witchcraft. The investigation of witchcraft in village, *bustee*, and town not only provides observations of changing belief and practice in the two kinds of industrial communities, but also an opportunity to test hypotheses concerning the interconnections of witchcraft with other phenomena in the village.

Generally for the village, beliefs and practice regarding witchcraft have not much changed during the last fifty years, despite the fact that a few relatively well educated Santals there hold views radically different from those of their fellows. According to the traditional view held by most village Santals, disease may be caused and treated either by natural means or by a number of supernatural means, of which witchcraft is one of the most important. Almost all treatment is administered by a Santal medicine man who is a part time specialist (*ojhā*, as in Hindi). If natural methods such as root medicine fail to bring about a cure, the *ojhā* will attempt to exercise evil spirits or spells by various supernatural methods. If even this fails he may suggest that a witch[5] is responsible. While the *ojhā* does not have the power to find out who the witch is, he can perform certain rites to eliminate the effects of the witchcraft. If these also fail, it becomes necessary to go to a *sok̲ha*, who has the power, through divination, to find out the guilty witch.

Witches are always women. They obtain their power to cause sickness through certain malevolent spirits (*boṅga*) who instruct them in return for various offerings. It is believed that witches are motivated by *hĩsạ*, a concept with a variety of meanings. In Hindi the word means 'injury,' 'malice,' 'robbery,' or 'murder.' The essence of the Santali meaning is 'envy' and/or 'concealed malicious intent.' The witch who harbors such feelings harms her victims by either eating the victim's internal organs or luring away his life spirit (*jiwi*; Hindi *jīv*).

Every Santal woman is regarded as a potential witch, and this belief, plus women's ritual impurity during menstruation, are the justifications for their exclusion from all forms of worship. As in many societies with the ideal of the patrilineal extended family, it is the women who are invariably blamed for schisms leading to the fragmentation of this unit into its component nuclear families. This projection of tension within the extended family onto women, especially wives, contributes toward the general denigration of the character of women. They are said to be of weak character, easily attracted by a shiny trinket, and hence persons in whom one cannot place trust. I suggest the hypothesis that this projection of tension is intimately connected with the view that all Santal women are potential witches.

The actual naming of a witch by a *sok̲ha* occurs only during serious illness or after an unexplained death. The penalties inflicted on the alleged witch vary in seriousness depending upon circumstances. She may merely be chastised by the *sok̲ha* and villagers, made to promise to discontinue her evil practices, and forced through her husband to pay a fine. If she does not confess and her husband will not testify to her guilt, they may both be beaten to extract the needed confession. In very serious cases she and her husband may be driven out of the village or even outcasted. If all of these community punishments prove unsatisfactory to the alleged victim or his family, they may themselves take action and do violence to or even take the life of the witch. For a variety of technical reasons connected with detection of crime and legal technicalities the "murderer" is seldom convicted even if brought to court. In addition the villagers may frequently take his side.

The Santals are, on the whole, a notably neat people. Unfortunately, the clean appearance of both their homes and persons is not often a hygenic cleanliness—for example, they frequently scrub their cooking and eating utensils to a fine polish with obviously contaminated water. Hence, like their Hindu neighbors, they suffer severely from a number of more or less endemic diseases. Particularly devastating are malaria and a variety of dysenteries, as well as the common epidemic diseases of the area such as cholera and smallpox. A large number of illnesses are attributed to witchcraft, but it is rare that a *sok̲ha* will be consulted and a witch named. The restraints operating are the serious repercussions which may follow with their danger to village solidarity, and the fact that consulting a *sok̲ha* is an expensive procedure.

Although any innocent looking Santal woman may secretly be a witch while the community remains unaware of it, it is possible to see witches in action. Almost every Santal has seen unexplained lights emanating from witches and a good number have actually seen a witch or two making offerings or even dancing in the sacred grove (*jaher*) where worship is held. It should be remembered that these beliefs and practices are not fundamentally different from those of many of the Santal's Hindu neighbors.

In general, belief and practice in the *bustee* regarding witchcraft are much like those in the village. Certain beliefs almost never found in the village have been added, however, to the common stock. One added belief which proved quite a surprise to me is a new idea about the elimination of witchcraft. I was told by a Santal in the *bustee* where I did most of my work that witchcraft is a bad thing, and the reason it is so prevalent among the Santal is ignorance. He added, "the educated *diḵu* don't have it, and with education it will disappear from our community also." As I thought this answer implied a disbelief in witchcraft, and as he was the first Santal to have indicated such an opinion to me, I fortunately decided to press the point further. When I then asked him how education could eliminate witchcraft, he gave an answer showing quite clearly that he still firmly believed in witches, but thought the practice of witchcraft would decline with education. He explained that women practice witchcraft because of *hĩsạ*, and the reason they have this *hĩsạ* is that they are ignorant. "When they become educated," he said, "they will see that this *hĩsạ* is a bad thing and will give up the practice of witchcraft." I thought this to be a special instance of a peculiar viewpoint and was astonished to learn that it is the common view in the *bustee*.

A less common attitude, but one which is much more frequent in the *bustee* than in the village is skepticism about the existence of witches. A number of *bustee* Santals have told me, "Yes, I have seen lights from what are supposed to be witches, but who knows if they were really witches? I have never seen a witch myself although others say they have seen. Since I have never seen myself, how can I say whether they exist or not?"

As for accusations of witchcraft in the *bustee*, I do not yet have a record adequate for comparing the nature and frequency of such accusations in the *bustee* with those in the village. Only a couple of years ago, one woman in the *bustee* was named by a *soḵha* as a witch, and she and her husband were beaten, made to pay a fine, and forced out of the *bustee*. A few years prior to this, a woman from the same *bustee* was killed while returning from market. The murderer was never apprehended, and it may well be that whoever was responsible believed her to be a witch.

In the city there are a number of attitudes toward witchcraft either totally lacking or extremely rare in the *bustee* or village. The most common point of view is a kind of quasi-naturalistic interpretation. Such city dwellers hold that witchcraft motivated by *hĩsạ* does indeed exist, as demonstrated by many observations they themselves and their fellows have made. They argue, however, that this witchcraft is not, strictly speaking, a supernatural power conferred by malevolent spirits, but rather a magical technique passed on from one witch to another. The Hindi word *jadu* is used for magic. They make it clear that it is magic in the sense of "seemingly supernatural." It is a kind of mysterious scientific technique, and the word which they frequently use to convey their view of its nature is "mesmerism." They have a very limited idea of what mesmerism is supposed to be, but they do know that it is a kind of scientific magic. As one Santal put it, expressing his preference for a naturalistic point of view, "How can I believe that witches can eat one's internal organs? When people are sick I never see any holes in their skin through which the organs might have been removed.

If a witch really has caused the sickness it must be by the use of some kind of poison or *jadu.*"

Another Santal, who is a student in the Jamshedpur Cooperative College, is the only Santal I know who gives a totally naturalistic explanation of witchcraft and denies the existence of witches. In the course of his studies he came across a psychology book belonging to one of his Hindu schoolmates, in which he read that people frequently imagine that they see those things of which they are very much afraid. He accepted this as a convincing explanation of witchcraft congenial to his own general outlook. This young man is the son of a Seraikela Tata employee and lives in that part of town where a number of Seraikela Santal are domiciled. As he told me this, a few of these Seraikela workers sat about and listened. Since they were completely uneducated and uninitiated to the ideology involved, his explanation was totally unconvincing to them. The young student's father is also unwilling to accept his son's point of view.

To our knowledge there have been no identifications of witches among the city Santals. From this fact and the changes in belief described previously it should not be inferred, however, that fear of witchcraft has declined much among the city Santals. While they are not much worried about it when among their city brethren, a great deal of anxiety is aroused when they visit a village. One of the most important reasons for this persistence of fear is that the city Santals believe themselves to be particularly susceptible to the *hĩsạ* or envy of villagers. This envy is aroused because they are so much richer and more successful than the villagers.

Before attempting an interpretation of the variations in witchcraft beliefs and practices that have been described, one additional set of witchcraft beliefs must be mentioned which in some ways cuts across the village-*bustee*-city axis. The Santals have a religious teacher (guru as in Hindi) of high repute who has been given the title "spiritual leader" (*marañ gomḵe*). This guru, Rạghnạt Murmu, has founded an organization whose chief function is to ascertain the "true" beliefs of the Santals and to codify them. Only the witchcraft beliefs of this guru and his followers can be presented here.

According to the guru's view, there are witches who, because of *hĩsạ*, practice witchcraft. These witches, however, can cause sickness only in a person who has committed some sin (*pap*, Hindi; he also uses the English "sin"). He and his followers further believe that the *soḵha* cannot be relied on to find out who are witches. The solution to the problem of illness caused in part by witchcraft and in part by one's own sin is to live a virtuous life and to follow the traditional religious practices and beliefs. The members of his organization all share his belief in the inefficacy of consulting a *soḵha* and the value of following religious tradition, but many of them do not quite comprehend his doctrine of sin. One Santal who attended a meeting of the organization with me but who is not a member remarked, "How can sin in any way be a cause of sickness? I have sinned so much; still I am usually healthy!"

Rạghnạt Murmu lives today in his native village in Mayurbhanj, practicing agriculture and engaging in his teaching, which also includes the propagation of an original alphabet he has developed for Santali. He is a matriculate graduate and has served several years as a high school teacher. Having learned to read Sanskrit in high school, he became deeply interested in and influenced by the Hindu Great Tradition. He has also been noticeably influenced by Christianity through contact with a Catholic missionary. His organization is headed by two uneducated Tata employees who live in a *bustee* (president and treasurer), one young student who is a Tata apprentice (secretary), and one villager from Seraikela who is also uneducated, called the priest (*naeke*) of the organization. The treasurer, though totally illiterate, is a brilliant ecstatic religious teacher who tends to dominate the organization when the guru himself is not present.

It is too early yet to tell how influential the beliefs of this organization will become. The evidence seems to indicate that it has picked up a few converts in the various *bustees* and has indirectly influenced the opinions of some who are not converts. The more educated city Santals, however, look down on the uneducated leaders who dominate the organization, and find the guru's theory about witchcraft uncongenial.

In a very general way it seems that the increasing skepticism toward witchcraft in the *bustees* and the quasi-naturalistic attitude toward it characteristic of the city, are examples of what has earlier been called "modernism." The rather striking *bustee* view of the role of education in eliminating witchcraft is an example of the syncretism of modernism and Santal traditional culture, since it is a combination of the social uplift force of education in eliminating bad social practices, and traditional beliefs regarding witchcraft. It has been stated that the "sin" theory of witchcraft is the result of a syncretism of traditional views of the Santals with those of the Hindu and Christian Great Traditions. Something of the congruence of the various witchcraft beliefs with differing ideological viewpoints has also been discussed.[6]

It is not, however, solely ideological affinity which determines the varying Santal viewpoints on witchcraft. These affinities themselves develop in a matrix of social identification, social approval, and correlative self-approval. Although this is true of the beliefs of all people, it is especially true for the Santals, who traditionally regard the true and the good as inseparable from the shared views of their community. The idea of an internalized yardstick of the true and good, as distinct from the point of view of society, is almost totally lacking, and even among the most modernized and Hinduized it is weakly developed. The variations concerning witchcraft observed in the three kinds of communities under discussion are largely a function of differences of social identification.

The typical village Santal identifies almost exclusively with the Santal community. He is sensitive to the judgments of his fellow Santals primarily and almost exclusively—more particularly to those of his own village or region. He is satisfied with his own views and behavior if his fellow Santals approve of them. Even if he has an ideological proclivity to differ with his fellows, he will be reluctant to express this difference in his village, and he will do all he can to modify his own beliefs so as to bring them into line with those of the community. For these reasons he is the least affected by views of the non-Santal world, even if he is made aware of them.

The *bustee* Santal is less exclusively Santal than is the villager. One powerful influence in the direction of wider identification for both the *bustee* and the city Santal is the fact that Jamshedpur and its environs are great centers of political activity. Many *bustee* and city Santals have entered into the activities of the *ādibāsī* Jharkhand political party. These Santals frequently identify themselves first as *ādibāsīs* and then as Santals. From this organization particularly they have imbibed the notion of social uplift which has been shown to be connected with the *bustee* Santals' new notions about witchcraft. Both the *bustee* and city Santal have widened their social horizons even further through union activity, which causes them to recognize a common interest with their fellow workers of whatever community. The increasing skepticism of the *bustee* Santals toward witchcraft, and the increasingly naturalistic viewpoint evident among the city Santals, are not only the results of increased contact with these ideas through non-Santals; they are also the result of new forms of social interaction with non-Santals, leading to the wider identification necessary to the receptivity of ideas from the non-Santal world. The city Santals' beliefs and practices regarding witchcraft have been more influenced by the non-Santal world because their social interaction is more intensive and persistent with this world than is the case with the *bustee* Santals. Therefore their receptivity is greater.

With respect to the development of a more naturalistic viewpoint among the city Santals and to a lesser extent among the *bustee* Santals, the question might be raised of the possible effects of industrial labor itself. There are two great difficulties in determining an answer to this question. The first is that the creation and operation of an industrial establishment presupposes the existence in fair numbers of personnel who already have such a naturalistic viewpoint. These modernized individuals are observably spreaders of their point of view, making it difficult to isolate any possible effect of industrial labor itself. The second difficulty is that if there is such an effect, it is not directly observable and would have to be inferred from the evidence available with the aid of some general theory regarding the relations of various forms of labor to naturalistic or supernaturalistic orientations.

The fact that the *bustee* Santals are much less naturalistic in their orientation than the city Santals, although both perform industrial jobs, suggests that human contact is at least the more important determinant. This latter comparison, however, must be qualified by recognition that, on the whole, the city Santals hold jobs which require more skill than those held by *bustee* Santals. There can be little doubt that where more complex jobs are learned by formal training, some naturalistic orientation will be absorbed. Some Santals of the city have had such training. The question is how far they will generalize this orientation to embrace other spheres. Will it, for example, affect their attitude toward witchcraft? I do not know of an adequate general theory with which this question can be approached. It may be that, all other things being equal, the more a man knows his working life to be governed by naturalistic means, the more likely he is to extend naturalistic techniques and beliefs to his nonworking life. The Santal certainly knows that all physical problems in the steel mill where he works are solved in a mechanical fashion. It is also certainly true that his working life in the factory is far more controllable and controlled than his traditional agricultural life. It must be remembered, however, that a naturalistic attitude toward witchcraft, for example, will hardly solve the problems that have generated the belief in witchcraft, such as the tensions in the extended family and the displacement of these onto women.

It will be remembered that all specific accusations of witchcraft occur at the time of illness. All Tata workers and most employees of other firms in Jamshedpur are not only provided with free medical treatment but are required to see a doctor and obtain a health certificate whenever they absent themselves from work for health reasons. In the early days this medical care was not much appreciated, but today it is widely used. In line with differences already noted between the *bustee* and the city Santals, it is not surprising that the latter take much more advantage of this service than the former. The *bustee* Santals frequently employ a native practitioner even when they are receiving professional medical care.

In spite of the fact that the *bustee* Santals undoubtedly recover from illness more rapidly and oftener than villagers because of the professional medical care they do receive, sickness is, if anything, more frequent in the *bustee*. This is probably the result of the fact that the *bustee* is much more crowded than any village, while its physical facilities are in no way improved. The city Santals, on the contrary, not only receive better medical care but enjoy far better physical accommodations and are far healthier than either the villagers or the *bustee* dwellers. These circumstances are then perhaps another reason why belief in witchcraft and even witchcraft accusations persist in the *bustee*, while belief is greatly weakened and accusations unheard of in the city.

From the few hypotheses put forth in connection with witchcraft in the village, it follows that anything which tends to raise the status of women in Santal society or to weaken the ideal of the extended family will tend to weaken belief in witchcraft. In this connection the *bustee* Santal suggestion that the education of women will help to eliminate witchcraft may not be wrong. It is as yet too early to pronounce judgment on the persistence of the ideal of the extended family, but if industrial life does lead to its demise, this too should lead to a higher status for women and a weakening of witchcraft.

Quantitative variations in marriage forms. Of the many Santal ceremonies, perhaps none is so rich in symbolic representation and so moving both to the Santal and the outsider as those accompanying marriage. As the method to be applied here is concerned only with interpreting shifts in frequency of the various marriage forms prevalent in Santal society, most of the representations and the beauty characteristic of Santal marriages must be ignored. Only the four most common varieties of marriage occurring in the areas from which most Santal workers have been recruited will be considered. Workers from parts of Seraikela and from Midnapur have been excluded from the sample, as their marriage forms are significantly different from those in the rest of the area under consideration. The factors relevant to choice of marriage form are considered only from the point of view of the groom and his guardians, since they are generally the more active initiators of marriage and more influential in choosing a form.

The marriage form with the highest prestige and involving the greatest expenditure is known as *duạr itut' sindur* 'placing vermillion on [the bride] at the door,' *duạr bapla* 'door marriage,' or *diḳu bapla* 'Hindu marriage.' All these names call attention to the fact that in this form as distinct from all others, vermillion is applied to the bride before the door of the bride's house rather than the groom's. The term *diḳu bapla* reminds one in addition that application of vermillion at the bride's house is the Hindu way. It also points to the fact that this form is in general more like a Hindu marriage than any of the other forms. Unlike the other forms, a proper *duạr bapla* (DB) requires the hiring of a Hindu band and dancers, and the performance, before the application of vermillion, of the marriage of the bride to a tree. This latter rite is practiced by many neighboring Hindu castes. The DB is an arranged marriage in which, if the couple are mature, they are permitted, before preliminary arrangements are completed, to see each other and give or withhold consent. Such consent is almost always forthcoming, and in the case of the girl she really dares not go against the wishes of her parents. Nearly all the inhabitants of both the bride's and groom's villages will be involved at some point in the marriage ceremony or ensuing festivities. A very large party from the groom's village will accompany him to the village of the bride. Traditionally his family was required to hire (usually from some Hindu caste) a number of men to carry the groom on a palanquin to the bride's home. Today, especially if the groom happens to be a Tata worker living in or about Jamshedpur, he may be borne by a hired taxi instead.

The large number of participants not only gives testimony to the affluence of the families being united, but is indicative that the marriage establishes a bond between villages as well as between families and the couple itself. The bride price proper (*gonoṅ*) in all forms of Santal marriage is fixed at two cows if the bride's father is living and one cow if he is dead. There are, in addition, certain other payments made by the groom's guardians, such as the presentation of *dhotis* to the bride's guardians and to a number of her villagers; this payment is not fixed and will be greater in a DB than in any lesser form. The really heavy costs, however, stem from the necessity of transporting and feeding the large party which accompanies the groom's party to the bride's village, hiring the palanquin bearers or taxi as the case may be, and finally providing rice beer (*hạnḍi*) for all one's own villagers as well as food for many villagers and relatives from other villages. In a DB marriage a few non-Santal acquaintances may be invited, often with the intention of enhancing the prestige of the groom's guardians by displaying the important connections they have. Such non-Santals are rarely invited to any of the other forms. The total cost of such a marriage at the present time is between Rs. 800-1500, or, at the going price for rice, between about 3200-6000 lbs.

The second most expensive and prestigeful form of marriage is known as *saṅge bạriạt*[6] (many' *bạriạt*, i.e., members of groom's party). The name *saṅge bạriạt* (SB) suggests that, like DB, it is an arrangement between important people, hence a large number of people will participate. In bride price and other gifts and exchanges it involves almost the same expenditure as a DB. The critical ceremonial difference is that the vermillion will be applied before the house of the groom. The number of people invited will not be so many as in a DB, thus the cost will be substantially reduced. Several events take place at the bride's village which do not usually occur at a DB, e.g., the bride's villagers stop the groom's party on the way through their village and force them to answer a series of riddles (*epeset'*) before they may proceed, a recitation is given by both parties of the mythical origin of the Santals and their society (*binti*), and a drama is presented in a spirit of buffoonery in which a very miserable bride and bridegroom, played by two men, abuse each other in typical mock Santal fashion. The total cost of an SB marriage is between Rs. 200-500 or between 800-2000 lbs of rice.

The least prestigeful and least expensive of arranged marriages is known as either *ṭuṅḳi dipil* 'to carry a small basket on the head,' or *haṛam bạriạt* 'a groom's party consisting of old men.' Most Santals say these two names refer to the same form, but a few insist that *haṛam bạriạt* is a somewhat more elaborate form. For the purpose at hand it will be adequate to treat them as identical. The name *ṭuṅḳi dipil* (TD) suggests that the bride's possessions and gifts are so few as to be portable on her head. *Haṛam bạriạt* emphasizes the fact that the groom's party consists only of a few old men. TD is simply an attenuated form of SB with vermillion similarly applied at the groom's house. The obligation to pay bride price is less and payment is frequently postponed till long after the marriage ceremony. Its cost is generally between Rs. 25-100 or between 100-400 lbs of rice.

In addition to the three forms of arranged marriage, and unlike their Hindu neighbors, the Santals have a traditional form of unarranged or love marriage known as *ńapam bapla* 'to meet' or 'come together marriage,' or more simply as *ńapam* 'to meet' or 'come together.' In practice, this form may include public announcement, bride price, and celebration—or all these practices may be dispensed with. If ceremony and bride price, etc., are included, the form is much like that of an attenuated TD. The cost may vary between Rs. 0-75 or up to 300 lbs or rice.

There are, in addition, two other forms of unarranged marriage. As they are relatively infrequent, they will not be dealt with here in any detailed manner. They are known respectively as *itut' sindur* 'application of vermillion' and *or ạgu* 'to bring by force.' In theory, both forms involve the seizing by a man of a girl against her will with the intention of marriage. In practice they are often a bit of a ruse designed to allow a girl to marry a boy to whom her parents object. While both forms continue to enjoy a kind of quasi-legal status among the Santal community, there is growing opposition, especially among the richer and more educated Santals, against these forms. To have their daughters, who nowadays may be educated and hence refined, seized by any illiterate and uncouth Santal, goes strongly against the grain.

One further preliminary should be mentioned before presenting the frequency data itself, and the interpretation. The samples that have been used are obviously smaller than they should be. I have not meant by these samples to establish definitive conclusions; rather, these sample results are meant as checks on uncounted impressions. Fortunately for the reliability of the results, in no case did their relative magnitudes run counter to my previous impression, though in a few cases I had no anticipation of what the results would be. It should be confessed that had there been cases counter to my expectations derived from considerable other investigation, I would more readily have blamed the size of the sample than abandoned my previous impressions. Considerable care was taken to see that the questions asked of informants were ones they could answer accurately. The only data that is not very accurate, because the informants could not give accurate answers, concerns age and the years ago that certain events occurred. Cross checks were made to determine that answers given by informants were truthful and almost always they were found to be so. A half dozen cases were eliminated because contradictory answers were given which could not be cleared up.

First consideration will be given to Santals married in their native villages and practicing agriculture at the time of their marriage. The sample here is fifty Santals, nineteen of whom at no time after marriage became industrial workers. These nineteen were drawn from two villages in Mayurbhanj. Fifteen were drawn from the village where I have done most of my rural investigations and the other four from a village I have frequently visited for control purposes. In the village where I have done most of my rural work, data was collected from every male in one *tola* (section) of the village. More than half the males in this *tola* had at some time prior to their marriage worked in the surrounding mines and will be excluded from consideration. Thirty-one included in the sample did, after marriage, become industrial workers. They were interviewed in *bustees*, town *bustees* or in the town itself, but most were living in the *bustee* where I have done most of my work. They were not collected by a format random sampling method; we simply went from house to house at various times and questioned anyone who was at home. No one refused to give us the information we requested.

From these fifty Santals, all married while living in villages well away from Jamshedpur or in any other major city, the following frequencies of the different forms of marriage were obtained:

TABLE 2

DB	SB	TD	NB	Total Number
5(10%)	20(40%)	9(18%)	16(32%)	50(100%)

Since the four varieties of marriage are graded in terms of cost, it is reasonable to plot farmers' per capita income against marriage form chosen to determine the degree to which income determines the form chosen. The figures given below are in terms of maunds of husked paddy per person per year after taxation.

TABLE 3

Choice of marriage form by farmers by per capita income

	Marriage Forms				
Maunds per capita	DB	SB	TD	NB	Income Class Total
0-10	0	4	4	10	18
11-20	0	11	3	3	17
21-30	1	5	1	2	9
31-40	2	0	1	0	3
41	2	0	0	1	3
Total Number of Marriages	5	20	9	16	50

If these figures are converted to percentages, it will be seen, for example, that eighty percent of DB fall in the greater than thirty maund category, eighty percent of SB in the greater than ten maund category, fifty-five percent of TD in the greater than ten category and only twelve percent of NB in the greater than ten maund category. The association between marriage form choice and per capita income is obvious and this association, relating high per capita income to expensive forms, is reasonably consistent throughout the table. It is suggested that per capita income is the largest single determinant of marriage type choice.

Of the other possible countable determinants, the possibility has been considered that having either a father or a mother alive at the time of marriage might be a significant determinant since a few cases were known of comparatively well-off Santals without parents who had contracted NB, and who explained that there was no one to arrange a marriage for them. From the sample of fifty it was found that there were only six cases in which both parents were dead at the time of marriage. This indicates that having parents alive at the time of marriage is not a common determinant of marriage forms, at any rate. There are only three cases in which the father was living at the time of marriage and the mother not. This is probably not entirely an accident of sample size. It is partly accounted for by men marrying later than women but it is also probably true that the life expectancy of men is less than that of women. If the twenty-one cases where only the mother was alive at the time of marriage be compared with the remainder of the sample, no significant difference in marriage type frequency will be found. Since these cases in which the father was not alive at time of marriage show no difference in frequency of marriage type from the rest of the sample, it is concluded that having a father alive is not a significant determinant of marriage type choice.

One other kind of countable information about rural Santal marriage type choice had to be considered, i.e., whether there was a shift in frequency during the historical period under consideration. The period covered by these marriages is from 1913 to 1957. The data indicate that there were no significant shifts in frequency during this period, nor were there any appreciable changes in the distribution of per capita income. As there has been a population increase during this period, the near stability of per capita income distribution is the result of employment opportunities at the mines and in Jamshedpur.

Before turning to a consideration of the marriage type choices of the industrial workers, it is necessary to account for the remaining partial determinants of marriage choice in the rural environment so that comparison between these choices in the village, *bustee*, and city can be controlled. Arranged marriages are the occasion for great dancing, singing, drinking, and general merry-making, and a Santal of some standing in the community is expected to validate his status by treating his villagers to a first rate marriage. As there are a number of inherited offices that confer high status, and a number of ways of achieving high status which are partially independent of wealth, those prominent Santals whose incomes are not high nevertheless feel compelled to choose a more expensive form than their income alone would dictate. In addition, there are idiosyncratic differences in desire for status which lead to choosing marriage forms beyond a man's income. Finally, there is the Santal belief that the higher the form of marriage, the greater its chances of lasting. Santals with a greater regard for the stability of their children's marriages may resort to a more expensive form than they can really afford or than their social standing dictates.

For the *bustees* a sample of forty-seven was chosen, of whom the majority came from the *bustee* where I have done most of my work, a few lived in nearby *bustees*, and a few now live in company houses. All these were workers at the time of marriage and lived in *bustees*. They were selected by simply going house to house at various times. No one refused to give us information. It should be mentioned that about sixty percent of the Santals who come to Jamshedpur are unmarried when they arrive.

The figures for marriage type frequency among these *bustee* workers show a marked shift away from DB and SB toward NB.

TABLE 4

Bustee Workers

DB	SB	TD	NB	Total Number	Total Percentage
0(0%)	6(13%)	7(15%)	34(72%)	47	(100%)
Rural Farmers (repeated)					
5(10%)	20(40%)	9(18%)	16(32%)	50	(100%)

If a Santal is going to have an arranged marriage his parents or guardians must arrange it for him. Those workers who did have arranged marriages regularly sent large portions of their income to their parents back on the farm. Almost all these workers maintained a joint interest with their relatives on the farm in the family property. As it has already been shown in the section on recruitment and commitment that Santal industrial workers were not much poorer as a group in terms of their former agricultural per capita income than those who remained on the farm, it follows that lower per capita income cannot account for the shift to NB. Since this sample of forty-seven *bustee* Santals contains a number of informants who were not included in the sample used in the chapter on recruitment and commitment and excludes some used there, per capita farm income as shown in it has also been compared to the original sample of fifty farmers. It was again found that there was only a small difference between the two groups, with the workers a bit poorer while still agriculturalist than the farmers who remained on the farm. The important fact shown in the tables below is that if one includes the industrial income of the workers at the time of their marriage with the farm income of those with whom they still share ownership, the total per capita income of this group is higher than that of the sample farmers who did not become industrial workers. Hence the shift to NB is in spite of available per capita income greater than farmers'.

TABLE 5

Per Capita Income of *Bustee* Workers and their Farming Family[7]

Maunds	Percentage of families
0-10	21%
11-20	34%
21-30	28%
31-40	6%
40	11%
Total	100%

TABLE 6[8]

Per Capita Income of Farmers (repeat)

Maunds	Percentage of Families
0-10	44%
11-20	32%
21-30	14%
31-40	2%
40	8%
Total	100%

Before interpreting this shift in marriage type choice, two additional, relevant, measurable matters should be mentioned. Among the *bustee* Santals of the sample, the length of time in the *bustee* before marriage ranged from zero to twelve years, with a mean time of 3.9 years. No significant shift in marriage type frequency was found to be related to the length of time spent in the *bustee* before marriage. It has been mentioned that when Santal *bustee* dwellers wish to have an arranged marriage, they send home considerable money to their parents. The great shift to NB indicates then that most of them are unwilling to send such amounts home. Since the length of time spent in the *bustee* before marriage does not determine this attitude, it was inferred that it is not due to some new values slowly acquired.

A number of factors inherent in the *bustee* situation and in industrial labor are, in my view, responsible for the shift to NB. The most important of these are the result of moving out of the native village and into a different kind of community. Although the *bustee* Santal tends to maintain his connections with his family in the native village and almost never requests a division of the land, he now has an income of his own. If he had remained in the village, he would only have achieved such an independent income by asking for a division of the land. Therefore, while he formally maintains his connection with his extended family, he has achieved the independence from the extended family normally attained by a division of land. This independence leaves him free to spend his money much as he pleases. Another factor contributing to this independence is that he is physically distant from his extended family and hence daily free from their social control and the supporting authority of the villagers. The question is, why does he use this greater independence to choose an NB?

One important reason relates to his reaction to industrial labor. As discussed earlier, there are a number of things he does not like about industrial labor, the most important dislikes being the necessity of working throughout the year instead of about six months as on the farm, and the lack of freedom to work when and how he pleases. He feels that he has made a great sacrifice in coming and is especially reluctant to part with the only great reward, his increased income. One other important factor arising out of freedom from parental and traditional village restraint is the opportunity afforded to *bustee* Santal men and women to meet each other without restraint. There are a great number of unmarried women workers in the *bustees*. These women, whose parents are seldom with them, have many more opportunities to enter into sexual alliances than girls living in the village. The same is true of the men who, if they entered into such alliances in the village, would be sharply censored, especially if they came from at least a moderately well-off family. The record shows that eighteen of the thirty-four NB marriages of the *bustee* Santal were contracted with working girls; it is probable that a large proportion of the remaining sixteen were contracted with girls who, though not working, were living in *bustees* while searching for work.

Before turning to the city Santals, one most interesting tendency regarding the shift to NB must be mentioned. The evidence indicates that between eleven and twenty-one years ago about sixty-four percent of the marriages were NB, while in the period of zero to ten years ago eighty-one percent were NB. Since there is no appreciable income difference between these two groups, it is suggested that this shift may be a truly cultural one. What began as a shift due to circumstances which had changed, has become a recognized norm for the *bustees*. It is now easier to enter into an NB because the stigma of low status associated with it has lessened.

As a consequence of the length of service required to obtain a company house in town, there are only four cases of city Santals married after moving into a company house, excluding the city Santals of Seraikela origin. Of the four cases one was a DB, one SB, and two NB. From only four cases there is really nothing to be inferred, especially since the city Santals tend to be richer than those of the *bustees*. What can, however, be offered for comparison is the prevailing attitude of the city Santals to the various forms. Considering their greater identification with and sensitivity to the Hindu world, as compared to either the villagers or the *bustee* dwellers, it is not surprising that from the traditional Santal repertory they strongly prefer the more Hinduized DB marriage, and severely criticize the NB form.

In the section on witchcraft it was said that the *bustee* dwellers as well as the city Santals have increased their identification with the non-Santal world as, for example, by union membership. If this is true, one may well ask why there has been a shift to NB in the *bustees*, since this is a shift away from the dominant non-Santal Hindu pattern? The answer appears to be that the *bustee* Santal, still living predominantly among fellow Santals or other *ādibāsī*, weakly identify with the dominant Hindu society. Beyond the heightened identification with other *ādibāsī*, they have formed identification with their fellow workers as a common interest group. This interest group does indeed include Hindus, but the nature of the identification with this group is such that the sensitivity of the *bustee* Santals to its point of view is largely confined to its attitudes regarding labor's interests. It is, then, because of this weak increased sensitivity to the Hindu point of view per se and the circumstances within the *bustees* conducive to a high frequency of NB, that the shift in the *bustees* is away from the Hindu pattern. In the city, on the contrary, the new forms of intercourse with the non-Santal world have led to a much increased identification with and sensitivity to Hindu cultural patterns per se.

It has been mentioned that there is a relatively strong development of what has been called modernism in Jamshedpur. The disparaging of expenditure of wealth for traditional ceremonial purposes is a characteristic of this cultural current. The question might then be raised why this current has not induced the city Santals to accept the cheap and unceremonious NB. The answer is that the dominant Hindu community in Jamshedpur has not adopted this western modernistic viewpoint with respect to marriage, although that viewpoint has influenced this community to spend less on a number of other traditional ceremonies. When there is a conflict between modernism and traditional Hinduism, the city Santals are primarily motivated to choose a form of behavior and belief in conformity with that of their Hindu neighbors, i.e., to make the same choice between the two traditions that the Hindus do. There is little tendency for them to choose independently between the two traditions.

The shift to NB in the *bustee* raises a final important methodological point. Manning Nash has very cogently suggested that the best situation in which to study the relations between industry and culture in countries newly embarking on development of industry is where factories grow up within a village or small community.[9] In studying the effects of this industry on the culture of the village or small community where it has grown up, one can largely eliminate the superfluous effects of urbanization. There is no doubt that this recommendation is sound and that such studies are needed. However, apart from the fact that there is intrinsic interest in the effects of urbanization per se on tribal and peasant people, there are additional reasons why studies of such people removed from their traditional setting are required. Furthermore, the method used in this study indicates that there are ways of controlling for the effect of urbanization. The shift to NB in the *bustees* indicates that mere removal of a people from their traditional environment with its accompanying freedom from traditional restraint may be a significant factor in cultural change. In this case the weakening of restraint combines with the *bustee* Santal's attitude toward industrial work to bring about this change. Indeed, a comparison of this finding with Nash's findings in Cantel make this point more striking. In Cantel one of the most important findings was that the Cantelensi used their increased earnings largely "to implement old cultural needs and wants."[10] Among the Santal *bustees* on the contrary, it is found that there is a great unwillingness to spend increased income on a traditionally prestigeful form of marriage. The point to be made is that both kinds of studies are required if the total gamut of the possible effects of industrialization are to be learned.

Considerable control over the added effects of urbanization can be obtained in studies like this one, where the community under study lives not only in the industrial city but also includes industrial workers who live outside the city. To the extent that these two kinds of communities occupy the same position in industry one can, by comparing them, control for the factor of urbanization.

The case of the city Santals' increased identification with Hindu society raises the final point to be considered. What is it that keeps these city Santals out of the Hindu fold? While they have abandoned many of the traditional values and attitudes of their society, they cling to certain religious practices and other traditional behaviors which are distinctively Santal and will not identify themselves as Hindu. Among the most important bonds with his own society are the traditional and deeply rooted sentiments of obligation and emotional attachment to his kin. These bonds are made even more manifest for the city Santal by his dependence on kin in his native village to maintain his interest in the family land. Ordinarily these relatives cultivate his share of the land and periodically bring him rice in return for cash contributions. He is further bound to his own society by the belief or at least the fear that if certain traditional rites are not performed to ancestors and other deities he may be punished with illness. One of the most prominently mentioned dependences of the city Santal on his own society is for the traditional rites associated with death in the event that he or a member of his immediate family should die. This dependency when considered in terms of the traditional configuration of beliefs and practices concerned with death appears to be largely a symbolic representation of his ramified interconnection with the traditional Santal social order. Apart from these and a number of other internal bonds there are a number of particularly significant external institutions contributing to the maintenance of his Santal identity. One of the most important of these is the system of caste ranking. The much acculturated city Santals have decided, for the moment at least, that to become Hindu would mean to accept a low position in the caste hierarchy. They know of the movement to abolish caste but they are not yet convinced that it will triumph. As suggested earlier, the rise of the Jharkhand party has contributed to a strong new identification with all *ādibāsī*. In addition it has provided a new avenue of social mobility, i.e., election to public office. Through the Jharkhand party and other institutions for tribal welfare the Santal who is better educated than his fellows can gain status in an area less competitive than that of the wider Indian society. Finally there are significant practical reasons for maintaining their identity as members of a scheduled tribe. Among such benefits are scholarships, special governmental appointments, and preferential industrial appointment.

This cursory treatment of the conditions contributing to Santal self identification particularly among the city Santals is obviously far from exhaustive. I have only meant to indicate that not all recent developments have contributed toward the absorption of city Santals into the Hindu fold. The city Santal is far from considering the abandonment of his tribal identity. What he is very actively considering is the conflict between his accepted social identity and his dissatisfaction with various aspects of the traditional culture. Under the present conditions it is far more likely that he will continue his attempt to remold Santal culture to his own liking than abandon his social identity. Increasingly sensitive to the beliefs, practices, and criticisms of the general Indian society, his aim is to "raise" his own society to a level where it will command the respect of the non-Santal world.

NOTES

[1] For an excellent prior example of such anthropological treatment, see Manning Nash, "The Recruitment of Wage Labor and Development of New Skills," *The Annals* (May, 1956); or by the same author, "Some Notes on Village Industrialization in South and East Asia," *Economic Development and Cultural Change,* III, No. 3 (April, 1955); or his unpublished doctoral thesis on industrialization among the Cantelenos (University of Chicago). I should mention here the considerable theoretical debt that I owe especially to the last study.

[2] The orthography used for all Santal words in this article is the standard system of romanization of Santali as developed and presented by P. O. Bodding in *Materials for a Santali Grammar,* Part I, second edition (Dumka, 1930), with the few diacritical modifications employed by W. J. Culshaw, *Tribal Heritage, A Study of the Santals* (London, 1949).

[3] The farmers who emigrated were interviewed in the *bustee* where they live and where I have done much of my work, or in the homes of the city Santals. They do not properly constitute a random sample, as the information was collected simply by going from house to house at various times. Like other statistics which follow, these are meant to be only suggestive of certain tendencies and of various methods being employed.

[4] This attitude toward the *diku* is much more ambivalent than the attitude in the village. As will be discussed later, this increased ambivalence is partly the result of new identifications formed on the job and by greater and new forms of social interconnection with the non-Santal world.

[5] Santali, *ḍahṛi,* Hindi *ḍain.* There are actually a variety of witches, but only the most common is under consideration.

[6] As Datta-Majumdar states very clearly in *The Santal,* the numerous traits borrowed by the Santals in their long contact with the Hindu world have been almost entirely either simply

artifacts or forms of behavior adequately modified by the Santals to fit traditional patterns of meaning and value. I suggest that the recent changes reported here regarding witchcraft belief are of a more fundamental character and represent significant changes in traditional beliefs. See Nabendule Datta-Majumdar, *The Santal, A Study in Culture-Change,* Department of Anthropology, Government of India, Memoir No. 2, 1955 (Calcutta, 1956).

[7] Industrial cash income was converted into husked paddy according to the prevailing price of rice at the time of marriage and added to farm income in husked rice after taxation.

[8] This is the same farm sample used in the section on recruitment and commitment.

[9] Nash, 1955, 1956, and thesis.

[10] Nash, 1956, p. 29.

University of Chicago
Chicago, Illinois

CULTS OF THE DEAD AMONG THE NĀYARS

By E. Kathleen Gough

IN this paper I shall attempt both a sociological and a psychological analysis of Nāyar cults of the dead. That is to say, I shall try to relate the role-structure and social functions of the cults to those of legal and economic institutions, and to relate the emotional content of the cults to that of certain relationships among the living.

The Nāyars[1] are a high, matrilineal caste of landholders and salaried workers. Some four to seven matrilineal lineages of commoner Nāyars traditionally occupied the high caste area of a village. They served a Nāyar or Nambūdiri Brahman village headman, and had authority over tenants, artisans, and serfs of lower caste. The lineage was exogamous, had a depth of about ten to fifteen generations and was concerned in village government. But the more significant economic unit was a lineage segment (*taravād*), whose members jointly owned property including an ancestral house. The eldest man of this group was its legal guardian (*kāranavan*).

Before British rule began in 1792, the Malabar Coast comprised a number of kingdoms. I am concerned with Nāyars of villages in the former Cochin kingdom, in the center of the coast, and with those of villages in the former Kottayam kingdom in the north.

In Cochin, the country was relatively flat, fertile, and densely populated. The Nāyars were the professional military caste. For a part of each year they tended to be absent from the village in military training or war. Women remained on their ancestral estates under the legal guardianship of the *kāranavan* and were maintained by the work of tenants and serfs. Probably largely as a result of the relatively mobile military occupation of the men, plural marital unions were customary. A woman might have six or eight husbands of her own or a higher subcaste, and a man, any number of Nāyar wives of his own or a lower subcaste. Residence was duolocal: spouses lived separately in their natal homes and a husband visited his wife in her home at night. Exact physiological paternity was, clearly, often unknown, and in any case a man had no rights in nor obligations to his children. Among Nāyars of this area, therefore, contrary to Murdock's generalization,[2] the elementary family was not institutionalized as a legal, economic or residential unit.

In Kottayam, the terrain was mountainous and jungly, the area more sparsely populated, and the kingdom less centralized. The Nāyars were cultivating landowners and only occasional warriors. The hilly and jungly terrain and the sparsity of population made duolocal residence impracticable. In most cases a man took his wife to live in his ancestral household in avunculocal residence, and children were brought up until adolescence in the houses of their fathers. There was some polygyny, but polyandry was forbidden. Fathers had morally though not legally recognized rights in and obligations to their children and a strong affective bond with them. The *Karanavān* of their lineage segment was however the authority in important matters.

Both in Kottayam and in Cochin, Nāyar women were occasionally married to men of the highest, patrilineal caste of Nambūdiri Brahmans. Children of such unions were Nāyars, and rules of ritual pollution maintained distance between them and their higher caste fathers. The Nambūdiri father might not eat with his wife and children, and might not touch them during the daytime while in a state of ritual purity. Only the eldest son of a Nambūdiri house might marry a Nambūdiri wife and beget children for his own family.

British rule brought about the collapse of the Nāyar armies early in the nineteenth century. Probably as a result of this change, plural marriages gradually died out in Cochin. The lineage system persisted with little change until the turn of the century, but in both areas the employment of men in professional and wage work led to the development of privately owned property in addition to property owned jointly by the matrilineal group. The Malabar Marriage Act of 1896 permitted men to register their marriages and gave the children of such marriages rights in half the personal property of the father after his death. During this century, the greatly increased employment of men in salaried work, and the development of cash-crop farming, have brought about a partial disintegration of the matrilineage, and have tended toward the emergence of the elementary family as an economic and legal unit. Under the pressure of these changes, laws[3] were passed in 1933 and 1937 which required all men to register their marriages, gave rights of maintenance to their wives and children, and provided that the whole of a man's personal property be inherited by his wife and children. In addition, the laws permitted, though they did not require, equal division of the matrilineal estate on a per caput basis[4] between all members. Although some traditional households remain, it has now become fairly customary for a woman and her immature children jointly to separate their shares of property from those of the rest of their matrilineal group, and to set up a new establishment with the woman's husband. He, in turn, may have abstracted his single share of property from that of his own matrilineal group. Sometimes, the husband himself provides a new house for his elementary family from his own share of property and his private earnings. Sometimes the new house is provided from the property of the wife and children, who receive their husband and father into it as a resident and wage earner. Sometimes husband and wife pool their property and set up a joint establishment.

Given the modern heterogeneity of legal, economic, and residential arrangements, and given also variations in education, interests, and life experience, it is not surprising that cults of the dead reveal differential rates of change. I shall be chiefly concerned with the traditional cults, although these persist without change in only a few of the more traditionally patterned households—actually, in fifteen percent of Nāyar households in one Cochin village, and in thirteen percent in one village in Kottayam.

The Nāyars participate in three distinguishable categories of cults of the dead. The first comprises a collective cult, by the matrilineal property group, of the ghosts of matrilineal forebears, which I call lineage ghosts. This cult is non-Sanskritic. The second category comprises various kinds of offerings by individuals to the spirits of dead kinsfolk at funerals or on the anniversaries of deaths. These cults are Sanskritic in origin. The third category comprises various cults of the ghosts of persons who were not members of the Nāyar's own lineage; I call these alien ghosts. These cults, like the cult of lineage ghosts, are non-Sanskritic. I discuss the three categories of cults in that order, and then refer briefly to modern changes in the cults.

The Cult of Lineage Ghosts

Each traditional Nāyar house contains a room devoted to lineage ghosts. Within the shrine are placed small, low stools (*pīṭhams*). On each of these it is believed that a particular ghost comes to sit on the days when offerings are made.

In property groups of the aristocratic lineages of village headmen and district chiefs, which own more land than do commoner Nāyars, family histories recorded in palm leaf documents may contain the names and achievements of twenty or more *kāranavans* extending back over two or three hundred years. In such lineages, whose property groups divide less frequently than do those of commoner Nāyars, the *kāranavans'* spirits are housed in a special building in the courtyard south of the ancestral house. Commoner Nāyars care somewhat less for their ancestry. Sometimes they have only three or four stools for their lineage ghosts and remember by name only those who died within the last hundred years or whose lives were in some way remarkable. Remarkable *kāranavans* are those who fought bravely in battles or received honor from chief or king, those who earned property on behalf of their matrilineal groups, or those who died prematurely through accident, murder, epidemic or suicide.

Regular offerings are made only to *kāranavans*, for only *kāranavans* hold legal authority and only their names tend to appear in documents which survive for posterity. On the advice of the astrologer, however, a *taravād* may, in emergency, propitiate the ghost of an ancestress or of a man who died before becoming *kāranavan*. But such ghosts are always those who died within the lifetime of living members.

The lineage ghosts are regularly propitiated[5] on the new moon days of Karkidagam (July-August) and Tulām (October-November). Food is cooked in the kitchen by women of the matrilineal household, and a large portion is placed on a plantain leaf for each of the ghosts. It includes curried meat and vegetables, fried paddy, beaten rice, fuits, and sweet puddings of various kinds. Toddy and arrack were traditionally served along with the meal. If a dead *kāranavan* is known to have enjoyed special foods during life, he receives a large portion of these foods. Occasionally, even in the past, individual Nāyars have been vegetarians. The spirits of vegetarian *kāranavans* may not be served with meat and are housed in a separate shrine. When the dishes are prepared, they are carried quickly to the shrine so that the ghosts may partake of their essence before others have tasted or smelled them. The living *kāranavan* places the leaves before the stools in the presence of men junior to him in the property group and then closes the door of the shrine. Age-rank is observed in making the offerings. For each spirit, in addition to its own leaf, is briefly offered the food later placed before the stools of spirits junior to it. Similarly, the vegetables of vegetarian ghosts are first offered to meat eaters who were senior to them, and the vegetables (but not the meat) cooked for meat eating ghosts are first offered to vegetarian ghosts who were their seniors. After a few minutes the *kāranavan* reopens the door and distributes the food, to be eaten by all members of the *taravād*. Women take no part in offering the food and may not enter the ancestral shrine on this day. They are also forbidden to enter it during menstrual and birth pollutions, and all members are forbidden entry during the fifteen days of pollution following a death.

Traditionally, at the close of offerings to the ghosts, men of the *taravād* might become drunk with toddy and arrack. In this condition, one or more young men might undergo possession by one of the ghosts. He performed a frenzied dance and called out to the assembled members with the voice of the ghost, declaring its will and thanking or threatening the *taravād* on its behalf. I heard of only one *taravād* where this custom persisted. Shamanistic possession by the goddess Bhagavatī or by the god Aiyappan is, however, still prevalent among rural Nāyars, and such religious possession is still more common among the lower castes.

In some *taravāds*, propitiation of lineage ghosts accompanies that of various deities associated with the *taravād*. Chief of these is the lineage's patron goddess (*dharma devī*). The goddess, though known by different names in different *taravāds*, is always thought of as a species of the generic goddess Bhagavadi or Bhādrakāli, the chief deity of the Nāyars. Each group of Nāyar *taravāds* in a village usually possesses in common a temple dedicated to Bhādrakāli, but each *taravād* has, in addition, its own goddess. Cults of the village goddess are more important in Cochin, and of the *taravād* goddess, in Kottayam. The village goddess is believed capable of withholding or inflicting on the population wholesale misfortunes of a kind which strike all men alike—smallpox, cholera, flood, drought, cyclone, cattle epidemic, or defeat in an intervillage feud. Such inflictions result from failure to propitiate the goddess or failure to uphold the moral laws of caste. The *taravād* goddess concerns herself with its members' private morality and inflicts such individual misfortunes as fever, barrenness in women or cattle, or grave financial loss.

In aristocratic *taravāds*, the goddess and the lineage ghosts may nowadays be housed together in an ancient gynasium (*ḳalari*) near the ancestral house—a building formerly devoted to the military training of the *taravād's* youth. The ghosts may then be propitiated with cooked food on the same day on which a cock is sacrificed to the patron goddess. In such rites, propitiation of both spirits and goddess are associated with the *taravād's* former martial glory. In the rites there usually figure one or more ancestral swords which the male forebears used during their lives. These swords are the property of the goddess and are propitiated by the *ḳāranvan* as representatives of the deity.

Lineage ghosts have some concern with the *taravād's* internal morality. If its members fail in hospitality to guests, squander their income, or neglect their property, the ghosts may inflict misfortunes on one or more members of the group. However, failure to propitiate the ghosts correctly is the offence most likely to provoke retribution. Conversely, if offerings are made correctly to the ghosts, they will help to preserve the *taravād* from misfortune.

The ghosts vary in their severity and in the wrongs which they punish. A *ḳāranavan* who amassed much property is most likely to resent extravagance on the part of his successors. Forebears who died prematurely are more punitive than those who died peacefully in old age. All ghosts, however, are somewhat capricious: a small offense may provoke stern retribution, and misdemeanors on the part of one adult may result in the sickness of another or of a child of the property group. In particular, a forebear who was injured or insulted by his juniors during life or after his death may wreak vengeance on the *taravād* even down to the seventh or eighth generation. One instance from a village headman's lineage in Kottayam will illustrate such retribution. In 1798, the property group was dying out for lack of women, and the *ḳāranavan* adopted a woman and her children from a related segment of his lineage. After the *kāranavan*'s death, his adopted successor was too young to manage the property. This passed temporarily into the management of a man from still another branch of the same lineage. When the true claimant came of age he disputed his guardian's management. After a bitter lawsuit the guardian was deposed in a British court. He continued to live on the *taravād*'s land and to harass his young successor. When the guardian died, the young *kāranavan* in his anger failed to arrange for the cremation rites until several days had passed and the corpse had decomposed. The ghost of this proxy *kāranavan* has harrassed his successors ever since, causing many of them to die of diabetes. The present members regard this condition as a decomposition of the body during life. The ghost's anger is so great that propitiations do not wholly avert its vengeance, although special offerings temporarily delay the progress of the disease.

The misfortunes inflicted by lineage ghosts include many forms of sickness, mental disorder, female barrenness and miscarriages, all of which are attributed to actual bodily possession by a ghost. Financial loss, crop failure and the deaths of babies or cows may also result from the ghosts' displeasure. I could find no very clear distinction between the misfortunes inflicted by lineage ghosts and those brought about by the patron goddess, by malevolent alien ghosts, or by the witchcraft or sorcery of enemies. Indeed it is obvious that the Nāyars themselves do not clearly restrict particular misfortunes to particular agents. For on the occasion of a misfortune, the *kāranavan* must often consult the village astrologer (Kanisan) who makes calculations to discover the responsible agent. He then instructs the *kāranavan* how to carry out its propitiation or to accomplish its control.

However, my information suggests that some misfortunes may be more likely to be attributed to some agents than to others. Miscarriages, for example, seem to be often attributed to ancestresses, to female alien ghosts, or to the patron goddess. Barrenness is often attributed to the snake gods of the *taravād*, who are believed to guard the fertility of its women. These misfortunes seem to be less often attributed to male ghosts, although some instances are known. Perhaps most important, however, circumstances immediately preceding the misfortune may help to determine the agent. If a forebear has died recently, or if a *taravād* has failed to propitiate its lineage ghosts or patron goddess, the *kāranavan* may not even trouble to consult the astrologer, or the astrologer may merely corroborate his suspicions. Similarly, if a man has an enemy with whom he has recently quarreled and then himself falls ill with fever, he is like to assume that the enemy has engaged the services of a witch or sorcerer against him. In small villages whose population is stable, moreover, the astrologer makes it his business to know the affairs of his clients and thus to diagnose appropriate causes for their misfortunes.

Sociological analysis. A satisfactory analysis of the functions of lineage ghosts must take into account those of other supernatural agents and of secular authorities. Among the Nāyars, supernatural agents have played only a minor role in punishing offences against men, as distinct from those against themselves. This is undoubtedly because human authorities of various kinds had strong judicial functions, deriving from their incorporation in a kingdom. In the last analysis their authority was backed by the military power of the king or chief. Among Nāyars, civil disputes were tried by village headman or district chief. Certain major crimes against the kingdom's religious laws were tried in the Raja's court. They included the killing of a cow or a Brahman or fornication with lower caste persons. The killing or assault of a Nāyar outside the lineage led to feuds between lineages or between larger territorial units. In Cochin, the king had more power than in Kottayam to curtail such feuds or confine them to organized duels for which a fee must be paid. Minor offences against caste law, such as dining with low caste persons, were tried by the subcaste assembly of the village and resulted in temporary excommunication of the offender's property group and the payment of a fine to the village goddess's temple.

The *ḳāranavan* had the legal right to punish offences within the property group and also those offences against caste law for which the caste held the property group responsible until justice had been done. Incest and murder within the lineage appear to have been punished by expulsion from the *taravād* by the *ḳāranavan* and from the caste by the caste assembly. In cases of grave insubordination by a junior member, the *ḳāranavan* had the right to deny him maintenance or access to the ancestral house until he mended his behavior.

Thus the supernatural agents of the village and the *taravād* primarily acted to force the human authorities to carry out their judicial duties. If, for example, the caste failed to excommunicate the *taravād* of an individual who had sinned against its religious laws, it was believed that the village goddess would strike the village with epidemic, flood, or some such misfortune. Similarly, if incest within the lineage went undetected or unpunished, the lineage ghosts and the patron goddess might cause the offenders to die or might bring misfortune on the *taravād* as a whole.

The fact that any member of the *taravād* may suffer as a result of the misdemeanors of any other, carries into the realm of supernatural sanctions the collective responsibility of the *taravād* in social and legal affairs. If a man breaks a ritual rule of the caste, his whole *taravād* is polluted and liable for excommunication. If a death or birth occurs, the whole lineage is temporarily polluted and excluded from normal social life. At the back of these norms lies the fact that the *taravād* is an economic and legal corporation. Its property is owned jointly, and the *taravād* is responsible for the debts of any one member. Its male members must support each other in feuds against other lineages. It is not surprising that the concept of being members one of another in secular affairs is projected into the realm of mystical retributions.

The points at which supernatural agents might replace, or act instead of, human authorities, appear to have been those where a subordinate was wronged by one who was himself a powerful authority and could manipulate the law. Thus lineage ghosts were probably particularly effective in punishing or setting to rights misdemeanors of the *ḳāranavan* himself. I am uncertain whether, in traditional law, junior members could sue in court for the deposition of an erring *ḳāranavan*. They certainly possessed this right in British law, but even so, it was very difficult before 1933 to get rid of a *ḳāranavan*. The lineage ghosts appear to have provided important sanctions against a *ḳāranavan's* misdoings, for they brought misfortune on a *taravād* whose *ḳāranavan* disgraced its reputation for hospitality or squandered its property. I was told that the former custom by which a junior member might be possessed by a ghost and voice its threats to the *taravād* added force to the complaints of young men who were cheated by their *ḳāranavans*. The fact that only the *ḳāranavan* may propitiate the lineage ghosts points up both his responsibility to the ghosts to ensure good conduct and prosperity in his *taravād*, and also his responsibility to his juniors to ensure the favor of the ghosts.

I have myself recorded no case in which lineage ghosts were believed to have actually prevented a crime on the part of a *ḳāranavan*, as distinct from punishing one. V. K.

Raman Menon, however, records a legend of a mother's brother who deliberately betrayed a nephew, whom he hated, to the vengeance of a lineage currently feuding with his own.[6] The nephew was to have been killed by his enemies on the following day. But in the night his mother prayed for the return of her son's elder brother who was absent in a distant land. The lineage ghosts miraculously brought home the brother in time to save his junior's life. It must be remembered, moreover, that the belief that the deceased himself would become a lineage ghost capable of wreaking vengeance probably formed a sanction against intralineage murder.

Women are excluded from the ancestral shrine during their pollutions and may not enter it on the day of propitiations. The former prohibition is related to the whole concept of bad sacredness associated with emissions of the body, which prevents women from touching or eating with others or entering any sacred place during their pollutions. That women should be totally excluded from the shrine on days of propitiation seems also to relate to the general position of women in the society. As in most of the higher Hindu castes, women traditionally played a very minor role in economic production, for the work of production was done by the lower castes. A few women were scholars, and a few were even trained in arms, but the Nāyars' occupation as soldiers in general tended to exclude women from work outside the home. The bearing of children was by far the chief value of women. Correspondingly, women were subordinates in the legal sphere. They were throughout life under the legal guardianship of men, might not take part in public deliberations, and might not act as witnesses in the village court. The legal subordination of women may have been partly connected with their comparative lack of value in economic production, and perhaps partly, with the great moral authority they derived from childbearing—for female procreation was very highly valued and male envy of these functions was overt. The cult of lineage ghosts supports the correct operation of male legal authority within the *taravād*. The exclusion of women from participation in it, and their exclusion from the shrine on days when their procreative functions were most apparent, perhaps expresses in a formal manner the notion that the power which women derived from these functions was polar and even antipathetic to the legal and economic power of men.

Although the lineage ghosts had only subsidiary judicial functions, their cult served in several ways indirectly to maintain right relationships within the *taravād*. First, a *kāranavan* who respected and correctly propitiated his own forebears provided a role model of piety for his juniors in their relations with living elders. Second, the ghosts, as we have seen, provided some sanctions against a *kāranavan's* ill treatment of his wards. Levy,[7] in connection with the Chinese ancestor cult, has pointed out the importance of having supernatural agents to whom a human authority owes deference, in social units where the authority is not chosen by his subordinates and cannot easily be manipulated or removed by them. For the authority's good behavior toward his subordinates then becomes a part of his sanctioned duty toward his own supernatural authorities. In the Chinese cult, which in this respect resembles the Brahman, the head of a family must care for his patrilineal descendants because it is part of his duty to the ancestors to provide happy and prosperous offspring. For these, by their own later ancestral offerings, will save the forebears' spirits, and his own, from suffering in the life after death. In the Nāyar case, the *kāranavan* must keep his *taravād* in good order because if he does not do so the lineage ghosts may inflict suffering on all, including himself.

Third, the ghost cult obviously provides one explanation for the cause of misfortunes, and offers a course of action whereby these may supposedly be allayed. Further, the *taravād's* collective responsibility for its misfortunes in a sense makes the ghosts a common threat to its members, for all may suffer from their anger. The ghost cult thus enhances the sense of unity and common destiny of *taravād* members.

Psychological analysis. The problem of the circumstances under which cults of punitive ancestors arise does not seem to have been solved in culture and personality writing. Freud[8] derived all forms of fear of, and taboos relating to, the dead, from ambivalence felt to these kinsfolk during life. Mead[9] in 1930 granted a probable universality of ambivalence to the dead, but pointed out that whereas Western Europeans tend to emphasize affection and grief toward the dead and to suppress hostility, some societies give ceremonial emphasis to the hostility and suppress the expression of affection and grief. Others appear to permit an equal expression of both hostility and grief, and Mead thought that personal conflicts relating to the dead may be almost eliminated when both attitudes find ceremonial expression. She argued that the choice of which attitude should be uppermost in ceremonial expression was "a function of the civilization in which the individual lives," but did not at that time attempt to relate attitudes to the dead to specific types of relationships with the living.

Opler,[10] in an analysis of Chiracahua and Mescalero Apache usages relating to the dead, has shown that these exhibit mixed feelings of grief and hostility, and has derived these from ambivalence to living relatives engendered in the matrilocal extended family. But Opler's analysis, convincing though it is, leaves us again with the problem that probably all social relations, and especially all kinship relations, are to some extent ambivalent. Why then do some societies express ambivalence in mixed attitudes to the dead, others in predominantly hostile attitudes with the benevolent aspects suppressed, and still others in predominantly benevolent attitudes with the hostile aspects suppressed? A more intricate analysis of types of ambivalence is required. Attempts in this direction have been made by a number of recent writers, notably Kardiner, Fortes, Roheim, Hsu, Mead in later writings, and Whiting and Child[11] in a cross cultural survey of beliefs about evil spirits and demons. Building on the theories of these writers, I shall try to find meaningful connections between Nāyar attitudes to lineage ghosts and their attitudes to living matrilineal kinsfolk of the preceding generation.

Nāyar lineage ghosts are oriented toward the living. Although Nāyars state that good spirits go to a heaven of sensual pleasures and bad spirits to a hell of physical torture, they do not elaborate this belief or refer to it in connection with the cult of lineage ghosts. They believe that their forebears were sorry to die and are envious of the living. The forebears retain affection for their lands and houses and continue to be interested in tangible good things, particularly in food and drink. These attitudes appear to form part of a general this-worldly attitude among traditional Nāyars. As a caste, their chief interests have been in land and houses, political power, and military exploits. They are not ritual specialists. Most Nāyar men and many women were traditionally literate in Malayālam. Malayālam poems, dramas, and translations based on the great epics, the *puraṇas* and the *Bhāgavad Gītā*, brought the content of much Sanskrit literature to them in a comprehensible form. Nevertheless, comparatively few Nāyars were philosophers or scholars. Among the great majority, ascetic practices were oriented chiefly toward averting misfortunes in this life rather than to accumulating religious merit against the life to come. With regard to their interests in this world, the ancestors resemble their descendants.

Lineage ghosts are powerful beings who can help or harm the living. The effect which they exert on the fortunes of the living is much greater than that exerted by the living on their own. They can aid their descendants by preserving crops, cattle, houses, and children, but their punitive characteristics are those most emphasized. Offerings to ghosts are designed less toward seeking positive good than toward averting misfortune. There is no idealization of the ghosts as morally superior beings. They are human in their failings of envy and bad temper, and indeed, even more capricious than the living. They may punish wrongdoing with a degree of justice, but they do not look sympathetically into the hearts of propitiants, and are almost as likely to exact vengeance for accidental mistakes in the performance of rites as for wilful immorality. Nāyars do not attempt to enter intimate spiritual communion with them or to please them by inner suffering and renunciation. Rather, the ghosts are bought off with gifts of food in order that their envy may be appeased.

These attitudes to the ancestors[12] are, it seems, directly related to relationships with the senior generation among the living. A man's relationship with his mother's brother is, from childhood, one of stern discipline. All mother's brothers have authority over their nephews and in traditional households may inflict corporal punishment on adolescents. There is a marked lack of intimacy between senior and junior men within the *taravād*, and the sanction on a nephew's good conduct is fear of punishment rather than fear over loss of love. Good *ḵāranavans* are devoted to their juniors in a stern and dutiful manner. They are proud of their *taravād* as against the rest of the world, but they do not exhibit personal tenderness to their juniors. Power is vested in the senior generation; there is little feeling that a nephew could wield power over his uncle by withdrawing his emotional support. Great emphasis is placed on a formal etiquette of dignified and respectful behavior, amounting to partial avoidance, but neither party need feel that he loves the other in his heart. Nephews will not normally readily reveal hostility toward their uncles before outsiders, for they wish to preserve the dignity of the *taravād*. But they do publicly acknowledge hostility under provocation, and more frequently accuse the uncle of aggression toward themselves. That hostility is a normal component of relationships with mother's brothers is proverbial among Nāyars. They recognize this as the reason why a formal etiquette of behavior is indispensable. And even in spite of the stringent rules regulating the intercourse of mother's brother and sister's son, physical aggression between them may occur. In spite of the supernatural sanctions against violence within the lineage, I heard several stories of nephews who poisoned or stabbed their mothers' brothers. Aged *ḵāranavans* of large *taravāds* often complain of their loneliness. They may not behave intimately with their juniors and know in their hearts that they are hated and envied. "Indeed," as one Nāyar remarked, "in an old-fashioned *taravād* the position of the *ḵāranavan* is not safe." The office of *ḵāranavan* is, of course, much coveted. Junior men commonly number themselves off in order of age-rank as second, third, fourth men, etc., and with divided feelings await the demise of those above them which will raise them to higher rank. The relationship between older and younger brothers, own or classificatory, is only slightly less stern and formal than that between mother's brother and sister's son.

The relationship of a woman with her mother's brother is less harsh than that between males, for a woman does not offer the threat of a rival to her male superior. Difference of sex, however, makes this relationship even more formal than that between men. Women do not appear frequently in the presence of their mothers' brothers. They occupy separate wings of the house, and intercourse between the sexes is severely restricted. Toward older brothers a woman's relationship is restricted almost to the point of avoidance. If she commits a misdemeanor, especially a sexual one, a woman immediately fears men senior to her in the *taravād*. Formerly, she might be executed by her brothers if she had sexual relations with a lower caste man. In an orthodox household today, a girl who becomes pregnant by a low caste man will be either expelled from the house by her male seniors or, at best, will be thrashed and will receive much subsequent harsh treatment.

It may be wondered why, since women are excluded from legal authority and from participation in the cult, ancestresses are believed capable of harming *taravād* members. The explanation of this, too, seems to lie in the content of relationships with the mother and other natal kinswomen. Women have no legal authority over their juniors. Indeed, the mother of a *kāranavan* is herself under his jurisdiction. Women do, however, exercise great moral authority over their children throughout their lives. In Cochin with duolocal residence, the care of children under about the age of five is almost entirely in the hands of women in a traditional *taravād*. Their fathers have no rights over them, the *kāranavan* is too remote a figure to concern himself with details of child training, and junior men of the *taravād* are often absent from home. A mother commonly treats her small children with indulgence, but is necessarily also the source of many frustrations, while the maternal grandmother and women of her generation are strict disciplinarians.

In Kottayam, where residence was traditionally avunculocal, children were frequently brought up in the *taravād* of the father. In such households today, the child has an intimate, affectionate relationship with his father who undertakes a part of his personal care. When the father's *kāranavan* is also the mother's father (as fairly often occurs with cross-cousin marriage), he and his wife treat the child with indulgence. Otherwise, they tend to have only a slight relationship with him and may even resent his claim to temporary hospitality in their house. The mother is, in these circumstances, again the child's chief mentor and disciplinarian, and he learns very early that his mother's brothers, though living elsewhere, are the real authorities whom he must respect and to whom he will return at adolescence, as their heir. In both areas the reverence acquired for the mother is perpetuated throughout life. Her wishes and those of his elder sister take precedence over those of a man's wife, to whom he has a very subsidiary attachment. The relationship with the mother is clearly characterized by great depth of emotion and by greater tenderness than that toward male seniors. Even so, it appears that in this relationship too, the emotion is usually consciously ambivalent. I illustrate this statement briefly with reference to the relationship between only one man and his mother, but it is characteristic of many. This Cochin Nāyar, aged thirty-five, visited us stealthily in the evenings and kept his visits from his mother, telling her he had business in the town. He was afraid she would become jealous, and angry with him for eating Christian food. She watched over him, upbraiding him when he spent much time in the house of his wife and children. He took care to be prompt for meals, and although he found her food inadequate he would not complain in case he appeared to slight her cookery. He had had a high school education and disbelieved in much traditional Nāyar ritual. Yet he once arranged for the performance of a sacrifice to a minor malevolent deity, Kuttichāttan, because his mother thought that this demon had killed their calf. On this occasion he complained that he found her control irksome, and wished he had younger brothers who would care for her and allow him to travel more. "I love *and* fear her," he said, "Sometimes I am angry with her." "But you don't say anything?" "Ah, no, nothing!" Far more than in most of the patrilineal castes of South India, therefore, a man's mother remains the supreme, if somewhat resented, moral authority. There is no wonder that after death a woman should be believed capable of punishing her children and grandchildren if they displease her.

Even so, ancestresses play only a minor part in the cult of forebears, subordinate, as in life, to the spirits of *kāranavans*. For the cult of lineage ghosts too closely resembles everyday adult relationships in the *taravād* for women to be accorded a paramount place within it. In religion, the supreme moral authority of the mother finds its expression rather in the cult of the goddess Bhagavadi. Bhagavadi is lifted above the sphere of kinship relationships, yet as patron of the *taravād* and the village she is stated to be the supernatural counterpart of the mother. Her attributes are more awesome and archaic than are those of ancestresses, and it seems probable that in her are portrayed very early infantile fantasies of the mother, corresponding to those of the period when she was the only significant object in the child's world. She inspires devotion and tenderness but, in her aspect as Bhādrakāli, she is also a horrendous demon, having snakes for hair, talons for fingernails, fangs for teeth, brandishing weapons in her arms, and with her mouth dripping blood. Her oral aggression is emphasized, for she is a devourer of male demons who dare to oppose her power. Bhagavadi is the great deity of both men and women among Nāyars, but she is more concerned with men than with women. She is the goddess of war, she possesses men more frequently than women, and it is men who devote themselves intensively to her cult. Ancestresses, on the other hand, seem to be somewhat more likely to attack women than men. The different relationships of men and of women to their mothers may be relevant in this connection. For a woman, the relationship with the mother is less awesome, less inspiring, more intimate and realistic but also more irksome and rivalrous than for a man. A woman replaces her mother in the *taravād*, and as she grows up, rivalry, including sexual rivalry, is often apparent between them. Women retain the right to administer corporal punishment to their daughters until adolescence or marriage, whereas men earlier pass under the discipline of their mothers' brothers and appear to retain a more childlike image of the mother. Nuances in the cult of the ancestors and the great deities appear to reflect this differential relationship of men and women to the senior generation.

In Kottayam, with avunculocal residence, fathers traditionally had a protective and intimate relationship with their children. It might be expected that the father's ghost would figure in some way in the cult of ghosts. This is not the case. The cults are practically identical in Kottayam and Cochin, and although a woman and her immature children in Kottayam lived in the house of the woman's husband, the husband's lineage ghosts were not believed capable of affecting their welfare. This is apparently because, both in Kottayam and Cochin, the ancestor cult mirrors the legal structure and collective responsibility of the *taravād*, which are identical in the two areas. The father's ghost has no place among the lineage ghosts because, however intimately related to his children he may have been, he belongs to a different economic and legal corporation. In death as in life, he has no publicly supported authority over his children. Children do have a personalized relationship with their father's spirit in Kottayam, however, which is discussed below.

The emotional content of the relationships with lineage ghosts among the Nāyars does not depend upon the fact that they follow matrilineal descent, although of course the role-structure of the cult is determined by this fact. The Īravas[13] of this area, who are tenant cultivators of lower rank than the Nāyars, have small patrilineal lineages and patrilocal extended families, cross-cut, traditionally, by dispersed exogamous matrilineal clans. The Īrava patrilineage is called a *taravād* and is headed by its senior male member as *kāranavan*. The Īravas have a cult of dead patrilineal *kāranavans* almost identical in emotional and belief content with that of Nāyars. So also do the Coorgs, a patrilineal caste of the small province east of Kottayam, well described by Srinivas.[14] The common form of the cult and the similarity of detail in this general area must undoubtedly be attributed to diffusion or to a common historical origin. Nevertheless, the question then arises of why this cult was not diffused to all castes of the southwest coast, notably to the Brahmans. Conversely, we may ask why the Brahmanical cult of ancestors, which is quite different in form and content, did not entirely replace the ancestral cults of the non-Brahman castes centuries ago—for these castes have been exposed to Brahmanical culture probably for two thousand years and have in fact adopted many elements of that culture. Moreover, cults of punitive ancestors similar to the Nāyar cult are very widespread in the world. It seems certain that whatever their historical origin, the reasons for the perpetuation of these cults must be sought in the role-structure of the kinship system and the emotional content of relationships with major figures of the senior generation within it. I would suggest that cults of predominantly punitive ancestors are likely to be accompanied by kinship relationships in which the senior generation retains control over the junior until late in life, but in which major figures of the senior generation are not highly idealized. It seems probable that the chief sanction against value-violating behavior will be fear of some tangible form of punishment, rather than fear over loss of love, and that although open expression of aggression toward disciplinary figures is controlled, the aggressive component in the ambivalent relationship to seniors will be strong and not deeply repressed. Among Nāyars and Īravas of my acquaintance, at all events, a man may even be conscious of his ambivalence toward seniors, and to the extent that he is not able fully to accept his own aggressive feelings he seems to project these in the belief that his superiors are even more punitive than they may really be. A portion of this projected aggression his culture encourages him to displace on the figures of lineage ghosts, who can inflict even more serious punishments than can living superiors. As is frequently the case in our own society, the mechanism of projection seems to be closely allied with that of introjection, which appears in the belief that sickness and mental derangement are caused by the entry of a hostile ghost into the body of the patient.

The nature of traditional Nāyar relationships to their lineage ghosts may be clarified by contrasting them with those of Brahmans. I choose for this purpose the Tamil Brahmans of Tanjore,[15] with whom I am best acquainted. This caste of landowners and ritual specialists has patrilocal extended families and patrilineal lineages. Headship of the extended family does not, as among Īravas and Coorgs, pass down the line of brothers and then to the junior generation. At the death of a man, his eldest son becomes head of the household until all the sons are adult and can divide their property and move into separate homes. Within the extended family each man must have a son of his own, or an adopted son, who will be his heir, perform his funeral rites, and make offerings for his spirit after death. There is no collective cult of lineage ghosts as among the Nāyars, Īravas and Coorgs. Each son propitiates in his own home the ghosts of his father and mother, paternal grandfather and grandmother, and paternal great-grandfather and great-grandmother. Offerings of water are made thrice daily to these ancestors, of water and gingelly seeds on the new moon days of each month, and of cooked rice balls and other objects on the anniversaries of the parents' deaths. The ancestors are not thought to be interested in the material affairs of the living and cannot help or harm them. Offerings are not made ostensibly to propitiate them but to ensure their own safety in the life after death. If the deceased's sins were not expiated before death it is believed that his spirit must endure terrible physical torture in the abode of Yama, the god of death, before proceeding to *pithiru loḳam*, the world of the ancestors. The offerings strengthen the spirit if it is in hell and help it to escape therefrom. In any case, even a spirit already in the ancestral world can fall down into hell if offerings are not made by dutiful descendants. After a period in the abode of the ancestors the spirit is reborn, in high or low estate according to its merit or demerit during life and according to the degree of merit acquired for it by the piety and offerings of its descendants. After many rebirths and the acquisition of great merit, the spirit merges in the universal soul. Village Brahmans believe that the correct performance of ancestral ceremonies is instrumental to this end.

These beliefs appear to be associated both with the general philosophy of the Brahmans and with the emotional content of their kinship relationships. The Brahmans, unlike the Nāyars, are ritual specialists. Their religion teaches that the pleasures of this world are illusory. The aim of the soul is to escape the cycle of rebirths and find union with the divine. Only the spirits of those who died prematurely and violently are believed still interested in this life. Weighed down by sin and desire, they hover about the site of their deaths awaiting the summons of Yama when their appropriate life span has passed. Such spirits may inflict sickness upon those who cross their paths, but the spirits of normal ancestors are not at all punitive.

The relationship between a man and his paternal ancestors reflects the deep personal devotion and mutual dependence between father and son during life. From early childhood a son is taught that aggressive thoughts, let alone acts, toward the parents are gravely sinful and to be shunned. The parents are highly idealized and enveloped in an aura of sanctity. Children are taught that the father and the mother are the first gods to be worshipped. Among individual Brahmans, the expression of any form of aggression toward the father appears to be attended by deep guilt. Neither should a son permit himself the thought that his father is punitive toward him. In everyday etiquette the relationship is one of comparative intimacy and informality. Corporal punishment is very seldom inflicted, and the chief sanction against bad behavior seems to be not fear of punishment but extreme emotional dependence and fear of rejection. Individual Brahmans, on the occasion of the sickness or death of their parents, have exhibited to me great guilt, blaming themselves for youthful impiety, and fearing that the ill which has now come on their parents is the result of their own misdemeanor. From case histories there seems no doubt that the relationship with the father is highly ambivalent; for as head of the family he is the source of many frustrations. After death, aggressive elements do seem to appear covertly in the horrifying picture of hell and in the fear that by failing to perform the ancestral rites correctly, and to live piously, the son may imperil his ancestors' souls. But aggression against the parents seems to be too deeply repressed for them to be thought of, alive or dead, as themselves aggressive. Instead, the Brahman seems to effect a reaction formation against his aggression which appears in unusual concern for the ancestors' safety, and in the anxious need to perform numerous rites which will ward off from them the punishment of the god of death. I do not mean to suggest that every Brahman handles aggression toward elders solely and precisely in this way, or that every Nāyar handles the same troublesome impulses by projection. I would suggest, however, that both socialization and belief system encourage these different modes of handling aggression toward authorities, and that a change in any one of these areas would be likely to produce change in them all.

A more apt contrast with the Nāyar cult would be that of the Nambūdiri Brahmans, who live in contact with the Nāyars and from whom the Nāyars have derived many elements of their religion. Unfortunately, the religious orthodoxy of the Nambūdiris prevented me from studying them intimately. The information which I have from Nambūdiri informants and from literature[16] indicates however that their ancestral cult is similar to that of the Tamil Brahmans. Its role structure is different, for in the Nambūdiri patrilineal household only the eldest son may have Nambūdiri descendants. Younger sons may have Nāyar children, but these are totally excluded from the performance of rites for their dead fathers. Headship of the Nambūdiri family, like that of the Īrava, passes from the eldest son down the line of brothers and then drops to the eldest son of the junior generation. There is both a collective cult of dead patrilineal heads and also separate anniversary rites for individual dead. Both types of ritual take the Sanskritic form. If the deceased was a younger son, his eldest brother's sons perform these rites. Nambūdiris hold the same beliefs about the fate of the soul as do Tamil Brahmans and, like them, deny that the spirits of ancestors are punitive. The informal intimacy of behavior between men of senior and junior generations in the Nambūdiri household is also very similar to that among Tamil Brahmans, and contrasts with the formal etiquette of partial avoidance between Nāyar matrilineal kinsmen. It is somewhat extraordinary and interesting to note that the Nambūdiri Brahmans and the Nāyars, through centuries of close proximity and hypergamous marital unions, have retained totally different legal and emotional relationships within their respective unilineal units, with correspondingly different beliefs connected with their ancestral cults.

Although the Nāyars' relationships with ghosts are similar in important respects to those with living elders, they are significantly different in others. The ghosts' powers are not limited by the demands of reality, and they can magically protect and punish in fantastic ways in which human elders cannot. As Fortes points out for the Tallensi ancestors, the ghosts appear "as a standardized and highly elaborated picture of the parents as they might appear to a young child in real life—mystically omnipotent, capricious, vindictive, and yet beneficent."[17] It is while a child is comparatively helpless that his elders appear in this form. As he grows up and gains competence, the elders shrink to human proportions. But in some areas of living a Nāyar was traditionally helpless throughout life—with regard to flood and drought, many sicknesses, and crop and cattle blight. These he continued to explain in terms of a childlike picture of powerful supernatural elders.

It must also be noticed that although there are slight differences in the relationships of men and women to lineage ghosts, the ghosts are, in general, far more alike than are matrilineal elders. A man's relation with his mother is very different from that with his mother's brother, and his relations with different mother's brothers are by no means uniform. Yet the ghosts are collectively regarded as both protective and dangerously punitive. It seems probable, therefore, that a Nāyar reprojects his own supergo onto the standardized, institutionalized image of lineage ghosts which his culture provides him. For the superego, like the ghosts, is a composite of the prohibitions imposed by a number of elders. The superego is also formed in part from the individual's own aggression, which he defends against by projecting it upon the generalized parental image which he has internalized. If this view is correct, reprojection of the harsh superego onto ghosts in times of misfortune must serve to reduce guilt. For the offences which the ghosts ostensibly punish with sickness are often inadvertent or trivial ones, such as failure in the correct performance of rites. The astrologer's diagnosis may thus permit him to focus his generalized guilt (concerning deeper, unconscious aggressive impulses) upon a specific, minor lapse of duty on the part of himself or one of his kinsmen. He is then able to take practical steps to alleviate his guilt through propitiation of the supernatural agents. The Brahman's offerings on behalf of his ancestors also seem to serve as an alleviation of guilt, but in a different manner. For instead of reprojecting his harsh superego onto ancestral figures, the Brahman apparently projects it wholly outside the area of human relations onto a vindictive god of death, whose hell he believes endangers both his own and his parents' souls. He appears to alleviate his guilt through rites designed to preserve them and himself from this fate.

If it is true that the Nāyar reprojects his own superego upon the lineage ghosts, this would explain why the ghosts are so much more punitive than are living elders. They are thus fitting agents for the infliction of natural misfortunes, which in fact fall more heavily and capriciously than do the punishments of living elders. The fact that all members of the *taravād* are enabled to focus projected aggression and guilt feelings upon the ghosts probably enhances the internal solidarity of the *taravād*, by lifting a portion of these troublesome feelings from inside to outside the group. The cult thus brings together in rites of propitiation these very kinsmen who (in one aspect of their relationship) hate each other, and forges renewed bonds of mutual devotion in the appeasement of beings whom all of them fear.

Funerals and Anniversaries: The Sanskritic Cults

Although they retained the non-Sanskritic cults of ghosts, the Nāyars long ago adopted many Brahmanical usages in connection with funerals and with rites on the anniversary of a death. Such usages include cremation rather than burial of the dead, and offerings of rice balls (*bali*), water, and other oblations in the days of pollution following a death. As among Nambūdiri Brahmans, the chief heir, at the end of the period of pollution, enters a period of ascetic mourning (*dīkṣā*) for one year in Cochin and for forty-one days in Kottayam. At the end of this time he may dispose of the bones and ashes in a sacred river. He makes *bali* offerings to the spirit on each day of his mourning, and at its close, performs final offerings which unite the deceased with his forebears. Thereafter he offers rice balls and other oblations in a *śrāddham* ceremony on each anniversary of the death.

Many of these customs are of long standing among the Nāyars. Barbosa[18] reported in 1518 that Nāyar royalty observed *dīkṣā* for the dead in the same manner as Nambūdiris. Sheikh Zein-ud-Deen[19] recorded the custom for commoner Nāyars in 1579. Linschoten[20] reported in 1598 that Nāyars normally cremated their dead. Today, Nāyar death and anniversary rites are almost identical in form with those of Nambūdiris. During the period of death pollution they employ a lower matrilineal caste to instruct them in the rites. (In Cochin, Chīdigans fulfill this function; in South Malabar, Attikūrssis; and in North Malabar, Mārārs.) The same caste assists Nambūdiri Brahmans to prepare the ritual materials for their funerals, and has clearly transmitted the Brahmanical rites to the Nāyars. Similarly, at the end of the death pollution on the sixteenth day, during the *dīkṣā* period, and on anniversary days, Nāyars are instructed in their oblations by a priest of a degraded subcaste of Brahmans. (This subcaste is the Elayads in Cochin and South Malabar and the Nambidis in North Malabar.) A few peculiarly non-Brahmanical rites do, however, survive. In Kottayam, poorer Nāyars among commoners customarily bury their dead.[21] In both areas those who burn the dead bury the bones and ashes in a pot under a jack-fruit tree outside the ancestral house near the ancestor shrine. Some leave the bones there permanently and consider that the ghost remains near the bones and the ancestral house. Others dig up the bones after the period of mourning, dispose of half of them in a sacred river, and return the other half to the grave. The bones of *kāranavans* are sometimes placed on an open platform under a jack-fruit tree, to which food offerings are made on days of propitiation. Other rites spring from the Nāyar view that the ghost requires appeasement rather than mere assistance to another world. Brahmans, for example, pour holy water into the mouth of a dying man to purify him for entry into the world of ancestors. Old-fashioned Nāyars offer rice gruel as a last act of appeasement.

Even the Sanskritic rites are in fact so adapted to Nāyar requirements that they carry a quite different emphasis of meaning from that associated with them by Brahmans. First, the role-structure of the rites is, of course, completely adapted to the descent system. A Nambūdiri deceased's chief mourner is his or her eldest son, or, if there is no Nambūdiri son, the eldest brother's son. A Nāyar woman's chief mourner is her eldest son; that of a man, the man next junior to him in the property group. But all males of the *taravād* junior to the deceased make subsidiary *bali* offerings to him in the period of pollution. Brahman spouses observe mourning and death pollution for each other. Nāyar spouses traditionally observe no mourning or pollution for each other, for they belong to different *taravāds* and have no mutual legal obligations. If a Nāyar dies in a wife's house, his body must traditionally be returned to his *taravād* for cremation. Shortly before or after the death of her husband, a woman goes to view his body for the last time. She is then ceremonially conducted out of the house on the north side—the side opposite to that from which the god of death arrives. She is returned to her natal home, and after this she may never reenter her dead husband's house. In Cochin, where men traditionally had no obligations to their children, a child did not observe death pollution for his genitor. But in North Malabar, where children have an intimate relationship with the father in avunculocal residence during childhood, a man's sons make offerings for him during death pollution, and the eldest son is second-in-command to the chief mourner at the cremation. The eldest son also traditionally observed *dīkṣā* for his father along with the matrilineal heir.

Age-rank within the *taravād* finds expression in the rites. Among Nambūdiri Brahmans, if an unmarried but initiated boy dies, his father may perform his funeral and anniversary rites. For the souls of father and son are dependent upon one another for salvation. But among Nāyars, a man may not take part in funeral rites for one junior to him in the *taravād*, for respect toward juniors is inappropriate. A Nāyar who dies leaving no junior old enough to act as chief mourner is therefore buried without ceremony and no rites are performed for his ghost.

Nāyars have adopted the Brahmanical belief that funeral and anniversary rites assist the spirit in its passage to another world, and that immersion of the ashes in sacred water affords it peace. Like the Brahmans, they acknowledge the theory of rebirth, and hold that a spirit which is correctly propitiated after death is likely to be eventually reborn in a high estate. As in the case of the Brahmans, the theory of *karma* provides the Nāyars with a moral rationale for their high position in the caste system, and it is chiefly in this connection that I have heard it quoted. It is difficult to discover how old are Sanskritic beliefs concerning the soul among Nāyars, and they are not uniform at the present day. Most Nāyars use the word *pretam* to refer to the ghost or the soul in all contexts. This is a Sanskrit word (*preta*) for a malevolent ghost, but it is used by Nambūdiri Brahmans only for alien malevolent ghosts. A few Nāyars stated that that aspect of the soul which is reborn is the *ātmā*. This Sanskrit word is used by Brahmans for the soul in connection with rebirth and with union with the universal soul, called *paramātmā*. The *ātmā*, these Nāyar informants say, is neither malevolent nor beneficent. It cannot be understood by ordinary people and is a subject for philosophers. The *pretam*, by contrast, is the punitive ghost of an ancestor or of one who died violently. It can be only too easily understood even by the ignorant and does not require deep study. This belief in two souls, or in a soul and a ghost, may be modern, for it was given by only a few younger informants.

At all events, the Sanskritic rites of death are customarily adapted by Nāyars to belief in a malevolent *pretam*, for at every step fear of the *pretam* is referred to. Whereas Brahmans perform the rites ostensibly in order that the soul may be at peace, Nāyars have traditionally performed them in active fear of the ghost's retaliation should its comfort not be ensured. During the days of pollution, Nāyars offer rice balls before a palmyra stem set up in the yard before the ancestral house. The *pretam* of the deceased is believed to enter this stem, and it is believed that it will attack the *taravād* with further death or with sickness if the offerings are not satisfactorily performed. During the offerings each Nāyar propitiant in turn wears round his waist a piece of cloth torn from the wrapper of the corpse in order to associate himself with the spirit. But inside this cloth Nāyars also tuck a knife, blade uppermost, to ward off the spirit's attack. After the offerings are made, both Brahmans and Nāyars clap their wet hands to summon crows to eat the rice balls. If the crows do not come, it is believed that the spirit has not received the offering. This may then be repeated on the advice of the astrologer. In Tanjore, Brahmans seemed to regret the miscarriage of the offering only for the sake of the spirit. But Nāyars regard it as an extremely evil omen, and fear the ghost's retaliation in the form of a second death within the *taravād*. The Brahmanical ceremonies themselves contain rites of segregation from the deceased which are susceptible to the interpretation that those who perform them wish to be rid of him. Such, for example, is the rite of dashing a pot of water at the head end of the pyre toward the close of the cremation, and the disposal of the bones and ashes in a river far from the ancestral house. But among my Brahman informants in Tanjore these rites were carried out without explanation, and hostility to the dead seemed to find no conscious expression. Nāyars performed the same rites in full consciousness of fear and hostility to the ghost. Even at the end of the *dīkṣā* period when the chief mourner has deposited the ashes in a river, Nāyars believe that Bhairava and Kāla, messengers of the god of death, dog the mourner's footsteps back to his ancestral house. He is out of danger from them only after performing final offerings in the house which gather the ghost to its forebears and thus appease its wrath. Nāyars, like Brahmans, express grief at a death and engage in ceremonial weeping, although neither caste weeps with the loud vehemence characteristic of the lower polluting castes. But whereas Brahmans give full expression to grief and guilt, suppressing the hostile aspect of their ambivalence, Nāyars perform the same rites in consciousness both of grief and of hostile fear of the dead.

The traditional Nāyar rites and beliefs illustrate the common phenomenon of elements of symbolic culture being diffused from one group to another and endowed with a new emotional content and meaning in accordance with the needs of the receiving group. The Nāyars presumably adopted Brahmanical death rites centuries ago because of the prestige associated with certain distinctive customs of the highest group in the caste society. The extensive contact with Brahmans afforded to them by hypergamous marital unions gave them an unusual exposure to Sanskrit culture. But through centuries of exposure to Brahmanical custom the Nāyars retained such characteristically "low caste" features as animal sacrifice to punitive deities, religious possession, and propitiation of punitive lineage ghosts. I would argue that the Nāyars and lower castes retained these customs because the emotional dispositions engendered by their occupations and social relations—in particular, their ways of handling aggression and relationships to authorities—are different from those of Brahmans. Presumably also the Nāyars adapted the Sanskritic death rites to their own role structure and belief system, because these grew out of and served to uphold norms of relationships within the *taravād*.

The Cults of Alien Ghosts

In addition to lineage ghosts, Nāyars believe that the spirits of persons of any caste who died prematurely from epidemic, accident, murder, or suicide can bring misfortune to the living. Such ghosts, which I call alien ghosts, haunt the neighborhood where they died and are particularly malevolent. The misfortunes they inflict include many kinds of sickness; madness, female barrenness, cattle deaths, house fires, or poltergeist activities. Like lineage ghosts, most alien ghosts are called *pretams*. In Cochin, the Sanskrit word *piśāca* is sometimes used to distinguish them from lineage ghosts. In Kottayam, there is an elaborate cult of certain particularly important ghosts, which are called *teyyams* (a corruption of the Sanskrit word *deva* 'god').

In Cochin, one or more alien ghosts is sometimes attached to a Nāyar *taravād*, whose members are obliged to arrange for its regular propitiation. The ghost may be that of a person who is known to have died violently, within living memory, on the *taravād's* land. Alternatively, when a misfortune occurs in a household, the astrologer may newly discover that the ghost of some such person, long dead, is haunting the *aravād's* land. He may order a shrine to be built and propitiations to be made. Shrines to alien ghosts are built in the garden of the *taravād* house. They are propitiated annually or in emergency, usually with a cock sacrifice and an offering of toddy. Such alien ghosts are of a lineage other than that of the hosts and are usually of different caste. If a member of the *taravād* dies violently, his successors take care of his ghost in the course of their ancestral propitiations and do not commonly build a special shrine for it in their garden. They may fear such a ghost more than they fear the ghosts of forebears who died naturally, but they will not speak of this to outsiders. Rather, they are likely to deny to others that violent deaths have taken place in their lineage in the past, particularly if the deceased was a suicide or was executed in punishment for a crime. Such a ghost may however be regarded as a source of misfortunes by a Nāyar household of another lineage or by a household of one of the lower castes, expecially it the deceased died on its land or was in some way connected with it. It is then enshrined as an alien ghost in the garden of this house.

Most commonly, an alien ghost housed in a Nāyar garden is that of a former serf of the property group, of one of the "exterior" agricultural laboring castes of Pulayans, Parayans or Pānans. The legends of such ghosts are nowadays often forgotten, but several Nāyars told me that they are likely to be the ghosts of serfs who died after a quarrel with their masters or who were actually killed by them. The ghost is hostile to the *taravād* as a group and demands regular sacrifices if misfortune is to be averted. It is more hostile and capricious than are lineage ghosts, although it can also afford a certain vague protection to the *taravād* if it is correctly propitiated. Propitiations are made annually by a person of the ghost's own caste, often a Parayan or Pulayan of a family now serving the Nāyar property group. The propitiant's fee and the materials for the offering are provided by the *taravād*.

An alien ghost tends to be angered by persons who walk near its shrine at times other than those of propitiations. Some ghosts are angered only if people approach them round midnight or midday. At night, however, ghosts are able to wander some distance away from their shrines, so that it is possible to approach and offend them without being conscious of trespassing. In case of sickness or misfortune, the astrologer may diagnose that someone of the *taravād* has unwittingly offended the ghost and may order an emergency offering. After he has made the sacrifice, the low caste propitiant is likely to become possessed by the ghost and, while in a state of frenzy, to declare its satisfaction or to order further offerings. He may also take the opportunity to voice any grievances harbored by the *taravād's* low caste servants against its *k̠āranavan*.

A ghost of this kind may occasionally harm someone from outside its hosts' *taravād* who walks on their land at night. It could also harm its low caste propitiant if he failed in the correct performance of the rites. Usually, however, its attacks are confined to its hosts.

The ghost of such a hostile servant is to be distinguished from that of a servant who died heroically and voluntarily in the service of his Nāyar masters. Many Nāyar *taravāds* have legends of faithful serfs who died defending their masters' house during war, saved the lives of women and children, rescued their patrons from accidental death, or committed suicide in grief when a Nāyar patron had been killed. After death the ghosts of these servants are housed along with the *taravād's* lineage ghosts and are honored in ancestral propitiations. Nāyars point out that their heroism even makes the difference of caste irrelevant, for food is offered to them before it is offered to lineage ghosts who were junior to them in age. The living of the *taravād* themselves make offerings to them and do them obeisance, whereas the ghosts of hostile serfs are especially polluting and malevolent and can be propitiated only by persons of their own caste.

Even so, the ghost of such a lower caste person who is honored for heroism by the *taravād* of his masters may, if he died violently, be feared as an alien ghost by other *taravāds*. In Kottayam in the eighteenth century, for example, there lived a certain Nāyar village headman who had as his servant a man of the Tiyyar caste of cultivators. During the invasions of Malabar by the Mysorean Muslim general, Tippu Sultan, in the 1780's, the Nāyar's *taravād* was threatened with conquest and forcible conversion to Islam. Having sent the women and children of his house into hiding, the *kāranavan* prayed before his lineage's patron goddess until the Muslims were at his gates. He then persuaded his Tiyyar servant to kill him, being unwilling to face the disgrace of circumcision at the hands of the Muslims. Having slain his master, the servant hid himself in an outhouse of the *taravād*. In the night he went forth and attacked the Muslims single-handed, killing several of them to avenge his master, before he was himself put to death. The ghost of this servant is now propitiated along with the lineage ghosts of his master's *taravād*. It is also, however, propitiated as an alien ghost by several other *taravāds* in the neighborhood.

Occasionally, malevolent alien ghosts are those of Nāyars who died violently, often in expiation of some crime. They may have committed suicide after being outcaste for contravention of religious laws, or in the case of a woman, may have been killed by their matrilineal kinsmen after cohabiting with low caste men. A woman called Kadangōtt Makkam, also of Kottayam, became a ghost in this way. According to legend, she was suspected by her sister-in-law of having sexual relations with an Oilmonger. Her brothers banished her from the *taravād*. She was agonized at the thought of leaving her children, and drowned them in the *taravād's* well. Her *kāranavan* and brothers were then obliged to stab her to death—the customary penalty for fornication outside the caste, and perhaps, also, for murder within the *taravād*. She became an alien ghost particularly liable to prevent women from bearing children, and is established in the gardens of several local *taravāds*.

Such alien ghosts, although Nāyar, are also propitiated by an officiant of the lower caste. The propitiant is usually from some caste which specializes in exorcism and counter-magic, such as Mannāns (washermen), Kanisans (astrologers, who in any case diagnose the misfortune and advise the propitiation) or Pānans (umbrella-makers, exorcists and agricultural workers). The mode of propitiation is the same as in the case of a low caste ghost.

Finally, an alien ghost is occasionally that of a Brahman who died violently. Brahman ghosts, or Brahmarākṣas, unlike all other ghosts, must be propitiated with vegetarian offerings by a Brahman priest hired for the purpose. But Brahman priests, unlike low caste officiants, never enter a state of voluntary possession by ghosts. Religious possession is particularly a low caste institution. It is not practiced by Brahmans, and when found among Nāyars, it is practiced by young men, women, and other persons who lack secular power. Brahmans do not need to become possessed by their ghosts and deities, for they have the power to demand whatever offerings and fees they require. Low caste propitiants need the authority of a supernatural agent in order to make demands on their high caste masters.

No clear distinction is made between alien ghosts and minor malevolent deities, or demons, which are also sometimes called *pretams* in Cochin. Some demons are found throughout Malabar. Chief of these is Kuttichāttan, a spirit capable of all kinds of poltergeist activities. Sometimes, on the advice of an astrologer, a *taravād* privately sets up a shrine to Kuttichāttan and arranges for his annual propitiation by a low caste person in the same manner as an alien ghost. Often, indeed, local myths of particular Kuttichāttans suggest that they have been derived from alien ghosts, whose legends became fancifully embroidered with miraculous elements. The story of one Kuttichāttan, in this case enshrined in a Nambūdiri Brahman garden and propitiated by a washerman, will illustrate this process. The god was said to have been born from a sacrificial fire during ancestral ceremonies in a Brahman house. The Brahman house-owner brought him up, and when he was adult sent him to graze cattle as a serf. One day the Brahman's red-horned bull was missing, and the serf admitted that he had killed and eaten it. The Brahman tied him to the rafters of the cowshed and had him beaten to the point of death. Afterwards, the serf turned into a Kuttichāttan and disappeared, but hovered above the Nambūdiri household bringing misfortune until a shrine was set up for him. Educated Nāyar informants surmised that the spirit had originally been that of an executed serf, later glorified by his propitiants as Kuttichāttan. Similarly, Kadangōtt Makkam, whose story was related above, is spoken of as a form of Bhagavadi in some *taravāds* where she is propitiated.

I have so far mentioned the kinds of alien ghosts which may be attached to individual *taravāds* in Cochin. In fact, however, cults of spirits and deities of the village are grander and more numerous in Cochin than are those of the *taravād*. This parallels the fact that the Cochin village was traditionally highly centralized as a unit of local government. In this area, the temple of the village goddess Bhagavadi is managed either by a Nāyar village headman's lineage or collectively by a village community of commoner Nāyars. Only the Nāyars and castes above them might traditionally enter the temple, but all castes owed allegiance to the deity and took part in her annual festival. The lowest castes of former serfs, and some other polluting castes such as washermen, took part in the festival through the medium of one or more minor malevolent deities or particularly important local ghosts which occupied small shrines at a distance from the main temple. Such spirits were thought of as servants of the goddess, and at her will could "sow the seeds" of smallpox or other misfortunes in the village. To avert such misfortune not only must the Nāyars and other high castes propitiate the goddess herself, but the lower castes must also assemble, bringing imitation bullocks and horses—the vehicles of the deity's demon servants—and make offerings to these demons. Selected persons from these lower castes became possessed by the village ghosts or demons and, in masked dances, made oracular pronouncements both to their own and the higher castes. During the festival, and for several weeks before it, Nāyar households must also entertain these shamans privately in the courtyards of their houses and make gifts of grain to them which warded off the demons' wrath.

In Kottayam, the village was traditionally less centralized. Each Nāyar *taravād* was an independent landowning body owing only tenuous allegiance to a chief. Cults of deities and ghosts associated with particular *taravāds* are therefore more prominent than are those of village temples, and it is in the former rather than the latter that ritual cooperation between high and low castes is most prominent. Whereas a Cochin *taravād* may enshrine only one or two alien ghosts particularly associated with it, leaving the majority of local ghosts to be propitiated at the central village temple, a wealthy Nāyar *taravād* in Kottayam builds shrines in its garden for six or eight alien ghosts and finances elaborate propitiations on their behalf. Such spirits are in Kottayam called *teyyams*. As in Cochin, the spirits are often the ghosts of Nāyar or low caste persons who died violent deaths—for example, girls who died violently before marriage, women excommunicated or executed for sexual offences, persons killed by lightning, servants executed by their masters, or warriors who died in battle. Usually, miraculous elements are interwoven into their legends. Sometimes, they become merged with common minor deities such as Vettakkorumagan, Kandhā-karanan, or some species of Bhagavadi. In a few cases, they have become associated with some episode from the puranic myths and their human origin is lost sight of. As in the village temple rites of Cochin, these ghosts in Kottayam are propitiated, on behalf of the Nāyar *taravād*, by selected persons from the lower castes. These are chiefly Vannans (washermen) and Malayans (exorcists).[22] Annually, the propitiants assemble in the Nāyar courtyard and recite the myths of origin of their spirits. Later, they make and receive blood sacrifices to the spirits, and finally, while possessed by them, perform spectacular masked dances and declare the spirits' satisfaction to an assembled company of many castes. These festivals take place throughout the whole of several nights in the month of January to February and draw vast crowds from the surrounding neighborhood.[23]

I have so far dealt with modes of propitiation of, and possession by, alien ghosts. In addition, both in Cochin and Kottyam, Nāyars believe that certain persons can, through appropriate rites and spells, gain private control over alien ghosts and minor deities and engage in witchcraft or sorcery through their power. In what I call witch-craft,[24] the individual uses the power of his patron spirit in order to take the form of a bull, dog, jackal, or other animal. In this form he touches his foe in the night, causing him to fall ill with fever, to become insane, or even to die. Witches always belong to one of the lowest castes of Parayans, Pulayans, Pānans or (in Kottayam) Malayans. They usually attack persons of Nāyar or other high caste whom they themselves hate. Occasionally, however, a normal person of any caste, even a Nāyar, may hire a witch to attack a personal enemy.

A sorcerer performs rites and recites spells to an alien ghost or minor deity over which he has control and causes it to pass magically into the body of an enemy, thus bringing about fever, miscarriages in women, insanity or death. Sorcerers can also bring about the deaths of cattle. Nāyars attribute sorcery chiefly to lower caste persons. For whereas the Nāyars predominantly worship Bhagavadi and certain Sanskrit deities, the castes below Nāyars specialize in the propitiation of evil ghosts and minor deities, and it is solely with these lower supernatural beings that witchcraft and sorcery are associated. Washermen, astrologers and umbrellamakers, who specialize in exorcising ghosts from the bodies of patients, are particularly suspected by Nāyars of themselves engaging in sorcery. Nāyars do, however, occasionally suspect Nāyars of other lineages, particularly affines with whom they have quarreled, of practicing sorcery or of hiring low caste witches or sorcerers to attack them.

Witchcraft does not usually require the diagnosis of an astrologer. A Nāyar of nervous disposition simply suspects that a low caste man has bewitched him if he falls ill after encountering an animal in the night. Sorcery is usually diagnosed by an astrologer, who, however, normally leaves his patient to guess which of his enemies has injured him. Public accusations of witchcraft and sorcery are theoretically not permitted, although Nāyars have been known to take the law into their own hands and inflict beatings on Pānans and Parayans whom they believed to have attacked them through witchcraft. Normally, sickness resulting from possession by a ghost or demon as a result of witchcraft or sorcery is counteracted by exorcism. Local specialists of the castes of washermen, astrologers or umbrellamakers are hired to attend at the patient's house. There they make sacrifices to patron spirits whom they themselves control. Later, they voluntarily become possessed by these spirits and perform frenzied dances in hideous masks before the patient, calling upon the alien malevolent spirit to leave him. The patient usually goes into a hysterical fit, after which the sickness may subside. Exorcism by masked dancing of this kind is known as *k̄ōlam tullal.* Any form of rites or spells to control ghosts or minor deities, whether evil or beneficent, is covered by the general term *mantravādam.*

Analysis

The analysis of beliefs and practices centering about alien ghosts involves the following questions: 1) Why are alien ghosts appropriate objects of fear? 2) How do these fears fit into the general pattern of Nāyar handling of aggression? 3) What psychic and social functions are fulfilled by the institutions surrounding alien ghosts? The answers to these questions will relate the alien ghost patterns to the functioning of the local community and its subgroups, and to the expressive needs of individuals.

Alien ghosts as objects of fear. Alien ghosts are individuals who suffered unusual or premature death. People expect them to be especially malevolent. This expectation is based on their presumed envy of the living, and in some instances on the fact that, having found death through violence and hatred, they can be expected to continue to be violent and hateful. Hence they are appropriate targets of fear.

Alien ghosts are the focus of more violent fears and hatreds than are the ghosts of matrilineal forebears, for they can be even more capricious and wantonly punitive. As we have seen, Nāyars do express a limited amount of aggression against lineage ghosts, and I have suggested that this is because their aggression training is not so strict as to prevent them from acknowledging to themselves some degree of hostility toward living matrilineal elders. Their projected aggression toward lineage ghosts, however, is constrained—like their aggression toward living elders. These ghosts, although punitive, are more protective than alien ghosts.

Alien ghosts are congenial objects for more violent aggression and fear, precisely because they *are* alien. They are securely outside the individual's most significant set of personal relations—those of the lineage. Even Brahmans, whose aggression training is so severe that they are unable to acknowledge hostility between themselves and their own ancestral ghosts, express fear and hatred of alien ghosts.

I assume that the fear and hostility which is directed at alien ghosts really has its source elsewhere. My reason for this assumption is that, although the fact that they died unnaturally provides a plausible reason why alien ghosts should be thought of as generally hostile, there is in most cases no ostensible reason in the individual's own personal relationships to alien ghosts which would account for their being chosen as the targets of hatred and fear. Presumably, if we follow psychoanalytic theory, the ultimate sources of these fears lie in familial relationships. This would seem reasonable in the Nāyar case, for in spite of the institution of lineage ghosts there are serious limitations on the expression of aggression within the matrilineage. It is therefore logical to hypothesize that a residuum of unexpressed aggression is displaced outside the lineage toward outgroups and toward supernatural agents which represent these groups. However, there are also, as we shall see, realistic reasons, issuing from the political and economic structures, why individuals should feel aggressive toward outgroups of various categories. It seems probable that the institutions surrounding alien ghosts absorb some of these aggressions as well.

Alien ghosts in the general context of Nāyar handling of aggression. The role-structure of alien ghost cults is that of the wider community, and to understand them we must see how they are interwoven with political and economic relationships between lineages and between castes. For political and economic factors limit both the form and the direction which the expression of aggression can legitimately take in these various relationships.

Within the lineage, as I have suggested, the Nāyars' aggression training permits them to acknowledge to themselves a certain degree of hostility in their relations with matrilineal kin. It does not, however, permit physical aggression between matrilineal kin, nor does it permit the expression of projected aggression in the form of accusations of witchcraft or sorcery between matrilineal kin. For the *taravād* is the smallest corporate unit in Nāyar society. Its members are bound by the closest ties of economic cooperation. They must present a united front to the world, and such forms of aggression would be incompatible with the smooth functioning of their group. A degree of aggression can, however, be safely projected outside the *taravād* on to lineage ghosts, whose cult, as we have seen, actually strengthens the solidary bonds between living matrilineal kin.

Turning to wider relationships within the Nāyar caste, we must note that the political organization traditionally permitted the open expression of organized physical aggression against peers outside the lineage, in controlled feuds between lineages of the same village, villages of the same chiefdom, and chiefdoms of the same kingdom, and in warfare between kingdoms. Such physical aggression within the caste was possible because the internal organization of the caste was segmentary. Conflicts within it therefore balanced each other. Lineages opposed each other within the village but combined against other villages. Villages opposed each other within the chiefdom but combined against other chiefdoms. Chiefdoms opposed each other within the kingdom but combined against other kingdoms in war.

In this system, the most severe limits on intersegment conflict were those on feuds within a village. Such feuds arose in response to grave disputes—often, it appears, involving charges against a Nāyar woman of immorality with a low caste man. But, particularly in Cochin, these feuds were of short duration. They were controlled and curtailed by the authority of village headman and district chief. Hence interlineage disputes were limited in their mode of expression. Moreover, it was possible for individuals of different lineages to quarrel, yet to be unable to persuade their *kāranavans* and the rest of their lineages to enter a feud with them. It is here that suspicions of sorcery came into play, chiefly through beliefs in the use of hired sorcerers who controlled alien ghosts. Affines were particularly suspect, for, outside the lineage, affines were the persons with whom one had closest relationships and with whom disputes could most easily arise. If, for example, a *kāranavan* seemed particularly fond of a wife, his matrilineal juniors were believed to be especially likely to hire sorcerers to harm her. For they would fear that their *kāranavan* might secretly convey to his wife gifts and cash which belonged to his *taravād*. Yet without their *kāranavan's* support they would be unable to enter an open group conflict with the *taravād* of his wife. The belief that affines might practice sorcery, and the existence of ritual remedies against such attacks, therefore provided for the expression of projected aggression against persons of other lineages within the caste. I do not know whether Nāyars did, in fact, hire sorcerers to harm their affines, or merely suspected this of others, but it seems very probable that they did. If so, sorcery also provided a covert mode for the expression of direct aggression outside the lineage too. It must be noticed that although, in the case cited, these hostilities arose as much in the conflict of interests between the *kāranavan* and his matrilineal kin as between the *kāranavan's* wife and her husband's *taravād*, their institutionalized expression was not allowed to disrupt the *taravād*. For the *kāranavan's* matrilineal kin could not practice, and could not be suspected of practicing, sorcery against the *kāranavan* himself. Instead, members of the *kāranavan's* lineage were believed to move (and probably did move) against his wife's lineage as a group, thus endangering the solidarity of the marriage but indirectly promoting unity within each lineage.

Turning to the relations between castes, it is obvious that as endogamous groups of different rank, occupation and wealth, castes were in many contexts outgroups to each other whose interests were opposed. As landlords and noncultivating tenants, the Brahmans and Nāyars wished to exploit the lower castes for their labor; conversely, the lower castes wished to obtain as much compensation as possible from the higher castes. In these circumstances there was great realistic potential for hostility between castes, quite apart from the fact that the internal unity of each caste probably required the displacement of considerable additional aggression toward outgroups in other castes. Organized physical aggression between castes was, however, not feasible. For castes were economically and politically interdependent and linked by hereditary, interhousehold service ties. The lower castes could not rise up against the higher castes who employed them and held political power, and the higher castes could not wantonly harrass the lower castes on whom they depended for services. Instead, it was in the relations between castes that the institutions of witchcraft and sorcery were most prominent. The general tendency was for the Nāyars to accuse the lower castes of these evils. This is understandable, for the Nāyars with their wealth and authority had particular reason to suspect the lower castes of envy and hidden hatred. This generalized projection of aggression toward the lower castes served to enhance the internal unity of the Nāyar caste. At the same time, the open expression of aggression against particular low caste persons was institutionally controlled. For the astrologer did not customarily name his client's enemy, and even if the Nāyar had his own suspicions, open accusations of witchcraft and sorcery were not permitted.

The lower castes were considered peculiarly appropriate propitiants for alien ghosts, and only low caste people could voluntarily undergo possession by them. This suggests that the Nāyar fear of direct attack from an alien ghost, like the fear of witchcraft and sorcery, expressed in a disguised manner the Nāyars' projected aggression against the lower castes. The association between lower castes and alien ghosts was, for Nāyars, indeed appropriate, for both were ritually polluting. Among Nāyars, the corpses of persons who die violently or from epidemic are unusually polluting and their ghosts unusually dangerous. Instead of being burned by their matrilineal kin, the corpses of these persons are buried hastily by men of the washermen's caste—a caste particularly associated with demon propitiation and voluntary ghost possession. The spirits of these victims become alien ghosts. In their anger they may possess and cause injury to persons of any caste in their community. But only the lower castes can induce shamanistic possession by them, and it is chiefly (some say only) the lower castes who can control them to work good or ill. Appropriately, Nāyars believe that low caste witches perform additional rites connected with highly polluting objects and places in order to enhance their evil power. Witches, for example, are believed to procure a magical substance by abstracting the foetus from the body of a pregnant woman and boiling it in a cremation ground, to the accompaniment of spells to a favorite ghost or patron demon.

There is, however, a qualitative difference between the Nāyar fear of direct attack from an alien ghost and the fear of witchcraft or sorcery. An element of morality enters into the former fear, even though alien ghosts are more wanton and capricious than lineage ghosts. Although they are malevolent and hateful, alien ghosts must, like lineage ghosts, be respected and propitiated, and there is a feeling that they have the right to be as they are. When they are associated with regular cults of the *taravād* and the village, moreover, alien ghosts can also afford some vague measure of protection from misfortune to those Nāyars who conscientiously arrange for their propitiation. It follows, therefore, that the alien ghost attached to a *taravād* or a village temple acts in some measure as a kind of conscience for the Nāyar in his relations with low caste people. For a Nāyar *taravād* which arranges grand festivals for its alien ghosts, lavishing gifts on the low caste officiants who propitiate them and represent them as oracles, is also likely to be a *taravād* which has good relations with its lower caste servants in all contexts of living. In the case of the Nāyar relation to alien ghosts of his *taravād* and his village, as in the case of his relation to lineage ghosts, the concept of reprojection of the superego may therefore be appropriate, as well as that of the simple projection of aggressive id impulses. For while there seems no doubt that the Nāyar projects on to alien ghosts some of the aggression which he has toward the lower castes, just as he projects onto lineage ghosts some of the aggression he feels toward matrilineal elders, these ghosts act also as stern monitors of his conduct in relationships, respectively, with the lower castes and with matrilineal kin.

The situation is somewhat different with regard to beliefs in witchcraft and sorcery. It is true that a Nāyar who has recently wronged an untouchable or an affine may be one most likely to suspect untouchables or affines of attacks by sorcery. But he does not—at least openly—phrase the attack in terms of justifiable retaliation for his own wrongdoing. Instead, he speaks of some anonymous affine or low caste person who, out of his own envy and wickedness, has used his evil power over a patron ghost in order to harm an innocent person. Nor does the Nāyar respond to the attacks of witches and sorcerers by humble propitiation of the possessing demon. Instead he engages a low caste practitioner of his own to exorcise the demon with the help of a superior ghostly power. Thus, while both the belief in sorcery and the public cults of alien ghosts probably reveal, indirectly, the projection of Nāyar aggression against out-groups, they operate in different social contexts. Witchcraft and sorcery are regarded, by Nāyars who are the recipients of these attacks, as the evil work of envious persons against those more successful than themselves. They are seen as covert substitutes for forms of direct aggression which would be condemned by law. I am uncertain whether low caste people actually practice sorcery, but it seems very probable that they do. If they do, it is also very probable that they regard their actions as forms of ṛetaliation which are morally justifiable, although outside the framework of the law. By contrast, alien ghosts institutionally attached to the *taravād* and the village have the support of all right-minded persons and are more comparable to institutionalized secular authorities. For they are concerned with the overall maintenance of interdependent and harmonious relations between castes of the community, and their cults are a public, collective acknowledgement of the need for these relationships.

A complete analysis of alien ghost cults would, of course, require full discussion of their role in the lives of the lower castes themselves. I lack space here for such a discussion but will make one or two relevant points. In each of these lower castes there were cults of familial ghosts. These, though less elaborate than the Nāyar cult of lineage ghosts, fulfilled similar intrafamilial functions. Some lower caste households also erected one or more unhewn stones in their gardens which were believed to enshrine male or female alien ghosts or minor deities. These spirits seem to have fulfilled, for the household itself, similar functions to those of the *dharma devī* of a Nāyar *taravād*. They were propitiated by the low caste householder. Nāyars believed that a low caste man could also control such a household spirit, or some personal spirit over which he had gained individual sway, to bring harm on an enemy through sorcery. Lower caste persons certainly believed that some members of their castes possessed these powers, and it seems probable that some persons did try to employ them. Household or personal spirits could also be used by powerful owners to exorcise other harmful spirits from the bodies of high or low caste people suffering from attacks by sorcery.

The Nāyar's relationship to these lower castes was therefore one of secular authority combined with some ability to oppress them in the economic and political spheres. In addition, the Nāyar projected his aggression against them in the belief that they might harm him through witchcraft or sorcery. The lower caste man's relationship to the Nāyar was one of submission. He could not express direct aggression toward the Nāyar. He probably did, however, express aggression toward a Nāyar enemy covertly through sorcery. It is possible that a few low caste persons in addition believed themselves capable, through witchcraft, of assuming the form of an animal and bringing harm to an enemy of higher caste. It must also be mentioned that low caste persons believed others of their caste to be capable of sorcery against themselves. Witchcraft, however, seems to have been confined to relationships between low and high castes.

The lower castes of the village also owed allegiance to the Nāyar goddess Bhagavadi, who was enshrined in Cochin in the village temple, and in Kottayam in small temples attached to particular *taravāds*. The lower castes could, however, approach Bhagavad, only through the propitiation of alien ghosts attached to the *taravād* or the temple. In the context of these propitiations, the lower caste officiant's relationship to his Nāyar hosts was a complex combination of aggression, authority, cooperation, and submission. In the *teyyam* festival of a Nāyar *taravād* in Kottayam, for example, lower caste officiants must first humbly gain permission from the living Nāyar *ḳāranavan*i the Nāyar lineage ghosts and the *taravād* goddess before starting their own propitiations. In the offerings to the *teyyams* which follow, the officiant's attitude to these minor deities is ostensibly one of humility, although the actual performance of the blood sacrifices permits considerable expenditure of aggression. Later, when the officiant dons his mask and becomes possessed by his *teyyam*, he may adopt an authoritative or aggressive attitude to his Nāyar hosts, demanding gifts or threatening them with misfortune before conferring his blessing. He may not, of course, physically attack the Nāyars. Indeed, he is, while possessed, likely to solicit admiration by inflicting physical suffering on himself, usually by burning himself with torches or rolling in the red hot ashes of a fire. After the oracular pronouncements, having doffed his mask, the officiant again becomes the servant of the *taravād* and humbly accepts his fee. For the low caste officiant, therefore, these festivals permit a limited, stylized expression of aggression and a temporary assumption of authority toward their high caste masters. At the same time, the festivals underline both the need for interdependence between the castes, and ultimately, the lower castes' permanent, secular role as submissive servants.

Functions of the cults of alien ghosts. My discussion of alien ghost institutions in the general context of Nāyar handling of aggression has necessarily pointed to some of their social and psychic functions. These may, it seems, be summarized as follows. First, the cults permitted, in a harmless manner, the handling of aggression which arose in relations between castes. Second, whether or not witchcraft or sorcery were actually practiced, the belief that those whom he wrongfully harassed could arm themselves with these ritual weapons must have acted as a deterrent to the Nāyar authority who was tempted to oppress low caste subordinates, or to favor his affines at the expense of his matrilineal juniors. Through witchcraft and sorcery, alien ghosts, therefore, might help to prevent injustices which could not readily be brought before a secular authority.

Third, these institutions brought together in ritual cooperation the very categories of persons whose mutual ambivalence provided the ultimate motive force for the institutions themselves. In the case of witchcraft and sorcery, there existed a complicated interplay of hostilities and alliances which, over time, balanced each other. All Nāyars feared the harmful supernatural power of the lower castes, and this gave unity to their caste. In a particular instance, however, a Nāyar who believed himself attacked by an individual low caste practitioner, or by another Nāyar with the help of such a practitioner, could obtain relief only by engaging the ritual assistance of some other officiant from one of the suspected castes. In the case of the cults of alien ghosts institutionally attached to his *taravād* and his village temple, it seems that the Nāyar's generalized fear of and hostility to outgroups was turned outside the area of human relations and focussed upon supernatural agents feared by all. But again, only willing and friendly ritual cooperation with lower caste officiants could ward off supernatural attacks from the whole community, including the Nāyars.

It seems probable to me that one of the most important functions of all religious ritual, if not the important, is this resolution of conflict within individuals and within groups. The manner in which this is achieved varies greatly. The rituals of rebellion[25] and the initiation rites[26] analyzed by Gluckman, for example, on the surface bear little resemblance to Nāyar cults of the dead. But as Gluckman has shown, their broad social functions are the same. Institutionalized religious ritual, like the private rites of obsessional neurotics, permits to the individual a disguised expression of his aggression, while at the same time reassuring him that his control over the direct physical expression of aggression is unimpaired. But institutionalized ritual does far more than this. It has not only temporary therapeutic value for the individual, but is also interwoven with social, legal, and economic institutions in such a way that it resolves recurrent conflicts within them and thus affords them support. For institutionalized ritual draws into cooperation, in common acts and a common belief system, the very categories of persons upon whose mutual ambivalence the rites are founded. More than this, by bringing home to the participants a sense of their common helplessness in face of the dangers and mysteries which confront man both in his own nature and in his world, ritual appears to transmute their very hatred into sentiments of mutual dependence and love.

Modern Changes in Cults of the Dead

At the present day the cult of lineage ghosts tends to be retained in its traditional form only in the most traditional households—those having residential and economic norms most closely approximating the traditional pattern, and living in the old style of ancestral house. In the new houses built in the past twenty years there is no ancestral shrine, and varying degrees of modification and attrition are observable in ancestral and death rites in these modern types of household.

In households comprising an elementary family or a congerie of mixed matrilineal, cognatic, and affinal kin, the cult of lineage ghosts has died out in its traditional form. In some families emergency propitiations are still made to the ghosts of kinsfolk on the advice of an astrologer. But such a ghost may now be that of any relative who died in the house, and the propitiation may be carried out by any adult male resident. In one Cochin house, for example, lived an old woman, her elder widowed daughter, and her children, and her younger daughter, daughter's husband and their children. The old woman's son, who would traditionally have been *ḳāranavan*, had taken his share of property and gone to live with his wife. When the younger daughter's small girl fell ill with fever, the astrologer advised a propitiation of the ghost of the elder daughter's husband, who had died in this house and been buried near it three years previously. The food offering was made by the child's father in a corner of the living room. In this case neither ghost nor propitiant were members of the *taravād*. Fifty years ago neither one of them could have been concerned in this *taravād's* ancestral rites.

In some households, regular collective offerings to lineage ghosts are still made in July and October, but the form of the rites has changed. Cooked rice balls are offered as in *śrāddham* instead of the old offerings of cooked food. In Cochin in 1952 there was no prohibition of alcohol. But even so, many modern families despised the old offerings of toddy, meat, and arrack and substituted vegetarian food with coconut juice, or else performed the Sanskritic rites. Even in traditional *taravāds* whose members have not yet divided their property, educated *ḳāranavans* are now often unwilling to perform the old-fashioned rites. Such was the case in one wealthy *taravād* of a Kottayam village headman. The *ḳāranavan*, a university graduate and a politician, felt that he must maintain the old ceremonies for the sake of his *taravād's* local reputation, but would not perform them himself. Instead he persuaded his younger son to carry out the offerings to the lineage ghosts and the annual cock sacrifice to Bhagavadi. This youth was, of course, of another *taravād*. Traditionally he would not even have been permitted to enter his father's ancestral shrine. In many households there are now no ancestral propitiations, for many now deny to lineage ghosts the power to bless or harm.

Funeral and *śrāddham* rites persist in a fuller form, but these, too, are often curtailed. This is especially the case in *taravāds* which have lost their ancestral wealth. Rice balls are sometimes offered only on the two last days of the pollution period. Only close kin, and not the whole Nāyar community, are invited to the sixteenth day feast. Often no *dīkṣā* is observed at all. Alternatively, twelve sets of *dīkṣā* rites, for the twelve months of the year of mourning, may be performed in succession on the sixteenth day. Often the bones are not taken to a sacred river. If they are taken, it may be believed that the ghost is thenceforth appeased and that no further *śrāddham* or ancestral rites are required.

The role-structure of death rites has also changed. In most households only immediate younger brothers and maternal nephews, or the own children of a deceased woman, take part in the offerings, instead of the whole *taravād* as heretofore. On the other hand, women, as well as men, now offer rice balls to the ghosts of their parents or matrilineal elders. This reflects a change in the legal status of women, and the fact that women are now the legal heads of many recently partitioned households. In elementary family households, spouses now frequently observe death pollution for one another. At the same time, each may now even refuse to attend the funerals of matrilineal kin. Both in Cochin and Kottayam, the son of a man now often replaces the matrilineal heir as chief mourner, especially if he has inherited his father's property. Nāyars indeed say that "the rites go with the property." If there are disputes over the property, sons and nephews may dispute the right to perform the ceremonies, feeling that their performance gives the chief mourner the right of inheritance. Some men perform rites for both father and mother's brother; others, for neither, if neither bequeathed wealth. The beliefs which accompany funeral and *śrāddham* rites have also suffered attrition. In general, the belief that death rites are performed solely to give rest to the spirit is triumphing over the belief in the necessity to propitiate punitive ghosts. On the other hand, the Nāyars do not dwell on the traditional Brahmanical belief in the tortures of hell which await unpropitiated souls. Many state that they now disbelieve in any form of afterlife. These perform rites only as a mark of respect for and commemoration of the dead. A very few refuse to observe death pollution or to perform funeral rites at all. One educated Nāyar, for example—a medical doctor—stated that on the deaths of his parents he would merely cremate their bodies and invite a few like-minded friends to a meal to commemorate them.

Analysis. Behind these changes lie several separable though related kinds of change in Nāyar social structure and culture. With regard to changes in the cults of dead kinsfolk, the collapse of the *taravād* as a legal and economic corporation is of major importance. With the loss of collective legal responsibility which this entails goes a loss of the sense of collective moral responsibility. Nāyars who are no longer legally responsible for one another, who no longer share land, a common house, and a common destiny, no longer think it probable that their misdemeanors can bring misfortune to each other.

The collapse of the *taravād* is also, of course, accompanied by a total change in the relationships between matrilineal kin. Mother's brothers whose property is divided from that of their nephews no longer have authority over them. Indeed, the mother's brother is now often absent in his wife's house when a child is growing up and exerts no discipline over him. In any case the change which takes place in matrilineal relationships after a modern division of property is very marked. One man whose *taravād* was still undivided commented to me on this change. "In my *taravād*," he said, "I dare not speak before the *kāranavan* without standing and placing my hand before my mouth. But in K. *taravād*, after their partition, I have seen the nephews sitting to play cards with their uncle and passing the cigarette from their mouth to his. When I saw this I knew that relationship means property, and without property there is no relationship."

Moreover, the change to elementary family households does not merely entail a shift of the same disciplinary functions from the mother's brother to the father. Nāyar fathers have a tradition of indulgent tenderness toward their children and are loth to discipline them. Even when they are forced to do so, the techniques of discipline differ from those in a traditional *taravād* house. In the intimate atmosphere of the small elementary family household, traditional etiquette is abandoned. Children learn to obey both parents from love more than from fear. There appears to be a much deeper repression of aggression than in the traditional setting, and correspondingly, many young Nāyars cannot entertain the notion that their parents' ghosts could act punitively toward them. It seems probable that such changes in the modes of handling aggression—affected also by the collapse of the military tradition and the modern legal ban on all forms of physical aggression—may also lie behind the repugnance of modern Nāyars for such other traditional religious forms as blood sacrifice and spirit possession.

Also important in the abandonment of ghost cults is, however, an increased tendency toward the adoption of Sanskrit rites. This tendency, which has marked all the non-Brahman castes during the past hundred years or so, I would associate with increasing mobility within the caste system and, most recently, with its gradual collapse. For the Nāyars, as for the lower castes, the Brahmans are no longer a group with whom they have fixed status relationships. Instead, the Brahmans are now a reference group whom the Nāyars emulate and with whom they compete in the struggle for high rank and respectability. Some Nāyars who still hold their traditional beliefs in ancestral spirits and deities deliberately "purge" their rites of non-Sanskritic elements in order to gain respectability. Others have changed both rites and beliefs toward a modified form of the Brahmanical religion, even while they are busy repudiating the religious authority of the Brahman. Yet others, whose number is probably increasing, repudiate both Brahmanical and non-Sanskritic religions in their orthodox forms. Instead, they work out for themselves a more or less agnostic world view with humanitarian ideals, in which ceremonies, if they figure at all, figure only as acts of piety toward respected persons.

The cults of alien ghosts are also changing their form and gradually dying out. This change accompanies the gradual collapse of the caste system as a system of ranked occupational groups linked by hereditary service ties. The collapse of the caste system itself results from the growth of the capitalist market economy and the democratization of political institutions. Some Nāyars retain their beliefs in witchcraft and sorcery, but the categories of persons whom they suspect are no longer solely caste determined. They are as likely to include fellow factory workers or competitors in government service, irrespective of caste. Professional exorcists of appropriate caste are often no longer available, for many have left their traditional work. So also have many of the low caste families who formerly propitiated ghosts and minor deities associated with village temples or with Nāyar *taravāds*. Since the passing of the Temple Entry

Act of 1947, moreover, low caste persons in general wish to enter the main court of the temple along with the higher castes and to propitiate the great deity. Alternatively, they build modern temples of their own dedicated to Sanskrit gods. They begin to shun the outer courtyards of temples populated by ghosts and devils and to leave these unpropitiated. Some Nāyars still believe that the lower castes have supernatural powers as sorcerers and lycanthropic witches, but believe that as the lower castes acquire education and "civilization" they voluntarily give up these powers. Others now deny that ghosts, witches, or sorcerers ever possessed powers at all.

All of these changes in belief and ritual are probably linked not only specifically to the collapse of *taravād* and caste as small birth-status groups, but more generally to the widening range of Nāyar social relations and to the relaxing of their former tight interdependencies in face-to-face relationships. As they move into a heterogeneous, mobile, urban setting composed partly of impersonal relationships with strangers, the Nāyars cease to regard the natural order as in all respects a moral order and cease to seek personal motives as the ultimate causes of misfortunes. The growth of scientific knowledge in schools and the spread of medical facilities also obviously influence beliefs about illness. This does not, of course, mean that the Nāyars and lower castes no longer require institutionalized modes of handling their aggressive impulses and their uncertainty in face of cosmic mysteries. In a few areas of living, new religious institutions have developed, which are outside the subject of this paper. In general, however, I think it is true to say that the scope of ritual beliefs and activities is shrinking[27] for Malabaris as a whole, and that as technology develops and new social arrangements become feasible, they concentrate more on the "how" of misfortunes, leaving the "why" to chance. Correspondingly, of course, conflict is increasingly handled through modern secular institutions (the law-court, the trades' union, the political party, the democratic election, etc.), which produce continuing social structural changes rather than serving to maintain harmony within traditional birth-status groups.

NOTES

[1] For a brief analysis of social change among the Nāyars, see E. K. Gough, "Changing Kinship Usages in the Setting of Political and Economic Change Among the Nāyars of Malabar," *Journal Royal Anth. Institute,* LXXXII (1952), 71-88.

[2] George P. Murdock, *Social Structure* (New York, 1949), p. 2.

[3] The Madras *Marumakkattayam* Act of 1933, and the Cochin Nāyar Act of 1937.

[4] Before the date of this Act, all division of ancestral property in a Nāyar *taravād* had been stirpital.

[5] For accounts of Nāyar propitiations of lineage ghosts, see E. Thurston, *Castes and Tribes of Southern India* (Madras, 1909), V, 362-3; F. Fawcett, *The Nāyars of Malabar,* Bull. Madras Govt. Museum (Madras, 1901), III, No. 3, 245-253; K. M. Panikkar, "Religion and Magic Among the Nayars," *Man,* XVIII, No. 7 (1918); V. K. Raman Menon, "Ancestor Worship Among the Nayars," *Man,* XX, No. 3 (1920); R. K. Pisharodi, *Ancestor Worship in Kerala* (1923).

[6] Menon, 1920.

[7] M. J. Levy, Jr., *The Family Revolution in Modern China* (Cambridge, 1949), pp. 168-9.

[8] F. Freud, *Totem and Taboo,* trans., Jas. Strachey (New York, 1950), pp. 51-63.

[9] M. Mead, *Male and Female* (New York, 1949), pp. 297-304.

[10] M. E. Opler, "An Interpretation of Ambivalence in Two American Indian Tribes," *Journal of Social Psych.,* VII (1936), 82-115.

[11] A. Kardiner and Associates, *The Psychological Frontiers of Society* (New York, 1945), pp. 112, 118ff, 167; M. Fortes, *The Web of Kinship Among the Tallensi* (Oxford, 1949), p. 234ff;

G. Roheim, *Psychoanalysis and Anthropology* (New York, 1950), pp. 134, 135, 432; F. L. K. Hsu, *Under the Ancestors' Shadow* (New York, 1948), pp. 240-243; Mead, 1949, pp. 40-41; J. W. M. Whiting and I. L. Child, *Child Training and Personality* (New Haven, 1953), pp. 263-304.

[12] Nāyar *Kāranavans* are of course not ancestors in the strict sense. However, I use this term for convenience as they fulfill roles similar to those of ancestors in many patrilineal societies.

[13] For an account of Īrava social organization and culture, see A. Aiyappan, *Iravas* and *Culture Change*, Bull. Madras Govt. Mus., 5 (1945).

[14] M. N. Srinivas, *Religion and Society Among the Coorgs* (Oxford, 1952), pp. 158-165.

[15] For a brief account of Tamil Brahman kinship, see E. K. Gough, "Brahman Kinship in a Tamil Village," *American Anthropologist*, XVIII, (1956), 826-853.

[16] See, e.g., Thurston, V (1909), 152-240.

[17] Fortes, 1949, p. 235.

[18] H. E. J. Stanley, trans., Duarte Barbosa, *A Description of the Coasts of East Africa and Malabar in the Beginning of the Sixteenth Century* (Hakluyt, 1886), p. 15.

[19] R. Rowlandson, trans., Sheikh Zein-ud-deen, *Tohfut ul Mujahideen*. An Offering to Warriors Who Shall Fight in Defence of Religion Against Infidels (Hakluyt, 1883), p. 63.

[20] A. C. Burnell, trans., *The Voyage of John Hughyen Van Linschoten to the East Indies* (From the Old English Translation of 1598) (Hakluyt, 1885), p. 284.

[21] All castes on the southwest coast bury or cremate the dead in the southwest corner of the ancestral garden. This custom contrasts with that of Hindus in the eastern districts, who burn or bury the dead on communal sites, each owned jointly by a caste community, outside the residential area of the village.

[22] The castes of agricultural serfs are absent in Kottayam, agricultural labor being done by Īrava tenants or by the Nāyars themselves.

[23] This form of propitiation of alien ghosts in Kottayam is called a *teyyam tira*. It closely resembles the *kāranava tērē* of the neighboring Coorgs (Srinivas, 1952, pp. 158-165.) In Coorg, however, lower caste officiants impersonate the Coorg *taravād's* own ancestors. In Malabar, lower caste propitiants impersonate only alien ghosts attached to the Nāyar *taravād*.

[24] Witchcraft (*odi*), a witch (*odiyan*). For a more detailed account of witchcraft, see Thurston, VI (1909), 36-41, 122-127.

[25] M. Gluckman, *Rituals of Rebellion in South-East Africa* (Manchester, 1954).

[26] Gluckman, *The Role of the Sexes in Wiko Circumcision Ceremonies. Social Structure*, M. Fortes, ed. (Oxford, 1949), pp. 145-167.

[27] All of these statements apply to conditions in 1947-9. I observed no major changes in ritual activities during a brief revisit in 1952. The Malabar Coast, as the newly formed State of Kerala, elected a Communist government in April 1957, and I have little information on conditions after that date.

University of Michigan
Ann Arbor, Michigan

A SIKH VILLAGE

By Indera P. Singh

SIKHISM has often been described by scholars as a way of life, one that can be best understood by studying the life of the people professing it. With this end in view, we selected Daleke, a village in Amritsar district in the Majha area, known as the cradle of Sikhism.[1] The holiest temple of the Sikhs, the Golden Temple, is situated in this area, and most of the followers of the faith come from here abouts. Most of the fighters in the forces of the Gurus came from Majha, and because of the sanctity attached to the Golden Temple, the land of the whole district of Amritsar is considered sacred by the Sikhs. The leaders of the various movements of reform or political emancipation in Sikhism were invariably drawn from this area. The premier educational institution of the Sikhs, Khalsa College, is also located in Amritsar. The region is full of reminiscenses of Sikh history—each second village having been visited either by one of the Sikh gurus or one of the Sikh heroes, and having some historical temple in commemoration of the visit or event.

Daleke is a small village situated at a distance of twenty miles from Amritsar. It was founded about three hundred years ago by Dalā Singh, who, along with his father, embraced Sikhism in the days of Guru Gobind Singh. Only five miles away is the Golden Temple of Taran Taran, where the Fifth Guru, Arjan (1563-1606, A.D.), established a second center of the Sikh faith. Daleke was unconnected with Taran Taran by road or rail until three years ago. The only approach was a small bridle path winding through the fields, allowing the use of horses or camels as alternative means of transport. The villagers have now built a twenty foot wide road, in cooperation with the Community Projects Administration. Most of the families living in the village are Jāṭs and Mazhbīs. Others are Brahmans, Kāmbhos, Tarkhāns, Mehrās, and Nāīs. Before "partition" (the villagers refer to India's independence in 1947 as 'partition' because the Panjab was partitioned into two parts—East and West Panjab—the latter going to West Pakistan), some Muslim families also resided in the village. They were by caste Arains (vegetable growers), Sakkās (water carriers), Julāhās (weavers), Telīs (oilmen) and Lohārs (blacksmiths). They migrated to Pakistan, and twenty Hindu families came from West Pakistan to settle in this village. They are mainly Kāmbohs (farmers), a Tarkhān (carpenter), and a Nāī (barber). All of them had emigrated from Daleke in 1918, when they were awarded lands in Lyallpur by the British government in recognition of their services in the army. Some of them have now been allotted lands in the next village in compensation for land they lost in Pakistan. They either have occupied the former Muslim houses or live in their old houses with holdings which have been extended with the help of the land left behind by Muslims. All the families belonging to castes like Jāṭ, Kāmboh, Ḳumhār, Tarkhān, Cīmbā, and Nāī, profess faith in Sikhism; all the Mazhbīs are also Sikhs. There are three Brahman families professing Hinduism. Four other families are Christian, having been converted to Christianity only one generation ago.

Castes and occupation. Jāṭs are, by tradition, agriculturists, and the Jāṭs of Daleke are no exception. They occasionally work also as laborers on road building, etc. Most of them have sufficient land, and about half of them employ *kāmīn*, or *sepī*, i.e., farm laborers, to help them in their work. Those not having enough land for cultivation either till the land of others on a half-and-half basis or work elsewhere as clerks or laborers. A few have joined the army. Five families possessing large tracts of land are called Jagīrdārs. They also receive rents from their Jagīrs in Ambala district. The Jagīrdārs are direct descendants of the founder of the village, Dala. All of them employ *sepīs* to work on their lands, and are considered higher in status than any others in the village.

The Kāmbohs, too, are mainly agriculturists, but are considered lower in status than the Jāṭs. They usually have much smaller land holdings than the Jāṭs, but are famous for tilling their lands in the most economical way and for producing much more from a given piece of land. They are very industrious and do all the work in their fields by themselves. They rarely engage a *sepī* to help them in their work or rent out their land for cultivation to someone else. They can, however, take to any other work. Unlike the Jāṭs, who would hate to open a shop, Kāmbohs run shops selling general merchandise, medicines, etc. Some Kāmbohs even add to their income by selling milk—a practice which is much looked down upon by Jāṭs.

Tarkhāns are traditionally carpenters and they are also called Rāmgaṛhīyas (after the name of the fort Rāmgarh and a Sikh *Misal* founded by Sardar Jasa Singh). The main work of the Tarkhāns is to make or repair ploughs, sickles, and the wooden parts of agricultural implements, as well as household articles like beds, spinning wheels, churns, stools and chairs, etc. With the migration of Muslim blacksmiths to Pakistan, the Tarkhāns now have taken to their work also. For his services to the farmer, a Tarkhān is paid in kind in the form of a certain quantity of grain at each harvesting time. But when his services are required as a mason or as a carpenter to build a house, the Tarkhān is paid a wage of Rs.4/-per day in cash. His Sardārs also give him fodder for his milk cattle. The Tarkhāns are more mobile than any other caste group in the village. One of their members has gone to Nairobi (Africa), another to Hirakud, and still another to Bombay. One Tarkhān from Daleke village works as an automobile mechanic in Amritsar. A mill for grinding flour locally is also owned by one of the Tarkhān families. The charges are one seer of grain per maund of grain ground by the mill. Tarkhāns also sometimes work as farm laborers in harvesting crops to supplement their income.

Tarkhāns also do minor services for castes other than the farmers and free of any cash charge. They are repaid by these castes through services rendered when the Tarkhān needs more persons to help him in threshing and winnowing or carrying loads.

While the Kumhārs are traditionally earthen potmakers, none of them practices this occupation today in Daleke. They are now all engaged in trade. They carry grain and husks on their donkeys from the village to the market in the nearby town, and they are paid the cartage charges by the farmer sending his grain. They also buy grains from the farmer on their own account and sell it at a profit in the town. The richer Kumhārs buy grain when it is cheap, hoard it, and sell it in the town only when prices are high. But this necessitates their paying the price of grain to the farmer at once. Generally, however, they carry grain on the same day to the market and pay the farmer its price when they return to the village after deducting their profit. The Kumhārs' services are very much in demand during the harvesting season, when the farmer has no time to carry his grain to the market himself. Moreover, the farmer is afraid of falling prey to the treachery of the market businessmen, a mishap which is less likely in the case of the Kumhārs, who have more frequent dealings in the town.

Six young men among the Kumhārs learned the craft of weaving from Muslim weavers who have now left the village. They were weaving cloth until 1955, but are now employed in an Amritsar textile factory which uses power looms. Nevertheless, the three families maintain hand looms in their houses and weave cloth for their own use and occasionally for the other villagers. Another Kumhār family deals in the trade of selling and buying cattle and horses.

The Mehrās are traditionally water carriers, as they carry water from the village well to the houses of the farmers. They also supply drinking water to their clients in the fields during harvesting. They serve all the castes except the Mazhbīs and the Sansīs. They also are given a certain amount of grain by each family so served by them. In addition, they get one loaf of bread and some vegetables daily from each house. The number of families engaging their services has now decreased considerably owing to installation of hand water pumps (tube wells) in many houses.

The Cīmbās are traditionally washermen; occasionally, they also work as tailors. The only Cīmbā family in Daleke does not have much work, as the village women prefer to wash their own clothes and pass on only thick bed clothes to him for cleaning. He sews clothes also for the simpler village folk. Others get them stitched in the nearby town or in their own homes. There are as many as twelve sewing machines, and recently thirty young women of the village attended classes in sewing and embroidery at a Training Center opened for this purpose by the Community Project Block in the village.

The Nāīs are traditionally barbers and are also nicknamed "Rājās" 'Kings.' They profess Sikhism and do not cut their own hair. Their presence in a Sikh village seems strange, but they form as important an element of the village community as any other. Instead of cutting hair or shaving beards, they cut nails of their clients. They act as messengers at marriages, deaths or births. They are entrusted with duties like collecting beds, sheets, mattresses, and utensils, etc., on occasions of marriages and other ceremonial gatherings. They also help in cooking meals on various ceremonial and festive occasions. Their wives groom the hair of the ladies of the house. They receive a certain amount of grain at each harvest from all the families they serve. For services rendered on occasions of marriages, deaths, or other ceremonial occasions, they are paid separately. Some of their clients also get their hair and beards trimmed to look younger. The Nāīs are also called upon sometimes to cut the hair of children when too many lice in the hair trouble the child, and other remedies to get rid of them prove useless.

The Nāīs are also traditional matchmakers. Formerly they used to arrange marriages and we find many folktales and folksongs that relate the entreaties of a mother to a Nāī to find a good husband for her daughter. About fifty years ago the Nāī's position in arranging matches was very significant, but now this task has been taken over by the relatives and friends of the parties concerned. "People no longer want to let a mere Nāī 'decide' the fate of their darling children"—as one of our witty respondents in the village remarked.

The Nāīs were famous for their skill in curing boils and sores, and one of the four barber families still practices this profession. Because of the loss of trade as matchmakers and haircutters, one of them is now engaged in cultivation. Others are engaged in trade in cattle and horses. One of them even rears mules and horses to sell in the market.

Mazhbīs, meaning the 'devoted,' form about half the population of the village. They were originally Chuhṛās (sweepers and scavengers) and were converted to Sikhism at the time of the tenth Sikh Guru, Gobind Singh. They work as farm laborers on yearly wages; and can change their master or Sardār every year after the *haḍ* 'wheat' crop. They are not bound to their Sardār as a family. In fact, the husband may be working for one family, and his wife, who cleans the courtyard and makes dung cakes, may be working for another family. Each is paid separately for his or her work. If they have sons, these also may work for different families and are paid for their services individually, depending on the amount of work done by each of them. The wages of a Mazhbī vary from forty maunds of grain to eighty maunds per year, or he may get one fifth of the total crop if the farmer has one plough. Besides his wages, he gets his food and tea also from his Sardar, when working for him.

Many Mazhbīs have joined the army as soldiers and in two families at present three generations are receiving pensions as ex-army personnel. Such families usually do not work as *sepīs* or farm laborers, but till the land of others on a contract basis.

The danger of losing their lands, under pending land reforms which seek to do away with intermediaries on land, has led all the Jagīrdārs to till their land themselves. This has rendered more than half the population of Mazhbīs in the village unemployed; they now either enlist in the army or have already left the village to work as laborers as far away as Hirakud Dam. They are well paid as laborers in construction work because of their good physique and stamina.

Some of the Mazhbīs depend for their livelihood on selling milk. For this purpose they usually maintain a couple of buffaloes. Fodder can always be had free from the Sardār even if one of the family members is working for him.

Besides those engaged in work for the whole year for one family, others work as farm laborers during the harvest season. In fact those working away from the village also return to Daleke to work in the harvest season. The women folk of the Mazhbīs supplement the income of their husbands by cleaning the houses of various families and spinning cotton. They also pick cotton during the season.

The Sansīs are traditional shepherds and are considered lower in status than the Mazhbīs. They are also members of the former criminal tribes. The Sansīs earn their livelihood by selling the wool of their sheep, which are clipped twice a year. The only family of Sansīs in the village had about eighty sheep. They died last year because of an epidemic. Now two out of the three brothers work as farm laborers on an annual wage basis for a Jāṭ. Another works as a hired laborer in the village. One of them knows the genealogies of all the Sardārs and recites them at the time of marriages. He also carries messages from one village to the other. The genealogies of the Muslims used to be kept by the Mīrāsīs, who left for Pakistan along with the Muslim farmers. The Sansī women occasionally indulge in prostitution with fields as their locale for this purpose. The clients are usually unmarried farmers and poor laborers.

The Sunārs are traditionally goldsmiths, and one such family resides in Daleke. The family came here from Pakistan after partition. The head of the family makes gold and silver ornaments, for which he is paid in cash or in grain, according to the amount of work done. The modern notions of not wearing many ornaments, and the Akali movement (1921-26), discouraging altogether the use of ornaments by men, have resulted in less demand for the work of the goldsmith. Being old and not knowing new designs used in the town, the Sunār prefers to stay in the village and lives a hand-to-mouth existence.

The Brahmans are traditional priests who conduct marriages, make horoscopes, and predict auspicious days for performance of certain ceremonies, for tilling the land, or for other important occasions. They used to occupy a very high position because of their sacred functions. In Daleke today they are shopkeepers selling vegetables, grains, and medicines. One of the two Brahman families residing in the village knows sorcery and witchcraft and is often called upon to cure persons "possessed" by various spirits or suffering from snake-bite. The common father of the two Brahman families, who came only forty years ago from Ambala District with some of the Jagīrdārs, commanded as great a respect as any Brahman in other orthodox Hindu villages. He was granted land by the Jagīrdārs on the birth of their sons, which he usually rented out to others for cultivation. His influence among the people was so great that at one time when the villagers wanted to give a contract on dead cattles' bodies to a Mazhbī Nāī, who intended to skin the animals, this Brahman managed to restrain them from so doing. He insisted that during his lifetime he would not allow the sacred cattle, which should be buried, to be desecrated.

Decline of the Brahmans. The decline of the Brahmans came in 1922-23 after the reform movement among the Sikhs, i.e., after the Singh Sabhā and Akali movement had begun. These movements aimed at removing the Brahmanical influence from the Sikh *gurdvārās* (temples) and the Sikh masses. This influence had slowly crept in after the fall of the Sikh Kingdom. The social life of the Sikhs, i.e., their births, marriages, and deaths, could not be performed without the help of Brahmans. Sikhism was gradually becoming a branch of Hindu protestants, owing allegiance to Hindu deities and gods. Even in the premier Sikh temples, like the Golden Temple at Amritsar, there were idols of Rāma and other Hindu gods and goddesses. The Rām Līlā used to be performed in the Golden Temple at Taran Taran. The other impetus to this reform movement was a reaction against the efforts of the Christian missionaries to bring Sikhs into their fold.

An Anand Marriage Act was passed in the Central Assembly to regulate marriages performed according to Sikh rites. This made the services of Brahmans unnecessary; the Sikh marriage rites could now be conducted by a *granthī*, a Sikh priest, who could be of any caste. The *granthī* of Daleke belongs to the Cīmbā (washermen) caste. The Sikh *granthī*, who was trained at the Sikh Missionary College run by the Gurdvārā Prabhandak Committee at Amritsar, replaced the Brahman at birth and death ceremonies. In fact, giving a Sikh child his baptism at birth, with sweetened water on the tip of a *kirpān* 'dagger' seems to have been adopted after the Christian custom. Such a practice is not known among Hindus of this area. The functions of a *granthī* can, moreover, be performed by any Sikh who knows what to do regarding each ceremony.

The Akali movement discouraged belief in horoscopes and astrology and pointed out that such beliefs were against Sikh precepts. And though there are still a few Sikhs in Daleke who will not till their land without asking for an auspicious day from the Brahman, there are many who do so now without asking him. Consulting the Brahman is considered an unnecessary expense which can be avoided without any danger of losing the crop. Only when a farmer has been unsuccessful in cultivation for two or three successive years will he take recourse to the Brahman in order to find an auspicious day and avoid misfortune next time.

Formerly the Brahmans were invited to feast in farmers' houses on certain ceremonial occasions, for example, *śrāddhas* (rites in honor of ancestors). The Sikh reform movements discouraged this practice too, and, today, though a few families still celebrate *śrāddhas*, they do not feed the Brahmans or ask them to perform any ceremony in honor of their ancestors. Instead, they just invite a few Sikhs of any caste and feed them.

To justify a break with the Brahmans, the story of betrayal by a Brahman cook of the Tenth Guru, Gobind Singh, was revived. Gangū, the Brahman cook, betrayed the two youngest sons of the Guru and their grandmother to the Muslim ruler of Sirhind, who had them put to death. Similarly, the defeat of the Sikhs at the hands of the British was attributed to the treachery of the Brahman generals of the Sikh Army.

The conversion of a Muslim woman to Sikhism and her marriage to a Jāṭ of Daleke broke the last link between the Brahmans and others in the village. The Brahmans threatened that they would not have anything to do with the villagers if the village permitted the conversion of a Muslim. The Sikhs were in no mood to heed this threat and went ahead with the conversion in the presence of the whole village. Again, one of the sons of the Brahman began to drink wine and to eat meat, and this was cited as another reason for not showing any special respect to the Brahmans. The Brahmans, therefore, are held in no great respect today in village Daleke, and are referred to in quite derogatory terms by Jāṭs and others.

Sikhism versus Brahmanism. It is worth mentioning here that Sikhism itself was one of the many reform movements in the fifteenth century during the period of Muslim domination in India. These aimed at preventing the masses from being converted to Islam. To achieve this, the leaders attacked the extreme rigidity of Brahmanism and advocated abolition of caste and removal of some of the social restrictions. The radical element of this movement broke away from Hindu orthodoxy. The founder of this wing of the movement was Bāsava, a Brahman. He gave up the caste-polity and permitted marriages even between the Brahmans and caṇḍāls.

Nānak (1469-1539 A.D.)—the founder of Sikhism, and a Kṣatriya by caste—preached in the North the equality of all men irrespective of their caste. He declared that distinctions based on caste and pedigree are vain and that no caste is acknowledged in the next world. He further said that by remembering Him, all—whether Kṣatriya, Brahman, Śūdra or Vaiśya—can attain salvation. In order to bring equality among all castes in Sikhism, the Third Guru, Amardās (1479-1574), opened a free kitchen and would not see any person unless he had eaten in his kitchen where people, irrespective of their caste, status or rank, ate together. Even Emperor Akbar was not given an audience by the Guru until he had eaten in the kitchen attached to the Guru's house. Other successive gurus also continued to emphasize the futility of being proud of one's caste, declaring that only the actions of the individual in this world would decide for or against his or her salvation. The Tenth Guru, Gobind Singh (1668-1708 A.D.), who organized the Sikhs into a distinct fraternity by ordaining them to keep the five symbols—1) uncut hair, 2) comb, 3) iron ring, 4) underwear and 5) the sword—also laid great stress on the equality of various castes. The Five Beloved, whom he had chosen from an assembly of thousands of Sikhs gathered at Anandpur to celebrate the Vesākhī festival, were drawn from all castes—Kṣatriya, Śūdra, Jāṭ and other lower castes. When these five were initiated into the new fraternity of the Khālsās 'the pure,' he made them drink from the same bowl and gave them new names with the suffix "Singh" 'lion.' He had himself initiated by these Five Beloved and, following him, many thousands of Sikhs present, irrespective of their castes, were thus initiated by the Five Beloved, drinking from the same bowl and eating from the same plate. All those so initiated took on the name "Singh," signifying one common brotherhood. This practice of eating from the same plate and drinking from the same bowl is followed today at the time of initiation of a Sikh into a Khālsā. The ceremony is known as Amṛt Chakna. The holy book of the Sikhs, the *Granth*, which succeeded the Tenth Guru as the Guru of the Sikhs, contains writings not only of the Sikh Gurus, but also of Hindu and Muslim *bhagats* belonging to different castes—tailor (Nāmdev), butcher (Sādhan), Vaiśya (Trilocan), barber (Sain), Jāṭs (Dhannā), Brahmans (Gīta Govind and Surdās), weaver (Kabīr), cobbler (Ravidās), Sheikh Farīd, and Bhikan (sūfīs).

Equality of castes. It is not only historically that the Sikh Gurus advocated the equality of castes. Even now, the villagers of Daleke point to this as one of the superior qualities of their faith. The social relations of various castes in Daleke are therefore worth noting. The people belonging to various castes professing Sikhism have been divided broadly into two groups: the Sardārs (the upper castes) and the Mazhbīs (the scavengers). The first group includes Jāṭs, Kāmbohs, Tarkhāns, Kumhārs, Sunārs, and Nāīs. These castes visit each others' houses, interdine, and attend marriage functions and other festive occasions. They go to the fairs together, and celebrate most of the festivals communally. These caste groups can be identified, however, in the same manner as in a Hindu village. The higher group of Sardārs is further subdivided into agriculturists and nonagriculturists, the latter including traders and artisans. The agriculturist group considers itself higher than the nonagriculturists. The houses of persons belonging to these various castes in the Sardār group adjoin each other. No clear-cut demarcations exist to signify separate quarters for separate castes. This cannot be said for the houses of the Mazhbīs, the scavenger caste. They live on one side of the village, and a long wall of the backs of the houses of the higher caste group separates them from others in the village. About twenty families live a hundred yards away on the land given to them for residence by the father of the Sarpanc on the birth of his first son. Mazhbīs work as farm laborers, while their wives clean the courtyards, collect cow dung and make cow dung cakes. The work of both Mazhbī men and women necessitates their entering into the houses of the Sardārs for whom they work. More than half of the farmers who employ them allow them house entry and some even let them milk their buffaloes. There is no feeling of pollution attached to their touch, person, or clothing. Some of the Kāmboh and Kumhār families, who do not let the Mazhbīs enter their houses beyond the cattleyard, give a very interesting legend to support their action. They say that when the Five Beloved were entering the tent of the Guru on his invitation, the Mazhbī among them asked Guru's permission to enter his tent also. The Guru told him that he need not have asked and, since he had done so, Mazhbīs would have to wait for three hundred years until they had free access to all places. This legend is not supported by any historical facts and seems to have been invented by some clever interested person. It is very similar to the other common legend of Bālmīki, the Guru of Cuhṛās (sweepers—converts to Sikhism from this group are called Mazhbīs) who happened to arrive late at a party given by Lord Viṣṇu and had to eat only the leftovers.

The Mazhbīs have a separate well while all other castes use the same well. Two years ago, the Sarpanc allowed the Mazhbīs to draw water from the well of the Sardārs. They have done so only occasionally, as many people still do not like Mazhbīs to draw water from the same well as themselves.

Mazhbīs and other Sikhs have a common *gurdvārā* (Sikh temple). They assemble together and sit there intermixed. Those high caste Sikhs, especially women, who do not allow Mazhbīs to enter their houses, usually sit away from the place where Mazhbīs are sitting. They all get the same *parsād* 'offerings' and eat food from the same kitchen. Food is prepared from grains gathered from families irrespective of any caste distinction.

The *gurdvārā* is used as a school during the day and is also used as the *Janj ghar*—a place where the bridegroom's marriage party stays for two or three days. Since village exogamy is the rule, the *gurdvārā* is always in demand for putting up the marriage parties on occasions of girls' marriages in the village. This courtesy is given to members of all castes. The Mazhbīs, until very recently, had a separate small room of their own for this purpose in their part of the village. No *granth sāhib* (the holy book) had been installed there and, when not in use for marriage parties, it was used as a common room where Mazhbīs used to gather, smoke, and talk. This room was washed away in the recent floods, and has not since been rebuilt. Mazhbīs have been allowed to put up their marriage parties in the *gurdvārā* only twice during the last ten years. The reason given by others for not allowing the Mazhbīs' marriage parties to stay in the *gurdvārā* is that the Mazhbīs smoke tobacco and opium (which is prohibited by Sikhism) and thus they desecrate the sanctity of the *gurdvārā*. The Mazhbī parties which were allowed to stay in the village *gurdvārā* are reported to have been "clean" people who did not smoke. In fact, they were military men.

Mazhbīs accompany marriage parties only of persons for whom they work. The Sardārs may come to the houses of a Mazhbī on festive occasions but they do it as a benevolent gesture to their farm laborers, who may, after all, feel greatly honored by such visits. Persons belonging to other castes also participate in each others' festive occasions, but they are mostly personal friends.

All persons, irrespective of their castes, go to attend fairs together and in these fairs no special food shops are erected for the use of Mazhbīs, although until about fifteen years ago Mazhbīs were not given food in the same utensils as others. Separate glasses and plates which the Mazhbīs had to clean themsleves were kept in a corner. Today they drink and eat from the same utensils at Sikh shops in the nearby town, Taran Taran, as are used by others. That is why orthodox Hindus sometimes do not buy eatables from a Sikh *halwāī* 'confectioner's' shop.

The Mazhbīs are traditional brewers of country wine. Whenever a villager needs wine (which he does quite often) he gives some *guṛ* (brown sugar prepared from sugar cane) to his Mazhbī, who gives him the prepared wine and keeps part of it for himself. Mazhbīs and Sardārs often drink wine together at the fairs and occasionally in the fields too. Those preaching equality of caste today refer convincingly to the fact that all the wine drunk by the Sardārs is brewed at the hands of Mazhbīs whom they would not like to touch otherwise.

Intermarriage by castes is one of the important tests as to abolition of caste system, but in Daleke no single case of intermarriage has occurred in its history. Marriages have taken place strictly within the caste. A religious reformer came to the village *gurdvārā* during our stay and profoundly advocated the abolition of caste distinctions, favoring intercaste marriages. One of the Mazhbīs listening to him got up and requested the speaker to solve his problem of finding husbands for his four daughters. The speaker asked those wishing to accept his daughters in marriage to raise their hands. Practically everybody in the audience, consisting of all castes, raised his hand. Apparently being satisfied with the result, the Mazhbī asked for girls to marry his sons. This time no hand went up. People were ready to accept wives from lower castes, but were not willing to give their daughters in marriage. The answer to this riddle lies probably in the prevalence of hypergamy among Jāṭs of all areas and, even in Daleke, there are fifteen women whose caste is not known. They were brought from outside by men who could not get a wife by regular means. These women are accepted as equals, and their children have the same status as children of a woman of known caste. However, such marriages are never allowed to be performed as regular marriages with all the ceremonies symbolizing the "essentials" of a marriage as conceived by the village community.

The solitary case of interreligious marriage, in which the whole village participated, was that of a Jāṭ Sikh with a Muslim woman. But this marriage was performed only after the woman had been converted to Sikhism. Her son married into a Jāṭ family on attaining adulthood.

Another important factor reflecting the social relations within the caste structure is the role of the priest. The village *gurdvārā* is looked after by a *granthī* (reader of the Holy Book) who is usually addressed as "Sant" 'Saint.' He serves persons belonging to all castes equally. He performs all Sikh marriages in Daleke irrespective of any caste distinction. At births and deaths he prays for all. He collects bread and flour everyday from each house, some of which he eats himself; the rest is distributed among the travellers staying in the *gurdvārā*. The poor people also gather near the *gurdvārā* to get some food from the Sant. This food is collected from the houses of all castes and distributed among persons belonging to all castes.

Often the Sant is called upon to perform *Akhaṇḍ Pāṭh*, the continuous reading of the Holy Book in its entirety in forty-eight hours, or *Sādhāraṇ Pāṭh*, reading of the entire Holy Book in a week or at leisure), in the homes of different people. In the case of *Akhaṇḍ Pāṭh* or *Saptāhik* 'weekly' *Pāṭh*, the Sant naturally cannot read the Holy Book alone. He invites three or four others who can also read the Granth to help him in this task. Among the usual three *pāṭhīs* (readers of the Granth) in Daleke, one is a Tarkhān (carpenter), another a Jāṭ and the third a Mazhbī. All the *pāṭhīs* take their meals at the house where an *Akhaṇḍ Pāṭh* is being conducted. All of them, irrespective of their caste, are fed by the inviting families. Such occasions were many during our stay in the village.

The end of the reading of the holy book is followed by *kīrtan* (singing of hymns). The traditional singers of Sikh hymns until the period of the tenth Guru were "Masands." They became corrupt and started demanding huge sums as their share of the offerings on various Sikh festivals. The tenth Guru dismissed them and enjoined his Sikhs to sing hymns themselves. In Daleke, there are four persons who usually sing hymns on these occasions. One of them is the Sant who sings to the accompaniment of a harmonium. The Tarkhān is a famous Ḍhādhī (the Panjābīs' traditional Sikh bards) and plays on a *sārangī*. Another is a Mehrā. One Jāṭ and a Mazhbī play on drums. These four singers are often joined by the whole congregation in singing hymns. In fact, some hymns, sung near the end of the meeting, are to be sung in unison only.

Mostly the prayers are led by the Sant in the *gurdvārā* or the house, but usually an elderly person, who knows how to read the Granth, is asked to sit near it and reads the verse of the day from it.

The acceptance of a low caste Cīmbā as their priest, and the admittance of another Mazhbī to dine in their houses when performing *Akhaṇḍ Pāṭh*, may be due to the reverence paid to all persons connected with supernaturals and gods, irrespective of their castes and religion. Sikhs, as well as Hindus, worship the tombs of Muslim saints and make promises to offer clothes or food if a certain wish of theirs is fulfilled. The worship of these Muslim saints has not died out with the exodus to Pakistan of all Muslims from Daleke and other adjoining villages. Festivals are arranged to commemorate the anniversaries of Sher Shāh Valī, Hājī Shāh Pīr, and Jogī Pīr. Jogī Pīr is now called Joga Singh, and a Sikh holy book has been installed in his shrine. The Nihangs (a sect of warrior Sikhs) have replaced the Muslim Mīrāsīs as the priests. Instead of *qawālīs* (hymns sung in praise of Prophet Mohammad in a special manner), Sikh hymns are now sung. Similarly, Sher Shāh is now called Bābā Sher Singh, and his Sikh followers organize a fair on his anniversary. In the days of the Muslims there were always two kitchens; one for Muslims and the other for non-Muslims, and believers of different faiths ate from different kitchens, although now such separation is not practiced.

It is worth mentioning here that the worship of tombs by the Hindus and Sikhs of the Panjab (especially the western part) is due to the influence of Muslims, and although Sikh gurus and the Singh Sabhā Movement of 1921-26 discouraged the worship of tombs, the practice has remained common. The various Muslim *fāqirs* worshipped are considered to possess some supernatural powers by virtue of which they can bestow sons, cure some chronic disease, or even cure the cattle of their ailments. The strong faith of the Sikh villagers in the power of these *fāqirs* is evident from the fact that they have not demolished these shrines, although no mosques are to be seen. This may be due to fear of the Pīrs' wrath, as it is well-known that these Pīrs can inflict calamities on the village if they are not satisfied or when they get angry.

The campaign of the Singh Sabhā and Akali movements against the worship of tombs and graves and belief in Pīrs has not resulted in the extinction of the practice but in the assignment of similar powers to some Sikh shrines. Sangrānā Sāhibā *gurdvārā*, at a distance of fifteen miles from Daleke (where according to a prevailing legend the sixth Guru, Hargobind, bestowed seven sons on a devotee woman), is now believed to be possessed with the power of bestowing children, and an annual fair is organized there. Similar powers are connected with another Sikh temple, Bidh Sāhib, twelve miles east of Daleke.

In fact, when a man leaves this world and becomes a saint, every Hindu, Muslim, of Sikh considers him to be sacred and thenceforth belonging to no caste or creed. Not only do Hindus (from whom most of the Sikhs have been converted) frequently visit various Sikh places of worship reputed to possess supernatural powers, but

Muslims too have been known to go to these places for favors. Equal respect has been paid to the saints by persons belonging to different faiths, irrespective of their religion, who are believed to possess supernatural powers. The reason given for this attitude by the villagers was that all of the saints should be kept contented so as not to let them bring wrath on the villagers, and while it takes nothing to respect them, doing so may do some good; if they are not respected, however, a calamity is almost certain. Probably the primitive man's fear of the supernatural explains the behavior of the people in this respect.

Fairs and festivals. Celebrations by the villagers also provide an insight into the social and religious life of the people. Fifteen of the thirty-one festivals are celebrated commonly by both Sikhs and Brahmans in Daleke. Two of these, Bābā Sher Shāh Vālī and Melā Hājī Shāh, are in honor of two Muslim *fāqirs*, who were well-known for their spiritual powers. The legend goes that once Sher Shāh went to a shop and asked for *misrī* 'crystal sugar.' The shopkeeper, who did not sell any (*misrī*), told the Pīr that he had none. When implored by him to go inside his shop, the shopkeeper found *misrī* lying everywhere. People ask for favors and, if these are fulfilled, they come to offer cloth sheets for the grave or distribute sweets to those present. These fairs are not now so well attended as in the days of Muslims, but the villagers of Pallasor two and a half miles away from Daleke, where their shrines are situated, still try to maintain their importance, and all contribute towards the expenses of the free kitchen provided on these occasions. This is probably the case because Pallasor was predominantly populated by Muslims before partition.

Four other common festivals—Vesākhī, Sāvanī, Lohṛhī, and Basant—are connected with the change of seasons and with agriculture. Vesākhī marks the beginning of the harvest season (wheat) and big cattle fairs are held all over the Panjab. The oldest, biggest and most famous cattle fair is that of Amritsar. Transactions amounting to hundreds of thousands of rupees are conducted every year in this fair. This festival, not much known in other parts of India, was made popular by the Fifth Sikh Guru, Rāmadās. Since his time, cattle fairs have been organized along with this festival. Wrestling bouts, cattle competitions, physique tests, and sports matches are organized by the government for the benefit of the visitors. People by the thousands go to the Golden Temple, at Amritsar, for a dip in the holy water, and the streets are full of village folk.

Vesākhī is also the day when the Tenth Sikh Guru converted the Sikhs 'disciples' into Singhs 'lions' at Keshgarhi, 200 miles away from Daleke.

Sāvanī marks the beginning of the rainy season, and is celebrated all over North India, being known as Tīj in Uttar Pradesh and Delhi. On all Sundays of the month of Sāvan (Śrāvaṇa, August-September), girls set up swings under the trees near the village and sing. They sing especially *giddha* (clapping songs) and also dance. Usually persons belonging to all the castes except Mazhbīs swing together. Occasionally Mazhbī girls who wear clean clothes also join the group of higher caste Sikhs.

Lohṛhī marks the severity of winter and comes usually in the month of January. Daughters are invited to visit their parent's houses and are given clothes and sweets to carry with them. An especially large sweet containing a silver coin is sent for the daughter's mother-in-law. It resembles the custom in the Hariānā (Delhi State and Hindi speaking Panjab) of giving gifts to the parents-in-law on Saṃkrānti Day to please them. The children begin to demand *lohī* 'coins' from the beginning of the month and also collect firewood from all the houses. A bonfire is burnt on Lohrhī Day in the evening. Lohrhī is a special occasion for families with a newly born boy or a newly married bride. Such families distribute popcorn and *guṛ* (a kind of brown sugar candy) to all the guests and to the poor. Meat is cooked on this day and people indulge freely in wine drinking.

Basant marks the beginning of spring, and young and old tie yellow turbans on their heads to herald its coming. This color coincides with the color of the *sarsom* 'mustard' flowers in the fields. A big *melā* 'fair' is organized at Chehherta *gurdvārā*, twenty-two miles from Daleke, and many villagers go there to participate in the celebrations. One can buy all sorts of household articles in the *melā* organized around the temple.

Holī, which is celebrated with great gusto in some parts of India and in the towns of Panjab, is not much celebrated in Daleke. Only children throw colored water on each other. Formerly Mirāsīs (musicians) used to come to the village and stage dramas during these days. Each family contributed a dish of grain towards their expenses. As the throwing of colored water had caused many quarrels, it was discouraged by the Singh Sabhā and Akali Movement. Instead, some Sikhs go from Daleke to a *gurdvārā* at Anandpur (200 miles away) to participate in the celebration of Hola which falls on the next day after Holī. At Anandpur, since the time of the Tenth Guru, Gobind Singh, annual competitions in sports, wrestling, sword fighting, stick fighting and other sports of warfare, have been held and hundreds of thousands of Sikhs come from all parts of India to witness these sports every year.

Dīwālī, which marks the beginning of winter, is celebrated with great pomp and show in the village. People clean their houses, light candles, and place small lighted earthen lamps on their house tops. Many of them go to witness Dīwālī in Amritsar where the Golden Temple is profusely illuminated. A big cattle fair is also organized at Amritsar. In the Sikh homes in Daleke, goddess Lakṣmī is not worshipped in any form, neither cattle nor cow dung being worshipped as is the practice in Hindu Jāṭ homes. The only persons who worship Lakṣmī, the goddess of wealth, are the Brahmans. The day is celebrated by Sikhs to commemorate the release from prison and return of their Sixth Guru, Hargobind, to Amritsar on this day.

Another common festival of the Brahmans and Sikhs in the village is Māghī. It is considered as a very auspicious day by Hindus for giving charity. Usually rice and *dāl* 'pulses' and *til* seeds are given to Brahmans, but the Sikhs give these to the *gurdvārā*. This day has a special significance for the Sikhs of this area (Majha). When the Tenth Guru, Gobind Singh, and his forces were being badly pressed on all sides by the Mogul forces, a group of forty Majha Sikhs in his forces told the guru that they were neither his Sikhs nor he their guru, and they left for their homes. On return to their homes their womenfolk ridiculed them and told them to wear bangles and stay at home while they (the women) would go and fight for the guru. The Majhails (as men from Majha are called), as at all times, could not stand a *bolī* 'ridicule' from their women and marched back to the field to die fighting to the last man. On this site now a big *gurdvārā* has been built, where an annual fair is held on Maghi day. Some ten to fifteen people go from Daleke to attend this festival every year.

Daśahrā is another festival connected with the *Rāmāyaṇa* and its hero, Lord Rāma, which is celebrated in Daleke commonly. However, the sowing of barley seeds and the distribution of seedlings by a Brahman is not practiced in every house. Daśahrā marks the harvesting season for sugar cane, and people bring new sugar canes into their homes for the first time. A few sugar canes are now sent to the *gurdvārā*, though formerly they were given to the Brahmans. The Sikhs also kill goats on this day and eat their meat.

Rakhṛī, commemorating the love of brothers and sisters, is also celebrated commonly by all. On this day sisters tie a piece of colored thread on the wrists of their brothers, who give them some money and other gifts. It is a very old custom and signifies that brothers must protect their sisters in time of peril and difficulties. The love between brother and sister is proverbial in Panjab, and many instances are cited of brothers having sacrificed their wealth and lives to save the honor of their sisters. Formerly the Brahman used to tie a thread around the wrists of his Jajmāns (heads of the families) and used to be given money and grains. This practice has practically died out in Daleke since the Akali movement. Instead some villagers go and tie *rakhṛīs* 'threads' to the legs of the wooden cot on which the holy book is laid. They also offer money and grains in the *gurdvārā*.

Nirātā and Śrāddha are the other typical Hindu festivals celebrated by Sikhs also. Nirātā is in honor of goddess Durgā, while Śrāddha are held in the memory of ancestors. The Sikh Gurus preached against both. They considered that the food given to Brahmans at Śrāddhas did not reach the ancestors as claimed. Many Sikhs in Daleke do not celebrate Śrāddhas and the others, who do, feed only Sikhs and not Brahmans. No ceremony as prescribed by Brahmans is performed. In the case of Nirātā also, only a few Sikh families worship the goddess Durgā or keep fasts. But most of them feed virgin girls on the Aṣṭamī (eighth day). This festival is celebrated with great enthusiasm by the Kumhār Sikhs, who even organize singing for the whole night in honor of the Mātā (Mother Durgā). Most of the Kumhār families belong to the Rādhā Svāmī sect, which is nearer to Hinduism in its beliefs and ceremonies.

Another common festival is Gugā Navamī, which is celebrated in honor of the snake god. The women carry some milk and grains and pour it over the Gugā's shrine (a mound of earth having a hole signifying the abode of a snake) and request Gugā not to show himself to them or other members of their family. The area is infested with snakes and once, when the mother of the Sarpanc did not worship the Gugā, her son was bitten by a snake. Since then she never fails to worship Gugā. The legend about Gugā, his mother, Kacālī, and aunt, Bacālī, is the same as is prevalent in other parts of North India.

The only other festival celebrated by all the persons living in the village is a secular festival marking Republic Day on 26 January. The Community Projects Administration annually organizes a big fair in the *tahsīl* headquarters, Taran Taran. Exhibitions on the subjects of handicrafts and embroidery, seeds, manures, and health are organized by them. Wrestling bouts, races and *kabaḍḍī* matches are also conducted. The other highlight of the program is the award of certificates recognizing the services of different people in helping the work of the community projects and their achievements in the field of growing bumper crops or raising good breeds of cattle. The Chief Minister and the Speaker of the Panjab Legislative Assembly, both of whom belong to this *tehsīl*, come to participate in these functions. The fair lasts for three days and many persons from Daleke go to attend it.

Two Hindu festivals—Janmāṣṭamī and Śivrātrī, not celebrated by Sikhs but celebrated by the Brahmans—concern the Hindu gods Kṛṣṇa and Śiva. The other two, celebrated only by the Brahmans, are Ṭīkā and Karvā Cauṭh. On Ṭīkā, sisters put a vermillion mark on the forehead of their brothers and are given some money in exchange. Karvā Cauṭh is celebrated by married women for the safety of their husbands. This also involves keeping a fast and listening to the story of Sāvitrī who managed to win back life from the gods for her dead husband Satyavān, because of her virtuous devotion as an ideal Hindu wife. This is related by a Brahman woman who is given some grains by all the women assembled to listen to the story.

Ten of the eleven festivals celebrated exclusively by Sikhs mark the birthdays of their Gurus or commemorate the Gurus' accession to the *gaḍī*, or their martyrdom day. The birthday of Nānak (the First Guru and founder of Sikhism) and that of the Tenth Guru, Gobind Singh (who formed the Sikhs into the Khālsā Community), are celebrated with great enthusiasm in the village. Religious meetings are held in the village *gurdvārā*, and famous musicians or Ḍhāḍhis (bards) are invited to sing for the assembly. Discourses and lectures are held on the life of the Gurus and on Sikhism. An Akhaṇḍ Pāṭh (continuous reading of the Holy Book from beginning to end in forty-eight hours) is conducted in the *gurdvārā*, which is decorated with bunting and given a whitewash. The houses and the *gurdvārā* are illuminated as on Dīwālī nights. Special and extra food is cooked in the *gurdvārā* and most of the villagers and passersby take their meals in the *gurdvārā*. Money and grains are collected for this purpose from each house in the village. The amount of donations is decided by the village *pancāyat*.

Melā Bābā Bakale and Khadur Sāhib are held at Bakale and Khadur in the memory of the accessions of the second and the Ninth Guru respectively to guruship. Many villagers go to these fairs, where the program is practically the same as described for a guru's birthday in the village. On these days, early in the morning, the musicians begin to sing special hymns called "Asa di Var." This is followed by phrasing in simple Panjabi of a verse from the Holy Book. Later on, *rāgīs* 'musicians' and lecturers sing hymns and give discourses on the life of the Guru in whose memory the celebrations are being held. These meetings are also used for making political speeches by Sikh political leaders. Many times rival groups organize separate meetings, but the political speeches always follow the religious celebrations.

The martyrdom day of the Fifth Guru, Arjun, is celebrated with great pomp and show in Taran Taran (five miles from Daleke). A big *gurdvārā* and a large tank exist in Taran Taran commemorating his memory. He had, himself, founded this temple to serve as a center of Sikhism in Majha. His martyrdom took place in Lahore, which is now in Pakistan, and Sikhs come from all parts of the country to Taran Taran to celebrate it. Arjun was beheaded for refusing to accept Islam. On this day, which falls at the height of the June heat, the Sikhs serve sweetened milk water to all and sundry. Many *shabīls* 'posts' are set up for this purpose in all the bazaars and villages, and the sweetened water is given—rather, it is forced in quite an aggressive way—even to the unwilling. Buses, tongas, bullock carts and cycles are stopped and passengers are given *lassi* (sweetened water and milk) to drink. A *shabīl* is set up by the villagers of Daleke on the roadside also and all passersby and others in the village are served iced *lassi*. Every family donates all the milk in its house for this purpose. Some money is collected for buying ice and sugar. The serving of *lassi* is also customary on the Hindu festival Ekādaśī which comes a few days before the

Sikh festival. On Ekādaśī, grains and melons are given to Brahmans, but Sikhs do not celebrate Ekādaśī.

Two of the remaining three exclusively Sikh festivals commemorate the death anniversaries of the two Sikh heroes—Bābā Dīp Singh and Vīr Singh. Bābā Dīp Singh belonged to this area and took a vow not to be killed before reaching the Golden Temple at Amritsar. While fighting the Mogul forces, he lost his head seven miles away from Amritsar, but he did not give up courage and, lifting his head on his left palm, kept on fighting and advancing towards his destination. When he reached the outskirts of Amritsar, he could not proceed any further and threw his head with all his strength into the city. It fell in the precincts of the Golden Temple. There are many tales of the bravery and strength of Bābā Dīp Singh. His sword is said to have weighed twenty seers (kilos). An annual fair is held on the anniversaries of both the heroes, and many people from Daleke go to attend these functions.

The other exclusively Sikh festival is the anniversary of the birth of Bābā Gurdittā, a Sikh saint, who lived for more than a hundred years and wrote the Sikh holy book by hand as related to him by the Tenth Guru. This volume has been preserved and people come to pay their respects to it. A legend describes him as "the giver of a son to the wife of the Tenth Guru," and many people come here to ask for the boon of a child.

Many villagers go to Taran Taran to attend the anniversaries of the martyrdom of the four sons of the Tenth Guru. Two of them died fighting in the field, while the younger two are reported to have been buried alive in a wall for refusing to embrace Islam.

The other festival celebrated by Sikhs only is in honor of Jogī Pīr, who is believed to have had supernatural powers regarding rain. A monument has been built over the grave of the Pīr, who had both Sikh and Muslims followers. Near his monument stands a high mound of earth, which has been raised by the devotees pasting on a handful of mud every time they visit the shrine. Jogī Pīr is worshipped as a *Jaṭherā* (ancestral god) too, and all newly married couples pay their respects to his shrine before entering the village of Manochal where it is situated. The Muslim priests of this shrine left for Pakistan after partition and Nihang Sikhs have now occupied it. The Sikh holy book is at present kept in the shrine and the name has been transformed from Jogī Pīr to Joga Singh. A well attended annual fair accompanied by wrestling bouts (of all-India level), is held here even at present.

Besides these festivals, Sikh villagers go occasionally to Taran Taran and Amritsar to attend the birth and death anniversaries of all their Gurus and of Maharaja Ranjit Singh.

The only festival celebrated by the five Christian families in Daleke is Baṛha Din 'Big Day'—Christmas Day—signifying the birth of Christ. They dress themselves in their best clothes and go to attend the church in Taran Taran or Palasor village (two miles from Daleke) where many Christian families live. They organize a contributory tea party or a big dinner on this occasion. If the meeting is held in Palasor, the preacher comes from Taran Taran to deliver the service. They do not know whether they are Catholics or Protestants, and say that formerly they were under the British Church and now they are under the American Church.

Apart from these festivals, there are four monthly festivals celebrated by the villagers of Daleke. The most important of these is Masyā (new moon day). It was made popular by the fifth Sikh Guru, Arjun, after building the big Sikh temple and tank at Taran Taran. People come from far and near to take a dip in the holy tank and pay their respects to the guru. A cattle fair is also organized on this day on the *melā* ground. It is typical of most Sikh festivals in being also connected with agriculture. All over India, farmers do not yoke their oxen on Masyā and observe it as a holiday. Masyā is also connected with a Moslem petty government official, Massa, who donated the land on which Guru Arjun built the temple and the tank. He returned the money paid to him as the price of land by the Guru on imploration of his mother's entreaty, and instead, asked for his name to be remembered forever in the world. It is believed that it is after his name that the festival is called Masyā. The number of people coming to Taran Taran on Masyās is enormously large, as whole families come to celebrate it. Special religious and political meetings are organized on this day. The crowd is so thick in the path around the holy tank that thieves have a field day, though posters all around the paths are displayed telling people to beware of thieves and pickpockets. The crowds also provide a chance for lovers to run away unnoticed, and often rendezvous are fixed for this day. This festival also provides the surrounding villagers with an opportunity to meet each other, and many marriages are arranged on this day. Also many disputes are settled. The educated young man, who today often insists on seeing the girl before marriage, usually gets a chance to see the prospects on Masyā when the girls go to the temple. Such a procedure does not involve any criticism by the neighbors, which is otherwise unavoidable in the village.

Many temporary shops selling sweetmeats, particularly *jalebīs*, a favorite of the villagers, are set up in Taran Taran on this day. Shopkeepers selling merchandise and cloth also do a good business.

The second monthly festival is Puṇya, which falls on the full moon day. The full moon day has assumed special importance because of the birth of the First Sikh Guru on this day in the month of Kārttika (October-November). It is celebrated in Goindwal (eight miles from Daleke), and many villagers go there to pay their respects to the Guru and visit their relatives. On this day also, religious and political meetings are held in the *gurdvārā* and food is distributed to all free of charge. There is a big well attached to this temple with eighty-four steps signifying the eighty-four stages of life one has to pass through before attaining salvation. It is believed that if one takes a dip in the well after reciting *Japjī* (the Sikh morning prayer) at each step, he will attain salvation without having to go through the various stages. Many attempt to do this but only some succeed, while others give up due to exhaustion.

The third monthly festival is Samgrānd, which marks the first day of every Indian month. This is celebrated in the village. People go to the *gurdvārā* where the *granthī* reads to them the Guru's word for the month from the holy book. It contains verses especially written for each month and depicts the conception of the soul as "the bride seeking the bridegroom, Hari." A handful of grains is offered at the *gurdvārā* by each devotee. All the villagers do not go to the *gurdvārā*. Many come to know what has been told about the new month from a person who had been to the *gurdvārā* or from the *granthī* when he comes to their houses to collect food for the *gurdvārā's* kitchen (*laṅgar*).

The Brahman families celebrate Aṣṭami—eighth day—in honor of Mātā Rānī (goddess Kālī). They prepare special food and distribute it among virgin girls. They join the Sikhs in celebrating Masyā and Sangrānd. While on Masyā they also go to the Taran Taran temple; Sangrānd is celebrated in their homes. Similarly, Christian families go the Taran Taran temple on Masyā.

Thus we find that most of the exclusively Sikh festivals are different from those of the Hindus and those Hindu festivals which are celebrated by Sikhs have been given added importance due to their connections with some events of Sikh history. One thing is certain, however, and this is that the part played by the Brahman in their religious life has been completely wiped out. A similar situation is noted among the Hindu Jāṭs of Ranikhera but, although the Jāṭs make no use of the Brahman in their festivals, they still have to depend upon him for conducting their marriages and the functions connected with the life cycle. These functions are performed by the *granthī* in Daleke or, in his absence, by any other elderly person knowing the procedure. The Brahman in Daleke has completely lost his superior position because of a change in his function, and he now sells merchandise and medicines to make his living. He is now at the mercy of the villagers who even brought a Kāmboh refugee compounder to open a shop in the village when the Brahman "doctor" left the village last year. When he came back this year to resume his business, he found that many of his customers were already patronizing the new doctor.

This drifting away from the hold of Brahmans, which became very strong after the fall of the Sikh kingdom, was caused mainly by the revival movements of Sikhism—Singh Sabhā and Akali. The Daleke villagers know more about the Akali movement than that of Singh Sabhā. One of the villagers, Hukam Singh, participated actively in the movement. He joined the band of Sikhs who went to jail to protest against the dethroning of the Sikh ruler of the Nabha State. Besides that, many groups of volunteers (they were called *jatthās*) passed through this village on their way to offer Satyagraha at various places. Such *jatthās* were fed by the villagers in the *gurdvārā*. They were helped with money and grain. The *jatthās* organized religious meetings, explained the purposes of the *morcās* 'front,' and advocated the removal of Brahmanistic rituals and customs among the Sikhs. The *morcā* was mainly against the priests of the Sikh *gurdvārās* who had become corrupt and had been behaving as if the *gurdvārās* were their personal property. The British government sided with them to protect their rights. The villagers remembered the *morcās* of Guru Ka Bagh, Amritsar, Taran Taran temple and of Nankana Sahib (the birthplace of Nānak). The Sikh volunteers were beaten mercilessly and sometimes even fired upon. The *morcās* resulted in the formation of a *gurdvārā* management committee consisting of 271 members elected by the adult Sikh electorate every five years. A member from a nearby village represents Daleke also in the Gurdvārā Committee.

The predominance among the Sikhs of Jāṭs, whose hatred against Brahmans seems to be traditional, has been another cause of the break away from Brahmans. As long ago as the Vedic period, Jāṭs were degraded from their position of Kṣatriyas to "Sat Śūdras" by Brahmans as a punishment for defying Brahmans. The Jāṭs of the Hindi speaking part of the Panjab, of Delhi, and of Uttar Pradesh do not seem to have much respect for Brahmans either.

The Sikhs—a martial group. Sikhism began as a movement of nonviolence, but after the martyrdom of the Fifth Guru, Arjun, it began to transform itself into a martial group. Sikhs fought their first battles against the Moguls under the leadership of their Sixth Guru, Hargobind. Since his time Sikhs have been encouraged to present to the guru good horses, swords, guns and other weapons of warfare instead of grains, clothes, and money. The Sikhs who performed feats of bravery were greatly honored by the guru. This drift from nonviolence to belief in the "efficiency of the sword" was complete by the time of the Tenth Guru, Gobind Singh (after the Ninth Guru had sacrificed his life for refusing to embrace Islam). He changed the Sikhs 'disciples' into Singhs 'lions' by giving them a special initiation ceremony, *amṛit cakhnā* (the drinking of nectar prepared by stirring a double edged sword in the water contained in an iron bowl). Sugar was added by his wife to this water, and five Sikh hymns were recited while preparing this *amṛit* 'nectar.' Those so baptized were required to keep five symbols: uncut hair, iron ring, comb, underwear, and a dagger. The Guru built fortresses and organized Sikhs into a regular army and fought many battles against the Moguls. The struggle against the Moguls was carried on after him by his followers. It became strong when the government happened to be weak and was suppressed when the government happened to be strong. Often the Sikhs were driven into the forests for refuge, and their only home was on their horses. They used to pounce upon the Mogul and Afghan armies and run away with the loot. This went on for quite awhile, and finally, when the government of Delhi became very weak, the Sikhs became rulers, and different bands of Sikhs, under their chiefs, reigned over certain territories. Thus twelve *misals* were formed which were later amalgamated by Maharaja Ranjit Singh into one kingdom.

Channels of communication of Sikh history. The villagers of Daleke remember these events of Sikh history vividly and speak of the days when a price of forty rupees was laid on each Sikh head. The main source of knowledge of their history is the presence of hundreds of *gurdvārās* in the Panjab commemorating their gurus and heroes. This is particularly true for the Majha area, comprising the districts of Amritsar, Ferozepore, and Gurdaspur. Annual religious meetings accompanied by cattle fairs and other fairs are organized in these *gurdvārās* and many villagers go to attend these. On these days, special discourses and lectures relating the deeds of the particular guru or hero are held. Other channels of communication of their history are the meetings held in the village *gurdvārā* to celebrate various monthly and annual festivals. Pracāraks (preachers), trained in the Sikh Missionary College, Amritsar, are sent by the *Gurdvārā* Prabhandak Committee to address these meetings. The well known *rāgīs* 'musicians' are also invited to sing the gurus' hymns and they also relate certain events from the life of the gurus and Sikh history. The most liked singers are the Ḍhāḍhīs—the traditional folk bards. They sing folk tunes and have the *sārangī* and small drums as their musical instruments. They used to sing the various *rāgs* of warlike nature during the battles of the Sikhs. One of the villagers, a carpenter, plays the *sārangī* and is often a member of the group of Ḍhaḍhīs. His knowledge of Sikh history seems to be very wide and he possesses about twenty books on it.

Occasionally, some famous *sant* 'saint' comes to the village and people go to listen to him. His discourses are usually concerned with the Sikh scriptures. Often political meetings are organized by various candidates seeking election. The Akali party's political meetings are always preceded by religious discourses, and their political speeches are punctuated and embellished with events of Sikh history. This procedure is followed by other political parties also, but to a lesser extent. The Sikh prayer read at the close of all religious and social functions in a Sikh *gurdvārā* or home contains verses composed by Guru Gobind Singh invoking God and the first nine gurus, as well as rhythmic prose composed by generations of Sikhs relating the various events of their history. This prayer has been gradually extended to include the recent events of Sikh history. A reference is made in suitable terms to the Sikhs killed during the partition of the Panjab, and to the present-day difficulties. This prayer helps greatly to keep the Sikhs informed regarding their history through the present.

The *gurdvārā's granthī* also served as a schoolteacher before a government school was opened. He taught his pupils elements of Sikh history, along with the alphabets. Daleke children going to the high school at Taran Taran attend the Khalsa (Sikh) High School. One hour is alloted daily to the teaching of the Sikh holy book. A competitive examination is conducted throughout the Panjab by the *Gurdvārā* Prabhandak Committee to test the ability of Sikh students in their history and scriptures. Prizes and scholarships are awarded to the successful candidates.

Besides the schools and *gurdvārās*, Sikh children learn about their history in their homes and the *sāth* (a common meeting place near the *gurdvārā*). Grandmothers and grandfathers usually relate the stories of the brave deeds of the Sikh Gurus and heroes to their children at bedtime. Similarly, the children often surround an old man in the *sāth* and implore him to tell them stories. On festive occasions and celebrations in the village *gurdvārā*, children are encouraged to read poems, sing hymns, and make speeches relating to the heroic and saintly virtues of the gurus.

The Mīrāsīs, the Moslem musicians who used to live by begging, were another channel of communication of Sikh history. When begging before a Sikh house, they sang the praises of the Sikh gurus or related events from the Sikh rule. The verses composed in Panjabi by a Moslem poet, Mohammed Shāh, in connection with the Sikh wars against the British, were great favorites of the villagers. The Mīrasīs left for Pakistan in 1947 following partition. Some of them, however, still are invited to India to sing hymns from Sikh scriptures in the *gurdvārās*.

Another source of information is the written literature. All houses which have at least one person who can read have some books. Most of these books concern the lives of Sikh Gurus, Sikh generals and other heroes. Mostly the villagers read small pamphlets of twenty or thirty pages costing only two to four annas, and these are written in folk tunes to be sung easily by the villagers. Occasionally a farmer is heard singing the praises of the guru when ploughing his fields. The most popular pamphlets, as is evident from the sales of a shopkeeper in the fair of Jogī Pīr, are poems regarding Guru Gobind Singh, Guru Nānak, the martyrdom of Guru Arjan and the subsequent concern of Candu's daughter-in-law (Candu had issued orders to torture the Guru), the stealing of horses by Bidhi Cand (from a Mogul provincial governor who had forcibly taken them), the Birth of the Khālsā, the martyrdom of Guru Teg Bahādur, and the martyrdom of the four sons of Guru Gobind Singh, etc. Pamphlets containing the famous Panjabi folktales like Hīr Ranjhā, Sohnī Mahīval, and Pūran Bhagat, as well as tales about famous dacoits and modern fashions, are also sold in large number at these fairs.

Stress on health. The transformation of the Sikh community from a band of peaceful disciples into a warrior race created new values among the people. A high premium is placed on good health and manliness. A coward is the most despised person in Daleke. In order to "measure" a new visitor to the village a few jerks are administered to him for endurance and strength, and, if he can stand them, he is considered really worthy of friendship. The main topic of discussion among the young and the old is health. If someone can tell them how to improve their health, the villagers will listen for hours. The first thing looked at in a prospective son-in-law is his health, and, similarly, one wants to know when selecting a wife whether she is strong enough to cook food for ten to fifteen people.

The hardy work of a farmer provides enough opportunity for developing muscles and body, but sports form an especially integral aspect of a Sikh village life. In Daleke *kabaḍḍī* is played daily either in the fields or near the school. This game is very popular in all parts of Northern India. A group of men divides itself into two, and each half stands on either side of a line. One person from one group crosses the line to enter the other group's "territory" and chants "*kabaḍḍī, kabaḍḍī*" while holding his breath throughout. The members of the other group try to catch him and he tries to get away to his side after touching one or two persons of the other side without stopping his utterance of "*kabaḍḍī*" or losing his breath. This game calls for great stamina. Young men of Daleke also practice wrestling, and their best wrestlers enter in the intervillage wrestling competitions. On such occasions the village men accompany their wrestlers or *kabaḍḍī* teams to encourage them by shouting and betting. If a wrestler or a *kabaḍḍī* team of the village is victorious in a competition, it becomes an occasion for rejoicing, and meat and wine are taken in plenty.

Another game which is not very common now involves still greater stamina. A man goes running half a mile towards another and strikes hard with both his hands on another's chest. Then comes the turn of the second person to strike the first on his chest with both hands. They go on doing so until the first person, who has to run backwards, reaches the starting point.

Often the young men of Daleke organize weight lifting competitions. In the harvesting season, when the harvested crop is carried home on the heads, bets are laid as to who can lift a particularly heavy bundle. The usual stakes are either a bottle of wine or cash money, or both. Sometimes, when a donkey or a horse carrying a heavy load passes through the *sāth*, those assembled there place a bet as to who can lift it singlehanded or with both hands. Once bets were laid on lifting a concrete electric pole lying in the *sāth*. Jeeps of the community projects or heavy ploughs or even heavy persons are some of the other objects that are used for weight lifting competitions.

Cycle races are also held among Daleke villagers, with the objective of reaching Taran Taran earlier. They usually carry one and sometimes three persons on their cycles. One carrying more people and taking less time is considered to be a hero and is much talked about in the village. Once a young man was carried by a lady teacher of the village embroidery school on her cycle from Daleke to Taran Taran. While the people praised the strength of the lady school teacher, the man who was carried was much laughed at for many days after the incident.

People love to keep good horses and usually go to marriages and to visit friends on horseback. Competitions are held among the horseriders. There were twenty-four horses in Daleke before the floods, and at present only six horses remain in the village. Most of them have been sold due to lack of fodder and the need for money for other necessities of life. Moreover, cycles also have replaced horses, but most of these cycles are like "unbridled horses," as they have no brakes, bells, or lights.

The accent on health is evident from childhood. The children, especially boys, are given hard slaps on their backs and are given other jerks. They are encouraged to play games requiring considerable stamina and are even encouraged to fight while others simply watch. When children try to ride on the rear of the jeep or a tractor, nobody stops them from doing so. Many happened to be thrown over because of a loose hold. But when their parents were asked why they had not tried to stop them to avoid such injuries, their reply was that this experience would make them strong and hardy and would enable them to stand such falls in the future. Two Daleke children are in the school "elevens" in hockey and volley ball at Taran Taran.

The Community Projects Block also organizes intervillage competitions in races, *kabaḍḍī* wrestling, and volley ball on the Republic Day. These competitions are enthusiastically welcomed and fully participated in. The Community Project Block has also opened recreation centers and organized youth clubs along the lines of the 4-H Clubs. There is no such club at Daleke, but one exists at Pallasor, which has a good membership.

Other pastimes for the young and the old are the ability to twist each other's arm or opening each other's tightly closed fists.

Good health is so much prized by the Daleke villagers that they openly criticize the police for having recently killed the three dacoits who had been terrorizing the area for six months. The villagers had to keep vigil for all these months and were kept awake for many nights for fear of an attack by these dacoits on the village. The explanation given for being sorry was at the destruction of such nicely built bodies. They would have liked the police to capture them and despatch them with a small force to conquer Pakistan or Kashmir or any other rebellious part of the country like the Nagas, as would have been done by Maharaja Ranjit Singh.

Good food. Good food accompanies good health, and one often hears in Daleke, "Eat this, it is good for your health." The daily food of an average villager consists of *chapattis* prepared from wheat in summer and from maize in winter, with plenty of buttermilk and one green vegetable or pulses. Tea is very common and is drunk at least twice a day; but this tea contains plenty of milk. Butter and ghee are added in plenty to the vegetables or pulses. Butter and ghee are also eaten alone. The *prasād* distributed in the Sikh *gurdvārās* also requires equal quantities of ghee, flour, and sugar. It is often prepared at home on festive occasions. The people of Majha have been well-known for their possession of highly bred buffaloes. The number of buffaloes giving milk in Daleke is 345. Even the poor tenants try to buy a buffalo in order to have enough milk and ghee for their family. Meat, usually goat, is eaten on festive occasions. Once a month the Mehrā kills a goat in the Sikh manner (i.e., at one stroke) and sells the meat to the villagers. A few bring meat occasionally from Taran Taran. No one except two Brahman brothers in Daleke claims to be vegetarian. One of the Brahman brothers also eats meat and drinks wine.

The quantity of food eaten is also large. An average villager eats *chapattis*, made often from about half a seer of wheat or maize flour, and drinks half a liter of tea at one time. During the summer he drinks at least three liters of buttermilk in one day. Bets are laid on the number of *chapattis*, meat, or sweets eaten, or sugar cane juice or milk drunk. People who can drink ten liters of milk or sugar cane juice at one time are well-known in the village. Food given to males and females in the house is similar, although the boys studying in schools are occasionally given a larger helping of butter and ghee in order to help their brain.

Drinking of wine is very common among the Daleke villagers. The number of persons (males) who have never drunk any wine is only two in the whole village, while about fifteen persons drink wine daily. Others drink on festivals; at marriages, wine is not only provided by the bridegroom's and bride's parents, but the members of the marriage party buy wine at their own cost and drink together. At one Jāṭ marriage, the members of the party spent forty rupees each on wine. Whenever a guest comes to visit, he is offered wine. In fact, offering of wine to a guest signifies respect for him, and sons-in-law and brothers-in-law are always treated to a feast of wine and meat. Some visitors bring a bottle of wine with them and the host then has to offer them more wine. On Lohrī day, when Daleke is facing extreme cold, the villagers drink wine in plenty and one often hears the challenging voices of men from each house. Disputes and fights are common on this day.

Wine is not drunk alone, but in groups. These groups usually consist of relatives and friends. Persons belonging to a hostile group or enemies never drink wine together. They may be sometimes invited and murdered, and the murderers enter a plea of having killed them while intoxicated.

Most of the wine drunk in the village is country made. It is usually distilled by the Mazhbīs from *guṛ* 'brown sugar.' For a special guest, distilled wine may be bought from the government licensed shop. Foreign liquor has been tasted by only a few, and they prefer to drink wine made from *guṛ*, to which they have added many spices. It is drunk, usually, mixed with water or aerated water. One of the shopkeepers sells aerated water, which he gets daily from Taran Taran. A person who can drink more wine than others and still remain in his senses is considered to be very brave and superior to others.

The stress on military qualities has created a love for arms. There are six licensed guns owned by rich Jagīrdārs of Daleke. Every home possesses a number of large swords and spears. Nobody goes to Masyā or any other festival without arms. A person having no arms is ridiculed by his friends as being effeminate. He may not wear a gold necklace (which he likes to do) but is sure to be carrying a weapon which may be a sword, spear, pistol or gun. These arms are freely used during fights in the fairs, fields, or in the village.

Many persons from Daleke have joined the Indian army. Sikhs have always been regarded as good soldiers and even today are reckoned among the first of the Indian Army. Most of the villagers from Daleke serving in the army are Mazhbīs. There are twenty-seven pensioners, and fifteen young men are still serving in the army among them. Ten Jāṭs have also served in the army. The highest rank attained in the army by any Daleke villager has been that of Havildār (Sergeant), although in the surrounding villages many have been commissioned and risen to the rank of colonels and captains. Military service was the first preference of school children regarding occupation. The next preference was for police. Nobody from Daleke works in the Police Department, although two Jāṭs have served as policemen in Shanghai.

The Daleke villagers are very adventurous and often leave their village in search of better jobs or to supplement their earnings in the village. Their wanderlust (typical of Sikhs) has carried sixty-five of them overseas during the last forty years, thirty of these being soldiers who visited Africa, the Middle East, and Europe during the last two World Wars. One of them, a Jāṭ, lived for seven years (1914-21) in Canada and the United States. He worked there as a farm laborer and speaks some English. His brother worked as a policeman in Shanghai. A Tarkhān has settled in East Africa as an engineer. The Brahman brothers at one time opened shops in Burma and stayed there for over ten years. Another Tarkhān is working on Hirakund Dam (1,200 miles away) while one Tarkhān works in Bombay (1,100 miles away). About twenty Mazhbīs have left Daleke to work as laborers on Bhakra Dam and other dams where strong people are well paid. Most of them maintain their families in the village. Six of the Kumhar boys who have learned weaving now work in Amritsar textile mills.

The reason given by the villagers for leaving the village every now and then to make their living was a desire on their part to live like Sardārs (chiefs). They want to maintain a good standard of living, and to attain it they do not hesitate to do any work.

Sikhism gives equal importance to all occupations and lays unequivocal stress on the dignity of labor. There is nothing which a Daleke villager is ashamed to do. The removal of cow dung and other refuse is considered to be the work of Mazhbīs, but poorer Jāṭs, Kāmbohs, and others make cakes from cowdung for their own use. Similarly it is women's duty to bring water from the well if the family has not engaged a Mehrā, but men are also often to be seen carrying water on their heads. Food is usually carried for the Sepīs and others in the fields by children or servants, but often we find a Sardār (the employer) taking food himself to his workers in the fields. Food for everybody in the house, including the family members as well as Sepīs and other servants, is cooked by the mistress of the house. A great stress is laid on service. The master of the house takes pride in serving his guests himself, even though when alone he himself is served by servants. When they visit the *gurdvārā* they willingly fan those assembled there, clean, and take care of the shoes of the visitors, prepare *prasād* and food for the *laṅgar* 'kitchen.' If any construction work is going on, every one gives a helping hand. The artisan Sikhs work for a day or two free of charge, while others help carry bricks and mortar. A number of Daleke villagers participated in the cleaning of the tank around the Golden Temple and at Taran Taran. Recently an approach road was built connecting the temple Bidh Sabib (fifteen miles away) with the main road, through voluntary labor. This was one of the most successful projects of the Community Project Block in the area. The example has been put to good use by them to build other roads through voluntary labor.

No infringement of freedom. The Daleke villagers are of a very independent frame of mind, and do not stand any infringement of their freedom. One author has remarked that the Sikhs of this area neither fear God nor the law, if they are carrying a weapon, even a stick. This is probably true if we add, "if the Sikh has a bottle of wine inside him." Most of the quarrels resulting in murders are caused by trifles like, "I will shout, who are you to stop me?" or "I shall go through this field, who are you to stop me?" They do not bother about others' opinion, and will go on doing as they like. The only persons whose opinion, or rather ridicule, matters are their women.

Every one in Daleke, or, for that matter, in the whole of Majha, wants to become a leader, and Majha has produced some of the best leaders of all types—politicians, reformers, saints, sportsmen and dacoits. Their aggressive nature combined with good physique and an enormous power for creating intrigues prepares them well for this role. Other factors helping them are discipline and organization, which have been inculcated into them by their military tradition. The *Sarpanc* of the village is one of the most ambitious persons and is working assiduously on a five year plan of serving the people of his area. His ultimate aim is election to the Panjab Legislature and a

Ministership in the Panjab Government. Others are less ambitious, but none of them wants to become a clerk. All aspire to be officers.

Women of Daleke. The women of Daleke are as upright and manly as the men. They ride horses admirably and are often seen on horseback going to Masya at Taran Taran. The men walk on foot if they do not have an extra horse. Many folktales describing the bravery of women warriors are current in the area. Although division of labor has resulted in the polarization of duties of men and women—men work in the fields while women work in the house—many women give a helping hand to their husbands in the fields. Most of the women do not observe purdah, but it is very strictly observed in the Jagīrdār families and by young brides. Women are not allowed to keep their faces veiled in the *gurdvārā* according to Sikh tradition, and there they usually sit a little farther away from the persons from whom they should hide their faces, i.e., father-in-law and elder brother-in-law. As a woman grows older (about thirty-five to forty years) she discards purdah and moves in and out of the house very freely. Fifteen families among various castes were known to have women as their heads. In one case a widow has kept one of her daughters and her husband in her home. She employs *sepīs* and sees to every detail of agriculture from sowing to harvesting herself. She is quite fearless and goes alone with a stick to watch over the watering of her fields through the irrigation channels. She has often rounded up her son-in-law from a group of wine drinkers. Another widow runs a petty shop selling sugar, spices, etc. The cases of two other widows in the village are similar. In eleven other families, although the husbands are living, nothing important is decided without prior consent of their wives.

In the remaining families men are undisputed heads, and whether they consult their women folk or not depends on their discretion. The wives are usually consulted in matters concerning marriages or giving gifts to relatives on various festive occasions. They are even consulted on matters concerning agriculture or disputes. In fact, in most of the families, the men do most of the shopping for their women. Occasionally an elderly woman of the house may accompany men (usually grown-up sons) to help in the selection of clothes and cosmetics. The daughters-in-law apprise her or their husbands of their wishes.

However, the woman, particularly the eldest, is the supreme ruler inside the home. She divides the household work among the daughters and daughters-in-law. She supervises the work of the servants in the house, stores the grain, cotton, and other agricultural products. Her opinion is sought in the selection of brides or sons-in-law. She also decides the daily menu. She is invariably the cashier of the house; this task may be assigned to a younger woman in the family if she is literate and can keep written accounts. But the woman cannot spend the money deposited with her, and must always ask the permission of her husband or son, whichever is the head of the family.

Women are not allowed to participate in the meetings of the *pancāyats*, and none of them has been elected as a member of the *pancāyat*, but they wield a great influence through their husbands, brothers and sons. A lot of lobbying goes on behind the scenes, and women play a great role in it. Their usual method is a constant repetition of their request accompanied by weeping, threats to leave the house, or demanding what they want as a favor after having pleased their men with their charms. It is worthwhile to note that even though most of the men interviewed in Daleke declared that they did not listen much to the advice of women, most of the joint families have broken up into smaller units because of fights between different women of the house. When the interviewees were asked to explain this anomaly, they said that even a hard stone breaks when it is struck constantly by clothes, and that they were only human beings. They try to pacify their wives in the beginning, but when the women constantly insist on separation, the men accede to their request.

In fact, there are not more than three joint families in Daleke. The brothers may till their lands cooperatively, but they live and cook their food separately. Even in the case of two out of the three joint families, it is only one brother who resides in the village, the others living in another village. Also a definite trend toward the shifting of stronger ties from consanguineal to affinal relationships was noticed. The old men described this change as a shift from "turban-relationships" to those of "skirts." This is happening because bitter feelings are created, usually among brothers, on distribution of land and other property, while the wife's relatives have nothing to lose although they may give him something.

Female infanticide was very common among Jāṭs about forty years ago. This practice was condemned by the Sikh Gurus, but persisted for some time as girls were considered to be a burden on the family on account of the dowry system. The last case of infanticide in this village occurred about fifty years ago.

NOTE

[1] This paper is dedicated to my "guru," Oscar Lewis, University of Illinois, who initiated me into village studies. It is based on the field work in Daleke (Amritsar District) from July 1956 to November 1957. Fieldwork was carried on with the assistance of Shris A. S. Sethi, Ram Narain, M. G. Oswal, Darshan Singh and Mrs. Balbir K. Singh. Fieldwork was supported by a grant-in-aid by Robert Redfield of the University of Chicago. I am indebted to P. C. Biswas, Head of the Anthropology Department, Delhi University and Milton Singer for their valuable guidance and advice in fieldwork and preparation of this paper. I am thankful to R. N. Bansal for valuable comments on this paper. I owe grateful thanks to S. Dilbagh Singh, Sarpanch of Daleke, for his hospitality and assistance in fieldwork. The assistance of G. S. Malhi, Block Development Officer, Taran Taran in the selection of the village, making contacts and in providing secretarial work is also acknowledged. To all those mentioned above I wish to express my deep appreciation and gratitude, and to extend my sincere thanks and best wishes.

Delhi University
Delhi, India

TRIBAL CULTURES OF PENINSULAR INDIA AS A DIMENSION OF LITTLE TRADITION IN THE STUDY OF INDIAN CIVILIZATION: A PRELIMINARY STATEMENT

By Surajit Sinha

Introduction

THE Genesis and functioning of indigenous civilizations has been conceived by Redfield and Singer as involving continued interaction between a Great Tradition, as abstracted and systematized by the specialist literati, mainly in urban centers, and the Little Traditions of little communities.[1] A social group that perpetuates Little Traditions in relation to a civilization is labelled a "peasant community,"[2] as distinguished from the isolated self-sufficient "folk-society" which Redfield conceived as an ideal type in his earlier work.[3] Unlike the ideal folk society, the peasant society is in continuous interaction with "country-wide networks" tied to one or more urban centers. The urban dimension of a primary civilization is mainly a product of elaboration and systematization of a core culture pattern shared by the peasant hinterland. Thus, in the course of a specific study of the peasant community at Kishan Garhi, Marriott finds it articulated with the Indian universe through various aspects of its social structure and also through its religious culture.[4] Such persistent and numerous channels of communication between the peasant's village and the larger culture community of the Great Tradition of India are a general characteristic of peasantry all through North India, and to a somewhat limited extent, also in other parts of India.[5]

In this paper, we are concerned with conceptualizing the socio-cultural position of the little communities forming the so-called tribal belt of peninsular India[6] in relation to the study of Indian civilization. These communities demand special consideration, for here we find communication with the larger universe of Indian civilization relatively more restricted and interrupted, although in not a single case is the community completely shut off from contact with what we call the great culture community of India.

The tribal belt of central and southern India comprises about fifteen million people, of whom about forty-eight percent did not declare themselves as Hindu during the 1931 census. We can conjecture with a reasonable degree of certainty that the bulk of the remaining fifty-two percent, a large majority of whom declared themselves as Hindu, were not consciously Hindu at a time one, two, three, four, five, or some more hundred years back. If, for the sake of operational advantage, we take "consciousness of being a Hindu" as the diagnostic criterion of a persisting link with the Great Tradition of India, then we may be prompted, by taking a middle range perspective of history, to exclude this group from the scope of our main interest, namely, the study of the development of Indian civilization.

Aside from this picture of isolation, however, we have also another set of observations. Although these tribal communities are relatively more isolated in their active contact with the larger culture community of the Great Tradition, compared to a traditional Hindu peasant community, it is still important to note that everywhere within the Indian mainland, these tribal communities have been in touch with the traditional network of weekly markets whereby they are involved in economic symbiosis with at least ten or more Hindu castes. This has been going on for at least a hundred years in most cases. Besides this participation in the organized market system, the tribal communities are, in most areas, in intimate contact with at least four Hindu or Hinduized artisan castes: the blacksmith, the basketry maker, the potter, and the weaver. Interaction with these artisan groups extends beyond economic symbiosis to other aspects of social life, such as ceremonial friendship, participation in common festivals, and so on.

Leaving the problem of genesis aside, and restricting ourselves to an observation of the contemporary scene, these little tribal communities would thus fall within the "social field" of the Great Tradition of India. Whether they fall within the "ideological field" of the Great Tradition or not demands closer examination.

If we look at this tribal belt in a broad impressionistic manner, three points strike our attention: 1) the overall characteristics of the socio-cultural system of these tribal communities are distinguishable from those of the traditional Hindu peasant communities; 2) there are significant elements of continuity between the two kinds of socio-cultural systems; 3) all over central and southern India we find the tribal communities in a process of transformation which brings them closer to peasant Hindu communities—there is not a single tribe in this belt that is completely unaffected by Hinduism.

Keeping the above impressions in mind, we can perhaps conceptualize the position of the Little Traditions of these tribal communities in one of the following three ways.

Firstly, these tribal cultures seem apparently to be outside the main historical current of the development of Indian civilization. The only way to study them in relation to that civilization will be in terms of numerous particular acculturation studies involving the contact of tribal cultures with already formed centers of Indian civilization.

Secondly, following Kroeber's paper on "The Ancient Oikumene," the tribal cultures may be conceived of as a backward branch of traditional Indian civilization:

> The primitives in the area, or adjoining it, derive their cultures mainly from the civilizations characteristic of the *Oikumene* as a whole through reductive selection. They preserve old elements which their retardation make them unable or unwilling to accept. Basically, however, these retarded or primitive cultures in or adjacent to the *Oikumene* are fully intelligible only in terms of 'oecumenical civilizations'. They usually add to what they share some lesser measure of their own proper peculiarities and originations and they have developed a distinctive style of their own. But in the main these backward cultures depend and derive from the greater ones whose nexus we have been considering.[7]

Lastly, the tribal cultures give us an idea of the initial primitive level of cultural raw materials that contributed to the development of Indian civilization. The contemporary tribal cultures represent a relatively untransformed section of the original primitive culture, arrested in its development mainly as a result of ecological factors of isolation and also perhaps because of some unknown series of historical accidents.

The first one of this series of conceptualizations is the safest and most noncommittal but analytically the least incisive. I am inclined to keep it in reserve only as the last alternative, if other more bold and committed approaches fail.

The second approach suggested by Kroeber is appealing and in a way very similar to our third approach, but with a reversed starting point. Here we are looking from the top, namely, from civilization down to the primitive isolate. Kroeber's assumption, that ". . . in the main these backward cultures depend and derive from the greater ones . . .," appears true if we look at the contemporary, recent or middle range historical scene, when civilization is dominantly established for a major area of the Indian mainland.

But taking a long range perspective of history, we are led to the third approach, reminiscent of the old-fashioned evolutionary approach. Here we see the problem of genesis starting from the primitive isolate and looking upwards. Such an approach seems to the author to be the most promising and in conformity with available data. There is, however, no way of providing long range historical documentation in support of this last approach. We shall examine the data mainly on a synchronic level by examining socio-cultural systems at different levels of integration, and thus try to reach the middle range of historical depth wherever possible.

As an essential first step, we will attempt to isolate a series of functionally related characteristics that distinguish the tribal communities as a whole from the Hindu peasant communities. This will be the main concern of the present paper. Later on, we may take up a comparative study of the transformation scene, with a view to isolating some of the persistent processes of change in the social-structural and ideological dimensions in the cultural system.

In Redfield's writings, again, I find a favorable pointer to my selection of the third way of conceptualization. He puts it remarkably well when he describes Indian peasant society as follows: "It is as if the characteristic social structure of the primitive self-contained community had been dissected out and its components spread about a wide area. Rural India is primitive or tribal society rearranged to fit a civilization."[8] He characterizes the growth of indigenous civilization as a "conversion of tribal people into peasantry." Evidently, the conversion cannot be conceived as a quick process reached in one step with equal intensity throughout precivilized tribal India.

There were, in all probability, multiple focal points (spatially speaking) of development of civilization—with urban or urbanlike centers and peasant hinterland—from which acculturative influences spread out to the as yet untransformed, but genetically related, outlying tribal groups. This process of transformation has not reached its logical limit in contemporary India. The primitive tribal belt of today may thus be conceived as the yet untransformed residue of tribal cultures; and in the acculturation or transformation scene of tribal cultures of today we are likely to discover some of the basic processes involved in the building up of the indigenous civilization of India.

Among the earlier workers seriously interested in the relation of tribal cultures to the traditional Hindu cultural system, we may mention Risley, Hutton, Roy, O'Malley, Elwin and numerous census commissioners. On the one hand, they have indicated numerous elements of similarity between tribal religions and popular

Hinduism, while, on the other, they have, with the possible exception of Hutton, implied or stated that tribal cultures are essentially unrelated to the core pattern of classical Hinduism which was imported by the Aryan conquerors. This latter hypothesis, however, is being modified in the light of excavations connected with the Indus valley civilization. John Marshall clearly shows many roots of puranic or classical Hinduism in the Indus valley civilization.[9] Although there is a general consensus of opinion that the builders of that civilization were pre-Aryan, we are still on no sure ground about their actual identity. It is possible, as some speculate, that they were related to the ancient progenitors of the contemporary Dravidian culture of South India. In any case, the system of religious belief of the above mentioned primitive tribes needs to be more carefully compared with the Hinduism of the peasants, as also with classical Hinduism.

A general limitation of the earlier approaches is that they have uniformly used religious belief as an isolated topic for comparison, instead of using a more holistic, functionally integrated framework. Marriott's Master's thesis entitled "Growth of Caste in India" (1949) is a refreshing departure from this procedure. Here he examines eleven tribes of the central Indian belt with the hope of isolating some of the major persistent processes involved in the growth of the caste system. He uses the "acculturative or synthetic approach" to the study with exclusive reference to social structure. His approach is of special interest to us; for here he examines, from the available literature, rudiments of the process of development of the caste system, mainly as a result of interactions within the tribal zone. Marriott, however, is not entirely satisfied with his social-structural framework: ". . . the significance of a general background of Hindu cultural influences, especially the influence of religious ideas, may have been unduly neglected in this thesis . . . ." Following his lead we may approach the material in a broader perspective.

In our discussion of tribal India, we roughly limit ourselves to fifteen million people living in and around Peninsular India, covering the hills, plateaus and the neighboring plains of Bombay, Madhya Pradesh, Hyderabad, Orissa, southern Bihar and West Bengal. In order of their numerical importance, the principal tribes are the Gond, Santal, Bhil, Oraon, Kondh, Munda, Bhuiya, Ho, Savara Kol, Korku, Pahariya and Baiga. They represent communities at various levels of economic efficiency: the Birhor and the Hill Kharia live by dependence on hunting and collecting; the Baiga or Hill Bhuiya similarly depend on shifting cultivation, while the Munda, Ho, Santal, and Bhumij practice settled agriculture. Some of these tribes living in relatively interior areas have been very lightly touched by Hinduism, namely, the Baiga or the Ho of Kolhan, while at the other extreme there are tribes such as the Bhumij of Manbhum or the Raj Gond of Madhya Pradesh, who declared themselves as Hindu in the census of 1931.

The languages of these tribal groups of Peninsular India belong primarily to two stocks, the Munda or Kherwari and the Dravidian. The Munda speaking tribes, such as the Ho, Kharia, Munda, and Santal, are restricted in their distribution to Chotanagpur plateau and surrounding areas, while the major habitat of the Dravidian speaking tribes, such as the Gond, Khond, Bison-horn Reddi, Kadar, etc., is in central and southern India. A few of these tribes, again, like the Bhil of central India and the Bhumij of Manbhum, have used Indo-Aryan languages in place of their original tongue for quite some time.

Physical anthropologists of the past have specified the physical features of the group as follows: short to medium stature, wavy black hair, dark skin color, dolichocephalic head and platyrrhine nose. Guha labels them Proto-Australoid as distinguished from the Mediterranean type of South India, represented mainly by the Dravidian speakers. With the exception of narrower nose, the latter's physical features are almost identical with those of the so-called Proto-Australoids.[10] (Guha 1937).

Hutton, since the census operation of 1931, has made a somewhat arbitrary and neat speculation about racial migrations and cultural developments in India. In Hutton's view, there have been successive waves of migration of peoples into India, bringing in different cultures. Contemporary Indian population and civilization, according to Hutton, is an amalgam of all these. The successive series, as he sees them, are Negrito, Proto-Australoid, Early Mediterranean, and finally, the Later Mediterranean, Alpine, and Nordic, all these having come through the northwestern gateway. From the northeast came the various Mongoloid groups, about whose relative date of entry Hutton is not certain.[11]

Arthur Keith questions Guha's and Hutton's hypothesis that the early population of India was entirely received through immigration: "Yet, strange to say, all or nearly all, who have sought to explain the differentiation of the population of India into racial types have sought the solution of this problem outside the Peninsula. They have never attempted to ascertain how far India has bred her own races. . . . No doubt India has been invaded over and over again; certain racial types are of extraneous origin. But one would venture the opinion that eight-five per cent of the blood of India is native to the soil. At least it is urgently necessary that our eyes should be focussed more directly on the possibility of India being an evolutionary field—both now and in former times."[12] Following this lead of Keith, S. S. Sarkar prefers to use the term "Veddid" for the Dravidian speaking, mainly forest dwelling, tribes of South India who are, according to him, the true autochthones of India. Within this group, he tentatively includes the Urali, Kanikkar, and Muthuvan of Travancore; the Paniyan of Wynad, Malabar; the Sholga, the Kurumba and the Irula of the Nilgiris; the Chenchu of Hyderabad and the Kadar and the Malsar of Cochin. Sarkar distinguishes the autochthonous Dravidian speaking Veddid racial stock from the Munda speaking tribes, who are regarded by him as later immigrants to the Indian soil.

In the absence of datable fossil human remains and adequate cultural data, we are not yet in a position to take too definite a stand on this controversial issue, particularly with reference to the chronological aspect of it.

We can perhaps say with some confidence that the Aryan speakers are later arrivals on the Indian scene compared to the main carriers of Munda and Dravidian languages.[13] In all probability the basic orientation of India's primary civilization was laid before the Aryan intrusion, through prolonged interaction of the Little Traditions of the Munda and Dravidian little communities. If the measurements on the Mohenjodaro skeletal remains published by Marshall, Mackay, Sewell and Guha are taken at their face value, we find evidences both of "Proto-Australoid" and "Mediterranean" types in the urbanized population.[14] If the Mediterranean type be identified with the ancestors of modern "non-Proto-Australoid" "non-Veddid" Dravidian speakers in South India, then we may assume that the interaction started as early as about the third millenium B. C.

Leaving these historical speculations aside, let us turn to a synchronic structural comparison between the tribal cultures and the cultures of the Hindu peasantry. The data on tribal cultures is provided by various published materials and my own field work among the Munda, Bhumij, Ho, and Oraon. Broadly speaking, we shall restrict ourselves to the following communities: 1) mainly hunters and gatherers, the Hill Kharia, Pahira and Birhor of Chotanagpur; 2) mainly shifting cultivators, the Hill Bhuiya, Juang and Khond of Orissa; the Korwa, Baiga, and Hill Maria Gond of Madhya Pradesh; the Chenchu and Bison-horn Reddi of Hyderabad; 3) settled agriculturists, the Munda, Ho, Santal, Dudh Kharia, Bathuri, Bhumij, Oraon and Savara of Southern Bihar and Orissa; the Raj Gond of Madhya Pradesh and Hyderabad.

The generalized characteristics of the Hindu peasant communities will be derived partly from my general impression of Hindu village communities in West Bengal, Bihar, and Orissa, as I have seen them, and also from the recent publications on Indian peasant communities in the *Economic Weekly* (1951-54), and from the various articles published in *Village India*, edited by Marriott (1955).

The Two Kinds of Cultural Systems[15]

In the following pages, we shall describe in broad terms some implicitly functionally related aspects of the culture pattern of the two kinds of societies, referring only occasionally to a single community or tribe. The totality of the culture pattern and its settings has been broken down into the following aspects, namely, habitat, economy, social structure, and ideological system. Our characterization will perhaps be more applicable to preindustrial India, i.e., the India of the middle of the nineteenth century, than to contemporary India; although in all essentials it fits the contemporary picture as well.

1.1. Habitat: *tribals.* A major portion of the tribal habitat of central India is hilly and forested. Tribal villages are generally found in areas away from the alluvial plains close to rivers.

1.2. *Hindu peasantry.* A large portion of Hindu peasant villages are in deforested plateaus or plains. Many of these villages are crowded in the river plains.

2.1. Economy: *tribals.* The subsistence economy is based mainly on either hunting, collecting, and fishing (e.g., the Birhor, Hill Kharia), or a combination of hunting and collecting with shifting cultivation (e.g., the Juang, Hill Bhuiya, etc.). Even the so-called plough using agricultural tribes have the tradition of having subsisted mainly by means of shifting cultivation in the past.

Specialization of crafts includes iron smelting and smithery, basket and bark rope making, and weaving. It is difficult to say whether they had wheel made pottery and brass work traditionally. Some of the tribes, like the Juang or the Chenchu, have the tradition of never having used pottery in ancient times. In all probability, initially, most of the crafts were not confined to full time specialists. There is evidence that the Lohār blacksmiths and iron smelters once formed a part of the Munda tribe, and that the Mahālī basketmakers once formed a part of the Santal tribe.

The local village community is nearly self-sufficient. Circulation of goods is based entirely on barter. There are, however, rudiments of interethnic cooperation in the circulation of goods within a limited area. The wandering Birhor supplied bark ropes and honey to the Ho and Munda and other neighboring peoples. The Munda procured iron implements from the Asur and various types of basketry from the Mahali. Mandelbaum describes the socio-economic symbiosis among the aboriginal Kota, Badaga,

Kurumba and Toda in the Nilgiri area.[16] There are no specialist traders among them.

There is very little incentive towards the accumulation of capital on an individual level, although a sense of individual ownership is quite developed with reference to hunted animals or collected vegetables. The hunting or collecting territory roughly belongs to the village community; and it is customary for any group not to poach upon the territory of another. Among the tribes that practice shifting cultivation, and have ample scope for expansion, there is very little competition for the covering of more land individually. Among the settled agriculturists, like the Ho, Munda, and Bhumij, however, we find a distinct incentive towards accumulation of capital in the form of land and a store of paddy.

2.2 *Hindu peasantry.* The main subsistence economy is intensive agriculture with the help of the plough drawn by bullocks or buffaloes. There is also an intricate full time specialization in crafts, with the development of a sophisticated tradition of artistic excellence supported mainly by a feudal aristocracy. Among the full time specialists associated with Hindu villages, not to be found in the traditional tribal communities, may be mentioned gold and silver smiths, weavers of fine silk cloth, bell-metal workers, etc.

Beyond a limited degree of local self-sufficiency, the village community is tied to a country-wide network of markets, ultimately related to commercial towns. Incentive towards the accumulation of capital is quite strong. Capital is mainly defined in terms of land, store of grains, cash, valuable metals, and jewelry.

3.1. SOCIAL STRUCTURE: *tribals.* The largest significant reference group is the tribe or a segment of it, the "sub-tribe," i.e., a single, endogamous, ethnic group occupying a more or less contiguous territory. In many cases, we find tribes like the Santal, Munda, or Ho describing themselves as *Hor* 'men,' while others are *Diḳu* 'aliens.' In actuality, we find that, among the same tribes, the latter term is not actually used with reference to a few ethnic groups with whom they have set up traditional symbiotic relatiônships of long standing. Thus, the Ho do not use this term for the Lohār 'blacksmith,' Mahālī 'basketmaker,' or Gaur 'cattle tender' within their village community.

The tribe is segmented into exogamous (patrilineal in most cases), (often) totemic clans, frequently with territorial cohesion and strong corporate identity. Clans are segmented into lineages which serve as important corporate groups.

The kinship system may be labelled as "tempered classificatory" (maximal lineage setting the limit to the application of kinship terms, although terminologies often extend to members of the village as a whole). In terminology, we find that the emphasis lies on the unilineal principle, generation and age. There is an emphasis on patrilineal descent and patripotestal authority in most groups.

The village is the most important territorial unit. Among many of these tribes, nearly twelve villages form a socio-political federation with its own council. Among a few (the Munda and the Bhumij) we also find a tendency to form even larger federations.

There is very little specialization of social roles. With the exception of role differentiation in terms of kinship and sex and some specialization in crafts already referred to, the only other role specializations are headman, village priest, and medicine man.

There is very little rigid stratification in society. (This is especially so among the tribes who practice hunting and collecting and shifting cultivation.) There is, however, a tendency towards stratification along the following lines, especially among the settled agricultural groups: relative political supremacy of the numerically dominant clan, compared to other settlers; superiority in land holding of the earlier settlers, relative to later settlers; symbolic ritual superiority of one group over another, due to ritual degradation of the other in traditional terms, and tendency of the priest-headmen to form an endogamous class.

Secular and religious leaderships are combined in one person. The headman is a chief amongst equals, with no special privilege in property. He is assisted in his work by a democratic council of village elders formed by all the adult members of the village. The council's decision is final.

3.2. *Hindu peasantry.* The largest significant reference group expands beyond the village or the caste group to the linguistic province or even farther, covering the total Hindu social universe and comprising numerous distinct ethnic groups. The bases of such extended ties beyond the little village community are varied and numerous, including connection with central administrative townships, network of markets, marriage and caste relations, and network of religious centers and religious fairs.

The caste is usually segmented into exogamous clans which are often nontotemic. The clans are usually nonterritorial and do not have any corporate identity. Clans or *gotras* are segmented into lineages which serve as important corporate groups.

The kinship system may be labelled as "tempered classificatory" (maximal lineage setting the limit to the application of kinship terms, although terminologies often extend to members of the village as a whole). In terminology, we find the emphasis on the unilineal principle, generation and age. There is an emphasis on patrilineal descent and patripotestal authority among most groups.

The village is the most important territorial unit. But territorial relations extend beyond the village on various different bases, such as democratic federation of villages under a superior council, connection with a hierarchy of administrative towns, network of markets, and relationships through marriage, ties of caste, and participation in religious fairs and pilgrimages. Territories organized under such varied principles make up a complex interpenetrating country-wide network.

We have already spoken about intensive specialization of crafts and the existence of full time traders. There is similar specialization in political roles within a feudal setting which touches the village. Religious aspects of culture demand the service of various specialists, e.g., priests (for usual life cycle rites and festivals), astrologers, genealogists, *sādhus* of repute and also medicine men or *ojhās*. Among such specialists, we may also mention teachers belonging to traditional schools.

Intricate stratification into hierarchically arranged, endogamous castes whose ranking refers itself to the classical ideal pattern of four orders or *varṇas* is evident; while specific rank as a caste within a region seems to be determined by a combination of the following objective factors: relative economic position, especially with reference to land holding, relative political dominance, relative numerical strength, and symbolic validation in ritual habits in relation to the Great Tradition.

Besides caste ranking, there are also other principles of stratification current in society, e.g., ranking in terms of wealth or economic class, political power and literary education. These various principles of stratification largely overlap and partially interpenetrate, making the overall ranking system extremely complicated.

Although secular leadership is provided with direct and indirect ritual sanctions, the two functionaries, secular and religious, are clearly differentiated. Here we often find a combination of democratic leadership by elders and direct control by the feudal aristocracy from the top, with its center at the capital township, having its court of justice as final reference of law and order, supported by a police force and military reserve.

4.1.1. IDEOLOGICAL SYSTEM: *Tribals. Supernaturalism.* The pantheon consists of one Sun God and a lower hierarchy of gods. Next to the Sun God, the important deities are village tutelary gods and ancestral spirits. Almost of equal importance are some nature spirits, for example, the spirits of the hills and the presiding deities of the waters.

Gods are conceived of as powerful beings. They are classified into two classes, namely, those who are habitually friendly or benevolent, and those who are malevolent. But even the benevolent gods are not considered to be repositories of ethical qualities. Gods do not necessarily demand noble or generous action from their devotee; they demand only personal loyalty.

Supernatural rites are explicitly directed towards happiness and security in this world, abundance of crops and children and avoidance of sickness and death being the supreme considerations.

There is no concept of "heaven" or "hell" or of rewards or punishments for moral or immoral acts. The soul is called back to join the ancestral spirits in the sacred domestic tabernacle. Thc soul turns into a malevolent spirit only in the case of an unnatural death.

There is a belief in reincarnation and transmigration of souls into various forms of life, namely, trees, birds, animals, etc. But there is no connection between ethical action and the form of reincarnation. The concept of reincarnation is not arranged in an ascending hierarchy of superior forms of life (as traditionally determined), nor is reincarnation considered inevitable.

No idol or temple in well-defined form is found; although we do find rudiments of idolatry in the worship of unworked stones and also rudiments of the concept of the temple in the institution of the sacred grove. There is, however, no erection of a house for the deity among most of these tribes.

Animal sacrifice is an essential part of rituals, and magic and witchcraft predominate.

4.1.2.1. *Some aspects of value systems and world views*: *Man-nature.* The natural universe is charged with impersonal and personalized supernatural power. The natural universe is significantly continuous with the human world of sentiments and social interaction. Thus man, nature, and the supernatural are connected in terms of intimate relationship. (This is true with reference to both tribal and non-tribal Hindu peasant communities.)

4.1.2.2. *Man-man.* The human universe is practically limited to the tribe or, at the most, extends to a few local ethnic groups having long standing traditional symbiotic relationship. Equality and reciprocity are emphasized in human relationship. Morality of social action is always judged in terms of corporate kinship or territorial reference groups. Elders are respected. There is significant male dominance in social life, and the desire for children is strong. The good life is conceived of as a life with ample scope for indulgence in pleasure, while maintaining social obligations to corporate group or groups. We find little emphasis on cautious accumulation of wealth at the cost of pleasure.

4.2.1. *Hindu peasantry. Supernaturalism.* This is a combination of monotheism, pantheism and polytheism. Sun worship is a very important element of Brahmanical tradition; although the Sun God is not regarded as the Supreme Being or *Bhagavān*.

The pantheon is much more elaborate in peasant Hinduism, which has some limited access to written sacred literature. It contains some of the gods of the Great Indian Tradition, as well as local spirits and deities. Reverence for mountains, ancestral spirits and village tutelary spirits is an important element in peasant Hinduism. The peasant is accustomed to classifying his gods with special reference to caste, village, lineage, family, and individual, each unit having its special presiding deity.

In peasant Hinduism, magical or power connotation of the deities predominates. But, in addition, there is an emergent overtone of the gods occasionally standing for high ethical quality, *dharma*, rewarding moral behavior and punishing sinful or immoral behavior. When he uses the term "religious" (*dhārmika*), the villager may mean a rather mechanistic concept of one who observes the traditional rituals correctly. But there is also a parallel concept of one leading a generous and selfless life, not speaking untruth, being above greed, and so on. It is believed that such moral behavior is favored by the gods, and is also good for the soul.

Along with the predominance of concern about happiness in terms of material prosperity and health in this world, there is also a pragmatic concern about a similar kind of happiness in the other world. Austerity and renunciation are directed towards this goal.

The concepts of "heaven" and "hell" are very important. Belief in reincarnation is highly systematized through the concept of an ascending series of forms, and is loaded with ethical connotation; the form of reincarnation being determined by the ethical value of an action.

Both temples and idolatry are very important. Animal sacrifice forms an essential part of the rituals of many sects; while abstention from killing of all kinds is associated integrally with other sects. There is a predominance of magic and witchcraft.

4.2.2.1. *Some aspects of value systems and world views*: *Man-nature*: same as in 4.1.2.1.

4.2.2.2. *Man-man.* The human universe, after accentuation of narrow range social affiliations like lineage, local group or village, caste, and so on, expands outwards to encompass the state or even farther. Superordination and subordination is the keynote of social interaction. The morality of social action is usually judged in terms of corporate kinship, territorial, or other reference groups. Respect for elders is even more intense than in the case of the tribals, this being especially so among upper castes. Male dominance is even more marked among most groups, and the desire for children is strong. Tribal hedonism is mixed with a cautious concern for economic prosperity through strenuous and steady labor, the latter attitude being supported by the puritanical streak of abstention that we find in supernaturalism.

5. *Aspirational level.* Impressionistically, we can state that relative to the peasantry, the level of aspiration among tribal communities is comparatively lower. Even within the bounds of indigenous civilization, the peasant's world view is affected by ideals coming from the elites of the city, creating in him the desire for more land and wealth, more political power, superior social status for his family, lineage, or caste group, artistic and intellectual excellence which is recognized by an expanded audience, and so on. These surplus desires hit the peasant's mind, which is otherwise marked by a relatively passive acceptance of what he is.

5.1. *The common denominators.* A cursory review of the above comparison reveals significant elements of continuity between non-Hindu tribal and Hindu peasant socio-cultural systems. Among these may be mentioned the following:

Economy: Emphasis is on local self-sufficiency, with barter as an important element in trade, corporate kinship reference in economy, and symbiotic relationship with ethnic groups.

Social Structure: "Caste" and "tribe" have almost identical structural features as social units, with a belief in common descent and endogamy, exogamous clans segmented into functional lineages, a tempered classificatory kinship terminology whose maximum limit of applicability is set by the maximal lineage; relative age and generation are very important in the kinship system; the village is the most important territorial unit; there is patrilineal and patripotestal emphasis (in most cases), and finally democracy in leadership.

Ideological System: 1) Supernaturalism: There exist a polytheism, belief in a supreme being, pantheon including village tutelary gods, ancestral spirits, spirits of the hills and waters, belief in reincarnation, corporate social reference in religion; pragmatic considerations of fertility in crops and women, and avoidance of sickness, rule supreme in rituals and animal sacrifice. 2) Value-system and world-view: The natural universe is charged with personal and impersonal supernatural powers; it is contiguous with the human world of sentiments and social interactions; there is respect for elders, desire for children, male dominance in social life, and an underlying hedonism.

One question, however, arises in these pursuits of common denominators: to what extent is their commonness "apparent" or "real"? How can we be sure, for example, whether animal sacrifice, transmigration and reincarnation of the soul and the like have the same meaning in the two cultural systems under comparison? It is the contention of the writer that while a final definite answer cannot be given to such queries in the present state of our knowledge, existing literature and the writer's ethnographic field experience point to the plausibility of such a comparison.

Many of the earlier students of tribal cultures in India were aware of this fact of continuity, especially in the field of religion. Risley described Hinduism as "animism more or less transformed by philosophy," or as "magic tempered by metaphysic," and finally expressed the opinion that, "No sharp line of demarcation can be drawn between Hinduism and animism (i.e., tribal religions). The one shades away insensibly into the other." E. A. Gait, Census Commissioner of 1911, found it extremely difficult "to say at what stage a man should be regarded as having become Hindu."[17] J. J. Marten, Census Commissioner of 1921, observes: "There is little to distinguish in the religious attitude of an aboriginal Gond or Bhil from that of a number of lower Hindu castes. Both are essentially animistic." Verrier Elwin suggests that all the aboriginal tribes except those of Assam "should be classed in the census returns as Hindu by religion as their religion belongs to the Hindu family."

Reviewing previous comments on the cultural position of the aboriginal tribes of central India, Ghurye remarks:

> It is clear from this discussion that the proper description of these peoples must refer itself to their place in or near Hindu society . . . while sections of these tribes are properly integrated in the Hindu society, very large sections, in fact the bulk of them, are rather loosely

assimilated. Only very small recesses of hills and depths of forests have not been more than touched by Hinduism. Under the circumstances, the only proper description of the people is that they are imperfectly integrated classes of Hindu society. Though for the sake of convenience they may be designated as tribal classes of Hindu society, suggesting thereby that they retained much more of the tribal creeds and organizations than many of the castes of Hindu society, yet in reality they are backward Hindus.[18]

6. *The emergent aspects.* Now let us summarily isolate and list the "discontinuous" or "emergent" aspects in peasant cultures.

Economy: Intensive agriculture is the basis of economy, with an incentive towards accumulation of capital, a currency and intricate network of markets tied finally to commercial towns, multiple specialization of roles in production, emergence of the specialist trader group, and the differential possession of wealth leading to economic stratification.

Social Structure: There is a highly formalized stratification into castes and the development of other principles of stratification, more complex specialization of social roles, widening of social ties involving multiethnic groups, interpenetrative network of territorial structure, tied to townships and cities, priestly class and literati, and the presence of formal educational institutions.

Ideological System: 1) Supernaturalism: There exist idol worship and temples, an organized priestly class, moral connotation of supernaturalism with concepts of sin heaven and hell, and reference to a written sacred tradition. 2) Value system and world view: emphasis is placed on superordination and subordination in social life. There is an intensive supernaturally oriented drive for moral life supported by puritanical concepts of asceticism and renunciation, and the human universe extending beyond caste, lineage or local group.

Among the above emergent items, a surplus economy based on settled agriculture, the development of social stratification, and the growth of ethical religion, appear to have been most comprehensive in scope.

7. *The transitional aspects.* We should also note some of the transitional elements in tribal cultures in the direction of our general characterization of the peasant level of culture. In economy, for example, we find a tendency towards full time specialization in the following crafts: basketmaking, smithery, ropemaking and weaving. We also find interethnic exchange of goods and services in the aboriginal setting, for example, the case of the Birhor and the Ho, and also of the Kota, Kurumba, Badaga, and Toda. In social structure, we spoke of some tendencies towards stratification, defined by the factors of relative numerical strength, priority of arrival, ritual purity, and so on. We also found tendencies towards feudalization of leadership among the Bhumij and the Munda.

In supernaturalism, however, we cannot identify elements of transition from "ethnically neutral supernaturalism" to "ethical supernaturalism."

Conclusion

It may be argued that our characterization of the tribal cultures appears to be much too general to be useful; it might fit in well with the picture of primitive cultures anywhere in the world. This is indeed so when we refer to such items as lack of stratification, limiting the social and moral universe to one's own ethnic group, intimate integration of man, nature and supernatural in the world view, and lack of personal ethics in supernaturalism. We emphasized these aspects deliberately in order to point out that tribal cultures of Peninsular India do share certain characteristics common to primitive cultures all over the world. Beyond these, however, we also find certain specific items among the tribal cultures of India which are not necessarily universally shared by primitive tribes in other parts of the world. Among these, we may mention the existence of a hierarchic pantheon with the Sun God at the top; and belief in reincarnation and transmigration of the soul.

David G. Mandelbaum commented, on a preliminary version of this paper, that most of the distinctions put forward in characterizing the peasant Hindu vis-a-vis the tribals would hold ground if we restrict the comparison only to the highest among the Hindu castes. On the other hand, he argued, very few significant differences in cultural patterns and in value systems would be found between the lower Hindu castes and the tribals. There is indeed some validity in Mandelbaum's criticism; for many of the lower castes in India seem to share with the tribals the following characteristics: emphasis on equality in social behavior within one's own ethnic group, considerable freedom of cultural participation for the women, and a value system little burdened by puritanical asceticism. Further, the supernaturalism of these lowest castes has some similarity with that of the tribes, in that their pantheon primarily consists of local gods, while their supernaturalism is rarely accompanied by ethical considerations. Through economic backwardness, social segregation, and a general lack of direct access to literate Hindu traditions, the lowest Hindu castes are in comparative isolation from the central current of the development of sophisticated Hinduism—a position more or less similar to the situation among the tribes. Yet, even with these important similarities, the main feature that distinguishes the cultures of the lowest castes from those of the tribals is that while the former accept, perhaps somewhat grudgingly, their inferior status in a larger social system, the tribals live in a comparatively more easily defined, self-sufficient, social and ideological world. The latter consider their culture as being unique to themselves, and do not feel that they are in any way subservient to a larger system. Also, while it is true that the lowest castes are primarily illiterate, they are not completely free from the influence of the ethically loaded, partly puritanical theology and world view of literate upper caste Hindus, whose messages they receive through verbal communication of wandering *sādhus* and through cultural performances, such as the dance, drama, etc. These considerations prompt us to maintain our initial distinction between the cultures of the tribals and those of the Hindu peasantry, taken as a whole. We should, however, be prepared to make a future attempt at characterizing the lower Hindu castes as a special dimension of Hindu peasantry, with a view to examining whether the latter come nearer to the tribals or to the upper caste Hindus.

Our lumping together of the Dravidian and the Mundari speaking tribes into one whole, and the exclusion of the Assam group of tribes, may be justified only on the plea of a preliminary effort at systematization. The next step will obviously involve examining in detail the cultures of the so-called tribal groups vis-a-vis those of the Hindu castes, higher and lower, taken separately, in the different major regions of India. This will have to be done both in terms of synchronic structural comparison and in terms of the key processes of interaction between the tribals and the Hindu peasantry. This latter aspect needs to be studied in as great historical depth as possible. Furthermore, it is important to make overall comparisons of the cultural patterns of the Munda, Dravidian, and Assam group of tribes.

Within the limitations of our present endeavor, as mentioned above, we may say that we have been able to demonstrate the possibility of orthogenetic development of civilization in India from a primitive cultural level roughly comparable to cultures of the less acculturated tribes of Peninsular India. We have pointed out vital elements of continuity between tribal cultures and Hindu peasant traditions. We have also been able to isolate some potential elements of transition in the direction of peasant cultures in tendencies towards feudalization, stratification, specialization of roles, and so on.

If we leave aside the problem of specific historicity for the time being and try to look upon the total social field of India touched by the Great Tradition, the tribal cultures fall within this field in terms of structural comparison. We have also seen that within this field they represent a distinctive level (relatively the lowest) of complexity. In order to make this distinction clear, it seems best to describe the tribal cultures as a special dimension, namely, the "primitive" or "folk"[19] dimension of the Little Traditions of India. On a formal level of abstraction, at least, the folk (or tribal), peasant, and urban dimensions of Indian tradition and culture community represent a series of increasingly complex levels of socio-cultural integration with evidence of continuity in core pattern.

A comprehensive understanding of the development of the primary civilization of India will thus inevitably involve a clear understanding of the primitive level of manifestation of core traditions and their supporting social organization, as they are still partially preserved among contemporary tribes.

Students of classical Indian philosophy and art like A. Coomaraswamy have been struck by its essentially nonpuritanical and expressedly joy oriented sensual core.[20] Life is conceived of as a great festivity where spiritual qualities are to be attained by intensive participation. This is, in a way, a synthesized and abstracted version of a primitive, hedonistic world view. The slow rate of technological development in India allowed the classical dimension of the Great Tradition to maintain a nourishing contact with the primitive core of community life.

NOTES

1 Robert Redfield and Milton Singer, "The Cultural Role of Cities," *Economic Development and Cultural Change* (Chicago, 1954), III, 53-73; Redfield, *Peasant Society and Culture* (Chicago, 1955).

2 Redfield, 1955.

3 Redfield, *The Folk Culture of Yucatan* (Chicago, 1941).

4 M. Marriott, "The Little Communities in an Indigenous Civilization," in Marriott, ed., *Village India* (Chicago, 1955).

5 A preliminary version of this paper was prepared by the author for a seminar on "Comparison of Cultures: Little and Great Traditions of India—Interaction of Tribal, Peasant and Urban Dimensions," conducted jointly by Robert Redfield, Milton Singer, and the writer at the University of Chicago in the spring of 1956. The project was financed by the Ford Foundation. The author acknowledges his indebtedness to Redfield and Singer for many kind suggestions during the preparation of this essay. With some minor changes, this paper was published in *Man in India,* XXXVII (1957), and is reprinted with the permission of the editor.

6 This includes the entire area south of the Indo-Gangetic plains.

7 A. L. Kroeber, "The Ancient Oikumene," *The Nature of Culture* (Chicago, 1952), p. 392.

8 Redfield, 1955.

9 Sir John Marshall, *Mohenjodaro and the Indus Civilization* (London, 1931).

[10] B. S. Guha, "An Outline of the Racial Ethnology of India," in *An Outline of the Field Sciences of India* (Calcutta, 1937).

[11] J. H. Hutton, *Caste in India* (London, 1951), pp. 1-7.

[12] S. S. Sarkar, *The Aboriginal Races of India* (Calcutta, 1954), p. 19.

[13] C. F. Haimendorf, however, questions the priority of the Dravidians on the Indian scene relative to the Aryans on grounds which are not yet very convincing. See Haimendorf, "Problems and Prospects of Indian Anthropology," *Man in India,* XXIX (1949), 152-157.

[14] M. Wheeler, *The Indus Civilization* (Cambridge, 1953), p. 51.

[15] The author wishes to acknowledge here his indebtedness to Tarak Chandra Das of the University of Calcutta, from whom he imbibed many of his ideas regarding the characteristics of the tribal communities as distinguished from the Hindu peasantry. Das, however, is not responsible for the details of the present characterization or for the general developmental implications in this paper.

[16] D. G. Mandelbaum, "Culture Change Among the Nilgiri Tribes," *American Anthropology,* XXXXIII (1941).

[17] E. A. Gait, Census of India (1913), I, Pt. 1, 129-130.

[18] G. S. Ghurye, *The Aborigines—"so called"—Their Future* (Poona, 1943).

[19] The writer is inclined to use "folk" in place of "primitive" to avoid the popular derogatory connotation of the latter term.

[20] A. K. Coomarswamy, *The Dance of Shiva* (Bombay, 1948).

Indian Museum
Calcutta, India

INDEX

INDEX